Strategies for Successful Writing

A Rhetoric, Research Guide, Reader, and Handbook

Strategies for Successful Writing

A Rhetoric, Research Guide, Reader, and Handbook

James A. Reinking

Robert von der Osten

Sue Ann Cairns
Kwantlen Polytechnic University

Sixth Canadian Edition

PEARSON

Toronto

Editorial Director: Claudine O'Donnell
Acquisitions Editor: Jennifer Sutton
Marketing Manager: Euan White
Program Manager: Emily Dill
Project Manager: Jessica Mifsud
Manager of Content Development: Suzanne Schaan
Developmental Editor: Rachel Stuckey
Media Editor: Lise Dupont
Media Developer: Tiffany Palmer
Production Services: Garima Khosla, iEnergizer Aptara®, Ltd.
Permissions Project Manager: Alison Derry
Photo Permissions Research: iEnergizer Aptara®, Ltd.
Text Permissions Research: iEnergizer Aptara®, Ltd.
Art Director: Alex Li
Interior and Cover Designer: Anthony Leung
Cover Image: Evgeny Karandaev / Shutterstock

Vice-President, Cross Media and Publishing Services: Gary Bennett

Credits and acknowledgments for material borrowed from other sources and reproduced, with permission, in this textbook appear on the appropriate page within the text or on page 590.

Original edition published by Pearson Education, Inc., Upper Saddle River, New Jersey, USA. Copyright © 2017 Pearson Education, Inc. This edition is authorized for sale only in Canada.

If you purchased this book outside the United States or Canada, you should be aware that it has been imported without the approval of the publisher or the author.

3   16

Library and Archives Canada Cataloguing in Publication

Reinking, James A., author

Strategies for successful writing : a rhetoric, research guide, reader, and handbook / James A. Reinking, Robert von der Osten. — Sixth edition.

Revision of: Strategies for successful writing : a rhetoric, research guide, reader, and handbook / James A. Reinking . . . [et al.]. —Canadian ed. — Scarborough, Ont. : Prentice Hall Allyn and Bacon Canada, ©2000.

Includes bibliographical references and index.

ISBN 978-0-205-96989-0 (paperback)

1. English language—Rhetoric—Handbooks, manuals, etc. 2. English language—Grammar—Handbooks, manuals, etc. 3. Report writing—Handbooks, manuals, etc. 4. College readers. I. Von der Osten, Robert, author II. Title.

PE1408.R45 2015   808'.0427   C2015-906444-9

ISBN 978-0-205-96989-0

CONTENTS

PART TWO
RESEARCH GUIDE

PART THREE   READER

PART FOUR   HANDBOOK

Preface

The sixth Canadian edition of *Strategies for Successful Writing: A Rhetoric, Research Guide, Reader, and Handbook* is a versatile, all-in-one text that offers ample material for either a full-year or a one-term composition course.

While informed by current rhetorical theory, the text engages students directly through a clear, conversational style that invites them into the text, lessens their apprehension about writing, and provides a model for their own prose. This style complements our practical, student-based approach to writing.

The organization of *Strategies for Successful Writing* reflects a view of writing as a process that is rarely linear. This edition emphasizes the interrelationship of critical reading, thinking, and writing. It helps students move along a developmental continuum as they learn, practise, and consolidate their writing skills, while also helping them gain insight into the recursive and fluid nature of the writing process. Students learn how to generate ideas in the early prewriting stages; how to arrange these ideas in the drafting stage, employing rhetorical devices such as analysis, comparison, or argument; and how to make strategic changes in the editing stage. Lively and relevant professional and student model essays help students observe and internalize the strategies of effective writing. Practical classroom-tested activities engage students in and give rise to stimulating class discussions.

CHANGES IN THE SIXTH CANADIAN EDITION

The sixth Canadian edition of *Strategies for Successful Writing* has been carefully streamlined, but retains the many strengths of previous editions while incorporating improvements suggested by readers and reviewers. Many new readings, updated excerpts, the inclusion of new sections on new media, the use of visuals, and examples of different genres such as literacy narratives along with two literary analyses, appear throughout the text. Among the many changes we have made in this edition, the following are noteworthy.

- **A record number of 21 new essays, many with a Canadian focus.** The new essays include not only 15 new professional essays, but also 6 new student-authored essays. The essays that have been selected have high interest and relevance for students in diverse communities, focusing on areas such as language differences, climate change, and community issues such as homelessness.
- **More inclusion of student voices.** Since many instructors and students find student prose models especially practical, this edition includes three student essays with MLA documentation, as well as a sample student outline, and a sample student essay based on an interview.

- **More samples of substantial academic and other documented essays.** These in-depth essays include one on food politics from the independent magazine *The Walrus*, highly relevant pieces on climate change and on the coming North American water crisis from a book by Chris Wood, and one on homelessness adapted from the scholarly journal *Anthropologica*.
- **Inclusion of essays that work synergistically.** In addition to paired arguments on nuclear energy, food politics, and Canadian policies on inclusion, many other essays, such as the two paired literacy narratives by Canadian students, can be taught together. In Chapter 10, two essays offer extended definitions of ethno-cultural or post-racial identities, and blend personal history with reflection and critical questioning in authentic ways. Many essays can be profitably taught together because they are linked thematicially.
- **New section on writing for new media.** New material on writing in multiple genres and for changing online environments such as blogs, websites, and social media has been added to Chapter 1.
- **Revision of argument chapter.** This chapter (Chapter 13) now contains a section on visual argumentation and includes a sample scholarly article that serves as a model for the use of graphic visuals. This article also demonstrates an effective blending of sources from both secondary research and primary research, such as interviews.
- **Enhancement of research and documentation chapters.** Updated guidelines on conducting research now focus more heavily on electronic research. Chapters on the MLA style and the APA systems of documentation based on the 2009 edition of the Publication Manual of the American Psychological Association and current updates have been separated for purposes of clarity.

THE RHETORIC

The Rhetoric is a streamlined 13 chapters, which may be used independently or sequentially. The first five chapters are grouped together under the heading Writing Strategies: A Writing Process. These chapters help students learn and practise writing strategies for planning, drafting, revising, and editing. Chapter 1 gives an overview of the principles of effective writing: awareness of purpose; awareness of audience, including conventions in different discourse communities; the qualities of strong writing; and ethical concerns in writing. Chapter 2 offers strategies for active reading, including summaries and critiques. Chapter 3 looks at strategies for prewriting, drafting, and finding a thesis. Chapters 3 and 4 are unified by an unfolding case history that includes the first draft of a student paper, the initial revision marked with changes, and the final version. Notes in the margin highlight key features of the finished essay. Students can relate the sequence of events to their own projects as they work through the various stages. Chapter 4 focuses on more global revision strategies, while Chapter 5 focuses on local revisions, helping students to look closely at paragraphs, sentences, and words, and to think about their editing in more subtle ways as they consider style, tone, diction, sentence rhythm, variety, and emphasis. Sets of checklists pose key questions for students to consider.

The remaining eight chapters in the Rhetoric feature various strategies, or modes such as illustration, cause and effect, definition, and argument that can be used to develop an essay. While we point out that these strategies do not usually exist in isolation and may overlap considerably, these rhetorical modes can be considered natural ways of organizing our thoughts and ideas. Each of these eight chapters includes a mini-reader, which contains at least one student essay and one professional essay employing the relevant rhetorical mode. The first essay in each strategy section is annotated in the margin to highlight aspects of the rhetorical strategy under discussion.

The rhetorical strategies move progressively from more personal writing closer to home to more analytical writing and eventually to more research-based, formal writing. These strategies also move from relatively straightforward to more complex kinds of writing, culminating with persuasion and argument. In Chapter 6, which focuses on narration, we have provided new material, and sample student essays, including the literacy narrative that invites students into a metacognitive reflection on their own learning about literacy. Strategies for using illustration follow, since illustration is commonly used to strengthen both personal and formal writing. The next three rhetorical modes—process analysis, cause and effect, and definition—all represent types of analytical writing. Chapters 11 and 12 introduce the organizational patterns of comparison and classification. Finally, Chapter 13, Strategies for Convincing Others, shows how argument often subsumes many rhetorical modes such as definition, illustration, and analysis. Because argument is an important focus for many writing instructors, we have included two pairs of model essays in Chapter 13, in addition to the five argument essays in the Reader. These essays pair arguments on the politics of food and on cultural diversity, and instructors can use them separately or together.

THE RESEARCH GUIDE

Chapters 14 to 17 constitute the Research Guide. Chapter 14 shows how to narrow down a topic requiring secondary research, choose and evaluate sources, take notes, and blend in sources. This chapter includes examples of a topic and sentence outline for a research paper, and sample student research arguments using MLA and APA styles. Chapter 15 explains and illustrates the most common primary research strategies: interviews, questionnaires, and direct observations. Student models, annotated with margin notes, embody the key features of these strategies. Chapters 16 and 17 show how to blend in external sources using the two main styles of documentation in common use: the Modern Language Association (MLA) system, favoured by English and humanities instructors, and the American Psychological Association (APA) system, used by most social science and psychology instructors. These chapters also show the correct formats for references within the body of the paper.

THE READER

The third section of the text is the Reader, organized according to broad rhetorical categories of personal writing, analysis, and argument. Within these broader categories instructors will find examples of other rhetorical strategies, such as comparison or definition. Instructors may also choose to approach the essays thematically (see the Thematic Table of Contents in the Instructor's Manual), for example by examining different points of view on cultural identities, popular culture, or health. A brief biographical note about the author precedes each selection, and stimulating questions designed to enhance student understanding of structure and strategy follow it. In addition, a section titled Toward Key Insights poses one or more broad-based questions prompted by the essay's content. Answering these questions, either in discussion or in writing, can help students engage more deeply with their writing as they gain more insight into important issues. Finally, we include one or more writing assignments related to each essay's topic.

THE HANDBOOK

The fourth and final section of the text is a concise grammar and mechanics handbook, which features tab indexing on each page for easy access to all material and consists of five parts: Sentence Elements, Editing to Correct Sentence Errors, Editing to Correct Faulty Punctuation and Mechanics, Spelling, and Glossary of Word Usage. Explanations avoid using unnecessary grammatical terminology and are reinforced by sets of sentence exercises in the first three sections. The section Sentence Elements explains how students can use sentence structure to improve their writing skills. We also include connected-discourse exercises—unfolding narratives that engage and retain student interest while they correct errors—in the sections Sentence Errors and Editing to Correct Faulty Punctuation and Mechanics. The Spelling section presents four useful spelling rules and an extensive list of commonly misspelled words. The Glossary of Word Usage offers a similarly comprehensive coverage of troublesome words. Instructors can use the Handbook either as a reference guide or as a basis for class discussion.

SUPPLEMENTS
MyWritingLab

MyWritingLab is a state-of-the-art interactive and instructive solution designed to help students meet the challenges of their writing courses and to assist them in all their future writing. MyWritingLab enables students to use a wealth of resources, all geared to meet their learning needs. **MyWritingLab** will give users access to the Pearson eText—a feature that allows students to refer to the text whenever and wherever they have access to the Internet. The eText pages look exactly like the printed text, offering powerful new functionality for students and instructors. Users can create notes, highlight text in different colours, create bookmarks, zoom, click hyperlinked words and phrases to view definitions, and see the text in single-page and two-page views.

Instructor's Resource Manual *Strategies for Successful Writing*, Sixth Canadian Edition, offers an Instructor's Resource Manual with teaching strategies, additional classroom activities, suggested answers to the text's exercises, and additional readings for instructors. The manual is available to instructors from the Pearson Canada online catalogue at **http://catalogue.pearsoned.ca**.

Learning Solutions Managers Pearson's Learning Solutions Managers work with faculty and campus course designers to ensure that Pearson technology products, assessment tools, and online course materials are tailored to meet your specific needs. This highly qualified team is dedicated to helping schools take full advantage of a wide range of educational resources, by assisting in the integration of a variety of instructional materials and media formats. Your local Pearson Canada sales representative can provide you with more details on this service program.

ACKNOWLEDGMENTS

I am very grateful to reviewers for their helpful suggestions that assisted me in finding a new shape for and perspective on this sixth Canadian edition:

Elizabeth Gooding	Kwantlen Polytechnic University
Gene Homel	British Columbia Institute of Technology
Rachel Mines	Langara College
Jennifer Read	Capilano University
Lauralynn Tomassi	George Brown College

Like all textbook writers, I am indebted to many people: colleagues, reviewers, and the outstanding team at Pearson Canada, whose editorial expertise, genial guidance, and promotional efforts have been vital to this project. Joel Gladstone and David Le Gallais, the acquisitions editors, provided helpful direction at the early stages of the project. A special note of appreciation is due Rachel Stuckey, the developmental editor who was so very responsive and efficient, even when she was travelling in Asia, shepherding this project from beginning to end. Thanks also to the copy editor, Susan Broadhurst, and proofreaders Garima Khosla and Rachel Stuckey again; they worked hard to make things consistent throughout the book; and to the Pearson marketing team, whose efforts will help this book reach its audience. I would like to express my appreciation to colleagues Greg Chan, Mark Cochrane, Elizabeth Gooding, Ranjini Mendis, and Jennifer Williams, for suggestions on aspects of this text, and to friends/colleagues Ross Gordon and Barry MacDonald for permission to use their writing.

Finally, a special salute to the students from Kwantlen Polytechnic University whose essays and excerpts appear in this edition for the first time: Filza Ahmar, Kyle Butt, Kimberly Florendo, Jessie Foley, Kiran Heer, Gurminder Khun Khun, Jamie Lockrey, Alexander Mcilwain, and Sheridan Taylor for their contributions to this text; thanks also to James Greenhalgh, whose sample research project proposal appears in the Instructor's Manual for this text.

Dr. Sue Ann Cairns

CHAPTER I

Writing: An Overview

Why write? Hasn't the Digital Revolution made ordinary writing unnecessary? Is the popularity of texting, online chat, email, and status updates making us, as some have feared, less and less literate?

Actually, the younger generation is writing more, not less, than previous generations, especially outside the classroom. Most people reading this have probably written some kind of message today—most likely a text or two at the very least. The ease of online communication offers people more chances than ever to play with written language. How, why, and when we write may be changing, but one thing is certain: The need to communicate with others through writing is more vital than ever.

Writing offers very real benefits to both writers and readers:

1. It allows us to share thoughts, information, and ideas with others.
2. It gives writers time to reflect on and research what they want to communicate, and then allows them to shape and reshape the material to their satisfaction.
3. It makes communication more precise and effective.
4. It provides a permanent record of thoughts, actions, and decisions.
5. It saves the reader time: We absorb information more swiftly when we read it than when we hear it.

Many people will expect you to write for them. Instructors ask you to write reports, summaries, reflective pieces, critiques, research papers, and essay exams. If you're looking for a job, you'll need to write resumés and cover letters. And once you're hired, writing will probably figure in your job duties. You might be asked to discuss the capabilities of new computer equipment, report on a conference you attended, or write a progress report on a client with whom you have worked. The ability to write will help you earn better grades, land the job you want, and advance in your career.

Writing also yields personal benefits. Sometimes people find that private writing, as in a journal, can help them sort out their emotions and achieve greater clarity about their decisions. At university, taking notes in class or writing summaries of lecture material can help you understand, remember, and integrate information. Informal, exploratory writing can help you uncover ideas you didn't know you had. In your personal life, writing can bring social and even financial benefits. You might have to write a tactful letter of apology to mend a broken relationship. Or you might need to defend a reimbursement claim you filed with your dental insurer or document a request to replace a faulty product. Being comfortable with these different writing challenges will help you to be more effective in the world.

Although we may write for ourselves in order to explore ideas, to make knowledge our own, or to communicate privately with our inner selves, we usually write in response to situations that involve other people. When we write, we adapt our tone, style, and message to the situation or environment in which we are writing. We follow different writing conventions when writing journal entries, texts to our friends, emails, status updates, policy briefs, memos, letters of reference, reflective critiques, and formal research-based essays. To write effectively in different social, business, or academic contexts, we need to be aware that readers have different expectations and values in different situations. If we are dashing off a text message to a friend, we might leave out commas and periods, partly to save time but also because using complete sentences might seem overly formal in that casual situation. However, before we submit an academic essay to be graded, we would be wise to check our punctuation very carefully.

PURPOSE IN WRITING

Whenever you write, a clear purpose should guide your efforts. If you don't know why you're writing, neither will your reader. Writing simply to fulfill an assignment doesn't qualify as a real writing purpose. Faced with a looming deadline for a research paper or report, you may tell yourself, "I'm doing this because I have to." However, an authentic purpose requires you to answer this question: What do I want this piece of writing to do for both my reader and me? As you might expect, purpose grows out of the writing situation.

Here are four *general writing purposes*. Remember that a single piece of writing may have more than one purpose.

To Inform   Presenting information is one of the most common writing purposes. The kayaking enthusiast who writes about how to manoeuvre a kayak plays the role of teacher, as does the researcher who summarizes the results of an investigation for co-workers. In school, you will often be asked to demonstrate your understanding of concepts in exams and papers so that instructors can gauge how well you have mastered the course material.

To Persuade   You probably have strong views on many issues, and these feelings may sometimes impel you to try to sway your reader's views. You might write a letter to a newspaper editor about the need for more bicycle lanes in your community. Or, alarmed by a sharp jump in provincial unemployment, you might write to your member of provincial Parliament or member of the legislative assembly and argue for a youth employment program.

To Express Yourself   Expressive writing includes personal essays, fiction, plays, and poetry as well as journals and diaries. Self-expression has a place in other kinds of writing, too. Almost everything you write offers you a chance to enjoy playing with words and to use fresh turns of phrase to enliven your prose.

To Entertain   Some writing merely entertains; other writing links entertainment with a more serious purpose. A lighthearted approach can help your reader absorb dull or difficult material. Satire allows you to expose the shortcomings of individuals, ideas, and institutions by poking fun at them. An intention to entertain can add flair to many kinds of writing.

Besides having one or more general purposes, each writing project has its own specific purpose. Consider the different papers you could write about Canada's refugee policy. You could explain how the process works, compare and contrast it with the U.S. policy, or argue why and how it should be reformed.

Having a specific purpose assists you at every stage of the writing process. It helps you define your audience; select the details, language, and approach that best suit the needs of the people who will read your writing. The following example from the Internet has a clear and specific purpose.

Marianne Halavage

Turn Down Your iPod Volume (Or Go Deaf)

1   I have had a Walkman, CD Walkman or iPod surgically attached to my ears via headphones since about the age of about five (anatomically strange. But true).

2   So chances are that I'm a case in point for the recent *LA Times* article. It says that one in every five teens has at least a slight hearing loss. Many experts think the culprit is the use of headphones to listen to portable music.

3   *LA Times* said:

Most teens think they are invulnerable and for most of them, the hearing loss is not readily perceptible so they are not aware of the damage. But the bottom line is, "Once there, the damage is irreversible," said Dr. Gary C. Curhan of Brigham and Women's Hospital.

4   Irreversible, you HEAR him. Gone. NEVER to return.

5   The idea of losing my hearing, even a little bit, terrifies me. Struggling to hear my music: my first love, my passion and my therapist; unable to hear my family and friends. I don't even want to think about it.

6   But for my hearing's sake in the future, I will. I'm 28, long out of teeniedom, so no doubt some damage has been done. But I will, from now on, keep the volume on my iPod at an ear-friendly level, as the experts advise:

"The message is, we've got to stop what we are doing," said Dr. Tommie Robinson Jr., president of the American Speech-Language-Hearing Assn. "We have to step back and say: OK, turn down the volume on iPods and earbuds and MP3 players. Wear ear protection at rock concerts or when you are exposed to loud noises for long periods of time," like when using a lawn mower.

7   Um, not so sure that many teens will take to wearing ear protection at concerts. They'd probably rather lose their hearing than have their pals laugh at them for looking a bit naff in it.

8   But, no ear protection now, hearing aid later . . .

9   Suddenly ear protection never sounded so good.

To draw readers' attention in the highly distractible Internet environment, Marianne Halavage announces her purpose boldly in her title. In the rest of the piece, the author alternates claims by authorities that listening to loud music may result in hearing loss with her own speculations and reactions. The last two single-sentence paragraphs present a stark choice and reinforce the essay's purpose.

Now examine this paragraph, which does *not* have a specific purpose:

> Imagine people so glued to their computers that they forget to eat or sleep and even miss work. It is like a strange version of a zombie movie. What could have eaten their brains? Video games can be addictive as players struggle to get to the next level. Still, this negative effect is exaggerated. But there are a number of qualities that make a video game player want to keep coming back to the game and any good game designer needs to know those qualities.

Is the essay for game addicts to get them to quit, is it meant to entertain, or is it serious recommendation for game designers? Once the writer decides on a purpose, the paragraph can be focused.

> The stereotype of gamers is that they are so glued to their computers that they forget to eat, sleep, or work. While this is a gross exaggeration, game designers do want their players to be hooked on their games. There are in fact many qualities that make video players want to keep returning to a favorite game, and any good game designer needs to know those qualities.

THE AUDIENCE FOR YOUR WRITING

Except for personal free writing or journaling, most writing we do has at least one purpose and is directed to an audience—a person or people you want to reach. Some real-world writing such as job and grant applications may be addressed to more than one audience, as people at different levels of the application process may be evaluating the merits of the application. Some writing also has more than one purpose. For example, an essay that argues for more strict enforcement of local fishing regulations might be directed to a general educated audience such as an English professor, but also could address fellow recreational fishers and perhaps a wider audience of the public.

Since the ultimate purpose of all writing is to have an effect on a reader or readers, purpose and audience are closely linked. Whether you are writing to inform *someone* of something, to persuade *someone* to believe or do something, to express feelings or insights to *someone*, or to entertain *someone*, you will write better if you know or can at least imagine a particular someone as the audience for your writing.

In any kind of writing you do, you can't assume that the reader is able to read your mind and understand what you really meant to say. It is important to recognize that writing, even texting, is very different from face-to-face conversations.

Face to Face	Writing
You can observe body language and vary what you are saying in response.	You don't get to see how people are responding.
You can respond to immediate questions.	It would be difficult for people to get questions to you.
There is little record of what you say.	Readers can reread your text.

In face-to-face conversations, you can observe your listeners' reactions and instantly respond to signs of confusion, boredom, or anger. You can clarify your meaning by offering examples. You can alter your tone, ask a question, or even change the subject. You can use gestures and facial expressions to emphasize your main points. When you write, however, the words on the page are all that carry your meaning. Once written or sent into cyberspace, your written work is on its own, even if the tone is wrong and the message is garbled or incomplete. Readers will not charitably fill in gaps in meaning and you will not be there to explain what you really meant. Of course, when you write to friends or others you know well, you may be able to anticipate how they might respond to what you say, but when you write for people you know only casually or not at all—such as employers, customers, or the general public—you need to assess your audience before starting to write. What do they already know? What do they need to know? How can you appeal to their interests? The more you understand your readers' assumptions, expectations, needs, and desires, the more you can tailor your writing to their needs and interests.

One way to assess your readers is to develop an audience profile. This profile emerges gradually as you answer the following questions:

1. What are the educational level, approximate age, and cultural outlook of the audience I want to reach?
2. Why will this audience read my writing? To gain information? Learn my views on a controversial issue? Enjoy my creative flair? Be entertained?
3. What attitudes, needs, and expectations do they have?
4. How are they likely to respond to what I say? Can I expect them to be neutral? Opposed? Friendly?
5. How much do they know about my topic? Do they need certain background information to follow my argument? (Your answer here will help you gauge whether you're saying too little or too much.)
6. What kind of language and tone will reach them most effectively?

Assignment instructions sometimes ask you to envision a reader who is intelligent but not an expert, someone receptive to new ideas but unwilling to put up with boring, rambling, or confusing material. Another assignment may ask you to write for a certain age group, especially one with particular interests. These differences affect what you say to each audience and how you say it.

Discourse Communities

In university, as at work, people often write as members of specific communities that have their own conventions, values, shared assumptions, and background knowledge. This shared understanding affects how they write. For example, professional and scholarly writing often begins with a section linking the content to previous research projects and articles that will be of interest to that specialized community of study. Environmental biologists with similar interests engaged in dialogue about policies related to climate change in the Arctic can safely assume that their audience is familiar with current research findings. In specialized discourse communities, custom often dictates what information must be included, what pattern of organization should be used, and what style the paper should follow. In formal academic writing, documentation of sources follows different conventions in the humanities (such as English) than in the social sciences (such as psychology).

In addition, different academic disciplines and discourse communities may emphasize different writing structures and forms. In a marketing class, you might be asked to do a case study; in a communications class, you might be asked for a technical report and PowerPoint presentation; and in an economics class, you might be asked to analyze an economic problem and explore a hypothetical solution to the problem. A chemistry instructor might expect you to write a lab report in such a way that someone with your background could repeat the experiment exactly as you did. In a literature class, an instructor will probably be more interested in your in-depth analysis or interpretation of a story than in an accurate recounting of the plot. So, throughout your studies you will discover that learning to write well means becoming familiar with the values and conventions of different discourse communities. To do this, you need to read carefully in a particular field, acquainting yourself with its current issues and concerns and learning how to write about them. Ask yourself these questions as you start reading in any professional area:

1. What are the major concerns and questions in this discourse community?
2. What seems to be common knowledge?
3. To what works do writers regularly refer?
4. How do those in the field go about answering questions?
5. What methods do they follow?
6. Which kinds of knowledge are acceptable? Which are not?
7. What values seem to guide the discourse community?
8. What kinds of information must writers include in papers?
9. How are different writing projects organized?
10. What conventions do writers follow?

Of course, we all belong to many different communities, but the more comfortably you can move from one discourse community to another, the more you will be in a position to exert influence in your world. At university, as you gain familiarity with the language, conventions, and expectations of different academic audiences such as psychology, philosophy, or marketing, you will find it gets easier to write papers for these different discourse communities.

EXERCISE *The three excerpts below deal with the same subject—antigens—but each explanation is geared to a different audience. Read the passages carefully; then answer the following questions:*

a. What audience does each author address? How do you know?

b. Identify ways in which each author appeals to a specific audience.

1. The human body is quick to recognize foreign chemicals that enter it. "Foes" must be attacked or otherwise got rid of. The most common of these foes are chemical materials from viruses, bacteria, and other microscopic organisms. Such chemicals, when recognized by the body, are called *antigens*. To combat them, the body produces its own chemicals, protein molecules called *antibodies*. Each kind of antigen causes the production of a specific kind of antibody. Antibodies appear in the body fluids such as blood and lymph and in the body's cells.

   L.D. Hamilton, "Antibodies and Antigens," *The New Book of Knowledge*

2. [An] *antigen* [is a] foreign substance that, when introduced into the body, is capable of inducing the formation of antibodies and of reacting specifically in a detectable manner with the induced antibodies. For each antigen there is a specific antibody, the physical and chemical structure of which is produced in response to the physical and chemical structure of the antigen. Antigens comprise virtually all proteins that are foreign to the host, including those contained in bacteria, viruses, protozoa, helminths, foods, snake venoms, egg white, serum components, red blood cells, and other cells and tissues of various species, including man. Polysaccharides and lipids may also act as antigens when coupled to proteins.

   "Antigen," *Encyclopaedia Britannica*

3. The substance which stimulates the body to produce antibodies is designated antigen (antibody stimulator). . . .

   Most complete antigens are protein molecules containing aromatic amino acids, and are large in molecular weight and size. . . . Other macromolecules, such as pure polysaccharides, polynucleotides, and lipids, may serve as complete antigens.

   However, certain other materials, incapable of stimulating antibody formation by themselves can, in association with a protein or other carrier, stimulate antibody formation and are the antigenic determinants. . . . Referred to as *incomplete antigens* or *haptens*, . . . they are able to react with antibodies. . . .

   However, before an antigen can stimulate the production of antibodies, it must be soluble in the body fluids, must reach certain tissues in an unaltered form, and must be, in general, foreign to the body tissues. Protein taken by mouth . . . reaches the tissues of the body as amino acids [and] no longer meets the requirements for antigenic behavior.

   Orville Wyss and Curtis Eklund, *Microorganisms and Man*

WRITING AND READING IN MULTIPLE GENRES

Our writing necessarily has certain constraints—that is, certain limitations within which we must work. The most obvious constraint in a university class is that our writing must fit within limitations such as the recommended length and focus of the assignment. Our writing must also consider the surrounding environment and situational climate. For example, if you were writing an argument about changing Canada's energy policies, you would need to demonstrate your awareness of the most recent debates and policies on this issue. You would also need to reflect on what the reader's expectations and habits of mind are likely to be.

In addition to considering your rhetorical situation, another constraint in writing is the conventions of the genre, or the communication form with which you are working. Readers who are skimming a website or social media update do not have the same expectations of formality and verbal precision as readers who are reading academic papers. Conventions around length, format, levels of formality, and documentation styles are not always spelled out, but they still influence the reader's expectations.

Whatever genre of communication you are working within, you will be more successful in attracting readers, listeners, or viewers if you keep your purpose and audience in mind as well as the expectations and assumptions the audience is likely to have.

New Media Genres

The processes and principles for effective writing apply to any genre, including new media, for which you may write. On campus and on the job, you will email, text message, tweet, blog, and write text for web pages. If you are texting your boss to let him know why you will be late to work, you know you have to be polite and clear about the reasons you are delayed. Clearly, "Dude, traffic jam" won't do. If you are creating a website that presents your restaurant, you are likely to write a description of the restaurant, revising the text several times to make it as effective as possible. If you are writing a blog on your favourite musical group, you may identify what has caused the band to be successful. Some of your university instructors may encourage you to use other media to complete assignments, and most careers will require you to work with a wide range of communication media. Consider the following points:

Email   While in school, you will email faculty and advisers. Email has the advantage of giving both you and your reader a written record of the exchange. If you ask a faculty member for permission to vary an assignment, it might be better to ask using an email, as a face-to-face conversation will soon fade from people's memories. An email provides you with a written record of your request and, hopefully, the permission you received.

Even though emails are usually informal, you should still be as clear as possible when writing them. The following email to a professor is clearly too informal and incomplete. It also establishes the wrong tone.

Hey Prof

Sorry missed class. Car trouble. I'll turn my assignment in Monday when I see u, OK.

Thanks tons.

Who is writing the message? Was the car trouble sufficient for an extension on the assignment? Is the person simply using the car trouble to stall for extra time? Why didn't she jump the car or get a ride to campus? The informal tone makes it seem that the student does not take the class or the professor seriously.

A more formal communication sensitive to both the situation and the audience would be received much better.

Professor von der Osten

I am very sorry I missed class today. I live an hour's drive from campus; unfortunately, this morning my car would not start because the distributor is broken. This is my first absence, and I notice from the syllabus we are allowed five unexcused absences. If you wish, I can bring in the estimate from the garage. I have emailed Tim Sullivan for notes from today's class.

Attached you will find a copy of the assignment due today, Friday, September 25. Thank you for allowing us to submit our work electronically in case of an emergency. I will also bring in a hard copy on Monday in case that would be helpful.

I look forward to seeing you in class on Monday.

Susan Miller

ENGL 150: 9:00 A.M.

This more complete email recognizes the relative formality of the situation, uses an appropriate form of address, provides a clearer explanation, indicates a serious attitude about the work in question, takes clear steps to meet the demands of the situation, and clearly identifies the writer in a way that recognizes the reader may have many classes and students.

Your email, like all writing, should be appropriate to the situation and the audience. An email in response to a formal situation or sent to an important audience should be appropriately serious and respectful. Since you and your readers are busy, try to write clearly and completely so that follow-up exchanges are unnecessary. Use a subject line that clearly identifies what the email is about. Avoid abbreviations, slang, emoticons, or other informal devices except with close friends. Be sure to clearly identify who you are, your position, and why you are writing; not all email addresses clearly identify the writer. Most important, remember that your email can be forwarded to other readers, so make sure your messages reflect well on you.

EXERCISE *Below are sample emails sent by students either to an instructor or an adviser. In each case, point out the problem with the email and explain how it could be written to be more effective for the audience.*

1. Here. (The only message on an email that submitted an attached paper)
2. Hey, sorry I won't be in class. Family trouble. (A student with excessive absences.)
3. Can I drop my chemistry class? The teacher sucks. (An email from an advisee to her adviser.)
4. I really don't understand this assignment. Can I do it differently. I have lots of ideas. (From a student beginning a class assignment.)

Text Messaging   Text messaging has some dangers. It is easy to respond too quickly to a question and to strike the wrong note. Because messages are necessarily short, they can often lack necessary information or context. Since people text from their phones, it is easy to be excessively informal or make careless mistakes in spelling or grammar. Even if you are in the habit of sending unedited text messages to your friends, you should be aware that sloppiness in grammar and spelling will create a negative impression in less casual situations where you might be judged.

As with all writing, you should know your audience. If you are writing to your BFF, you can LOL ☺. If you are writing to someone you don't know well or with whom you have a professional relationship, however, avoid abbreviations and symbols and be as clear and concise as you can while still providing any necessary reminders or cues the reader might need. The short text message "Go ahead with 3 copies to Halifax" will be confusing unless the context is clear. Even if something is on the top of your mind, the receiver of your text may be too busy or distracted to recall what you talked about last week, so you may need to be more complete. "Please send 3 copies each of the editions of FemSpec from 4.1 to 10.2 to our address at 245 Milsom St., Halifax, NS B3N 2C2."

Twitter   There are some fields, such as media studies or business, where you may be required to follow the Twitter feed for an industry or area. Twitter is simply a system for sending short messages of 140 characters maximum. Most tweets are not very consequential. However, if you are writing or responding to a tweet, the goal is to have an interesting message in very few words, and you will need to assume some context. Writing tweets, like writing telegrams in the previous century and even before, can provide practice in distilling words and characters to their absolute essence.

EXERCISE *Rewrite the following messages so that they would be suitable as a tweet.*

1. Katherine Briggs has done it again and in *River Marked* produced another compelling Mercy Thompson story with magic, mystery, and romance. She is on her honeymoon with husband, a werewolf, but their getaway doesn't last long as she ends up in a battle for her life with a river monster that threatens humankind. (Create a tweet for Katherine Briggs fans.)

2. This semester our online registration system will allow interested students to sign up for two semesters instead of just one, locking in their schedule for not just the fall but also the spring semester. Students are not required to schedule the second semester. If they do so, they will have to do an online drop and add process to change schedules. However, students who do not register for two semesters may find the classes they want closed for the spring semester. (Create a tweet that could go to students.)

Blogs The term *blog*, one that blends the two words *web* and *log*, is a web-based record of a writer's personal ideas, opinions, observations, interests, and experiences, often including hyperlinks to other sites. Many learning platforms allow you to blog so you can share your ideas with your class. Some teachers have students create blogs using an easy blog-based program such as WordPress or Blogger. Blogs allow you to share an enthusiasm, and you can incorporate images or video files to draw people's interest. Since bloggers have to compete with busy Internet traffic, you need to grab a reader's attention quickly and use vivid, economical language to say something interesting.

Web Pages Having your own website or web page, a kind of online portrait, can help you in your job hunt and also help you network with others who might have similar interests. More and more students applying for jobs provide an address for their web page on their resumé or even use a web page as a resumé. A web page allows you to post more information about your experience, show samples of your work, and shape the professional impression you want to make. Employers often look for the websites of applicants, not only to get more information about a job candidate, but also to find out whether the prospective employee has initiative and necessary skills. In many careers, writing for a web page can be a regular responsibility. A nurse might write for a hospital web page on standard post-operative care. An engineer may write technical information about the company's product line. To help you prepare for your web-based future, a number of university courses have students work on a web-based project.

Web pages need to be attractive, easy to use, and appealing to multiple audiences. Clarity and conciseness are vital; if you need to provide more in-depth information, you can insert hyperlinks to additional material. You also want to make it as easy as possible for the reader to understand and process information. When appropriate, use headings, subheadings, and bullet points to guide your reader's attention, as well as pictures or other visuals that illustrate your point and make your site stand out. Of course, as a public document that helps you establish an online presence, your web page should be free of grammatical and spelling mistakes.

Graphics and Text Many writers incorporate graphics, charts, and images along with text. As a student, you may have used graphics such as pictures, charts, or diagrams in your PowerPoint or other kinds of presentations; such graphics can sometimes be combined with text to enliven a piece of writing, to show patterns and relationships, and to add credibility. If you do use graphics in your communication, keep in mind a few key points:

1. The images need to clearly make the point or support the point.
2. The writing needs to be very clear and concise, with precise vocabulary.
3. The graphics need to fit the available space without overrunning the text.

EXERCISE *Find two examples of communication that you find interesting and that are from genres other than essays—for example, you could find a photograph; a YouTube clip; a letter, legal document, or business memo; a blog; an advertisement; a poem; or a website. Bring these two examples to class and note three strategies the author or artist uses to draw in the reader, viewer, or listener. Reflect on how these strategies to are similar or different from strategies that you or others use in essay writing.*

Level of Diction

How does a writer choose the right level of diction, or word choice, for a particular audience, genre, and situation? It depends on the writer's purpose as well as the expectations and conventions in the discourse community the writer is addressing. Think about a safety engineer who investigates a serious industrial accident on which she must write two reports: one for the safety director of the company, who represents a technical audience, and another for the local newspaper, which represents a general audience. Although the two accounts will deal with the same matter, the first case calls for more specialized, formal language while the second case would require more ordinary, relaxed prose. In both cases, the language needs to reflect the background of the audience. As you write, always choose language that is suited to your audience and purpose.

Edited standard English follows the familiar grammatical rules maintained in most formal and academic writing. Generally, everything you write for university courses or on the job should be in edited standard English. *Nonstandard English* refers to any version of the language that deviates from these rules, as illustrated in the following example from Dionne Brand's short story "Blossom: Priestess of Oya, Goddess of Winds, Storms and Waterfalls":

> This was Blossom's most successful endeavour since coming to Canada. Every once in a while, under she breath, she curse the day she come to Toronto from Oropuche, Trinidad. But nothing, not even snarky white people could keep Blossom under. When she first come it was to babysit some snot-nosed children on Oriole Parkway. She did meet a man, in a club on Henry Street in Port-of-Spain, who promise she to take care of she, if she ever was in Toronto. When Blossom reach, the man disappear and through the one other person she know in Toronto she get the work on Oriole.

As this example shows, nonstandard English does have a place in writing, especially in narratives. Fiction writers use it to narrate the talk of characters who, if real, would speak that way; journalists use it to report eyewitness reactions to accidents and crimes; and people who compile oral histories use it to record the recollections of people they interview.

Edited standard English includes four levels of usage: formal, informal, formal–informal, and technical. Another commonly recognized category is colloquial language and slang.

Formal Level   The formal level, which is dignified and serious, suits a more public discourse and is commonly used on official occasions. Its vocabulary is marked by many abstract and multisyllabic words but no slang or contractions. Long sentences and deliber-ately varied sentence patterns help give it a strong, rhythmic flow. The more formal cadence of these sentences comes, in part, from relatively complex parallel or balanced structures. Overall, formal prose impresses the reader as authoritative, stately, and graceful.

The following excerpt from the introduction to the third edition of Susanna Moodie's *Roughing It in the Bush* illustrates the formal level:

> In most instances, emigration is a matter of necessity, not of choice; and this is more espe-cially true of the emigration of persons of respectable connections, or of any station or position in the world. Few educated persons, accustomed to the refinements and luxuries of European society, ever willingly relinquish those advantages, and place themselves beyond the protective influence of the wise and revered institutions of their native land, without the pressure of some urgent cause. Emigration may, indeed, generally be regarded as an act of severe duty, performed at the expense of personal enjoyment, and accompanied by the sacrifice of those local attach-ments which stamp the scenes amid which our childhood grew, in imperishable characters upon the heart. Nor is it until adversity has pressed sorely upon the proud and wounded spirit of the well-educated sons and daughters of old but impoverished families, that they gird up the loins of the mind, and arm themselves with fortitude to meet and dare the heart-breaking conflict.

In this address to readers of the third edition of her journals recounting expatriate life in Canada during the nineteenth century, Moodie formally expresses her sense that "emigration is a matter of necessity, not of choice." This initial parallelism is characteristic of the contrast throughout the passage as Moodie notes the dire circumstances of life in the colony, removed from "the protective influence of the wise and revered institutions" of Europe. All of the sentences use complex causal relationships and modification. The sense that the European emigrant performs a noble task in an ignoble place is reinforced through elevated diction—longer words such as *educated, protective, revered, sacrifice, imperishable, impoverished,* and *fortitude,* along with shorter abstract words like *duty, proud, spirit,* and *mind.* The carefully controlled language and syntax lend an earnest tone to this passage directed toward a largely European audience.

Informal Level   Informal writing resembles orderly, intelligent conversation. Earmarked by relatively ordinary words, loose sentences (sentences in which the main clause comes at the beginning), shorter, less varied sentence structures than formal prose, informal writing may include contractions or even slang, and it is more likely than formal writing to use the pronouns *I, me, my, you,* and *yours.* Casual and familiar rather than dignified and rhythmic, informal writing does not usually call attention to itself. Nevertheless, the language is precise and effective. Consider the following example, taken from a newsletter addressed to parents:

Lead By Example

> It is not through our singular effort that we learn to become optimistic, but through our relationships with others. Children of all ages are like sponges, listening to what you say and watching what you do. Tune into the subtle everyday messages you give your child about how you manage setbacks. When you are running late, and have become flustered and even self-critical, reframe your thinking out loud so that your child can hear and learn from your own process. Emphasize that you are trying to change by saying something like, "It looks like I misjudged the timing for today and we'll be arriving late. I'm disappointed

in myself but I will do my best to make up time. I also just realized that we won't be as late as last time and that I have improved on the last time I made us late by 20 minutes."

When we face our own setbacks and admit mistakes, children will follow our lead. When we talk openly about our own struggles with motivation—especially with the tasks we dislike—children will learn that yes, life is sometimes hard and we still work to fulfill our responsibilities by taking charge of our motivation. Be real. Let your kids know that you too are always learning, maybe saying something like, "I know I messed up today. I am doing my best to fix this problem and believe that I can get better. I would be grateful if you to hang in there with me while I'm on this learning curve."

Barry MacDonald, "Help Your Son Think Positively"

Unlike the Moodie excerpt, this excerpt has relatively uncomplicated sentences. The passage also includes several contractions, as well as casual phrases and colloquial expressions ("tune in," "running late," "messed up," "learning curve"). Most of the words are short and none would be out of place in an ordinary conversation.

Formal–Informal Level   As life has become less formal, informal diction has become increasingly widespread. Today, many articles and books, even ones on relatively serious topics, mix informal and formal elements. Here is an example:

We can credit scientists with creating the wonder of the whole new cyber world out there, but as a society we haven't begun to assess its unintended consequences. Thomas L. Friedman in his latest book, *The World Is Flat*, does a brilliant job of telling us what we now have the capabilities to do—and it's scary. What he can't tell us is what all this outsourcing, in-sourcing, instant worldwide communication and so on is going to mean for societies and members of those societies. Thanks to scientific development we now have a communications system that is brilliant but utterly out of control in the sense that nothing but one's innermost thoughts (and who knows about them one day) is private any more. Everywhere we go we're on "Candid Camera." We have no secrets.

Rafe Mair, *Hard Talk*

Although a few expressions in this excerpt—*unintended consequences, capabilities, scientific development*—echo formal diction, most of the words have an informal ring and three phrases—*it's scary, out of control*, and w*e're on "Candid Camera"*—skirt the edges of slang.

Technical Level   A specialist writing for others in the same field, or for sophisticated nonspecialists, writes on the technical level, a cousin to the formal level. Technical language uses specialized words that may be unfamiliar to a general audience. Its sentences tend to be long and complex, but unlike formal diction, the writing doesn't lean toward periodic sentences, parallelism, and balance. Read this example from the field of entomology, the study of insects:

The light organs of fireflies are complex structures, and recent studies using the electron microscope show them to be even more complex than once supposed. Each is composed of three layers: an outer "window," simply a transparent portion of the body wall; the light organ proper; and an inner layer of opaque, whitish cells filled with granules of uric acid, the so-called "reflector." The light organ proper contains large, slablike light cells . . . filled with large granules and much smaller, dark granules, the latter tending to be concentrated around the numerous air tubes and nerves penetrating the light organ. These smaller granules were once assumed by some persons to be luminous bacteria, but we now know that they are mitochondria, the source of ATP [adenosine triphosphate] and therefore of the energy of light production. The much larger granules that fill most of the light cells are still of unknown function.

Howard Ensign Evans, *Life on a Little-Known Planet*

Note the specialized vocabulary—*granules, uric acid, mitochondria,* and *adenosine trihosphate*—as well as the length and complexity of the five sentences. Note also how the writer gives very precise descriptions and definitions in this technical piece. Every field has *jargon,* specialized terms or inside talk that provides a convenient shorthand for communication among its members. For example, for an audience of biologists, you may write that two organisms have a *symbiotic relationship,* meaning that they are "mutually beneficial"; for psychology majors, you might use *catalepsy* instead of "a temporary loss of consciousness and feeling, often accompanied by muscular rigidity." As a general rule, use technical terms only if you can be fairly certain that your audience will know their meanings. If you use technical words when writing for a general audience, define them the first time they appear.

Colloquial Language and Slang   *Colloquial* originally meant "the language of ordinary conversation between people of a particular region." According to the *Canadian Oxford Dictionary, slang* is defined as "words, phrases, and uses that are regarded as very informal and are often restricted to special contexts." These two categories blend into each other, and even authorities sometimes disagree on whether to label a term *colloquial* or *slang.* The word *bender*—meaning an extended drinking spree—seems to fall firmly in the colloquial camp, while the word *hype*—meaning excessive and exaggerated publicity—could be considered either colloquial or slang. If someone mentions getting "busted" for doing something forbidden, that person is using slang. Sometimes words such as *guy* and *kid* start off as slang but are used for so long that they become colloquial.

While colloquial and slang terms may serve a useful purpose in informal narrative writing by creating a sense of authenticity or increasing audience appeal, their use is almost never appropriate in more formal academic and professional writing.

EXERCISE   *Identify the level of diction in each of the following passages. Support your answers with examples from the passages. Point out slang or colloquial expressions.*

1. My brother excelled at any physical activity, but his best sport was hockey. From the time he was a little kid, people called him a natural. When he joined his first real team, he went to practise in his jeans with nothing to protect his lower legs. The other players, boys from around our neighbourhood, had hockey pants and shin pads. He asked Mom to buy a set of pads for him, she said we couldn't afford it. She flushed and fidgeted when the coach of the team knocked on our door and spoke to her in the kitchen about her son's talents and the likelihood of injuries if he wasn't properly equipped. My brother never knew how she got the money out of our father or what it cost her, but before his next game at the rink he strapped shin pads over his jeans.

Lorna Crozier, *Small Beneath the Sky*

2. I have just spent two days with Edward T. Hall, an anthropologist, watching thousands of my fellow New Yorkers short-circuiting themselves into hot little twitching death balls with jolts of their own adrenalin. Dr. Hall says it is overcrowding that does it. Overcrowding gets the adrenalin going, and the adrenalin gets them queer, autistic,

> sadistic, barren, batty, sloppy, hot-in-the-pants, charred-in-the-flankers, leering, puling, numb—the usual in New York, in other words, and God knows where else. Dr. Hall has the theory that overcrowding has already thrown New York into a state of behavioral sink. Behavioral sink is a term from ethology, which is the study of how animals relate to their environment. Among animals, the sink winds up with a "population collapse" or "massive die-off." O rotten Gotham.
>
> Tom Wolfe, *The Pump House Gang*

Whether you choose a relatively formal or casual level of diction depends on your audience, purpose, and situation. Moreover, as you shape your paper, the writing must please you as well as your audience—it must satisfy your sense of what good writing is and what the writing task requires.

THE QUALITIES OF GOOD WRITING

Good writing is essential if you want your ideas to be taken seriously. Just as you would have trouble listening to an argument of a speaker who looked scruffy and was wearing a ragged shirt inside out, most readers dismiss out of hand writing that is disorganized, poorly worded, or marred by errors in grammar and spelling. In a world where most people are drowning in a flood of information, few have the time or inclination to hunt through bad writing for quality ideas. Unclear, poorly worded cover letters get tossed in the wastebasket, as do other kinds of applications that are written sloppily.

Fresh Thinking   You don't have to astound your readers with something never before discussed in print. Genuinely unique ideas and information are rare, but you can bring your own special slant or perspective to what you are writing about and, depending on the situation, perhaps freshen your writing by exploring personal insights and perceptions. But be careful not to strain too desperately for originality or your writing will seem contrived.

Sense of Style   Whatever context you are writing in, once you have figured out what you want to say, say it as clearly as you can. Sometimes students think that vague, mysterious writing intrigues readers; however, most readers do not want to play guessing games. Write to communicate, not to impress. Good writing is clear, with a style appropriate for the particular situation, audience, and purpose. It may be quite appropriate to write without capital letters or apostrophes in an online chat room, but not in an academic essay. In technical, scientific, or legal documents, readers expect a neutral tone. If you are writing a narrative essay or persuasive argument, well-chosen verbs and nouns and vivid examples or metaphors can help to draw your reader in. Your style should be suited to the writing situation, whether informal or formal.

Effective Organization   While some personal writing and online writing may not have a linear structure, readers expect formal writing to have a beginning, a middle, and an end—that is, an introduction, a body, and a conclusion. The introduction sparks interest and acquaints the reader with what is to come. The body delivers the main message and exhibits a clear connection between ideas so that the reader can easily follow your thoughts. The conclusion should not suddenly drop the reader off a cliff, but end in such a way that the reader feels satisfied. Overall, your paper should follow a pattern that is suited to its content.

WRITING AND ETHICS

How do you build trust in your readers? Like you, readers expect that what they read contains dependable information. If you are writing a report, a brief or abstract, or a review or recommendation, you do not want to skew your conclusions by failing to mention important evidence that contradicts your conclusions. In research writing, you establish credibility when you give credit to authorities and clarify the sources of your information. Few readers would bother with a carelessly presented or even deliberately deceptive piece of information. As a writer, you earn the trust of your reader through accuracy, fairness, and honesty.

Think for a minute about how you would react in the following situation. You decide to vacation at a Canadian country resort after reading a brochure that describes its white-sand beach, scenic trails, fine dining, and peaceful atmosphere. When you arrive, you find the beach overgrown with weeds, the trails littered, and the view unappealing. The gourmet restaurant is a greasy-spoon cafeteria. Worse, whenever you go outside, swarms of vicious blackflies attack you. Wouldn't you feel cheated? In addition, think how you'd feel if you decided to attend a university because of its distinguished faculty members, only to discover on arrival that they rarely teach on campus. The university uses the scholars' reputations to attract students, even though these scholars are usually unavailable. Hasn't the university done something unethical?

Ethical writing, which is accurate, fair, and honest, reflects the integrity of the writer.

The Principles of Ethical Writing

Accuracy Writing that is perceived as truthful should *be* truthful. Granted, a writer may use humorous exaggeration to make us laugh, and some sales pitches may stretch the truth a bit to entice buyers ("Try Nu-Glo toothpaste and add sparkle to your life"). Most readers recognize and discount such embellishments as harmless. However, deliberate distortions and falsehoods may hurt not only the reader but also the writer. If you were angered by misrepresentations in the vacation brochure, you would likely warn your friends against the resort; you might even take legal action.

No Deliberate Omissions To be perceived as truthful, a document should tell the whole truth, omitting nothing the reader needs to know in order to make an informed decision. The text should not be deliberately incomplete so as to mislead. Suppose that a university's recruitment brochure stresses that 97 percent of its students get jobs upon graduation, but omits the fact that only 55 percent of these jobs are in the graduates' chosen field of study. Certainly, these brochures are deceptive, perhaps attracting students who would otherwise choose schools with better placement records.

Clarity Writing should be clear to the reader. All of us know the frustration of trying to read an important legal document that is impossible to comprehend. Moreover, a person who writes instructions so unclear that they result in costly or harmful mistakes is partially (and often legally) responsible for the consequences. An annual report that deliberately obscures information about its yearly losses is not fair to potential investors.

Honest Representation   Writing should not present itself as something different from what it is. It would be unethical for a drug company to prepare an advertisement in the form of an unbiased news story.

No Intentional Harm   Writing should not be intended to harm the reader. Certainly, it is fair to point out the advantages of a product or service that readers might not need. However, think about how unethical it would be for a writer to encourage readers to follow a diet that the writer knows is not only ineffective but also harmful. Think about the harm a writer might cause by deliberately attempting to persuade readers to try crack cocaine.

Good writing is also ethical writing. A good test of the ethics of your writing is to determine how you would react after you had read your own work and acted on the basis of the information. Would you feel comfortable with it, or would you feel cheated, manipulated, belittled, or deceived? By practising the principles of ethical writing, you show respect to your readers and to yourself.

Academic Honesty and Avoiding Plagiarism

Often our writing draws on the work of others. After we get information from an article, we might summarize what the authors have to say, and perhaps paraphrase their wording or use quotations that help to reinforce a point. In any kind of writing you do, academic honesty is essential. If you have taken material from sources (including the Internet) without using the proper documentation, even if you have recast some of it in your own words, you must give credit to the original author. Sometimes high school students get into the habit of cutting and pasting information from an essay, however, if you use another writer's language, even in part, without using quotation marks and giving credit to the original source, you are plagiarizing. Sometimes students think that it is adequate to cite sources at the end of a paragraph only, but each sentence or partial sentence that comes from someone else must be clearly credited and separated from your own ideas. Most faculty members check carefully for plagiarism and many automatically fail a paper for academic dishonesty. Some even give the student an F for the entire course. Before using information from sources, review the discussion of documentation that appears in Chapters 16 to 17.

Why is academic honesty an important issue?

1. Other people have worked hard to develop ideas, do research, and write effectively. They deserve credit for their work when someone else uses it. The authors of this text, for example, pay fees to use the essays of others. You would probably not like it if others used material from your papers without giving you credit.
2. Proper documentation shows that you have done your homework and strengthens your work, since the source, if recognized, can add credibility to your claims.

3. Taking some material from a source and using it in your paper without documentation is a form of cheating, since you are falsely presenting another writer's work as your own.

4. You are in the process of being trained to do professional work. Professionals need to be ethical. You wouldn't want someone to take credit for the computer program you wrote, charge you for repairs they didn't make, or write you a ticket for a traffic violation you didn't commit. Journalists have been fired, politicians have lost elections, and companies have been sued because they have been involved in plagiarism.

How can you avoid plagiarism and the failing grade that often comes with it?

1. Be committed to honesty and accuracy. You should make certain that your writing is your own work.

2. If an assignment does not ask you to use sources but you believe that information from sources would be useful, talk to your instructor. There may be a reason that you are not asked to use sources. If sources are acceptable, you may be asked to follow a specific procedure for that assignment, such as turning in copies of your sources.

3. Take very careful notes as you read and research a topic. Be meticulous in documenting your sources, even if you are paraphrasing the material in your own words. Be careful when quoting and documenting anything, even a phrase, that comes from another writer.

4. Carefully double-check to ensure that all content in your text is your own and that you document any source you have used at all.

5. Ensure that you use quotation marks if you have used another writer's words, even only a brief phrase.

6. Although you do not have to document something that is widely known and found in a variety of sources, be careful when you decide about what counts as common knowledge. No one is expected to document what a reasonably educated person would know: that water consists of H_2O or that the Dominion of Canada was formed on July 1, 1867. However, if you didn't know it before you read the source or if you have to have your notes open as you write, you probably should not count it as common knowledge and should document the information.

You must make a conscious effort to avoid plagiarism. Ignorance and carelessness are rarely accepted as an excuse by professors trying hard to make certain that students are graded fairly and that no one gets credit for work that is not their own. If you follow the guidelines in this text and ask your teacher for help when you are confused, you will easily avoid the embarrassment and the often dire consequences of being accused of plagiarism.

If you are struggling with citation formats and have not yet studied the documentation chapters, you can get initial help with formatting entries from Citation Machine at www.citationmachine.net. This website assists users with the styles of documentation most commonly used in university: MLA and APA (discussed in Chapters 16 to 17) and even Chicago style, which is often used in classes such as history. Be aware, though, that just as spell-check can help you find some spelling errors, it is not infallible, and neither is a website such as this one. You still need to do your own checking and refining, as everything you hand in bears your signature of responsibility.

A First Look at Your Writing

Know your discourse community.

- What are shared questions?
- What counts as knowledge?
- What conventions do they follow?

Know your purpose.

- Are you going to inform, persuade, express yourself, entertain?
- What specific purpose do you want to accomplish?

Know your audience.

- What do they already know?
- Why will they read my writing?
- How are they likely to respond?
- How can I best reach them?

Apply principles of good writing.

- Write with fresh thinking that offers your own slant.
- Use a clear style in your own voice.
- Use effective organization.

Make certain your writing is ethical!

- Is your writing truthful, unslanted, complete, clear, helpful rather than harmful?
- Is your writing your own? Have you carefully avoided plagiarism?

CHAPTER 2
Strategies for Active Reading

Good writing requires good reading. You get ideas, information, a feel for language, and ideas for writing from what you read. As a writer, you are a part of a knowledge community that learns from reading and responds to the texts of others. Careful reading involves bringing your knowledge and experience to bear on a piece of writing in order to understand and assess its ideas. For example, the experience of going to a farmers' market or growing a garden can help you connect with and comprehend an article that explores the politics of food sustainability. As you read, take the time to reflect on each point that's made, consider how the various parts fit together, and anticipate the direction the writing will take. Active reading requires attention. Using specific reading strategies can help you take in more of what you read.

ORIENTING YOUR READING

Just as you write differently for different purposes, you also read in different ways, depending on whether you are reading for entertainment or for more thorough understanding. When reading for pleasure, you can relax and proceed at your own pace, slowing down to savour a section you especially enjoy, speeding up when you encounter less interesting material, and breaking off when you wish. However, reading for academic purposes requires more focused attention. Sometimes you read specifically for material or arguments that you can use in your own writing. Below are some useful questions to guide your reading:

- **Why am I reading this material?** Is it for a project you are working on? Is it for a class or an exam? Is it to understand material more thoroughly?

- **How well do I need to know the material in the article?** Can you look back to the article as a reference? Is there only one main point you need to know? Are you going to be tested on the material in depth?

- **Is some material in the article more important to me than other material?** Sometimes in doing research, you may be looking for a specific bit of information that is located in one paragraph of a long article. If so, you can skim for the information. In most documents you read, some sections are more important than others. At times you can often read to get the main points of the article and slide over the details. Other times, of course, you need to understand the whole piece in depth.

- **What will I do with the information in the article?** If you are looking for ideas for your own writing, you might read quickly. If you are responsible for writing a critique of the article, you need to read carefully and critically.

- **What kind of reading does the material suggest?** The significance, difficulty, and nature of the writing can all influence how you read. You may read an easy, humorous narrative quickly, but you may need to slow down when you read an argument for or against an important issue, paying careful attention to the main points put forward, perhaps even asking questions about them.

EXERCISE

Reading Activity

Look briefly at "Teen Angst, RIP" on pages 25–26. Identify three purposes you could have for reading this essay. Identify how these purposes would affect how you would read the essay and what you would look for in the essay.

A FIRST READING

When going on a trip or an outing, you don't just jump in your car and take off. Usually you take some time to think about where you want to go. Sometimes you even have to check your route. The same is true of active reading. Because of the challenging nature of most university-level reading assignments, you should plan on more than one reading. The goal of a good first reading is to orient yourself to the material.

Orient Yourself to the Background of the Essay   Before you begin, examine information accompanying the essay for clues about the essay's relevance. Scan the accompanying biographical sketch (if available) to determine the writer's expertise and biases on the topic. Read any notes by the author or editor about the process of researching or writing this essay. For professional essays, look for an abstract that provides a brief summary of the article. At this point, you may want to judge the credibility of the source, a topic discussed in Chapter 14.

Use the Title as a Clue   Most titles identify the topic and often the author's viewpoint as well. So, a title such as "Ten Reasons Why New Nuclear Was a Mistake—Even Before Fukushima" (in Part Three's "Reader") reveals that the essay will argue against the use of nuclear power.

Skim to Get the Gist of the Article   Sometimes you can just read the introductory and concluding paragraphs and the topic sentences (often the first or last sentences of paragraphs) to get the overall meaning of the article. Other times you will need to read the whole essay quickly. In your first reading, you can skim the more difficult sections without trying to understand them fully. Simply try to get an idea of the essay's main thrust, the key ideas that support it, and the ways in which they are organized.

Make Connections   Once you have skimmed the essay, think about what you have learned and then express it in your own words. Until you can state its essence in your own words, you don't really understand what you've read, and you will be unlikely to remember it. Then make connections between the ideas. Go back and underline what you consider to be the thesis statement (a statement of the main point of the essay) or, if one is not included, try to formulate one in your own words. Reflect on what you already know or think about the topic. You will read more effectively if you can connect what you read to your own knowledge and interests. Finally, jot down questions that the first reading raises in your mind.

EXERCISE

Reading Activities

1. Using the author biography statement at the beginning of the article "Teen Angst, RIP" (page 25), identify what you can about the author's background, interests, and biases.

2. Before reading, write what you expect to be the essay's main idea based on its title.

3. After skimming the essay, identify the main points of the essay and the thesis. Jot down at least two questions you have at the end of your first quick reading.

A SECOND READING

If you find the material difficult or you need to absorb information thoroughly, a second or even third reading may be necessary. On the second reading, take more time so that you can really absorb the writer's ideas.

Read Carefully and Actively   Read at a pace suitable to the material. Underline significant topic sentences as well as other key sentences and ideas or facts that you find important, but keep in mind that underlining or highlighting doesn't ensure comprehension. Restating the ideas in your own words is more effective. Depending on your purposes, you may also want to write down the main points in your own words or jot down ideas in the margins. As you proceed, examine the supporting sentences to see how well they back up the main idea. Keep an eye out for how the essay fits together.

Consider Reading as a Kind of Conversation with the Text

Develop the habit of asking questions about facts, examples, logic, and ideas—practically anything in the essay. Jot down your queries and their answers in the margins. (On pages 25–26, you can see how a student interacted with Adam Sternbergh's essay "Teen Angst, RIP.") Careful readers anticipate questions and find answers later in the essay. Moreover, because you have posed the questions yourself, you are more likely to see the connections in the text. If the author hasn't answered your questions anywhere in the essay, you may have discovered some weaknesses in the writing and research.

Master Unfamiliar Words

Although we typically infer the meaning of words by reading them in context, sliding over unfamiliar words can sometimes hinder your grasp of the material. When you are reading very thoroughly and encounter a new word, circle it, use context to help gauge its meaning, check the dictionary for the exact meaning, and then record the meaning in the margins or some other convenient place. If the writing is peppered with words you don't know, you may have to read the whole piece to figure out its general drift, then look up key words, and finally reread the material. When you read academic writing, you may need to learn some unfamiliar vocabulary in order to understand the professional or disciplinary discourse.

Take Conscious Steps to Understand Difficult Material

When the ideas of a single section prove difficult, write down the points of those sections you do understand. Then experiment by stating in your own words different interpretations of the problem section to see which one best fits the writing as a whole.

Sometimes, large sections or entire texts are extremely difficult to understand. Use the following strategies to improve your comprehension:

- State the ideas that are easier for you to understand and use them to unlock more difficult (but not unintelligible) meanings in related sections. Save the most difficult sections until last. However, don't assume that you have to understand everything completely, as some particularly dense works may challenge even highly skilled readers.
- Discuss the essay with others who are reading it.
- Read simpler background material on the topic if it is unfamiliar or difficult to understand.
- Ask your instructor for help. Your instructor may help you find background material that will make the selection easier to understand.

Pull the Entire Essay Together

Whenever you finish a major section of a lengthy essay, express your sense of what it means. Depending on your learning preferences, you might choose to translate your understanding into words, pictures, charts, or diagrams. Say it out loud or write it down. If you have difficulty seeing connections between the ideas, try representing them visually. You might make an outline that states the main points followed by subpoints (see pages 47–49 in Chapter 3 for ways to outline). For a comparison essay, you might create a table with the main points of the comparison side by side. In addition, you can draw a diagram, list the steps of a process, or write out main facts.

You can also use different strategies to strengthen your grasp of any material you may need to remember for a long time. Try restating the main points a couple of days after the second reading to test your retention. Sometimes, it is helpful to explain the material to a sympathetic listener; then, if anything has become hazy or slipped your mind, reread the appropriate sections. If you really must know the material, try making up your own test and giving it to yourself. Writing in your own words about what an essay meant can give you ideas for an essay that develops the reading, contradicts it, or takes a part of it and launches in a new direction. To retain information and make sense of it, some people who find it easier to talk than to write might experiment with speech-to-text apps that they have installed on their tablet or smartphone.

Adam Sternbergh

emotional suffering and fear that life is pointless

Angst is a word often associated with teens. So angst is dead?

rest in peace

Teen Angst, RIP

He writes for urban North American magazines. He is clearly writing from an adult perspective, removed from adolescence but still close enough to remember it clearly.

Adam Sternbergh, an author and journalist who has written a number of articles on popular culture and the entertainment industry, is the co-founder of Fametracker.com, which satirizes celebrity culture. He writes for New York magazine and also has a weekly column in the National Post. He has written several articles for The Walrus, from which this article is taken.

1   Are you happy? Are you a teenager? These two questions might seem contradictory, even oxymoronic. For, as we all know, teenagers aren't happy. They're sullen, moody, impulsive, dramatic, pimply, gangly, and wracked with angst. They mope, wear black, write bad poetry, and doodle dark thoughts on their binders.

Is he making fun of depressed teens?

2   How do we explain, then, that when Statistics Canada set out to measure the happiness of Canadians, it found that teenagers (aged twelve to nineteen) are not only very happy but are, in fact, the happiest people in the country? It's true. Every year since 2002, the Canadian Community Health Survey has asked Canadians to rank their life satisfaction, among other things, and every year teens overwhelmingly claim to be either satisfied or very satisfied with their lives. In 2008, the exact figure was a shocking 94 percent; 2009 results will be published this June.

How did StatsCan find these teens? Are they representative? Are the findings similar in the U.S. or is there something about Canadian culture that makes teens happier?

3   As a former teenager myself, I have to ask: what is going on here? Personally, I don't remember being happy at that age; I remember listening to the Smiths. I remember that, in John Hughes's *Breakfast Club* taxonomy of teens, he called Anthony Michael Hall the Brain, which seemed like an act of mercy to me because it meant I didn't have to self-identify with someone called the Dweeb. (Because, let's face it, I was not the Athlete, the Criminal, or the Princess. Maybe the Basket Case, though she had terrible dandruff.) I remember various people back then, from my school guidance counsellor to

Bryan Adams, trying to convince me that these were the best years of my life. And I remember thinking, "If that's true, then I don't have much to look forward to."

So he took pleasure in misery and resented teens who acted happy?

4   Not only was I an unhappy teen, but I've often retrospectively revelled in that unhappiness, treasuring it as a kind of emotional forge. To me, way back when, the teenage world was a tug-of-war between the Morrissey "sixteen, clumsy, and shy" types on one side and the Bryan Adams "18 'Til I Die" types on the other. With their swaggering optimism, confounding confidence, and obediently well-styled hair, the latter clearly weren't to be trusted. So it's with some dismay that I discover that, apparently, 9.4 out of every ten Canadian teenagers are people who, in high school, I would have considered the enemy.

5   On closer analysis, the statistics make more sense. For starters, Canadians as a whole are exceptionally satisfied (with a life satisfaction rate of 91 percent, as of 2009). Also, StatsCan argues that the two factors most likely to erode life satisfaction are health issues, and life stress, i.e., "managing multiple roles associated with career and family responsibilities." These are two areas, not coincidentally, that teens aren't particularly worried about. Teens may be likely to have a million little stresses (OMG I can't BELIEVE that just HAPPENED txt me back!!) but neither of the two really big ones.

Two big ones? Does he mean death and financial worries? Don't teens have these worries at times — and aren't they even less equipped to deal with them?

6   Even so, it's pretty clear that the best-years-of-your-lifers are winning the tug-of-war. Perhaps it's fitting that Hughes, the patron saint of teenage melodrama, died last year. A phenomenon like *Twilight* suggests that there's still a market for tales of brooding boys and heartsick girls, but it also reinforces the fact that teens themselves have become a formidable market. What's to be glum about when the entire entertainment industry is falling over itself to service your desires?

So being able to program your parents' DVD player edges up your happiness quotient?

7   Not to mention that as a teen today you're part of the first generation in human history that's more adept with technology than its elders are. (I can't imagine that 200 years ago there were many fifteen-year-olds explaining to their dads how to work a plow.) Today's parents, for their part, tend to be much more capable, or at least more fun, caregivers than the generation of parents who came before them. If all of that helps alleviate some clichéd teenage misery, who am I to stand in opposition?

8   Yet looking over this wasteland of teenage happiness, I'd like to say a word in favour of old-fashioned angst. Just as the child is the father of the man, I'd argue that the teen is the father (or the mother) of the grown-up and that the process of becoming a grown-up should involve at least a little, you know, growth. Which in turn should probably involve some unhappiness. As an adult, I ascertained pretty quickly that I could never truly be friends with anyone who claimed to love and miss their high school years, because it reliably meant that, on some level, he or she was still stuck there. It's no doubt fun, and perhaps even healthy, to want to be eighteen till you die when you're, say, eighteen. It's another thing to be that same guy at forty, no matter how satisfied (or very satisfied) he imagines himself to be.

MASTERING READING PROBLEMS

Master the Problems That Interfere with Reading   If your environment is too noisy, if you are too tired, or if you have something on your mind, you may have difficulty reading. Do your reading at the time of day when you are most alert. Be sure you are in a well-lit environment that allows you to concentrate. Try to be rested and comfortable.

If you get tired, take a break, go for a short walk, or have a drink of water and a nutritious snack. If something is bothering you, try to resolve the distraction or put it out of your mind. To avoid boredom, read more actively by asking questions or relating the topic to your interests.

If you have extensive problems with your course reading, ask for help. Most universities offer courses in reading and provide tutors and workshops. Higher education usually requires a lot of reading, so take the steps necessary to become the most effective reader possible.

EXERCISE

Reading Activities

1. Reread "Teen Angst, RIP." Write more questions and notes in the margin as you deepen your understanding of the main points.

2. Test the author's claims about teenage emotional states, or the value of social pain, against your own experiences and observations.

3. Find three difficult or unusual words in the essay. Try to determine their meaning from the context before checking them in a dictionary.

4. Try to explain the main ideas of the article to a friend or roommate. Ask a question related to the article that can stimulate debate or discussion.

READING ASSIGNMENTS CAREFULLY

Many students could get better grades simply by reading their assignments more carefully. In assignments, instructors often indicate possible topics, suggest additional readings, identify the kinds of information that should and *should not* be included, set expectations on style and format, and establish requirements for the assignment, such as the due date and approximate length. You should read the assignment several times. Carefully note any specifications on topic, audience, organizational strategy, or style and format. Be sure to jot down due dates in an assignment log or calendar. Do not make assumptions. If you are not clear about a part of the assignment, ask your instructor.

Below is a very specific assignment; read it over carefully to determine what it requires.

OBJECTIVE DESCRIPTION
SHORT ASSIGNMENT (50 POINTS)

Typed final draft following the class format guide is due in class September 12. This assignment page should be turned in with your completed description:

The corner of Perry and King streets, near the Starr building, has been the scene of a terrible accident. The insurance company has asked you to write a brief objective description (approximately two pages double spaced) of the intersection for a report for possible use in court. Your description should not try to take a position about the relative danger of the intersection but rather provide as clear a picture as possible of the situation. The description should include the arrangement of the streets, including the number of lanes, the businesses located immediately around the intersection, traffic and pedestrian flow, and the timing of traffic lights and its effect on traffic.

Checklist:

The description should:

1. Provide the general location of the intersection.
2. Indicate the streets' traffic function—i.e., major route from 131 into downtown Big Rapids.
3. Describe the actual roads.
4. Identify the businesses and their locations.
5. Describe traffic and pedestrian flow.
6. Detail the timing of traffic lights.
7. Maintain objective language.
8. Use clear, nontechnical language.

The assignment specifies the topic (a specific intersection), an audience (a court of law and an insurance company), key elements that are required as part of the description, a general style of writing (objective without taking a stance), and procedures, including a deadline and format constraints. Clearly, a short paper about the accident would not be acceptable since the assigned topic is the actual structure of the intersection. A style of writing that stresses the "horribly short traffic lights that force students to scurry across the intersection like mice in front of a cat" would lose points since it takes a position and is not objective. Descriptions that leave out any of the required elements (such as the timing of traffic lights) would also lose points.

READING TO CRITIQUE

In university, you usually read not only to understand but also to evaluate what you read. You may be asked about the extent to which you agree or disagree with a writer's argument. Sometimes, you are asked to write a critique of what you have read.

Your instructors want to see if you can make judgments about the relative merits of an argument or distinguish facts and well-supported arguments from opinions and assumptions. Merely because information and ideas are in print does not mean that they cannot be questioned. An essay that looks professional might still have faulty logic, far-fetched claims, questionable facts, or unreliable authorities, despite its professional look. Don't hesitate to dispute the writer's information. Ask yourself these questions:

- Does the main point of the essay match your experience or prior learning about this subject?
- Does the evidence support the claim?
- Do the ideas seem clear, reasonable, and logical?
- Are there internal contradictions or other pieces of evidence that contradict these claims?
- Do the ideas connect in a logical way?

Knowing the principles of argumentation and various reasoning fallacies, discussed later in a chapter on argument and persuasion, can also help you critique pieces of writing—even your own.

EXERCISE

Reading Activities *Prepare your critique of "Teen Angst, RIP" by doing the following:*

1. Identify where and how the claims fail to match your experience.
2. Indicate where the evidence does not support the claims.
3. Indicate at least three places where the ideas do not appear reasonable.
4. Identify any evidence that seems to contradict the author's claims.
5. Evaluate whether the ideas connect in a logical way.

READING AS A WRITER

All of us who write can use reading as a springboard for improving our writing. You can do several things to make your reading especially useful.

As you read, the views of others, the experiences they relate, and the information they present often deepen your understanding of yourself, your relationships, and your surroundings. In turn, this broadened perspective can supply you with writing ideas. When possible topics surface, be sure to record them. Some writers keep a reading journal in which they summarize what they've read and jot down writing ideas that come to mind. In addition, you can jot down specific ideas, facts, and perhaps even a few particularly telling quotations that you discover. You may want to weave this material into your writing at a later time. Carefully record the source so that you can document it later if you use it.

When you read several sources that explore the same topic or related topics, you may notice connections among their ideas. Since these connections can be fertile ground for an essay of your own, be sure to record them. Once you have jotted down these ideas, circle or label the ideas to which they connect. You can also draw lines linking different thoughts to each other and back to the main point. Then express your view of how these ideas fit together as a thesis statement. Interacting with multiple sources and using their ideas to advance the purpose of your writing is a form of synthesis.

When you synthesize ideas into a new essay, review your information, determine the points you want to make, and experiment until you find the order that works best. As you write, use the material from your sources, taking care to credit the authors properly to avoid plagiarism.

You can also learn new techniques and strategies from other writers. If you find an organizational pattern or a style you like, study the writer's technique. Perhaps you can use it yourself. Similarly, observe when a piece of writing loses you and try to determine why.

EXERCISE

Reading Activities

1. Identify at least two strategies used in "Teen Angst, RIP" that you would find useful.
2. Identify at least two phrases that you find effective.
3. Identify at least two ideas that spark approaches you could use in your own writing.

WRITING ABOUT WHAT YOU READ

Before you can analyze or interpret or critiique what you have read, you must be able to digest it. Summarizing the main ideas of a piece of writing in your own words will help you internalize it. Summaries do not simply parrot what someone else has written, and they also do not use a piece of writing as an excuse to go off on a tangent. When you summarize a longer piece of writing, such as an essay, you distill what you have read into its essence, rather as a cook will reduce a sauce by cooking liquids until their flavour intensifies. Unlike a critique, a summary is a no-value-added assignment, as you are expected to be neutral and not make assumptions, jump to conclusions, or add your own examples and opinions at this stage. In university, summaries will be useful when you write research papers, but you may also be asked to write summaries as stand-alone shorter assignments focused on testing your ability to understand what you read.

Writing a Summary

A summary states the main points of an essay in your own words. A good summary allows someone who hasn't read the essay to understand what it says. It does not go into specific details or examples, but rather includes only main ideas. A summary reduces the length of the original piece considerably, and may be only one or more paragraphs. It should:

- Provide a context for the essay.
- Introduce the author of the essay. You may want to start with an introductory author tag, such as "According to the author Adam Sternbergh . . ."
- State the thesis.

These first three elements often form the introduction of a multiparagraph summary.

- Then state the main points of the essay (sometimes but not always based on the topic sentences).
- Conclude by summarizing the author's final point. Remember, this is not your opinion of the author's ideas, but rather expresses what the author is aiming to communicate.

To prepare to write a summary, follow the steps in active reading.

- Underline the main points of the essay.
- Write in the margins or on a separate sheet of paper those main points in your own words.
- Decide the order that would make sense for your reader. Usually a summary follows the order of the orginal.
- Prepare a brief outline.
- Use your own words unless a phrase is particularly memorable. If you do need to use the author's words, be sure to use quotation marks, even if you are quoting only a brief phrase.
- Don't insert your own views. A summary should include only the original author's ideas.

A Sample Single-Paragraph Summary of "Teen Angst, RIP"

In his article "Teen Angst, RIP," Adam Sternbergh points out that despite their reputation for being moody, Canadian teens are surprisingly happy. Could it be that teens are happier today because the entertainment industry caters to them, because they do not have the same stresses about health and finances as older people do, or even because they have so much technological savvy? The writer remembers his own adolescence as being filled with feelings of misery, but StatsCan reports that teens are the happiest people in the country. Nevertheless, Sternbergh claims that suffering can help people grow.

Writing a Critique

Instructors often ask you to give your views on an essay, indicating where you agree and disagree with the author's position. Keep in mind that you can agree with some points and disagree with others. A critique combines a summary of the article with your thoughtful reaction. Most critiques consist of several paragraphs. A critique usually includes the following elements:

- A description of the context of the essay.
- An introduction of the author.
- A statement of the essay's thesis.
- The thesis for your critique.

- A summary of the essay's main points.
- A statement of the points with which you disagree.
- A statement with reasons and evidence for your disagreement.
- A conclusion.

You are well prepared to write a critique if you follow the steps for reading effectively and reading critically.

A Sample Multiparagraph Critique of "Teen Angst, RIP"

1   The title of the article, "Teen Angst, RIP," sets the rather flippant tone that Adam Sternbergh sustains throughout—the notion that the stereotype of the moody, depressed teenager is now dead. The word *angst* implies suffering, but it suggests more a kind of romantic pose than actual anguish; Sternbergh himself admits that he took a perverse kind of pleasure in his youthful misery. He expresses surprise about the finding reported by Statistics Canada that Canadian teens, those aged 12 to 19, are supposedly the happiest people in Canada. He recalls his own gloomy adolescence in which he identified with the morbid singer Morrissey, who sang about being "16, clumsy, and shy," and not the optimistic, upbeat Bryan Adams, who sang about the joys of being 18.

2   A possible weakness in this article is the unquestioning way it reports the finding from StatsCan that "every year teens overwhelmingly claim to be either satisfied or very satisfied with their lives." The word *claim* itself is a red flag—how can anyone, especially a teen whose moods may be up and down and up again, accurately report "life satisfaction"? Has a representative cross-section of teens been consulted in the surveys? Do teens who feel disenfranchised participate in such surveys? What about teens who live below the poverty level; who are Aboriginal or people of colour; who are gay, lesbian, or transsexual; or who are homeless, stoned, or too cynical to care about surveys?

3   Finally, the tone of the article seems condescending toward teens. Sternbergh refers to the death of film director John Hughes, who directed films about high school dramas, as the "patron saint of melodrama." Why is the suffering of high school teens, which sometimes ends in suicide, necessarily associated with melodrama? And Sternbergh's hypotheses about why teens are reportedly so happy seem flimsy, to say the least. While many teens may not be as preoccupied with health issues as older people, many others have significant physical and mental health worries, including depression related to body image, sexual confusion, bullying, and substance abuse. The speculation that teens may

be happier because of their relative technological expertise seems far-fetched. Are computer programmers in Silicon Valley happier than people who have minimal contact with technology? Finally, the idea that teens are happier because their parents are more fun-loving than parents in previous generations seems highly questionable. Many parents today seem very stressed about their own careers and marriages, as well as the direction or lack of direction they see their kids taking.

4   Despite its questionable logic, the article does raise interesting questions about the emotional lives of adolescents and the possibility that the experience of unhappiness is necessary for growth into maturity. Reflecting on this article can make adult readers grateful to be out of adolescence, free of the pressure to fit into stereotypes that the culture prescribes for teens.

Active Reading

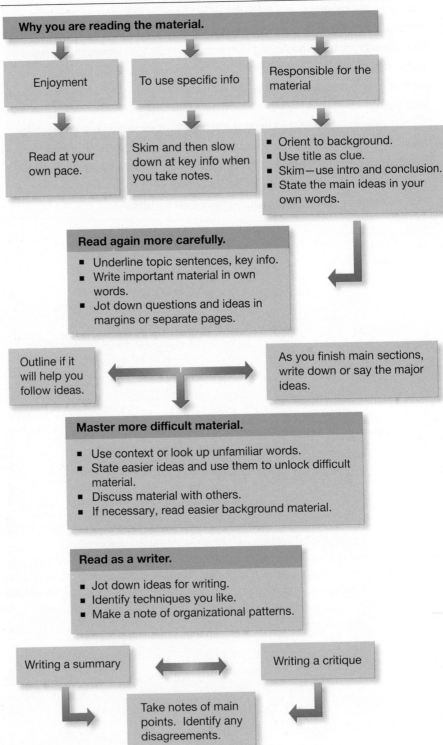

Why you are reading the material.

Enjoyment

To use specific info

Responsible for the material

Read at your own pace.

Skim and then slow down at key info when you take notes.

- Orient to background.
- Use title as clue.
- Skim—use intro and conclusion.
- State the main ideas in your own words.

Read again more carefully.

- Underline topic sentences, key info.
- Write important material in own words.
- Jot down questions and ideas in margins or separate pages.

Outline if it will help you follow ideas.

As you finish main sections, write down or say the major ideas.

Master more difficult material.

- Use context or look up unfamiliar words.
- State easier ideas and use them to unlock difficult material.
- Discuss material with others.
- If necessary, read easier background material.

Read as a writer.

- Jot down ideas for writing.
- Identify techniques you like.
- Make a note of organizational patterns.

Writing a summary

Writing a critique

Take notes of main points. Identify any disagreements.

CHAPTER 3

Strategies for Planning and Drafting Your Writing

Many students believe that good essays are dashed off in a burst of inspiration. Students themselves often boast that they cranked out their best papers in an hour or so of spare time. Perhaps this is true. For most of us, however, writing is a messy process that takes time and work. Don't confuse your planning and drafting with a final version. If your computer's grammar check and spell-check slow you down, turn them off until you are revising a later draft or proofreading your work.

Writing is a flexible process. Some writers establish their purpose and draft a plan at the start of every project, while others begin with a tentative purpose or plan and discover their final direction as they write. Very few writers can proceed in an orderly, straightforward sequence; more commonly they leapfrog backward and forward. For example, partway through a first draft a writer may think of a new point to present, then pause and jot down the details needed to develop it. Similarly, part of the conclusion may come to mind as the writer is gathering the details to support a key idea.

Regardless of how the writing process unfolds, most writers use some combination of the six stages listed below. If you have no plan, or if you run into snags while using your approach, advancing through each stage will help you get your essay under control. Once you're familiar with these stages, you can combine or rearrange them as needed.

- Understanding the assignment
- Zeroing in on a topic

- Gathering information
- Organizing the information
- Developing a thesis statement
- Writing the first draft

Types of Writers

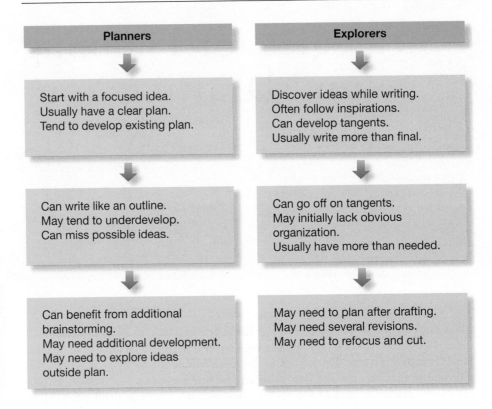

Planners	Explorers
Start with a focused idea. Usually have a clear plan. Tend to develop existing plan.	Discover ideas while writing. Often follow inspirations. Can develop tangents. Usually write more than final.
Can write like an outline. May tend to underdevelop. Can miss possible ideas.	Can go off on tangents. May initially lack obvious organization. Usually have more than needed.
Can benefit from additional brainstorming. May need additional development. May need to explore ideas outside plan.	May need to plan after drafting. May need several revisions. May need to refocus and cut.

UNDERSTANDING THE ASSIGNMENT

Different instructors give different kinds of writing assignments. Some specify the topic, some give you several topics to choose from, and still others offer you a free choice. Likewise, some instructors dictate the length and format of the essay, while others do not. Whatever the case, be sure that you understand the assignment before you start.

Think of it this way: If your boss asked you to report on ways to improve working conditions at your office and you turned in a report on improving worker benefits, would you expect the boss's approval? Following directions is crucial. So, if you have any questions about the assignment, ask your instructor to clear them up right away. Also make sure that you understand the instructor's expectations for a particular assignment. For example, some assignments require formal academic writing, while others may call for a more informal and personal style. An essay for a sociology class will follow different conventions than an essay for an English class. Don't be timid; it's much better to ask for clarity than to receive a low grade for failing to follow directions.

Once you understand the assignment, consider the project *yours*. Whether you are writing for a local newspaper, for a friend, or for your instructor and classmates, this is your chance to tell others about something important to you. By asking yourself who your audience is and what the assignment allows you to accomplish, you can find your purpose.

ZEROING IN ON A TOPIC

A subject is a broad discussion area, such as sports, academic life, or Canadian popular culture. A topic is one small segment of a subject. For example, if you are interested in public education, you might explore a topic within this larger category—perhaps standardized testing in the province's public schools, school policies related to the use of laptops, or ways of dealing with school violence. If you choose your own topic, pick one narrow enough that you can develop it adequately within the length limitation. Avoid sprawling, slippery topics that result in a string of trite generalities.

In addition, choose a topic that you can learn enough about in the time available. Avoid overworked topics such as an argument about the legal drinking age. Instead, select a topic that allows you to offer readers something they did not already know.

Strategies for Finding a Topic

Students sometimes think that having a larger, more general area to write about will be easier than having a more focused topic. However, writing is usually easier—and more interesting for you and your reader—if you take on a topic that is more specific and manageable. Would you be more interested in an essay titled "Hockey in Canada" or one titled "Why Hockey Is No Longer Canadian"? When your instructor assigns a general subject area, you need to stake out a limited topic within that broad area suitable for your essay. If you're lucky, the right topic will come to mind immediately, but usually you'll need to dig deeper. The following are six strategies that many writers use. Not all of them work for everyone, so experiment to find those that work best for you.

Tapping Your Personal Resources If your instructor asks for writing that draws from personal experience, you may be able to uncover a suitable topic by tapping into your memories of family gatherings, school activities, movies, concerts, plays, parties, jobs, books you've read, TV programs, dates, discussions, arguments, and so on. Suppose that you've been asked to write about some aspect of education. Recalling the difficulties you had last term at registration, you might argue for better registration procedures. Or if you're a hopeless TV addict, why not analyze advertising techniques for a specific consumer item you have seen on TV, such as a hybrid car or a new health product?

Anything you've read in magazines or journals, newspapers, novels, short stories, or textbooks can also spark an idea. Dan Greenburg's "Sound and Fury" (see Chapter 6), in which a potentially explosive situation is defused, might suggest an essay on some dangerous encounter in your past. Alice Munro's short story "Boys and Girls," in which a girl growing up in rural Canada comes to accept the gender role she is assigned, might suggest an essay on gender socialization in rural areas. Possibilities crowd our lives, waiting for us to recognize and seize them. But one word of caution: When using personal experience, ensure that it fits the assignment and the instructor's expectations. Some instructors who ask for formal academic papers may want a more objective approach throughout, while others may appreciate personal reflections that are woven into the overall essay. As always, the key is to determine your audience and the situation or context for your writing.

EXERCISE *Select five of the subjects listed below. Use your personal resources to come up with one topic for each. Then for each topic, list three questions that you might answer in a paper.*

Public transit	Water
A particular field of work	Contemporary forms of dancing
Drugs	Youth gangs
Saving money	Trendiness
Home ownership	Human rights

Keeping a Journal   Many writers record their experiences in a journal—a private gathering of entries accumulated over a period of time. In addition to helping writers remember and reflect on their experiences, journal keeping provides an abundance of possible writing topics and a valuable opportunity for writing practice.

The hallmark of the journal entry is the freedom to explore thoughts, feelings, responses, attitudes, and beliefs. In your own private domain, you can express your views without reservation, without concern for being judged. *You* control the content and length of the entry without being held to a specified topic or number of words. Journal writing does not represent a finished product, but rather an exploration. In addition to personal journals, learning journals—where you reflect on what you've learned in your classes—can yield interesting topics for formal research papers.

A few simple guidelines can help you to write effective journal entries:

1. Write on the computer or in any kind of notebook that appeals to you; the content, not the package, is the important thing.
2. Write on a regular basis—at least five times a week, if possible. In any event, don't write in fits and starts, cramming two weeks of entries into one sitting.
3. Write for 10 to 20 minutes, or longer if you have more to say. Don't aim for uniform entry length, such as three paragraphs or a page and a half. Simply explore your reactions to the happenings in your life or to what you have read, heard in class, or seen on television. The length will take care of itself.
4. If you have multiple pages of journals in your computer files, you can use "Find" to search for key words and discover related ideas.

Let's examine a typical journal entry by Sam, a first-year composition student.

Last week went back to my hometown for the first time since my family moved away and while there dropped by the street where I spent my first twelve years. Visit left me feeling very depressed. Family home still there, but its paint peeling and front porch sagging. Sign next to the porch said house now occupied by Acme Realtors. While we lived there, front yard lush green and bordered by beds of irises. Now an oil-spattered parking lot. All the other houses on our side of the street gone, replaced by convenience stores and low-rise office buildings. All of them dingy and rundown looking, even though only a few years old.

Other side of the street in no better shape. Directly across from our house a used-car dealership with rows of junky looking cars. No trace left of the park that used to be there. Had lots of fun playing baseball and learned meaning of sportsmanship. To left of the dealership my old grade school, now boarded and abandoned. Wonder about my grade 5 teacher, Ms. Wynick. Is she still teaching? Still able to make learning a game, not a chore? Other side of dealership the worst sight of all. Grimy looking plant of some sort pouring foul smelling smoke into the air from a discoloured stack. Smoke made me cough.

Don't think I'll revisit my old street again.

This journal entry could spawn several essays. Sam might explore the causes of residential deterioration, define sportsmanship, explain how Ms. Wynick made learning a game, or argue for stricter pollution-control laws.

EXERCISE *Write journal entries over the next week or two for some of the following items that interest you. If you have trouble finding a suitable topic for a paper, review the journal entries for possibilities.*

Pleasant or unpleasant conversations	Cultural or sporting events
Developing relationships	Academic life: myth vs. reality
Parents	Looking for a job

Sorting out a Subject　All of us sort things. We do it whenever we tackle the laundry, clear away a sinkful of dishes, or tidy up a basement or bedroom. Consider how we might begin organizing a cluttered basement. We might sort the contents according to type: books in one place, clothing in a second, toys in a third. That done, chances are we'd do still more sorting, separating children's books from adults' and stuffed animals from games. As we look over and handle the different items, long-buried, bittersweet memories might start flooding from our subconscious: memories of an uncle, now dead, who sent this old adventure novel . . . of our parents' pride when they saw their child riding that now battered bicycle . . . of the dance that marked the debut of the slinky dress over there.

Sorting out a subject is similar. First, we break our broad subject into categories and subcategories; then we allow our minds to roam over the different items to see what topics we can turn up. The chart on the next page shows what one student found when she explored the general subject of Internet communication.

As you'll discover for yourself, some subjects yield more topics than others; some yield no topics at all.

EXERCISE *Select two of the following subjects and then subdivide them into five topics each.*

Advertising	Movies	Transportation
Computers	Occupations	Camping
Fashion	Popular music	Television programs

Asking Questions   Often, asking questions such as those listed below can lead you to a manageable topic.

How can this subject be described?

How is this subject accomplished or performed?

What is an example of my subject?

Does the subject break down into categories?

If so, what comparisons can I make among these categories?

If my subject is divided into parts, how do they work together?

Does my subject have uses? What are they?

What are the causes of my subject?

What is the impact of my subject?

How can my subject be defined?

What case could be made for or against my subject?

Let's convert these general questions into specific questions about a broad general subject: telescopes.

Narration:	What is the story of the telescope?
Description:	How can a telescope be described?
Illustration:	What are some well-known telescopes?
Process:	How did the Hubble telescope take pictures of Mars?
Analysis:	What are the parts of the telescope, and how do they work together?
Functional analysis:	How is a telescope useful?
Causal analysis:	Why did the telescope come about?
Analysis of effects:	What effects have telescopes had on human life and knowledge?
Classification:	What are the different kinds of telescopes?
Comparison:	How are they alike? How are they different?
Definition:	What is a telescope?
Argument:	Why should people learn to use telescopes?

Each of these questions offers a starting point for a suitably focused essay.

Results of Sorting out the Subject of Internet Communication

Personal		Community		Large Community of Followers	
Texting	Chat	Discussion Boards	Facebook	Blogs	Tweeting
The reasons texting is replacing email	The growing use of chat for online support	Fan boards	Why FB became so popular	Political blogs	Celebrity tweets
The style of texting	The role of chat in higher education and online classes	Professional discussion boards	The challenges of keeping FB profitable	Corporate blogs	Political tweets
The extent to which texting influences language use	A comparison of online chat and phone calls	Discussion boards in the classroom	Effects FB has on the social relations of university students	Personal blogs	Tweeting friends
The dangers of texting and driving; the effects of texting on attention		Frequently asked questions		How to write a successful blog	Product tweets
		The problem of civility in discussion boards		The way blogs may keep us in our personal information bubble	The ways tweeting is increasingly used in political campaigns
		The growing use of discussion boards with online news media		The extent to which blogs give average citizens a political voice	The ways tweets are used to manage a celebrity's image
					A classification of the different kinds of people who tweet and follow tweets

EXERCISE *Convert two of the general subjects below into more manageable topics. Then, drawing from the list of questions suggested on page 40, ask specific questions about the topics. Finally, come up with two essay topics for each of the two subjects you selected.*

> *Example:* Take a general subject, such as music, and then narrow it to a more manageable topic, such as downloading music. After running through the list of questions above, you might choose an essay topic such as "How to Download Music onto Your Phone."

Tourism	Games	Fitness
Sports	Violence	Restaurants
Languages	Television	

Freewriting   The freewriting strategy, in which you write nonstop for a brief period without editing, can help you snare thoughts or ideas as they race through your mind. To begin, turn your pen loose and write for about five minutes on your general subject or in response to a prompt. Put down everything that comes into your head, without worrying about grammar, spelling, or punctuation. What you produce is for your eyes alone. If you start to feel blocked, write "I'm stuck, I'm stuck. . ." until you break the mental logjam. When your writing time is up, go through your sentences and see if you can find any potential topics—or even a promising phrase that sparks your interest. If you draw a blank, or would like to use the idea that you extracted as a prompt for a new freewrite, write for another five minutes and look again.

The following example shows the product of one freewriting session. After Drew's business instructor had assigned a two- or three-page paper on technology, Drew finds himself writing about the cellphone.

> Technology, huh. What do I know about technology? Cellphones are technology. What about them? I love my iPhone. It does everything I want it to do. The pictures it takes are amazing. I can Google anything I want to find out about, and can check out YouTube in a flash. Music too. These phones change people's lives. How? Well, we are always on them talking to friends, to anybody, and parents and teachers never get it. What did people do before cellphones? What if their car broke down, or they couldn't make an appointment on time? Or they couldn't find where they wanted to go? I'm glad I got the one with the GPS so I hardly ever get lost now. Stuck, stuck, stuck. Well, I keep in touch with friends. Some are away at university. My girlfriend is always texting me. Is she trying to keep tabs on me? Sometimes I feel too tied to my phone.

This example suggests at least three papers. For people shopping for a new cellphone, Drew could write about the advantages of different types of phones. He could write to those perplexed by student behaviour to explain why students use cellphones so extensively. He could also write a warning to young people not to become too tied to their phones.

Brainstorming   Brainstorming, a close cousin of freewriting, captures fleeting ideas in words, fragments, and sometimes sentences, rather than in a series of sentences.

Brainstorming generates ideas faster than the other strategies do. But unless you move immediately to the next stage of writing, you may lose track of what some of your fragmentary jottings mean.

To compare the results of freewriting and brainstorming a topic, we've converted our freewriting example into this list, which typifies the results of brainstorming:

Types of cellphones	Why young people use cellphones so much
Advantages of iPhones	Organizing life and keeping in touch
Pictures	GPS function
Text messages	Possible overdependence on cellphones
YouTube and music	

EXERCISE *Return to one of the five-topic sets you devised for the exercise on page 40. Freewrite or brainstorm for five minutes on each topic, then choose one that is suitable for a two- or three-page essay. State your topic, intended audience, and purpose.*

Narrowing a familiar subject may yield not only a topic, but sometimes also the main divisions for an essay on this topic.

More commonly, the main divisions will emerge only after you have gathered material to develop your topic. After considering his options, Drew decides he doesn't know enough about types of cellphones and might get carried away when writing about the iPhone. He decides to write about the reasons that university students are so attached to their cellphones.

Identifying Your Audience and Purpose

You can identify your audience and purpose at several different stages in the writing process. Sometimes, both are set by the assignment. For example, you might be asked to write to your university president to recommend improvements in the school's registration system. At other times, you may have to write a draft before you can determine either your audience or your purpose. Usually, though, selecting audience and purpose occurs when you determine your topic. Think of the different types of information Drew would gather if he wrote for (1) university students to break them of their cellphone habits, (2) professors and parents to make cellphone use seem less peculiar, or (3) a sociology professor to demonstrate how common behaviours can be explained through sociological theories.

GATHERING INFORMATION

Once you have a topic, you need things to say about it. This supporting material can include facts, ideas, examples, observations, sensory impressions, and memories. Without this kind of support, essays lack force, vividness, and interest, and they may confuse or mislead readers. The more support you can gather, the easier it will be for you to write a draft. Time spent gathering information is never wasted.

Strategies for Gathering Information

If you are writing on a personal topic for a creative writing class, much of your supporting material may come from your own head. Brainstorming is the best way to retrieve it. However, with academic, professional, and fact-oriented topics, you have to use research for your supporting material. But whatever the topic—personal or academic—using friends, parents, and neighbours as sounding boards and talking to local experts can also produce useful ideas.

Brainstorming   Brainstorming a topic, like brainstorming a subject, yields a set of words, fragments, and occasionally sentences that furnish ideas for the paper. Drew has decided that he wants to demonstrate to professors and parents that there are good reasons for student cellphone use. He generated the following list through brainstorming.

students open cellphones after class	weather updates
coordinating a life	sending emails
meeting friends for study sessions	sending pictures by email
arranging a lunch date	holding up a phone at a concert
getting a ride	calling when something funny
coordinating a team project	happens
getting things done	keeping in touch
resolving bill disputes	old friends in different schools
scheduling car repairs	boyfriends or girlfriends
finding babysitters	text messaging
GPS function	playing music

You can see how some thoughts have led to others. For example, the fourth jotting, "arranging a lunch date," leads naturally to the next one, "getting a ride," and "keeping in touch" leads to "old friends in different schools."

Clustering and branching are helpful and convenient extensions of brainstorming that allow you to add details to any item in your list. In clustering, you place ideas in bubbles and generate associations from there. Refer to the accompanying figure to see how you might use the technique of clustering for "cellphone use."

Don't worry if your brainstorming or clustering notes look chaotic and if some seem irrelevant. Sometimes, the most unlikely material turns out to be the freshest and most interesting. As you organize and write your essay, you'll probably combine, modify, and omit some of the notes, as well as add others. Drew decides from his brainstorming that "GPS function" and "weather updates" are too specific and should not be part of his paper.

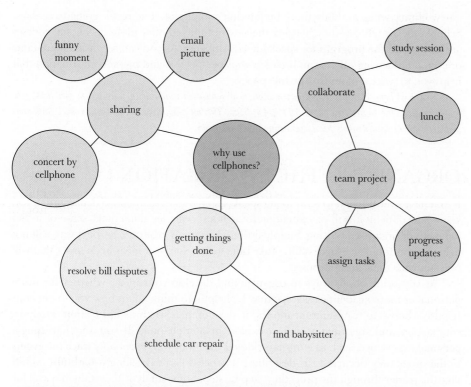

Sample Clustering Diagram on Cellphone Use: One common strategy is clustering, where you place ideas in bubbles and make as many connections as come to mind.

EXERCISE *Prepare a brainstorming sheet or a cluster diagram of supporting details for the topic you developed for the exercise on page 43.*

Reading, Listening, and Talking with Others

In addition to getting ideas from reading, as discussed in Chapter 2, we may get ideas from face-to-face or online conversations. Imagine that you're writing a paper about a taxpayers' revolt in your province. After checking the leading provincial newspapers at the library, you find that most of the protest centres on high property taxes. You then decide to supplement what you've read by asking questions about the local tax situation in your town.

Your parents and neighbours tell you that property taxes have jumped 50 percent in the last two years. The local tax assessor tells you that assessed valuations have risen sharply and that the law requires property taxes to keep pace. She also notes that this situation is causing some people on fixed incomes to lose their homes. A city council member explains that part of the added revenue is being used to repair city streets, build a new library wing, and buy more firefighting equipment. The rest is going to schools. School officials tell you they're using their extra funds to offer more vocational courses and to expand the program for special-needs students. As you can see, asking questions or even interviewing others can broaden your perspective and provide information that helps you to write a more worthwhile paper.

Note: *Whenever you use a direct quotation or rephrased material in your paper, you must give proper credit to the source (see pages 341–343; 395–396 on plagiarism). You should check with your instructor about requirements for documenting what others have said.*

ORGANIZING THE INFORMATION

If you have ever listened to a rambling speaker spill out ideas in no particular order, you know how difficult it is to pay attention to such a speech, let alone make sense of it. So, too, with disorganized writing. Simply listing ideas in an arbitrary, garbled way will not help you communicate successfully. Take time to arrange your ideas in an order that will best suit your topic and purpose.

As you think about ways to organize and develop your ideas, whether for more personal or more academic essays, it may be helpful to think about how you might consciously choose to use different modes of development such as illustration, analysis, comparison, and argument, which we explore in later chapters. If you were narrating a personal experience, such as a mishap-riddled vacation, you'd probably trace the events in the order they occurred. In describing a process—say, caulking a bathtub—you'd take the reader through the procedure step by step. Some analytical writing may call for patterns, such as cause and effect, definition, and comparison (which we discuss in more detail in Chapters 9, 10, and 11, respectively).

It's important to remember that these modes of developing ideas usually do not occur in isolation. For example, an argument may use some narrative and illustration, and an essay that is primarily a comparison may also analyze the causes or effects of something. A comparative essay is often an argument as well.

The Flexible Notes System

While formal outlines can be useful road maps for longer pieces of writing, especially research-based writing, for shorter essays a simple, informal system of *flexible notes* will probably suffice.

To create a set of flexible notes, write each of your key points at the top of a separate sheet of paper. If your essay requires a thesis statement (see pages 49–51), refer to it to keep your key points on track. Next, list under each heading the supporting details that go with that heading. Drop details that don't fit and expand points that need more support. When your sheets are finished, arrange them in the order you expect to follow in your essay.

Drew uses his flexible notes to draft a plan for his essay, according to their probable importance—starting with coordinating activities, something he imagines that the audience will consider as the most important reason for using cell phones.

Since coordinating activities, getting things done, sharing, and keeping in touch are equivalent reasons, this listing arranges them according to their probable importance—starting with the most important reason from the point of view of the audience.

Now you're ready to draft a plan showing how many paragraphs you'll have in each part of the essay and what each paragraph will cover. Sometimes, the number of details will suggest one paragraph; other times, you'll need a paragraph block—two or more paragraphs. Here's a plan for Drew's cellphone essay:

Coordinating Activities

Meeting for study session

Arranging a lunch date

Getting a ride

Coordinating a team project

Getting Things Done

Resolving bill disputes

Scheduling car repairs

Finding a babysitter

Sharing

Sending pictures by email

Holding up phone at concert

Calling about a funny event

Keeping in Touch

Old friends in different schools

Boyfriends and girlfriends   } By voice

Text messaging   } By text

These groupings suggest one paragraph about coordinating activities, one about getting things done, one about sharing, and two about keeping in touch.

EXERCISE *Organize into flexible notes the supporting details that you prepared for the exercise on page 45. Arrange your note pages in a logical sequence and draft a plan showing the number and content of the paragraphs in each section.*

CREATING A FORMAL OUTLINE

Many writers do not write outlines until they have gathered material and even begun writing a draft, since they do not always know what direction they want to take until their ideas have started to unfold. Others prefer more structure early in the writing process, and a formal outline creates a visual overview of how to order ideas and shows at a glance the logical relationships between ideas. If you are writing a longer essay or if you have been asked to submit a formal outline, creating a formal outline can show you how to organize your material.

Most text programs such as Word have templates that you can use to create two kinds of formal outlines: a topic outline, which simply states the main topic to be addressed in a section, and a more elaborate full sentence outline. The following example of a topic outline illustrates how larger chunks of material, identified by Roman numerals (I, II, III), are then broken down into smaller divisions identified by letters (A, B, C), with those divisions further subdivided and identified by numbers (1, 2, 3).

I.   Coordinating Activities
  A. Meeting friends for study sessions
     1. Setting the time
     2. Making certain everyone gets there
  B. Arranging a lunch date
     1. Deciding where everyone is meeting
     2. Arranging a ride to lunch

II. Getting Things Done
  A. Coordinating a team project
     1. Assigning tasks
     2. Monitoring progress
  B. Resolving bill disputes
     1. Calling during business hours

Topic outlines quickly let you know if you have enough information for a paragraph. If you have only one letter or, under a letter, only one number under a major heading, as in II B in the example above, you may need to do more brainstorming.

In a sentence outline, you make full statements or sentences that often can be used in your paper. A sentence outline makes you think about what you really want to say.

I.   Cellphones can be used to coordinate activities that otherwise would be difficult to coordinate given students' busy schedules.
  A. Cellphones can help students to find out where a study session is being held.
  B. Often there is a complex schedule of classes, work, meals, and meetings to organize.
  C. Cellphones can let members of a team collaborate on a project.

To develop your outline, you take your brainstorming or notes and mark the major units as I, II, III, and so on based on the main ideas they demonstrate. Then you start to develop your outline, identifying the major points for each major heading

(I, II . . .) and the next major points (A, B, C). You can use your outline to goad additional planning as you see holes in it. You should rarely have an A without a B or a 1 without a 2.

DEVELOPING A THESIS STATEMENT

A thesis statement—one or two sentences that express the main idea in your essay—can help you stay on track. If you do not have a thesis, or central point you are heading toward when you write, your reader will probably feel bored or frustrated. Even if it is not spelled out explicitly, the thesis statement governs and unifies the entire essay. The thesis statement points you and your reader in a specific direction and prepares your reader for what to expect.

Finding an interesting thesis statement can take time, and one may emerge at several points in the writing process. If an instructor assigns a controversial topic on which you hold strong views, you may immediately know what you want your thesis statement to be. Usually, though, a thesis statment emerges gradually, after you have examined, assessed, and gathered relevant material and supporting information. As you examine your information, search for the central point, the idea that seems to have the most interesting potential, and the key points that back it up. Try blending, narrowing, or modifying claims to develop your thesis statement.

For example, one student was writing about the way in which Disney movies she had seen as a child still haunted her imagination. As she started writing about her recollections of *Bambi*, *The Little Mermaid*, *Babe*, and *Finding Nemo*, it seemed at first that she was getting off track. Then, as she thought about how other people might relate to what she had to say, she decided that she would combine her ideas and write an essay on how Disney movies may actually help children become more sensitive to environmental concerns. She was able to draw on her own experiences of watching Disney movies to support her thesis.

If you convert a topic to a question, the answer to this question may be your thesis statement. Consider the following example:

Topic:	The commercial advantages of computerized data storage systems.
Question:	What advantages do computerized data storage systems offer business?
Thesis statement:	Computerized data storage systems offer business enormous storage capacity; cheap, instant data transmission almost anywhere; and significantly increased profits.

Thinking of your thesis statement as an answer to a question can help you focus.

The following are some key strategies that can help you to develop a thesis statement.

- Identify your topic and the scope of your concern.
- Formulate a question about this topic that interests you.
- Brainstorm ideas, review notes, or skim research related to this question.
- Formulate an answer to the question that will become your preliminary thesis.
- Brainstorm and formulate major claims related to this preliminary thesis.

- Identify and select those claims that will become the main points of your paper.
- Blend those major claims into the preliminary thesis. You will then have your overarching idea (the thesis statement) as well as a map to develop these points.

Requirements of a Good Thesis Statement

Unity   Unless it is intended for a lengthy essay, a thesis statement *focuses on just one central point or issue.* Suppose that you prepare the following thesis statement for a two- or three-page essay:

> New Generation College should re-examine its policies on open admissions, vocational programs, and aid to students.

This sprawling statement would commit you to address three separate issues. At best, you could make only a few general remarks about each one.

To correct matters, consider each issue carefully in light of how much it interests you and how much you know about it. Then make your choice and draft a narrower statement. The following thesis statement would suit a brief essay. It shows clearly that the writer will focus on *just one issue:*

> Because of the rising demand among high school graduates for job-related training, New Generation College should expand its vocational programs.

If you find your essay splintering into two seemingly unrelated directions, you may be able to reformulate your thesis to blend the two ideas by showing how they are related to each other. Using the example above, you might write the following:

> New Generation College needs to increase its financial aid program in order to attract more students to its vocational programs.

Tailored Scope   A good thesis statement also *tailors the scope of the issue to the length of the paper.* No writer could deal adequately with "Many first-year university students face crucial adjustment problems" in two or three pages. The idea is too broad to yield more than a smattering of poorly supported general statements. But paring it down to "Handling free time in responsible, disciplined ways challenges many first-year university students" results in an idea that could probably be developed adequately as a thesis.

Indication of Writer's Attitude   An essay is not simply a statement of fact or a bland report, but a piece of writing that reflects a particular point of view. The thesis statement implies purpose by suggesting the writer's attitude toward his or her subject. A thesis statement such as "Ethanol is an alternative fuel composed of oxygen, hydrogen, and carbon" simply states a fact but does not indicate the writer's attitude or position. Consider instead how the following thesis statements suggest the writer's point of view: "The use of wind turbines creates more environmental problems than it solves" or

"Although there are potential challenges with disruption of bird migration patterns, wind turbines are a viable renewable energy source that the Canadian government should encourage."

Accurate Forecasting   A good thesis statement further provides *an accurate forecast of what's to come*. If you plan to discuss the effects of overeating, don't say, "Overeating stems from deep-seated psychological factors and the easy availability of convenience foods." Because this statement incorrectly suggests that the paper will focus on causes, not effects, it would only mislead and confuse your reader. On the other hand, the statement "Overeating leads to obesity, which can cause or complicate several serious health problems" accurately represents what will follow.

Preview of Organization   Finally, a good thesis statement is precise, often previewing the organization of the paper and indicating a strategy of development. Assertions built on fuzzy, biased words, such as *fascinating, bad, meaningful,* or *interesting,* or vague statements like "My paper is about . . ." do not let the reader know how you intend to proceed. Look at these two examples:

> Montreal is a fascinating city.
> My paper is about health benefits in Canada.

These thesis statements raise too many questions. Why does the writer find Montreal fascinating? Because of its architecture? Its nightlife? Its restaurants and shops? Its museums and theatres? Its cultural diversity? And what about health benefits? Will the writer explain how to apply for health benefits? Or defend the current system of benefits, trace its history, or suggest ways of improving it? Without a clear road map sentence suggesting the writer's direction, readers must labour through the paper, hoping to find their way.

Now look at the rewritten versions of those vague, imprecise thesis statements:

> Montreal's ethno-cultural diversity offers visitors the chance to sample cuisine from every continent.

> Canada's national health care system should be a two-tier system that allows patients the options of receiving medical treatment from private clinics and hospitals at their own expense or from public clinics or hospitals at public expense, because such a system would reduce waiting lists and lower the costs of health care paid for by the Canadian government.

These thesis statements not only tell the reader what points the writer will make, but also suggest the order and strategy of development they will follow. The Montreal essay will proceed by way of illustration, offering examples of dishes from different parts of the world that a visitor might sample. The health care thesis statement suggests that the writer will argue why a two-tier health care system would be desirable. Note that the second thesis statement could easily be broken into two sentences, with the first sentence stating the writer's position and the second sentence providing the road map—a preview of the writer's main points.

Placement of the Thesis Statement

Although the placement of the thesis statement can vary, in most academic papers the thesis statement appears at the end of the first or sometimes the second paragraph of the paper. Many essays take two or three sentences to lead into the thesis, but some, such as an essay for an in-class mid-term exam, may state the thesis immediately in the first sentence. On the other hand, in persuasive essays, the writer may state off stating the thesis until close to the end of the first paragraph or even later in the essay, especially if it is controversial. Moreover, some essays—narratives in particular, or those by professional writers—may have only implied thesis statements. *Nonetheless, a core idea underlies and controls all effective writing. Usually it is best to state that core idea in a thesis statement, especially in more formal academic pieces.*

Changing Your Thesis Statement

Before your paper is in final form, you may need to change your thesis statement several times. If you draft the thesis statement during the narrowing stage, you might change it to reflect what you uncovered while gathering information. Or you might amend it after writing the first draft so that it reflects your additions and deletions. In his first rough draft, Drew thought that "In the end, this cellphone mania is a necessary part of university life" was an adequate thesis statement. In revising his draft, however, he realized that it was not precise enough to direct his readers. He added a more focused statement that identified the main reasons addressed in his paper to serve as his thesis: "They use cellphones to coordinate the day's activities, to get some business done, to share life's events, and to keep in touch."

Whether tentative or final, formulated early or late, the thesis statement serves as a beacon that spotlights your purpose.

EXERCISE

1. Write a thesis statement for the flexible notes you developed for the exercise on page 47.

2. Using "Requirements of a Good Thesis Statement," explain why each of the following does or does not qualify as an effective thesis statement for a two- or three-page essay.

   a. My paper discusses the impact of globalization in China.

   b. There should be more competition among Canadian cellphone companies.

   c. Although I don't know much about running a business, I know that PDT Accounting Inc. is not run well.

   d. Ecotourism in the sensitive ecosystem of Antarctica needs to be managed much more carefully than it has been for many reasons.

   e. People may be able to improve their writing skills with the aid of electronic media: blogging, texting, and using social networking sites.

3. **Revise the following weak thesis statements by narrowing them in focus.**

   Example: Pollution affects all of us in negative ways. (This thesis is too broad. What kind of pollution? What kind of effect?)

Revised thesis for personal essay: *Stores and restaurants in the city should reduce the decibel level of their music so that customers can shop and dine in relative peace.*

Revised thesis for a paper using research: *Noise pollution, which stresses animals and humans, should be strictly regulated in Canadian cities.*

a. Learning to manage money is a good thing.

b. Facebook offers many features.

c. My paper discusses the importance of a university education.

d. Climate change is affecting the economy.

e. Many young people are drawn to video games.

WRITING THE FIRST DRAFT

Of course, sometimes when you sit down to write a first draft or even notes for a draft, the words won't come. All you can do is doodle or stare at the blank page. Perhaps the introduction is the problem. Many writers are terrified by the thought of the opening paragraph. They want to get off to a good start but can't figure out how to begin. If this happens to you, additional brainstorming or freewriting can make you more comfortable and may suggest an opening. Keep in mind that any lead-in you write now can be changed later. If these suggestions don't solve your problem, skip the introduction for now. Once you have drafted the body of the paper, an effective opening should come more easily.

The following are some suggestions for writing a first draft:

1. Reread your thesis statement, notes, brainstorming, and written plan. They will start you thinking.
2. Rewrite your thesis statement at the top of your first page to break the ice and build momentum.
3. **If it helps, start writing without worrying about anything but getting ideas down; you can reshape everything later.**
4. Write quickly; capture the drift of your thoughts. Concentrate on content and organization, but recognize that you can easily change the organization later. Don't spend time correcting grammatical or punctuation errors, improving your language, or making the writing flow smoothly. You might lose your train of thought and end up doodling or staring again.
5. If you have ideas that may not fit the flow, you can open another page to jot down those ideas so they are not lost and save the page under a different file name. If you don't know what to say about a section, you can mark that place "xxxxx" and fill it in later.
6. If you have ideas while writing for earlier sections, you can either go back and write them or keep a separate page you can open to jot down any additional ideas that come to you.
7. Take breaks at logical dividing points, such as when you finish discussing a key point. Before you start to write again, scan what you've written.

Now, here are some specific suggestions that will help you with the actual writing:

1. Write your first paragraph, introducing your essay and stating your thesis. If you get stuck here, move on to the rest of the paper.

2. Follow your plan as you write. Begin with your first main point and work on each section in turn.

3. Look over the supporting details listed under the first heading in your flexible notes. Write a topic sentence stating the central idea of the paragraph.

4. Turn the details into sentences; use one or more sentences to explain each one. Add other related details, facts, or examples if they occur to you.

5. When you move from one paragraph to the next, try to provide a transitional word or sentence that connects each paragraph.

6. Write your last paragraph, ending your essay in an appropriate fashion. If you get stuck, set your conclusion aside and return to it later.

Writing a draft isn't always so systematic. If you are inspired, you may want to abandon your plans and simply use your first draft to explore ideas. You can always revise, so don't be overly concerned if you get off track. You might uncover some of your best material during this type of search.

EXERCISE *Using the plan you prepared for the exercise on page 47, write the first draft of an essay.*

Drew now uses his thesis statement and paragraph-by-paragraph plan to write the following draft. Notice that Drew, like many writers, gets off track. That is a common occurrence at this stage and can even be a step in generating new ideas. It isn't something to reject. Drew knows even as he writes that he will need to make significant revisions. We focus on the revision process and Drew's revisions in Chapter 4.

Case History

Cellphone Use Rough Draft

1   Students open their cellphones almost before they are out of the room. It confuses professors and parents. My parents complain that young people are so wrapped up in their cell conversations that they completely miss the world around them. Why are students such non-stop cellphone users? It's crazy how so many students wander around talking into their phones, ignoring the people around them. In the end this cellphone mania is a necessary part of student life.

2   It is hard to imagine how people managed their lives without cellphones since there seems to be so much to get done. Weren't friends going to meet after class for a study session? Where is everybody? Life in school can be crazy. We juggle complex schedules, work, meals. A quick phone call can organize it all. We arrange study sessions, confirm a lunch date, get a ride, coordinate a team project for class, and maybe even make time for a date.

3   Students, like everyone else, need to call about possible jobs, resolve disputes over bills, arrange to have their car fixed, find out the results of medical tests, and even, in some cases, find babysitters. Sometimes walking back to the dorm from a night class, students are on the phone simply to feel safer so that if anything happens they can let someone else know and perhaps get help. Cellphones let them get all this done.

4   Cellphones let us be together at the same time, even if we are in different places. Part of the reason for such widespread cellphone use is that instead of having to wait. A quick phone call has one person getting out of bed while another is getting out of class. Two friends seated at different ends of a stadium can enjoy the blow by blow of the action at the same time.

5   Everyone likes to share. Cellphones let people share. I love the way it's so easy to take pictures and post them on the phone. You have to be careful, though. Cellphones are banned in some locker rooms and why it is dangerous to be caught in an embarrassing situation at a party. You never know what can be emailed to your friends or even posted to the Internet. At concerts some in the audience call up friends and then hold up the phone so that they can hear part of a concert. When something really funny is happening, anyone can with a quick call share it with someone else who would appreciate the moment. L.O.L. Cellphones allow an instant connection, a voice instant messenger.

6   Cellphone calls let people reach out and touch each other. Most phone calls are very short. "Hey, what's up?" "What are you doing?" "How are you?" Little information is exchanged. "Nothing much," in fact, is a common answer. What do such phone calls accomplish? They let people keep in touch with each other.

7   Texting is really a very handy way to keep in touch. Social media like Facebook lets friends know what is going on with each other's lives, even long lost friends. Facebook can even be a great space for sharing since you can post pictures, blog your ideas, identify your favourite group or more. I can't imagine how out of touch I would feel without a cellphone.

8   It must have been weird to wait an entire day before bragging to friends and family about getting the only A on a Chemistry test. It is almost impossible that students managed the complex schedule of their days before cellphones. It should not be surprising that students talk on their cellphones over nothing.

This essay is revised in Chapter 4.

Drafting: Let Yourself Explore

When you are writing a draft, you know you will revise later, so you can afford to experiment. If you are writing and want to return to a section later to develop an idea or try
a different approach, mark it with an asterisk and continue to write. You can leave gaps
to fill in later. If you have more than one idea for a section, write down the other
approaches, either bracketed on the same page or in a separate file. Always save each
draft in a separate file, if not in a hard copy. You may want to use parts of an early draft
in a later version.

Planning and Drafting Your Paper

Understand the assignment.

- Understand the topic.
- Identify key expectations.
- Make the project yours.

Find your topic.

- Talk with others.
- Keep a journal.
- Sort the subject into categories.
- Brainstorm.

Identify audience, purpose.

Develop details.

Read, talk to others, and brainstorm.

Organize the information.

- Create labelled, flexible notes.
- Develop a rough plan: a list of points in order.
- Write a quick draft to find your focus and pattern.

Develop a focused thesis.

- Focus on just one central point or issue.
- Provide an accurate forecast of what is to come.

Draft to capture your thoughts—expect to revise.

CHAPTER 4

Strategies for Global Revisions: Working with the Whole

At one time or another, all of us have said something careless to a friend, date, or partner and then spent the rest of the night regretting our words. When we speak, we cannot cut and paste, add and delete. When we write, however, we can use revision skills to work toward getting the wording right, so that it says exactly what we mean. Even professional writers don't express themselves perfectly on the first try, but they can relax, knowing that writing is a process.

Just what is revision? Don't confuse it with proofreading, the final stage of the writing process, when you carefully inspect your word choices, spelling, grammar, punctuation, and overall sentence structure and variety. The word *revision* means "re-seeing." Revision is much more drastic than proofreading, often involving an upheaval of content and organization as you become more certain about what you want to say. The writer E.M. Forster once asked, "How can I know what I think until I see what I say?" Revising can help writers bring their own ideas into sharper focus.

Most of what you read, including this text, has been considerably altered and improved as the writers progressed through early drafts. This fact shouldn't surprise you. After all, a rough draft is merely a first attempt to jot down some ideas in essay form. No matter how well you gather and organize your material, your ideas evolve only as you write. Sometimes, the best ideas come toward the end of your first or second draft, and you could end up sacrificing entire chunks of your first draft. You might even discover an entirely different approach buried within the first draft. During revision, you keep changing things—your focus, approach to the topic, supporting material, thesis statement, and topic sentences—until the results satisfy you.

Inexperienced writers often mistakenly view initial drafts as nearly finished products rather than as experiments to alter, or even scrap, if need be. As a result, they often approach revision with a defensive attitude. To revise effectively, you need to control your ego and fear and become your own first critical reader. Set aside natural feelings of accomplishment ("After all, I've put a great deal of thought into this") and dread ("Actually, I'm afraid of what I'll find if I look too closely"). Instead, recognize that revision offers an opportunity to communicate more effectively with your audience. Think of your early drafts simply as works in progress.

PREPARING TO REVISE

To distance yourself from your writing and sharpen your critical eye, set aside your first draft for half a day or longer if time permits. When you return to it, gear up for revision by jotting down your intended purpose and audience before you read your paper. These notations will help to keep your changes on track. As well, note any additional ideas that have occurred to you. Here are some tips:

- Set aside your draft for at least half a day—longer if possible.
- Write down your purpose and audience for your essay.
- Write down possible alternate directions for your essay.
- Write down any ideas or phrases that have come to you since writing the essay.

Many inexperienced writers are tempted to rush through the revision stage, hastily skimming their essays to reassure themselves that "everything sounds okay." Avoid such a quick-fix approach. If your draft appears fine on first reading, read it again with a more critical eye. You can also read your writing out loud so that two senses—hearing and seeing—are involved during revision. Reading aloud can also help you gain distance from your writing. Look at the paper globally, checking for overall focus, before you begin checking sentences and words. Can you sum up your main idea in a sentence (or two), and is that sentence interesting and clear? Try putting yourself in your reader's place. Will your letter home asking for money really convince parents who might think they've already given you too much? Will your recommendation of a new policy to address homelessness convince a cash-strapped community council? If you aren't critical now, anticipating confusion and objections, your reader(s) will be later.

Read your essay at least three times, once for each of these reasons:

To improve the focus and development of the essay as a whole

To strengthen paragraph structure and development

To sharpen sentences and words

GLOBAL REVISIONS

If you inspect your draft only sentence by sentence, you can easily overlook how its parts work together. Take a step back when you begin to revise so that you can view the overall essay rather than its separate parts. Consider big-picture elements, such as the essay's focus and direction, audience, organization, and development. Ask questions such as "Does the beginning mesh with the end?" "Does the essay wander?" and "Has anything been left out?" In this way, you can gauge how the parts relate to each other and to the whole. Use the acronym *FACT* to guide this stage of your revision.

F Ask yourself first whether the whole essay FITS together, presenting a central point for a specific audience. Have you delivered what the thesis statement promises? First drafts often include paragraphs or even large sections that have little to do with the main point. Some drafts even contain ideas for different possible essays, threads that pull in different directions. Furthermore, one section of a draft might be geared to one audience (parents, for example) and another section to an entirely different audience (students, perhaps). As you read each part, verify its connection to your purpose and audience. Don't hesitate to remove sections that don't fit, redo stray parts so they accord with your central idea, or alter your thesis statement to reflect better your supporting material. Occasionally, you might even expand one small, fertile section of your draft into an entirely new essay.

A Whenever we write first drafts, we may know what we mean, but we often do not think about what the reader needs to know. We tend to assume that readers know what we know and can somehow read our minds. Unwittingly, we leave gaps. As we revise, we try to locate and fill in these gaps where we have left out essential background information or material. Ask yourself, "Where will the reader need more information or examples to understand my meaning?" Then ADD the appropriate sentences, paragraphs, or even pages.

C First drafts often contain material that relates to the thesis but doesn't contribute to the essay. When writing quickly, we tend to repeat ourselves, include trite or uninformative examples, and crank out whole paragraphs when one clear sentence would suffice. As you revise, CUT away this clutter with a free hand. Such paring can be painful, especially if you're left with a skimpy text, but your final message will emerge with much greater clarity. As you've probably guessed, revising a draft often requires both adding and cutting.

T Carefully TEST the organization of your essay. The text should flow smoothly from point to point, with clear transitions between the various ideas. Test the organization by outlining your major and minor points, and then check the results for logic and completeness. Alternatively, read the draft and note the progression of its paragraphs and points. Look for places where you can clarify connections between ideas and thus help your readers to understand.

Chapters 6 to 13 explain different writing strategies for personal, analytical, and argumentative writing, and conclude with revision questions geared specifically to each strategy. Use these questions, together with the *FACT* of revision, to help you revise more effectively.

Now let's apply the *FACT* approach to Drew's essay on cellphones, which you read in Chapter 3 on pages 54–55. Like most early drafts, this one needs work.

FIT. While most of Drew's paper fits his audience and thesis, the material concerning the misuses of the cellphone to email pictures and instant messenger slang like "L.O.L." doesn't match his audience or purpose. It is off track, raises unnecessary suspicion about cellphone use, and is too informal for the audience.

ADD. If Drew really wishes to convince a skeptical audience that student cellphone use is necessary, he needs to make his examples more detailed. The material on using cellphones as a way of being together at the same time and keeping in touch is especially scanty, but each paragraph could be better developed with more detailed examples.

CUT. The paragraph on text messaging may fit the topic, but it is different in kind from using cellphones for voice communication. Cutting that paragraph will allow the paper to be more focused on a single type of cellphone use.

TEST. If the paper is going to be organized according to the order of importance to the audience, it would make sense to put a paragraph on sharing after "getting business done" and to put a paragraph on "keeping in touch" before "together at the same time." A careful review of the flow of the paragraphs shows that the third paragraph lacks a clear transitional topic sentence.

Decide if you revise better from the computer screen or using a printout. Sometimes, essays look different in print than on the screen, and you will likely find it helpful to have a printout of your essay if you are doing a major revision. As you read your own essay, note on a separate sheet of paper or computer page problem areas or ideas to add and changes to try. You can insert ideas directly into your draft by using a symbol such as < > or a different colour font. Some writers paste revision ideas with Post-it notes, which you can do either on paper or on a computer screen with a software program. If you are revising directly on the computer, you can also track your changes so that you do not lose them.

Keep backup copies of drafts, using the *Save As* function and renaming and possibly dating each revision. Accidentally erasing a file or losing your work to an electrical power surge is not uncommon. In addition, consider backing up copies of your earlier drafts; selected parts of these drafts may prove useful later, and new papers sometimes sprout from old drafts. Regardless of the medium you use, be willing to write three or more versions of the same idea to find out which works best. When you approach the actual essay, make your job easier by using these basic techniques:

1. To delete something, cut it and track the changes or cross it out lightly; you may decide to resurrect the deleted material later.
2. When you are working with a draft, you may have ideas or questions that could prove helpful. On the computer, you can insert these into your text, marking them with a special symbol, such as < >. Delete them later if they serve no purpose. To add a section of text on a print copy, place a letter *(A, B, C, D)* at the appropriate spot; then create the new material in a new file or at the bottom of your draft file, clearly marked with the letter. Make smaller changes within sections by crossing out on the hard copy what you don't want and writing the replacement above it or nearby. You can wait to move blocks of new text into place until you have finished reviewing the entire draft, as you may end up changing your mind.
3. On a computer screen, you can simply cut and move sections to rearrange the organization of your essay. After you have moved material, you will need to make certain it fits into the new context. If there is a problem with coherence, you can rearrange the organization to improve the flow. To rearrange the organization on a print copy, draw arrows showing where you want things to go, or cut up your draft and rearrange the sections by taping them on new sheets of paper. Use whatever method works best for you.
4. When you finish revising, check the coherence of this draft. The writing must flow smoothly at the points where you have added, deleted, or moved sections of text. Using transitions and topic sentences that focus the main idea of the

paragraph, or provide a bridge from one paragraph to the next, can help you stitch together different parts of the essay more seamlessly. In addition, altered sentences must be clearly written and logically constructed. You can best check the essay's flow using a printout.

5. When you are satisfied with your changes, enter them in a *new copy* of your draft file. Always keep separate files for draft versions in case you need to go back to them.

It is crucial that you view revision not simply as a quick sweep through your draft just prior to handing it in. Instead, revision should be an ongoing process that often involves an upheaval of major sections as you see your draft through your reader's eyes and strive to write as well as you can.

EXERCISE

1. List Drew's other options for revising this draft; then indicate the necessary changes if he had decided to write for fellow students.

2. Use the *FACT* acronym to revise the first draft you created for the exercise in Chapter 3 on page 54.

Case History

Cellphone Use
Rough Draft Marked Up

At the end of their class,
Students open their cell phones almost before they are out of the room. It con-
flip ~ *are greatly confused by this practice and*
fuses professors and parents. My parents complain that young people are so
^ Some
wrapped up in their cell conversations that they completely miss the world
Most wonder *are compulsive*
around them. Why are students such non-stop cell phone users? It looks
The *ing*
ridiculous when large numbers of college and university students wander ~
may seem ridiculous to
around talking into their phones, ignoring the people around them. In the end
outsiders. However,
this cell phone mania is a necessary part of student life.
There are many reasons students wander around campus talking into the air. They use
cell phones to coordinate the day's activities, to get some business done, to share
life's events, and to keep in touch.
　　It is hard to imagine how people managed their lives without cellphones

since there seems to be so much to get done. Weren't friends going to meet
Add Ⓐ
after class for a study session? Where is everybody? Life in school can be
hoctic as students *of classes* *and a social life.*
crazy. We juggle complex schedules, work, meals. A quick phone call can

organize it all. We arrange study sessions, confirm a lunch date, get a ride,

coordinate a team project for class, and maybe even make time for a date.

Add Ⓑ

   Students, like everyone else, need to call about possible jobs, resolve dis-

putes over bills, arrange to have their car fixed, find out the results of medical

There is often a lot to get done that has to be squeezed into a busy day.

tests, and even, in some cases, find babysitters. Sometimes walking back to

the dorm from a night class, students are on the phone simply to feel safer so

that if anything happens they can let someone else know and perhaps get

help. Cellphones let them get all this done. *in the time between classes or even while*

walking back to their dorm, leaving them with more time for other things like studying or

going out with friends.

   ~~Cellphones let us be together at the same time, even if we are in different~~

~~places.~~ Part of the reason for such widespread cellphone use is that instead

We can be part of the immediate now.

of having to wait. A quick phone call has one person getting out of bed while

another is getting out of class. Two friends seated at different ends of a

Anyone can know what almost anyone else their call list is doing at any moment.

stadium can enjoy the blow by blow of the action at the same time.

   Everyone likes to share. Cellphones let people share. Many phones

moments of delight, success, and even failures with others who care.

even let you take a picture and email it to a friend. ~~It is because of this~~

When a baby is expected, the soon to be grandparents can't wait for

~~practice that cellphones are banned in some locker rooms and why it is dan-~~

the call.

~~gerous to be caught in an embarrassing situation at a party. You never know~~

~~what can be emailed to your friends or even posted to the Internet.~~ At con-

certs some in the audience call up friends and then hold up the phone so that

they can hear part of a concert. When something really funny is happening,

anyone can with a quick call share it with someone else who would appre-

to let people experience what you are experiencing, whether it

ciate the moment. L.O.L. Cellphones allow an instant connection. a ~~voice~~

is excitement over a success, an idea, the finals of

~~instant messenger.~~

a sporting event, or a newscast.

Add Ⓒ

   Cellphone calls let people reach out and touch each other. Most phone

calls are very short. "Hey, what's up?" "What are you doing?" "How are you?"

Little information is exchanged. "Nothing much," in fact, is a common answer.

What do such phone calls accomplish? They let people keep in touch with

each other.

Continued on next page

Continued from previous page

~~Texting is really a very handy way to keep in touch. Even if you can't reach the other person, you can leave a message to let them know that you are thinking about them. Other people keep in touch through social media such as Facebook which lets friends know what is going on with each other's lives, even long lost friends. Facebook can even be a great space for sharing since you can post pictures, blog your ideas, identify your favourite group or more. If anything, students of today can be considered the in touch generation.~~

It must have been weird to wait an entire day before bragging to friends and family about getting the only A on a Chemistry test. It is almost ~~impossible~~ *incomprehensible* that students managed the complex schedule of their days before cellphones.

It should not be surprising that students ~~talk~~ *snap open* on their cellphones ~~over nothing.~~ *at the drop of almost anything. The surprise would be if they kept their cell phones in their pockets and waited.* ↗ Add ⓑ

What did a student do if a ride didn't show up? How did a couple share the excitement of a concert in the moment or a good joke if they had to wait days? Earlier generations who seem puzzled by the cell phone fever that has hit campuses might wonder how they might have felt without a phone, having to wait for weeks for the mail or longer for a visit.

A.　　A quick cellphone call to a friend reveals that the study session was moved to the student centre. Does everyone have his or her part ready for the presentation speech class at 3:00 p.m.? A flurry of cellphone calls makes certain everyone is ready. Will Collin be able to meet his girlfriend this afternoon? He needs to call to see if she is still free. Where is Jennifer since she said she was picking me up in front of the Science Building?

B.　　Sometimes cellphone calls get important business done. Heather needs to convince her parents that she really, really needs more money to cover the cost of books. Tim needs to contact his adviser so he can schedule for the next semester.

C.　　If you got an A on a paper that you thought would get an F, you can quickly spread the celebration to anyone who would echo your joy while the feeling was still hot. Sometimes a cellphone call can make the sharing very concrete, getting someone to go outside to look at a spectacular meteor shower, getting a friend to change channels so they can see an interview with a favourite rock star, or letting family know about a terrible earthquake in China.

D.   Contact is what helps keep people close. Parents like their children to visit. Couples need to make time for each other. When people keep in touch, it lets them know that others care, lets them keep each other as important parts of their lives. Some students call their parents every day keeping the family ties tight, getting the emotional reassurance of those loving connections. Sometimes it seems like couples seem to be holding electronic hands as they walk across campus, with little room for some interloper to break up their relationships. Friends may not be able to see each other since they are going to different schools, but a simple cellphone call lets them each know the others are still friends.

After letting his draft sit for a day, Drew was able to come back to it with fresh eyes. In the next draft, Drew works to on clarifying, organizing, and cutting material that does not fit.

Case History

Cellphone Use
Second Draft

At the end of their class, students flip open their cellphones almost before they are out of the room. Professors and parents are confused by this practice. Some complain that young people are so wrapped up in their cell conversations that they completely miss the world around them. Most wonder why students are compulsive cellphone users. There are many reasons students wander around campus talking into the air. They use cellphones to coordinate the day's activities, to get some business done, to share life's events, and to keep in touch. The large number of college and university students wandering around talking into their phones, ignoring the people around them, may seem ridiculous to outsiders. However, in the end this cellphone mania is a necessary part of student life.

It is hard to imagine how people managed their lives without cellphones since there is so much to coordinate. Weren't friends going to meet after class for a study session? Where is everybody? A quick cellphone call to a friend reveals that the study session was moved to the student centre. Does everyone have his or her part ready for the presentation in Speech class at 3:00 p.m.? A flurry of cellphone calls makes certain everyone is ready. Will Collin be able to meet his girlfriend this afternoon? He needs to call to see if she is still free.

Continued on next page

Clarified that Drew means classroom by adding "class."	
Added thesis statement that maps paper order.	
Provided more detailed account of cellphone use. Placed academic material first for audience.	

Continued from previous page

Where is Jennifer since she said she was picking me up in front of the Science Building? Life in school can be hectic as students juggle complex schedules of classes, work, meal times, and a social life. A quick phone call can organize it all; arrange study sessions, confirm a lunch date, arrange a ride, coordinate a team project for class, and maybe even make time for a date.

Clarified what was complex.

Sometimes cellphone calls get important business done. Heather needs to convince her parents that she really, really needs more money to cover the cost of books. Tim needs to contact his adviser since he needs to lift his holds so he can schedule for the next semester. Students, like everyone else, need to call about possible jobs, resolve disputes over bills, arrange to have their car fixed, find out the results of medical tests, and even, in some cases, find babysitters. There is often a lot to get done that has to be squeezed into a busy day. Sometimes walking back to the dorm from a night class, students are on the phone simply to feel safer so that if anything happens they can let someone else know and perhaps get help. Cellphones let them get all this done in the time between classes or even while walking back to their dorm, leaving them with more time for other things like studying or going out with friends.

Added a transitional thesis statement. Added more specific examples to appeal to audience.

Everyone likes to share moments of delight, success, and even failure with others who care. When a baby is expected, the soon-to-be grandparents can't wait for the call. Cellphones let people share. Many phones even let you take a picture and email it to a friend. At concerts some in the audience call up friends and then hold up the phone so that they can hear part of a concert. When something really funny is happening, anyone can with a quick call share it with someone else who would appreciate the moment. If you got an A on a paper that you thought would get an F, you can quickly spread the celebration to anyone who would echo your joy while the feeling was still hot. Sometimes a cellphone call can make the sharing very concrete, getting someone to go outside to look at a spectacular meteor shower, getting a friend to change channels so they can see an interview with a favourite rock star, or letting family know about a terrible earthquake in China. Cellphones allow an immediate connection to let people experience what you are experiencing, whether it is excitement over a success, an idea, the finals of a sporting event, or a news event.

Added context that relates to understanding of reader. Moved sharing paragraph earlier in the essay to improve clarity and coherence. Cut material on inappropriate use of phone picture that might offend audience. Added more concrete examples appropriate to target audience.

Cellphone calls let people stay in touch with each other. Most phone calls are very short, over before students have gotten from the classroom to the door of the building. "Hey, what's up?" "What are you doing?" "How are

Adds more detailed examples appropriate to target audience.

you?" Little information is exchanged and little is really shared. "Nothing much," in fact, is a common response. What do such phone calls accomplish? They let people keep in touch with each other. Contact is what helps keep people close. Parents like their children to visit. Couples need to make time for each other. When people keep in touch, it lets them know that others care, lets them keep each other as important parts of their lives. Some students call their parents every day keeping the family ties tight, getting the emotional reassurance of those loving connections. Sometimes it seems like couples seem to be holding electronic hands as they walk across campus, with little room for some interloper to break up their relationships. Friends may not be able to see each other since they are going to different schools, but a simple cellphone call lets them each know the others still are friends.

> Cut paragraph on text messages.

Part of the reason for such widespread cellphone use is that instead of having to wait, we can be part of the immediate now. A quick phone call has one person getting out of bed while another is getting out of class. Two friends seated at different ends of a stadium can enjoy the blow by blow of the action at the same time. Anyone can know what almost anyone else in their call list is doing at any moment.

> This paragraph still needs improvement.

It must have been lonely to wait an entire day before bragging to friends and family about getting the only A on a Chemistry test. It is almost incomprehensible that students managed the complex schedule of their days before cellphones. What did a student do if a ride didn't show up? How did people share the excitement of a concert in the moment or a good joke if they had to wait days? Earlier generations who seem puzzled by the cellphone fever that has hit campuses might wonder how they might have felt without a phone, having to wait for weeks for the mail or longer for a visit. It should not be surprising that students snap open their cellphones at the drop of almost anything. The surprise would be if they kept their cellphones in their pockets and waited.

STRENGTHENING PARAGRAPH STRUCTURE AND DEVELOPMENT

Once you finish considering the essay as a whole, examine your paragraphs one by one, applying the *FACT* approach that you used for the essay as a whole. Make sure that each paragraph *FITS* the paper's major focus and develops a single central idea. If a paragraph needs more support or examples, *ADD* whatever is necessary. If a paragraph contains ineffective or unhelpful material, *CUT* it. *TEST* the flow of ideas from paragraph to paragraph and clarify connections, both between and within paragraphs, as necessary. Ask the basic questions in the checklist that follows about each paragraph, and make any needed revisions.

REVISION CHECKLIST FOR PARAGRAPHS

- ■ Does the paragraph have one, and only one, central idea?
- ■ Does the central idea help to develop the thesis statement?
- ■ Does each statement within the paragraph help to develop the central idea?
- ■ Does the paragraph need additional explanations, examples, or supporting details?
- ■ Would cutting some material make the paragraph stronger?
- ■ Would reorganization make the ideas easier to follow?
- ■ Can the connections between successive sentences be improved?
- ■ Is each paragraph clearly and smoothly related to those that precede and follow it?

Don't expect to escape making any changes; some readjustments will undoubtedly be needed. Certain paragraphs may be stripped down or deleted entirely, others beefed up, and still others reorganized or repositioned. Chapter 5 contains more detailed information on writing effective paragraphs.

EXERCISE *Below are two sample student paragraphs. Evaluate each according to the Revision Checklist for Paragraphs and suggest any necessary changes.*

1. For hours we had been waiting under the overhang of an abandoned hut. None of us had thought to bring ponchos on our short hike through the woods. Soon it would be dark. Earlier in the day it had been a perfectly clear day. We all agreed that we didn't want to stand here all night in the dark, so we decided to make a dash for it.

2. Canadians are beginning to become more and more conscious about the ingredients and production that goes in the food that they are ingesting. There are many reasons that Canadians are choosing to buy organic food whenever possible. With free-range chicken products, customers know exactly where their food is coming from. Free-range chickens are not raised in factories. They can run around. Vegetables that are grown organically in a garden taste better. People who want to have optimal health should also avoid unnecessary exposure to airborne chemicals, and should get plenty of exercise.

WRITING THE INTRODUCTION AND CONCLUSION

Even when you do not have time to revise extensively, you can almost always improve your writing by going back to the introduction and sharpening your focus. After you have finished a draft or two, you are usually more clear about what you want to say than when you first sat down to write. Sometimes, students actually benefit by starting a whole new draft, using what they thought to be a conclusion as a new starting point.

Generally, short papers begin with a single paragraph that includes the previously drafted thesis statement, which sometimes needs to be rephrased so that it meshes smoothly with the rest of the paragraph. An effective introduction acquaints the reader with your topic, clearly signals your intention, and sparks the reader's interest.

The conclusion should follow from the rest of your essay, reinforce your purpose, and fit with the type of writing you are doing. If you are writing to inform someone about a business plan, a summary may be the best type of conclusion. For an illustration or persuasive piece of writing, you might want to leave the reader with a thought or question to ponder. For a persuasive piece of writing, you might conclude with warnings, recommendations, or hopes.

SELECTING A TITLE

Like writing an introduction, choosing a title can wait until you finish the paper. Since the reader must see the connection between what the title promises and what the essay delivers, a good title must be both accurate and specific.

Titling the student essay "Cellphone Use" would mislead the reader, since it would seem to suggest that the essay is on how to use a cellphone. A specific title suggests the essay's focus rather than just its topic. For example, "The Reasons for Student Cellphone Fever" is clearer and more precise than simply "Cellphone Use." The essay is about why cellphones are used so extensively, not about how they are to be used.

To engage your reader's interest, you might try your hand at a clever or catchy title, but don't get so carried away with creativity that you forget to relate the title to the paper's content. Here are some examples of catchy titles where word play is effective at drawing the reader in and signalling the focus of the essay:

Common "Handling a Hangover"
Clever "The Mourning After"
Common "Selecting the Proper Neckwear"
Clever "How to Ring Your Neck"

Use a clever title only if its wit or humour doesn't clash with the overall purpose and tone of the paper. A specific title suggests the essay's focus rather than just its topic.

SHARPENING SENTENCES AND WORDS

Next, turn your attention to sentences and words. You can improve your writing considerably by finding and correcting sentences that convey the wrong meaning or are stylistically deficient in some way. Consider, for example, the following sentences:

Just Martin was picked to write the report.

Martin was just picked to write the report.

Martin was picked to write just the report.

The first sentence says that no one except Martin will write the report, the second says that he was recently picked for the job, and the third says that he will write nothing else. Clearly, each of these sentences expresses a different meaning.

Now let's look at a second set of sentences:

Personally, I am of the opinion that the results of our membership drive will prove to be pleasing to all of us.

I believe the results of our membership drive will please all of us.

The wordiness of the first sentence slows the reader's pace and makes it harder to grasp the writer's meaning. The second sentence, by contrast, is much easier to grasp.

Like your sentences, your words should convey your thoughts precisely and clearly. After all, words are your chief means of communicating with your reader. Examine the first draft and revised version of the following paragraph, which describe the early-morning actions of the writer's roommate. The underlined words identify points of revision.

First Draft

Coffee cup in hand, she <u>moves</u> toward the bathroom. The coffee spills <u>noisily</u> on the tile floor as she <u>reaches</u> for the light switch and <u>turns</u> it on. After <u>looking</u> briefly at the face in the mirror, she <u>walks</u> toward the bathtub.

Revised Version

Coffee cup in hand, she <u>stumbles</u> toward the bathroom. <u>Spilled</u> coffee <u>slaps</u> on the tile floor as she <u>gropes</u> for the light switch and <u>flips</u> it on. After <u>squinting</u> briefly at the face in the mirror, she <u>shuffles</u> toward the bathtub.

Note that the words in the first draft are general and imprecise. Exactly how does she move? With a limp? With a strut? With a spring in her step? And what does *noisily* mean? A thud? A roar? A sharp crack? The reader has no way of knowing. Recognizing this fact, the student revised her paragraph, substituting vivid, specific words. As a result, the reader can visualize the actions more sharply.

Don't confuse vivid, specific words with pretentious or flowery words. Write to communicate, not to impress.

Reading your draft out loud will force you to slow down, and you will often hear yourself stumble over problem sections. You'll be more likely to uncover errors such as missing words, excessive repetition, clumsy sentences, and sentence fragments. Be honest in your evaluation; don't read in virtues that aren't there or that exaggerate the writing quality.

Chapter 5 discusses sentences, diction, and style in detail.

PEER EVALUATION OF DRAFTS

At various points in the writing process, your instructor may ask you and your classmates to read and respond to one another's papers. Peer response often proves useful because even the best writers cannot always predict how their readers will react to their writing. For example, magazine articles designed to reduce the fear of an economic downturn have in some cases increased anxiety about a recession. Furthermore, writers often have difficulty seeing the problems with their own drafts because so much hard work has gone into them. What seems clear and effective to you can be confusing or boring to your reader. Comments from peers can help you to see your writing from a reader's point of view.

Just as the responses of others help you, so, too, will your responses help them. Since you don't have the close, involved relationship with your peers' writing that you do with your own, you can assess it with greater objectivity. Eventually, the practice of doing peer reviews will help you develop the critical eye you need to become your own editor.

Responding to Your Peers' Drafts

Responding to someone else's writing is easier than you might imagine. The most helpful way to respond is to let the reader know how you understand what you have read, what draws you in, and what loses or confuses you. It's not your job to spell out how to make the draft more effective, how to organize it, what to include, and what language to use. The writer must make these decisions. Your job is not to *solve* problems, but to *identify* them. You can do that best by letting the reader know what goes on in your mind as you are reading.

Some responses are more helpful than others. For example, saying that the draft "looks fine" does not help the writer. Such a response suggests that you have not read carefully and critically. It can take courage as well as attention to give specific, constructive feedback, but it is far more helpful in the long run than polite, generic praise. In addition, critical but vague comments, such as "The introduction is uninteresting," are not helpful either. Point out *why* it is uninteresting. For instance, you might note, "The introduction loses me because it's very technical. I ask myself why I should read on." Below is another example of an ineffective response and a more effective counterpart.

Ineffective:

> The paper was confusing.

Effective:

> Paragraphs 2, 3, and 4 confused me when the subject kept jumping around. First you wrote about your experience on the first day of university, then you went on to how much you enjoyed junior high school, and finally you wrote about what you want to do for a career. I don't see how these ideas relate or why they are in the order that they are.

Here are some steps to follow when responding to someone else's draft.

1. You can read the essay from beginning to end without interruption. If time allows, it can also be a helpful exercise to read the paper while listening to the writer reading it aloud. This way, writers are more likely to hear awkward or unclear sentences themselves.
2. On a separate sheet of paper, indicate what you consider to be the main idea— what you hear the writer saying. The writer can then see whether the intended message has come through.

3. Identify the greatest strength and the greatest problem or weakness of the paper. Writers need suggestions for improvement, but they also need to hear about what is working. What stays with you after reading the piece, and what would you like to hear more about?

4. Reread the paper and write either specific responses to each paragraph or your responses to general questions such as the ones in the checklist that follows. In either case, don't comment on spelling or grammar unless it really inhibits your reading. If you are tempted to make suggestions about grammar, check with your instructor for an expert opinion.

PEER RESPONSE CHECKLIST

■ What is the main point of this essay?

■ What is the greatest strength? What is the greatest problem?

■ What material doesn't seem to fit the main point or the audience?

■ What questions has the author not answered?

■ Where should more details or examples be added? Why?

■ At what point does the paper fail to hold my interest? Why?

■ Where is the organization confusing?

■ Where is the writing unclear or vague?

As you learn more strategies for successful writing, you will be able to recognize more weaknesses and strengths in peer papers above.

As you read the final version of Drew's paper on cellphones, carefully examine the margin notes, which highlight key features of the revision. Drew added an example to the introduction to make it more interesting, added a section on how the common use of cellphones has an impact, and clarified the paragraph on "the now." He has cut the material on babysitters and walking across campus that his readers found inappropriate. He has tightened his language by sharpening his sentences and his word choices in a few places and by using more consistent pronouns.

Changed title to make it more focused.

Added short conversation to make more interesting.

Case History

The Reasons for Student Cellphone Fever
Final Draft

At the end of their university classes, students turn on their cellphones almost before they are out of the room.

"Hey, just got out of English."

"What ya goin' to do?"

"Get some coffee and study before Biology. You?"

"Got Intro to Business in 10 minutes."

"Well, see ya."

These conversations seem far from necessary. Yet students plow their way from class to class with their cellphones glued to their ears. Professors and parents are confused by this practice. Some parents complain that young people are so wrapped up in their cell conversations that they completely miss the world around them. Many wonder why students are compulsive cellphone users. There are many reasons students wander around campus talking into the air. They use cellphones to coordinate the day's activities, to get business done, to share life's events, and to keep in touch. Part of this trend, undeniably, is that many others are also doing it. The large number of university students who wander around talking into their phones, ignoring the people around them, may seem ridiculous to outsiders. However, in the end this cellphone mania is a reasonable, pleasurable, and vital part of student life.

It is hard to imagine how people managed their lives without cellphones since there is so much to coordinate. Weren't friends going to meet after class for a study session? Where is everybody? A quick call reveals that the study session was moved to the student centre. Does everyone have his or her part ready for the presentation in Speech class at 3:00 p.m.? A quick call or text makes certain everyone is ready. Will Colin be able to meet his girlfriend this afternoon? He needs to call to see if she is still free. Where is Jennifer since she said she was picking me up in front of the Science Building? School life can be hectic as students juggle classes, work, meal times, and a social life. A quick phone call can organize it all: arrange study sessions, confirm a lunch date, arrange a ride, coordinate a team project for class, and maybe even make time for a date.

Sometimes, cellphone calls get important business done. Heather needs to convince her parents that she really, really needs more money to cover the cost of books. Tim needs to ask his adviser to lift his holds so he can schedule next semester's classes. Students, like everyone else, need to call about possible jobs, resolve bill disputes, arrange to have their car repaired, and find out medical test results. Cellphones let them get all this done in the time between classes or while walking back to their dorms, leaving them with more time for other things like studying or going out with friends.

Continued on next page

Marginal annotations:

Added sentence with more active verbs to capture scene.

Clarified the "some."

Added trend that is a later paragraph.

Clarified "necessary" by expanding idea.

Simplifies language since calls are obviously made from cellphones" would be clearer. Throughout, changed language so consistently "student" and "they," not "we."

Tightened sentence by cutting wordiness.

Tightened language.

Cut the line about walking across campus at night.

Continued from previous page

Changed pronouns to be consistent.

Cut unnecessary phrase "while the feeling was still hot."

Changed "from any idea" to "a great idea" more likely to be shared.

"Answer" was chosen as a better word than "response."

Provided a context for the paragraph. Reworded to be clearer.

Everyone likes to share moments of delight, success, and even failure with others who care. When a baby is expected, the expectant grandparents can't wait for the call. Cellphones let people share. At concerts, some in the audience call up friends and then hold up the phone so that they can hear part of a concert. When something really funny is happening, anyone can with a quick call share it with someone else who would appreciate the moment. If students get an unexpected A, they can quickly spread the celebration to those who would echo their joy. Sometimes, a cellphone call can make the sharing very concrete, getting someone to go outside to look at a spectacular meteor shower, getting a friend to change channels to see an interview with a favourite rock star, or letting family know about a terrible earthquake in China. Cellphones allow an immediate connection to let people experience what callers are experiencing, whether it is excitement over a success, a great idea, the finals of a sporting event, or a news event.

Cellphone calls can let people stay in touch with each other. Most calls are very short, over before students have gotten from the classroom to the door of the building. "Hey, what's up?" "What are you doing?" "How are you?" Little information is exchanged and little is really shared. "Nothing much," in fact, is a common answer. What do such phone calls accomplish? They let people keep in touch with each other. Contact is what helps keep people close. Parents like their children to visit. Couples need to make time for each other. When people keep in touch, it lets them know that others care, lets them keep each other as important parts of their lives. Some students call their parents every day to maintain family ties while getting the emotional reassurance of those loving connections. Couples hold electronic hands as they walk across campus. Friends may not be able to see each other since they are going to different schools, but a simple cellphone call confirms their continued friendship.

A sociology professor told her class that she thought that the cellphone "created a virtual society of now." Cellphones create a feeling that all are in it together at the same time, even if in different places. Instead of having to wait to find out what might be happening, students can be part of the same now. A quick phone call has one person getting out of bed while another is getting out of class. Two friends seated at different ends of a stadium can enjoy the blow by blow of the action at the same time. Anyone can know what almost anyone else in their call list is doing at any moment. A clip from a news story on television about cosmetic surgery conveyed this perfectly. A woman is talking on her cellphone while she is undergoing liposuction. "Yeh," she declares, "I am undergoing surgery right now. No, I don't feel much, maybe just a tickle." It is hard to get more immediate than that.

> Added a very specific example to make the idea clearer.

All of this is made possible because others are doing it. Teenagers are notorious for doing what others are doing. Parents ask, "If your friends jumped off a bridge, would you do it too?" The answer is an embarrassing "yes," especially if the jumpers were attached to bungee cords. It would be embarrassing not to have a cellphone, ideally a Razr or an iPhone or whatever is the latest trend. Everyone else seems to be talking while walking. So using cellphones right after class, between classes, during lunch, or at a concert just seems to be normal behaviour—and most people want to be normal. Besides, if students are lucky enough to have good friends, their friends are probably calling them; and if friends are calling, it is important to call them back.

> Added section on "how everyone is doing this" has an impact in response to peers.

> Added a phrase to be memorable.

> Added specific idea to explain concept.

It must have been lonely to wait an entire day before bragging to friends and family about getting the only A on a Chemistry test. It is almost incomprehensible that students managed their complex schedules before cellphones. What did a student do if a ride didn't show up? How did people share the excitement of a concert in the moment or a good joke if they had to wait days? Earlier generations who seem puzzled by the cellphone fever that has hit campuses might wonder how they might have felt without a phone, having to wait for weeks for the mail or longer for a visit. It should not be surprising that students snap open their cellphones at the end of class. The surprise would be if they kept their cellphones in their pockets and waited.

Acting on Your Peers' Responses

Sometimes, you need strong nerves to act on a peer response. You can easily become defensive or discount your reader's comments as foolish. Remember, however, that as a writer you are trying to communicate with your readers, and that means taking reader feedback seriously. Of course, you decide which responses are appropriate, but even an inappropriate criticism sometimes prompts a train of thought that leads to good ideas for revision.

ACTING ON PEER RESPONSE CHECKLIST

- Did the reader understand my main point? If not, how can I make it clearer?
- What did they see as the main problem? Can I solve it?
- What strengths did they identify that I can keep?
- What didn't fit that I need to cut or make clearer?
- Which reader's questions should I answer more completely?
- Where should I add details or examples?
- How could I make sections that lose my reader's interest more engaging, or should I cut those sections?
- Why did my reader find some sections confusing? How could I reorganize those sections?
- Where could I rewrite sections to make them clearer?

THE FINAL STAGE: PROOFREADING YOUR DRAFT

Proofreading is the final stage of writing. Check carefully for errors in grammar, punctuation, and spelling, as well as syntax, diction, tone, and style. Since we often slide over our own errors simply because we know what we mean, or because we are so familiar with the work that we see what we think it says, some writers find that they catch problems when they read their own writing out loud. Others inch through the draft deliberately, moving a finger slowly under every word. You can repeat this procedure several times, looking first for errors in grammar, then for sentence errors and problems in punctuation and mechanics, and finally for mistakes in spelling. Be especially alert for problems that have plagued your writing in the past.

Although a spell-check tool can be useful for a quick review, you cannot rely on it blindly. For example, spell-check can't judge whether you used the wrong word (*form* instead of *from*) or confused identical sounding but differently spelled words (*to, two, too,* or *their, there, they're*). *You* are still the ultimate proofreader.

Effective proofreading calls for you to assume a detective role and probe for errors that weaken your writing. If you accept the challenge, you will certainly improve the quality of your finished work.

To help guide proofreading, Chapter 5 discusses local revisions for paragraphs, sentences, diction, and style.

COLLABORATIVE WRITING

At many workplaces and in university, you will likely be asked to engage in collaborative projects that involve others. While writing as part of a group offers some advantages, it also poses some interesting challenges. A group can draw on many different perspectives and areas of expertise, split up the work, and enjoy the feedback of a built-in peer group. At the same time, to create a collaborative project, people in the group must develop the interpersonal and teamwork skills needed to coordinate several efforts, work through differences of opinion, deal with people who may not do their fair share, and integrate different kinds of personalities into a functional and productive unit.

How can you increase the likelihood of success for your collaboration? In the first meeting, the group should decide how each member will contribute to the project, plan how to approach the assignment, work out a schedule or timetable for meetings, decide how group members will communicate with each other, and discuss ground rules. What happens if one group member tries to dominate too much or if a member does not show up or participate? It can be helpful to assign roles to people early on, and to designate a group leader. Decide beforehand whether it is the group leader's responsibility to contact anyone who misses a meeting or does not contribute. You could also select one or two final editors who can blend different contributions and materials into a final product that reads smoothly, as though it were written by one person.

Here are some suggestions for successful collaborative work:

1. Select a leader with strong organizational skills.
2. Make sure that each person has every other group member's phone number and email address.
3. Analyze the project and develop a work plan with clearly stated deadlines for each step of the project.
4. Assign roles to group members based on their interests and strengths.
5. Schedule regular meetings or check-in times to keep everyone on track.
6. Encourage ideas and feedback from all members at each meeting.
7. If each member is working on a different portion of the paper, submit each contribution to other members of the group for peer input.
8. To ensure that the finished product is written in one style and fits together as a whole, assign one person to compile the submissions and write the complete draft.
9. Allow plenty of time to review the complete draft so that necessary changes can be made.

If a serious problem develops despite these efforts, in some cases you can contact your instructor. Keep in mind, however, that working through the group's challenges is part of the assignment, and some instructors expect groups to solve these problems on their own.

Online Collaboration

When it is difficult to find common meeting times for all group members, online collaboration offers several advantages. You can use digital tools such as Google Docs and wikis to exchange material and comments at every stage of the writing process. Google Docs allows you to create and edit documents in Word, Excel, and PowerPoint, so that group members can edit online simultaneously and do not need to trade file attachments back and forth. Many online collaborative writing platforms, such as PrimaryPad or PiratePad, can provide a common writing space for you to edit in real time. Examples of online collaboration include the following:

1. Post a general idea on Facebook so that others can add comments on possible topics.
2. Email each other information you find, possibly as an attachment in an agreed-upon format such as Word.
3. Use online chat or Google Docs to discuss ideas for the project.
4. Text message your thesis statement to friends to see if it is effective, and get their feedback.
5. Copy sections of the project into Notes in Facebook or email the sections as an attachment.
6. Share the final document as an attachment.
7. MindMeister and other web programs allow you to build mind maps and brainstorms with others.

Whenever you use email or other media for collaborative writing, it's helpful to designate a project leader who will ensure that all members participate and who will receive and distribute all materials. Your instructor may request copies of the email exchanges so that he or she can follow your work.

MAINTAINING AND REVIEWING A PORTFOLIO

Some instructors may require you to compile an organized collection of your writing in a paper binder or electronic portfolio. They will probably specify both what is to be included and how the portfolio is to be organized. Portfolios can give both you and your instructor a complete picture of all of your work. If you are asked to keep a portfolio, be sure to retain all of your work for each assignment, including the instruction sheet, your prewriting notes, and all of your drafts, in case the instructor asks to see them. Organize this material either in the order of completion or by type of assignment.

Keeping a portfolio has benefits for you. It may provide a source of ideas for future writing that you can play with or build on later. As well, it allows you to review the progress of your writing. Practically speaking, the contents of your portfolio could help clarify any confusion about a grade or an assignment. Most importantly, you can gain a deeper understanding of your writing strengths and learning over time.

As you review your portfolio, answering the following questions can help you identify your own writing strengths, as well as areas that need more work.

1. With what assignments or topics was I most successful? Why?
2. What assignments or topics gave me the most problems? Why?
3. How has my planning changed? How can I make it more effective?

4. What makes my best writing effective? How does this writing differ from my other work?

5. What are the problem areas in my weakest writing? How does this writing differ from my other work?

6. Did I make significant changes in response to my own critical review, a peer evaluation, or my instructor's comments? If not, why not? What kinds of changes did I make? What changes would improve the quality of my work?

7. What organizational patterns have I used? (See Chapters 6 to 13.) Which ones have been effective? Why? Which ones have given me trouble? Why?

8. What kinds of introductions have I used? What other options do I have for effective introductions?

9. What kinds of conclusions have I used? What other options do I have for effective conclusions?

10. What kinds of grammar or spelling errors get in the way of my effectiveness as a writer? (Focus on these errors in future proofreading.)

MyWritingLab

How Do I Get a Better Grade?

Go to **www.mywritinglab.com** for additional help with your grammar, writing, and research skills. You will have access to a variety of exercises, instruction, and videos that will help you improve your basic skills and help you get a better grade.

Revising Your Paper

Prepare to revise.

- Distance yourself from your writing.
- Jot down your initial plans for your writing and ideas that came to mind.
- Talk about your paper with others.
- Read peer response and judge what makes sense.

Revise your whole essay.

- To discover new directions.
- Find what *FITS* and doesn't.
- *ADD* to develop and clarify.
- *CUT* what doesn't help.
- *TEST* the organization and restructure and add transitions.

Read out loud if it is helpful. Pay attention to where you stumble and what doesn't sound good. Slow down your reading to revise so you don't skim.

Revise your paragraphs.

- Fit the thesis.
- Focus on central idea.
- Add detail as necessary.
- Cut what doesn't fit.
- Reorganize for easier flow.

Strengthen words and sentences.

- Use more precise and vivid words.
- Make sure sentences mean what you want.
- Avoid wordiness.

Repeat entire process or parts as needed.

Now proofread your paper.

Strategies for Local Revisions: Paragraphs, Sentences, Diction, and Style

The process of editing and revising sometimes requires you to stand back and look at the essay as a whole. However, even after making larger, global revisions related to your thesis, organization, and development, you will want to zoom in and consider parts of your essay—playing with paragraphs, sentences, and words. You can learn to get rid of clutter in sentences, stitch ideas together more smoothly, and divide ideas that have run together. One way that you can provide clarity, emphasis, and guidance for your reader is through strategic paragraphing.

STRATEGIES FOR WORKING WITH PARAGRAPHS

Imagine the difficulty of reading a magazine article or book if you were faced with one solid block of text. How could you sort its ideas or know the best places to pause for thought? Paragraphs help guide readers through longer pieces of writing. Some break lengthy discussions of one idea into segments of different emphasis, thus providing rest stops for readers. Others consolidate several briefly developed ideas. Still others begin or end pieces of writing or link major segments together. Most paragraphs, though, include a number of sentences that develop and clarify one idea. Throughout a piece of writing, paragraphs relate to one another and reflect a controlling purpose. To make paragraphs fit together, you can't just sit down and dash them off. Instead, you first need to reflect on the entire essay and then channel your thoughts toward its different segments. You'll often have to revise your paragraphs after you've written a draft.

CHARACTERISTICS OF EFFECTIVE PARAGRAPHS

Effective paragraphs have some key characteristics: unity, a topic sentence, adequate development, organization, and coherence.

Unity

A paragraph with unity develops one, and only one, key controlling idea. To ensure unity, edit out any stray ideas that don't belong and fight the urge to take interesting but irrelevant side trips—they only create confusion about your destination. The following paragraph *lacks unity*.

> You can start a Registered Retirement Savings Plan (RRSP) as soon as you are 18 years old. You may need to pay off student loans. It is hard to be financially disciplined.

What exactly is this writer trying to say? We can't tell. Each statement expresses a different, undeveloped idea:

1. Starting a Registered Retirement Savings Plan
2. Paying off student loans
3. Financial discipline

In contrast, the following paragraph develops and clarifies only one central idea: the advantages of starting an RRSP early.

> You can start a Registered Retirement Savings Plan (RRSP) as soon as you are 18 years old. Of course, you may need to pay off significant student loans when you are young, but you can start an RRSP before you buy a car or even real estate. Ideally, you should maximize your RRSP contributions, even if you have to cut back on some discretionary spending. Making RRSP contributions will save you money since you can reduce your taxable income and defer paying taxes. Retirement may seem a long way off when you are young, but starting an RRSP early will help you gain financial discipline while your savings grow.
>
> Paul Johnson, student

Because this paragraph focuses entirely on a discussion of the advantages of starting a Registered Retirement Savings Plan, it has unity. To check your paragraphs for unity, ask yourself what each one aims to do and whether each sentence helps that aim.

EXERCISE *Read the following two paragraphs and then answer the questions below.*

1. The legend—in Africa—that all elephants over a large geographical area go to a common "graveyard" when they sense death is approaching led many hunters to treat them with special cruelty. Ivory hunters, believing the myth and trying to locate such graveyards, often intentionally wounded an elephant in the hopes of following the suffering beast as it made its way to the place where it wanted to die. The idea was to wound the elephant seriously enough so that it thought it was going to die but not so seriously that it died in a very short time. All too often, the process resulted in a single elephant being shot or speared many times and relentlessly pursued until it either fell dead or was killed when it finally turned and charged its attackers. In any case, no wounded elephant ever led its pursuers to the mythical graveyard with its hoped-for booty of ivory tusks.

Kris Hurrell, student

2. Mental health practitioners need to be sensitive to the influence of labels and diagnoses. When those in power label the "other" who makes them uncomfortable as deviant in some way, this labelling depersonalizes and objectifies the labelled person. My cousin who was bipolar found it difficult to find and keep a job because of his major mood swings. Educators can be too quick to say that a child who is restless or inattentive has attention deficit disorder, and should take Ritalin. The pharmaceutical industry has a vested interest in getting as many people as possible to take prescription drugs. In the medieval period, women were easily labelled as witches, as madwomen, or as victims of emotional instability.

Sue Johnston, student

1. Which of these paragraphs lacks unity? Refer to content in the paragraphs when answering.
2. How would you improve the paragraph that lacks unity?

The Topic Sentence

The topic sentence states the main idea of the paragraph. Think of the topic sentence as a rallying point, with all of the supporting sentences developing its core idea. A good topic sentence is general enough to express the controlling idea of the paragraph, yet specific enough to alert your reader to the point you will be making.

Placement of the topic sentence varies from paragraph to paragraph, as the following examples show. As you read each one, note how supporting information develops the topic sentence, which is italicized.

Topic Sentence Stated First   The most common placement of the topic sentence
is at the beginning of the paragraph. The writer reveals the central idea immediately
and then builds from a solid base.

> *Ours is a whimsical, loud and very social cuisine that practically begs you to share it with as many
> people as possible.* Its aromas will go through your entire home, the floor of your apartment
> building or your entire neighbourhood block. Meeru remembers childhood picnics at the
> Washington Monument and recalls how non-Indians would often follow the smell of curry
> and ask her parents what they were eating. Every time Meeru's parents would invite the
> inquisitors to try the food. They always had more than enough, since Indian food tastes
> even better as leftovers.
>
> Meeru Dhalwala and Vikram Vij, *Vij's at Home*

Topic Sentence Stated Last   Just as music sometimes swells toward a crescendo, a
paragraph may build momentum gradually toward a conclusion—the topic sentence
that comes at the end of the paragraph. Since this position creates suspense for the
reader, who anticipates the climactic or summarizing point, it can be particularly useful
in personal or narrative writing.

> It is a terrible thing to lose a home or a job; the human costs of the financial
> collapse of 2008, measured in ruined lives and collapsed communities and multivalent
> social decay, will surely outweigh even those catastrophic trillion-dollar losses in the
> long term. The prospect of permanently rising oil prices threatens not only to amplify
> such problems at every gas pump but also to fundamentally alter the economic
> equations by which we feed and clothe and house ourselves using goods delivered to us
> over immense distances by oil's grace (and often made from the byproducts of its
> refining). The disastrous BP oil spill in the Gulf of Mexico in 2010 provided a graphic
> illustration of the staggering size of the modern energy economy and the profound risk
> involved in its everyday operations. Still, these problems remain comprehensible in
> human terms. Losses can be calculated, compensation paid out, leaking wells sealed.
> *But there is simply no tabulating the cost of the loss of an entire ecosystem and the permanent altera-
> tion of the chemistry of every drop of sea water on the planet—and all the money in the world can't
> begin to repair the damage.*
>
> Chris Turner, *The Leap: How to Survive and Thrive in the Sustainable Economy*

Topic Sentence Stated First and Last   Some paragraphs lead with the main idea
and then restate it, usually in different words, at the end. This technique allows the
writer to reinforce an especially important idea.

> *You often hear that water is life.* And if water in its molecular essence—a pair of hydro-
> gen atoms bonded to one of oxygen—is not itself life, it is, nonetheless, essential to it. We
> can find simple life in a remarkable range of environments. We've found bacteria in the
> deepest oceans, sustained by sulphurous exhalations from volcanic vents. Microbes
> endure and replicate at temperatures approaching absolute zero in the frozen crevices of
> Antarctic glaciers. We've found life on the highest mountains and beneath deserts that
> get only millimetres of rain annually. *The only place we've never found it is in the absolute absence
> of water.*
>
> Chris Wood, *Dry Spring: The Coming Water Crisis of North America*

Topic Sentence Stated in the Middle   Occasionally, the topic sentence falls between background information and sentences that develop the central idea. This midpoint positioning of the topic sentence can be a kind of well-oiled hinge that allows the writer to shift the emphasis and at the same time continue to build on the original idea. It can be particularly useful in longer, complex paragraphs.

> In the world of modern food manufacturing, Kraft Dinner Original remains a fairly simple formula, with only ten ingredients. (My own recipe also calls for ten, if you lump together the natural flavours, as labellers do.) *But KD has spawned generations of mac and cheese dinners, each one a greater feat of engineering than the last, and each one less recognizable as something we could make in our own kitchens.* In 1999, the company launched Kraft Dinner Cup, a line that now includes Kraft Dinner Triple Cheese in a microwaveable package. It contains twenty-one ingredients, including "cheese flavours." Cheddar is eighth on the list. A version sold only in the US, described as Triple Cheese Cheesy Made Easy, contains forty-two ingredients, depending on how you count them.
>
> Sasha Chapman, "Manufacturing Taste"

Topic Sentence Implied   Some paragraphs, particularly in narrative and descriptive writing, have no topic sentence. Rather, all sentences point toward a main idea that readers must infer for themselves.

> I spent my college holidays researching the past. I read Chinatown oral histories, located documents, searched out early articles. Those early citizens came back to life for me. Their long toil and blood sacrifices, the proud record of their patient, legal challenges, gave us all our present rights as citizens. Canadian and American Chinatowns set aside their family tongue differences and encouraged each other to fight injustice. There were no borders. "After all," they affirmed, "Daaih ga tohng yahn. . . . We are all Chinese!"
>
> Wayson Choy, "I'm a Banana and Proud of It"

The details in this paragraph collectively suggest a clear central idea: that Barclay had incredible physical endurance. In most academic writing, however, clearly formulated topic sentences will help focus and unify your paragraphs.

EXERCISE *Identify the topic sentences in the following paragraphs and explain how you arrived at your decisions. If the topic sentence is implied, state the central idea in your own words.*

1. The immigrant dream—of financial and social success; of carving out a place within the larger society—is grand in its simplicity. Requiring great courage, it is self-limiting on no level. All one asks is the freedom and fairness—through anti-discrimination legislation, if necessary—to fulfill one's potential. A vital part of that freedom is the latitude to recognize and welcome inevitable change in society and the migrant. One may treasure a private, personal identity built from family lore and experience, all the while pursuing the public integration vital to wider success. To be put in the position of either obliterating the past or worshipping it is, for the individual, an unnecessary burden that leads to a false and limiting theatre of the self.

Neil Bissoondath, "No Place Like Home"

2. What my mother never told me was how fast time passes in adult life. I remember, when I was little, thinking I would live to be at least as old as my grandmother, who was dynamic even at ninety-two, the age at which she died. Now I see those ninety-two years hurtling by me. And my mother never told me how much fun sex could be, or what a discovery it is. Of course, I'm of an age when mothers really didn't tell you much about anything. My mother never told me the facts of life.

Joyce Susskind, "Surprises in a Woman's Life"

3. It was funny how everyone in the second half of the twentieth century suddenly started buying these large, lumpy, sculptured, multicolored shoes. It was as though people discovered overnight that their footwear didn't have to be black or brown, and didn't need to conform to what was streamlined and quietly tasteful. The traditional shoe was challenged, and it collapsed at the first skirmish. Shoes could trumpet their engineered presence, their tread, their aggressive padding; they could make all manner of wild claims, converting whole populations to athletic splendor and prodigious fitness. Larry's running shoes are red and white, with little yellow insignias located near the toe. Each of the heels has a transparent built-in bubble for additional comfort and buoyancy when running on hard pavement.

Carol Shields, *Larry's Party*

4. That empty building on the left was once a school. Here in Cutback World we have discovered that the educational system operates far more efficiently if schools are not open. You should not conclude from this that we have closed all our schools. That would be foolish. There is a school downtown somewhere. Every city of at least 100 000 people in Cutback World is entitled to have a school. Ours has 15 000 students in it, which enables it to offer a full range of courses. When we pass it, you might notice some students hanging out the open windows. We regard this as a sign that classroom space is being fully utilized.

Charles Gordon, "A Guided Tour of the Bottom Line"

EXERCISE

1. **Develop one of the ideas below into a topic sentence. Then write a unified paragraph that is built around it.**

   a. The career (or job or profession) I want is _____.

   b. The one quality most necessary in my chosen field is _____.

   c. The most difficult aspect of my chosen field is _____.

   d. One good example of the Canadian tendency to waste is _____.

   e. The best (or worst) thing about fast-food restaurants is _____.

2. **Write a topic sentence that would control a paragraph on each of the following:**

   a. Preparations for travelling away from home

   b. Advantages of having your own room

   c. A landmark in the community where you live

   d. A favourite way to relax and refresh

   e. Choosing what university courses to take

Adequate Development

Students often ask for guidelines on paragraph length: "Should I aim for 50 to 60 words? Seven to ten sentences? About one quarter of a page?" The questions are natural, but the approach is wrong. Instead of targeting a particular length, ask yourself what the reader needs to know. Then supply enough information to make your point clearly. On the one hand, skimpy, undeveloped paragraphs frustrate readers by forcing them to fill in the gaps for themselves. On the other hand, a rambling paragraph stuffed with useless padding dilutes the main idea and often loses the audience. Paragraph length and development are influenced by the reader's expectations, as well as the conventions of the writing genre or publication medium. A newspaper article might feature short paragraphs that include only key facts, whereas a scientific journal might have lengthy paragraphs that offer detailed explanations of facts and data. Personal narrative writing is more likely to use short paragraphs to control dramatic pacing, while formal academic writing usually contains well-developed paragraphs of several sentences each.

The details you supply can include facts, figures, thoughts, observations, steps, lists, examples, and sometimes personal experiences. Individually, these bits of information may mean little, but combined, they clearly illustrate your point. Keep in mind, however, that development isn't an end in itself, but instead advances the purpose of the entire essay.

Here are two versions of a paragraph, the first inadequately developed:

Underdeveloped Paragraph

Many sports have peculiar injuries associated with them. Repetitive use of certain body parts can cause chronic injuries in athletes who play baseball, football, or basketball. All of these common sports injuries are a result of the overuse of specific body parts. However, these injuries can be greatly reduced if athletes train properly, rest fully, and respect their bodies.

Adequately Developed Paragraph

Many sports have peculiar injuries associated with them. Repetitive use of certain body parts can cause chronic injuries in athletes who play baseball, football, or basketball. *Baseball pitchers can throw up to 150 pitches per game. This repetitive throwing action can cause pitchers' elbows to swell. Over time, tendonitis often develops. Similarly, football linemen also suffer chronic injuries related to their sport. The constant jarring pressure during physical contact can cause severe back pain. Many linemen struggle with spinal disc injuries throughout their lives. In addition, basketball players often suffer from shin splints because of the repetitive pounding on their legs when running and jumping on a hard surface.* All of these common sports injuries are a result of the overuse of specific body parts. However, these injuries can be greatly reduced if athletes train properly, rest fully, and respect their bodies.

The first paragraph lacks examples of particular sports injuries, whereas the second one provides the needed information.

Readability also helps set paragraph length. Within a paper, paragraphs signal natural dividing places, allowing the reader to pause and absorb the material presented up to that point. Too little paragraphing overwhelms the reader with long blocks of material. Too much creates a choppy Dick-and-Jane effect that may come across as simplistic or even irritating. To counter these problems, writers sometimes use several paragraphs for an idea that needs extended development, or they combine several short paragraphs into one.

EXERCISE

1. **Indicate where the ideas in this long block of material divide logically. Explain your choices.**

   During the summer following graduation from high school, I could hardly wait to get to university and be on my own. In my first weeks at university, however, I found that independence can be tough and painful. I had expected the kind of raucous good times and a carefree collegiate life depicted in old beach movies and suggested by the selective memories of sentimental alumni. Instead, all I felt at first was the burden of increasing responsibilities and loneliness. I discovered that being independent of parents who kept at me to do my homework and expected me to accomplish certain household chores did not mean I was free to do as I pleased. On the contrary, living on my own meant that I had to perform for myself all the tasks that the family used to share. Studying became a full-time occupation rather than a nightly duty to be accomplished in an hour or two, and my instructors made it clear that they would have little sympathy for negligence or even for my inability to do an assignment. However, what was more troubling about my early university life than having to do laundry, prepare meals, and complete stacks of homework was the terrifying sense of being entirely alone. Although I was independent, no longer a part of the world that had seemed to confine me, I soon realized that confinement had also meant security. I never liked the feeling that people were watching over me, but I knew that my family and friends were also watching out for me—and that's a good feeling to have. At university, no one seemed particularly to be watching, though professors constantly evaluated the quality of my work. I felt estranged from people in those first weeks, desperately needing a confidant but fearful that the new and tenuous friendships I had made would be damaged if I were to confess my fears and problems. It was simply too early for me to feel a part of the university. So there I was, independent in the fullest sense, but feeling like a person without a country.

2. **The following short, choppy units are inadequately developed. List some details you could use to expand one of them into a good paragraph.**

   Teachers should have strong interpersonal skills. When teachers fail, they usually fail in relationships.

> The commercialism of Canadian society affects children from an early age. When they watch television, they are bombarded with commercials that reinforce the message that happiness comes from buying things.

Organization

An effective paragraph unfolds in a clear pattern of organization so that the reader can easily follow the flow of ideas. Usually when you write your first draft, your organization reflects the flow of your thoughts. Sometimes this logic of association makes sense, but when you revise, you will often see how you can organize paragraphs more effectively. Writers do not ordinarily stop to decide on a strategy for each paragraph, but when you revise or are stuck, it's useful to understand the available choices. Here are some options:

1. The strategies discussed in Chapters 6 to 13, including narration, illustration, process analysis, cause and effect, definition, comparison, classification, and argument
2. Commonly used sequencing patterns, including time sequence and space sequence
3. Order of climax

Six example paragraphs follow. The first, organized by *time sequence*, traces the sequence of a horrifying failed rescue attempt at sea.

> I once read a story about a sailor who was washed overboard while round the Horn on a clipper ship. His shipmates immediately lowered a boat, and a few of them rowed to the rescue while the remainder of the crew dropped sail and brought the ship into the wind. The boat crew plucked the hapless sailor out of the sea, but the small boat broached on a steep breaking wave and capsized. As the men clung to the upturned keel, a flock of albatrosses circled overhead. The lookout on the main ship watched with horror as one of the birds dove, landed on a man's head, and plucked out his eyes. Then a second bird dove, and a third. Another rescue boat was dispatched, but the lines became tangled in the davits as the mother ship drifted downwind. The lost time was fatal. Blinded and bloody, the men in the water untied their life vests and one by one dove to their deaths rather than face the continued assaults.
>
> Jon Turk, *Cold Oceans: Adventures in Kayak, Rowboat, and Dogsled*

Common *spatial arrangements* used to organize paragraphs include top to bottom, left to right, right to left, nearby to far away, far away to nearby, clockwise, and counter-clockwise. Consider how the following descriptive paragraph moves from outside to inside.

> Next to the laundry, across the alley, which ran like a sparkling river of broken glass and urine produced by the hordes of feral cats, giant rats and stumbling drunks who waded therein, was the Jewish Tailor. His narrow house, barely a door and a window wide, extended backwards from his work room and housed his wife and daughter, a sewing machine and a steam iron. An air of sadness, like the tape measure he wore around his neck, enveloped the place.
>
> Moses Milstein, "Memories of Montreal—and Richness"

The next paragraph, which contrasts a simpler life with a more ambitious one, illustrates development by *comparison and contrast*. As in many descriptive or narrative paragraphs, the topic sentence is implied.

> We've been raised to believe that you must go as far as you possibly can in life, and that distance is measured by how busy you are, how hard you work and how much you've accumulated. This is still a compelling dream for many who are happy to buy in and do what it takes to maintain the upgradeable lifestyle. But now there is also a new alternative lifestyle emerging that neither rejects the affordable luxuries of life nor yearns for more. It is a satisfaction with less, in the sense that less of one thing, pressure, intensity, busyness or affluence means a trade for something else, such as self-determination, personal satisfaction, spiritual fulfillment or other things not valued so highly on the trading floor.

John Shepler, "What Thoreau Knew: Walden and the Meaning of Voluntary Simplicity"

The following paragraph illustrates *development by process*:

> The extraction method being used is known as hydraulic fracturing, otherwise known as fracking. Fracking involves pumping between one and eight million gallons of water, proprietary chemicals, and sand under high pressure into a well. This causes the shale or coal bed to fracture, releasing the desired natural gas from the well. Between 80 and 300 tons of chemicals may be used each time a well is fracked, which can happen up to 18 times during its lifetime.

Elle-Máijá Tailfeathers, "Fractured Land"

The next paragraph employs a common pattern of development used in argument, *cause and effect*:

> We behave differently (read: more irrationally) when we're behind the wheel of a car, which—especially if it's a big SUV—can create a sense of isolation and invincibility. The anonymity of riding in a living room on wheels, an extension of the anonymity of suburban life, can weaken common sense and self-discipline so much that even upstanding citizens can act in ways they never would in a grocery store lineup. "Road-ragers are an unpredictable group," Sgt. Cam Woolley, who recently retired from the Ontario Provincial Police, told me. "They've timed their commute down to the last second, and if anybody goes too slow or doesn't drive the way they'd like, they go nuts."

Tim Falconer, "Autoholics"

Climactic order, often used in personal writing, creates a crescendo pattern starting with the least emphatic detail and progressing to the most emphatic. The topic sentence can begin or end the paragraph, or it can remain implied. This pattern holds the reader's interest by building suspense. Here is a paragraph illustrating climactic order:

> The speaking errors I hear affect me to different degrees. I'm so conditioned to hearing "It don't make any difference" and "There's three ways to solve the problem" that I've almost accepted such usage. However, errors such as "Just between you and I, Arnold loves Edna" and "I'm going back to my room to lay down" still offend my sensibility. When hearing them, I usually just chuckle to myself and walk away. The "Twin I's"—irrevelant and irregardless—are another matter. More than any other errors, they really grate on my ear.

Whenever I hear "that may be true, but it's irrevelant" or "Irregardless of how much I study, I still get C's," I have the urge to correct the speaker. It's really surprising that more people don't clean up their language act.

Valerie Sonntag, student

EXERCISE *From a magazine or newspaper article, select four paragraphs that illustrate different patterns of organization. Identify the topic sentence in each case, or if it is implied, state it in your own words. Point out the organization of each paragraph.*

Coherence

If you do not want to take your readers on a bumpy ride where they lurch from one idea to another, you need to guide the reader to see how ideas fit together. Coherent writing flows smoothly and glides easily from one sentence and paragraph to another, so that readers can easily grasp relationships among ideas. Incoherent writing, which does not follow a logical order and fails to make connections clear, can confuse and even irritate readers. Consider how the following paragraph jumps around confusingly.

> At certain times counselling can be extremely beneficial. People should be committed to becoming healthy. They should never be forced to go to counselling. Sometimes people do need to be told in a gentle way that maybe they should consider seeking counselling. A person who decides to try counselling should do some research. They have to find a counsellor who is suited to their specific needs. Sometimes it is hard for people to reach out and admit they need help. Mental health is as important as physical health. Finding a counsellor with whom a person feels safe and comfortable is important. Now that you have found a good counsellor, therapy can begin and your mental health is on its way to recovery.

This paragraph has some degree of unity, because most of its sentences relate to the writer's interest in the benefits of counselling. Unfortunately, though, its many gaps in logic create questions rather than answer them, and in very bumpy prose. How does the third sentence relate to the fourth? And what do the seventh and eighth sentences have to do with the writer's main purpose—to explain how people can benefit from counselling at certain critical moments?

Now read this rewritten version. Note what has been deleted, and what has been added to improve coherence. Transitions and content additions are italicized:

> People who *are in emotional crisis or who have experienced trauma* can benefit from counselling. They should not be forced to go into counselling, *because forced treatment is not likely to be effective. Although* it can be hard at times for people to reach out and admit that they need help, counselling is

most effective *when people come to it on their own and feel committed to the process. After* they decide to seek counselling, they should do some research in order to find a counsellor who is suited to their specific needs, and with whom they feel safe.

As this example shows, changing the order of sentences and inserting connecting words or phrases can make paragraphs smoother and more coherent.

EXERCISE *Rewrite the following student paragraph to improve coherence. You may rearrange sentence order, combine and condense sentences, or add any connecting words that seem appropriate.*

> Many elderly people, as well as people who can no longer care for themselves, are placed in long-term care facilities. These surroundings can be unpleasant for many, and can cause residents to become very depressed. Within the last few years, animal therapy has become recognized as a way to improve health. Many care facilities arrange weekly visits from a local handler and their best friend, which is usually a well-trained dog. These visits provide patients with something to look forward to. The presence of a loving animal companion can comfort lonely people. Visiting with animals helps to lower blood pressure. It also can reduce stress. In turn, many patients generally become more responsive to their treatment. Residents seem happier overall and feel better when animals are allowed to visit their facility.

If your writing seems choppy and hard to follow, you may need to stitch your ideas more effectively by supplying different kinds of connections between sentences and between paragraphs. There are four primary strategies that will help you improve the coherence of your writing:

1. Transitions—connecting words and phrases
2. Repeated key words
3. Pronouns
4. Parallelism

Transitions—Connecting Words and Phrases   These connectors clarify certain kinds of relationships—similarity, contrast, elaboration, and so on—between ideas at the sentence level.

> *Showing similarity:* like, in like manner, likewise, just as, similarly

> *Showing contrast:* at the same time, but, even so, however, in contrast, instead, while, whereas, nevertheless, still, on the contrary, on the other hand, otherwise, yet

> *Showing results or effects:* accordingly, as a result, because, consequently, hence, since, therefore, thus

Adding ideas: also, besides, first (second, third . . .), furthermore, in addition, in the first place, moreover, and then, again, too

Drawing conclusions: as a result, finally, in brief, in conclusion, in short, therefore

Pointing out examples: for example, for instance, to illustrate

Showing emphasis and clarity: above all, after all, again, as a matter of fact, besides, in fact, in other words, indeed, of course, nonetheless, that is

Indicating time: at times, after, afterwards, from then on, immediately, later, meanwhile, next, now, once, previously, subsequently, then, until, while

Conceding a point: granted that, of course, to be sure, admittedly, certainly

Do not overload your paper with transitions, and do not use them arbitrarily. For example, if you insert "on the other hand," you need to be drawing a clear, balanced contrast between two ideas. Use these connectors only when they help the reader move naturally from one point to the next. In the following excerpt, which clarifies the difference between workers and workaholics, the transitions are italicized:

My efforts to define workaholism and to distinguish workaholics from other hard workers proved difficult. *While* workaholics do work hard, not all hard workers are workaholics. Moonlighters, *for example*, may work 16 hours a day to make ends meet, but most of them will stop working when their financial circumstances permit. Accountants, *too*, seem to work non-stop, but many slow down after the April 30 tax deadline. Workaholics, *on the other hand*, always devote more time and thought to their work than their situation demands. Even in the absence of deadlines to meet, mortgages to pay, promotions to earn, or bosses to please, workaholics still work hard. What sets them apart is their attitude toward work, not the number of hours they work.

Marilyn Machlowitz, "Workaholism: What's Wrong with Being Married to Your Work?"

DISCUSSION QUESTIONS

1. What ideas do each of the italicized words and phrases above connect?

2. What kind of relationship does each transition show?

Repeated Key Words Repeating key words, especially those that help to convey a paragraph's central idea, is another way to smooth the reader's path. The words may appear in different forms, but their presence keeps the main issues before the reader. In the following paragraph, coherence is achieved through repetition of simple phrases ("it adds," "it is") along with the word *blandness*.

What is the point of the battered fry? *It adds* crunch. *It adds* weight. *It adds* calories. *What it* does not *add* is flavour. *What it* removes *is* potato-ness. *It is* a blandifier.

And *it is* its very *blandness* that makes it popular. *Blandness* is more tenacious than any virus: *It* will always conquer a host population, wherever *it is* introduced.

Russell Smith, "Battered by Blandness"

EXERCISE *Write a paragraph using one of the following sentences as your topic sentence. Insert the missing key word and then repeat it in your paragraph to help link your sentences together.*

1. _____ is my favourite relative.

2. I wish I had (a, an, some, more) _____.

3. _____ changed my life.

4. _____ is more trouble than it's worth.

5. A visit to _____ always depresses me.

Pronouns   Pronouns stand in for nouns that appear earlier in the sentence or in previous sentences. Mixing pronouns and their nouns throughout the paragraph prevents monotony and promotes clarity. We have italicized pronouns that aid coherence in the following excerpt from an address about Canadian literature by Robertson Davies.

> In psychological terms, Canada is very much an introverted country, and *it* lives cheek by jowl with the most extroverted country known to history. Let me explain the terms. In personal psychology, the extrovert is *one* who derives *his* energy from *his* contacts with the external world; for *him*, everything lies outside and *he* moves outward toward *it*, often without much sensitivity to the response of that toward which *he* moves. The introvert, on the other hand, finds *his* energy within *himself*, and *his* concern with the outside world is a matter of what approach the outside world makes to *him*. It is absurd to say that one psychological orientation is superior to the other. Both have *their* values, but difficulties arise when *they* fail to understand one another.

> Robertson Davies, "Living in a Country without a Mythology"

Some words such as *this, that, those,* and *these* also may contribute to coherence, or flow, by referring to something that has come just before. Sometimes, they function as pronouns; at other times, they function as demonstrative adjectives.

> If climate displays itself in weather, it is through water, above all, that we notice both. *This* is most evident when it rains or snows. But it is equally true when day after day of clear, dry, sunny skies draw the last beads of moisture out of soil, bodies and plants. Wind may do damage on its own, but the wreckage is far greater when wind drives sheets of rain before it, or pushes waves into storm surges that overwhelm beaches and dikes. Both wind and rain (or snow) are, moreover, creations of heat distributed unevenly through the atmosphere. Water's capacity to absorb, hold and release enormous quantities of *that* heat is central to the forces that keep the clouds and breezes in perpetual motion. The physics that drive all of *these* also determine whether there will be enough water—or too little, or too much—to meet the needs of ecology and humanity on any day in any given spot of earth.

> Chris Wood, *Dry Spring: The Coming Water Crisis of North America*

Notice how the repetition of certain pronouns aids coherence in the following paragraph:

> In fact, hope just is. You can't run through a checklist to get to *it*. Yes, *it* is absurd and irrational. But, like love, *it* is human. Like laughter, hope catches and spreads. *It* works logarithmically, like the changes now under way on our planet, like our growing understanding of *them* and like our powerful collective human ability to start coping with *them*.

> Alanna Mitchell, "Reading the Vital Signs: Adaptability"

EXERCISE *In a magazine, newspaper, textbook, or some other written source, find two paragraphs that use pronouns or demonstrative adjectives to increase coherence. Copy the paragraphs, underline the pronouns, and explain what each refers to.*

Parallelism   Parallelism uses repetition of grammatical form to express a series of equivalent ideas. Besides giving continuity, the repetition adds rhythm and balance to the writing. Note how the following italicized constructions tie together the unfolding definition of poverty:

> *Poverty is staying up* all night on cold nights to watch the fire, knowing one spark on the newspaper covering the walls means your sleeping children die in flames. In summer *poverty is watching* gnats and flies devour your baby's tears when he cries. The screens are torn and you pay so little rent you know they will never be fixed. *Poverty means* insects in your food, in your nose, in your eyes, and crawling over you when you sleep. *Poverty is hoping* it never rains because diapers won't dry when it rains and soon you are using newspapers. *Poverty is seeing* your children forever with runny noses. Paper handkerchiefs cost money and all your rags you need for other things. Even more costly are antihistamines. *Poverty is cooking* without food and cleaning without soap.

> Jo Goodwin Parker, "What Is Poverty?"

PARAGRAPHS WITH SPECIAL FUNCTIONS

Special-function paragraphs include introductions, transitional paragraphs, and conclusions. Although introductions and conclusions may be more than one paragraph, one-paragraph introductions and conclusions generally appear in shorter essays. Transitional paragraphs may function like hinges, helping the writer to swing into a different section of the essay—perhaps a different time frame in a narrative essay, or a different argument in a more formal essay.

Introductions

A good introduction acquaints and coaxes. It announces the essay's topic and may directly state the thesis. In addition, it sets the tone for what will follow—a sombre, lighthearted, or angry introduction for personal writing, or an authoritative, confident, or persuasive introduction for an academic paper. The tone of the introduction should fit the purpose of the paper. Thus, an amusing anecdote would not be an appropriate opening for a paper about torture. With essays, as with people, first impressions are important. If your opening rouses interest, it will draw the readers into the essay and pave the way for their acceptance of your ideas. If your beginning is mechanical, plodding, and dull, you will likely turn readers away. Consider these weak openings:

In this report I intend to . . .

Wars have always afflicted humankind.

As you may know, having too little time is a problem for many of us.

In the modern world of today . . .

Are you yawning yet? Ask yourself that same question about every opening you write.

A Directly Stated Thesis   This is a common type of opening that orients the reader to what will follow. After providing some general background, the writer of our example narrows her scope to a thesis that previews the upcoming sections of her essay.

> An increasing number of midlife women are re-entering the workforce, pursuing degrees, and getting more involved in the public arena. Several labels besides "midlife" have been attached to this type of person: the mature woman, the older woman, and, more recently, the re-entry woman. By definition, she is between thirty-five and fifty-five years old and has been away from the business or academic scene anywhere from fifteen to thirty years. The academic community, the media, marketing people, and employers are giving her close scrutiny, and it is apparent that she is having a greater impact on our society than she realizes.
>
> Jo Ann Harris, student

A Definition   This kind of introduction works particularly well in an essay that acquaints the reader with an unfamiliar topic.

> You are completely alone in a large open space and are struck by a terrifying, unreasoning fear. You sweat, your heart beats, you cannot breathe. You fear you may die of a heart attack, although you do not have heart disease. Suppose you decide you will never get yourself in this helpless situation again. You go home and refuse to leave its secure confines. Your family has to support you. You have agoraphobia—a disabling terror of open spaces.
>
> "Controlling Phobias through Behavior Modification"

A Quotation   A beginning quotation, particularly from an authority in the field when writing a formal paper, can be an effective springboard for the ideas that follow. Make sure that any quotation you use relates clearly to your topic.

> Despair is the depth of hell, as joy is the serenity of heaven.
>
> John Donne, English poet (1572–1631)
>
> Quoted by Douglas Todd in "Combating the 'Culture of Despair'"

An Anecdote or Personal Experience   A well-told personal anecdote or experience can draw readers in. Like other introductions, this kind should bear on what comes afterwards. In the following example, an essay that decries the plight of foreign domestic workers in Canada begins with an anecdote about one typical morning for a struggling domestic worker.

> When Joyelle arrives at work, it is 7:45 on Monday morning and the bags of garbage from the weekend are stacked in the hallway of the Pintos' well-appointed condominium. The half-empty wineglasses are strewn around her employers' living room, and the faint odour of stale beer is in the air. Lugging the plastic bags down the hallway to the garbage chute and clearing up the dishes from the previous night's party have become rituals for Joyelle (all names have been changed to protect privacy).
>
> Marina Jiménez, "Domestic Crisis"

An Arresting Statement   Sometimes, you can jolt the reader to attention by using surprising or even shocking content, language, or both. An arresting claim may even consist of a single sentence that draws the reader in.

> Tell me what you think of Kraft Dinner, and I will tell you who you are.
>
> Sasha Chapman, "Manufacturing Taste"

Intriguing Claim   An essay about anger makes an initial claim that may puzzle and intrigue readers.

> We carry around a lot of free-floating anger. What we do with it is what fascinates me.
>
> Dan Greenburg, "Sound and Fury"

Unusual Slant on a Familiar Theme   It can be difficult to find a fresh approach to such a familiar subject as a simple walk in the woods, but consider how the following image helps to draw the reader in.

> The Japanese have a wonderful expression for spending time in the woods: *Shinrin-yoku*, or forest bathing.
>
> Joe Kelly, "Go Take a Walk"

Interesting Details   The following paragraph piques a reader's curiosity through its use of vivid, specific details.

> Sporting a green jacket, pants and a days-old beard, Andy wouldn't look out of place on the deck of a fishing boat back in the Maritimes. But this is a rainy February evening on the West Coast . . . He's out for a long night of blue-box binning in Kitsilano, an affluent Vancouver neighbourhood. One of his huge jacket pockets is stuffed with garbage bags, the other with a two-litre bottle of pink-grapefruit cider.
>
> Suzanne Ahearne, "Monday Night in the Nickel Fields"

A Question or Problem   Some pieces of writing set out a problem early on that the rest of the essay goes on to address.

> As individuals and as a society, we love our automobiles—even as we hate how they screw up our planet, our cities, and our lives. Environics Research Group, a Toronto-based research firm, found that 32 percent of Canadians see their wheels as an extension or reflection of their style and image. For the other 63 percent, it's an appliance, a tool used to get from A to B. Recreational driving may seem, in an age of climate change, to be a destructive pastime. But the auto collectors and recreational drivers aren't the problem, just as connoisseurs of fine wine, who prize quality over quantity, aren't necessarily problem drinkers. It's the people who drive (or drink) all the time—mindlessly, compulsively, because they can't help themselves— who do the real damage to themselves and others. That's addiction—and collectively, we're pretty close to hitting bottom. The automobile has wasted our time, choked our air, and destroyed many downtowns while spurring sprawl in the suburbs. Obviously, cars aren't about to go away completely (though we can certainly hope they change dramatically over the next few years). But let's never forget: the fault, dear drivers, lies not in our cars, but in ourselves.
>
> Tim Falconer, "Autoholic"

In a similar way, an essay may pose a thought-provoking question at the beginning:

> But what is the future of Canada's petroleum sector? Has our country done an adequate job negotiating resource rents that protect the interests of Canadian taxpayers? Ensuring worker safety or protecting the environment? Building a national consensus around the development of this globally important resource? Providing a lasting economic legacy for future generations?
>
> Mitchell Anderson, "Oil Wealth: Should Norway Be the Canadian Way?"

Blended Strategies　Many effective introductions contain more than one way to draw the reader in and frame the topic or argument. The following example blends a direct statement of the thesis with an unusual slant on a familiar theme and provocative questions.

> For what is unquestionably one of the classic folk fairy-tales, "Little Red Riding Hood" is more surprising for what it lacks than what it contains. There is no royalty, no enchantment, no romance—just a talking wolf with a big appetite. How then has the heroine of this tale become as famous a figure as her more glamorous cousins, Sleeping Beauty, Cinderella, and Snow White? What is so remarkable about this stark little tale that describes the dramatic confrontation between an innocent little girl and a wicked wolf? How has it come about that the line "Grandmother, what big teeth you have!" is one of the most anticipated and familiar moments in all of Western literature, let alone fairy tale?
>
> Martin Hallett and Barbara Karasek, eds., *Folk and Fairy Tales*, 3rd ed.

EXERCISE

1. Explain why each of the preceding introductions interests or does not interest you. Does your response stem from the topic or the way the author introduces it?

2. Find magazine articles with effective introductory paragraphs illustrating at least three different techniques. Write a paragraph explaining why each impresses you.

Transitional Paragraphs

At some point in a lengthy essay, you may need a short paragraph that announces a shift from one group of ideas to another. Transitional paragraphs may summarize previously explained ideas, repeat the thesis, or point to ideas that follow. They may also provide a kind of pause to allow the reader time to take a breath and prepare for something new. In the example below, Bruno Bettelheim has been discussing a young boy named Joey, who has turned into a kind of human machine. After describing Joey's assorted delusions, Bettelheim signals his shift of emphasis from the delusions to the fears that caused them.

> What deep-seated fears and needs underlay Joey's delusional system? We were long in finding out, for Joey's preventions effectively concealed the secret of his autistic behavior. In the meantime we dealt with his peripheral problems one by one.
>
> Bruno Bettelheim, "Joey: 'A Mechanical Boy'"

The following transitional paragraph looks back as well as ahead:

> Certainly these three factors—exercise, economy, convenience of shortcuts—help explain the popularity of bicycling today. But a fourth attraction sometimes overrides the others: the lure of the open road.
>
> Mike Bernstein, student

Conclusions

A conclusion rounds out a paper and signals that the discussion has been completed. Not all papers require a separate conclusion, however. For example, narratives and descriptions generally end when the writer finishes the story or completes the details. Although some papers, especially personal narratives, do not always require a separate conclusion, most essays benefit from at least one concluding paragraph that drives the point home or leaves the reader with something to reflect on. To be effective, a conclusion must mesh logically and stylistically with what comes earlier. A long, complex paper often ends with a summary of the main points, but other options may be used for shorter papers with easy-to-grasp ideas. Most short essays have single-paragraph conclusions, while longer papers may require two or three paragraphs.

Here are some suggestions for writing effective conclusions:

1. Don't introduce entirely new material that is irrelevant to your thesis. Draw together and round out, but don't branch off in another direction.
2. Don't tack on a trite ending in desperation when the hour is late and the paper is due tomorrow—the so-called midnight special. Your reader deserves better than "All in all, skiing is a great sport" or "Thus we can see that motorcycle racing isn't for everyone."
3. Don't apologize. Saying that you could have done a better job makes a reader wonder why you didn't.
4. Don't moralize. A preachy conclusion can undermine the position you have established in the rest of your composition.
5. Do go beyond a flat restatement of what you said at the beginning of your essay. Give the reader something to think about, a sense of why this issue matters.

The following examples illustrate several common types of conclusions.

Restatement of the Thesis   Andrew Beyak's conclusion reasserts his thesis that "the term *youth* has been co-opted by government and corporate interests." It also leaves the reader with something larger to think about—not only those "other issues" that government must address, but also the idea that language shapes the ways we think about public concerns.

> By replacing the term *adult* with *youth*, governments, corporations, and the media can offer the majority of the electorate and the majority of society (baby boomers, if you will) an easy explanation for why those aged 18–35 are not receiving what they as adults need—namely employment, a living wage, and a minimal level of independence. At the same time, those with a vested interest in the status quo are creating a diversion from a multitude of other issues that will inevitably have to be addressed. All of this with one word.
>
> Andrew Beyak, "The Sweet Bird of Youth Is Showing Signs of Age"

A Summary   A summary draws together and reinforces the main points.

> In conclusion, I believe that both products are better in a certain environment. PowerPoint, with its professional settings and vastness, is better in a corporate setting where money and time can be used to create amazing presentations. Prezi, since it is free, easy, and visually exciting, is better for students and smaller scope projects. Personally, I think Prezi is a better tool because anyone can use it anywhere. It is just on a browser and can be accessed and edited by anyone with a password. Its future looks relatively secure after landing a $14 million investment to accelerate the startup (Venture Beat).
>
> Jessie Foley, student

A Question   A final question often encourages the reader to think further on the topic. If your essay is meant to be persuasive, be sure to phrase a concluding question so that the natural answer prompted by your question emphasizes your point of view. The paragraph below concludes an argument that we should address the issue of bullying not as an isolated problem but within the context of a larger social framework.

> Before even posing the question—"How can we prevent this?"—that sparks so many anti-bullying campaigns, we wonder if it's more useful to ask ourselves whether we're open to the kind of change that far-reaching prevention requires. We can prevent these deaths and the injustice that leads to them. The question is, are we really willing to change not only ourselves but also the social systems in which we participate?
>
> Krissy Darch and Fazeela Jiwa, "Beyond Bullying"

A Quotation   A quotation can capture the essence of your thoughts and end the essay with authority or punch. Consider the way in which the final quotation in the brief paragraph below sums up the philosophy of Montreal-born philanthropist Seymour Schulich.

> When he is giving money away, an activity that currently occupies much of his energy and most of his thoughts, Schulich always recalls a marvellous French saying, which, translated, means: "You can't tow a safe behind your hearse."
>
> Peter C. Newman, "Seymour Schulich: Champion Philanthropist," in
> *Heroes: Canadian Champions, Dark Horses and Icons*

Ironic Twist or Surprising Observation   These approaches leave the reader with something to think about. The following paragraph highlights the irony of the writer's regret after he has fulfilled a seemingly desirable dream. Although now living in a premium Vancouver locale, the author regrets that his son is missing out on the cultural and economic diversity of his own youth in Montreal.

> When I grew up I bought a house in the gentle forests of the Pacific and my son walks to school among the cherry blossoms. And sometimes I am sad for him.
>
> Moses Milstein, "Memories of Montreal—and Richness"

In the following conclusion, the writer makes a surprising admission that leaves us thinking.

I'm glad I'm greedy. I would hate to be envious.

> Marilyn Baker, "Greed Works"

Clever or Lighthearted Ending   In humorous or otherwise light essays, clever twists of wording can make for effective endings. In this example, capitalizing on the essay's topic (clichés), the writer ends by exaggerating the fault being criticized.

> Because using clichés is as easy as falling off a log, it goes without saying that it would be duck soup to continue in this vein till hell freezes over. However, since that would be carrying coals to Newcastle, let's ring down the curtain and bid adieu to the fair topic of the cliché. (No use beating a dead horse.)

Personal Challenge   A challenge often prompts the reader to take some action.

> Although we should push the carmakers—and our politicians, who now own a chunk of them—to come up with more fuel-efficient products, even the cleanest vehicles will do nothing to fix sprawl. So we need to convince developers, politicians, and urban planners that we actually want to live in mixed-use walkable neighbourhoods. We can do that by moving to such places. And we must encourage walking, cycling, public transit, and car sharing, for ourselves and for others. Our credo should be: driving, if necessary, but not necessarily driving.

> Tim Falconer, "Autoholics"

Recommendation or Hope   Both a recommendation and a hope may restate points already made in the essay or suggest actions to take in order to arrive at a solution. Andreoni's conclusion recommends creative action for an entire generation.

> So how do we find the happiness that has eluded our generation? By drugging ourselves into mass status quo submission or by defeating the spectacle that robs us of our singular essence. Be unique. Use your hands. Go out and create.

> Jeffrey Andreoni, "Why Can't I Feel What I See?"

The following conclusion conveys not only a hope, but also a sense of warning urgency about the consequences of failing to heed the author's advice.

> It is not more time we need: it is fewer desires. We need to switch off the cell-phone and leave the children to play by themselves. We need to buy less, read less and travel less. We need to set boundaries for ourselves, or be doomed to mounting despair.

> Richard Tomkins, "Old Father Time Becomes a Terror"

EXERCISE

1. Explain which of the above conclusions appeals to you. Does your response stem from the topic or from the author's handling of it?

2. Collect effective concluding paragraphs from magazine articles, illustrating at least three different techniques. Then write a paragraph explaining why each impresses you.

STRATEGIES FOR WORKING WITH SENTENCES

Learning to write well means learning to revise in order to sharpen the effectiveness of what you want to say. By using more varied sentence structures, you will sound like a more mature and sophisticated writer. Getting rid of excess clutter in sentences also gives your writing a pleasing crispness and authority. Finding the right word, instead of the good-enough or almost-right word, is like putting the puck into the net—instead of almost doing it.

To gain control over your writing, you need to be able to recognize what a sentence is. A sentence is a group of words that begins with a capital letter; ends with a period, question mark, or exclamation point; and makes sense by itself. The elements that comprise sentences include subjects, predicates, direct objects, indirect objects, subject complements, object complements, phrases, and clauses.

Sentences take many forms, some straightforward and unadorned, others intricate and ornate, each with its own stylistic strengths. Becoming familiar with these forms and their uses gives you the option to:

- emphasize or de-emphasize an idea
- combine ideas into one sentence or keep them separate in more than one sentence
- make sentences sound formal or informal
- emphasize the actor or the action
- achieve rhythm, variety, and contrast

Effective sentences bring exactness and flair to your writing. However, effective sentence writing is not an accident; it requires practice and hard work. To create stronger sentences, use these strategies: avoiding wordiness; using clear diction; varying sentence length, complexity, and word order; building a rhythm for your reader; and selecting the right verb voice. Usually, it's best to work on these different strategies as you revise rather than pausing to refine each sentence immediately after you write it.

Avoiding Unnecessary Wordiness

In first drafts, it is common for people to write flabby sentences.

It is my considered opinion that you will make an excellent employee.

Joan will give a presentation on our latest sales figures to the CEO.

Mr. Headly, who was my grade 7 biology teacher, recently was honoured for the research he had done over the years with his classes.

My neighbour's Subaru that was old and rusty still could navigate the winter streets better than most other cars.

Although there may be stylistic reasons for these sentences, such as creating variety or adding a particular emphasis, a writer could sharpen them by reordering the sentence structure and eliminating unnecessary words.

You will make an excellent employee. (The fact that you write it makes it clear that it is your opinion.)

Joan will present our latest sales figures to the CEO. (Instead of saying "give a presentation" in the example above, we can change the phrase to the simple verb "present.")

Mr. Headly, my grade 7 biology teacher, recently was honoured for the research he had done over the years with his classes. (You can often delete redundant phrases to tighten your sentences; the phrase "who was" is not necessary in the example above.)

My neighbour's rusty, old Subaru still could navigate the winter streets better than most other cars. (Changing a relative clause to simple adjectives makes this sentence crisper. Often you can change word order to produce more emphatic sentences.)

What are some of the most effective strategies for tightening sentences? Cut out words that seem unnecessary, organize sentences in different ways, and let verbs do more of the work.

A type of wordiness referred to as *deadwood* can result from unconscious use of redundancies. Watch for redundant word pairs such as *advance planning, near proximity,* and *twelve midnight,* which can be written more simply as *planning, proximity,* and *midnight.*

Another type of wordiness, called *gobbledygook,* consists of long, abstract, or technical words that create unnecessarily long and complex sentences. Some people mistakenly believe that this fancy talk sounds more dignified. Others, who may be trying to dazzle the reader rather than communicate, end up clouding their meanings even from themselves. Consider how the following examples of gobbledygook can be clarified and simplified.

Original Version	**Revised Version**
The fish exhibited a 100 percent mortality response.	All the fish died.
We have been made cognizant of the fact that the experiment will be terminated in the near future.	We have learned that the experiment will end soon.

Gobbledygook can result from the practice of transforming verbs into their noun forms. The result is heavy text and sentences that drag. Wherever possible, use a verb in its verb form:

She had a *discussion* about methods for *improvement* of writing.	She *discussed* ways to *improve* writing.

Varying Sentence Complexity and Length

A string of simple sentences that all follow a subject–verb pattern creates a choppy, monotonous effect.

Janice hated pain. She had her nose pierced. She had her bellybutton pierced. She had her tongue pierced. She wanted to be different. She ended up just like her friends.

This string of simple sentences unnecessarily repeats word phrases and seems choppy. Combining these sentences and using a subordinate conjunction results in a smoother and more varied prose style.

Although Janice hated pain, she had her nose, bellybutton, and tongue pierced in order to be different. She ended up, however, just like her friends.

You can combine and condense sentences by learning to use coordinate and subordinate conjunctions that show the relationship between ideas.

Coordination   Coordinating conjunctions join phrases or clauses of equal weight or importance. They include *and, but, or, nor, for, yet,* and *so.*

> The audience was young, friendly, *and* responsive, *so* it cheered for each speaker.

> *Either* we hang together *or* we hang separately.

> A tornado ripped through our town, *but* fortunately it spared our house.

Subordination   Subordinate conjunctions can link a dependent clause to the main clause. *Because, since, although, if, unless, while, before, during, after,* and *instead of* can join clauses and create emphasis, for example. Subordinate conjunctions show the logical relationship of one idea to the other.

> Millicent swam 400 laps today *because* she was feeling unusually strong.

> Arthur collapsed on the sofa *after* the dance was over.

> *After* they had reached the lakeshore, the campers searched for a level spot *because* they wanted to pitch their tent there.

Relative Clauses   Sentences may also be combined and condensed using groups of words called *relative pronoun clauses* (clauses that contain pronouns such as *who, whose, which,* and *that*).

> Students work hard, and they usually succeed.

> Students *who* work hard usually succeed.

> You ordered books on the history of Crete, and they have finally arrived.

> The books on the history of Crete *that* you ordered have finally arrived.

Intentional Fragments   A fragment is a part of a sentence that is capitalized and punctuated as if it were a complete sentence. Fragments are often pieces of sentences that have broken off from the main clause, or what might be thought of as the "parent sentence." They may lack a main subject, a main verb, or both. Although fragments are seldom used in academic writing, they form the backbone of most conversations and thus are popular in fiction. Here's how a typical bit of dialogue might go:

> "Where are you going tonight?" (*sentence*)

> "Woodland Mall." (*fragment*)

> "What for?" (*fragment*)

> "To buy some shoes." (*fragment*)

Moreover, writers of non-fiction use fragments to create special effects. In the following passage, the fragment emphasizes the importance of the question it asks and varies the pace of the writing.

> Imagine waking up one day suddenly unconvinced by western society's founding myths. You realize human progress is a sham. Endless growth, impossible. Your

middle-class lifestyle? Built atop a battery of horrors: factory farming, rainforest destruction, mass extinctions and a dangerously warming climate. How would your world look if you admitted civilization is teetering on collapse?

Geoff Dembicki, "Four Tribes of Climate Change"

Once in a while, a writer uses a series of fragments. In the following paragraph, fragments create an impressionistic effect that mirrors the central kaleidoscope image.

The Jazz Age offers a kaleidoscope of shifting impressions. Of novelties quickly embraced and quickly discarded. Of flappers flaunting bobbed hair and short skirts. Of hip flasks and bootleg whisky, fast cars and coonskin coats, jazz and dancing till dawn. And overall a sense of futility, an uneasy conviction that all the gods were dead.

Elliott L. Smith and Andrew W. Hart, The Short Story: A Contemporary Looking Glass

A word of caution: Before using any fragment in your own writing, think carefully about your intended effect and explore other ways of achieving it. Unless only a fragment will serve your needs, don't use one; fragments are likely to be viewed as unintentional—and thus errors—in the work of inexperienced writers.

Gaining control over these techniques—coordination; subordination; relative clause use; and selective, intentional fragment use—can help you to create rhythm, pacing, and flow in your writing style. Note the variety in sentence length in this paragraph by a master stylist.

To protest that some fairly improbable people, some people who could not possibly respect themselves, seem to sleep easily enough is to miss the point entirely, as surely as those people miss it who think that self-respect has necessarily to do with not having safety pins in one's underwear. There is a common superstition that "self-respect" is a kind of charm against snakes, something that keeps those who have it locked in some unblighted Eden, out of strange beds, ambivalent conversations, and trouble in general. It does not at all. It has nothing to do with the face of things, but concerns instead a separate peace, a private reconciliation.

Joan Didion, "On Self-Respect"

Much of the appealing rhythm of this passage stems from varied sentence length. The first two rather long sentences (of forty-nine and thirty-six words) are followed by the very brief sentence "It does not at all," which gains emphasis by its position. The last sentence adds variety by means of its moderate length (nineteen words), quite apart from its interesting observation on the real nature of self-respect.

Varying sentence length can also help you to emphasize a key idea. Instead of burying a key point in a long sentence, you can highlight it as a separate, shorter sentence, giving it the recognition it deserves.

Original Version

Employers find mature women to be valuable members of their organizations. They are conscientious, have excellent attendance records, and stay calm when things go awry, *but unfortunately, many employers exploit them.* Despite their desirable qualities, most remain mired in clerical and retail positions. On the average, they earn two-thirds as much as men.

Revised Version

Employers find mature women to be valuable members of their organizations. They are conscientious, have excellent attendance records, and stay calm when things go awry. *Unfortunately, many employers exploit them.* Despite their desirable qualities, most remain mired in clerical and retail positions. On the average, they earn two-thirds as much as men.

Varying Word Order

By using more varied sentence structures, your writing will flow better, and you will sound like a more mature writer. Most independent clauses follow a similar arrangement. First comes the subject, then the verb, and finally any other element needed to convey the main message.

Barney blushed. (*subject, verb*)

They built the dog a kennel. (*subject, verb, indirect object, direct object*)

Samantha is an architect. (*subject, verb, subject complement*)

This typical order of sentences puts the emphasis on the subject, right where it's usually wanted.

However, the pattern doesn't work in every situation. Occasionally, you want to emphasize another part of the sentence, create a special effect, or give the subject unusual emphasis. In these situations, you may use inverted order and the expletive construction.

Inverted Order   To invert a sentence, move to the front the element you want to emphasize. Sometimes, the rest of the sentence follows in regular subject-then-verb order; other times, the verb precedes the subject.

Lovable he isn't. (*subject complement, subject, verb*)

This I just don't understand. (*direct object, subject, verb*)

Tall grow the pines in the mountains. (*subject complement, verb, subject*)

Sentences that ask questions typically follow an inverted pattern.

Is this your coat? (*verb, subject, subject complement*)

Since readers expect normal order and read it most easily, do not use inverted word order unless you have reason to.

Expletives   An expletive takes up room in a sentence and rarely contributes anything to the meaning. English has two common expletives, *there* and *it*. Ordinarily, *there* functions as an adverb, and *it* as a pronoun; either can appear anywhere in a sentence. As expletives, however, they alter normal sentence order by beginning sentences and anticipating the real subjects or objects.

Expletives are often used unnecessarily, and can be eliminated to reduce wordiness:

There were twenty persons attending the sales meeting.

This sentence errs on two counts: Its subject needs no extra emphasis, and it is very clumsy. Notice the improvement without the expletive and the unneeded words:

Twenty persons attended the sales meeting.

Sometimes, when the subject or object needs highlighting, leading off with an expletive calls it more forcefully to the reader's attention by altering normal order.

> *Normal order:*   A fly is in my soup. He seeks her happiness.

> *Expletive construction used to highlight subject:*   There is a fly in my soup.

> *Expletive construction used to highlight object:*   It is her happiness he seeks.

Once in a while, you find that something just can't be said unless you use an expletive.

> There is no reason for such foolishness.

Beyond the Single Sentence

Like players on a hockey team, your sentences need to work together to be effective. You need to vary sentence length, word order, and rhythm, but in a way that is not obvious or clumsy. This takes work. A good place to start is by studying the essays in the Reader of this text to see what kinds of combinations the authors use—a series of questions that are then answered; long sentences with modifiers leading up to and emphasizing a short sentence; a series of fragments followed by a long sentence. In your own writing, keep an eye on what kind of sentences you are creating and how those sentences create a pattern. Once you have finished a draft, read it to hear how its rhythms strike your inner ear, and mark sections that "sound" wrong. Play with your sentences to get the results that you want.

REVISION CHECKLIST FOR SENTENCES

- What sentences are not clearly expressed or logically constructed?
- What sentences seem awkward, excessively convoluted, or lacking in punch?
- What words require explanation or substitution because the reader may not know them?
- Where does the writing become wordy or use vague terms?
- Are there carelessly omitted or wrongly used words?

STRATEGIES FOR WORKING WITH DICTION AND TONE

Diction, or word choice, is an important part of successful writing. The words you use also help to set your tone for the reader, along with your style. Often, the writer's tone can convey as much meaning as the information itself.

Using Clear Diction

Clear diction stems from choosing words with the right meanings, using abstract and concrete words appropriately, and picking terms that are neither too specific nor too general.

Word Meanings   Make sure the words you use mean what you think they do, so that inaccurate word use does not distort your message. Sound-alike word pairs often trip up unwary writers. Take *accept* and *except*, for example. *Accept* means "to approve." *Except*, when used as a verb, means "to exclude or omit." If you want to indicate approval but you say, "The following new courses were *excepted* by the committee," think of the obvious consequences. Likewise, consider the distinction between *continual* (frequently or regularly repeated) and *continuous* (uninterrupted). If you illustrate your popularity by saying, "My phone rings *continuously*," your reader will wonder why you never answer it and how you ever sleep.

Concrete and Abstract Words   Sometimes, using more concrete words can bring to life a piece of writing that seems vague or dull. A concrete word names or describes something that we can perceive with one or more of our five senses. A thing is concrete if we can weigh it, measure it, hold it in our hands, photograph it, taste it, sniff it, add salt to it, drop it, smash into it, or borrow it from a neighbour. But if a thing is abstract, we can't do any of these things. *Anne of Green Gables* is a concrete term, as are *Swiss cheese*, *petroleum*, *maple syrup*, and *Halifax*. On the other hand, *jealousy, power, conservatism, size,* and *sadness* are all abstract terms.

Concrete words evoke precise, vivid mental images and thus help to convey a message. In contrast, the images that abstract terms create differ from person to person.

Specific and General Terms   One concrete term can be more specific or more general than another. As we move from *Lassie* to *collie* to *dog* to *mammal* and finally to *animal*, we become less and less specific, ending with a term that encompasses every animal on earth. With each step we retain only those features that fit the more general term. Thus, when we move from *collie* to *dog*, we leave out everything that makes collies different from terriers, greyhounds, and other breeds. The more specific the term, the less difference among the images it calls to mind. For example, if you say *animal* to a group of friends, one may think of a dog, another of a horse, and a third of a gorilla. *Collie*, on the other hand, likely triggers images of a large, long-haired, brown and white dog with a pointed muzzle.

Typically, a first draft will contain overly general words that are abstract rather than concrete. Ask yourself how specific you need to be and then revise accordingly. Often, the more specific term is the better choice. For example, you might characterize a wealthy jet-setter by noting that he drives a Ferrari, not just a car. However, if you're writing a narrative about your flight to Quebec City and your experience at the winter carnival, nothing is gained by naming the make of car you rented and used during your stay. Choose details that fit your purpose.

Listening for Tone in Writing

Tone reveals the author's attitude toward the topic and the reader. While it is relatively easy to pick up on a speaker's tone of voice—solemn, confident, ironic, or lightly humorous—tone in writing is conveyed largely through word choice, style, and sentence rhythm.

Word Meaning   Tone is conveyed partly through the words you choose. Use the exact word that you need for the job. It can sometimes take some thought to come up with accurate and precise words for what you want to convey; for example, a student who referred to a cyber-bully giving *naive* nicknames to celebrities realized that *naive* was not really the right word. She replaced the word with a more accurate one: *demeaning*.

Sometimes, you have words in your passive vocabularies—words that you have read or heard before but that you have not used yourself. If you are unsure of the meanings of a word, or if you want more information about a word, consult a good dictionary such as the *Oxford English Dictionary*, which is available online.

Dictionaries can help you learn about current and past meanings of a word. They identify parts of speech; variant spellings of a word; pronunciations; and the history, or etymology, of a word. If you are using a word extensively in your paper, including information about the word's etymology can help your reader understand the word's nuances.

Usage Labels   A dictionary's usage labels also help you to determine whether a word suits the circumstances of your writing.

Label	Meaning
Colloquial	Relatively casual usage characteristic of informal conversation
Slang	Informal, newly coined words and expressions or old expressions with new meanings
Obsolete	No longer in use but found in writing from the past
Archaic	Old, usually outmoded, but still finds restricted use; for example, in legal documents
Poetic	Used only in poetry and in prose with a poetic tone
Dialect	Used regularly only in a particular geographical region such as parts of Newfoundland or the Scottish Lowlands

Denotation and Connotation   Word meanings often extend beyond dictionary definitions, or *denotations*. Many words carry emotional associations, or *connotations*. For example, a word such as *medicine* denotes a "substance used in treating illness or disease." This definition is objective and neutral—it does not assign any special value or convey any particular attitude toward the word or what the word stands for. However, the word *medicine* could also carry strong positive or negative connotations, depending on how it is used. To say that going into the wilderness is just the "medicine" one needs sounds positive, but to say that something tastes "like medicine" sounds negative. Context—the parts of a passage that precede and follow a word—also affects connotation.

Some words—*death*, for instance—almost always carry strong connotations or emotional associations. The *Canadian Oxford Dictionary* defines it as "the final cessation of vital functions" or "the ending of life," but it means much more than that. All of us have hopes, fears, and memories relating to death, feelings that colour our responses whenever we hear or read the word. Likewise, we have personal responses to words such as *sexy*, *cheap*, *radical*, *politician*, and *mother* based on our experiences. Cultural connotations are even more important than personal connotations. Cultural connotations develop much as personal ones do, but on a much larger scale, as they grow out of the common experiences of many speakers and writers. As words are used in different ways through different circumstances, their connotations may also change over time. For example, the word *problem* literally means "a difficult matter requiring a solution"—a very neutral denotation. But its cultural connotation is negative in most social situations. Imagine if an instructor called you into her office and demanded, "Do you have a problem?" Imagine the reaction if a store clerk approached a hesitant customer and asked, "What is your problem?" In both situations, the listener would probably feel insulted and even angry, due to the negative cultural connotation of the word.

Denotation is sometimes called the language of science and technology, and connotation the language of art. But we need both to communicate effectively. Denotation allows us to convey precise, essential meanings. Connotation adds richness, warmth, and texture.

Types of Tone   Every piece of writing has combined characteristics that give it a special tone. The following excerpt conveys a *sophisticated, rather formal tone.*

> Unless you have led an abnormally isolated adulthood, the chances are excellent that you know many people who have at one time or another committed an act, or consorted with someone who was committing an act, for which they might have been sent to prison. We do not consider most of these people, or ourselves, criminals; the act is one thing, the criminality of it quite something else. Homicide, for example, is in our law not a crime; murder only is proscribed. The difference between the two is the intention, or to be more accurate, society's decision about the nature of that intention.

> Bruce Jackson, "Who Goes to Prison: Caste and Careerism in Crime"

The formal tone is suggested partly by words such as *consorted* and *proscribed* that do not form part of most people's everyday word kits. The complexity of the first sentence and the varied patterns of the others add to the air of sophistication.

An *objective* tone keeps the writer's personality and opinion out of the message. If you are writing a lab report or another kind of factual report, you will likely be expected to have an objective tone. Consider this example of a relatively neutral piece of prose:

> In 1867, the year of Confederation, Canada's population was close to 3.5 million. Since then, the population size has grown steadily and has doubled about every 40 years. In recent years, however, the increase in population has slowed. In July 2011, Canada's population was estimated at just under 34.5 million.

> Human Resources and Skills Development Canada,
> "Indicators of Well-Being in Canada"

The neutral tone here is businesslike and authoritative, the sentence patterns uncomplicated, and the person behind the words adequately concealed.

In persuasive writing, your tone will be determined by your purpose, your audience, the context of your writing, and your own attitude. In more personal writing, you might be quietly reflective, unemotional, or lightly humorous. In formal academic writing, your tone might be serious, subtle, and calm. If you have strong feelings about an issue, an *angry or impassioned tone* might be conveyed through choice of details and word selection, as shown in the following excerpt.

> Cans. Beer cans. Glinting on the verges of a million miles of roadways, lying in scrub, grass, dirt, leaves, sand, mud, but never hidden. Piels, Rheingold, Ballantine, Schaeffer, Schlitz, shining in the sun or picked by moon or the beams of headlights at night; washed by rain or flattened by wheels, but never dulled, never buried, never destroyed. Here is the

mark of savages, the testament of wasters, the stain of prosperity. Who are these men who defile the grassy borders of our roads and lanes, who pollute our ponds, who spoil the purity of our ocean beaches with the empty vessels of their thirst? Who are the men who make these vessels in millions and then say, "Drink and discard"? What society is this that can afford to cast away a million tons of metal and to make a wild and fruitful land a garbage heap?

Marya Mannes, "Wasteland"

Rhythm and word choice contribute equally to the tone of this passage. The excerpt opens with imagistic sentence fragments that create a panoramic word picture of littered roadways. Then complete sentences and sombre commentary follow. Words and patterns are repeated, mixing the dignified language of epic and religion with common derogatory terms—*testament, purity, vessels,* and *fruitful* set against *savages, wasters, defile,* and *garbage heap*—to convey the contradictions Mannes deplores. The rhetorical questions, used instead of accusations, add a sense of loftiness to her outrage, helping to create a tone both majestic and disdainful.

Erethizon dorsatus, an antisocial character of the Northern U.S. and Canadian forest, commonly called a porcupine, looks like an uncombed head, has a grumpy personality, fights with his tail, hides his head when he's in trouble, attacks backing up, retreats going ahead, and eats toilet seats as if they were Post Toasties. It's a sad commentary on his personality that people are always trying to do him in.

R.T. Allen, "The Porcupine"

The tone of the above passage is *affectionately humorous*. Allen sets this tone by noting the porcupine's tousled appearance, testy personality, and peculiar habits, such as eating outdoor toilet seats (for their salt content, as Allen later explains). The net effect is to personify porcupines, making them seem like eccentric, reprobate humans whom others regard with amused tolerance.

The next excerpt is an example of a *solemn tone* and begins by referring to "genuine love": the patience, sharing, forgiveness, trust, and acceptance necessary to reconcile Aboriginal cultures with the contemporary North American culture.

The only thing that can truly help us is genuine love. You must truly love us, be patient with us and share with us. And we must love you—with a genuine love that forgives and forgets . . . a love that forgives the terrible sufferings your culture brought ours when it swept over us like a wave crashing along a beach . . . with a love that forgets and lifts up its head and sees in your eyes an answering love of trust and acceptance.

Chief Dan George, "I Am a Native of North America"

This writing speaks honestly and passionately about love and reconciliation. Its most obvious rhetorical strategy is the personification of love. Love takes on human form when it "lifts up its head and sees . . . an answering love." This personification reinforces the basic humanity, mutual respect, and love that all people must recognize in each other for reconciliation to take place. The repetition of love throughout the passage reinforces the earnest, emotional plea. Eloquence comes through parallelism, repetition, and words like *truly* and *genuine*. Vividness comes through the simile describing the impact of colonization on First Nations cultures as akin to "a wave crashing along a beach." Chief Dan George uses both rhythm and diction to create a tone that infuses and invigorates his message.

STRATEGIES FOR WORKING WITH SPECIAL STYLISTIC TECHNIQUES

The style of a piece of writing is its character or personality. Like people, writing can be many things: dull, stuffy, discordant, sedate, lively, flamboyant, eccentric, and so on. Figurative language and irony can contribute to your own distinctive writing style.

Figurative Language

Figurative language uses concrete words in a non-literal way to create sharply etched sensory images that catch and hold the reader's attention. Besides energizing the writing, figurative language helps to strengthen the reader's grip on its ideas. Five figurative devices are especially important: simile, metaphor, personification, overstatement, and understatement.

Simile and Metaphor   A *simile* directly compares two unlike things through the use of *like* or *as*. "Todd is as restless as an aspen leaf in a breeze." "Her smile flicked on and off like a sunbeam flashing momentarily through a cloud bank." A *metaphor* also compares unlike things, but without using *like* or *as*. Some metaphors include a linking verb (*is, are, were,* and so on); others do not. "The moon was a wind-tossed bark" and "The curtain of darkness fell over the land" are both metaphors. Here is an excerpt that contains similes and metaphors:

> The field is a sea of deep, dark green, a sea made up of millions of small blades of grass blended together as one. Each blade is a dark green spear, broad at the bottom and narrowing to a needle point at the tip. Its full length is arched so that, viewed from one end, it looks like a shallow trough with paper-thin sides.
>
> Daniel Kinney, student

Keep in mind that similes and metaphors must be used well to be effective. Writers too often snatch hastily at the first similes and metaphors that come to mind and end up strewing their pages with overused and enfeebled specimens. Johnny is "as blind as a bat," Mary runs around "like a chicken with its head cut off"—and the writing slips into triteness. Other comparisons seem strained because they link items that are too dissimilar. For example, "The wind whistled through the trees like a herd of galloping horses" would only puzzle a reader.

Personification   *Personification* is a special sort of metaphor that assigns human qualities or traits to something nonhuman: a plant, an abstraction, an inanimate thing. Here are some examples:

The vine clung stubbornly to the trunk of the tree.
The waves lapped sullenly against the base of the cliff.

These sentences create a picture and a mood by assigning a different emotional quality—stubbornness or gloom—to their subjects: Vines aren't literally stubborn, of course, and waves aren't sullen, though they may seem that way to the human observer.

Overstatement   *Overstatement*, sometimes called hyperbole, deliberately and drastically exaggerates to make a point. In his humorous essay contrasting the stubby and long-necked beer bottles, Perry Jensen writes:

> Time to take a stand, Canada. Let's demand the return of our national beer bottle, the stubby, and refuse to drink from foreign containers until the brewers come crawling on their hands and knees.
>
> Perry T. Jensen, "Lament for the Short and Stubby"

Overstatement may contribute to a humorous effect. If it is used sparingly in persuasive essays, it can sometimes add force and punch.

Understatement   *Understatement* makes a quiet assertion in a matter-of-fact way, as when a sportscaster calls a team's 23–2 win–loss record "pretty fair." By drawing attention to the thing it appears to slight, this soft-spoken approach offers writers an effective strategy. Here is an example:

> To assume that Heidi Mansfield lacks the qualifications for this position is not unwarranted.

Without ever actually calling Mansfield unqualified, the statement suggests that she is.

Irony

Irony occurs when a writer intentionally states one thing but actually means something different or even opposite. The sportswriter who refers to the "ideal conditions" for a tennis tournament when rain has drenched the courts and forced cancellation of matches speaks ironically. In an article about government cutbacks, Charles Gordon uses irony to make a serious point.

> Welcome to Cutback World, ladies and gentlemen. We hope you enjoyed your flight. Sorry you had to walk so far in the rain, but spending reductions have made it possible for us to operate the same number of airplanes with fewer unloading ramps. You will notice complimentary newspapers on some of the seats of this bus. We hope you don't mind sharing them. While we wait to begin our tour, you might like to read some of the stories, just to get an introduction to the place we call home. If you turn to page 1, you'll see the little item about what we are doing for our homeless citizens. We have provided 300 beds for them in this city alone. According to the most recent estimates, this means that at least 10 percent of our homeless citizens will be able to find a bed tonight. So across the country, only 20 000 to 40 000 people are sleeping on the streets.
>
> Charles Gordon, "A Guided Tour of the Bottom Line"

The author never directly states that he disagrees with the government's spending reductions, but he uses details that highlight what he considers to be the injustice or absurdity of government spending cuts. When he states that "at least 10 percent" of the homeless have beds, he pretends to be congratulatory but is in fact emphasizing the relatively tiny portion of the homeless population that has shelter.

EFFECTIVE STYLE: SAYING WHAT YOU MEAN

As you become conscious of your writing style, you can work toward more directness and clarity. When you revise, stay alert to diction flaws such as euphemisms, clichés, mixed metaphors, and sexist language, and eliminate any that you find.

Euphemisms

Euphemisms are sometimes used to evade unpleasant realities. Familiar expressions include *pass away* for *die, pre-owned* for *used,* and *sanitation engineer* for *garbage collector.*

In most cases, the writer simply intends to cushion reality. But euphemisms also have grisly uses. Companies don't fire employees; they *restructure* or *downsize.* Mobsters don't *beat up* merchants who refuse *protection* (itself a euphemism); they *lean on* them. Hitler didn't talk about *exterminating the Jews* but about *the final solution to the Jewish problem.* These euphemisms don't just blur reality, but blot out images of horror: of merchants with broken limbs and bloodied faces; of cattle cars crammed with men, women, and children en route to death camps.

Any euphemism, however well intentioned, probably interferes with communication by obscuring an issue.

Clichés and Mixed Metaphors

Clichés   Clichés are expressions that have become stale from overuse. They weaken your prose, because these oft-repeated words or phrases stem from patterned thinking. It is natural that our early drafts will have the trite expressions that spring readily to mind, but when you revise, take the time to replace clichés, such as the following, with fresh, evocative language.

acid test	burn the midnight oil	green with envy
better late than never	cool as a cucumber	rears its ugly head
black sheep	easier said than done	set the world on fire

Mixed Metaphors   Clichéd writing often suffers as well from mixed metaphors—inappropriate combinations that startle or unintentionally amuse the reader.

> When he opened that can of worms, he bit off more than he could chew.

Did you visualize someone chewing a mouthful of worms? Beware of mixed metaphors.

Inclusive Language

Inclusive language is language that respects all communities. It does not single out traits such as gender, sexual orientation, abilities, age, or ethnicity when they are not relevant to the context or topic at hand. Non-inclusive language is often inadvertently offensive, as it may exclude some people, demean them, or assign them to limiting roles. As language evolves, it is best to use the descriptors that members of a particular community prefer.

Non-inclusive:	Please consult the chairman of your department.
Non-inclusive:	It's hard to find tradesmen these days.
Non-inclusive:	I'm hoping the mailman will bring me a surprise.
Inclusive:	Please consult the chair/chairperson of your department.
Inclusive:	It's hard to find tradespeople these days.
Inclusive:	I'm hoping the letter carrier will bring me a surprise.

Note how, in each case, the sentence has been rewritten as gender neutral.

CHAPTER 6

Strategies for Personal Writing: Narration

Clicking off the evening news and padding toward bed, Heloise suddenly glimpsed, out of the corner of her eye, a shadow stretching across the living room floor from under the drawn curtains.

"Wh—who's there?"

No response.

Edging backwards toward the phone, her eyes riveted on the shadow, she stammered, "I—I don't have any money."

Still no answer.

Reaching the phone, she gripped the receiver and started to lift it from its cradle. Just then she heard a noise. . . .

If you want to know what happens next, the above *narrative* has begun to weave its spell. A narrative relates a series of events that may be real—as in histories, biographies, or news stories—or imaginary, as in short stories and novels. Television sitcoms and mysteries, video games, movies, and even commercials use stories to draw us in, making us want to know what happens next. No doubt, you have responded to stories almost from the time you began to talk. As a child, as soon as you heard the words "Once upon a time," you probably leaned forward to listen closely, your eyes glowing. As adults, we gossip about people we may or may not know, tell friends about odd or distressing events we have experienced, and report stories we have read about on social media. Good speeches are usually enlivened with relevant stories.

The writing we do for school and work may use short narratives to hook the reader in or illustrate a point we are making. You might also be asked to write essays based on narratives. In an English class, you may be asked to research the story of how a novelist lived and wrote. In a psychology class, you might study or write a case history, or your history instructor might have you recap the events leading to a major war. At work, a police officer may record the events leading to an arrest, a scientist may recount the development of a research project, and a department manager may prepare a brief history of an employee's work problems.

PURPOSE

Most narratives do not simply tell what happened or recite a series of events, but instead they make a point or have a purpose. The point can be stated or implied, but it always shapes the writing. Narratives of history and biography delve into the motives underlying the events and lives they portray, while narratives of personal experience offer lessons and insights. Sometimes they reveal a change, or shift in perspective, from the beginning of the story to the end. In the following conclusion to a narrative about an encounter with a would-be mugger, the writer reveals his understanding of the meaning of self-respect.

> I kept my self-respect, even at the cost of dirtying my fists with violence, and I feel that I understand the Irish and the Cypriots, the Israelis and the Palestinians, all those who seem to us to fight senseless wars for senseless reasons, better than before. For what respect does one keep for oneself if one isn't in the last resort ready to fight and say, "You punk!"?
>
> Harry Fairlie, "A Victim Fights Back"

ACTION

Action plays a central role in any narrative. Some writing tells about action that has happened offstage. Sometimes, gaps remain to stimulate readers' imaginations:

> A hundred thousand people were killed by the atomic bomb, and these six were among the survivors. They still wonder why they lived when so many others died. Each of them counts many small items of chance or volition—a step taken in time, a decision to go indoors, catching one streetcar instead of the next—that spared him. And now each knows that in the act of survival he lived a dozen lives and saw more death than he ever thought he would see. At the time, none of them knew anything.
>
> John Hersey, *Hiroshima*

This passage suggests a great deal of action—the flash of an exploding bomb, the collapse of buildings, screaming people fleeing. However, because it does not recreate the action moment by moment, it does not pull the reader directly into the scene as the following narration from Charles Dickens' novel *Great Expectations* does:

> . . . Passing on into the front court-yard, I hesitated whether to call the woman to let me out at the locked gate of which she had the key, or first to go up-stairs and assure myself that Miss Havisham was as safe and well as I had left her. I took the latter course and went up.
>
> I looked into the room where I had left her, and I saw her seated in the ragged chair upon the hearth close to the fire, with her back towards me. In the moment when I was

withdrawing my head to go quietly away, I saw a great flaming light spring up. In the same moment, I saw her running at me, shrieking, with a whirl of fire blazing all about her, and soaring at least as many feet above her head as she was high.

I had a double-caped great-coat on, and over my arm another thick coat. That I got them off, closed with her, threw her down, and got them over her; that I dragged the great cloth from the table for the same purpose, and with it dragged down the heap of rottenness in the midst, and all the ugly things that sheltered there; that we were on the ground struggling like desperate enemies, and that the closer I covered her, the more wildly she shrieked and tried to free herself; that this occurred I knew through the result, but not through anything I felt, or thought, or knew I did. I knew nothing until I knew that we were on the floor by the great table, and that patches of tinder yet alight were floating in the smoky air, which, a moment ago, had been her faded bridal dress.

Then, I looked round and saw the disturbed beetles and spiders running away over the floor, and the servants coming in with breathless cries at the door. I still held her forcibly down with all my strength, like a prisoner who might escape; and I doubt if I even knew who she was, or why we had struggled, or that she had been in flames, or that the flames were out, until I saw the patches of tinder that had been her garments, no longer alight but falling in a black shower around us.

Charles Dickens, Great Expectations

Dickens' description of a struggle between a young man and a very disturbed elderly woman in flames conveys a vivid moment-to-moment replay of action that is so terrifying as to seem unreal. Of course, narrative action is not always this dramatic, and often refers to more ordinary events —such as a long, patient wait that comes to nothing, or an unexpected kiss after some friendly assistance. It may also convey the dramatic tension of an inner struggle. In all cases, the narrative action should contribute to a larger point.

CONFLICT

In narrative writing, conflict and its resolution, if any, usually motivate and often structure the action. Some conflicts pit one individual against another or against a group, such as a company or institution. In other cases, the conflict may be between a person and the elements of nature. Often, the conflict is an inner one that involves clashing impulses inside one person's mind.

In the following excerpt from the beginning of an essay, note how the student writer sets out an inner conflict that she has had about accepting and appreciating her name.

While I sit here at my desk, trying to think of something to write about for my English class, I begin by typing my name at the top right hand corner of the page. I frown as I read the words "Gurminder Khun Khun." All I can think of is past memories of children at school mocking my name as they chanted, "Gur-Hindu, and Gurbinder." I remember the unbearable feeling as the teacher would read out the list of names from the attendance list. She would call out "Jeremy Jingson, Brandon Klame," pause for a few seconds and call out, "Gurminder Khoon Khoon." As I stare at the computer screen, I notice that the Microsoft Word program underlines my name in pink, suggesting that my name is a typo. I enjoy being simple, so why on earth did I get such an embarrassing name? As I sit here pondering several negative thoughts about my given name, a flashback quickly fills my mind.

I am ten years old and sitting at the kitchen table. My mother is filling out passport application forms and our birth certificates are spread out on the wooden table. I pick up my green birth certificate that is in a plastic case. I sigh as I read the words "Gurminder Kaur Khun Khun."

As I rub my finger over the plastic cover, frowning, I say, "I hate my name. It's so embarrassing. Why couldn't I get a prettier name? Like Gurina, Sabrina, or Kelly, just like Mom did."

My grandmother, who is also sitting at the table, frowns, puts down her tea cup, and says, "You have a beautiful name. There is so much meaning and value attached to your name."

Gurminder Khun Khun, student, "What's in a Name?"

For some narrative writing, as in the essay excerpted above, it might be helpful to think of conflict in terms of an unresolved problem with which the narrator struggles. Tension builds until the ending, which may suggest a solution to the problem.

POINT OF VIEW

Narrative writers may adopt either a first-person or a third-person point of view. In first-person narratives, one of the participants tells what happened, whereas a third-person narrator tells the story from an outside perspective. Narratives you write about yourself use the first person, as do autobiographies. Biographies and histories use the third person, and fiction may employ either point of view.

In first-person narration, pronouns such as *I, me, mine, we,* and *ours* identify the storyteller. Often, the immediacy of first-person narration enhances reader identification. In contrast, the third-person narrator usually stays behind the scenes, quietly shaping events and selecting details. Although the use of third-person narration creates more distance between reader and characters, this narrator can move more freely in time and space.

First-Person Narration

It was a lovely and windless evening, and the birds were twittering, and the trees in the orchard near the road were golden in the late sunlight, and the purple milkweed flowers that grew beside the drive smelled very sweetly; and also the last few peonies beside the verandah, and the climbing roses; and the coolness came down out of the air, while Jamie sat and played on his flute. . . . After a while McDermott came skulking around the side of the house like a tamed wolf, and leant against the side of the house, and listened also. And there we were, in a kind of harmony; and the evening was so beautiful, that it made a pain in my heart, as when you cannot tell whether you are happy or sad; and I thought that if I could have a wish, it would be that nothing would ever change. . . .

Margaret Atwood, *Alias Grace*

Third-Person Narration

People driving by don't notice Spit Delaney. His old gas station is nearly hidden now behind the firs he's let grow up along the road, and he doesn't bother to whitewash the scalloped row of half-tires someone planted once instead of fence. And rushing by on the Island highway today, heading north or south, there's little chance that anyone will notice Spit Delaney seated on the big rock at the side of his road-end, scratching at his narrow chest, or hear him muttering to the flat grey highway and to the scrubby firs and to the useless old ears of his neighbour's dog that he'll be damned if he can figure out what it is that is happening to him.

Jack Hodgins, "Separating"

KEY EVENTS

Any narrative includes many separate events, enough to swamp your narrative boat if you try to pack them all in. Suppose that you wish to write about your recent attack of appendicitis to make a point about heeding early warnings of an oncoming illness. Your list of events might look like this:

Awakened	Greeted fellow	Ate lunch
Showered	employees	Returned to work
Experienced acute	Began morning's	Began afternoon's
but passing pain in	work	work
abdomen	Felt nauseated	Collapsed at
Dressed	Met with boss	workstation
Ate breakfast	Took coffee break	Was rushed to
Opened garage door	Visited bathroom	hospital
Started car	Experienced more	Underwent
Drove to work	prolonged pain	diagnostic tests
Parked in employee	in abdomen	Had emergency
lot	Walked to cafeteria	operation
Entered building		

A narrative that included all, or even most, of these events would be bloated and ineffective. Thus you need to be selective, building your narrative around key events that bear directly on your purpose. Include just enough incidental details or events to keep the narrative flowing smoothly, but sketch them in lightly. Key events, such as the first attack of pain in the example above, will be developed more fully.

My first sign of trouble came shortly after I stepped out of the shower. I had just finished towelling when a sharp pain in my lower right side sent me staggering into the bedroom, where I collapsed onto an easy chair in the corner. Biting my lip to hide my groans, I sat twisting in agony as the pain gradually ebbed, leaving me grey-faced, sweat-drenched, and shaken. What, I asked myself, had been the trouble? Was it ulcers? Was it a gallbladder attack? Did I have stomach cancer?

The vivid details in this passage help to recreate the experience in the reader's imagination.

USE OF TELLING DETAIL

To establish the setting, create a mood, or advance the storyline, a narrative often blends in specific details that appeal to the reader's senses. If you are telling a story about a dreamlike, disoriented moment in your life, you may use details that suggest a dreamlike setting—maybe a time when you were driving on a wet, foggy night, peering through the wipers swishing back and forth on your car's windshield. Rather than simply piling on adjectives and adverbs, search for accurate nouns and verbs. In one of the essays in this chapter, the writer Moses Milstein does not simply tell the reader that he lives with his son in a wealthy part of the city; instead he describes the "quiet punctuated by the thwonk of tennis balls" from nearby tennis courts. In his novel *In the Skin of a Lion*, Michael Ondaatje describes how "a blue moth had pulsed on the screen, bathed briefly in light, and then disappeared into darkness." The verb "pulsed" indicates the subtle movement of the moth while also evoking the brevity of the moth's life, and the image of a moth "bathing" in light is a simple but striking way to describe the attraction of the light for the moth. If you are writing a narrative and want to show that someone was angry with you, you might find a verb or a telling detail that implies anger: perhaps the person *glared* at you, *tightened their lips,* or *stomped out of* the room.

To give your narrative a sense of life, you need to pay close attention to details that appeal to all five senses. As you read the next passage, excerpted from a student essay, note which sensory details are most effective in conveying the harshness of a family's struggle to survive in urban poverty.

"It was about survival," Ken said, looking down at the table, as if he felt a twinge of guilt about what he was telling me. Saturdays were good for hungry kids looking to make money. They would be taken to the centre of town, near the bars. Rifling through the pockets of drunks sleeping off their Friday night paycheques earned them a few coins, which bought meat pies from the bakery on the corner.

Staring through the bakery window at the huge meat pies, Ken would enjoy the whiff of the aroma of fresh food. As he describes these pies to me, he stretches his hands out wide, like someone in a commercial barely able to hold an enormous burger with two hands.

After spending their hard-earned money in the bakery, the three siblings would take their meat pies behind the dry cleaner next door and hunker down. The warm steam silently drifting down brought shelter from Toronto's unforgiving cold.

Under the vent, wrapped in a blanket of stream, three children would stay warm eating meat pies. They relished what might be their first real food in days, but no matter how hungry they felt, they always saved one pie to take back to their mother.

Kyle Butt, student

Choose only those details that relate to your overall purpose, or the mood you are trying to create. As you read the following passage from an article about cleaning out an elderly parent's home, note how the writer has incorporated details that suggest a sense of loss and contribute to a larger point about the ephemeral nature of human life and memory.

On day one of all this, we had ducked into the basement, past wooden shelves of canned preserves that will never be opened, to check out the crawl space. And there we found the steamer trunk. It was a grimy, beaten-up old thing, the kind of container that once carried people's lives over from Europe. Dragged upstairs, its contents (all unused) started to tell a story: a frying pan with the label still on, a set of pea-green containers, eight tiny wine glasses, three pressed dresses from Woodward's, two pairs of men's socks and ten pairs of hose, still in their packaging. Why was it all untouched? Why abandoned there, wrapped in pages of a 1969 copy of the *Vancouver Sun*?

Michael Harris, "Clearing House"

EXERCISE *Spend some time in an environment such as a cafeteria or a city intersection. Concentrate on one sense at a time. Begin by observing what you see; then jot down the precise impressions you receive. Now do the same for impressions of touch, taste, smell, and sound.*

When you have finished, select four or five of these details that you could use to create a certain kind of mood in a narrative—perhaps anxiety, dread, excitement, boredom, delight, or security.

DIALOGUE

Dialogue, or conversation, animates many narratives. Written conversation, however, does not duplicate real talk. When speaking with friends, we repeat ourselves, throw in irrelevant comments, use slang, lose our train of thought, and overuse expressions like *you know*, *uh*, and *well*. Dialogue that reproduced actual conversation word by word would likely bore the reader.

Good dialogue resembles real conversation without copying it. It chooses economical sentences while avoiding excessive repetition of phrases such as *she said* and *he replied*. If the conversation unfolds smoothly, the speakers' identities are clear, as seen in the following excerpt from an essay based on an interview a young Canadian-born woman had with her mother, who was born in Pakistan.

Now I had the choice to continue with clichéd questions or meaningful ones. I chose quality over quantity. "So you had an arranged marriage? Would you want the same for me?" Since she and I frequently bickered about the value of arranged marriage vs. a love marriage, I thought that this was the perfect time for me to listen to her on this sensitive topic.

"It was time. I was twenty-two, educated, young, and I could cook. I was ready for marriage, I guess. I didn't have anyone in mind at that time. Time is everything and no man wants an old wife."

                                                            Filza Ahmar, student

Besides making your dialogue sound realistic, make sure that you punctuate it correctly. Here are some key guidelines:

- Each shift from one speaker to another requires a new paragraph.
- When an expression like *he said* interrupts a single quoted sentence, set it off with commas.
- When such an expression comes between two complete sentences, put a period after the expression and capitalize the first word of the second sentence. "I know it looks bad," she said. "But I didn't mean to blow up the lab."
- Put commas, periods, and other punctuation marks that come at the end of a direct quotation inside the closing quotation mark. "What do you want from me?"

ETHICAL ISSUES

Think what your response might be if you were surfing the Internet and came across a narrative about your first date that used your real name and cast you in an unfavourable light. At the very least, you would find it embarrassing. As you mull over any narrative you write, you'll want to think about several ethical issues, especially if you're depicting an actual event.

- Am I providing a truthful account that participants will recognize and accept? Deliberate falsification of someone's behaviour that tarnishes that person's reputation is libel and could even result in legal action.
- Would the narrative expose anyone to possible danger if it became public? Do I need to change any names to protect people from potential harm? Suppose that your narrative includes someone who cooperates with authorities behind the scenes to help solve a case. You should probably give that person a fictitious name.
- Does the narrative encourage unethical or illegal behaviour? For example, extolling the delights of smoking marijuana for a teenage audience is clearly unethical.

These guidelines don't rule out exaggerated, humorous, or painfully truthful narratives. As with any writing, however, narratives can affect people's lives; ethical writers consider the possible consequences of their work.

WRITING A NARRATIVE

Although you might use the third person if you are writing about something that happened to someone else, most narratives that you write for a composition class will use the first person because they will relate personal experience. In either case, your narrative needs to make a point, or go somewhere. In your first draft, you may start describing how you violated a friend's confidence, and as you continue writing, a point may emerge—for example, you may uncover an idea about the ethical obligations of friendship. Later, as you revise, you can shape and consciously select parts of the narrative that lead to this point.

Prewriting the Narrative

As you consider what to write about, do some guided brainstorming, asking yourself these questions. When you have pinpointed a topic, use further brainstorming to generate supporting material.

FINDING YOUR TOPIC

- What experience in my life or that of someone I know interests me?
- Is there an interesting problem—even a small one—that I have struggled with and would like to explore?
- Who was involved and what parts did they play?
- Is there a point to this story that I could state in one or two sentences?

Planning and Drafting the Narrative

Before you start to write, develop a plot outline showing the significant events of your narrative. Begin with the context—the details of where, who, and when. Then move on to the first, second, and subsequent events. For each one, jot down what you saw, heard, or did, and what you thought or felt. To create a **thesis statement**, ask yourself what important insight or discovery you made.

Consider the following tips for drafting and organizing your narrative.

Following are suggestions for organizing your narrative:

Introduction
- Sets the stage for what follows.
- Possibly tells when and where the action occurred.
- Provides useful background information.
- Notes the incident that started events.
- States main point here or in the conclusion.

Body
- Moves action forward to turning point.
- Establishes conflict.
- Provides sequence of main events.
- Usually resolves conflict.
- Uses time signals such as "now," "next," "finally," "when I returned" to help reader.
- Uses dialogue.

Conclusion
- Ties up loose ends.
- Gives a sense of completion.
- May include a reflective summary of events, note your reactions, offer a surprise twist, or discuss aftermath.

ELEMENTS TO KEEP IN MIND FOR A PERSONAL EXPERIENCE NARRATIVE

1. **Larger purpose**—similar to a thesis, it is the larger point, something the reader can ponder. It can be stated or implied.

2. **Action**—shows or recreates action; is not just a summary. Use energetic verbs (for example, instead of saying, "I walked slowly with heavy limbs," you could use a verb such as "trudged," "limped," or "strolled" to do the work).

3. **Conflict or problem**—provides tension and intrigue; may be subtle inner conflict, such as a moment when you were unsure about what to do.

4. **Point of view**—first person (I) or third person (he or she). Check later that you have used consistent pronoun reference; students often unconsciously switch from "I" to "you."

5. **Key event(s)**—should be selected as they relate to the overall purpose or point. Don't try to tell everything, but provide only what the reader needs to stay engaged, including any necessary background.

6. **Dialogue**—even if yours is a more reflective piece, such as the essay "Memories of Montreal—and Richness" later in this chapter, even a partial quotation or scrap of dialogue can add life.

   Note that you use a new paragraph each time someone new speaks. Therefore, if your essay has much dialogue, you could have many more paragraphs than are usual in your writing.

   - *Direct quotations:* "I'm coming. Don't worry. I won't be late," I murmured.

     "Well, that would be a first. You've been late all year so far," Mr. Miller snapped.

   - *Indirect quotation:* I promised Mr. Miller that I would not be late. He said that he didn't believe me.

7. **Paragraphing**—depending on what kind of story you tell, may have more paragraphs and shorter paragraphs than you normally do. Paragraph breaks in narratives can signal a change of scene or mood, and can help control the pace.

8. **Time signals**—use words or phrases that move the action forward: *then, next, immediately afterwards, a few days later, as soon as I, the next morning, when I returned, later that afternoon, before I had time to think*, and so on. Readers and listeners get frustrated if they are not oriented in time as well as space.

Revising the Narrative

As you revise, follow the guidelines in Chapter 4. With narratives, it is especially useful to brainstorm details for the events described in the narrative. You can also jot down additional dialogue. Sometimes, it is useful to freewrite briefly about the narrative from someone else's point of view. In addition, ask yourself these questions:

- Have I made the point, stated or unstated, that I intended?
- Do I need to supply necessary background information or context?

- What parts seem bland, vague, or overly obvious, and could be cut or greatly condensed?
- Have I made the most of key events, developing them with details or relevant dialogue?
- What about rhythm and pacing? Do I need to use more strategic paragraph breaks and time signals?
- What could help develop the conflict or build tension more effectively for the reader?
- What events that are important to the purpose of the narrative have been left out? What details would make the narrative more powerful and interesting?
- Does the point of view work for the reader? Are there any places where it changes and is confusing?
- Where is more dialogue necessary, where does it get in the way, and where does it seem artificial or boring?
- Where could paragraphs be better focused or developed?
- Is the conclusion satisfying, or does it simply trail off? What could be done to make it more memorable and leave the reader with something to think about? Do I need to cut something so that I do not belabour an obvious point—or do I need to add?
- Is the narrative ethical or are there sections that cause misgivings?

EXAMPLES OF STUDENT ESSAYS USING NARRATION

The following two student essays are responses to a special kind of narrative assignment called a literacy narrative. Students were asked to narrate a story related to their development of literacy—their process of learning to read and write and/or speak English, either in school or outside school.

I Found My Voice in Room 204

Kiran Heer

1   In elementary school, I was the kid who sat in the back corner of the classroom trying desperately to disappear into the white plastered walls. My fascination with chameleons—the way their bodies could change colour to adapt to changing environments and the way they could pass by unseen—began in kindergarten.

2   That year I had a teacher, Mrs. O'Connell, who liked to call on students to answer questions. She would walk around the classroom with small, measured steps, while her short brown curls bounced with invisible electricity. With her lullaby-soft voice, she would utter bits of wisdom until her sharp gaze settled on one student.

3   Once during science class, her gaze landed on me. I don't recall the exact question, but I know it had something to do with butterflies. I know because in class we were raising monarch butterflies. We kept them in little, cylinder-shaped habitats made of net. For weeks after school I watched as they slowly emerged from their cocoons, staggering on the plastic floors of their home, their orange and black wings too wet for them to fly. The time I spent watching the monarchs was the best of my kindergarten experience. The butterflies were content with my silence and didn't ask me to answer questions I wasn't sure about.

4   I never did answer the question my teacher asked me that day. I just shook my head sheepishly while staring at the vinyl floor of the classroom, hoping my body would slowly mutate into the scaly form of a chameleon. The seconds dragged by interminably until Mrs. O'Connell walked on. That day after school I was watching the butterflies as usual, when I saw my parents come in. They were talking to my teacher, but I didn't pay attention until I heard the phrase "Room 204." For kindergarteners in my school, Room 204 was a death sentence. Kids who didn't know how to speak English were sent to Room 204. These were the same children who sat separately during lunch, munching away on their strangely foreign foods.

5   "Room 2-0-," I remember my friend, Melissa whispering, her words stuttering before she actually got to the number four. "My brother told me that his friend Alex was tortured there in kindergarten. He said they tied him to a chair and made him rehearse 'Peter Piper' until his tongue was tied."

6   I tried to imagine what it would feel like to have my tongue tied.

7   "But he said that Alex wouldn't admit to being tortured," Melissa continued. "He said that Alex only told him that it was fine and they mostly sat around a table doing show-and-tell."

8   That night I remember telling my parents that I didn't want to go to Room 204. They only shook their heads, saying that it was probably for the best. When I tried to tell them about Alex and how he was tortured, my mom said that reciting nursery rhymes was hardly torture.

9   "You'll like ESL," she said. "It'll give you more practice speaking English. We don't speak it nearly enough at home."

10   What my mother called ESL, I called a nightmare. I already knew how to speak English and I got all the practice I needed when I watched television.

11   On my first day of ESL, it didn't take me too long to discover what all of us ESL children had in common—dead silence. No one in the ESL class liked to answer questions in class. We were all quiet and all foreign in some way. My friend, Lee was also in my class. His parents had been called in after I was and though he was one of the smartest kids I knew, Lee was also silent. Lee could

count to twenty, tie his own shoe laces, and write down the entire alphabet from memory. At home, Lee didn't speak too much English either since he was Chinese. He told me his grandmother didn't like it when he spoke English at home, because she couldn't understand what he was saying.

12   There was also a Portuguese kid named Aldo in my ESL class, who had a pet hamster named Skunk. I didn't know about his hamster until after our first show-and-tell practice. Aldo had brought Skunk with him to school in a cage, and during show-and-tell we got to feed him sunflower seeds. I quickly befriended Aldo after this because I'd never had a friend with a pet before. There were three more kids in my ESL; two were Chinese like Lee and another was of Indian descent like I was.

13   The first few weeks of ESL passed in agonizing silence. The ESL teacher, Miss Hadley, would try and encourage conversation, but after a few short replies that conversation would wither and die. It was nearly the third week in before a brave soul ventured to break the silence. It all started when Miss Hadley asked us about our favourite show.

14   "I like *Power Rangers*," said Lee. "The blue one's my favourite. He's the smartest."

15   I watched *Power Rangers* as well but I thought the yellow one was the smartest.

16   "No," said Aldo. "The red one is the smartest because he's the leader."

17   Then other children jumped into the debate, which soon became a loud symphony of sound.

18   I saw Miss Hadley glance at me. I knew what was coming—she was going to ask me a question.

19   "What about you, Kiran? Do you watch *Power Rangers*?" Her blue eyes looked at me expectantly.

20   Swallowing, I nodded and quietly said, "I do."

21   "Oh, and who's your favourite?"

22   "I like the yellow one. I think she's the smartest." Then I saw Lee looking at me like I had betrayed him so I added, "But I think the blue one is smart too."

23   Miss Hadley nodded her blonde head and smiled at me. I felt myself glow from the inside out and I knew why Mrs. O'Connell had sent me here.

24   For the rest of our ESL days, the six of us learned to speak out more, and answer more questions. Miss Hadley would paste a smiley-face sticker on our progress charts whenever we raised our hand and answered a question without being asked. I remember that Lee beat me for the grand prize chocolate bar by the sticker he got on our last day of ESL.

25   Even now, I remember my ESL experience with more clarity than anything else in that year. I remember hating Mrs. O'Connell for a while, thinking that she

must not have liked me very much and that was why she wanted to send me away to Room 204. It was a betrayal I felt keenly because I thought teachers were supposed to like all their students. It wasn't until much later that I found out that she had nothing against me personally, but it was the silence she couldn't fight. My not speaking meant she had no way of knowing that I was learning any of the material she was presenting. I know now that from her point of view, she was trying to help me as best she could. Though she wrongly assumed that my foreignness was the reason behind my silence, because I didn't give her any evidence to the contrary, I do not resent Mrs. O'Connell for what she did. I made more friends in ESL and answered more questions than I ever did in my homeroom. The smaller group of students in ESL made it easier for the painfully shy students like me to open up.

26   Room 204, with formerly silent students and their supposedly strange foods, taught me the power of speech.

DISCUSSION QUESTIONS

1. Identify two turning points in this narrative.
2. This narrative spans about one school year. At what points has the writer omitted events? Why?
3. How does the writer help you appreciate that some children of immigrants may feel like outsiders in Canada, even though they were born in this country?
4. What is the larger point of this essay? Is it stated or implied?

TOWARD KEY INSIGHTS

Were you surprised at the revelation that the writer ended up appreciating the dreaded ESL class? Why or why not?

Do you think the elementary school teacher was insensitive in sending a Canadian-born student to the ESL room, or do you think she made an appropriate choice?

What have been your experiences of speaking in class?

Have you ever been in situations where you have felt a shyness or fear similar to the writer's?

SUGGESTION FOR WRITING

After reading this essay and the next one, write your own literacy narrative that explores your identity as a reader, writer, and speaker. What early experiences shaped your identity as a literate person? What people, events, and literature shaped you as a writer, speaker, or student of English? Bring in some dialogue and focus on developing one or two key scenes with telling detail. Include at least one turning point that helps the reader to envision a change of perspective.

English as the Enemy

Kimberly Florendo

1   "You will have to take English." I cringed as the university counsellor spoke. The word "English" made my stomach churn.

2   The counsellor must have seen my expression. "You don't like English?" she asked kindly.

3   "Not at all." I rolled my eyes.

4   A flashback to high school quickly filled my mind.

5   I sat at my desk writing a newspaper article for our Grade 10 "New Westminster's Newsflash" newspaper. Everyone in our English class had to write one article. Our English teacher, Mr. Hodson, would grade our articles out of five and then select a few of the best to publish in our fictional newspaper.

6   I had no doubts about my writing abilities. Ever since I started receiving letter-graded report cards, I got straight A's. Not one subject posed a challenge for me, including English, so a prosaic newspaper article seemed like child's play. I continued scribbling away at my desk, writing about a woman who was robbed at Metrotown station by a man threatening to harm her.

7   Quite pleased when I finished, I walked up to Mr. Hodson's desk and proudly handed him my article. I stood for a moment by his desk, anticipating some delicious praise for my writing. I watched him scan the article until he reached the end. He then looked up and I looked away, hoping he did not realize I was staring at him. He grabbed his red pen and scrawled 3/5 in the top margin of the paper.

8   My heart sank. I stood there looking at the paper in his hands. The red ink seemed like blood. He handed me my article, saying nothing, and returned to his unfinished crossword puzzle. I slowly walked back to my seat, and by then my friends realized that something was wrong.

9   Concetta, my best friend, saw my stunned look. "What's wrong?"

10   "I failed," I said flatly, not meeting her eyes.

11   My friends rushed to my desk. They knew that I was a straight A student who scored A's on all her assignments and tests. They stared at my article in disbelief. The red ink stared back at them.

12   "Do you want me and Brittany to talk to Mr. Hodson?" Concetta offered. "We'll tell him to let you hand in another newspaper article so that you can get a higher mark."

13   I said nothing. Concetta and Brittany took my silence as a yes and marched themselves up to Mr. Hodson's desk. I kept my head down and my eyes fixated on the 3/5 veined in red. My vision of the red ink began to blur. "Don't cry, Kim.

Don't cry," I repeated sternly to myself. When I glanced at Mr. Hodson's desk, I saw Mr. Hodson and my friends looking back at me while they spoke. They were not so far out of earshot that I could make out the words: "Look how sad she is." I grabbed another sheet of paper and began writing another version of the newspaper article. Concetta and Brittany returned to my desk.

14   "Mr. Hodson said you can hand in a revision and he'll average your mark."

15   "Thanks Britt," I murmured, not looking up from my paper. Questions swirled in my mind. Why didn't I receive an A? What was wrong with my writing?

16   I half-heartedly wrote another version of the article and dropped in on Mr. Hodson's desk. As the lunch bell rang and the classroom emptied out, I lingered. When the last person left, I asked what I needed to know. "Mr. Hodson, was my article that bad?"

17   He looked up from his desk. "No," he said. "It's just that your word choices and sentence structure need improvement, but your ideas are good."

18   With a quiet inner shudder, I came back to the present moment, looking blankly at the counsellor behind the desk. She smiled politely and we continued our discussion on how I could pursue my goal of becoming a high school teacher.

19   After our talk, I walked out slowly, contemplating my options. It looked if I wanted to become a high school teacher, my best shot was to graduate with a double minor in math and English. That meant that I would have to take many English courses, courses that would require an abundance of writing. I thought I could completely elude all English courses in university, but that was not the case. I either had to switch career paths in order to avoid taking any English courses, or I had to face English and all its challenges.

20   Looking at my choices was like staring at my nemesis. I had two options: to fight or to flee.

21   I chose to fight.

DISCUSSION QUESTIONS

1. What is the main conflict or tension in this narrative, and how is it brought out?

2. How does the writer use dialogue to further the narrative? How does the writer identify the speakers without using too many tag phrases such as *she said* or *I replied*?

3. How does the writer dramatize key moments in the narrative that are also personal turning points?

4. What details are most effective, in your opinion, for conveying emotions and moods?

TOWARD KEY INSIGHTS

Were you able to empathize with the writer's intense disappointment about her mark on the high school assignment? Why or why not?

Have you ever experienced a similar deflation of your expectations—in school, sports, or family/social life?

SUGGESTIONS FOR WRITING

1. *Write a narrative about an encounter or experience in school where the outcome was not what you expected and you learned something new about yourself.*

2. *Write a narrative that shows how you were able to find resilience or a new perspective after having your expectations disappointed. Keep in mind all of the key narrative elements: purpose, action, conflict, point of view, key events, and dialogue.*

THE PERSONAL ESSAY: PROFESSIONAL MODELS

NARRATION READING STRATEGIES

1. Read each essay quickly to get a feel for the story and its main point.
2. Identify the main conflict that moves the story forward. Identify the major characters and what they may represent.
3. Don't get lost in the details. Note (possibly in the margins) the overall impression or mood the description is evoking.
4. Identify a thesis statement (possibly in the first or last paragraph—but in a narrative, it may be implied) and/or a statement of purpose. Read the essay with an anticipation of what the description is intended to accomplish.
5. Read each narrative again, more slowly, with the main point in mind. Keep an eye on how the narrative supports the main point.

READING CRITICALLY

1. Consider whether the narrative would seem different if told from another person's point of view. Consider how a scene or event might look very different if described from a different vantage point.
2. Examine what principle seems to have guided the selection of details. Has the writer created a certain mood or dominant impression by selecting certain kinds of details?
3. Ask whether the narrative really supports the author's main point. Consider what other possible perspectives or narratives could be included but are not. Would these contradict the writer's claims?

READING AS A WRITER

1. Identify the organizational pattern and decide whether it is the most effective arrangement for this piece of writing.
2. Determine the setting, conflict, characters, and development of the narrative. Note whether the writer gives enough information, or too much in places.
3. Notice any particularly effective movements in the plot. If you find a useful strategy, jot it down.
4. Observe how the writer uses dialogue. Make a note of any especially effective techniques.
5. Examine the essay for particularly effective examples of word choice.

Dan Greenburg

Sound and Fury

A native of Chicago, Dan Greenburg holds a Bachelor of Fine Arts from the University of Illinois and a Master of Fine Arts from UCLA. A prolific writer, he has authored 72 books, including such bestsellers as How to Be a Jewish Mother, How to Make Yourself Miserable, *and* How to Avoid Love and Marriage. *Greenburg has also written four different series of children's books, including* The Zack Files, *which were inspired by his son Zack. His articles have appeared in a wide and diverse range of popular magazines and been reprinted in many anthologies of humour and satire. He has been a guest on* The Today Show, Larry King Live, Late Night with David Letterman, *and other major TV talk shows.*

1   We carry around a lot of free-floating anger. What we do with it is what fascinates me.

2   My friend Lee Frank is a stand-up comedian who works regularly in New York comedy clubs. Not long ago I accompanied him to one of these places, where he was to be the late-night emcee and where I myself had once done a stand-up act in a gentler era.

3   The crowd that night was a typical weekend bunch—enthusiastic, hostile and drunk. A large contingent of inebriated young men from Long Island had decided that a comedian named Rusty who was currently on stage was the greatest thing since pop-top cans and began chanting his name after almost everything he said: "Rus-TEE! Rus-TEE!"

4   My friend Lee knew he had a tough act to follow.

5   Indeed, the moment Lee walked on stage, the inebriated young men from Long Island began chanting "Rus-TEE! Rus-TEE!" and didn't give him a chance. Poor Lee, the flop sweat running into his eyes, tried every trick he knew to win them over, and finally gave up.

6   When he left the stage I joined him at the bar in the back of the club to commiserate.

7   "You did the best you could," I told him.

8   "I don't know," he said, "I could have handled it better."

9   "How?"

10   "I don't know," he said.

11   As we spoke, the young men who'd given him such a tough time trickled into the bar area. One of them spotted Lee and observed to a companion that Lee might want to do something about their heckling.

This familiar expression comes from the title of a famous novel by William Faulkner and is originally taken from Shakespeare's *Macbeth*: "[Life] is a tale/ Told by an idiot, full of sound and fury,/ Signifying nothing." The reader may be intrigued: What does the title signify here?

The brief opening paragraph suggests a larger purpose and point for the story that is about to unfold. Paragraph 2 identifies who, when, where, and why. Paragraphs 2 and 3 set up tension, conflict, and even suspense.

Sound impression

Touch impression

Time signal

Dialogue: The off-stage exchange between the writer and his comedian friend helps draw readers into the story.

Conflict arises in key event

12   Lee thought he heard the companion reply, "I'm down," a casual acknowledgment that he was willing to have a fistfight. Lee repeated their remarks to me and indicated that he, too, was "down."

13   Though slight of frame, Lee is a black belt in Tae Kwon Do, has had skirmishes with three-card monte con men in Times Square, and once even captured a robber-rapist. I am also slight of frame but have had no training in martial arts. I did have one fistfight in my adult life (with a movie producer), but as Lee's best friend, I assumed that I was "down" as well.

14   Considering that there were more than a dozen of them and only two of us, the period of time that might elapse between our being "down" and our being down seemed exceedingly brief.

15   The young man who'd made the remark drifted toward Lee.

16   The eyes of everyone in the bar shifted slightly and locked onto the two men like heat-seeking missiles. Fight-or-flight adrenaline and testosterone spurted into dozens of male cardiovascular systems. Safeties snapped off figurative weapons. Red warning lights lit up dozens of DEFCON systems; warheads were armed and aimed. In a moment this bar area might very well resemble a saloon in a B grade western.

17   "How ya doing?" said Lee, his voice flat as unleavened bread, trying to make up his mind whether to be friendly or hostile.

18   "Okay," said the guy, a pleasant-looking, clean-cut kid in his mid-20s.

19   I was fascinated by what was going on between the two of them, each feeling the other out in a neutral, unemotional, slightly bemused manner. I saw no hostility here, no xenophobic loathing, just two young males jockeying for position, going through the motions, doing the dance, willing to engage at the slightest provocation. I had seen my cat do this many times when a stranger strayed onto his turf.

20   And then I had a sudden flash of clarity: These guys could either rip each other's heads off now or they could share a beer, and both options would be equally acceptable to them.

21   I'd felt close to critical mass on many occasions myself. But here, feeling outside the action, I could see clearly that it had to do with the enormous reservoir of rage that we men carry around with us, rage that seethes just under the surface and is ready to be tapped in an instant, with or without just provocation.

22   "What're you in town for?" asked Lee casually.

23   The guy was watching Lee carefully, making minuscule adjustments on his sensing and triggering equipment.

24   "It's my birthday," said the guy.

25   Lee mulled over this information for a moment, still considering all his options. Then he made his decision.

26   "Happy birthday," said Lee finally, sticking out his hand.

27   The guy studied Lee's hand a moment. Then, deciding the gesture was sincere, he took the hand and shook it.

28   "Thanks," he said, and walked back to his buddies.

29   All over the room you could hear safeties snapping on, warheads being unarmed. The incident was over, and in a moment it was as if it had never happened.

30   I felt I had just witnessed in microcosm the mechanism that triggers most acts of aggression, from gang fights to international conflagrations. It was so simple: a minor act of provocation. A decision on how to interpret it. Whether or not to escalate. And, in this particular case, a peaceful outcome. What struck me was how absolutely arbitrarily it had all been decided.

Sight impression

His stance as a first-person observer allows the writer close positioning to the drama, as well as the distance to reflect on it from a somewhat detached point of view.

Larger point of narrative: The reader draws a larger significance about men's "reservoir of rage" from this incident, thus reminding us of his larger point.

Turning point: Lee takes a risk by saying "happy birthday" since the words could be taken as provocative, but instead the potential confrontation is defused in this instant.

The writer returns to the larger purpose of the essay—to get us to reflect on the ways we can choose to deal with conflict. The last sentence leaves readers thinking, perhaps wondering whether they might choose to de-escalate conflict when a potential crisis arises.

DISCUSSION QUESTIONS

1. Discuss the appropriateness of Greenburg's title.
2. Does this essay have a stated or an unstated point? If it is stated, indicate where. If it is unstated, express it in your own words.
3. The expression *our being down* occurs twice in paragraph 14. Explain what it means in each instance.
4. Discuss the effectiveness of the figurative language in paragraph 16.
5. In paragraph 21, Greenburg credits "feeling outside the action" for helping him understand the rage involved in this situation as well as in others. Explain what he means.
6. How often do you think that the "equally acceptable" options mentioned in paragraph 20 occur in confrontations?

TOWARD KEY INSIGHTS

What reasons can you give for the "free-floating anger" that Greenburg mentions at the outset of the essay? How frequently and in what ways is this anger manifested?

What are some effective strategies for coping with this anger?

SUGGESTION FOR WRITING

Write a narrative about a small incident that turned into a serious confrontation. Possible incidents include an improper or reckless action of another driver, a minor disagreement with a friend or spouse, or retaliation for an action at a sporting event. The outcome can be peaceful or otherwise. Make sure your essay makes a larger point that could be stated or implied throughout the essay.

Moses Milstein

Memories of Montreal—and Richness

Moses Milstein was born in 1947 in Austria and grew up in Montreal. He received degrees from McGill University, Université de Montréal, and Guelph University, and worked in British Columbia as a veterinarian. In this essay, originally published in The Globe and Mail, *Milstein recounts memories of growing up in Montreal. He reflects with subtle nostalgia on how his experience of urban, economic, and cultural diversity growing up in Montreal will not be duplicated for his son, who is growing up in a more homogeneous, upper-middle-class area of Vancouver. The essay may prompt discussion of generational, class, or ethnic differences, or of gains that may entail losses.*

1   In the April of his youth, my son walks to school in a gentle shower of cherry blossoms. Down the slopes of West Vancouver's Hollyburn Mountain he can see the houses nestled among tall cedars. Bursts of rhododendrons guard the yards and over their tops

he can see the sun glinting on the placid waters of Howe Sound. He walks through this serene neighbourhood unmolested, the quiet punctuated by the thwonk of tennis balls coming from cozy courts nearby.

2   And I blame myself.

3   In the April of my childhood in the Montreal of the fifties, the way to school was still studded with chunks of sandy moraine from winter's retreating ice. With the threat of blizzards gone, I could shed my heavy winter boots, and feel the sidewalk strangely close beneath the thin soles of my shoes.

4   The corners of our street, like every street then, were held by the four corner stores. The one we used, the "Jewish" store, could be counted on for an emergency box of matzohs, or kosher Coca Cola during Passover. Although Mr. Auerbach practically lived in his store, he did, in fact, go home at night. His French competitors across the street, though, lived amidst their crowded displays of potato chips, soft drinks and fly-paper rolls—cooking, sleeping, arguing, watching TV, just behind the curtain in the back of the store.

5   You could buy a tiny bag of potato chips for a penny. My mother insisted that it was filled with sweepings.

6   Around the corner was Wing Ling, the Chinese laundry, like all Chinese laundries painted green on the outside. Within, great vats seethed with steam where Mr. Lee and his family washed and ironed our sheets, which he would then hand to me in a package wrapped in brown paper and string.

7   Next to the laundry, across the alley, which ran like a sparkling river of broken glass and urine produced by the hordes of feral cats, giant rats and stumbling drunks who waded therein, was the Jewish Tailor. His narrow house, barely a door and a window wide, extended backwards from his work room and housed his wife and daughter, a sewing machine and a steam iron. An air of sadness, like the tape measure he wore around his neck, enveloped the place.

8   His old, thick-legged wife shared his melancholic mien. Their daughter was my age and wore braces on her legs. I often wondered whether they were her parents or her grandparents, so great was the difference in their ages. According to rumour, they were, like our family, survivors of the "Krieg," the Holocaust. The tailor and his wife had each had families of their own, children and spouses. They perished somehow, I don't remember the details. Every family I knew then had a story of death and they were all mixed up in my mind. In a DP camp after the war, the tailor met and married this woman and she was able to give birth to one more child, with crippled legs, and then no more.

9   I would rush by their sad house, and in one block was on St. Lawrence Street, noisy and bursting with commerce. Two long blocks before I reached my school.

10   My father worked on St. Lawrence Street at the Junior Trend Factory, which he pronounced "Jooniohtren." One April, when school was closed for Passover, I brought him his lunch. The elevator in his building passed floor after floor of angrily buzzing sewing machines. On some floors anonymous contractors were making clothes under other manufacturer's labels; on others I could see fancy offices where men with cigars, manicured fingers and pomaded hair struggled for ascendancy in the *shmatte* business.

11   My father worked among his friends from back home. They would usually greet me with jokes, smiles and much cheek-pinching. But when I saw them at their sewing machines their faces were closed and dark and they worked feverishly at

piecework, sewing linings, sleeves, buttonholes under the critical eyes of the fore-man. I left quickly.

12   Between these rows of tall, brown brick buildings, I would pass the restaurants that fed the workers. Delicatessens beckoned, their windows steamed from the smoked meat briskets waiting within, festooned with hanging salamis, rows of jars of pickled toma-toes and long banana peppers, green and red. Inside, the esteemed smoked-meat cutter stood resplendent on his pedestal, dispensing thick, greasy, spicy slices of meat onto golden rounds of rye bread. A good cutter was rumoured to be worth his substantial weight in gold and was held in reverential awe by my friends and me. Unhappily, the price of 25 cents, an hour's wages for my father, was beyond our reach.

13   The smells of the delicatessen mixed with the forest of urban smells welling out of each block—fruit stores, bakeries, taverns (for men only), poultry and egg stores, fish stores, bagel bakeries, steak houses, all of which would have me slavering until I reached that pinnacle of sensual delights, the Rachel Market. Here, the smells and sights merged as the French farmers, some able to speak Yiddish, backed their trucks up to the wide sidewalks where they set up their tables and displayed their produce. Beneath the market, down a spiral of stone steps slicked with blood, was a subterra-nean chamber of death. If you stood halfway down the stairs, you could see the hell waiting for the birds below. An open fire to singe their pin feathers burned in an alcove. Hooks covered the walls from which the chickens were suspended by their feet while men in bloodied aprons cut their throats, drained their blood and plucked their feathers which floated in the air until they settled among the clots of gray droppings on the floor and walls.

14   Across the street, the large bakery, Richstones, held a secret known only to the few. On Fridays, if you went to the door at the top of the loading bays, you could ask for the seconds, the crumbled cakes, broken doughnuts, smeary cupcakes. Sometimes they would give you some and sometimes they would chase you away angrily. Another example of the incomprehensible capriciousness of adults.

15   As if to remind me of my destination, I would ultimately come to the offices of *Der Kanader Adler*, one of three local Yiddish papers. Occasionally, one of my teachers would publish a poem there, truly the last song of the Last of the Mohicans. The Jewish Peretz School was just around the corner on Duluth Street. We were educated in Yiddish, spoke to each other in English and lived in a French neighbourhood.

16   I can recall every building and business along the two blocks to school. Many of the proprietors knew me and my family. I felt as safe and happy on the streets as in my own home and would often linger until dusk on the return home.

17   When I grew up I bought a house in the gentle forests of the Pacific and my son walks to school among the cherry blossoms. And sometimes I am sad for him.

DISCUSSION QUESTIONS

1. What contrast does the writer introduce in the first three paragraphs? What details are especially effective in highlighting the contrast? Why do you suppose that the second paragraph is only one sentence long?

2. Point out sensory details that reflect sight, sound, taste, smell, and touch. Comment on the effect of these sensory impressions.

3. What does the description of the Jewish tailor and his small family (paragraphs 7 to 9) add to the essay?

4. An adult writer who is trying to evoke the reality of childhood experiences in the here and now often blends the child's perspective with the adult's. How does Moses Milstein reveal a kind of double perspective, as a child and an adult? Consider the fragment that ends paragraph 14, where the writer clearly uses vocabulary he would not have known as a child: "Another example of the incomprehensible capriciousness of adults." What does the writer mean here? Can you find other examples where the adult is able to articulate something the child sensed, but probably could not have put into words?

5. In the last paragraph, the father states that he is sad for his son sometimes, even though his son "walks to school among the cherry blossoms." What is the paradox here? Do you think the boy would understand if his father tried to explain to him that he was missing something?

6. Does this essay have a stated or an unstated point? If it is stated, indicate where. If it is unstated, express it in your own words.

TOWARD KEY INSIGHTS

What are the advantages of living in a place of cultural and economic diversity? Are there any disadvantages?

What are the possible losses and gains associated with moving away from the place where you grew up?

What does Moses Milstein reveal about the nature of parent–child relationships?

Whose childhood would you prefer—the father's or the son's? Explain.

SUGGESTIONS FOR WRITING

1. *Create a sense of paradox by recounting a memory of a time or place that at first glance seemed perfect, until you gradually discovered what was missing. Conversely, you could narrate a memory of a time or place that at first seemed far from perfect, but has given you riches that you have come to appreciate over time.*

2. *After reading "Memories of Montreal—and Richness" (pages 135–137), read two other essays about place and identity—"No Place like Home" (Chapter 13) and "I'm a Banana and Proud of It" (Chapter 10)—and then write a narrative that focuses on what has been lost or gained by staying in or moving away from a particular community or ethno-cultural group you know well. If you want to incorporate actual material from any of these essays, be sure that you understand the documentation conventions covered in Chapters 14 to 17.*

MyWritingLab

How Do I Get a Better Grade?

Go to **www.mywritinglab .com** for additional help with your grammar, writing, and research skills. You will have access to a variety of exercises, instruction, and videos that will help you improve your basic skills and help you get a better grade.

CHAPTER 7

Strategies for Using Illustration: Making Yourself Clear

"It doesn't pay to fight City Hall. For example, my friend Josie . . ."

"Many intelligent people lack common sense. Take Dr. Brandon . . ."

"Predicting the weather is far from an exact science. Two winters ago, a surprise snowstorm . . ."

Have you ever noticed how often people use *illustrations* (examples) to clarify general statements?

Ordinary conversations teem with "for example . . ." and "for instance . . ."—often in response to a furrowed brow or puzzled look. A Korean rapper's "Gangnam Style" is an example of a viral YouTube hit; the joining of retailers Loblaw and Shoppers Drug Mart illustrates a successful Canadian megamerger. Teachers, researchers, and writers often present an abstract principle or general claim, then supply concrete illustrations or examples to bring it down to earth. An economics instructor might illustrate compound interest by showing how much $100 earning 5 percent interest would appreciate in 10 years.

Examples are also used in business and in the world of work to clarify ideas and to persuade. Advertisers show satisfied users of their products to induce us to buy, and websites marketing a service commonly include testimonials from happy clients. A teacher who is asking for more counselling staff might describe particular students who need help but can't get it. A nurse who is advocating a new method for distributing medication might provide examples of where the current system failed patients.

The use of vivid illustrations helps people absorb what you are saying, and enlivens personal writing as well as more formal academic writing. When writing a personal essay about the effects of stress, you might draw examples from your experience or observations. When writing a more formal research essay about the effects of stress, you might include examples from psychological or medical research studies.

Like pictures and other visuals, specific examples help readers grasp ideas that might otherwise seem too fuzzy and abstract.

SELECTING APPROPRIATE EXAMPLES

You need to ensure that your examples actually support the points you are trying to make. Sometimes, in a first draft, writers get sidetracked by intriguing side issues. For instance, in making the point that the lyrics in a rap group's latest download were not in good taste, a writer might begin ranting about the thuggish lifestyle of one of the singers. In a revision, however, that writer should substitute more relevant material to support the thesis, such as several excerpts from song lyrics that illustrate the writer's claim.

Furthermore, ensure that your examples display all the chief features of whatever you're illustrating. Don't offer a country as an example of a democracy if, even though elections are held, there is only one party on the ballot and the results are rigged. Consider the following student example that describes the symptoms of someone suffering from depression.

> Carl wasn't just sad. Nothing really bad had happened in his life. But he had lost all interest in his past favourite activities. His skateboard had been discarded in a corner of his room. He no longer bothered to play his video games. Simple things like getting tickets to a rock concert seemed to be too much effort for him. Some days he stayed in bed and missed his classes. Often he irritably snapped at anyone who talked with him. Friends could easily see the difference in him when he shuffled to the dining room, his head down. Without a doubt, Carl was depressed.

This short example demonstrates that Carl meets many of the key characteristics of depression: a lack of interest in normal activities, a sense that ordinary things aren't worth the effort, an inability to attend to ordinary responsibilities, and irritability.

NUMBER OF EXAMPLES

How many examples do you need? One long one, several fairly brief ones, or a large number of very short ones? Look to your topic for the answer. Use one long example for a topic where traits are combined in a single person or object. To illustrate that a good nurse must be compassionate, conscientious, and competent, one extended example would probably work best.

With trends or broader claims, however, use several examples. To show that parents have been raising children more and more permissively in the last few decades, at least three examples from different decades would be appropriate: one example from an earlier time, around 1980; a second example from about 2000; and a third example from the present time. In addition, if you are claiming that an attitude or characteristic is typical of people in a certain group, you will need more than one example to support your claim.

Finally, some topics require a whole series of examples. If your thesis argues that many everyday expressions originate from the world of gambling, use several examples to illustrate your point.

EXERCISE

1. **Choose one of the following topic sentences. Select an appropriate example and write the rest of the paragraph.**

   a. Sometimes, a minor incident drastically changes a person's life.

   b. _____'s name exactly suits (her/his) personality.

   c. I still get embarrassed when I remember _____.

   d. Not all education goes on in the classroom.

   e. I learned the value of _____ the hard way.

2. **Explain why you would use one extended illustration, several shorter ones, or a whole series of examples to develop each of the following statements. Suggest appropriate illustrations.**

   a. Many parents I know think for their children.

   b. More and more people are trying to buy local food and products.

   c. Flying on a plane is more stressful than it used to be.

   d. Different university students manage their expenses in different ways.

   e. The quality of youth hostels ranges from excellent to shabby.

ORGANIZING THE EXAMPLES

Your organizational strategy will depend on your topic and the number of examples.

A single extended example suggests that something is typical or represents a general trend and often traces a narrative, following events in a time sequence such as the course of a day.

- May describe something spatially—moving, for example, from top to bottom, or from the outside to the inside.

Multiple examples illustrate degrees of something or change *over time:*

- Often proceeds in order of importance or desirability—for example, from a hostile sales clerk, to a neutral one, to a highly considerate one.

- Trends offer examples over time. An exploration of how phones got smarter may move from a discussion of early rotary dials, to touch-tone phones with caller ID, to today's smartphones.

If you have multiple examples, you might first group them into categories, and then arrange the categories in the most logical or rhetorically effective order. For example, if you were writing a paper on types of expressions associated with casino games, you might group together expressions from table games, electronic gaming machines, and random-number games. Within each paragraph, you might move from older to more recent expressions, or from common expressions to less common ones. After considering your categories, you can decide on the most effective way to order them.

ETHICAL ISSUES

In writing an illustration, we try to show readers something truthful about our understanding of the world. Readers won't take us seriously if they think we are skewing our evidence by choosing only the evidence that fits our thesis and ignoring examples that challenge it. If we have a strong bias, we may be tempted to distort our examples. For instance, parents trying to talk their teenager out of pursuing an acting career might mention only examples of failed or struggling performers, and omit any examples of successful performers. Such a distortion is not really fair to the acting profession or the teenager. Moreover, some distortions can be outright lies. In past debates about welfare, some commentators cited examples of people who were living like millionaires while on welfare. It turned out that the examples had been falsified, and no real instances of such massive abuse could be found. To help avoid distortion and deception in examples, ask yourself the following questions:

- Are the examples truthful and representative, or are they slanted and one-sided?
- Could my illustrations have harmful consequences? Do they stereotype an individual/group or harm someone's reputation unjustly?
- Will my examples promote desirable or undesirable behaviour?

WRITING AN ILLUSTRATION
Prewriting and Planning the Illustration

If you are writing an essay that draws from personal experience or observation, you could do some freewriting to uncover possibilities for a starting point. Perhaps you will decide to write about something you know well, such as experiences related to school, work, or family life. If you are writing a more formal paper, you can get ideas from reading as well as from talking to others.

You can begin your illustration paper at either end of the telescope—with the larger point you are trying to make, or with the smaller examples that take you and the reader to a larger point that emerges as you write. Don't forget that you can revise your paper later—editing, deleting text, and developing the paper so that it relates more clearly to your larger point.

FINDING YOUR TOPIC

- Keep a journal and record basic patterns or trends you have observed or read about.
- Brainstorm a list of observations you have made about the world.
- Write down some main points you want to make.
- Think about what impact you want your paper to have on readers.
- Decide if you need one extended example or multiple examples.

Once you have your topic, you can easily develop your illustration.

DEVELOPING YOUR ILLUSTRATION

- Brainstorm a list of examples.
- Compile supporting details for each example.
- Decide which examples and details would be best for your audience.
- Review and add examples and details as necessary.
- Create a chart or use branching as shown below.

Once you've picked your topic, ask yourself, "What example(s) will work best with my audience?" Then brainstorm each one for supporting details. Use a chart patterned after the one below to help you.

Example 1	Example 2	Example 3
First supporting detail	First supporting detail	First supporting detail
Second supporting detail	Second supporting detail	Second supporting detail

Here is an example of brainstorming on the difficulty of running a small store.

Drafting the Illustration

A **thesis statement** for an illustration usually states the main point that the rest of the essay will develop. If you were writing an essay on the perils of digital distraction, your examples would relate to your larger point about these dangers. It is often helpful to clarify and sharpen your thesis statement in the revision stage. Here are suggestions for organizing your illustration:

Introduction
- Introduce topic and give the reader a reason to read paper.
- Possibly create an arresting or unexpected statement.
- "Immigrants work harder than any other employees in Canada."
- Or indicate the stake a reader has in the essay. "Every student can learn from those who have been successful."

Body

- Present the examples that achieve your purpose.
- Use an order for examples that fit your topic.
- Often there are separate paragraphs for each example.
- An essay on how phones got smarter might have a paragraph for each phone type you discuss.

Conclusion

- Summarize the examples and re-emphasize the main point.
- Or issue a warning or challenge, as might follow from a paper on binge drinking.
- Or offer a hope or recommendation, as in a paper on how to become the employee of the future.
- Or discuss broader implications, as in a paper on how people have brought about social change.

Revising the Illustration

Think about the following questions and the general revision guidelines discussed in Chapter 4 as you revise your paper:

- Exactly what idea am I trying to express? Have I chosen relevant examples to support it?
- Do I need additional examples or details to make my paper more engaging for my reader?
- Do any examples or details need to be cut because they fail to fit my main point?
- Are my examples arranged in the most effective or logical order?
- Where could I better focus or develop my paragraphs around key examples?
- Is my paper ethical, with honest examples that are selected fairly?

SAMPLE STUDENT ESSAY: USING ILLUSTRATION

The Cleanse Cycle

Jamie Lockrey

1   Hoarding is not really something to joke about. It is actually a serious clinical disorder in which a person cannot control the impulse to collect and keep things: old newspapers, clothes, used gum wrappers, porcelain figurines—it doesn't really matter. The collection swells until it fills an entire house or apartment until the clutter makes the space barely livable. These are extreme cases of being unable to part with possessions, but almost all of us

can relate to some degree. We all have stuff—that soft fringed shawl that was a present from an ex-partner; the jigsaw puzzle that holds fond memories and which may or may not be missing pieces; old Archie comics that used to be a favourite escape. We may not have used or thought about these things in years, but we cannot manage to throw them out—after all, they were precious once, and might be once again. It is all too easy to fall into the habit of hoarding, almost as if saving for scarce times comes instinctively to us. Yet purging our lives of useless items is a necessary cycle to find balance and space in our lives.

2   Many of us grow up believing that throwing things away is wasteful. Why throw out that flannel shirt, even if it does have a few holes, when it could be kept for those grubby cleaning days—or a camping trip? When you have more time, you will be able to consult those numerous websites that show you how to repurpose almost anything: socks without a partner could be turned into rags, toilet paper rolls can be made into art, and broken jewellery can always be made into something new. So we begin to put things aside, convinced they will be used again. We think we are being practical, but we are really being senti-mental as the boxes begin to pile up in our closet or spare room: birthday cards from years gone by, old books that you had to spend good money on for school, cords and more cords, jeans and sweatpants from lost decades. Our space gets smaller, overwhelmed by things that we cannot bring ourselves to get rid of, knowing we will need it the minute we have said good-bye to it. Besides, if we throw out items from our past, it feels as if we are discarding parts of ourselves. The old file folders, retired or broken jewellery, photos and letters that remind us of foolish times continue to take up room on the shelf, because simply we feel a sense of comfort knowing the stuff is there.

3   Yet just as people have learned to hoard, they can also learn to purge, or de-clutter. Most of us, after all, do want to have more space and simplicity in our lives. At some point, when all the clutter makes it hard to move around freely, the fear of getting rid of stuff may turn into an urgent need to organize it, or get rid of it—recycling it if we can, throwing it out if we can't. On the show *Consumed*, normal people have let their collecting get out of hand, and they can't take control of the rest of their lives until they clear the clutter. In the episode "The Hoffer Family," "Debby Hoffer has never met a pair of shoes—or a purse—that she did not like. Her passion for material things makes the small townhouse that she shares with her three daughters look more like a warehouse than a home. Her house is so packed that her oldest daughter has nowhere of her own to sleep. De-cluttering expert Jill Pollack's challenge to Debby is for her to

Uses specific examples to show how we may all have similarities to hoarders when we cannot let go of possessions.

Offers a clear thesis in the last sentence of the first paragraph.

Uses more examples to illustrate reasons why we might find it difficult to let go of clutter.

Details the effects of letting too much clutter pile up.

Uses a more extended illustration from popular culture.

recognize that mere things do not represent security—it is her relationship with her daughters that has true value" (IMDb). Since Debby applied to be on the show, she was obviously compelled to purge her cherished belongings. At the end of the show, Debby is happier with her simplified life. Purging the unnecessary material things from our lives is a way to cleanse, and it allows us to focus on bettering other areas of our lives, such as improving our relationships with family and friends.

4   We collect things because they once seemed useful, or attractive, or fun—or we simply grew attached to them. These items may take up space for years before you notice that they are more oppressive than comforting. Do you still really need that Disney memorabilia or old PlayStation or Wii game that you used to play whenever you felt bored? Maybe it's time to get rid of the things that haven't been hauled out in years, and let go of old memories that don't cause a positive emotional stir any more. There is often a way to recycle these things so that we can imagine them having new life and energy in someone else's life.

Offers reassurance to reader after admitting that de-cluttering can be difficult.

5   It can be hard to remember that this cleanse cycle is never a one-time process, as we are regularly buying the items we think we need to replace the ones that seem obsolete. The birthday cards keep coming; the formerly favourite baggy shirt goes out of fashion; and maybe it's time to admit that you never will wear those expensive leather boots with the high, uncomfortable heels.

WORK CITED

IMDb. "IMDb: *Consumed*, 'The Hoffer Family: But They're All Nice!'" September 2011. *IMDb*. Web. 20 February 2012.

DISCUSSION QUESTIONS

1. Identify several of the concrete examples of clutter that the writer uses throughout her paper (pick the example from each paragraph that resonates the most with you). Why do you suppose she uses so many examples?

2. In the first four paragraphs, the writer gives four possible reasons why we hold on to stuff for far too long. What reasons does the writer identify? Are there any other reasons that you can imagine for why we might hold on to things for too long?

3. Why did the writer include an example of hoarding from TV in her essay?

4. How does the writer conclude in the last paragraph? How does the final sentence follow from what has come before, but go beyond a flat restatement of the thesis and leave the reader with something to think about?

5. This essay contains a persuasive angle. Does it persuade you? If so, how? If not, why not?

SUGGESTIONS FOR WRITING *Just as the student writer uses familiar, everyday examples to show the negative effects of having too much clutter, write your own essay illustrating the dangers of excess with something that at first seemed desirable but turned into a negative when taken too far. This could be any number of things—too much exercise, too much work, or too much time spent in trying to make a decision. Draw examples from your own life or observations.*

After reading this essay, also read the essay titled "Clearing House" in the Reader (pages 416-418) and then think of a concrete experience you have had with getting rid of stuff. Was the experience liberating, sad, or both? What do you want to say to others about this process? Decide whether you want to focus, as this writer did, on the benefits of de-cluttering, or the sadness of clearing house at times—or some other idea. Use either one or two extended examples or several.

This writer mentions recycling, but only in passing. Write an essay showing the benefits of recycling or repurposing items that are no longer needed—and that we don't usually think about—such as e-waste, electrical or personal care items, kitchenware, or food waste from our homes or from restaurants. Be specific, drawing from your experience or the experiences of others.

STEPPING UP TO SYNTHESIS

When we write an illustration paper, we don't always draw our examples from personal experience. As we reflect on a topic, we may talk with other people and read various source materials to broaden our understanding. We explore differing perspectives and determine the connections between them en route to arriving at our own views and insights.

Prewriting for Synthesis   If you are interested in sustainability and environmental issues, you might read two or three essays in this text on environmental issues ("The Four Tribes of Climate Change" in Chapter 12, "Autoholics" in the Reader, and an abridged excerpt from *Dry Spring: The Coming Water Crisis of North America* in Chapter 9) and then, after drawing on your own observations, focus on a specific environmental issue that concerns you—perhaps the way that emissions from automobiles in the city where you live are reducing the quality of life. You could synthesize others' illustrations and your own to produce a paper that presents this insight. Although very few people have truly original ideas, when we synthesize we can create something fresh and interesting by combining some of what we learn from others with our own perspectives.

Planning and Drafting Your Synthesis   Whether you draw on material from informal resources, conversations, or notes from reading, the process for planning and drafting your synthesis follows a familiar pattern. Determine how many examples you will use to illustrate your point. Check to be sure those points fit. Determine an appropriate order for them and build paragraphs around your key point. For example, if you were trying to illustrate how video games interfere with studying, you might start a paragraph with data from a source followed by your own personal observations. Sometimes, in representing conflicting viewpoints, you may want to organize the paper based on those viewpoints leading to the position you support the most. You will need to clearly shift any changes in the point you want to make with effective transitions.

Of course, if your paper draws on published information or media sources, be sure to read the sections on research in Chapter 14 and 15 and those in Chapter 16 on handling quotations and avoiding plagiarism. As always, follow your instructor's guidelines for documenting sources.

GETTING STARTED

1. Read several issues of a Canadian magazine such as *Maclean's*, *Chatelaine*, or *Canadian Living* and determine what the articles suggest about a particular aspect of Canadian life. Then write an essay that illustrates your conclusions and incorporates relevant material from the articles.

2. Read two or three essays in this book that raise questions about Canadian cultural identities. Drawing from essays such as "Memories of Montreal—and Richness" (pages 135–137), "I'm a Banana and Proud of It" (pages 216–217), "No Place Like Home" (pages 303–307), and "Getting Schooled by My Pakistani Mother" (pages 369–373), as well as your own observations or experiences, write an essay that gives one extended example, or several shorter examples, of the ways in which diverse ethno-cultural traditions shape values or personal identities.

ILLUSTRATIVE ESSAYS: PROFESSIONAL MODELS

READING STRATEGIES

1. Read the introductory and concluding paragraphs quickly to determine the thesis for the illustration. Then read the essay quickly to get the main point of the essay. Jot down the key points of the illustration.

2. Based on your purpose for reading and the level of difficulty of the essay, determine if it is necessary to read the essay more carefully.

3. If a more careful reading is warranted, read slowly, noting any key details of the illustration that make a more general point.

READING CRITICALLY

1. Test whether the illustration really demonstrates the main point.

2. Determine whether the illustrations seem representative of the larger point being made. Has the writer chosen typical, realistic examples or unusual, unlikely examples that are difficult to trust?

3. Test the point by thinking of examples that would argue against the writer's position.

READING AS A WRITER

1. Identify and evaluate the kinds of examples used in the illustration.
2. Notice the strategies used to link the illustrations to a main point.
3. Identify and evaluate how the illustrations were organized (e.g., as short narratives, as descriptions) and jot down any strategies you found useful.

Marc Zwelling

The Blended Economy

After graduating with a B.Sc. degree in journalism from Northwestern University in 1968, Marc Zwelling worked for Canadian Press and the Toronto Telegram, and as a public relations official for the United Steelworkers of America. He is currently president of Vector Research and Development, Inc., conducting opinion surveys and completing feasibility studies. A Toronto consultant, he has facilitated numerous workshops and written extensively about future trends. In this selection, he examines the changing nature of the business marketplace.

1   The traditional way to innovate is to carve a specialized niche. Some building contractors specialize in renovating nineteenth-century homes. Lawyers practice trade law, criminal law, family law, labor law, immigration, copyright, or libel. Doctors can be ear-nose-throat specialists, gerontologists, or pediatricians. Specialization is efficient; specialists do their jobs faster because they know them better than non-specialists. And a niche is usually more profitable than the mass market from which someone sliced it. The trouble with a niche is that when competitors recognize it's profitable they rush in.

> Examples help define the concept of specialization.

2   Blending is the opposite of specialization. Instead of burrowing deeper into a field or product to specialize, blending creates a new market category. The secret in the technique is to unite different, not similar, ideas, products, or services. Minivans and sport-utility vehicles, for example, grew from blending cars and trucks, creating whole new categories of consumer vehicles.

> Examples of blending to create a new market category.

3   Companies can continually generate new ideas by blending. Most new products today are simply extrapolations of successful products, such as a faster microprocessor, a cheaper airline ticket, a smaller camera, and so on. These innovations eventually run out of possibilities. Blending different ideas instead produces limitless new directions for innovative products.

4   A food company searching for a new product for kids might think of blending different items from a list of opposites like "frozen or unfrozen," "milk or cola," "peanut butter or peanuts," "salad or soup." Perhaps kids who love peanuts would savor them in a soup. And perhaps a cola could be frozen so it would stay cold longer, requiring no ice. The ideas may prove impractical, nonsensical, or just plain awful, but the point is to generate more ideas because they can lead to practical products.

> Examples of blending different food items.

5   Blending also operates within social and economic trends. For instance, barriers are falling between work and leisure, devastating some retail clothing chains and department stores as employees *don* the same outfits at home and the office.

> Example of how blending may blur social and economic categories.

6   In the job market, there is vast potential to create opportunities by combining apparently unrelated occupations. Consider the number of specialists you must work with to

buy or sell a house: There is a real estate agent, the loan officer, the building inspector, an insurance agent, and the mover. One specialist hands you off to another. The blending opportunity here is for, perhaps, a "home transitions" professional who can manage all these different steps.

Example of blending opportunity in real estate.	

7   Some employees may have over-specialized. Specialization narrows a worker's opportunities in a slowly growing economy and causes bottlenecks in a booming economy. Blending avoids these problems.

8   The *New York Times* recently reported unprecedented growth in the new profession of legal nurse consultant. From none a decade ago, there are more than 4,000 in America today. Blending the skills of nurses and lawyers, legal nurse consultants help lawyers in medical-related lawsuits. Blending professions is not the same as stacking one university degree on another. The legal nurse consultant is still a nurse, not a lawyer. Nurses learn enough law in training institutes to become legal nurse consultants.

Example of a blended profession.

9   Another example of a blended career opportunity might be an ergonomic architect— a designer and engineer with special training in child development to make safer houses for families with small children.

10   Try mixing and matching completely dissimilar occupations, such as carpenter, receptionist, software writer, investment adviser, security guard, dentist, chemical engineer, lifeguard, teacher, embalmer, chef, hairstylist, pharmacist, actor.

Examples of different jobs that might be mixed and matched.

11   A list like this may yield few blended jobs in the literal sense, but it triggers thinking about ways to add value to products and services and differentiate businesses in super-competitive markets. For instance, a funeral home could offer caskets carved by its own carpenters. A supermarket could build customer loyalty if its meat cutters demonstrate cooking techniques. A chef with pharmaceutical training or a pharmacist with cooking skills could help customers create healthier meals using herbs and other natural supplements.

Examples of how blending could help businesses offer added value.

12   Career blending is most likely to develop among entrepreneurs, as attempts to blend work in traditional settings have historically met with resistance: Unions protest that management wants to make one employee do two jobs for one worker's pay. Management says unions obstruct change and efficiency.

Writer acknowledges potential problems with blending.

13   Indeed, most fields resist merging and consolidating because of tradition. But since nobody can predict what the market will bear, the greater the number of innovations you can generate in products, services, and careers, the greater your chance of success.

Ends with positive suggestion.

DISCUSSION QUESTIONS

1. In the first two paragraphs, the author contrasts blending with specialization. What might be his reason for such an approach?

2. Identify the different categories of blending that the author provides. Why does the author provide so many examples within the different categories? Which examples are most helpful for you? Explain.

3. In paragraph 11, the author offers a list of different jobs which he admits "may yield few blended jobs in the literal sense." Does this list get you thinking about new job combinations, or does it seem too unlikely? What other jobs might you imagine blending?

TOWARD KEY INSIGHTS

We are often trapped by limiting our thinking to established categories. Can you think of examples—in marketing or advertising; in the media or arts; in cooking, fitness, or home design—where blending has helped to refresh a way of thinking about an established category?

SUGGESTIONS FOR WRITING *Imagine that you are writing to an employer or a company about their need for a new job category that would be a unique blend of skills or roles. Use concrete examples that illustrate how these different skills can be combined to add value to the company.*

Just as Zwelling uses a number of examples to illustrate an economic trend called blending, write an essay that uses several examples to explain a new trend in an area you know well—perhaps a fashion, cultural, or technological trend—to an audience unfamiliar with this trend.

Sasha Chapman

Manufacturing Taste

Sasha Chapman has been writing about Canada's culinary culture for more than a decade. She is a senior editor at The Walrus, *the magazine from which this article, slightly abridged, has been taken. She has also been an independent food writer for* The Globe and Mail, Reader's Digest, Saveur, *and* Toronto Life *magazine.*

1   Tell me what you think of Kraft Dinner, and I will tell you who you are. If you belong to Canada's comfortable class, you probably think of the dish as a childish indulgence and a clandestine treat. The bite-sized tubular noodles are so yielding and soft, you will say a little sheepishly, and next to impossible to prepare al dente. The briny, glistening orange sauce tastes a little bit sweet and a little bit sour—at once inter-esting, because of the tension between the two flavour poles, but not overly challenging or unfamiliar. And its essential dairyness connects it to that most elemental of foods: a mother's milk. KD is the ultimate nursery food, at least if you were born and raised in Canada, where making and eating cheese has been a part of the culture since Champlain brought cows from Normandy in the early 1600s—a tradition nearly as venerable as the fur trade. It may be the first dish children and un-nested students learn to make ("make," of course, being a loose term; "assemble" may be more accurate). This only strengthens its primal attractions.

2   If you recently immigrated to Canada, you will have a very different association with KD, as a dish that polarizes family meals. Your children nag you for it, having acquired a taste for it at school, or at the house next door. And if you count yourself among the 900,000 Canadians who use food banks each month, you may associate the iconic blue and yellow box with privation: a necessary evil while you wait for your next cheque to arrive, bought with your last dollar, and moistened with your last spoonfuls of milk.

3   The point is, it's nearly impossible to live in Canada without forming an opinion about one of the world's first and most successful convenience foods. In 1997, sixty years after the first box promised "dinner in seven minutes—no baking required," we celebrated by making Kraft Dinner the top-selling grocery item in the country.

4   This makes KD, not poutine, our de facto national dish. We eat 3.2 boxes each in an average year, about 55 percent more than Americans do. We are also the only people to refer to Kraft Dinner as a generic for instant mac and cheese. The Barenaked Ladies sang wistfully about eating it. In response, fans threw boxes of KD at the band members as they performed. This was an act of veneration.

5   True, Canada is just one outpost in Kraft's globalized food system. The company's iconic brands are on the rise in emerging markets, which is to say in the ancient cultures beyond the borders of North America, Europe, and Australia. In China, another Kraft product, the Oreo, has been re-engineered for the Asian market, with such success that it is now the country's number one cookie. But this is history repeating itself: our own food system was colonized long ago by Kraft, a company that has always striven to give us (or at least our consumer, magpie selves) what we want: cheaper food that is faster to prepare. We have been only too happy to drink the Kool-Aid, another Kraft brand.

6   KD's popularity is a symptom of a world that spins distressingly faster and faster. We devote a total of forty-two minutes to cooking and cleaning up three meals a day—six fewer minutes than we spent in 1992. Over half the dinners we consume at home involve a prepared or semi-prepared food. As the clock ticks, we spend more of every food dollar on these shortcuts.

7   But what does it mean if a national dish is manufactured, formulated by scientists in a laboratory in Glenview, Illinois, and sold back to us by the second-largest food company in the world? Kraft Foods employs 126,000 people worldwide, and raked in $54.4 billion in 2011. By the end of this year, it will formally split into two divisions— North American groceries and global snacks—no doubt to go forth and multiply. Kraft Canada isn't just manufacturing 120 million boxes of powdered cheese and noodles at its factory in the desolate Montreal suburb of Mont-Royal. It is manufacturing taste. In so doing, it has left an indelible mark on what and how we eat, and therefore how we live.

8   Despite our ever-present nostalgia for the foods of childhood, tastes and recipes are always evolving. We have no definitive version of macaroni and cheese, or any dish for that matter. The word "macaroni," first coined in Italy, describes any short tubular pasta; there, the cheese of choice was often Parmesan. Although I have yet to uncover a primary source to prove the point, I would wager that macaroni, which first became fashionable in England in the eighteenth century, most likely reached Britain in the trunks of travellers. The dish soon grew so popular among anglophones that "macaroni" became slang for a dandy who favoured outlandish wigs, which is why Yankee Doodle "stuck a feather in his cap and called it macaroni."

9   The Italian recipe typically featured the noodle, rather than a cheesy sauce, in the starring role, but English cooks inverted this relationship, adding English cheeses, such as cheddar, and egg yolks, to create a creamier, more pudding-like dish. An early domestic iteration, published in *Modern Practical Cookery* in 1845, calls for puff pastry to line the baking dish. Its author, Mrs. Nourse, gives instructions to stew the noodles in a cream thickened with egg yolks, with a little "beaten mace" and "made mustard" to sharpen the flavours before grating Parmesan or Cheshire cheese over top.

10   Liz Driver, the culinary historian who introduced me to the recipe, believes the macaroni Mrs. Nourse used would have been imported from Italy, and was probably far superior to much of the Canadian-made pasta available today, which Italians consider too soft for their taste. Driver is the curator of Campbell House, a Toronto heritage building where she teaches open-hearth cooking in the nineteenth-century kitchen, and keeps a collection of vintage cast iron pots piled under her desk.

11   She showed me into the formal drawing room, where we sat like museum pieces, surrounded by a games table and a writing desk. "Macaroni and cheese was considered sophisticated, as proven by the fact that it was served in a puff pastry–lined pan," she noted in the hushed, measured tones of someone who has spent her life in libraries. Mrs. Nourse's Cheshire cheese notwithstanding, there was plenty of local cheddar for making macaroni puddings in the nineteenth and early twentieth centuries. At the time, Canada was known for little else, food-wise, perhaps one reason we remain so enamoured with mac and cheese. Commercial cheese making in Ontario took off in the mid–nineteenth century, helped along by a depression in the wheat market, and the prevalence of the wheat midge, which was devastating crops. In the age before pasteurization, cheese was often safer—and much longer lasting—than fluid milk. More plentiful than the English original, Canadian cheddar soon became a staple among the English working class. By the turn of the twentieth century, there were 1,242 cheddar factories in Ontario, where the bulk of Canadian cheese making happened, and cheddar exports—some 234 million pounds in 1904—were second only to timber. More than a century later, we export only 19 million pounds of cheese, five million of which is cheddar, while we import more than 55 million. Although we cannot wholly lay the decline of cheese craft in Canada at the feet of James Lewis Kraft, it did correspond with the rise of Kraft's processed cheese empire.

12   In 1893, the Chicago World's Columbian Exposition displayed the blueprint for the century of middle-class consumerism that followed. North American society was changing rapidly: cities such as Chicago had sprung up seemingly overnight, and industry, not agriculture, was in ascendance. Following two decades of social, economic, and political upheaval, the public hungered for the rosy promise of progress. One cannot overstate the fair's influence on the North American imagination: it drew 30 million visitors when only 63 million people lived in the US. Model houses touted the new middle-class lifestyle, featuring electric stoves, washing machines, doorbells, and fire alarms. Exhibitors hawked new refrigeration technology, canned meats, desiccated soups, synthetic lard substitutes, and saccharin derived from coal tar. New food preparation technologies were marketed as more sanitary, more efficient, and more economical than anything nature or home cooks could provide on their own.

13   J. L. Kraft, who had grown up on a dairy farm in Ontario, headed off to Chicago a decade after the world's fair. Fascinated by the promise of innovation, he resolved to find a modern, more profitable way to distribute cheese. He arrived in the US with $65 and a plan to launch a wholesale cheese business.

14   There he joined the ranks of dairy experts who were searching for ways to make cheese production more efficient. All cheese is an ancient expression of "milk's leap towards immortality," as Clifton Fadiman so poetically put it, and an extremely effective method for preserving a dairy surplus. You need just three main ingredients: milk, rennet (to curdle it into a solid), and microbes (to convert lactose into acid, which deepens the flavour and prevents the curds from spoiling or harbouring disease).

15   Emulsifying salts help stabilize processed cheese by taking calcium from the milk protein and exchanging it with sodium. This allows the proteins to hold water, thickening the cheese. Early attempts to make processed cheese resembled a kind of re-solidified, long-keeping fondue; the Swiss, not surprisingly, were the first to figure out that these "melting salts" would keep the cheese stable (i.e., emulsified).

16   By the beginning of World War I, J. L. Kraft was experimenting with a similar process, which he developed over a double boiler. His formula hinged on a combination of citric acid and phosphates (the emulsifying salts). While not the first to develop a processed cheese, he was the first to win a patent (in 1916) and, eventually, to capitalize on it. His method paved the way for Velveeta (1928), Kraft Dinner (1937), Cheez Whiz (1952), and Kraft Singles (1965). The discovery that emulsifying salts could be used to make processed cheese turned out to be the great innovation—and some would say tragedy—of twentieth-century cheese making. It standardized the process and ruled out variation, good or bad, at every stage.

17   The idea for boxed macaroni and cheese came during the Depression, from a salesman in St. Louis who wrapped rubber bands around packets of grated Kraft cheese and boxes of pasta and persuaded retailers to sell them as a unit. In 1937, the company began to market them as Kraft Dinner, promising to feed a family of four for 19 cents (US). The boxes had a good shelf life and could be kept in a pantry for about ten months; back then, many Canadian households did not yet own a refrigerator.

18   In 1939, two years after KD launched in Canada and the US, Kraft's Canadian sales had already reached $8 million. A mere six years later, at the end of World War II, sales had nearly doubled to $14 million, helped in large part by government requisitions for the armed forces, and at home by war rationing and general privation, which made meatless entrees more common. Demographic shifts also played a part: as fewer families retained servants and more women went to work, they had less time to prepare meals. Corporate cookbooks rose to prominence in Canadian kitchens at this time. It is significant that expert cooking advice took hold when life was uncertain: the Depression, and then the war, shook the nation's confidence, and people felt comforted by instructions from professionals.

19   Meanwhile, the Canadian cheese industry began to flounder. Exports to its biggest market, the UK, dropped off in the '20s as the standard of living rose for the British worker, which meant families could afford more meat. And the world wars, which all but halted exports, nearly killed the industry. Even so, Heather Menzies believes it would have rallied in the '60s, had political leaders chosen to protect craft cheese. They even had a report telling them how. Instead, they chose to favour the interests of large-scale producers, a group dominated by American corporations such as Kraft. Canada's local cheese factories watched as the British market collapsed and their own milk supply dried up.

20   Big American companies signed contracts with local dairies, effectively binding the suppliers to sell most if not all of their production to them. This squeezed out the smaller cheese factories, and more dairy went to making processed cheese instead of artisanal types. At the height of its influence, in 1971, Kraft controlled more than 50 percent of cheese production in Canada.

21   Meanwhile, demographics continued to shift. Canada's population was growing, thanks to the baby boom and immigration. The middle class was moving to the suburbs, and still more women went to work outside the home. Food manufacturers saw opportunity in this, and flogged their products on television and in magazines and

newspapers, promising status and convenience. Sales of processed cheese took off. By 1973, Kraft Canada was the largest single advertiser in Canadian magazines and, with General Foods, the biggest advertiser on television. Tom Quinn, a former Kraft Canada president, told Menzies, "If we did anything right, it was merchandising and advertising. We created the demand."

22   In the world of modern food manufacturing, Kraft Dinner Original remains a fairly simple formula, with only ten ingredients. (My own recipe also calls for ten, if you lump together the natural flavours, as labellers do.) But KD has spawned generations of mac and cheese dinners, each one a greater feat of engineering than the last, and each one less recognizable as something we could make in our own kitchens. In 1999, the company launched Kraft Dinner Cup, a line that now includes Kraft Dinner Triple Cheese in a microwaveable package. It contains twenty-one ingredients, including "cheese flavours." Cheddar is eighth on the list. A version sold only in the US, described as Triple Cheese Cheesy Made Easy, contains forty-two ingredients, depending on how you count them.

23   Yet KD Original has not changed much in seventy-five years, from the consumer's point of view. What has changed is how it is engineered and manufactured. "The early sauces would have been nearly all cheese, except for the emulsifying salts," says Art Hill, a cheese scientist at the University of Guelph, in Ontario. But as dairy became a commodity in the intervening years, profits came from manufacturing it for the lowest cost and the highest volume possible, and from developing new "cheese products" that over time were made with less and less cheese.

24   Manufactured foods originally appealed to consumers because they were beacons of progress—which they were, if you bought in to the premise that food is just fuel, and if you measured success by how cheaply and quickly a meal could be prepared. But as convenience foods became more common and cooking from scratch less so, people began to miss the connection they once had to how food was produced, on the farm and in the kitchen. They craved the meals their mothers once cooked, the real mac and cheese, homemade. So Kraft cannily adjusted its marketing strategy, creating an ersatz nostalgia for the very thing KD had supplanted. "Mama's in the kitchen making mac and cheese," ran one American marketing slogan. Another announced: "Two new Kraft home cooked dinners, the quick kind you cook up fresh."

25   People feel a strong emotional connection to the KD label, says Jordan Fietje, senior brand manager for Kraft Dinner, who takes pains to highlight his company's sacred covenant with matriarchs. Like many other Kraft employees, he is inordinately fond of the phrase "our promise to moms." The slogan makes sense. Food is about ritual, tradition and conviviality, and what your mother made for Sunday dinner, which means it is also about identity. The cliché is not wrong: we are what we eat, and our choices both reflect and shape who we are.

26   Manufactured food has its attractions: it is cheaper and lasts longer, and engineers can manipulate moisture, salt, and sugar content to appeal to a broader market, or to target a social group's preferences. But as much of our food production has shifted to manufacturing—44 percent of Canadian agricultural output is now destined for processing—products, especially the ones dreamt up by scientists and nutritionists in corporate labs, are made a long way from the consumer. We increasingly rely on professionals to teach us how to cook (if we ever learn), dieticians and nutritionists to tell us what to eat, and scientists to engineer the food we buy.

27   By the early twentieth century, manufacturers had begun using professional tasters to help ensure quality control. Technology enabled new ways of delivering nutrition, but the food developed by scientists and produced by machines didn't always taste good. "You can break down food into protein, fat, carbohydrates, but you can't tell just from the chemical properties what it will taste like," says Chris Findlay, the garrulous CEO of Compusense, a consultancy in Guelph. He has spent a lifetime advising multinationals on how to launch and refine food products so they will appeal to consumers. This proved especially troublesome for the US military, which had been working to develop cheap, nutritious, and easy-to-store rations for soldiers.

28   In the '40s and '50s, the US Army Quartermaster Food and Container Institute began studying "food acceptance," and so began the field of sensory analysis, or the study of perception. Corporations were quick to discover its uses in evaluating consumer goods. Most large food companies now have sensory analysis labs; many also employ consultants like Findlay to learn more about a product and whether there might be room for something new in its market category.

29   What is true elsewhere holds up in the food industry: try to please everyone, and you'll end up pleasing no one—or, as Findlay remarks in his faint Scottish brogue, "Between two stools, fools fall through." He boasts that if he gives test subjects three samples to taste, he can predict where on the sensory map they will fall. The universal product and the average consumer do not exist, which is why, in addition to Kraft Dinner Original, you will find dozens of KD products on grocery shelves, from extra creamy to white cheddar, whole wheat, and even versions fortified with vegetables, fibre, or flax seed.

30   Sensory analysis relies heavily on trained testers rather than consumers to dissect the sight, smell, and taste of a product and its competitors by developing a list of attributes to describe them. At Compusense, this data is entered into a computer program that uses statistical methods to create a sensory map of the various traits and where each product falls on the graph. To illustrate how this works, Findlay offers to make me a map for the boxed macaroni and cheese category, with one condition: first I must spend the day as a human detector, trained (rather like a bomb-sniffing dog) to use my senses for one of his panels.

31   A few days later, I find myself at a table in a room full of strangers, staring at a hospital tray that holds my tools for the next two hours: a cup of distilled water, a few crackers, another empty cup with a lid, a white napkin, and a plastic spoon. The first sample arrives: a Styrofoam cup labelled number 943. One of Findlay's employees, Sheila Fortune, stands in front of a blank whiteboard in a lab coat and demonstrates the procedure. Opening the plastic cup by a centimetre, she takes quick "bunny sniffs" to detect the aroma of the steam that billows out. Each of the testers scribbles down descriptions: butter, brine, starch, the tang of processed cheddar, a sweet aromatic. Next, we remove the lid and note the visuals: straight, thin noodles in an unctuous slick of saffron orange. A few bubbles cling to the pasta. Following Fortune's instructions, we taste and expectorate the sample. We will have eleven more macaroni and cheese dishes placed before us over the next two hours.

32   By the time the session ends, we have covered the whiteboard with a list of traits to describe the product. Fortune will feed sixteen of them into software that generates a new survey for us to fill out as we taste the products again. This time, though, we dine alone, in front of a computer screen in a white booth, under bright white light. Portions

appear like clockwork in the hatch in front of us as we click through the computer survey. In the afternoon, Fortune generates a sensory map of the products we tasted, to show where on the taste spectrum each one falls. KD Original is the cheesiest, yellowest, and saltiest. KD Smart Vegetables Original, made with half a serving of freeze-dried cauliflower, is distinctly pungent and sour, with overtones of boiled brassica.

33   From inside the belly of the food-producing beast, one thing becomes clear: this is not a way to make food, but a way to manufacture fuel—for our bodies, and for the hungry consumer market. The food industry, like any empire, depends on expansion for success: to survive, it must continue to increase both its output and its consumer base.

34   Outside the lab, at the dinner table, taste remains the physical manifestation of memory; it is impossible to eat something without relating or comparing it to an earlier, often a childhood, experience. Taste's relationship to memory becomes especially poignant after you leave home—as immigrants, caught between two worlds, know well. Helen Vallianatos, an anthropologist at the University of Alberta, who studies the food habits of the province's South Asian and Middle Eastern communities, notes that many of her subjects remark on how their sensibilities change almost imperceptibly over time. On trips back home, she says, some are surprised to discover that the dishes they once loved now seem too rich, too spicy, too strange, now that they have become accustomed to a different way of eating. She has a special interest in how food and identity are intertwined, and how food helps construct identity: when you cannot eat the food you remember, who are you?

35   Another common observation among new arrivals to Canada concerns the fast pace of life. Ask immigrants to define Canadian food, and they most often name hamburgers, pizza, and pasta. But one brand turns up again and again in field studies: Kraft, as in "Dinner" and "Singles."

36   Canada's emerging markets reflect similar realities to global ones: as our South Asian and Chinese populations have risen, Kraft Canada has rolled out ethnic-specific programs to appeal to immigrants, who may arrive here with traditional recipes and expectations of leisurely, old-fashioned meals, but soon discover that our food culture doesn't leave much time for tradition at the table.

37   Visible minorities represent the fastest-growing segment of our population—they comprised 16.3 percent of Canadians in 2006—and they may offer Kraft its best chance to expand the domestic market. Our foreign-born population is projected to increase four times faster than the rest by 2031. Because most product development takes place south of the border, Kraft Canada lacks the resources to create products specific to our country's changing demographics. Instead, it hires anthropologists and other researchers to find "modern families" (i.e., visible minorities and immigrants) and send sheltered executives to observe them. The corporation has also hired spokespeople to develop and promote recipes within their own communities, and to bring new perspectives to the team of home economists who cook in the 6,000-square-foot kitchens at its headquarters in Don Mills.

38   As befits a company that trades in nostalgia, Kraft's corporate office feels like a step back in time. Four important-looking men in suits huddle outside the concrete building, BlackBerrys drawn and at the ready. The "girls," as everyone calls the group of middle-aged women who are the face of Kraft products, are inside working away in the kitchen. These are the home economists and dieticians who develop recipes for the company's magazines, websites, and newsletters. The North American Kraft

Recipe Library contains about 30,000 entries, enough to fill 300 cookbooks. Michele McAdoo, who has spent seventeen years cooking for Kraft, pushed out 1,000 recipes to nearly one million Canadians in her email blasts last year, to promote home cooking with Kraft products.

39   Today cumin and coriander waft through the demonstration kitchen. Smita Chandra, an elegant South Asian immigrant in a gold-embroidered fuchsia top, is browning ground chicken in a wok for keema, a spiced meat dish. In a girlish voice that channels Glinda the Good Witch, she recalls how exotic macaroni and cheese seemed when she was growing up in India. She drops a spoonful of cumin from a round stainless steel tin, just like the ones you see in kitchens all over the subcontinent, and says, "Dad would make us mac and cheese when Mother didn't feel like cooking. We so looked forward to those nights." The keema she is preparing will be mixed with KD instead of the usual basmati rice.

40   The recipes Chandra prepares taste pretty good and are quick to throw together. But they could be done just as well without Kraft products, as in the case of a chicken dish that calls for Miracle Whip, a completely unnecessary and less healthful ingredient than the traditional yogourt. Then there's the processed aftertaste KD lends to her chicken keema, which would have been simpler, anyway, to make with rice; even the best spices and an extra dose of cayenne can't mask it.

41   While promoting its products to specific ethnic groups, Kraft Canada discovered another market: Canadian cooks who grew up in a multicultural environment, exposed to many styles of cuisine at home, in restaurants, and through travel. A year after Chandra joined the demonstration team, Kraft hired renowned Toronto chef Susur Lee as a spokesperson for the Chinese community, an idiosyncratic choice if ever there was one. Lee's cooking is notoriously cerebral and complicated, and when the announcement came out last year it was hard to imagine him writing recipes that any home cook—let alone those in search of convenience—could duplicate. Yet it turned out to be an inspired choice. Omnivorousness may define modern Canadian cuisine, and the open-mindedness that accompanies it makes for one of the most exciting aspects of our burgeoning food culture. If anyone can speak to the fusion that informs Canadian cuisine, and the multiculturalism of cooking, it is Lee. He stands out among an elite group of chefs who succeed at fusion, the overexposed cooking fad of the '90s. The style has its critics (including me); when new combinations seem rootless and random, it devolves into "confusion" cuisine. Lee, however, keeps an open mind in the kitchen, and borrows freely from different cultures to create his dishes without ever bewildering (or, worse, boring) his guests. He demonstrates a deep knowledge of various cuisines, and an ability to uncover the connections between seemingly disparate styles, which is why he can successfully pair a Shanghai lion's head meatball with Alsatian cabbage and potatoes from Lyons.

42   "When I think of fusion, I think of culture, of the deep root of recipes," he says, sitting on a black leather couch at his eponymous restaurant in Toronto. "Like Peking duck." As Lee well knows, even the most classic dish begins with an adaptation.

43   I ask him how immigration changed his approach to cooking. "When you arrive in Canada, you start to reflect on who you are," he replies.

44   Tastes are always changing. Lee does not eat Kraft Dinner, but his three sons do. It's one thing for tastes to develop organically, however, and quite another for them to be influenced by government or corporate interests. A few years ago, the Martin Prosperity

Institute, at the University of Toronto's Rotman School of Management, published a paper by geographer Betsy Donald entitled "*From Kraft to Craft: Innovation and Creativity in Ontario's Food Economy,*" a rosy, if at times unrealistic, report about the economic benefits of an artisanal cheese renaissance in Canada. As part of her research, she interviewed Lee, who told her, "True innovative cooking comes from a deep understanding of, and respect for, different cultural roots and certain openness to new ideas. . . . What I find so exciting about Toronto, and North American urban society in general, is the possibility for the betterment of the human condition through experiencing on a daily basis differentness and diversity."

45   Differences—whether in people, cultures, or even cheese—are Canada's greatest strength, and life would be exceedingly dull without them. They shape and define who we are. But differences can never be manufactured in any meaningful way by a large food conglomerate, which always seeks to standardize. So the question is: are we content to have our national dish come from a laboratory in Illinois, or do we want to have a hand in its (and our) creation? If we can't be the authors of our own meals, who are we? To cook and live life to the fullest, Lee tells me, "I need a good foundation. I have to know who I am."

DISCUSSION QUESTIONS

1. In the first two paragraphs, how does the author try to draw in readers from the dominant culture as well as readers from diverse backgrounds?

2. What does the author mean when she claims that Kraft Dinner is the "ultimate nursery food" (paragraph 1)?

3. How does the writer support her claim in paragraph 4 that KD is the "de facto national dish"? (You may want to look up the meaning of the term *de facto*.)

4. How does the writer support her claim in the topic sentence of paragraph 5 that "Canada is just one outpost in Kraft's globalized food system"? What tone or attitude is revealed when she ends that paragraph by saying, "We have been only too happy to drink the Kool-Aid, another Kraft brand"? (If you do not recognize the reference to drinking the Kool-Aid, look it up.) Since this article is not just an information piece, but also an argument, what other words has the writer used up to this point that reveal her tone?

5. Paragraphs 8 to 12 explore some of the culinary history of the macaroni and cheese combination that Kraft later exploits. What are two specific sensory details that stand out for you in these paragraphs? What contrast is implied between the macaroni and cheese of the nineteenth century and that manufactured by Kraft today?

6. In paragraph 24, the author writes that the desire for quick, cheap food gave way to nostalgia for foods made from scratch once convenience foods became plentiful. How did Kraft then adjust its marketing strategy?

7. Toward the end of the article, the writer discusses the way memories of the taste of food are among our earliest: "Outside the lab, at the dinner table, taste remains the physical manifestation of memory; it is impossible to eat something without relating or comparing it to an earlier, often a childhood, experience. Taste's relationship to memory becomes especially poignant after you leave home." Why would this relationship become "poignant" after one leaves home? Can you think of examples of significant food memories that define a part of your identity?

8. In addition to using Kraft Dinner as an extended example of manufactured food and making an argument, this article uses other strategies of development, such as definition, process, cause and effect, comparison and contrast, narrative, and illustration. Find one example of each of these strategies of development, and explain how the writer blends these strategies to further her argument.

9. Examine the last paragraph. How does the writer broaden the significance of her discussion far beyond the question of food preferences?

TOWARD KEY INSIGHTS

What is your experience of Kraft Dinner or other convenience foods that the author considers to be manufactured foods? What is your experience of eating or cooking food made from scratch? If you were to say that you have certain values around food, what would they be?

What does the writer mean when she says, "Omnivorousness may define modern Canadian cuisine, and the open-mindedness that accompanies it makes for one of the most exciting aspects of our burgeoning food culture"? How would you characterize a food culture in Canada or elsewhere?

The article ends with the idea that "to cook and live life to the fullest" we need to know who we are. What, in your view, might be the connections between cooking and living fully, and knowing who we are?

SUGGESTIONS FOR WRITING *Using one or more extended illustrations, write an essay that shows how a particular food, beverage, or, if you prefer, consumer item could be an emblem of a particular community or a particular kind of person. If you know enough about a dish or food from Canada or from another country to discuss it in depth, you could choose to begin with the following statement: "Tell me what you think of . . . , and I will tell you who you are." If you decide to do research, you must cite your sources; see Chapters 14 and 16 for help with documentation and with avoiding plagiarism.*

In her essay, the author claims that "food is about ritual, tradition and conviviality, and what your mother made for Sunday dinner, which means it is also about identity" (paragraph 25). Write an essay that illustrates what a particular food you grew up with reveals about your identity. Make sure your essay leads to a larger point—for example, you might show how certain family or ethno-cultural rituals strengthen a sense of community, or disappear over time; or you could show how childish preferences give way to sophisticated adult tastes.

MyWritingLab

How Do I Get a Better Grade?

Go to **www.mywritinglab.com** for additional help with your grammar, writing, and research skills. You will have access to a variety of exercises, instruction, and videos that will help you improve your basic skills and help you get a better grade.

CHAPTER 8

Strategies for Analytical Writing: Process Analysis

EXPLAINING HOW

Drat, you can't get your course software to run at all. After getting out of your browser and trying all over again, you call your school's technical support. The person on the help desk walks you through several steps. She has you check to see if your browser is up to date and compatible with the software. Next, she has you run a diagnostic to determine if you have the appropriate, up-to-date software, including something called Java. You discover that your Java Script is not up to date. The technician then talks you through the steps of going to the website, identifying the version appropriate for your computer, downloading the software, and finally eliminating older versions of Java. You try again.

Every day, we perform processes almost constantly, ranging from brewing a pot of coffee to taking a picture, preparing for work, or replacing a light switch. We often share our special technique for doing something—for example, making chicken cacciatore—by passing it on to a friend.

Many popular publications feature process analyses that help readers sew zippers in garments, build canoes, fill out tax forms, and improve their wok cooking techniques. Many YouTube clips are actually process analyses that teach a range of skills: how to remove a film on your windshield; how to change the screen saver on your desktop; how to tie a scarf, use chopsticks, or play guitar.

Process analysis also frequently helps you meet the writing demands of your courses and future careers. For biology, you may need to explain how bees find their way back to the hive. A nurse may need to provide home-care instructions for diabetes patients. An IT specialist may need to explain to employees how to use the new software. A process can be technical, nontechnical, historical, scientific, or natural, and it can have audiences with very different levels of expertise.

Process papers fall into two categories: those intended for readers who will perform the process and those intended to explain the process to nonperformers. Papers in either category can range from highly technical and sophisticated to nonspecialized and simple.

Processes for Readers Who Will Perform Them   The audience for these papers may be technical and professional personnel who need the information to carry out a work-related task or individuals who want to perform the process for themselves.

A how-to-do-it paper must include everything the reader needs to know in order to ensure a successful outcome. Its directions take the form of polite commands, often addressing readers directly as "you." This approach helps involve readers in the explanation and emphasizes that the directions must, not merely should, be followed. Here is an illustration:

> To prepare a bacterial smear for staining, **first** use an inoculating loop to place a drop of distilled water on a clean glass microscope slide.
>
> **Next**, pass the loop and the opening of the tube containing the bacterial culture to be examined through a Bunsen burner flame to sterilize them.
>
> From the tube, remove a small bit of culture with the loop and rub the loop in the drop of water on the slide until the water covers an area one and one-half inches long and approximately the width of the slide.
>
> **Next**, reflame the opening of the culture tube **to** <u>prevent contamination of the culture,</u> and then plug it shut.
>
> Allow the smear to air dry, and **then** pass the slide, smear side up, through the flame of the burner until it is warm to the touch. The dried smear <u>should have a cloudy, milky-white appearance.</u>

Darryl Williams, student

> Warning of possible risk.

> Feedback on what will be seen with a successful completion.

Each separate step is often represented as a step in a separate paragraph or a numbered list to make it easier for the reader to see the separate actions that need to be completed. In a process, each step must be signalled by key words that let the reader know a shift took place. The key words are highlighted above in green. Also, it is important to provide readers with warnings when there are risks, either from the procedure or in making a mistake, as well as feedback that will let them know if they have been successful, noted above with underlining.

Processes for Readers Who Won't Perform Them   These papers may tell how some process is or was performed or how it occurs or occurred. For instance, a paper might detail the stages of grief, the procedure involved in an operation, the role of speech in the development of children's thinking, or the sequence involved in shutting down a nuclear reactor. These papers serve many purposes—for example, to satisfy popular curiosity; to point out the importance, difficulty, or danger of a process; or to cast a process in a favourable or unfavourable light. Even though the writers of such papers often explain their topic in considerable detail, they do not intend to provide enough information for readers to carry out the process.

Papers of this sort present the needed information without using polite commands. Sometimes a noun, a pronoun like *I, we, he, she,* or *it,* or a noun–pronoun combination identifies the performer(s). At other times, the performer remains unidentified. Three examples follow, using green to identify the performer.

Pronouns Identify Performer

Thus, when **I** now approach a stack of three two-inch cinder blocks to attempt a breaking feat, **I** do not set myself to "try hard," or to summon up all my strength. Instead **I** relax, sinking my awareness into my belly and legs, feeling my connection with the ground. **I** breathe deeply, mentally directing the breath through my torso, legs, and arms. . . . When **I** make my final approach to the bricks, if **I** regard them at all they seem light, airy, and friendly; they do not have the insistent inner drive in them that **I** do.

Don Ethan Miller, "A State of Grace: Understanding the Martial Arts"

Noun–Pronoun Combination Identifies Performers

Termites are even more extraordinary in the way **they** seem to accumulate intelligence as **they** gather together. **Two or three termites** in a chamber will begin to pick up pellets and move them from place to place, but nothing comes of it; nothing is built. As **more** join in, **they** seem to reach a critical mass, a quorum, and the thinking begins. **They** place pellets atop pellets, then throw up columns and beautiful, curving, symmetrical arches, and the crystalline architecture of vaulted chambers is created.

Lewis Thomas, "Societies as Organisms"

Performer Unidentified

The analyzer was adjusted so the scale read zero and was connected to the short sampling tube, which had previously been inserted into the smokestack. The sample was taken by depressing the bulb the requisite number of times, and the results were then read and recorded. The procedure was repeated, this time using the long sampling tube and sampling through the fire door.

Charles Finnie

EXERCISE *Examine your favourite newspaper or magazine for examples of process analysis. Bring them to class for group discussion of which kind of process analysis each represents and the writer's purpose.*

ETHICAL ISSUES

Unclear, misleading, incomplete, or erroneous instructions written for someone to follow can create unwanted consequences. Often frustration and lost time are the only results. Sometimes, though, the fallout is more serious, as in the case of a lab explosion. And in extreme cases, the outcome can be potentially catastrophic, as when an accident occurs in a nuclear power plant. As writers, we have an ethical obligation to write clear and complete instructions. To help you do this, ask yourself the following questions when you're writing a process that the reader will perform.

- Have I used clear and unambiguous language so the reader will not encounter unnecessary frustration and inconvenience?
- Have I clearly indicated all requirements, such as time needed or additional supplies that have to be purchased?
- Have I clearly warned readers about any possible harm they could face?

WRITING A PROCESS ANALYSIS

Planning and Drafting the Process Analysis

When the choice is yours, write about something you know well. If you're not the outdoor type and prefer to stay at a Holiday Inn rather than in the north woods, don't try to explain how to plan a camping trip. Muddled, inaccurate, and inadequate information will result. On the other hand, if you've pitched many a tent, you might want to share your camping knowledge with your readers.

FINDING YOUR TOPIC

- Use the strategies discussed in Chapter 3.
- Select a familiar topic, not something you don't know well.
- List the things you know how to do or have observed.
- Decide why the readers may find the process interesting or useful.
- Decide if you want to provide directions for the reader to follow, describe the process, or explain how others perform it.
- Test to see if it can be explained within the assigned length.

Processes for Readers Who Will Perform Them

Prewriting for the Process Analysis   Follow these steps to develop an essay that clarifies a process for readers to follow:

> ■ Brainstorm the steps and details in the steps.
> ■ Check to make certain you didn't miss a step.
> ■ Identify the reasons for each action.
> ■ Test each action to determine if any warning is necessary to keep readers safe.
> ■ Build a chart like the one shown below.
> ■ Review the chart and add needed material.
> ■ Group related actions to form steps, the major subdivisions of the procedure.

DEVELOPING YOUR PROCESS

Planning and Drafting the Process Analysis   When you have your answers, you could record them in a chart similar to this one:

Action	Reason for Action	Warning
First action	First reason	First warning
Second action	Second reason	Second warning

Sometimes, a reason will be so obvious that no mention is necessary, and many actions won't require warnings. When you've completed the chart, review it carefully and supply any missing information. If necessary, revise your chart.

Once you've listed the actions, group related ones to form steps, or the major subdivisions of the procedure. The following actions constitute the first step—getting the fire going—of a paper explaining how to grill hamburgers.

remove grill rack   light briquettes
stack charcoal briquettes   spread out briquettes

EXERCISE

1. **Develop a complete list of the actions involved in one of the following processes, then arrange them in an appropriate order.**

   a. Cleaning out a garage

   b. Assembling or repairing a common household device

   c. Giving an effective PowerPoint presentation to a class

   d. Breaking a bad habit

2. **Locate a set of instructions for a new product that requires the purchaser to do something: assemble furniture, activate a phone, use a cappuccino maker, and so on. Evaluate the clarity and helpfulness of these instructions.**

The **thesis statement** for a process paper identifies the key process that is being explained and a key point you may want to make about that process. "CPR is easy to perform and can save lives." "Grilling hamburgers outdoors is a simple process."

"Geothermal energy is simply a way of using the temperature of the earth to heat or cool a building through very basic techniques."

Here are strategies for drafting your process paper.

Introduction

■ Identify the process and arouse interest.

■ Possibly note importance, usefulness, or ease of process.

■ Indicate the list of items needed for the work.

■ Note any special conditions required for a successful outcome.

Body

■ Describe the process in detail.

■ Present each step in a distinct paragraph clearly and accurately.

■ If two steps must be performed simultaneously, tell the reader at the start of the first step.

■ In some places, offer feedback to let readers know what to expect if they completed the instructions properly. This lets them know if they are on track.

■ Note the reason for each action unless it is obvious.

■ Flag with a warning any step that is difficult, dangerous, or in need of special care.

■ Check to make certain you included everything readers need.

Conclusion

■ Provide a few brief remarks on the process.

■ With longer processes, summarize the steps.

■ Evaluate the result of the process.

The paper explaining how to grill hamburgers might begin as follows:

> Grilling hamburgers on an outdoor charcoal grill is a simple process that almost anyone can master. Before starting, you will need a clean grill, charcoal briquettes, charcoal lighter fluid and matches, hamburger meat, a plate, a spatula, and some water to put out any flames caused by fat drippings. The sizzling, tasty patties you will have when you finish are a treat that almost everyone will enjoy.

DISCUSSION QUESTION

1. How does the writer try to induce the reader to perform the process?

Let's see how the first step of the hamburger-grilling paper might unfold.

> The first step is to get the fire going. Remove the grill rack and stack about twenty charcoal briquettes in a pyramid shape in the centre of the grill.

Stacking allows the briquettes to burn off one another and thus produces a hotter fire.

Next, squirt charcoal lighter fluid over the briquettes. Wait about five minutes so that the fluid has time to soak into the charcoal. Then toss in a lighted match. The flame will burn for a few minutes before it goes out. When this happens, allow the briquettes to sit for another 15 minutes so that the charcoal can start to burn.

Once the burning starts, do not squirt on any more lighter fluid. A flame could quickly follow the stream back into the can, causing it to explode.

As the briquettes begin to turn from pitch black to ash white, spread them out with a stick so that they barely touch one another. Air can then circulate and produce a hot, even fire, the type that makes grilling a success.

DISCUSSION QUESTIONS

1. At what points has the writer provided reasons for doing things?
2. Where has the writer included a warning?

Some processes can unfold in *only one order*. When you shoot a free throw in basketball, for example, you step up to the line and receive the ball before lining up the shot, and you line up the shot before releasing the ball. Other processes can be carried out in an *order of choice*. When you grill hamburgers, you can make the patties either before or after you light the charcoal. If you have an option, use the order that has worked best for you. The paper on hamburger grilling notes the results.

Once the patties are cooked the way you like them, remove them from the grill and place them on buns. Now you are ready to enjoy a mouth-watering treat that you will long remember.

E.M. Pryzblyo

Processes for Readers Who Won't Perform Them

Prewriting the Process Analysis Like how-to-do-it processes, those intended for nondoers require you to determine the steps—or for natural processes, the stages—that are involved and the function of each before you start to write.

- Brainstorm steps or, with natural processes, stages.
- Since readers won't perform the process, identify your purpose or why readers would be interested.
- Identify steps that fit your purpose.

DEVELOPING YOUR PROCESS

Planning and Drafting the Process Analysis   If you're trying to persuade readers that animal testing should be discontinued in the cosmetics industry, the choices you make in developing your steps should reflect that purpose, including some of the painful consequences for the animals.

The thesis statement for a process that won't be performed by the reader often identifies the process and either the main point or the reasons for the reader to know the process. Drafting this type of process paper has some differences. You can arouse your reader's interest by offering an historical overview, summarizing the whole process, or explaining its importance. But because the reader will not perform the process, rather than including detail, supply just enough information for a basic understanding of each stage. Present each stage in a distinct paragraph with clear transitions and demonstrate how the stage fits in the overall process. Conclude by providing some perspective or evaluating the results. You can also assess the importance of the process and identify further consequences.

Revising the Process Analysis

To revise, follow the guidelines in Chapter 4 and the suggestions below.

- Have I written consistently for someone who will perform the process or who will merely understand it?
- If my paper is intended for performers, have I included every necessary action, offered reasons where necessary, and provided necessary warnings? Brainstorm briefly to determine additional details that might be necessary.
- Test the process following the instructions to see if they work or help understand the process.
- Are my steps in the appropriate order? Would any other order be more helpful?
- Is my paper ethical?

SAMPLE STUDENT ESSAY: USING PROCESS ANALYSIS

Basic Songwriting Techniques

Hannah Hill

Tyler Junior College

Faculty Member: Dr. Linda Gary

Establishes reader point of interest. Establishes thesis with main points discussed in paper.

1   When listening to a song, one always wonders where the idea of the song comes from. What was the singer thinking, and what provoked him or her to write such a song? Songwriting is a simple technique that anyone can do if they put their hearts into it. Songs are stories put to music through the process of emotion, thought, and rhythm.

2   <u>Emotional feelings are important when composing a good song.</u>
<u>Start by finding a comfortable place to relax and to think freely. Perhaps</u>
<u>a favorite room or an outdoor getaway could rid the mind of distractions.</u>
Once settled and comfortable, begin jotting down notes. Focus on
feelings and emotions that are current to life or thoughts from the past
that weigh heavily on the mind. For example, express how a certain
situation feels or affects day-to-day life. Make it either dominantly
positive or negative, but avoid mixing the emotions. Allow the
mysterious secrets to flow freely. Do not be afraid to let go. Expression of
the heart and mind is the most coveted form of music because it is so
real. "To take an emotion and make it mean something, take other
people into the feeling" is famous country singer/songwriter Kenny
Chesney's initial form of songwriting ("Kenny Chesney" 1). He puts his
true life on the line to create amazing music for country fans to enjoy.
Ultimately, personal experience will always draw the listener in with the
passion that comes from loving to write and listen to music.

> Explains parts of how to connect to emotional feelings.

> Offers concrete practices and clearly marks steps.

3   <u>After putting feelings into words, a clear thought process helps to</u>
<u>organize and put these emotions into a clear composition. Don't worry</u>
<u>about rhyme scheme yet until all the ideas are put down and arranged.</u>
Processing through the jotted notes of life will add organization. This
assembling will, in turn, add clarity of understanding for the listener. <u>Add</u>
<u>description and detail that brings insight of the writer out to the listener.</u>
Although life experience is the best writing utensil, it is not the only one.
Add fantasy or exaggeration to liven up and add spice. Be overly
emotional in certain and pertinent areas. The most important situation
should show the most drama to the listener. It is common for depressing
lyrics to be favored over upbeat ones. For instance, twists and turns are
always more interesting than perfectly happy endings. Always
remember, less is more. Take out the unnecessary, so there's not an
overload of information. Leave mystery to be interpreted by the listener.

> Offers transition to next step.

> Foreshadows next step, rhyme, and indicates that the next step should be delayed.

> Offers sequences for ordering and developing initial idea.

4   <u>After modifying thoughts and before moving onto rhyme,</u> put all
information in an organized structure. Assembling begins with determining
the order of the writing. Pick out the writing and separate it into sections.
The first paragraph part becomes the introduction or verse one. Next is the
chorus, which will repeat in between each verse. <u>Add the second section,</u>
<u>which becomes verse two, and repeat the chorus.</u> If necessary, add a
bridge, which is the part that intertwines but differs from the rest of the
song. Then repeat the chorus one more time. Organization puts an
intellectual tweak on mainstream emotions on which the song is based.

> Offers transition to next step.

> Offers concrete actions. Uses verbs at start of sentence to indicate action.

Offers transition to next step: rhythm.

Offers concrete strategies that might be completed in multiple order.

5   Finally, thoughts and feelings are translated into a potential rhythmic pattern. This is where the mainstream thinking turns into a complete thought. The story is then formed into a poetic framework. Manipulate words and sentences to contrast the feelings in the most exciting way. Be sure to avoid clichés, but add interest and uniqueness. Determine a pattern of rhyme as one would in poetry. Rhyming every other line is the most popular style of rhyme, but this is where the exotic twist of the writer can step in. However, avoid overrhyming and nonsense rhyming. Make certain that the rhyme has a reasonable flow. Form the song around individuality. This distinguishing and poetic step perfects the complete thought and finishes the writing step of song formation.

Conclusion summarizes the centre of the process—emotional release.

Ends by encouraging reader to act.

6   Writing songs can be a subtle attempt to make a statement. Songwriting is an emotional release that can be personal to both writer and listener for many different reasons. Writing of any kind should be emotionally sincere and can be very therapeutic for both writer and reader. Honest writing is always the easiest and best procedure. A passionate realization can openly interpret thoughts and feelings in an indescribable way. So get out there, write, and discover the hidden truth.

WORK CITED

"Kenny Chesney: Here Comes His Life." *Cincinnati Post* 8 July 2004: T14. *Infotrac Newspapers.* Web. 20 Sept. 2007.

DISCUSSION QUESTIONS

1. What is the purpose of this process essay? How does this purpose influence the way the process is explained?
2. Identify the key steps the writer recommends for writing a song.
3. Identify places where the writer offers clear warnings.
4. There are many possible ways to write a song, yet the writer suggests only one approach. What are the advantages and disadvantages of focusing on only one approach?
5. What changes could the writer provide to make this essay even more effective?

SUGGESTIONS FOR WRITING *Write a process analysis on one of the topics below or one approved by your instructor. The paper may provide instructions for the reader to follow, tell how a process is performed, or describe how a process develops. Prepare a complete list of steps, arrange them in an appropriate order, and follow them as you write the body of your essay.*

1. A natural process, such as erosion, that you observe or research
2. Breaking a bad habit, such as procrastination

3. Getting a tattoo

4. The stages in a student's adjustment to university

5. Buying or selling on eBay

6. Locating and renting an apartment, or buying a house

7. Planning a personal budget

8. The stages in developing an argument

9. Carrying out a process related to your hobby

10. Throwing a successful small party

11. Overcoming a fear or phobia

12. Reducing clutter

Stepping up to Synthesis

Is there only one way to study effectively, develop a marketing campaign, or cope with a demanding supervisor? No, of course not. As you've already learned, not all processes unfold in a single, predetermined order. The writing process itself illustrates this.

If you were to think about how you write and talk with other students about their writing processes, you would learn that different writing occasions call for different approaches. When you write a letter to a good friend, you probably spend little or no time on preliminaries but start putting your thoughts on paper as they occur to you. By contrast, other kinds of correspondence, such as inquiry and claim letters, require careful planning, drafting, and perhaps rewriting.

For this reason, there are many different approaches to writing about processes.

Imagine you are writing a process paper about the writing process itself. The steps in the process would be determined by the nature of the writing situation—the purpose and audience for the writing. Informal writing to a friend would require fewer steps than formal, academic writing. For example, when you write an email to a good friend, you probably just start typing and then press the Send button as soon as you are finished. However, in formal writing such as job applications or academic research essays, the writing process involves careful planning, drafting, revising, and editing.

PREWRITING FOR SYNTHESIS

Sometimes, the same writing occasion may allow for differing procedures, so you may need to take notes on multiple kinds of writing that people do. If you're writing an essay for your English class, you might brainstorm for ideas, develop a detailed outline, rough out a bare-bones draft, and add details as you revise. In talking to other students with the same assignment, you might find that they prefer to write a much longer draft and then whittle it down. Still other students might do very little brainstorming or outlining but a great deal of revising, often making major changes over several drafts. Research papers present a more complex challenge, requiring that the student find and read source material, take notes, and document sources properly. Here again, variations are possible: One student might prepare the list of works cited before writing the final draft, while another might perform this task last.

CRITICALLY EVALUATING YOUR SOURCES

Some important processes have been disputed in print, and if you wanted to investigate them you would need to consult written sources rather than talk to others. Informed disagreements exist about how the human species originated, how language developed, and how children mature. Police officers debate the best way to handle drunks, and management experts determine the best way to motivate employees. When you investigate such controversies, determine which view is supported by the best evidence and seems most reasonable. Then, as a writer, you can present the accounts in an appropriate order and perhaps indicate which one you think merits acceptance.[1]

PLANNING AND DRAFTING YOUR SYNTHESIS

If you decided to synthesize your findings about student writing practices, you would, of course, need to organize your material in some fashion. Perhaps you might focus on the differences that distinguish one writing occasion from another. You could develop each occasion in a separate section by presenting the practices followed by most students while ignoring variations. A second possibility would be to report different practices used for the same writing occasion, first considering the most common practice and then describing the variations. The result might be likened to a cookbook that gives different recipes for the same dish.

SUGGESTIONS FOR WRITING

1. Drawing on your own experience and/or interviews with others, write an essay explaining how to make decisions about an area that is important in some way to you right now.

   —a decision about what courses to take

   —a decision about what car to buy

   —a decision about what kind of job or career to pursue

   —a decision about where to travel

   —a decision about whether to break up with someone

2. Write an essay explaining how to manage money, or get out of debt, while one is a student.

PROCESS ANALYSIS ESSAYS: PROFESSIONAL MODELS

READING STRATEGIES

1. Determine the reason you are reading the process essay. If it is to follow instructions, you need to read in one way; if it is to understand a process, you need to read differently.

---

[1] If you rely on information obtained through interviews, read pages 367–373 in Chapter 15. If you rely on published sources, read the sections on library and Internet research in Chapter 14 and those on handling quotations and avoiding plagiarism in Chapter 16. As always, follow your instructor's guidelines for documenting sources.

2. If you are going to follow the instructions, read over the process first to get an understanding of the whole. Look for specific warnings or feedback you should consider. Get an idea of what the end result should look like. Gather any equipment you need. Then follow the process step by step, checking after each step to make certain the results you are obtaining match those described in the process.

3. If you want to understand the process thoroughly, first read it quickly to get an overview. As you read through again more slowly, take notes outlining the major steps of the process.

READING CRITICALLY

1. Check to see if the process could be completed differently or more effectively. Are there any cautions or warnings not included in the essay that should be there?

2. If the writer is explaining a process, is there evidence that his or her account is correct? Verify that there is good reason to believe the given account. If you believe there might be competing accounts of the process, test your suspicion by doing some research.

READING AS A WRITER

1. Observe how the writer uses verbs to indicate actions.

2. Notice how the writer gets from step to step in the process. If there is a strategy you could use, make note of it.

Bruce Jay Friedman

Eating Alone in Restaurants

Bruce Jay Friedman (born 1930) is a native of New York City and a 1951 graduate of the University of Missouri, where he majored in journalism. Between 1951 and 1953, he served in the U.S. Air Force and for the next decade was editorial director of a magazine management company. He now freelances. A versatile writer, Friedman has produced novels, plays, short stories, and non-fiction, earning critical acclaim as a humorist. In our selection, taken from The Lonely Guy's Book of Life *(1979), he offers the urban male who must dine out alone witty advice on coping with the situation.*

1   Hunched over, trying to be as inconspicuous as possible, a solitary diner slips into a midtown Manhattan steakhouse. No sooner does he check his coat than the voice of the headwaiter comes booming across the restaurant.

2   "Alone again, eh?"

3   As all eyes are raised, the bartender, with enormous good cheer, chimes in: "That's because they all left him high and dry."

4   And then, just in case there is a customer in the restaurant who isn't yet aware of the situation, a waiter shouts out from the buffet table: "Well, we'll take care of him anyway, won't we, fellas!"

Illustration in narrative form gets reader interest.

5   *Haw, haw, haw,* and a lot of sly winks and pokes in the ribs.

6   Eating alone in a restaurant is one of the most terrifying experiences in America.

7   Sniffed at by headwaiters, an object of scorn and amusement to couples, the solitary diner is the unwanted and unloved child of Restaurant Row. No sooner does he make his appearance than he is whisked out of sight and seated at a thin sliver of a table with barely enough room on it for an hors d'oeuvre. Wedged between busboy stations, a hair's breadth from the men's room, there he sits, feet lodged in a railing as if he were in Pilgrim stocks, wondering where he went wrong in life.

8   Rather than face this grim scenario, most Lonely Guys would prefer to nibble away at a tuna fish sandwich in the relative safety of their high-rise apartments.

9   What can be done to ease the pain of this not only starving but silent minority—to make dining alone in restaurants a rewarding experience? Absolutely nothing. But some small strategies *do* exist for making the experience bearable.

Before You Get There

> First step in process: preparation for going out.

10   Once the Lonely Guy has decided to dine alone at a restaurant, a sense of terror and foreboding will begin to build throughout the day. All the more reason for him to get there as quickly as possible so that the experience can soon be forgotten and he can resume his normal life. Clothing should be light and loose-fitting, especially around the neck—on the off chance of a fainting attack during the appetizer. It is best to dress modestly, avoiding both the funeral-director-style suit as well as the bold, eye-arresting costume of the gaucho. A single cocktail should suffice; little sympathy will be given to the Lonely Guy who tumbles in, stewed to the gills. (The fellow who stoops to putting morphine in his toes for courage does not belong in this discussion.) En route to the restaurant, it is best to play down dramatics, such as swinging the arms pluckily and humming the theme from *The Bridge on the River Kwai*.

Once You Arrive

> Second step in process: entering the restaurant.

11   The way your entrance comes off is of critical importance. Do not skulk in, slipping along the walls as if you are carrying some dirty little secret. There is no need, on the other hand, to fling your coat arrogantly at the hatcheck girl, slap the headwaiter across the cheeks with your gloves and demand to be seated immediately. Simply walk in with a brisk rubbing of the hands and approach the headwaiter. When asked how many are in your party, avoid cute responses such as "Jes lil ol' me." Tell him you are a party of one; the Lonely Guy who does not trust his voice can simply lift a finger. Do not launch into a story about how tired you are of taking out fashion models, night after night, and what a pleasure it is going to be to dine alone.

> Humorous warning.

12   It is best to arrive with no reservation. Asked to set aside a table for one, the restaurant owner will suspect either a prank on the part of an ex-waiter, or a terrorist plot, in which case windows will be boarded up and the kitchen bomb-swept. An advantage of the "no reservation" approach is that you will appear to have just stepped off the plane from Des Moines, your first night in years away from Marge and the kids.

> Third step in process: promenade to table.

13   All eyes will be upon you when you make the promenade to your table. Stay as close as possible to the headwaiter, trying to match him step for step. This will reduce your visibility and fool some diners into thinking you are a member of the staff. If you hear a

generalized snickering throughout the restaurant, do not assume automatically that you are being laughed at. The other diners may all have just recalled an amusing moment in a Feydeau farce.

14   If your table is unsatisfactory, do not demand imperiously that one for eight people be cleared immediately so that you can dine in solitary grandeur. Glance around discreetly and see if there are other possibilities. The ideal table will allow you to keep your back to the wall so that you can see if anyone is laughing at you. Try to get one close to another couple so that if you lean over at a 45-degree angle it will appear that you are a swinging member of their group. Sitting opposite a mirror can be useful; after a drink or two, you will begin to feel that there are a few of you.

> Cautions reader about where to sit.

15   Once you have been seated, and it becomes clear to the staff that you are alone, there will follow The Single Most Heartbreaking Moment in Dining Out Alone—when the second setting is whisked away and yours is spread out a bit to make the table look busier. This will be done with great ceremony by the waiter—angered in advance at being tipped for only one dinner. At this point, you may be tempted to smack your forehead against the table and curse the fates that brought you to this desolate position in life. A wiser course is to grit your teeth, order a drink and use this opportunity to make contact with other Lonely Guys sprinkled around the room. A menu or a leafy stalk of celery can be used as a shield for peering out at them. Do not expect a hearty greeting or a cry of "huzzah" from these frightened and browbeaten people. Too much excitement may cause them to slump over, curtains. Smile gently and be content if you receive a pale wave of the hand in return. It is unfair to imply that you have come to help them throw off their chains.

16   When the headwaiter arrives to take your order, do not be bullied into ordering the last of the gazelle haunches unless you really want them. Thrilled to be offered anything at all, many Lonely Guys will say "Get them right out here" and wolf them down. Restaurants take unfair advantage of Lonely Guys, using them to get rid of anything from withered liver to old heels of roast beef. Order anything you like, although it is good to keep to the light and simple in case of a sudden attack of violent stomach cramps.

> Fourth step in process: ordering food.

Some Proven Strategies

17   Once the meal is under way, a certain pressure will begin to build as couples snuggle together, the women clucking sympathetically in your direction. Warmth and conviviality will pervade the room, none of it encompassing you. At this point, many Lonely Guys will keep their eyes riveted to the restaurant paintings of early Milan or bury themselves in a paperback anthology they have no wish to read.

18   Here are some ploys designed to confuse other diners and make them feel less sorry for you:

19 ■ After each bite of food, lift your head, smack your lips thoughtfully, swallow and make a notation in a pad. Diners will assume you are a restaurant critic.

20 ■ Between courses, pull out a walkie-talkie and whisper a message into it. This will lead everyone to believe you are part of a police stake-out team, about to bust the salad man as an international dope dealer.

21 ■ Pretend you are a foreigner. This is done by pointing to items on the menu with an alert smile and saying to the headwaiter: "Is good, no?"

22 ■ When the main course arrives, brush the restaurant silverware off the table and pull some of your own out of a breastpocket. People will think you are a wealthy eccentric.

23 ■ Keep glancing at the door, and make occasional trips to look out at the street, as if you are waiting for a beautiful woman. Half-way through the meal, shrug in a world-weary manner and begin to eat with gusto. The world is full of women! Why tolerate bad manners! Life is too short.

The Right Way

24 One other course is open to the Lonely Guy, an audacious one, full of perils, but all the more satisfying if you can bring it off. That is to take off your dark glasses, sit erectly, smile broadly at anyone who looks in your direction, wave off inferior wines, and begin to eat with heartiness and enormous confidence. As outrageous as the thought may be—enjoy your own company. Suddenly, titters and sly winks will tail off, the head-waiter's disdain will fade, and friction will build among couples who will turn out to be not as tightly cemented as they appear. The heads of other Lonely Guys will lift with hope as you become the attractive center of the room.

25 If that doesn't work, you still have your fainting option.

> Final step in process: eating and enjoying one's own company.

DISCUSSION QUESTIONS

1. What details does the writer use to illustrate each step? Consider especially paragraphs 10, 14, and 15 to 23. Are there any details you find especially effective or amusing?

2. Consider the brevity of the paragraphs in this essay, especially the introductory and concluding paragraphs. Why do you think the writer has written such short paragraphs? What do you understand by the final sentence? Why do you think the writer did not take the process further—such as paying the bill and leaving the restaurant?

3. How and where does the writer use exaggeration for humorous effect? Does the humour work for you?

4. The article is mainly a how-to, focusing on the steps of eating alone in restaurants. Identify places where the writer employs other methods of development also, such as narration and description, illustration, and effect.

5. Although this is a light article, how does it also offer a bit of wisdom that the reader might take away?

TOWARD KEY INSIGHTS

This essay seems directed toward males who might go out to dine alone. Would women who might dine alone be likely to find it interesting? Why or why not? Does it seem plausible to you that the "Lonely Guy" would go out alone to eat at such a relatively high-end restaurant?

Have you ever felt self-conscious or anxious in going to a restaurant, party, movie, or other event by yourself? If so, how did you manage your discomfort?

SUGGESTION FOR WRITING *Think of a social situation where many people experience anxiety. Write an essay explaining how to be at ease in this situation.*

Tara Lee

Knife Skills: How to Choose the Right Knife and Wield it Like a Pro

Tara Lee teaches English at the University of British Columbia, and is a freelance food and restaurant writer who contributes to publications such as The Vancouver Sun, Northwest Palate, and The Georgia Straight, from which this article is adapted.

1   Does cutting up veggies with your kitchen knife make you slightly nervous? If so, it might be time to learn how to show your knives who's boss.

2   First of all, confident knife use requires a blade that is capable of making clean, efficient cuts. "Number one is to make sure your knife is sharp. A dull knife is your worst enemy," explains chef Curtis Webb of the Northwest Culinary Academy of Vancouver during a phone chat. He recommends realigning the edge of your blade by using a honing steel every 15 minutes during chopping sessions and having your knife professionally sharpened several times a year.

3   Webb teaches a knife skills class that covers honing and sharpening as well as a variety of cutting techniques. When tackling round fruits and vegetables, he suggests, slice off a side to make a flat surface to place on the cutting board so those suckers don't roll around as you're trying to cut them. If students are intimidated, Webb tells them to breathe deeply: "Try and relax. It's about being slow and steady. Work on your consistency, and then you can move on to speed afterwards."

4   Giulia Vendramin, director of admissions at the Pacific Institute of Culinary Arts, says it's important for home cooks to learn standard cutting techniques, such as a basic dice, brunoise (an 1/8-inch dice), julienne cut (matchsticks), and chiffonade (raglike strips of herbs), and to aim for uniformity when cutting. "That way, the pieces all cook at the same rate," she says.

5   Vendramin also emphasizes the importance of protecting the hand gripping the food by shaping it into a claw, tucking those fingers out of harm's way. She gives another safety tip over the phone: "When your knife drops, just let it fall. Don't try to catch it." As well, make your cutting board slip-proof by putting a damp kitchen towel or paper towel underneath it.

6   David Robertson, chef and owner of the Dirty Apron Cooking School and Delicatessen, emphasizes that gaining strong knife skills takes consistent practice. "It's homework that you need to take home with you," he says over the phone.

7   And that bad habit of constantly lifting up the tip of your knife and hacking downward? Robertson says your knife should always move in a fluid, rocking motion. "You need to treat your knife like a wheel moving forward. Always try to keep your knife on

the cutting board as you're cutting through something," he instructs. Robertson adds that using a knife is easier if you invest in a decent one.

8   Cookware stores like Ming Wo are good places to get a feel for what's right for you. "You can't buy a knife by just reading about it. You need to come in and hold them, and see what feels good in your hand. That's the most important thing," explains Ling Tao, a sales associate at Ming Wo.

9   "A lot of chefs on the Food Network and a lot of local chefs like the Japanese knives because they're very sharp and the blades are very thin," Ling Tao adds. "They do a lot of precision cutting." The bottom line on choosing the right knife? "Don't buy a knife because it looks cool. Buy it if it feels comfortable in your hand," says Robertson. With the perfect knife and the correct skills, you can cut with confidence.

DISCUSSION QUESTIONS

1. Characterize the kind of audience the writer is addressing. How do you know?
2. What does the writer do at the beginning to get the reader's attention, and how does she conclude? What order does she follow through the article?
3. Explain how the writer brings in quotations from others she has talked to about using knives in the kitchen, and what these quotations add to the article.

TOWARD KEY INSIGHTS

Did you learn anything new from this article that you may not have thought about before?

Can you think of a skill that seems very simple and clear at first glance, but in fact is more complicated than it seems to be? What would you focus on if you were writing a guide to this skill?

SUGGESTIONS FOR WRITING

1. Write an essay that explains an online process such as how to join a social media group to a member of the older generation who has never done anything on the computer except use email and conduct basic searches.
2. Interview several students about the stages they experienced in learning to adapt to university, get a job, or get their debt under control. Then write a paper discussing these stages, including relevant quotations to illustrate your points.
3. Explain to a student who wants a vacation break how to use the Internet to plan an affordable two-week vacation.

MyWritingLab

How Do I Get a Better Grade?

Go to **www.mywritinglab .com** for additional help with your grammar, writing, and research skills. You will have access to a variety of exercises, instruction, and videos that will help you improve your basic skills and help you get a better grade.

CHAPTER 9

Strategies for Analytical Writing: Cause and Effect

EXPLAINING WHY

Cause and effect are inseparably linked. Together they make up *causation*. Cause probes the reasons why actions, events, attitudes, and conditions exist. Effect examines their consequences. Causation can help explain historical events, natural happenings, and the actions and attitudes of individuals and groups. It can also help us anticipate the consequences of personal actions, natural phenomena, or government policies.

Everyone uses questions of causation in daily life. For example, Scott wonders why Gina *really* broke off their relationship, and Alysha speculates on the consequences of changing her major. Many wonder why homeless populations are on the rise in Canadian cities, and millions worry about the causes and effects of climate change on our planet.

At work, an employer might want an analysis of the reasons why a certain product is sometimes malfunctioning, or an analysis of the reasons why a new product is not selling. At school, your instructors might ask you to write on topics such as the political or social consequences of a terrorist incident, the effects of the fluctuating U.S. dollar on the Canadian economy, or the effects of attending residential schools on Aboriginal peoples and their descendants.

Since you will need to analyze causes and effect in papers and reports that you write, consider some possible organizing patterns.

PATTERNS IN CAUSAL ANALYSIS

Several organizational patterns are used in a causal analysis. Sometimes, a single cause produces several effects. For instance, poor language skills prevent students from keeping up with required reading, taking adequate notes, and writing competent papers and essay exams. Below, the outline on the left shows a pattern for a paper that traces a single cause with multiple effects; on the right, you can see how this pattern could be used for a paper analyzing the effects of having poor language skills in school.

I. Introduction: identifies cause	I. Poor language skills
II. Body	II. Body
A. Effect number 1	A. Can't keep up with required reading
B. Effect number 2	B. Can't take adequate notes
C. Effect number 3	C. Can't write competent papers or exams
III. Conclusion	III. Conclusion

Alternatively, you might discuss the cause after the effects are presented.

On the other hand, several causes may join forces to produce one effect. For example, if you were looking at a university student's large debt load, you might note several causes: tuition fees are higher than ever before, the student finds it easy to use credit and debit cards to purchase things, the student's parents have not modelled good money management, and the student does not have training in financial literacy. Note how the outline on the left below shows a pattern for analyzing how multiple causes may contribute to a single effect; on the right, you'll see how this pattern could be used to outline the reasons for a particular student's large debt load.

I. Introduction: identifies effect	I. High student debt
II. Body	II. Body
A. Cause number 1	A. High tuition fees
B. Cause number 2	B. Easy access to debit cards, credit cards, and online shopping
C. Cause number 3	C. Poor parental modelling
D. Cause number 3	D. Lack of training in financial literacy
III. Conclusion	III. Conclusion

As an alternative, you might discuss the effects after presenting the causes.

Often a set of events forms a causal chain, wherein each event is the effect of the preceding one and the cause of the following one. For example, a student sleeps late and so misses breakfast and ends up hungry and distracted, which in turn results in a poor performance on an exam. Interrupting the chain at any point halts the sequence. Such chains can be likened to a row of falling dominoes. The entry of the United States into the Vietnam War illustrates a causal chain: One major cause of the war was a widespread belief in the domino theory, which held that if one nation in Southeast Asia fell to the communist enemy, all would fall, one after the other.

Causal chains can also help explain how cultural and social changes proceed. The popularity of ebooks and ereaders, for example, has led to a softening of the market for paper books and magazines, which in turn has led to a crisis in traditional publishing in North America. This crisis has then motivated publishing companies to launch new digital publishing platforms. In many situations, the sequence of causes and effects is too complex to fit the image of a chain. Suppose you are driving to a movie on a rainy night. You approach an intersection screened by bushes, and because you have the right of way you start to drive across. Suddenly, a car with unlit headlights looms directly in your path. You hit the brakes but skid on the slippery pavement and crash into the other car, crumpling its left fender and damaging your own bumper. Later, as you think through the episode, you become aware of its complexities.

Obviously, the *immediate cause* of the accident was the other driver's failure to heed the stop sign. But other causes also played roles: the bushes and unlit headlights that kept you from seeing the other car sooner; the starts and stops, speedups and slowdowns that brought the two cars to the intersection at the same time; the wet pavement that made you more likely to skid; and the movie that brought you out in the first place.

You also realize that the effects of the accident go beyond the fender and bumper damage. After the accident, a police officer ticketed the other driver. As a result of the delay, you missed the movie. Further, the accident unnerved you so badly that you couldn't attend classes the next day and therefore missed an important writing assignment. Because of a bad driving record, the other driver lost his licence for 60 days. Clearly, the effects of this accident, like the causes, are complex.

Here's how you might organize a multiple cause–multiple effect essay:

I.	Introduction	I.	The accident
II.	Body	II.	Body
	A. Cause number 1		A. Driver ran stop sign
	B. Cause number 2		B. Bushes and unlit headlights impaired vision
	C. Cause number 3		C. Wet pavement caused skidding
	D. Effect number 1		D. Missed the movie
	E. Effect number 2		E. Unnerved so missed classes next day
	F. Effect number 3		F. Other driver lost licence
III.	Conclusion	III.	Conclusion

In some situations, you might first present the effects, then turn to the causes.

EXERCISE

1. **Read the following paragraph and then arrange the events in a causal chain.**

Although some folk societies still exist today, similar human groups began the slow process of evolving into more complex societies many millennia ago, through settlement in villages and through advances in technology and organizational structure. This gave rise to the second level of organization: civilized preindustrial, or "feudal," society. Here there is a surplus of food because of the selective cultivation of grains—and also because of the practice of animal husbandry. The food surplus permits both the specialization of labor and the kind of class structure that can, for instance, provide the leadership and command the manpower to develop and maintain extensive irrigation systems (which in turn makes possible further increases in the food supply).

Gideon Sjoberg, "The Origin and Development of Cities"

2. **Brainstorm about the possible effects of an aging population on the Canadian labour force, economy, or health care system. Then do a quick web search to see what other effects you might identify.**

REASONING ERRORS IN CAUSAL ANALYSIS

Ignoring Multiple Causes

An effect rarely stems from a single cause. The person who believes that an upsurge in sexually transmitted infections is due to media portrayals of sex or who blames video game violence for a child's aggression oversimplifies these situations. While media images and video game violence may be contributing causes, numerous other factors undoubtedly contribute as well.

Mistaking Chronology for Causation

Don't assume that, just because one event follows another, the first necessarily causes the second. Therese breaks a mirror just before Wade breaks off their engagement; then she blames the cracked mirror. Youth crime rates may have declined in Canada since the Youth Criminal Justice Act was introduced, but does this necessarily mean that the introduction of the Act has caused the decline? Don't misunderstand: One event *may* cause the next event, but before you go on record with your conclusion, make sure that you're not dealing with mere chronology.

Confusing Causes with Effects

Young children sometimes declare that the moving trees make the wind blow. Similarly, you may assume that Tara's relationship breakdown caused her depression, but perhaps her undiagnosed depression caused her relationship breakdown. Scan your evidence carefully to avoid such faulty assertions.

EXERCISE *Which of the following statements point toward papers that focus on causes? Which point toward papers that focus on effects? Explain your answers.*

1. There are many reasons why more immigrants than working-age people from the general Canadian population are earning university degrees.

2. While offshore oil exploration will produce new jobs, it may also damage the marine environment in a number of ways.

3. Children who live in poverty are twice as likely as other children to have poor health, low scores on school readiness exams, and high remediation needs.

ETHICAL ISSUES

We need to be thoughtful and honest when we ascribe causes and effects; they can be abused either accidentally or deliberately. When the causes of something difficult to understand are obscure and complex, it can be tempting to latch on to an untested theory of causation that may, if accepted, result in great suffering. In the 1940s, the term so called *frigid mother* was coined when autism and schizophrenia were blamed on cold, rejecting parents, especially a frigid mother. It is also common to confuse causation with correlation—just because two things happen at the same time, we cannot assume that one thing causes the other. If there is a major bank crisis soon after a particular politician comes into office, one cannot automatically assume that the politician has caused the crisis. Skewing evidence so that some effects are ignored can also be an ethical violation. Imagine the consequences of an article that touts a new medication but fails to mention several serious side effects that could harm many users. Asking and answering the following questions can help you meet the ethical responsibilities of writing a cause-and-effect paper.

- Have I tried to uncover all of the causes that might result in a particular outcome? A report blaming poor instruction alone for a high failure rate in a town's public schools almost certainly overlooks such factors as oversized classes, inadequate facilities, and economic deprivation.

- Have I carefully weighed the importance of the causes I've uncovered? If only two or three of the classes in the school system are oversized, the report should not dwell on the significance of class size.

- Have I tried to uncover and discuss every important effect, even one that might damage a case I'm trying to make? A report emphasizing the beneficial effects of jogging would be negligent if it failed to note the potential for injury.

- What would be the consequences if people acted on my advice?

Careful evaluation of causes and effects shows that you have taken your ethical obligations as a writer seriously.

WRITING A CAUSAL ANALYSIS

> - For more personal essays, brainstorm or freewrite about circumstances in your life with effects that could interest others, such as "why I decided to participate in a tough obstacle race" or "the effects of a reading disability on my life."
>
> - For more research-based essays, keep notes on current social trends or news events. You might read editorials or watch shows such as CBC's *Doc Zone* to get ideas.
>
> - Note topics that may be of interest and broad appeal, such as why people become addicted to video games or the reasons why university students cheat in courses.

PREWRITING: FINDING YOUR TOPIC

DEVELOPING YOUR CAUSE AND EFFECT

- Identify the audience and purpose for your paper. What do you want to accomplish and why would people be interested?
- Decide whether you would be better off focusing on causes, effects, or both.
- Brainstorm causes and effects. Research examples and details.
- For causes, identify how significant each cause is, what role it played in producing the effect, and whether it is part of a chain.
- For effects, identify the importance of the evidence and how the cause produced the effects.

The strategies discussed on pages 37–43 in Chapter 3 can also help you find several topics. Answer these questions about each potential candidate:

What purpose guides this writing?

Who is my audience? Will the topic interest them? Why or why not?

Shall I focus on causes, effects, or both?

Brainstorming your topic for supporting details should be straightforward. If you're dealing with causes, consider these questions about each one:

How significant is this cause?

Could it have brought about the effect by itself?

Does it form part of a chain?

How does it precisely contribute to the effect?

For papers dealing with effects, ask these questions:

How important is this effect?

What evidence will establish its importance?

Charting your results can help you prepare for writing the paper. You might tabulate causes with an arrangement like this one:

Cause	**Contribution to Effect**
First cause	Specific contribution
Second cause	Specific contribution

For effects, use this chart:

Effect	**Importance**
First effect	Why important
Second effect	Why important

A **thesis statement** for a cause-and-effect paper often identifies the event to be explained or the effects to be considered, explains the importance of understanding the causes or effects, and sometimes offers a summary of the major causes or effects.

For example, "In the last 35 years North Americans started consuming significantly more calories partly because of greater food availability, more snacking, larger average food portions, and increased consumption of carbohydrates."

To aid in forming your thesis statement, identify the reasons you think the topic is important and the major causes or effects you need to discuss. Your thesis statement can be a question that the paper answers and often signals whether the paper concerns causes, effects, or both. Use the opening of your paper to identify your topic and indicate whether you plan to discuss causes, effects, or both. You can signal your intention in a number of ways. To prepare for a focus on causes, you might use the words *cause*, *reason*, or *stem from*, or you might ask why something has occurred. To signal a paper on effects, you might use *effect*, *fallout*, *consequence*, or *result*, or you might ask what has happened since something took place. Read these examples:

Signals causes: Sudbury's recent decrease in street crime stems from its expanded educational program, increased job opportunities for young people, and a falling rate of drug addiction.

Signals effects: Climate change has affected global food production in several ways.

Signals effects: How has my social life changed since my marriage?

How you organize the body of the paper depends on your topic. Close scrutiny may reveal that one cause was indispensable; the other causes merely played supporting roles. If so, discuss the main cause first. For example, when analyzing your car accident, start with the failure of the other driver to yield the right of way; then fan out to any other causes that merit mentioning. Sometimes, you'll find that no single cause was at fault but that all of them helped matters along. Combinations of this kind lie at the heart of many social and economic concerns, such as depression and urban crime rates. Weigh each cause carefully and rank the causes in importance. If your topic and purpose would profit from building suspense, work from the least important cause to the most important one. For analyzing causal chains, chronological order works most effectively.

If space won't permit you to deal adequately with every cause, pick out the two or three you consider most important and limit your discussion to them. To avoid giving your reader an oversimplified impression, acknowledge that other causes exist. However, ensure that you stay on topic. Even with no length limitation, don't attempt to trace every cause to more remote causes and then to still more remote ones. Instead, determine a sensible cut-off point that fits your purpose.

Treat effects as carefully as you treat causes. Keep in mind that effects often travel in packs, and try to arrange them in some logical order. If they occur together, consider order of climax. If one follows the other in a chain-like sequence, present them in that fashion. If you are close to the maximum length permitted, limit your discussion to the most interesting or significant effects. Whatever order you choose for your paper, don't jump helter-skelter from cause to effect to cause in a way that leaves your reader bewildered.

It's important to remember, however, that you're not just listing causes and effects; you're showing the reader their connection to serve a larger purpose. Let's see how one student handled this connection. After you've read "Why Students Drop Out of University," the student essay in this chapter, carefully re-examine paragraph 3. Note how the sentence beginning "In many schools" and the two following it show precisely how poor study habits develop. Note further how the sentence beginning "This laxity produces" and the three following it show precisely how such poor habits result in "low grades and failure." University students who read this causal analysis are better armed to avoid poor study habits and their consequences.

Causal analyses can end in several ways. A paper discussing the effects of the mountain pine beetle infestation on Canada's forests might specify the far-reaching consequences of failing to address the problem, or it might recommend strategies for dealing with it. Frequently, writers use their conclusions to emphasize the larger implications of causes or effects. Here are strategies for drafting a cause-and-effect paper.

Introduction

- Employ an attention getter that ties the topic to a reader's interest. "Your home may be hazardous to your health."
- Identify the topic that will be explored.
- Clearly signal whether the paper will focus on cause or effect.
- In a longer paper, possibly mention the major causes or effects that will be discussed.

Body

- Determine if you are going to discuss all the causes or effects or narrow them.
- Determine the best organizational strategy: main cause followed by causes with a supporting role, or multiple causes discussed in order of importance, or chains leading to an effect.
- Support causes or effects with examples, details, or statistics.
- Paragraph according to key causes or effects, with clear transitions.

Conclusion

- Stress the consequences of not taking such action, such as the impact of acid rain on Canada's lakes.
- Or suggest something will be done or encourage the reader to act.
- Or evaluate the importance of their causes or effects.

Revising the Causal Analysis

Follow the guidelines in Chapter 4 and answer these questions as you revise your causal analysis:

- How could the paper better achieve its purpose or reach its audience?
- Does the focus on causes, effects, or both accomplish the goal of the paper?
- Does the paper address the important causes and effects necessary for its purpose? Brainstorm or do additional research.
- Does the paper address the right relationships? Check your brainstorming to determine if the paper needs to address a causal chain, an immediate cause with several supporting causes, or multiple causes and effects.
- Are there any mistakes in reasoning? Test to see that other causes aren't neglected, chronology is not mistaken for causation, and causes are not confused with effects.

- Where could the order and relationship between causes and effects be clearer or placed in a better order?
- Where could the discussion be supported with better explanation, details, examples, or statistics?
- Where could the paragraphs be better focused or developed? Too many causes or effects in a paragraph can be confusing.
- Where could the transitions be made clearer?
- Does the paper accurately and ethically represent the causes or effects and their relationships without distortion?

EXAMPLE OF A STUDENT ESSAY USING CAUSE AND EFFECT

Why Students Drop Out of University

Diann Fisher

1   Each fall, a new crop of first-year university students, wavering between high hopes for the future and intense anxiety about their new status, scan campus maps searching for their classrooms. They have been told repeatedly that university is the key to a well-paying job, and they certainly don't want to support themselves by flipping hamburgers or working at some other dead-end job. So, notebooks at the ready, they await what university has in store. Unfortunately many of them—indeed, over 30 percent—will not return after the first year. Why do so many students leave? There are several reasons. Some find the academic program too hard, some lack the proper study habits or motivation, others fall victim to the temptations of the environment, and a large group leave for personal reasons.

> Identifies importance of topic and area of concern. Identifies primary question and main causes to be discussed.

2   Not surprisingly, the academic shortcomings of university students have strong links to high school. In the past, a high school student who lacked the ability or desire to get postsecondary education or training could still find a job with decent pay, perhaps in the resource sector. Now that possibility scarcely exists, so many poorly prepared students feel compelled to try college or university. Getting accepted by some schools isn't difficult. Once in, though, the student who has taken nothing beyond general mathematics, English, and science faces serious trouble when confronted with advanced algebra, first-year English, and biological or physical science. Most universities do offer remedial courses and other assistance that may help some weaker students to survive. In spite of everything, however, many others find themselves facing ever-worsening grades and either fail or just give up.

> Transition identifies first major cause. Provides detail of related causes producing lack of preparation. Offers qualification, but links major cause with effect.

Transitions to second
cause.
Provides details that lead
to poor study habits.
Explains relationship
between cause and result.

3   Like academic shortcomings, poor study habits have their roots in high school, where even average students can often breeze through with a minimum of effort. In many schools, outside assignments are rare and so easy that they require little time or thought to complete. To accommodate slower students, teachers frequently repeat material so many times that slightly better students can grasp it without opening their books. And when papers are late, teachers often don't mark them down. This laxity produces students who can't or don't want to study, students totally unprepared for the rigorous demands of university. There, courses may require several hours of study each week in order to be passed with even a C. In many programs, outside assignments are commonplace and demanding. Instructors expect students to grasp material after one explanation, and many won't accept late papers at all. Students who don't quickly develop disciplined study habits may face low grades and failure.

Provides transition to
next cause.
Details relate sequence
of events that result
in effect.

4   Poor student motivation aggravates faulty study habits. Students who thought high school was boring find even less allure in the more challenging university offerings. Lacking any commitment to do well, they shrug off assigned papers, skip classes, and avoid doing required reading. Over time, classes gradually shrink as more and more students stay away. With final exams upon them, some return in a last-ditch effort to salvage a passing grade, but by then it is too late. Eventually, repetition of this scenario forces the students out.

Offers a transition to the
next cause.
Provides supporting
details.
Links cause to result under
discussion.

5   In addition, the wide range of freedoms offered by the university environment can overwhelm even well-prepared newcomers. While students are in high school, parents are on hand to make them study, push them off to class, and send them to bed at a reasonable hour. Once away from home and parents, however, far too many students become caught up in a constant round of parties, dates, and other distractions that seem more fascinating than school work. Again, if such behaviour persists, poor grades and failure result.

Offers transition to final
cause discussed.
Provides supporting
examples.

6   Personal reasons also take a heavy toll on students who might otherwise complete their programs successfully. Often, money problems are at fault. For example, a student may lose a scholarship or grant, fail to obtain needed work, or find that the family can no longer afford to help out. Some students succumb to homesickness; some are forced out by an illness, injury, or death in the family; and yet others become ill or injured themselves and leave to recuperate. Finally, a considerable number become disillusioned with their programs or the size, location, or atmosphere of their schools and decide not to return.

7   What happens to the students who drop out? Some re-enrol later, often in less demanding schools that offer a better chance of academic success. Of the

remainder, the great majority find jobs. Most, whatever their choice, go on to lead productive, useful lives. <u>In the meantime, campus newcomers need to know about the dangers that tripped up so many of their predecessors and make every effort to avoid them.</u>

> Identifies effects of item under consideration. Challenges the reader.

DISCUSSION QUESTIONS

1. Identify the thesis statement in this essay. Who is the audience and what is the larger purpose for this essay?

2. How do paragraphs 2 and 3 show the relationship between cause and effect in a causal chain?

3. Note how the author uses transitions to move into discussion of the first cause (paragraph 2) and the second cause (paragraph 3), as well as the next several causes (paragraphs 4 to 6). Why do you think the author chose to focus more on causes than effects until the final paragraph?

SUGGESTIONS FOR WRITING *Use one of the topics below, or another that your instructor approves, to develop a causal analysis. Determine which causes and/or effects to consider. Scrutinize your analysis for errors in reasoning, settle on an organization, and write the essay.*

1. Effects of cellphones use on family life, social life, or work life

2. Causes and/or effects of a particular kind of stress or pressure on university students

3. Causes and/or effects of bullying in public schools or elsewhere

4. Reasons for the popularity of a particular trend among teenagers (gaming, marijuana use, text messaging, gang culture) or another group of people

5. Positive and/or negative consequences of a recent change in public policy regarding health care, education, law, or an other field

6. Effects of media coverage of a recent incident of violence that has occurred in Canada or elsewhere

7. Effects (or mixture of causes and effects) of a particular obsession or minor addiction (worry, gossip, video games, energy drinks, etc.)

8. Benefits of participating in a particular healthful practice or sport

Stepping Up to Synthesis

Although nearly everyone recognizes the role of causation in human affairs, people's opinions differ about the causes and effects of important matters. What factors contribute to the North American habit of eating fast food? Why are women more likely than men to leave management jobs? What are the causes and/or effects of child poverty in Canada? What impact does identity theft have on society? Obviously, such questions lack simple answers; as a result, even when investigators agree on the causes and effects involved, they often debate their relative importance.

PREWRITING FOR SYNTHESIS

Suppose that your business instructor has asked you to investigate the departure of women from managerial positions. Library and Internet searches reveal several articles on this topic that identify a number of causes. Some women leave because they find it harder to advance than men do, and as a result they seldom attain senior positions. Others leave because they receive lower salaries than their male counterparts. Still others leave because of the stifling effects of corporate rigidity, unrealistic expectations, or the demands of raising a family. Although most articles cite these causes, the relative importance of each cause is debatable. For example, one researcher emphasizes family concerns by discussing them last and at greatest length. Another puts the chief blame on obstacles to upward mobility—the "glass ceiling" that blocks women from upper-level positions along with an "old-boy network" of entrenched executives that parcels out jobs among its members.

CRITICALLY EVALUATING YOUR SOURCES

Once you've finished your research, your job is to sift through all of these causes and synthesize (see pages 323–331) the views of your sources with your own views. Before you start to write, though, take some time to consider carefully each cause and effect you've uncovered. Obviously, you should ground your paper with well-supported and widely acknowledged causes and effects, but you can also include more speculative ones as long as you clearly indicate their hypothetical nature. For example, one researcher who mentions corporate rigidity as a reason that women leave management jobs clearly labels this explanation as a theory, yet she backs it up with only a single example. As you examine your research, ask yourself these critical questions as well as any others that occur to you: Does any researcher exhibit obvious bias? Do the studies cited include a sufficient number of examples to be meaningful? Do the statistics appear reliable, or are some out of date, irrelevant, or skimpy? Have the researchers avoided reasoning errors? Whenever you find a flaw, note where the problem lies so that you can discuss it in your writing if you choose. Such discussions often clear up common misconceptions.

PLANNING AND DEVELOPING YOUR SYNTHESIS

There are various possibilities for organizing your paper. If your sources substantially agree on the most important cause of a particular issue, you might begin with that cause and then take up the others. A second possibility, the order-of-climax arrangement, reverses the procedure by starting with secondary causes and ending with the most significant one. You can use the same options for organizing effects. When no clear consensus exists about the relative importance of the different causes and effects, organize the material in a way that is easy to understand and interesting to read.[1]

---

[1]Because this type of paper draws on published information, it is important to read the sections on research in Chapters 14 and 15 and those on handling quotations and avoiding plagiarism in Chapter 16 before you start to write. As always, follow your instructor's guidelines for documenting sources.

SUGGESTIONS FOR WRITING

1. Read three articles on the causes of a major social controversy, such as First Nations land claims, Canadian drug policies, or an enterprise such as the oil sands exploration project in Alberta, and incorporate those causes and your own views in a paper. Be sure that you have read Chapters 16 and 17 on documentation, and cite appropriately where needed.

2. Write an essay that corrects a common misconception about the causes or effects of a matter in your community about which you feel strongly. Possibilities might include the causes of homelessness in your region or the effects of zero-tolerance policies in schools.

CAUSE AND EFFECT ESSAYS: PROFESSIONAL MODELS

READING STRATEGIES

1. Identify the central event of the essay around which the causes and effects are organized.
2. Determine whether the writer is identifying a chain of causes that yields a single result or multiple causes for the same event.
3. Read carefully before determining the writer's main point. In more sophisticated academic writing, writers often first present several causes or effects, both worthy and unworthy. Only after ruling some out with key explanations do they reveal which ones they think are most plausible.
4. It can be helpful to make a diagram showing the connection between the causes and the effects.

READING CRITICALLY

1. Evaluate the evidence the writer gives for the relationship between cause and effect. How does he or she prove that the causes link to the effects as described?
2. Determine whether there could be other causes or effects that the writer hasn't mentioned.
3. Writers often confuse *correlation* and *causation*. Just because something happens close to the same time as another event (correlates) doesn't mean that it is the cause of the event. Does the writer confuse correlation and causation?

READING AS A WRITER

1. Note how the writer organizes the causes and effects to keep them clear and distinct.
2. Observe what devices the writer uses to demonstrate the connection between the causes and the effects.
3. Examine how the writer pulls his or her ideas together in the conclusion.

Kristine Nyhout

Send in the Clowns

Kristine Nyhout is a freelance writer living in London, Ontario. She frequently writes on family issues, particularly the joys and challenges of raising a special-needs child. "Send in the Clowns" traces the physical and emotional benefits of laughter.

1   You exercise, eat the right foods and take vitamins. If you really want to stay healthy, try laughing more each day. It may sound silly, but health professionals are taking laughter seriously and using it to help people heal. Twenty years ago, the best-seller *Anatomy of an Illness* inspired the first research. When author Norman Cousins was diagnosed with a rare arthritis-like disease, he refused to accept pain as a fact of life. With his physician's approval, he checked in to a hotel and watched funny movies. He timed the effects: a belly laugh kept pain at bay for two hours. Now mainstream scientists are investigating humour's effects on health: it's no joke because jocularity has real psychological and physiological effects—from reducing stress to affecting production of hormones.

2   So the next time you visit a hospital, you may well see a red-nosed therapeutic clown or humour specialist—health professionals trained to get laughs—among white-coated doctors. Comedy carts filled with doses of satirical verse or slapstick films roll down the corridors. Consultants even bring the comedy preventive to workplace wellness seminars—apparently laughter also boosts creativity and productivity. Regina therapist Catherine Ripplinger Fenwick recognized the importance of humour when she battled breast cancer eight years ago. "I didn't laugh enough." She outfitted herself with a laughter first aid kit, took up clowning during her chemotherapy, and noticed the "wows" of life. Now she lectures government employees and others in the benefits of mirth.

3   Bringing humour into hospital helps defuse patient anxiety and change attitudes. One of the new healing clowns, registered nurse Dee Preikschas of Kitchener, Ont., tuned in to humour's healing power when her husband became ill. Now she's one of a number of therapeutic clowns in Canada who often work with children. Once Preikschas was dispatched to the bedside of a 10-year-old boy recovering from an appendectomy—he hated his IV and wasn't eating. By giving the kid a "magic" hammer that made a smashing noise at the offending IV, the clown got the boy to laugh—and cooperate. Clowns also bring comfort. Joy Van Herwaarde, who calls herself Joybells when she's clowning, says, "Humour can make someone less aware of the pain and can make them feel less lonely." Indeed, when a 101-year-old woman at Good Samaritan Hospital in Edmonton neared death, she asked for Joybells's brand of comfort. In Hamilton, Ont., nurse Sharon Orovan is using and studying humour to fend off panic attacks.

4   Humour also packs a physical punch. A sort of pharmacist of silliness, humour specialist Barbara Wetmore-Patel of London, Ont., dispenses videos and joke books from her comedy cart. How does it work? The laughing response can lower both heart rate and blood pressure, increase T-cell activity to fend off illness, and may improve digestion. Wetmore-Patel has seen how humour helps seniors in retirement homes and palliative care hospitals feel better physically. Laughing may release endorphins—chemicals in the brain responsible for the feeling of well-being known as runner's high—into the bloodstream, taking the edge off pain.

5   What's more, laughter may actually help keep you from getting sick. When you laugh, an antibody called immunoglobulin A travels from the bloodstream to the salivary glands where it blocks viruses from their usual port of entry, explains Herb Lefcourt, a psychology professor at the University of Waterloo. Lefcourt's research found that people who used humour more in their daily lives had higher levels of immunoglobulin A in their saliva. And when your body is under stress (as in a fight-or-flight confrontation), your immune system is suppressed. Lefcourt found humour defuses that state of arousal, allowing the immune system to continue doing its job.

> Writer further develops the idea that laughter has physical health benefits.

6   Laughter can also lead to deeper breathing and relaxed muscles, according to physiologist David Garlick at the University of New South Wales in Sydney, Australia. Tense muscles can mean increased heart rate and blood pressure. Adrenaline levels and mental stress may also go up, Garlick adds. You may not be able to meditate during a meeting, but as Garlick points out, "Laughter is the usual way of helping to relieve muscle tension."

> More physical benefits.

7   You don't have to be a stand-up comic to reap the health benefits of a chuckle—just look on the light side of life.

> Simple, brief, light-hearted conclusion mirrors the theme of entire essay.

DISCUSSION QUESTIONS

1. Study the introductory paragraph and the concluding paragraph. What is the relationship between them?
2. Identify five or six positive effects of laughter that are discussed in paragraphs 3 to 6.
3. How are paragraphs 4, 5, and 6 related? On what basis did the writer make the decision to separate these paragraphs?
4. What examples, or brief anecdotes, does the writer use to illustrate the benefits of laughter?
5. While this essay focuses on the effects of laughter, it also has a persuasive, or argumentative, slant. What strategies does the writer use to persuade you that laughter is beneficial for health? Why do you suppose the writer does not cite statistics to strengthen her argument?

TOWARD KEY INSIGHTS

To what extent do you agree with Kristine Nyhout that physical health and emotional health may be related?

Some people go to classes such as "Laughter Yoga," dedicated to promoting laughter. Could you imagine seeking out opportunities to laugh in this way? Why or why not?

How can humour help with other stressful situations besides physical illness?

Are there ever times when humour could strike the wrong note? Explain.

SUGGESTION FOR WRITING *Interview three or four people who are knowledgeable about some aspect of health, and write an essay persuading your reader of the positive effects of a specific healthful practice, such as weight lifting, vegetarianism, or meditation. Explain the benefits with short anecdotes, examples, and quotations from your interviewees.*

Chris Wood

Dry Spring: The Coming Water Crisis of North America

Chris Wood is an international journalist and former Maclean's *magazine editor who has written for many Canadian publications, such as* The Globe and Mail, *the* Financial Post, *and* The Walrus. *He has also won two National Magazine Awards for his work on water. His most recent book on water is* Down the Drain: How We Are Failing to Protect Our Water Resources, *co-authored with Ralph Pentland. He lives on Vancouver Island, where he contributes to local efforts toward sustainability. The following essay is a slight abridgement of the prologue to a book by the same title.*

1   You often hear that water is life. And if water in its molecular essence—a pair of hydrogen atoms bonded to one of oxygen—is not itself life, it is, nonetheless, essential to it. We can find simple life in a remarkable range of environments. We've found bacteria in the deepest oceans, sustained by sulphurous exhalations from volcanic vents. Microbes endure and replicate at temperatures approaching absolute zero in the frozen crevices of Antarctic glaciers. We've found life on the highest mountains and beneath deserts that get only millimetres of rain annually. The only place we've never found it is in the absolute absence of water.

2   That fact seems to reside in the pre-conscious memory of our species. It emerges in the many ways that water is enlaced in the sacred. A practitioner of no particular religion, I've always found it easier to feel a Creator's presence when I visit the shore and watch the waves come in. Christians exercise the sacrament of baptism by immersing believers in pools or streams, or anointing them with water made holy by prayer. Hindus are called to bathe at least once in their lives in the sacred Ganges River. "We made from water every living thing," Allah reveals in the Qur'an, which further instructs the faithful to wash with water before each daily prayer.[1] Jews seek ritual purification in the *mikvah*, a specially built pool of natural water.

3   If life and the sacred strike you as insufficiently pragmatic considerations, then look at the economy. Nothing—absolutely *nothing*—is made, sold, traded or supplied without water. That is most obviously true for food. The 11,000 litres of water used to grow the ingredients of a single hamburger (bun, beef and condiments) would fill more than 75 bathtubs.[2] This is less evident but just as true for every other product. It would require two large tanker trucks to deliver the 33,000 litres of water needed to manufacture an ordinary desktop computer.[3] Now picture a convoy of 22 such tankers and you have the 400,000 litres that go into the average new car.[4] Many policy analysts describe the trading of the invisible but necessary water that goes into farm and factory products as the sale of "virtual" water. By this thinking, Canada sends between two and five *Exxon Valdez*–size shiploads of virtual water to the United States every day in the form of synthetic crude oil, which takes up to four-and-a-half barrels of water for each barrel of crude extracted from boreal "tar" sands.[5]

4   Toward the end of the 1990s, the same newsmagazine assigned me to write a story about the breathtaking new gadgets promised by the era's frenzied technology boom. As my research looked into the future, however, I became aware of an uncomfortable disconnect. At the same time that technophiles were imagining breathtaking capabilities

for new developments in computing, nanotechnology and genetic science, other fore-casts, no less rigorous and in some cases much more firmly footed on present-day trends, called attention to a variety of rising threats to our society's optimistic trajectory. Among them were the depletion of the world's oceans and an impending peak in oil production. How to feed the world's increasingly urbanized and prosperous billions of inhabitants from diminishing acres of farmland was another. A fourth was the water crisis looming in some of the planet's least stable regions, notably in Africa and the Middle East.[6]

5   Those pressures have only increased in the years since. It was mid-October 2006 when I negotiated the cliff-hanging curves of the mountain highway to Tofino. A few days earlier, an American group calling itself the Global Footprint Network had announced a gloomy precedent: the earliest-ever World Overshoot Day. The idea was a twist on "Tax Freedom Day," that date when the average taxpayer has earned enough income to satisfy all the various taxes he or she will pay during the year, and after which [h]e or she gets to keep anything earned over the rest of the year.[7] World Overshoot Day is when the human economy is estimated to have consumed all the ecological resources the earth can renew within the same year, and after which our species, in effect, borrows from future years of planetary productivity.[8] The Global Footprint Network calculates that humanity first went into "overshoot" in late December, 1987. By 1995, the day was arriving in late November. It crept into October around the turn of the millennium and is now heading toward September, as it takes the ecosystem about 15 months to produce all the natural services—food, fresh air, clean water—that the human economy consumes in 12.

6   Plainly, this cannot go on without end. And, as economist Herb Stein memorably observed, "If something cannot go on forever, it will stop."[9] If we don't change our "business as usual" voluntarily, events will change it for us, probably painfully. Gregg Easterbrook, a writer on climate policy and visiting fellow at The Brookings Institution in Washington, D.C., envisions a future decade when "huge numbers of people die, while chaos render[s] social progress impossible in many developing nations and armies of desperate refugees c[o]me to the borders of wealthy nations."[10] Even darker prospects condemn *Homo sapiens* to the fate of the woolly mammoth, put out of commission by a wave of extinctions that he himself unleashed. The bleakest forecasters even seem perversely to welcome this outcome.

7   The mountain rocks of Vancouver Island are over 80 million years old in places. If you look, you can find fossils of palm forests and alligator-like reptiles that flourished here then. Should humankind not survive, doubtless something else will be along in a millennium or two, with or without the faculty of intelligence.

8   That is not an inevitable outcome. There *are* things we can do to prevent these dystopic visions from becoming our future. And there is time to do them. But not limitless time.

9   Much of the literature of climate change looks to the end of the present century and beyond. That's too long a frame. I focus instead on a more relevant window: the next 25 years. Why? Because that's a span through which the great majority of us today can be reasonably assured of living. Whether we have enough water to sustain our diets, live-lihoods and styles of life over that period isn't an academic question. It will largely deter-mine whether we'll prosper, encounter adversity or—let us be candid—end disastrously.

10   Another reason to dwell on the next 25 years is that we're beginning to understand what kind of weather to expect, as a growing weight of real-world, real-time observa-tions bolsters increasingly comprehensive and powerful climate models to reinforce our confidence that some trends will continue over this forecast period.

11   A third reason is that if we continue our current habit of environmental overshoot, we'll quite simply run out of key resources within the next quarter century. Consider that by every measure, China is the emerging colossus of our new century. If business-as-usual continues uninterrupted, China should enjoy by 2031 a per-capita income and style of living equal to those of the United States in 2005. But Lester Brown of the Earth Policy Institute in Washington, DC, has pointed out the actual impossibility of this. If it comes about, he has said, "China would be consuming two thirds of the current world grain harvest. Their consumption of paper would be double current world production. It would have a fleet of 1.1 billion cars; the current global fleet is 800 million. And they would be consuming 99 million barrels of oil a day. The world is currently producing 84 million barrels a day and will probably never produce much more than that."[11] All of that takes no account of the rising lifestyle of India, close behind China in population, or of the continuing increase in material wealth that North Americans and Europeans expect to enjoy in the same period. To paraphrase Stein, what cannot go on forever will stop before the next 25 years are out.

12   But there would be little point in sounding an alarm if there were nothing to be done. So a fourth reason for thinking about the next quarter-century is that it's time in which we *can* do something. We know too little about our circumstances in 2040 or 2050 to plan usefully for then. Our time is now. Indeed, actions we take or fail to take in the next few years will largely determine whether circumstances later leave us with any choices at all.

13   And the final reason to think about the 25 years in front of us may be the most urgent of all. Response takes time. Just as water runs through everything we do, everything we do affects our water. Factories and farms aren't replaced or retooled overnight. Investments in communities, housing and utilities can't easily be abandoned. Habits, policies, laws and societies possess inertia: changing them takes a great deal of effort.

14   To provide enough water for our future, we must choose between two fundamental strategies. We can *build more things*: more dams and reservoirs, more impoundments and river diversions, more aqueducts and canals and pipelines, more wells, and more recycling plants or desalination facilities. Or we can *change how we use what we have now*: we can manage our watersheds differently, choose more ecologically sound appliances and irrigation techniques, and change how our markets, bookkeeping and laws treat the one asset that underwrites every other. Assuming hopefully that we will choose to do anything at all, we'll probably choose some of both. But either strategy takes time.

15   Utility planners estimate that at least 15 to 20 years, but often many more, pass from the day they decide to build a new reservoir to the day when water starts filling it. To change rules and attitudes takes just as long: health advocates worked more than two decades to convince North American society to ban smoking from public places, and in much of the rest of the world, offices and restaurants are as smoky as ever. Whatever we may need to build or change to assure ourselves of water by 2031, we must start soon: preferably within the next five years, certainly within 10.

16   There is no time to waste.

17   Tofino feels like a town at the end of the world. It is, quite literally, the town at the end of the Trans-Canada Highway. Beyond here there is nothing but ocean all the way to Japan. Tourists seek the place out for the very qualities that set it apart from the congested freeways and pressured calendars of their workaday lives. Here, a blackberry is a fruit, not an electronic tether to the office. A large part of Tofino's year-round population has sacrificed conventional careers in order to live under the eaves of a

primeval forest within the sound of the wild Pacific surf. Among the surfers and kayak guides, the artists and aging hippies and occasional leftover draft dodger, it is easy to find critics of the rest of the continent's all-consuming appetite for *more*.

18   There are many reasons to be apprehensive about the quarter-century ahead. Many things could go terribly wrong: religious and ideological fanaticism; militarization; poverty; material self-absorption; ultimately ecological overshoot and habitat collapse. Water, however, is at the heart of solving all of these other problems. If we can get the water part right, we will have the chance to apply our astonishing collective ingenuity and adaptive capacity to all the rest.

19   Fail on water, as individuals and communities, and little else we get right will matter much.

Notes

1   Qur'an, Al-Anbiyaa', 21:30.

2   "Running Dry: The Humanitarian Impact of the Global Water Crisis," UN Office for the Coordination of Humanitarian Affairs (October 2006), http://www.irinnews.org/InDepthMain.aspx?InDepthId=13&ReportId=62312.

3   "Ecological Comparison of PC and Thin Client Desk Top Equipment" (Study), Fraunhofer-Institut für Umwelt-Sicherheits und Energietechnik (UMSICHT), Oberhausen (Germany) (December 18, 2006), p. 26, http://files.thinstore.com/Fraunhofer_Report.pdf.

4   Mark Charmer, "New Cards versus Old Cars: CO_2 versus Recycling" (blog), The Movement Design Bureau (London, U.K.) (March 27, 2007), http://movementbureau.blogs.com/projects/2007/03/new_cars_versus.html; Fiona Harvey, "Business and Water: Virtual Use Casts Light on Inequality," *Financial Times* (U.K.) (March 22, 2007), http://www.ft.com/reports/water2007.

5   "Canada's Oil Sands: Opportunities and Challenges to 2015," Energy Market Assessment, National Energy Board (Canada) (May 2004), http://www.neb-one.gc.ca/clf-nsi/rnrgymfmtn/nrgyrprt/lsnd/pprtntsndchllngs20152004/pprtntsndchllngs20152004-end.pdf; Mary O'Driscoll, "Tar Sand Companies Try Balancing Oil Gains, Environmental Pains," *Energy and Environment Magazine* (August 17, 2005), http://www.eenews.net/special_reports/tar_sands/; Stephen Leahy, "Canada: Oil Production Strains Parched Landscape," Inter Press News Service (July 21, 2006), http://www.corpwatch.org/article.php?id=13924.

6   That article was titled "The Future, Will It Work?" The answer was, more or less, "Don't bet on it." It won that year's Accenture Award for business journalism.

7   Pioneered by the pro-market non-profit Tax Foundation, based in Washington, D.C., the concept of Tax Freedom Day has been adopted in numerous other countries. In Canada, the date is calculated by the market-oriented Fraser Foundation.

8   Martin Hickman, "Earth's Ecological Debt Crisis: Mankind's 'Borrowing' from Nature Hits New Record," *The Independent* (London) (October 9, 2006), http://www.commondreams.org/headlines06/1009-03.htm.

9   The late Herbert Stein, a senior fellow at the American Enterprise Institute, claimed in, among other places, *Slate*, May 16, 1997, to have first uttered this widely quoted aphorism in the 1980s.

10   Gregg Easterbrook, "Case Closed: The Debate about Global Warming Is Over," The Brookings Institution (May 2006), http://www.brook.edu/views/papers/easterbrook/20060517.htm.

11   In an online interview at http://www.alternet.org/story/31679/.

DISCUSSION QUESTIONS

1. How does the writer use many examples to support the opening claim that "water is life" in the bio-physical realm in the first paragraph? How do the next two paragraphs develop the idea of the vital importance of water in spiritual and economic realms?

2. How does the writer support the claim that water is necessary for trade and commerce? How does he explain the concept of "virtual water" (paragraph 3)?

3. What four threats to the environment did the writer begin to notice in the late 1990s—threats that have only increased since then?

4. In your own words, explain what is meant by "World Overshoot Day" (paragraph 5), and what has caused this day to arrive a bit earlier each year?

5. What are the two main strategies that the author says we must choose between to ensure that there is enough water for the future (paragraph 14)? What strategy does he seem to prefer?

6. What are five reasons that the writer argues we should focus on the next 25 years rather than a longer span of time (paragraphs 9 to 15)?

7. Why does the writer describe a relatively pristine place where he has travelled—Tofino on the west coast of Vancouver Island (paragraph 17)? How might Tofino be a stand-in for other remote places in Canada and throughout the world?

8. What are two or three strategies that the writer employs to convey a sense of urgency?

TOWARD KEY INSIGHTS

Discussion of something as frightening and consequential as the effects of climate change can sometimes be so overwhelming that people turn away or give up. How does the writer try to keep readers attending, and encourage positive change?

SUGGESTION FOR WRITING *Compare and contrast the point of view, tone, and rhetorical strategies in this piece of writing by Chris Wood, excerpted from a book, and the essay "The Four Tribes of Climate Change" in Chapter 12. Be sure to use MLA documentation as appropriate.*

CHAPTER 10

Strategies for Analytical Writing: Definition

The holiday movies were full of schmaltziness.

The landlord is taking his tenant to arbitration because of damage to the property.

That hockey player is a goon.

Do you have questions? You're not alone. Many people would question the sentences above: "What does *schmaltziness* mean?" "What is *arbitration*?" "What is a *goon* in hockey?" To avoid puzzling and provoking your own readers, you'll often need to explain the meaning of some term. The term may be unfamiliar (*schmaltziness*) or used in a specialized way (*arbitration*), or it may mean different things to different people (*goon*). Whenever you clarify the meaning of some term, you are *defining*.

Humans are instinctively curious. We start asking about meanings as soon as we can talk, and we continue to seek and supply definitions all through life. In school, instructors expect us to explain literary, historical, scientific, technical, and social terms. On the job, a member of a company's human resources department might prepare a brochure that explains the meaning of such terms as *corporate responsibility* and *product stewardship* for new employees. A special education teacher might write a memo explaining *developmental delays* to the rest of the staff. An accountant might define *statistical sampling inventory* in a report calling for a change in the inventory system.

When you define, you identify the features that distinguish a term, thereby establishing its boundaries and separating it from all others. Knowing these features enables both you and your reader to use the term appropriately.

Sometimes a single word, phrase, or sentence can settle a definition question. To clear up the mystery of *schmaltziness*, all you'd need to do is insert a brief phrase (*excessive sentimentality*) after the word. But when you're dealing with new terms—such as *cybersecurity*, *crowdfunding*, or *greenwashing*—brief definitions won't provide the reader with enough information for proper understanding.

Abstract terms—those standing for things we can't see, touch, or otherwise detect with our five senses—often require extended definitions, too. Terms such as *autism*, *colonialism*, or *courage* are too complex to capture in a single sentence, and people have too many differing ideas about what they mean. If you are using concrete terms—those standing for actions and things we can perceive with our five senses—you may also need to provide a longer definition to make sure your audience understands what you are talking about. For example, some people limit the term *drug dealer* to full-time sellers of hard drugs such as cocaine and heroin, others assume that the term applies to full-time and part-time sellers of any illegal or controlled substance, and still others believe that the term applies only to those involved in trafficking large quantities of controlled substances. Thus, writing an argument recommending mandatory sentences for convicted drug dealers would require you to explain just what you mean by the term.

TYPES OF DEFINITIONS

Three types of definitions—synonyms, essential definitions, and extended definitions—serve writers' needs. Although the first two seldom require more than a word or a sentence, an extended definition can run to several pages. Synonyms and essential definitions can be found in dictionaries, and they are starting points for extended definitions.

Synonyms

Synonyms are words with very nearly the same meanings. *Lissome* is synonymous with *lithe* or *nimble*, and *condign* is a synonym of *worthy* and *suitable*. Synonyms allow writers to clarify meanings of unfamiliar words without using cumbersome explanations. To clarify the term *expostulation* in a quoted passage, all you'd have to do is add the word *objection* after it in parentheses. However, since synonyms are not identical twins, using them as definitions puts a slightly different shade of meaning on a message. For example, to *protest* and to *object* have similar meanings, but saying that we *object* to the establishment of a toxic waste site in our area sounds much weaker than saying we *protest* against such a site. Still, synonyms may provide convenient shorthand definitions, if used judiciously.

Essential Definitions

An essential definition does three things: (1) names the item being defined, (2) places it in a broad category, and (3) distinguishes it from other items in that category.

Here are three examples:

Item Being Defined	Broad Category	Distinguishing Features
An ecosystem	is a community of living things	interacting with each other and their environment as a system.
An extrovert	is a sociable person	who gets energy from being around other people.
Blanching	is a cooking method	in which food is briefly immersed in boiling water or fat, then put into ice water.

Suppose that your instructor has asked you to write an essential definition of one of the terms listed in an exercise, and you choose *vacuum cleaner*. Coming up with a broad category presents no problem: A vacuum cleaner is a household appliance. The hard part is pinpointing the distinguishing features. The purpose of a vacuum cleaner is to clean floors, carpets, and upholstery. However, you soon realize that these features alone do not separate vacuum cleaners from other appliances. After all, carpet sweepers also clean floors, and whiskbrooms clean upholstery. What feature, then, does distinguish vacuum cleaners? After a little thought, you realize that, unlike the other items, a vacuum cleaner works by suction. You then write the following definition:

> A vacuum cleaner is a household appliance that uses suction to clean floors, carpets, and upholstery.

You will need to think carefully to uncover the distinguishing features in any essential definition.

Limitations of Essential Definitions   Essential definitions have certain built-in limitations. Because of their brevity, they often can't do full justice to abstract terms such as *cowardice, love, jealousy,* and *power.* Problems also arise with terms that have several settled meanings. The word *jam* when used as a noun would require at least three essential definitions: (1) a closely packed crowd, (2) a fruit preserve, and (3) a difficult situation. Nevertheless, despite these limitations, an essential definition can be useful by itself or as part of a longer definition.

Pitfalls in Preparing Essential Definitions   When you prepare an essential definition, guard against these flaws:

Circular definition. Don't define a term by repeating it or changing its form slightly. A definition of a psychiatrist as "a physician who practises psychiatry" will frustrate someone who's never heard of psychiatry. Avoid circularity and choose terms the reader can understand; for example, "A psychiatrist is a physician who diagnoses and treats mental disorders."

Overly broad definition. Shy away from loose definitions that cover too much territory. If you define a skunk as "an animal that has a bushy tail and black fur with white markings," your definition is not precise. Many cats and dogs also fit this description. But if you add "and that ejects a foul-smelling secretion when threatened," you will clear the air—of any misconceptions, at least.

Overly narrow definition. Don't hem in your definition too closely. The definition of a kitchen blender as "a bladed electrical appliance used to chop foods" is too restricted. Blenders perform other operations, too. To correct the error, add the missing information: "A kitchen blender is a bladed electrical appliance used to chop, mix, whip, liquefy, or otherwise process foods."

Omission of main category. Avoid using *is where* or *is when* instead of naming the main category. Here are examples of this error: "A bistro is where food and wine are served" and "An ordination is when a person is formally recognized as a minister, priest, or rabbi." The reader will not know exactly what sort of thing a *bistro* is (a bar? a party?) and may think that *ordination* means "a time." Note the improvement when the broad categories are named: "A bistro is a small restaurant where both food and wine are served" and "An ordination is a ceremony at which a person is formally recognized as a minister, priest, or rabbi."

EXERCISE

1. **Identify the broad category and the distinguishing traits in each of these essential definitions.**

   a. Gangue is useless rock accompanying valuable minerals in a deposit.

   b. A catbird is a small songbird with a slate-coloured body, a black cap, and a catlike cry.

   c. A soldier is a man or woman serving in an army.

2. **Indicate which of the following statements are acceptable essential definitions. Explain what is wrong with those that are not. Correct them.**

   a. A scalpel is a small knife that has a sharp blade used for surgery and anatomical dissections.

   b. Digital literacy is the ability to understand, use, and think critically about digital communication tools and resources.

   c. A rifle is a firearm that has a grooved barrel and is used for hunting large game.

   d. A drama queen is someone who acts dramatically.

3. **Write an essential definition for each of the following terms.**

   a. phishing

   b. body mass index

   c. telemark skiing

   d. consumerism

   e. fair trade

Extended Definitions

Sometimes, it's necessary to go beyond an essential definition and write a paragraph or whole paper explaining a term. Terms with differing meanings also frequently require extended definitions. New technical, social, and economic terms often require extended definitions. For example, a computer scientist might need to define *data integrity* so that computer operators understand the importance of maintaining it. Furthermore, extended definition is crucial to interpretation of the law when courts must clarify the meaning of terms such as *obscenity*.

Extended definitions are not merely academic exercises. A police officer needs to have a clear understanding of what counts as *reasonable grounds for search and seizure;* an engineer must comprehend the meaning of *stress;* a nuclear medical technologist had better have a solid grasp of *radiation.* As well, all of us are concerned with the definition of our *basic rights* as citizens.

Extended definitions commonly draw on other methods of development—narration, description, process analysis, illustration, classification, comparison, and cause and effect. Often, they also define by negation—explaining what a term *does not* mean. The following paragraphs show how one writer handles an extended definition of *sudden infant death syndrome*. The student begins by presenting a case history (illustration), which also incorporates an essential definition and two synonyms.

> Jane and Dick Smith were proud new parents of an eight-pound, ten-ounce baby girl named Jenny. One summer night, Jane put Jenny to bed at 8:00. When she went to check on her at 3:00 a.m., Jane found Jenny dead. The baby had given no cry of pain, shown no sign of trouble. Even the doctor did not know why she had died, for she was healthy and strong. The autopsy report confirmed the doctor's suspicion—the infant was a victim of the "sudden infant death syndrome," also known as SIDS or crib death. SIDS is the sudden and unexplainable death of an apparently healthy, sleeping infant. It is the number-one cause of death in infants after the first week of life and as a result has been the subject of numerous research studies.

DISCUSSION QUESTIONS

1. What synonyms does the writer use?
2. Which sentence presents an essential definition?

In the next paragraph, the writer turns to negation, pointing out some of the things that researchers have ruled out about SIDS.

> Although researchers do not know what SIDS is, they do know what it is not. They know it cannot be predicted; it strikes like a thief in the night. Crib deaths occur in seconds, with no sound of pain, and they always happen when the child is sleeping. Suffocation is not the cause, nor is aspiration or regurgitation. Researchers have found no correlation between the incidence of SIDS and the mother's use of birth control pills or the presence of fluoride in water. Since it is not hereditary or contagious, only a slim chance exists that SIDS will strike twice in the same family.

Finally, the student explores several proposed causes of SIDS as well as how parents may react to the loss of their child.

> As might be expected, researchers have offered many theories concerning the cause of crib death. Dr. R. C. Reisinger, a National Cancer Institute scientist, has linked crib deaths to the growth of a common bacterium, *E. coli,* in the intestines of newborn babies. The organisms multiply in the intestines, manufacturing a toxin that is absorbed by the intestinal wall and passes into the bloodstream.

Breast milk stops the growth of the organism, whereas cow's milk permits it. Therefore, Dr. Reisinger believes, bottle-fed babies run a higher risk of crib death than other babies. . . .

The loss of a child through crib death is an especially traumatic experience for the family. Parents often develop feelings of guilt and depression, thinking they somehow caused the child's death. To alleviate such feelings, organizations have been established to help parents accept the fact that they did not cause the death.

Trudy Stelter, student

ETHICAL ISSUES

How we define a term can have profound consequences. For centuries, the practice of defining Africans as *subhuman* helped justify slavery. During the 1930s and early 1940s, labelling Jews as *vermin* was used to fuel the attempt to exterminate them in both Nazi Germany and much of the rest of Western Europe. Even in the absence of malice, definitions can have far-reaching effects, both good and bad. Definitions of certain learning disabilities affect whether or not a student in the public school system is eligible for extra assistance. A word such as *terrorism* has critical political, legal, and military implications. Answering the following questions will help you think about the possible ethical implications of your definitions.

- Have I carefully evaluated all features of my definition? For example, a definition of *excessive force* by the police would be unfair if it included actions that constitute reasonable means necessary to subdue highly dangerous suspects.
- Have I slanted my definition to reflect a prejudice? Let's say a writer opposed to casino gambling is defining *gambling addicts*. The paper should focus on those who spend an excessive amount of time in casinos; bet and often lose large sums of money; and in so doing neglect family, financial, and personal obligations. It would be unfair to include those who visit casinos occasionally and strictly limit their losses.
- Have I avoided unnecessary connotations that might be harmful? A definition of *teenagers* that overemphasizes their swift changes in mood might be unfair, perhaps even harmful, since it may influence the reactions of readers.

WRITING AN EXTENDED DEFINITION
Planning and Drafting the Extended Definition

If you are writing an extended definition, choose an abstract term or one that is concrete but unfamiliar to your reader. For instance, why spend time defining *table* when the reader already knows what it is? An extended definition of an unfamiliar term that the reader may not understand, such as *fracking* or *carbon footprint*, might well prove interesting and informative for a reader.

PREWRITING: FINDING
YOUR TOPIC

- Brainstorm key words or phrases that interest you or you have disputed.
- Write down terms you have read that are points of contention.
- Identify a term you know about or that interests you.
- Determine what purpose would be served by defining the term. To clarify a specialized concept? To persuade the reader to adopt an attitude toward it? To discuss some neglected facet? To show what it means to you?
- Jot down ideas about audiences that would be interested in this term.

DEVELOPING YOUR
DEFINITION

- Select clear examples of what you wish to define, such as the United States as an example of a democracy.
- Brainstorm major identifying characteristics, such as majority rule, free elections, and a separately elected chief executive.
- Test these characteristics against other legitimate examples, such as Britain, which is a democracy but lacks a separately elected chief executive.
- Test your characteristics against clear counterexamples, such as the People's Republic of China, which the definition shouldn't fit.
- Chart the method you will use and brainstorm details.

Here's a helpful process to follow as you think through your definition. Imagine that you are defining an abstract term such as *democracy*. First, select a clear example that illustrates what you wish to define, then brainstorm to uncover major identifying characteristics. If you are brainstorming about the United States as an example for *democracy*, your list might include majority rule, free elections, a separately elected chief executive, a constitution, and basic human rights. Next, test these characteristics against other legitimate examples and retain only the characteristics that apply. Although Canada is clearly a democracy, it doesn't have a separately elected chief executive. Moreover, Canada was a democracy for more than a century before getting its own constitution. In addition, the People's Republic of China—which is not a democracy—has elections. What, then, truly constitutes a democracy? Finally, test your unfolding definition against a counterexample such as Myanmar (dictatorship) or Saudi Arabia (kingdom). Your definition should conflict with these examples.

Now evaluate what methods you might use to develop your definition. Each method has its own set of special strengths, as the following list shows.

Narration	Tracing the history of a new development or the changing meaning of a term: the history of Bitcoin and the digital economy
Description	Pointing out interesting or important features of a device, an event, or an individual: a blizzard
Process	Explaining what a device does or how it is used, how a procedure is carried out, or how a natural event takes place: Wi-Fi (wireless Internet)
Illustration	Tracing changes in meaning and defining abstract terms by providing examples: cybercrime

Classification	Pointing out the different categories into which an item or an event can be grouped: types of streaming media
Comparison	Distinguishing between an unfamiliar and a familiar item: food sovereignty distinguished from food security
Cause and effect	Explaining the origins and consequences of events, conditions, problems, and attitudes: causes of homelessness
Negation	Placing limitations on conditions and events and correcting popular misconceptions: why liberty isn't anarchy

Examine your topic in light of this list and select the methods of development that seem most promising. Don't hesitate to use a method because the purpose was not mentioned here. If you think that a comparison will help your reader understand some abstract term, use it.

Chart the methods of development you plan to use, and then brainstorm each method in turn to gather the details that will inform the reader. When you've finished, look everything over, rearrange the details as necessary, add any new ones you think of, and prepare a revised chart. The example that follows is for a paper using four methods of development.

Narration	**Classification**	**Process**	**Negation**
First supporting detail	First supporting detail	First supporting detail	First supporting detail
Second supporting detail	Second supporting detail	Second supporting detail	Second supporting detail

The **thesis statements** for extended definitions often focus on the reason that the readers may be interested in a term or concept combined with a major defining characteristic. "Many politicians claim the libertarian mantle, but few really accept the core idea that government and laws should be drastically limited." Look to your major defining characteristic and the reason in your brainstorming on why this term is important for ideas for your thesis.

Definition papers can begin in various ways. In writing the body of the paper, present the methods of development in whatever order seems most appropriate. A paper defining *drag racing* might first describe the hectic scene as the cars line up for a race, then classify the different categories of vehicles, and finally explain the steps in a race. If you're defining a term with no agreed-upon meaning (for example, *bullying*), you might note some differing views of it and then state your own.

Introduction

■ If no agreed-upon definition (as in "liberalism"), maybe note different views and then your own.

■ If the term reflects a new development (as in "the cloud"), possibly mention how it came to be.

- A definition of a colloquial or slang word ("chutzpah"), but other topics as well, can start with an example that grabs the reader.

- Sometimes a short dictionary definition can be useful, but this can often create a stale beginning.

Body

- Have a clear, logical order for your reader

- Select the strategies you use based on your purpose and audience. Don't use strategies just to use them.

- Develop each part of the definition with examples and details that will make it concrete for your reader.

- Provide clear transitions for your reader.

Conclusion

- If defining some undesirable condition (such as sudden infant death syndrome), maybe express hope for a speedy solution.

- Or if reporting a new development, discuss its impact.

- Or if defining a socially important term (such as "post-racial"), you might call for a certain action.

- Or if the paper is longer, summarize main points.

Revising the Extended Definition

Use the general guidelines in Chapter 4 and these specific questions and suggestions as you revise your extended definition:

- Where could the paper better fit your audience and purpose? If your definition of *drought* is to show the social impact and encourage action, you may need to strengthen your personal examples.

- If an essential definition was used, does it avoid the pitfalls?

- What other defining characteristics may be missing? Look for some additional examples and brainstorm.

- Where are additional examples and details necessary to make the definition clear and vivid for readers? Try brainstorming tied to specific paragraphs.

- What other strategies might have helped clarify the definition? Was any strategy unhelpful? Try writing some additional approaches on a separate page.

- Where could the organization of the paper be made more effective?

- Where could transitions be strengthened to more clearly signal shifts in focus to the reader?

- Where could paragraphs be more specifically focused? It can be helpful to label each paragraph to see what it is intended to contribute to the paper.

- Has the paper avoided being slanted by prejudice or presenting harmful and unnecessary connotations so that it is ethical?

EXAMPLE OF A STUDENT ESSAY USING DEFINITION

Lust and Gluttony

Bryan Wainwright

<table>
<tr>
<td>

Uses comparison and contrast to distinguish between two similar concepts.

Uses an arresting statement to get reader's attention and zero in on main idea.

Uses examples to illustrate.

</td>
<td>

1   If I had to choose between lust and gluttony, I would commit myself to a life of lust.

2   Although lust and gluttony may be sinful cousins of a sort, the lustful are full of joy, but the gluttonous are simply full. The lustful who fill their emptiness with all life's sensuous pleasures find unsurpassed happiness and delight. The gluttonous, however, who focus on filling their protruding stomachs with all that is fatty and sweet, live with a perpetual sense of anxiety—or guilty over-consumption. The lustful can anticipate the moment of pleasure, and revel in it when it comes. Whether they have been desiring a sexual experience or a high performance car, the lustful can experience true delight and fulfillment. The gluttonous, however, never really enjoy anything. They can't even taste that popcorn they are shovelling into their mouths at the movie. They gobble down their king crab and lobster slathered with buttery cream sauces as quickly as possible, as if they worried someone could take their food away. And before they have wiped the grease from their upper lip, they are already longing for that chocolate amaretto cheesecake with hazelnut crust.

3   One defining characteristic divides the lustful from the gluttonous. Drawing a chubby line in the sand of sins is the fact that the lustful being simply has no boundaries. The lustful may have immense amorous appetite for pleasure, but they are not limited by their physical capacities. They can enhance their pleasure through imagination. They feel delight before, during, and after the lustful experience. The gluttonous masses, however, are limited by their own earthly selves and their weak fleshy bodies. When the gluttonous finally sit back at the end of the meal, they rub their stomachs sadly, as if they wished they could keep eating forever. As they loosen their belt buckles as far as they possibly can, they may also feel a tinge of shame. The lustful, in contrast, reflect happily on their sexual encounters. Why else would Casanova have written his memoirs, except to re-live his amorous adventures with countless women in the pleasure palace of his imagination?

4   It's true that gluttony and lust are related. Gluttony is the fat, lethargic cousin of legendary lust. The glutton sleeps on the couch in lust's penthouse suite, leaving a lingering stench that all the Glade plug-ins of the world couldn't conquer. Gluttony is merely lust without imagination. Where lust strives to touch the stars

</td>
</tr>
</table>

and part the seas in hopes of a new high, gluttony waddles to the fridge and drinks milk from the carton to wash down the Twinkies.

5   The glutton is the hot dog cart of the sins: big and slow, full of saturated fat, and grease. Lust is the high octane muscle car that tears through the world at breakneck speeds in search of its next conquest. While lust evolves and discovers new forms of happiness, gluttony is stagnant and watches the world go by, flicking through the channels of life with chocolate-stained fingers and a gut full of trans-fatty acids. Every moment of the lustful life is an affront to the gluttons of the world, suggesting imagination need not be bounded by a kitchen. The desire to stimulate the senses with all the wonderful sensations life has to offer is not a real sin, but could even be considered a virtue that leads to fulfillment. While gluttony is focused on food and drink, lust encompasses much more than sexual pleasure. The lust for love leads to fiery passionate encounters; the lust for power drives people to glory and fame; the lust for blood creates champions and heroes who achieve greatness through sport and combat. To have lust course through one's veins helps one become a titan among mortals.

> Offers more comparisons to sharpen definition.

6   The glutton has great power as well: the power to waste the world's supply of food; the power to expand one's girth to the point of eruption; the power to make society pay for the disposal of a monstrously revolting corpse. While the lustful can channel their burning desires in many ways, the gluttonous are limited by their obsession with food and drink. While they may gain a small measure of glory in the so-called sport of food-eating competitions, most people are more disgusted than intrigued by stupendous feats of ingestion. Who would want to gain fame through the rapid consumption of 59 hot dogs, or 72 glazed doughnuts? The gluttonous also tend to die in undignified ways; in one strange *CSI (Crime Scene Investigation)* episode focused on extreme eating, a man who ate too many hot dogs is found in a dumpster after his gut literally exploded. The end of gluttony is not pretty.

7   The lustful contribute to society. They are the lovers, fighters, heroes, entrepreneurs, pioneers, and leaders of our world. The lust for knowledge, power and wealth command them to achieve greatness through innovation and revolution. The lustful know the world will not be inherited by the meek but by those who follow their passions.

> Identifies consequences of definition.

8   The gluttonous leave no legacy. The crooked, pitted headstone of the glutton has no story to tell, but the memorials of the lustful stand tall and proud, pronouncing grand tales and heroic deeds. As the gluttons lie six feet under, filling oversized caskets and extra-large graves, I, the lustful, will be setting out on one more passionate adventure.

> Evaluates clearly why one term is preferred over the other.

DISCUSSION QUESTIONS

1. What writing strategies does the writer use to develop an extended definition of lust and gluttony?

2. Find examples where the writer uses metaphors or figurative language to help define his terms.

3. How does the writer use transitions and topic sentences to help create coherence?

4. To what extent does this essay include a persuasive angle? Do you find yourself being persuaded? Why or why not?

SUGGESTIONS FOR WRITING *Write an extended definition using one of the following suggestions or one approved by your instructor. The term you define may be new, misused, or misunderstood, or may have a disputed meaning. Develop the essay using any combination of writing strategies.*

1. Literacy
2. Storm chaser
3. Refugee
4. Free speech

5. Emotional intelligence
6. Impaired driving
7. Biodiversity
8. EcoDensity

Stepping Up to Synthesis

Definitions are always social creations. The way that people in various communities understand and use a word determines what it means. Thus, writers who use abstract words such as *justice*, *love*, or *charisma* to convey a message may need to consult a number of sources to determine how others have used these words. With their findings of this research in mind, the writers can stake out their own meanings of the words.

PREWRITING FOR SYNTHESIS

If you were writing an extended definition of the word *dance* for a humanities class, you would probably discover that people have used the word in different ways. As you read *The Dance as an Artwork*, you might at first like Frank Thiess's definition of dance as the use of the body for expressive gesture. As you mull over that definition, however, you realize that it is both too broad and too narrow. While some forms of dance, such as ballet, feature expressive gesture, so does pantomime or even a shaken fist—and neither of these qualifies as dance. A square dance clearly qualifies, but does it represent expressive gesture? Then you turn to *Philosophy in a New Key*, in which Susanne Langer defines dance as "a play of Powers made visible" and stresses that dancers seem to be moved by forces beyond themselves. You recognize that this definition may apply to religious dance forms, that dancers sometimes appear swept away by the music, and that you yourself have experienced a feeling of power when dancing. Nevertheless, upon reflection you decide that people watch dancers for less mystical reasons, and that it's usually the dancer's skill and artistry that attracts viewers. Finally, you discover that Francis Sparshott, in *The Theory of the Arts*, defines dance as a rhythmical, patterned motion that transforms people's sense of their own existence according to the dance they do. As you evaluate Sparshott's contention, you decide that it has considerable merit, although you aren't convinced that every dance transforms our sense of existence.

CRITICALLY EVALUATING YOUR SOURCES

Carrying out this type of project requires you to look critically at the definitions of others. Do they accurately reflect the examples you know about? Do they describe examples that do not fit the definition? Are any parts of the definition questionable or unclear? Once you've answered these questions, you can then draw on the appropriate elements of the definitions to formulate your own.

PLANNING AND DRAFTING YOUR SYNTHESIS

When you think about the kinds of dance you know and the various definitions you have uncovered, you conclude that these writers, like the blind men who felt different parts of an elephant and tried to describe it, are each only partly correct. For your humanities paper, you decide to synthesize the different definitions. You might explain that all dance involves a rhythmical, patterned movement of the body for its own sake. Sometimes, such movement can transform our sense of existence, as in trance dances or even waltzes. Other dances, such as story ballets, use rhythmical movements as expressive gestures that tell stories or convey emotions. Still other dances may suggest the manifestation of powers beyond the dances themselves. You proceed to explain each of these features with details drawn both from your sources and from personal experience.

You might organize such a paper by developing each definition in a separate section, first presenting it in detail and then pointing out its strengths and weaknesses. In the final section, you could offer your own definition and support it with your reasoning and suitable examples.[1]

SUGGESTIONS FOR WRITING

1. Do some reading about an abstract term, such as *pornography*, *success*, *marriage*, or *happiness*, in at least three sources. Use the sources to develop your own definition of the term.

2. If you are familiar with a particular type of discourse from an area you know well (sports, computers, music, cooking, etc.), define the terms of this discourse for a reader uninitiated to this specialized language. This essay might blend different strategies of development such as illustration, for you need to provide examples and definitions along the way. Alternatively, you might choose to organize your essay mainly around one extended definition of a significant word or phrase.

---

[1]Because you need to draw on published sources, it is important to read the sections on research in Chapters 14 and 15 and those on handling quotations and avoiding plagiarism in Chapter 16 before you start to write. As always, follow your instructor's guidelines for documenting sources.

DEFINITION ESSAYS: PROFESSIONAL MODELS

READING STRATEGIES

1. Clearly identify the term being defined and the broad category to which it belongs.
2. As you read, note distinguishing characteristics of the concept.
3. If there is definition by negation, what terms or concepts are potential sources of confusion that are being ruled out?
4. Observe any analogies, similes, or metaphors that can help readers understand the concept by seeing what it resembles.
5. Consider whether you have unanswered questions or points of confusion.

READING CRITICALLY

1. Ask yourself whether the definition makes sense to you.
2. Test the definition to see if it is too narrow. If a person defines *literature* as works of fiction, the definition could leave out poetry, drama, creative non-fiction, and so on.
3. Test the definition to see if it is too broad. If a person defines *literature* as works that are in print, the definition would include phone books—a clearly unintended consequence of the definition.
4. Note whether the definition has a simple explanatory purpose or whether it is part of a larger argument.

READING AS A WRITER

1. Notice how the writer uses the introduction to explain the importance of the concept and the definition.
2. Identify the key strategies the writer uses to construct a definition—identifying the broad category and distinguishing characteristics, providing examples, arguing that it is not what people mistakenly have assumed, and/or drawing comparisons to similar ideas.
3. Observe how the writer limits the definition so that it is not too general.
4. Note whether the writer illumines a specialized concept, redefines a term in a new way, clarifies the meaning of the term for a particular context, or calls attention to an overlooked facet of the term.

Sadiqa Khan

Going Dutch: Reflections on Nation, Race and Privilege

Sadiqa Khan is a writer, poet, and artist. She published this article in the Canadian independent magazine Briarpatch.

i　*I stop at a roadside chip truck on a bright November afternoon. The chip truck worker is an older man leaning from an elevated window over a handful of customers.*
—A medium fries with mayo, please.

—You must be Dutch! Only the Dutch eat 'em that way.

—Yeah, I am Dutch.

—You know what else they like on their fries?

—Peanut sauce.

—What? No, mustard! Only the Dutch will ask for mustard.

—Oh, really?

—But you're not actually Dutch.

—Yes, I am.

—No, no. Come on, now.

> Conversational snippet illustrates problem with assuming people can fit into neat national categories.

ii   *I am volunteering at a festival, working the doors of an event with a fellow volunteer, a tall, friendly man. We are seated at a desk together, searching through a box of name tags for our own names.*

—Your name sounds Dutch, I say.

—Yes, my parents are Dutch.

—I'm from there, too. Do you speak Dutch at all?

—No, not really. A bit of German. But I've been to Holland. To a little town in the north called Stadskanaal.

—Oh, really. My aunt lives there. I've been to Stadskanaal lots of times. My mom's family is from the north.

—Hey, small world!

—Yeah.

—But you're not Dutch, are you?

> Second conversational snippet again illustrates a problem with assuming too much about what being Dutch means.

iii   *I walk into a Dutch vice-consulate office to renew my passport. There are photographs on the wall: Amsterdam's narrow row houses and boats with curved, dark sails. I speak to the secretary, a woman with square-framed glasses on a gold chain.*

—Hi, I'm here to renew my passport.

—This is the Dutch vice-consulate.

—I know.

—You need to have a Dutch passport.

iv   *At a crowded reception following a graduation ceremony, an acquaintance introduces me to a stylish, white-haired woman.*

—This is Sadiqa. She's Dutch, too.

—You mean Indonesian!

—No, Dutch.

The woman turns to my acquaintance. —How can she be Dutch?

1   I do not know how to divide myself into fractions when it comes to my ethnicity; I cannot say how much of me is my first language, or the food that was common on our family table, or where that food was grown. A genealogist might classify me as half Dutch and half Kenyan, and within the Kenyan half, several eighths and sixteenths Pakistani and Afghani.

> Examples show how difficult it is to classify and define ethnicity.

2   As is evident in the conversations transcribed above—a small selection from a growing compilation—that Dutch half sometimes turns into the whole story. It's not because I want to obscure any other parts of my background; my answer to where I am from differs with the context of who is asking, and why. But claiming to be Dutch, I have found, can draw out something ugly lurking below the surface of an interaction. When I suspect its presence, I say *Dutch*, and then it emerges: a monstrous little creature on a hook, writhing in the sudden light. *How can you be Dutch?*

3   The remarkable thing, to me, is not that the creature is there. It is undoubtedly a product of racist assumptions: I am Dutch under the standard definitions of birth and

citizenship, and I spent my childhood in the Netherlands. To question my claim is to imply that my appearance betrays my words (my hair, eyes and skin are all shades of brown). The image people hold of lightly pigmented homogeneity may be outdated, but it is not surprising. And it is easy to imagine how that assumption undermines the lives of residents of the Netherlands who are not white, even as the current Dutch government lays the blame with them, adopting increasingly hidebound integration laws. The difficulty, for me, is in understanding why people will persist in stating that I cannot be Dutch. It is as if we are watching that monstrous little creature approach suffocation, and they shout, *Wait, I need that thing!*

Reality of being a Dutch person of colour counters the stereotypical image. Connects the idea that people refuse to believe she is Dutch with racism.

4   What for?

5   There is no single, uncomplicated answer. But one motive could be our demand for material comfort. We, the wealthy minority in the global north, live in states of luxury that require many people to be subjugated, and race is one convenient way to invent divisions. Society's devalued peoples can then be forced from their own land so that we may inhabit or use it. They can assemble our jeans under abusive conditions or suffer pesticide poisoning to provide us with unblemished grapes. They can die from lack of money for medicines while we vacation in proximity. As one of the we, I inhabit a strange space; I am not white, but I have benefited from many of these warped relations, inheriting the profits of imaginary difference. Without that difference, how would we sleep at night?

Acknowledges being part of "the wealthy minority in the global north" even though she is not white. Contrast between the wealthy minority and "devalued peoples" that lead to an "imaginary difference."

6   I do not mean to draw too direct a line between these conversations and the bigger picture; our exchanges are twigs on a branch that grew from another branch, and that one from another, right down to the wide trunk that secures their privilege, old as the masts of the first colonizing ships. I doubt that they defended their assumption with the conscious intent of safeguarding their standard of living. But as an unwitting tradition, the practice makes sense historically. Not only did it bring Sri Lankan cinnamon to Dutch apples without the inconvenience of fair trade practices, but it continues to protect the comfortable Dutch from the very people who make their comfort possible.

Uses analogy between conversation exchanges and twigs on a branch that connect to a large trunk of an old tree.

7   For example, during the late 1950s and 1960s, there was a demand in the Netherlands for cheap, unregulated labour. Workers were actively recruited from Mediterranean countries, especially Turkey and Morocco. In the mid-'70s, when the Dutch economy slowed, and particularly when the *gastarbeiders* (guest workers) began to bring their families to the Netherlands, that recruitment was stopped. The Turkish and Moroccan families who stayed in the Netherlands continue to be treated as a threat by many white Dutch residents. The Dutch Party for Freedom, which advocates an immediate end to all non-Western immigration and the repatriation of non-Western residents to their countries of origin, currently holds nine parliamentary seats.

Synonym for unfamiliar word clarifies term *gastarbeiders*.

8   Of course, racist practices are common in Canada too, and are imposed most brutally on indigenous people. But this country is relatively welcoming to immigrants who are not white. Here, when I call myself Canadian, skepticism is the exception rather than the rule. Also, the question of confronting and reducing racism is at least part of the public discourse in this country. I would like to see added to that discourse the acknowledgment that working against racism is not just a matter of respect, acceptance or getting along. It involves being willing to fundamentally change our relation to material resources as well as to each other, refusing a lifestyle that sustains itself through the exploitation, displacement or dispossession of people imagined as different.

Historical example shows injustice of the socio-economic divide between non-Western immigrants in Netherlands and white residents.

9   In my own small sphere, I think saying *Dutch* can matter; because in a context where Dutch means white and white means human, subtly disrupting racist categories is a start.

Calls for a new definition of working against racism in a way that goes beyond talking and getting along. Her extended definition of Dutch identity challenges popular misconceptions and easy classifications.

DISCUSSION QUESTIONS

1. Sadiqa Khan begins her essay in an unusual way by remembering conversational exchanges she has had with ordinary people and officials about her ethnicity. What do the four scenes she sketches here seem meant to illustrate?

2. Khan recounts that many people seem skeptical when she claims to have Dutch ancestry. Why does she see, in their skepticism that she is Dutch, "something ugly" that she describes metaphorically as "a monstrous little creature on a hook"?

3. In your own words, explain the logic of the writer's causal chain in paragraph 5. What does race have to do with material comfort of people in the global north, and what does the writer mean when she says that she finds herself inhabiting a "strange space"?

4. How does the entire essay show not only the difficulties of trying to define and categorize people's racial and ethno-cultural identities at times, but also how the very attempt to do so may be damaging?

5. How does the writer suggest that she is "disrupting racist categories" by referring to herself as Dutch?

TOWARD KEY INSIGHTS

How do some Canadians justify having more resources than those who live in less developed countries of the global south that are popular vacation destinations for Canadians?

The writer alludes to how, once the Dutch economy began to slow in the 1970s, the guest workers who had been recruited from countries such as Morocco and Turkey were no longer needed, and a backlash against them ensued. What parallels or differences, if any, might you draw between attitudes toward guest workers in the Netherlands and attitudes toward those who are part of the Temporary Foreign Worker Program in Canada?

Toward the end of the essay, Sadiqa Khan challenges readers' willingness "to fundamentally change our relation to material resources as well as to each other, refusing a lifestyle that sustains itself through the exploitation, displacement or dispossession of people imagined as different." What does she mean here? What kind of response do you feel to her challenge?

SUGGESTIONS FOR WRITING

1. After reading this essay and two others related to identity and diversity in this text, write your own extended definition of covert or subtle racism.

2. If you have personally experienced prejudgments (prejudices) based on visible attributes such as race, ability, nationality, or age, write an essay showing how definitions and categories for people's identities may be restrictive, simplistic, or entirely off base.

Wayson Choy

I'm a Banana and Proud of It

Wayson Choy is a Canadian author, born in Vancouver in 1939. He is the author of the award-winning novel The Jade Peony *(1995) as well as* All That Matters *(2004), which was nominated for the Giller Prize. As the son of Chinese immigrants, Choy often writes on issues of multiculturalism, assimilation, and cultural hybridity and published his memoir* Paper Shadows: A Chinatown Childhood *in 1999. Choy has taught at Humber College in Toronto for more than 30 years and is currently on the faculty of the Humber School of Writers.*

1   Because both my parents came from China, I look Chinese. But I cannot read or write Chinese and barely speak it. I love my North American citizenship. I don't mind being called a "banana," yellow on the outside and white inside. I'm proud I'm a banana.

2   After all, in Canada and the United States, native Indians are "apples" (red outside, white inside); blacks are "Oreo cookies" (black and white); and Chinese are "bananas." These metaphors assume, both rightly and wrongly, that the culture here has been primarily anglo-white. Cultural history made me a banana.

3   History: My father and mother arrived separately to the B.C. coast in the early part of the century. They came as unwanted "aliens." Better to be an alien here than to be dead of starvation in China. But after the Chinese Exclusion laws were passed in North America (late 1800s, early 1900s), no Chinese immigrants were granted citizenship in either Canada or the United States.

4   Like those Old China village men from *Toi San* who, in the 1850s, laid down cliff-edge train tracks through the Rockies and the Sierras, or like those first women who came as mail-order wives or concubines and who as bond-slaves were turned into cheaper labourers or even prostitutes—like many of those men and women, my father and mother survived ugly, unjust times. In 1917, two hours after he got off the boat from Hong Kong, my father was called "chink" and told to go back to China. "Chink" is a hateful racist term, stereotyping the shape of Asian eyes: "a chink in the armour," an undesirable slit. For the Elders, the past was humiliating. Eventually, the Second World War changed hostile attitudes toward the Chinese.

5   During the war, Chinese men volunteered and lost their lives as members of the American and Canadian military. When hostilities ended, many more were proudly in uniform waiting to go overseas. Record Chinatown dollars were raised to buy War Bonds. After 1945, challenged by such money and ultimate sacrifices, the Exclusion laws in both Canada and the United States were revoked. Chinatown residents claimed their citizenship and sent for their families.

6   By 1949, after the Communists took over China, those of us who arrived here as young children, or were born here, stayed. No longer "aliens," we became legal citizens of North America. Many of us also became "bananas."

7   Historically, "banana" is not a racist term. Although it clumsily stereotypes many of the children and grandchildren of the Old Chinatowns, the term actually follows the old Chinese tendency to assign endearing nicknames to replace formal names, semicomic names to keep one humble. Thus, "banana" describes the generations who assimilated so well into North American life.

8   In fact, our families encouraged members of my generation in the 1950s and sixties to "get ahead," to get an English education, to get a job with good pay and prestige. "Don't work like me," Chinatown parents said. "Work in an office!" The *lao wah-kiu* (the Chinatown old-timers) also warned, "Never forget—you still be Chinese!"

9   None of us ever forgot. The mirror never lied.

10   Many Chinatown teenagers felt we didn't quite belong in any one world. We looked Chinese, but thought and behaved North American. Impatient Chinatown parents wanted the best of both worlds for us, but they bluntly labelled their children and grandchildren "*juk-sing*" or even "*mo no.*" Not that we were totally "shallow bamboo butt-ends" or entirely "no brain," but we had less and less understanding of Old China traditions, and less and less interest in their village histories. Father used to say we lacked Taoist ritual, Taoist manners. We were, he said, "*mo li.*"

11   This was true. Chinatown's younger brains, like everyone else's of whatever race, were being colonized by "white bread" U.S. family television programs. We began to feel Chinese home life was inferior. We co-operated with English-language magazines that showed us how to act and what to buy. Seductive Hollywood movies made some of us secretly weep that we did not have movie-star faces. American music made Chinese music sound like noise.

12   By the 1970s and eighties, many of us had consciously or unconsciously distanced ourselves from our Chinatown histories. We became bananas.

13   Finally, for me, in my 40s or 50s, with the death first of my mother, then my father, I realized I did not belong anywhere unless I could understand the past. I needed to find the foundation of my Chinese-ness. I needed roots.

14   I spent my college holidays researching the past. I read Chinatown oral histories, located documents, searched out early articles. Those early citizens came back to life for me. Their long toil and blood sacrifices, the proud record of their patient, legal challenges, gave us all our present rights as citizens. Canadian and American Chinatowns set aside their family tongue differences and encouraged each other to fight injustice. There were no borders. "After all," they affirmed, "*Daaih ga tohng yahn . . .* We are all Chinese!"

15   In my book, *The Jade Peony*, I tried to recreate this past, to explore the beginnings of the conflicts trapped within myself, the struggle between being Chinese and being North American. I discovered a truth: these "between world" struggles are universal.

16   In every human being, there is "the Other"—something that makes each of us feel how different we are to everyone else, even to family members. Yet, ironically, we are all the same, wanting the same security and happiness. I know this now.

17   I think the early Chinese pioneers actually started "going bananas" from the moment they first settled upon the West Coast. They had no choice. They adapted. They initiated assimilation. If they had not, they and their family would have starved to death. I might even suggest that all surviving Chinatown citizens eventually became bananas. Only some, of course, were more ripe than others.

18   That's why I'm proudly a banana: I accept the paradox of being both Chinese and not Chinese.

19   Now at last, whenever I look in the mirror or hear ghost voices shouting, "You still Chinese!" I smile.

20   I know another truth: In immigrant North America, we are all Chinese.

DISCUSSION QUESTIONS

1. Identify the essential definition that Choy gives at the beginning of the essay. To what extent is the rest of the essay an elaboration of this definition?

2. How does Choy use comparison or contrast in the essay? What purpose does the comparison or contrast serve?

3. How does the writer's view of Chinese culture and his Chinese heritage seem to change over time? Why does he decide that he needs "roots" (paragraph 13)?

4. Why does Choy say that he is "proud" to be a banana (paragraphs 1 and 18)? Why is his pride in this identity a "paradox" (paragraph 18)?

5. What does Choy mean with his closing statement, "In immigrant North America, we are all Chinese" (paragraph 20)? Could you substitute another group name for Chinese? Why or why not?

TOWARD KEY INSIGHTS

Comment on the significance of nicknames in your experience. Do you have a personal nickname now, or did you have one when you were younger? Do you belong to a group that has a nickname? If so, how do you feel about these nicknames?

Why do you think Wayson Choy is much better positioned to defend the term *banana* than an "anglo-white" person would be?

Wayson Choy writes that in every person, "there is 'the Other'—something that makes each of us feel how different we are to everyone else, even to family members." How do you understand this claim? Does it seem true in your experience? If so, explain.

SUGGESTIONS FOR WRITING

1. Just as Wayson Choy mounts a defence of a term (*banana*) that some might consider racist, write an essay explaining why a term such as *geek* that some consider offensive could be understood in a positive way—or, conversely, explaining why a descriptive term such as *lady* that some consider acceptable could be considered offensive.

2. Read the two essays in Chapter 13 related to Canada's multicultural policies, "No Place Like Home" by Neil Bissoondath and "Immigrants, Multiculturalism and Canadian Citizenship" by Will Kymlicka. Drawing from these essays and your own experience, write an extended definition of a term such as *social inclusiveness* or *cultural integration*.

CHAPTER 11

Strategies for Finding Patterns: Comparison

Which candidate for mayor should get my vote, Ali Randa or Kim Thompson?

Why do you prefer shopping online over going to the mall?

Doesn't this tune remind you of a Nelly Furtado song?

Is high school in Australia harder or easier than high school in Canada?

Everyone makes *comparisons*, not just once in a while, but day after day. When we compare, we examine two or more items for likenesses, differences, or both. Comparison has a purpose. Sometimes, when the similarities between two things are obvious, we may choose to emphasize how two things that appear at first glance to be similar are actually quite different. On the other hand, when the differences are obvious, we may choose to demonstrate how two things that impress us with their differences actually share underlying similarities.

Comparison often serves an evaluative purpose, showing why one person, thing, or plan of action is superior to another. It may help us clarify our preferences and decide on matters small and large. At a restaurant, we may compare the appeal and value of ordering a pasta dinner with the appeal and value of ordering a sub sandwich. Putting items side by side can help us weigh the relative merits of each item and choose between alternatives.

Comparison also influences our more important decisions. We weigh buying a Samsung against buying an iPhone, majoring in arts against majoring in sciences, renting a condo against buying one, working for a bank against working in the health care sector. An instructor may ask us to write a paper comparing the features of two behavioural organization models. An employer may have us weigh two proposals for decreasing employee absenteeism and write a report recommending one of them.

Comparison also acquaints us with the unfamiliar. To help uninitiated Canadian readers understand the sport of rugby, a sportswriter might compare its field, team, rules, and scoring system with those of North American football. To teach students about France's government, a political science textbook might compare the makeup and election of its legislature to that of the Canadian Parliament, and the method of selecting its president and prime minister to the Canadian method of selecting leaders.

Both academic assignments and jobs call for comparative analysis. A music instructor may ask you to compare and contrast the styles and complexity of music from the Baroque and Renaissance periods. A psychology instructor may want you to compare two different types of psychosis treatment and assess the legal and medical ramifications of each. A biology instructor might have you consider how the features of two different kinds of body cells enable them to perform their functions. A criminology instructor might ask you how a restorative justice model compares with a model of adversarial justice in a specific context. In the workplace, comparisons are also common because they help people make decisions. An office manager may compare several telephone systems to determine which one would be most useful for the company; a nurse may assess the condition of a patient before and after a new medicine is given; an insurance agent may point out the features of two insurance policies to highlight the advantages of one.

SELECTING ITEMS FOR COMPARISON

Any items you compare must share some common ground. For example, you could compare two golfers on driving ability, putting ability, and sand play, or two cars on appearance, gas consumption, and warranty; but you can't meaningfully compare a golfer with a car, any more than you could compare guacamole with Guadalajara or chicken with charcoal. There's simply no basis for comparison.

Any valid comparison, on the other hand, presents many possibilities. Suppose you head the music department of a large store and have two excellent salespeople working for you. The manager of the store asks you to prepare a one- or two-page report that compares their qualifications for managing the music department in a new branch store. Assessing their abilities becomes the guiding purpose that motivates and controls the writing. Rather than comparing irrelevant points such as eye colour, hairstyle, and religion, which have no bearing on job performance, you will focus on what managerial traits the job requires and the extent to which each candidate possesses them. Your thinking might result in a list like this.

Points of Similarity or Difference	Lee	Mike
1. Ability to deal with customers, sales skills	Excellent	Excellent
2. Effort: regular attendance, hard work on the job	Excellent	Excellent
3. Leadership qualities	Excellent	Good
4. Knowledge of ordering and accounting procedures	Good	Fair
5. Musical knowledge	Excellent	Good

This list tells you which points to emphasize and suggests Lee as the candidate to recommend. You might briefly mention similarities (points 1 and 2) in an introductory paragraph, but the report would focus on differences (points 3, 4, and 5) since you're distinguishing the relative merits of two employees.

EXERCISE *Compare two popular restaurants in order to recommend one of them. List the points of similarity and difference that you might discuss. Differences should predominate, because you will base your decision on them.*

DEVELOPING A COMPARISON

Successful comparisons depend on ample, well-chosen details that show just how the items under consideration are alike and different. Such support helps the reader grasp your meaning. Read the following student comparative paragraphs and note how the concrete details convey the striking differences between south and north 14th Street.

On 14th Street running south from P Street are opulent luxury stores such as Birks and Holt Renfrew, and small but expensive clothing stores with richly dressed mannequins in the windows. Tall, glass-covered skyscraping office buildings hold banks and travel bureaus on the ground floors and insurance companies and corporation headquarters in the upper storeys. Dotting the concretescape are high-priced movie theatres, gourmet restaurants, multilevel parking garages, bookstores, boutiques, and fancy gift shops, all catering to the wealthy population of the city. This section of 14th Street is relatively clean: The city maintenance crews must clean up after only a nine-to-five populace and the Saturday crowds of shoppers. The pervading mood of the area is one of bustling wealth during the day and, in the night, calm.

Crossing P Street toward the north, one notes a gradual but disturbing change in the scenery of 14th Street. A panhandler sits nodding on the sidewalk in front of a rundown hotel, too tired, or too drugged, to bother asking for money. A liquidation store promises bargains, but the window display shows an unattractive tangle of chains, watches, knives, and dusty tools. Outside a tavern with opaque windows, a homeless person is curled up, sleeping beneath a tattered blanket. On the opposite side of the street, a restaurant advertising curry competes for customers with the house of noodles and pizza-to-go restaurant. Sometimes, even when the air is chill, one sees young women in short skirts, low-cut tops, and high boots standing near the curb, or leaning into the windows of cars momentarily stopped, talking to the drivers.

Vivid details highlight the economic differences between the north and south ends of the street. These differences contribute to the writer's implied thesis: *The stark contrast between wealth and poverty on opposite ends of the same street is disturbing.*

ORGANIZING A COMPARISON

Comparison papers can be organized in two basic patterns: *block pattern*, also called comparison of wholes; and *alternating pattern*, also called comparison by points or by parts. Typically, a comparison paper uses some combination of these two patterns.

The Block Pattern   The block pattern first presents all points of comparison for one item and then all points of comparison for the other. Here is the comparison of the two salespeople, Lee and Mike, outlined according to the block pattern:

    I. Introduction: mentions similarities in sales skills and effort but recommends Lee for promotion
   II. Specific points about Mike
      A. Leadership qualities
      B. Knowledge of ordering and accounting procedures
      C. Musical knowledge
  III. Specific points about Lee
      A. Leadership qualities
      B. Knowledge of ordering and accounting procedures
      C. Musical knowledge
  IV. Conclusion: reasserts that Lee should be promoted

For a shorter paper or one that includes only a few points of comparison, the block pattern can work well, since the reader can remember all points from the first block while reading the second. Be careful, however, that you do not dwell too long on one half of the comparison without mentioning the other, or your essay might seem to break in two. The reader may often find it easier to follow a modified block pattern, in which you refer to the first item of comparison throughout the second block.

The Alternating Pattern   The alternating pattern presents a point about one item, then follows immediately with a corresponding point about the other. Organized in this way, the Lee-and-Mike paper would look like this:

    I. Introduction: mentions similarities in sales skills and effort but recommends Lee for promotion
   II. Leadership qualities
      A. Mike's qualities
      B. Lee's qualities
  III. Knowledge of ordering and accounting procedures
      A. Mike's knowledge
      B. Lee's knowledge
  IV. Musical knowledge
      A. Mike's knowledge
      B. Lee's knowledge
   V. Conclusion: reasserts that Lee should be promoted

If there are many points of comparison, the alternating method, which deals with each point in turn, can help your reader grasp similarities and differences. Be aware, however, that moving back and forth between two different poems or two different historical periods may become rather dizzying. To ground your reader, you may need to blend the two approaches. For example, when comparing protagonists from two works of fiction, you might give an overview of the two works' similarities in the block approach, and then use the alternating approach to focus on salient points of difference.

Once you select your pattern, arrange your points of comparison in an appropriate order. Take up closely related points one after the other. Depending on your purpose, you might work from similarities to differences or the reverse. Often, a good writing strategy is to move from the least significant to the most significant point so that you conclude with a punch.

EXERCISE *Using the points of comparison you selected for the exercise on page 221, prepare two different outlines for a paper, one organized according to the block pattern and one organized according to the alternating pattern.*

USING ANALOGY

An *analogy*, a special type of comparison, calls attention to one or more similarities underlying two different kinds of items that seem to have nothing in common. While some analogies stand alone, most clarify abstract or unfamiliar concepts in other kinds of writing. They are commonly used in political and business contexts. In the 1995 Quebec referendum on sovereignty, newspaper writers drew analogies comparing separation to divorce or major surgery. In trying to explain how social media can help with marketing, someone might compare the use of social media to networking at a party.

Drawing parallels through an analogy between seemingly unrelated things can help people get a picture in their mind's eye. Analogies that point out how cells may be like factories, or DNA molecules like ladders, may help people who are not scientists to get a mental picture that clarifies scientific concepts. Consider, for example, how the following passage provides insight by comparing something that is less understood (climate change) to something that is easier to visualize (a marble rolling around in a bowl):

> "Imagine a bowl," he told me, "with a marble in it. The marble is in constant motion, running up the side of the bowl and falling back down to the bottom and running up the side again. That's the normal variability of climate: hot . . . cold . . . wet . . . dry. Well, now imagine that the marble is gaining energy, running higher up the side of the bowl at the top of each roll. That's what's happening with the climate; it's becoming more energetic, more extreme." I could picture that: as the energy in the atmosphere amps up, the weather manifests that greater energy by becoming more pronounced. Rainy days get rainier. Hot days get hotter. Wind, windier. Droughts, drier.
>
> "What we don't know," Weaver said next, "is what happens when the marble goes right over the edge of the bowl. We know that sometimes in the past, the climate has changed from one more or less stable regime to another that may be quite different. We think that the closer the marble gets to the rim of the bowl, the closer we are to that kind of change. But we don't know just how close we are or what will happen when the marble

goes over. We just know that the marble is going higher higher up the side of the bowl as times goes on."

Chris Wood, *Dry Spring: The Coming Water Crisis of North America*

An analogy sometimes may also highlight the unfamiliar to help illuminate the familiar. The following paragraph discusses the qualities and obligations of an unfamiliar person, the mountain guide, to shed light on a familiar practice—teaching.

> The mountain guide, like the true teacher, has a quiet authority. He or she engenders trust and confidence so that one is willing to join the endeavor. The guide accepts his leadership role, yet recognizes that success (measured by the heights that are scaled) depends upon the close co-operation and active participation of each member of the group. He has crossed the terrain before and is familiar with the landmarks, but each trip is new and generates its own anxiety and excitement. Essential skills must be mastered; if they are lacking, disaster looms. The situation demands keen focus and rapt attention: slackness, misjudgment, or laziness can abort the venture.

Nancy K. Hill, "Scaling the Heights: The Teacher as Mountaineer"

When you develop an analogy, keep these points in mind:

1. Your readers must be well acquainted with the familiar item. If they aren't, the point is lost.
2. The items must indeed have significant similarities. You could develop a meaningful analogy between a kidney and a filter or between cancer and anarchy, but not between a fiddle and a flapjack or a laser and Limburger cheese.
3. The analogy must truly illuminate. Overly obvious analogies, such as one comparing a battle to an argument, offer few or no revealing insights.
4. Overextended analogies can tax the reader's endurance. A multipage analogy between a heart and a pump would likely overwhelm the reader with too much detail about valves, hoses, pressures, and pumping.

ETHICAL ISSUES

Although an old adage declares that "comparisons are odious," most people embrace comparisons except when they are unfair, which unfortunately happens all too often. For example, advertisers commonly magnify trivial drawbacks in competitors' products while exaggerating the benefits of their own merchandise. Politicians run attack ads that distort their opponents' views and demean the opponents' characters. And when scientific theories clash, supporters of one view have been known to alter their findings to undermine the other position. Your readers expect all comparisons to meet certain ethical standards. Ask and answer these questions to help ensure that the comparisons you write are solid.

- Have I avoided skewing one or both of my items in order to ensure a particular outcome?
- Are the items I'm comparing properly matched? It would be unethical to compare a student essay to a professional one in order to demonstrate the inadequacy of the former.
- If I'm using an analogy, is it appropriate and ethically fair? Comparing immigration officials to Nazi stormtroopers would trivialize the suffering and deaths of millions of Nazi victims and taint immigration officials with a terrible label.

WRITING A COMPARISON

Don't write merely to fulfill an assignment; if you do, your paper will likely ramble aimlessly and fail to deliver a specific message. Instead, build your paper around a clear sense of purpose. Do you want to show the superiority of one product or method over another? Do you want to show how sitcoms today differ from those of 20 years ago? Purpose governs the details you choose and the organization you follow.

Prewriting the Comparison

> - Brainstorm major areas of interest: movies, TV shows, teaching styles.
> - Brainstorm basic areas of comparison, or narrowing: e.g., "the representation of fathers on TV in the 1950s and now."
> - Identify your purpose for the comparison, such as to show progress or help consumers make a choice.
> - Identify what audience would be interested in your comparison.

PREWRITING: FINDING YOUR TOPIC

> - If possible, re-observe or use items to be compared and take notes of similarities and differences.
> - Brainstorm or create a chart of the major similarities and differences of the items being compared.
> - Branch or chart the details and examples.
> - Decide what points of comparison you will use based on audience and purpose.
> - Create a chart or create an outline that establishes an order for your comparison.

DEVELOPING YOUR COMPARISON

Planning and Drafting the Comparison

When you decide on an order, copy the points of comparison and the details, arranged in the order you will follow, into a chart like the one below.

Item A	Item B
First point of comparison	First point of comparison
First detail	First detail
Second detail	Second detail
Second point of comparison	Second point of comparison

A **thesis statement** for a comparison often stresses the major point or two of comparison and relates that point to the reader's interests. "While earthquakes in the East may be more infrequent and less severe than those in California, they may be more widely felt because they tend to be shallower and are not dampened by additional faults." To develop your thesis, review your brainstorming to identify the main points of comparisons that will interest your reader and consider why those points are important.

Here are some strategies for drafting a comparison:

Introduction

■ Connect to reader's interest, identifying reader's interest in making a choice or reasons for understanding something unfamiliar.

■ Identify items being compared and main points of comparison.

■ Sometimes preview the key points of comparison in the order they will be presented in the paper.

Body

■ Based on purpose, number of points you will make, and length, select organizational pattern: block or alternating.

■ If explaining something unfamiliar, start with something familiar.

■ If trying to demonstrate superiority of an item, go from less to more desirable.

■ Follow a consistent pattern throughout.

■ Provide details or examples to develop points of comparison.

Conclusion

■ Possibly end with a recommendation, like whether to buy Mac or PC.

■ Or make a prediction, such as the growing popularity of rugby at colleges.

■ Or stress the major point of the comparison and its importance: "Why the Maritimes also needs to be prepared for earthquakes."

■ Do not summarize all similarities and differences for a short paper. You may provide such a summary on a much longer paper.

Revising the Comparison

Revise your paper in light of the general guidelines in Chapter 4 and the questions and suggestions that follow.

■ What could help strengthen the achievement of the paper's purpose, whether to examine and weigh the advantages and disadvantages of two alternatives or acquaint the reader with something unfamiliar?

■ For something unfamiliar, where could the unfamiliar features be made clearer by a stronger comparison with something familiar?

■ Where could the paper be better directed to the audience? Cut or revise material not appropriate to the audience and purpose.

■ What additional points of similarity and difference might be included? Brainstorm.

■ Where would additional details or examples strengthen the paper? Brainstorm or use branching.

■ Does the organization of the paper not fit the purpose and audience? Where doesn't the paper follow a consistent pattern? Experiment with reorganization.

■ Where could the transitions be strengthened to better show the shifts in points of comparison?

■ Where do paragraphs lose focus or try to deal with too many points of comparison?

■ Where, if anywhere, does the paper unfairly distort the comparison unethically?

Write whatever kind of conclusion will round off your discussion effectively. Unless you've written a lengthy paper, don't summarize the likenesses and differences you've presented. If you've done a proper writing job, your reader already has them clearly in mind. Many comparison papers end with a recommendation or a prediction. For example, a paper comparing face-to-face poker with online poker might end with a recommendation to try the less familiar form of the game.

EXAMPLES OF STUDENT ESSAYS USING COMPARISON

Real vs. Fake Conversation

William Nichols

1   Have you ever been engaged in a conversation where you have no interest in the subject or who you are talking to? Of course. Now ask yourself what it feels like to be in a conversation that has your full attention. You are sure to notice many differences. For simplicity, <u>I will call these two types of conversations real and fake, the fake conversation being the one which you wish you were never part of.</u> These fake conversations are not limited to talks with teachers, parents, law enforcement officials, <u>but could in fact include even the closest people in your life, since it is the level of interest in the topic that determines engagement.</u> While real and fake conversations are very different, <u>they can be assessed by examining the degree of conversational engagement or disengagement, as the case may be.</u>

> Establishes point of view on topic and identifies major items to be compared and contrasted.

> Gives readers a reason this topic will be relevant to them.

> Establishes focus and purpose for comparison.

2   In a real conversation, the listener is genuinely interested in what the speaker has to say. This is not the case in a fake conversation, where the listener is not really listening, but usually either trying to get away or thinking only about what he or she wants to say. <u>If we examine the body language, eye contact, emotion, and overall interest displayed by the participants in both real and fake conversations, we will see that the differences are reflected in the type and level of engagement.</u>

> Identifies key points of comparison that will be discussed.

3   For a conversation to be real, all parties involved should show interest in what the others are saying and be aware of the messages that they are conveying through body language, eye contact, and emotion. <u>The use of body language and eye contact is integral to making good conversation.</u> Body language is often quite subtle, as even the slightest movement such as leaning toward someone or away from someone can be quite revealing. One obvious

> Topic sentence identifies first point of difference.

Develops the point on body language with example.	form of body language is the use of hands. <u>Our hands help us stay focused while conveying our message to the listener.</u> For example, consider how you might use your hands when you are on the phone talking to someone. When you are describing something, you might not even notice how much you are using gestures. If you are trying to describe a building or a shape, you may trace this shape with your hands, even though you are talking on the phone and no one can see you. It seems ridiculous in hindsight, yet most of us use our hands in such circumstances because we are fully engaged in conversation and genuinely interested in communicating our thoughts to others. Now imagine how you use your hands while talking person-to-person. Using your hands while talking person-to-person shows that you are thinking about what you are saying and that you are trying to get your message across by whatever means possible.
Topic sentence identifies second point that will be discussed.	4 <u>Another form of effective body language to use in conversation is eye contact.</u> In a real conversation all persons involved make eye contact quite frequently, but in a fake conversation, people often look off into the distance, or down at a newspaper. Eye contact tells people we are listening intently or that we are speaking directly to them. Both eye contact and the use of hands can directly show emotion.
Alternating pattern emphasizes contrast between signs of emotion in real conversation and lack of appropriate emotional response in fake conversation.	5 Showing emotion when speaking demonstrates that we care about what we are saying or about what is being said and that we are in fact engaged in a real conversation. <u>The emotion found in a fake conversation is very different from that of a real one. In a real conversation, the participants look animated and attentive; they may smile, laugh, frown, or widen their eyes as they speak and listen. In a fake conversation, sometimes one person is serious about what is being discussed and the other is bored.</u> While in a fake conversation, we may find ourselves becoming distracted by the smallest of things, such as the pattern on the other person's shirt. Obviously, when distracted, we fail to maintain eye contact and are not engaged in animated body language. Our disinterest is readily apparent to all . . . unless we are able to maintain the appearance of interest by staying in the conversation and sending enough body language cues to deceive our conversation partners. <u>By pretending or faking interest, we make the other person feel as if we are genuinely participating. In fake conversations, we may be engaged in a game with ourselves in order to keep us from admitting to the other person that we are in fact totally bored and distracted.</u>
Develops contrast in depth by showing that the line between real and fake conversations can be unclear.	6 When people are engaged in a fake conversation, they lack interest in those with whom they are conversing or the subject of the conversation. Fake conversations, which may occur with a teacher, parent, neighbour, or co-worker, are revealed not only by how we act but also by what we say. Clichéd statements

about the nice weather suggest that the person would probably prefer not to be talking at all. Fake conversation is often bland and lacks any real substance. Usually people stay in such conversations out of guilt and fear of offending. We don't want to admit to the other person—or sometimes even to ourselves—that we are completely bored by the conversation we are in.

> Develops by bringing in some causal analysis.

7   Although all conversations use similar tools of communication, the body language, eye contact, and degree of emotional engagement are different in real and fake conversations. In a real conversation, participants engage physically in many ways, and there is frequent, focused eye contact, but in a fake conversation, participants are disengaged and eye contact is uncommon. While we all can probably admit to being in a fake conversation, how many of us can really admit to knowing someone was trying to maintain a fake conversation with us? By remaining attentive to the real and fake conversational dynamics described above, next time you'll know.

> Includes brief summary of main points in concluding paragraph.

> Leaves readers with something to think about in the future.

DISCUSSION QUESTIONS

1. Comment on the significance of the rhetorical questions in the introductory and concluding paragraphs.
2. Point out effective supporting details for each major point in paragraphs 3, 4, 5, and 6. How do these details contribute to the writer's purpose?
3. What pattern of organization does the writer use? Examine how the whole essay and individual paragraphs are organized.
4. What reasons does the writer suggest to explain why people stay in fake conversations (paragraph 6)? What is the effect of his bringing in this causal analysis (exploration of reasons why)?

The following student essay was written for a literature class entitled Journeys in Literature: Land, Sea, Myth, and Imagination. In the essay, Alexandar McIlwain argues that the hero of a contemporary children's novel, an undersized mouse who goes on a quest to free a princess from a dungeon, is actually more heroic than the classic Greek hero Odysseus.

ZERO TO HERO: A COMPARATIVE ANALYSIS OF HEROISM IN *THE ODYSSEY* AND *TALE OF DESPEREAUX*

By Alex McIlwain

Humans have long been fascinated by tales of incredible exploits and epic journeys, and looked to models of heroism in literature for guidance and inspiration. While people in different cultures may have different attitudes about what constitutes heroism, most seems to agree that a hero must be an exceptional individual, with qualities that set them apart from their peers. In the west we often turn for models of heroism to ancient Greek epics such as *The Odyssey*. Other literary models such as the story in the Newbery award winning children's novel *Tale of Despereaux* show a different kind of contemporary hero than the tale of Odysseus. While it may seem unfair to compare the heroes of two very different literary traditions and genres, measuring the traditional epic hero Odysseus against the standards of heroism set by the mouse protagonist Despereaux in the children's fantasy illumines the flaws and merits of each. Although *The Odyssey* is often regarded as one of the finest works of western literature, and *Tale of Despereaux* is a popular children's novel, the titular protagonist of the latter proves to be a greater hero than Odysseus, more sympathetic, more consistent in his adherence to his principles and ideals, and ironically more wise and levelheaded than Odysseus, who is legendary for his supposedly great cunning.

Comparing the nature of their respective origins reveals Despereaux as a greater hero than Odysseus. At the beginning of *The Odyssey*, Odysseus is already a figure of great political and martial power, being the king of Ithaca, a skilled archer, and a cunning tactician. He is described as "beyond all mortals in wisdom" by none other than Zeus, the king of the Olympian gods (Homer, Book 1. 73). Furthermore, his virtues are likewise extolled by his ally Menelaus, the king who laments the loss of all the Achaeans lost at sea, but above all for Odysseus: "'And yet, though I often sit in my halls weeping and sorrowing for them all—one moment indeed I ease my heart with weeping . . . —yet for them all I mourn not so much, despite my grief, as for one only, who makes me to loathe both sleep and food, when I think of him; for no one of the Achaeans toiled so much as Odysseus toiled and endured'" (Book 4. 100). We hear much about Odysseus' prowess before we actually meet him.

While even the most cursory comparison between the two would indicate that Odysseus is the greater warrior, much admired by his compatriots, and even by the goddess Athena, it is precisely this elevated status which makes him the less compelling hero within the context of a journey narrative. Unlike Odysseus, Despereaux has few allies in his society, showing "no interest in the things a mouse should show interest in" (17) and is physically frail, "ridiculously small . . . . And he was sickly. He coughed and sneezed so often that he carried a handkerchief in one paw at all times. He ran temperatures. He fainted at loud noises" (DiCamillo 17). This attitude of disparagement is echoed by members of Despereaux's family. In contrast, Odysseus seems destined for success. Not only has Odysseus proven himself in events prior to the events of *The Odyssey*, having honed his skills as a warrior and tactician in the infamously bloody Trojan War, but also, as his heroic qualities are so repeatedly underlined, we have little doubt that he will succeed on his quest. After Zeus himself names him as "beyond all mortals in wisdom" (Book 1. 63), after he is praised by a major Greek general as the finest Achaean soldier of the Trojan War, *The Odyssey* is drained of the kind of taut narrative tension that runs through *Tale of Despereaux*. The reader expects Odysseus to accomplish his goals and defeat his foes, lest the lofty pedestal he has been placed upon seem false. Not even Odysseus' divine nemesis Poseidon poses any true threat to him, as the goddess Athena tells Odysseus, "'Cunning must he be and knavish, who would go beyond thee in all manner of guile . . . though it were a god that met thee'" (Book 13, 287). The critic Scott Richardson claims that "the second half of the Odyssey is essentially a grand performance, with Odysseus as director as well as lead actor, guiding the rest of the cast in what they might or might not realize to be roles in his show," but I would argue that it is more accurate to say, given the amount of divine aid Odysseus receives in his quest, that the gods are the directors, and Odysseus is the lead actor who is scripted to win (141). This interpretation is reinforced by Athena's revelation that it was she who made him "beloved by all the Phaeacians," and how he must endure woes before returning home but how she will help him (Book 13. 287). Readers, aware that Athena is pulling strings in the background, may think that the dangers Odysseus encounters thus seem less compelling than those endured by Despereaux.

Unlike Odysseus, Despereaux does not have divine allies or physical strength. His physical weakness presents a personal flaw for him to overcome as part of his journey, as well as a reason for readers to sympathize with him. Who has not wished to be able to do something, yet be held back by one's own inabilities? His physical limitations make Despereaux's acts of heroism throughout the novel seem even more remarkable, particularly when he, after having his tail violently chopped off, displays immense inner resolve through his ardent desire to save Princess Pea: "Alas, there was no one to comfort Despereaux. And there was no time, anyway, for him to cry. He knew what he had to do. He had to find the king" (DiCamillo 202). Likewise, as Despereaux descends into the dungeon to rescue Pea, he must conquer his terror, without the aid of any gods: "He stood very still. 'I'll go back,' he said. But he didn't move. 'I have to go back.' He took a step backward. 'But I can't go back. I don't have a choice. I have no choice.' He took one step forward. And then another" (241). Overall, Despereaux's determination to continue even after being maimed means that, while he may be beneath the notice of royals such as Pea's father, he is at the very least their equal in valour.

When we compare their respective characters, we also see ways that Despereaux's moral heroism surpasses that of Odysseus. Despereaux is a more morally consistent individual than Odysseus is, as he maintains his unwavering devotion to his ideals throughout his journey. Both protagonists are primarily motivated by their love for a woman—Odysseus for his wife Penelope—and Despereaux for Princess Pea— but the fidelity of Odysseus' love appears compromised by his sexual dalliances with other women during his journey home. Although we are told that he has been held captive against his will by the nymph Calypso, we may also notice a degree of pleasurable intimacy when Odysseus and Calypso "took their joy of love" in the hollow of a cave on their final night together (Book 5, 225).

This hint of an internal moral contradiction and even sexual double standard (we remember Penelope weeping and fending off suitors on Ithaka) might have been excusable given Odysseus' dire circumstances, yet the transgression is later repeated in his encounter with the goddess Circe. As the god Hermes warns Odysseus of Circe's powerful sorcery and provides him with a plan to face her, which in itself seems contradictory and unnecessary given Odysseus' status as a master tactician,

Hermes tells Odysseus that Circe" will be seized with fear" and will order him to lie wither her. "Then do not thou thereafter refuse the couch of the goddess, that she may set free thy comrades, and give entertainment to thee" (Book 10. 274). Once again, it would appear that Odysseus has little choice in the matter, but Odysseus neither protests this course of action nor asks if there is an alternate method of appeasing Circe. Indeed when the time comes he climbs into her "beautiful bed" (Book 10. 345) and proceeds to dally with her, feasting and drinking "sweet wine" (Book 10, 466) on her island for a full year, casting serious aspersions on the legitimacy of his love for Penelope. Scott Richardson even goes so far as to suggest that Odysseus deliberately uses charm and flirtation to achieve his ends, referencing Odysseus' encounter with the princess Nausicaa: "Odysseus delivers a masterful speech in which his hints and flattery impart all the characteristics of a potential husband without disclosing his identity or his true intentions toward her," a manipulative act that is done so lightly as to challenge the sincerity of his feelings for Penelope (134).

No such doubt can be found in Despereaux's earnest longing for Princess Pea, as the purity of his love seems to govern all his actions, for he "wanted to read those words. Happily ever after. He needed to say them aloud; he needed some assurance that this feeling he had for the Princess Pea, this love, would come to a good end" (DiCamillo 46-7). The fact that Despereaux feels compelled to utter these words aloud without any outside love is a mark of genuineness, a true display of courtly love. Furthermore, after Despereaux escapes the castle dungeons for the first time, he "crie[s] because he was happy . . . . His rescue had happened just in time for him to save the Princess Pea . . . . So Despereaux wept with joy and with pain and with gratitude. He wept with exhaustion and despair and hope" (181). Here, the sincerity and depth of Despereaux's love for Pea is evident; he is at once both overcome with worry for her safety as well as happiness that he might still use his own life to save hers. His relief at his rescue is explicitly tied to his capacity to aid Pea. Ironically, although the epilogue of *Tale of Despereaux* states that Despereaux and Pea will never be able to marry, their love feels far more substantial than Odysseus' affection for his human wife.

A second weakness in Odysseus' character that diminishes his own heroism in comparison to Despereaux's is in how they treat their defeated adversaries. As Odysseus fights the suitors who have invaded his home, one among their number, Eurymachus, attempts to surrender, pleading that they would give him full recompense for everything they had eaten and drunk in his house as well as adding "in requital the worth of twenty oxen" (Book 22, 42). However, Odysseus rejects these terms and continues his attack: "Then with an angry glance from beneath his brows Odysseus . . . answered him: 'Eurymachus, not even if you should give me in requital all that your fathers left you, even all that you now have, and should add other wealth thereto . . . not even so would I henceforth stay my hands from slaying until the wooers had paid the full price of all their transgression. Now it lies before you to fight in open fight, or to flee, if any man may avoid death and the fates; but many a one, methinks, shall not escape from utter destruction'" (Book 22. 60). Here Odysseus' aggression is problematic for two reasons. Although Odysseus has been trumpeted as a highly pragmatic tactician throughout the entire epic, yet his blunt refusal to accept Eurymachus' offer in spite of the obvious economic benefits it would bring to his household calls his pragmatism into question. It cannot be that Odysseus merely suspects duplicity on Eurymachus' part, as evidenced by his statement that he would still kill all of the suitors even if they donated all of their material wealth to him, but instead revenge appears to be a matter of honour for him. While the cultural mores around honour in ancient Greece may have justified the violence of Odysseus' revenge on the suitors, his treatment of them more is more bloody than necessary, especially as he knows that their families might seek vengeance. If Odysseus truly surpasses all mortals in wisdom, as Zeus claimed, then surely he would not allow his emotions to cloud his judgment, slaughtering the suitors and inciting further violence from their allies, but would instead make friends out of his enemies. In addition, Odysseus' anger over the suitors' flagrant violations of the laws of hospitality seems rather hypocritical, given how he invaded the homes of the Cyclops and Circe, could not stop his own crew from eating to Helios' sacred cattle, and, after dining on the bounty of King Alcinous, lets the Phaecians incur the curse of Poseidon by helping him. Odysseus' violations of the laws of hospitality may have been, unlike the suitors' gluttony, motivated at least in part by desperation, but his lack of critical self-awareness and generosity in his revenge shows him as rather self-serving.

Despereaux, in contrast, is far more level-headed when he confronts Roscuro, the villain of his story. He does not hesitate to take action against his foe, "plac[ing] the sharp tip of [his needle] where the rat's heart should be" the moment Roscuro lowers his guard, but even before Princess Pea orders Despereaux to stand down, Despereaux wonders "would killing the rat really make the darkness go away" (DiCamillo 261-2). This act of mercy seems not only generous but brave--given the very grave danger represented by Roscuro, who has already slain the jailor Gregory and caused the deaths of other knights who travelled to the dungeons. Further evidence of Despereaux's compassion can be found when, despite his father's "perfidy" in sentencing him to death, he declares "I forgive you, Pa" (208). Despereaux's willingness to consider other viewpoints and put aside his grudges for the greater good of all demonstrates that not only is he more generous than Odysseus, but wiser as well, as is reflected in the tone of the endings of each story. Whereas Odysseus recognizes that he must one day embark on a voyage of repentance to atone for his slights against Poseidon, implying that he has aired at least in some regard, Despereaux's tale ends on a much more optimistic note. He and Princess Pea go on to have "many adventures" which are ". . . another story," suggesting that Despereaux does eventually become the knight he has always dreamed of being (267).

If Odysseus is tested in his journey across the Aegean Sea on his way to Ithaka, Despereaux too is tested on his journey through the dungeon, back to the light of Princess Pea's castle. Arguably, however, while Odysseus is favoured by numerous advantages, the titular protagonist of *Tale of Despereaux* defies the disadvantages of his small stature and oppressive society to become a hero greater than one of the mightiest champions of Greek myth. Even discounting modern-day moral connotations of what it means to be a hero, Despereaux remains Odysseus' superior by virtue of his development from a sickly youth to a chivalrous knight, as well as his unflinching adherence to his principles. Odysseus' journey may be grander, but Despereaux's is the more remarkable. He embarks on a path of dangerous adventure for the sake of his ideals, while Odysseus' victory is all but assured from the very beginning due to having his destiny laid out for him by the gods. Thus it can be plausibly argued that Despereaux is a true hero who eclipses the wily Odysseus.

WORK CITED

Richardson, Scott. "Conversation in *The Odyssey*." *College Literature* 34.2 (2007): 132-149. Academic Search Premier. Web. 13 Aug. 2015.

Homer. *The Odyssey*. Trans. Murray, A T. Loeb Classical Library Volumes. Cambridge, MA, Harvard University Press; London, William Heinemann Ltd. 1919.Web. 15 Aug. 2015.

DiCamillo, Kate. *Tale of Despereaux*. Berryville: Candlewick Press. 2006. Print.

DISCUSSION QUESTIONS

1. How does the writer lead in to his discussion and provide a rationale for his comparison in the first paragraph?

2. What are the writer's main points of comparison and contrast in his analysis of the relative heroism of the epic hero Odysseus and the small mouse named Despereaux?

3. What is the main idea that the author is discussing in paragraphs 5 and 6? How does he support his argument with evidence and quotations from the two texts?

4. How does the writer tie the two threads of his comparison together in the final paragraph, and leave the writer with something to think about?

SUGGESTIONS FOR WRITING

1. Write a comparison essay on one of the topics below or another that your instructor approves. Determine the points you will discuss and how you will develop and arrange them. Emphasize similarities, differences, or both.

a. An arts education versus a trades education

b. The physical or mental demands of two jobs

c. Two advertisements for similar products

d. An online course and a face-to face course

e. A day-to-day relationship and a virtual one

f. Two different forms of exercise

g. Two cultures' approaches to dating

2. Develop an analogy based on one of the following sets of items or another set that your instructor approves. Proceed as you would for any other comparison.

a. Ending a relationship and leaving a job

b. Drug addiction and shopping addiction

    c. Troubleshooting a computer and writing an essay

    d. Learning to drive and learning a new language

    e. Taking an exam and going to the dentist

    f. A parent and a farmer

    g. A workaholic and an alcoholic

Stepping Up to Synthesis

Although you rely on your own knowledge or findings to develop many comparisons, in some cases you'll synthesize material from other sources.

PREWRITING FOR SYNTHESIS

Let's say that your business management instructor has asked you to prepare a report on the management styles of two high-profile chief executive officers (CEOs) at successful companies that manufacture the same kinds of products. You realize that you need to do some reading in business periodicals such as *Canadian Business*, *The Economist*, and *Fortune* to complete this assignment. Your sources reveal that the first CEO favours a highly centralized managerial structure with strict limits on what can be done by all employees except top executives. The company has pursued foreign markets by establishing factories overseas and has aggressively attempted to merge with or acquire its domestic competitors. The second CEO has established a decentralized managerial structure that allows managers at various levels of the company to make key decisions. The company has also established a strong foreign presence, but it has done so primarily by entering into joint ventures with foreign firms. Most of its domestic expansion has resulted from the construction of new plants rather than from mergers or takeovers. Both CEOs have borrowed heavily to finance their companies' expansion.

CRITICALLY EVALUATING YOUR SOURCES

After you've read the views expressed by your sources, examine them critically. Does any of the information about the two CEOs seem slanted so that it appears to misrepresent their management styles? For example, do any of the writers seem to exaggerate the positive or negative features of centralized or decentralized management? Do appropriate examples support the writers' contentions? Does any relevant information appear to be missing? Does any source contain material that isn't related to your purpose? Judging the works of others in this fashion helps you write a better report.[1]

PLANNING AND DRAFTING YOUR SYNTHESIS

The three differences and one similarity between the CEOs are your points of comparison, which you can organize using either the block or the alternating pattern. You could make a chart with each of the key points of comparison in order, with information from your sources. When you write your rough draft, you will want to decide in

---

[1]Because you rely on published sources for your information, it is important to read the sections on research in Chapters 14 and 15 and those on handling quotations and avoiding plagiarism in Chapter 16 before you start to write. As always, follow your instructor's guidelines for documenting sources.

advance whether you want an unbiased comparison or whether you will lead to a preference. If the latter, your introduction might focus on the challenges of determining a more effective management style; your paragraphs would compare the management styles point by point and lead to an emphasis on the qualities of the one you favour. You might conclude by indicating why you prefer one of the two management styles.

SUGGESTIONS FOR WRITING

1. Read at least two essays in this text that address a similar issue (for example, the essays on multiculturalism, "No Place Like Home" (pages 304–308) and "Immigrants, Multiculturalism and Canadian Citizenship" (pages 309–316); two essays on the politics of food, "Is Local Food Bad for the Economy?" (pages 298–303), "Canada Needs a National Food Strategy" (pages 296–297), or another essay you find online promoting the value of local foods; or the essays on the relative happiness of younger people, "Teen Angst, RIP" (pages 25–26) and "Why Can't I Feel What I See?" (pages 420–422).

2. Read the essays "Going Nuclear" by Patrick Moore and "Ten Reasons Why New Nuclear Was a Mistake—Even before Fukushima" by Alexis Rowell (in Part Three's Reader) and then compare the views of these two writers on the feasibility and safety of nuclear power. Also compare the different means by which they develop their arguments. In your comparison, make a case for what you consider to be the more effective or persuasive piece of writing, using examples to illustrate your claims.

COMPARISON ESSAYS: PROFESSIONAL MODEL

READING STRATEGIES

1. Identify your purpose for reading the comparison and the author's purpose for the comparison. Does the author compare in order to acquaint the reader with something new, or to suggest the relative merits of one thing over another?
2. Identify the items that are being compared, and identify the basis for the comparison.
3. Identify the pattern of organization (alternating point by point, block, or a blended approach) that is used in the comparison.
4. Read carefully to establish the points of similarities and differences. It can be helpful to create a table that matches similarities and differences, especially when the information might be necessary for future purposes.

READING CRITICALLY

1. Explore whether there are any biases underlying the comparison. Does the writer seem to give fair treatment to all items being compared? Test whether the basis for comparison is logically consistent.
2. Determine if the writer emphasizes similarities, differences, or both. Does the author go beyond ticking off similarities and differences and make a larger

point in the essay? Does the writer have something fresh to say and avoid dwelling on the obvious?

3. Identify whether there are other similarities or differences or more illustrative details that could have been used.

READING AS A WRITER

1. Examine how the author organized the essay. Was the organization effective in guiding the reader through the essay? Note what organizational pattern was most effective.

2. Notice transitional words and phrases such as *in contrast, on the other hand, while,* and *whereas* that indicate contrast, or words such as *just as, like, similarly,* and *both* that help the writer draw distinctions and parallels. Note also the sentences that the writer uses for transitions.

3. Observe how much detail was used to substantiate the comparison.

Ian Bullock

What Do You See? Is Your Brain East or West?

> Title sets up difference.

Ian Bullock is a Vancouver freelance writer who has published fiction and non-fiction in The Malahat Review, Vancouver Review, Vancouver Magazine, *and* Adbusters, *from which the following article is taken. He is currently at work on a novel.*

1   A plainclothes cop walks into a diner and finds no less than five gun-wielding criminals holding up the crowded joint. "We're not just going to let you walk out of here," the cop says. "Who's we, sucka?" says one of the criminals. "Smith and Wesson and me," says the cop. He draws his Smith & Wesson and—in a crowded diner—shoots four of the criminals and advances on the last gunman, who's holding a pistol to a hostage's head. One itchy trigger finger and the hostage could be dead. The cop glares at the criminal. "Go ahead, make my day." The cop is "Dirty Harry" Callahan, but really he could be any Hollywood hero. The movie is *Sudden Impact,* but really it could be any movie or book or manifestation of Western culture.

> The writer leads into his subject by describing a key scene in what he considers to be an iconic movie showing Western individualism.

2   With a few modern updates, Western culture has been re-creating the same story over and over again since Homer collected *The Odyssey* more than two and a half thousand years ago. Since the Greeks, the ideal of the unique and strong individual has become so prevalent in Western culture that we have stopped realizing that it is even part of our culture. Often we mistake our perceptions of the world for how the world really is.

> Thesis statement signals that writer will compare North American and East Asian cultural tendencies.

3   Psychologists have long known that North Americans overestimate their own distinctiveness, especially in comparison with East Asians. When asked to describe themselves, Americans and Canadians tend to talk about their individual personality and personal outlook more than Japanese do. North Americans tend to settle arguments in terms of right and wrong, whereas East Asians tend to seek compromises. Dirty Harry is an extreme and violent example, but he is emblematic of Western culture and he sums up our single-minded, goal-oriented behavior with aplomb. "When I see an adult male chasing a female with the intent to commit rape, I shoot the bastard. That's my policy."

4   New research shows that culture even affects our cognition. A study published in the *Journal of Personality and Social Psychology* claims that Americans and Japanese intuit the emotions of others differently based on cultural training. "North Americans try to identify the single important thing that is key to making a decision," explains Dr. Takahiko Masuda, the study's author, over the phone from his office at the University of Alberta. "In East Asia they really care about the context." He studied the eye movement of Americans and Japanese when analyzing a picture of a group of cartoon people. When asked to interpret the emotion of the person in the center, the Japanese looked at the person for about one second before moving on to the people in the background. They needed to know how the group was feeling before understanding the emotion of the individual. The Americans (and Canadians in subsequent studies) focused 95% of their attention on the person in the center. Only 5% of their attention was focused on the background, and this, Dr. Masuda points out, didn't influence their interpretation of the central figure's emotion. For North Americans the foreground is all-important.

5   Dr. Masuda is quick to point out that Americans and Japanese are physiologically the same. The difference in eye movement is tied to the roots of our respective cultures. When trying to explain the natural world, the Ancient Greeks—the founders of Western civilization—tended to focus on central objects and sought to explain their rules of behavior. Funnily enough, Aristotle thought a rock had the *property* of "gravity." It didn't occur to him that a *system* was working its powers on the rock. The Chinese on the other hand took a more holistic approach. They believed that everything occurred within a context, or a field of forces, and thus they unraveled the relationship between the moon and the tides.

6   These differences in philosophy can be explained, at least in part, by the environments that spawned them. "We are surrounded by socially created information, which affects our perception," Masuda explains. And perception affects our culture. Research shows that North American cities are less cluttered than East Asian cities, which means that North Americans can spend more time considering salient objects. When Americans or Canadians visit East Asia, they are often overwhelmed by the amount of information they have to process. I have experienced this phenomenon personally. The first time I bused from Incheon Airport into Seoul, South Korea, I was dumbfounded by the number of buildings, advertisements, lights, cars and people and had to turn away from the window to stop my head from spinning. Dr. Masuda first arrived in North America when he was 26. Compared to Japan, which was crowded with people and objects and "complex pieces of information," he felt North American cities to be lonely places.

7   Masuda stresses that no way of perceiving the world is better than another and refuses to interpret his studies too broadly. He has yet to conduct his tests in Africa or South America. But it seems to me that Masuda's study is important: It reminds us that there is more than one way of seeing the world.

8   North Americans have a tendency toward isolating singular goals and working doggedly towards them. And we have achieved some remarkable accomplishments. We put a man on the moon, invented the telephone and the airplane and achieved a thousand more seemingly impossible tasks. We congratulate ourselves on our individualism in our movies, our art, our personal relationships and, of course, our politics. But as we do so, we perpetuate this trait—perception informs culture, culture informs perception—until we mistake the way we see the world for the only way to see the world.

9   As alluring as the Dirty Harry approach may be, is it time to put away our Smith & Wesson and start considering the other customers in the diner? The problems we

face today—the environmental degradation of our planet, global recession, religious fundamentalism—don't fit inside borders or simple categories. Context is unavoidable. We need to start looking for it.

DISCUSSION QUESTIONS

1. In your own words, explain two cultural differences between North Americans and East Asians that the writer perceives (paragraph 3).

2. In paragraph 4, the writer describes a study that suggests Japanese and North Americans focus on different things when they look at a picture. How does the focus on the foreground, or central figure, versus the background, or group context, point to different cultural values?

3. What differences between North American and East Asian cities does the author note? How could these differences in urban environments lead to different habits of perception?

4. How is it clear that the writer is a Westerner addressing a North American audience rather than an East Asian one?

TOWARD KEY INSIGHTS

Can you find places where the writer seems to be criticizing the North American emphasis on single-minded individualism? Do these possible criticisms conflict with Dr. Takahiko Masuda's idea, cited by the author, that "no way of perceiving the world is better than another"? Explain.

What potential problems are there, in our increasingly "flat" world, with setting up a cultural dichotomy such as East and West?

SUGGESTIONS FOR WRITING

1. Ian Bullock remarks that "we mistake the way we see the world for the only way to see the world." Reflect on a time that you came to a similar understanding during a period of profound disorientation—perhaps while living or working in another country, or even while experiencing something radically new and different: parenthood, illness, or another shift in identity.

   Write an essay that contrasts the world or identity you once took for granted with a different one that challenged all of your previous assumptions. This essay will probably include personal examples and/or narrative.

2. If you have intimate knowledge of a culture outside the mainstream Western culture, compare and contrast these cultures in specific ways. Some areas you could consider looking at include different attitudes toward time, toward the family (especially the place of seniors or children), and toward the relative importance of the individual versus the group. While you should include enough detail and examples to support your claims, be careful not to overgeneralize, but use qualifying words if you need to (for example, *it appears that* or *it may be*).

CHAPTER 12

Strategies for Finding Patterns: Classification

Help Wanted, Situations Wanted, Real Estate, Personal. Do these terms look familiar? They do if you've ever scanned the classified ads of the newspaper. Ads are grouped into categories, and each category is then subdivided. The people who assemble this layout are *classifying*. Figure 12.1 shows the main divisions of a typical classified ad section and a further breakdown of one of them.

As this figure indicates, grouping allows the people who handle ads to divide entries according to a logical scheme and helps readers find what they are looking for. Imagine the difficulty of checking the real estate ads if all entries were run in the order that the ads were placed.

Our minds naturally sort information into categories. Within a few weeks after their birth, infants can distinguish the faces of family members from those of outsiders. Toddlers learn to distinguish among cats, dogs, and rabbits. In both cases the classification rests on physical differences, but as we mature, we start classifying friends, jobs, activities, and ideas in more abstract ways.

Classification helps writers and readers come to grips with large or complex topics. It breaks a broad topic into categories according to some specific principle, presents the distinctive features of each category, and shows how the features vary among categories. Segmenting the topic simplifies the discussion by presenting the information in small, neatly sorted piles rather than in one jumbled and confusing heap.

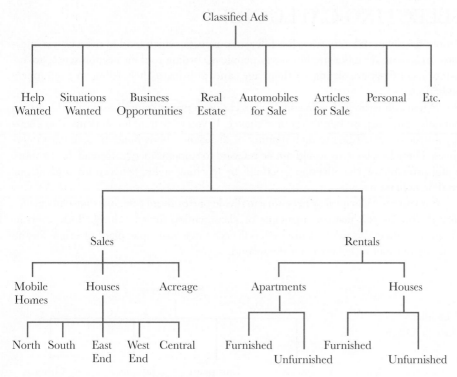

Figure 12.1 A Typical Classified Ad Section

Furthermore, classification helps people make choices. Identifying which groups of consumers—students, accountants, or teachers—are most likely to buy a new product allows the manufacturer to advertise in appropriate media. Knowing the engine size, manoeuvrability, seating capacity, and gas consumption of typical subcompact, compact, and intermediate-sized cars helps customers decide which one to buy. Examining the features of term, whole-life, and endowment insurance enables prospective buyers to select the policy that best suits their needs.

Because classification plays such an important part in our lives, it is a useful writing tool in many situations.

- For an accounting class, you might categorize accounting procedures for retail businesses.
- For a computer class, you might classify computer languages and then specify appropriate applications for each grouping.
- For an industrial hygiene class, you might categorize types of respiratory protective equipment and indicate when each type is used.
- On the job, a provincial health department employee may prepare a brochure grouping illegal drugs into categories based on their effects.
- A financial adviser might write a customer letter categorizing investments according to their degree of risk.
- An employee at Amazon might list new books under categories that interest readers.

SELECTING CATEGORIES

People classify in different ways for different purposes, which tend to reflect their interests. A clothing designer might classify people according to their fashion sense, advertising executives according to their age, and politicians according to their party affiliations.

When you write a classification paper, choose a principle of classification that suits not only your purpose but also your audience. If you're writing for students, don't classify instructors according to their manner of dress, their body build, or their car preferences. These breakdowns would not be relevant to students' needs. Instead, find a more useful principle of classification—perhaps by teaching styles, concern for students, or grading policies.

Sometimes it's helpful or necessary to divide one or more categories into subcategories. If you do, use just one principle of classification for each level. Both levels in Figure 12.2 meet this test because each reflects a single principle: place of origin for the first, and number of cylinders for the second.

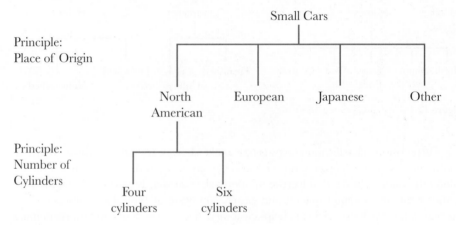

Figure 12.2   Proper Classification of Small Cars

Now examine Figure 12.3. This classification is not logical. Because it groups cars in two ways—by place of origin and by kind—it has overlapping categories, making it possible for one car to end up in two categories. For example, the German Porsche is both a European car and a sports car. When categories overlap in this way, confusion reigns.

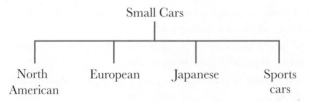

Figure 12.3   Improper Classification of Small Cars

EXERCISE

1. **How would each of the following people be most likely to classify the families living in a Canadian town?**

   a. The member of Parliament who represents the city

   b. A social worker

   c. The director of the local credit bureau

2. **The following lists contain overlapping categories. Identify the inconsistent item in each list and explain why it is faulty.**

Nurses	Winter Sports	Federal Political Parties
Surgical nurses	Sledding	Liberals
Psychiatric nurses	Hiking	Conservatives
Emergency room nurses	Snowboarding	Saskatchewan Party
Terminal care nurses	Skiing	New Democrats
Night nurses	Skating	Green Party

NUMBER OF CATEGORIES

Whether a classification paper discusses every category included within the topic or only selected categories depends on the purpose and scope of the discussion. Suppose that you work for a city finance department and you have been asked to write a report that classifies the city's major non-service industries and also assesses their strengths and weaknesses. Your investigation shows that food processing, furniture making, and the production of auto parts account for more than 95 percent of all non-service jobs. Two minor industries, printing and toy making, provide the rest of the jobs. Given these circumstances, you'd probably focus on the first three industries, mentioning the others only in passing. However, if printing and toy making were significant industries, they too would require detailed discussion.

DEVELOPING CATEGORIES

Develop each category using enough specific, informative details to provide a clear picture. The following excerpt from a student paper classifying public restrooms for women discusses two of the writer's three categories:

Luxurious washrooms are found in upscale department stores, chic boutiques, and the better restaurants. This aristocrat of public facilities usually disdains the term *washroom,* masquerading instead under the alias of *ladies' room.* Upon entering its plush environs, the user is captivated by its elegance. Thick carpet reaches up to cushion tired feet, wood panelled or brocade velvet walls shut the outside world away, and softly glowing wall sconces soothe the eyes. Inviting armchairs and gold-and-velvet tables add to the restful, welcoming atmosphere, and the latest issues of upscale magazines such as *Elle* and *Flare* entice customers to sit and read. Mirrors in carved frames, designer basins with gleaming gold faucets, and creamy scented soap suggest a spa-like luxury. Soft music, piped in through invisible speakers, may take patrons back in time, as if no one is waiting for them outside the door.

The adequate washroom offers utility without the swankiness of its lavish cousin. Typically located in a large shopping mall or mass-market department store, it is a stark world of hard, unadorned surfaces—tile floors, tile walls, and harshly glaring fluorescent lights recessed in the ceiling. For those who wish to rest, there is a garishly coloured Naugahyde couch and next to it a battered metal or wood table holding a few tattered copies of *Homemakers, People, Canadian Living,* and similar publications. The mirrors have steel frames; the sinks, set in a Formica counter, have plain chrome faucets; and the soap dispenser emits a thin stream of unscented liquid. There is no soothing music—just the relentless whining of someone's tired child.

The concrete details in these paragraphs effectively characterize each category and clearly distinguish between them. Imagine how vague and indistinct the categories would be without these details.

ETHICAL ISSUES

Classification can seem quite innocent, yet can cause great harm. In India, millions of people were once classified as *untouchables* and so were denied the rights of other citizens. In Canada during World War II, innocent people of Japanese descent were classified as a threat and were stripped of property and moved away from their homes. In many high schools, students are often lumped into categories with labels such as *preps, geeks, nerds, jocks,* or *druggies.* Clearly you have to evaluate the appropriateness and consequences of your classification scheme. To avoid problems, ask and answer these questions:

- Is my classification called for by the situation? It may be appropriate to classify students in a school environment according to their reading skills, but classifying factory workers in this fashion may be inappropriate and unfair to the people involved.
- Have I avoided the use of damaging classifications? People naturally resent stereotyping.
- Have I applied my classification without resorting to overgeneralization? In a paper classifying student drinkers, it would be a mistake, and even harmful, to imply that all university students drink excessively.
- Could my classification promote harmful behaviour? When classifying the behaviour patterns of young urban dwellers, it would be unethical to present favourably the lifestyle of a group that uses hard drugs and engages in criminal activities.

We are ethically responsible for the classification systems that we use in our writing. Always examine the ones you use for suitability, fairness, and potential harm.

WRITING A CLASSIFICATION

Prewriting for the Classification

Many topics that interest you are potential candidates for classification. If you're selecting your own topic, you might explain the different kinds of rock music, take a humorous look at different types of teachers, or, in a more serious vein, identify different types of discrimination.

> ■ Brainstorm areas where you and others make decisions or distinguish between types of things.
>
> ■ Keep notes on places where people you know make choices.
>
> ■ Branch from brainstorming why people might be interested in classification of topic.
>
> ■ Test topic by seeing if you can identify three or more distinct categories.

FINDING YOUR TOPIC

> ■ List the reasons readers may use classification.
>
> ■ List real examples of the topic and organize into categories.
>
> ■ Develop a table like the one below identifying the different categories and the features that distinguish the category.
>
> ■ Brainstorm examples and details for each category.

DEVELOPING YOUR CLASSIFICATION

Planning and Drafting the Classification

Once you have your details, create an outline or a second map of categories that distinguishes features and details in the order that you want to present them.

Category 1	**Category 2**	**Category 3**
First distinguishing feature	First distinguishing feature	First distinguishing feature
Second distinguishing feature	Second distinguishing feature	Second distinguishing feature

A **thesis statement** for classification often suggests why the classification will interest the reader, and names the major categories that will be discussed. For example: "The ecofriendly consumer needs to decide between fully electric, hybrid, flex-fuel, and fuel-efficient vehicles, each with its own advantages and challenges." To develop your thesis statement, review your brainstorming on how readers would use your classification and the major categories.

The following are some strategies for drafting a classification paper:

Introduction

- Capture your reader's attention and interest—for example, help the reader select among a confusing range of cellphones.
- Or stress the relevance of the topic—for example, classifying types of pollutants that have long-term effects on health.
- Or offer an interesting personal experience—for example, describing a course with an instructor that was wrong for you but might be exactly right for a different kind of student.
- Provide a thesis that identifies a reason for the classification, and names the major categories.

Body

- Organize the paper by categories in the order that makes sense to you (most common to least common; least desirable to most desirable).
- Clearly signal the shifts from category to category, not with common words like "next" but phrases that show your logic. "Though using traditional fuel rather than electricity, the hybrid . . ."
- Follow a logical pattern in the paragraphs such as noting majorcharacteristics in each category.

Conclusion

- Summarize key features of each category.
- Or provide warnings, recommendations, or something for the reader to reflect upon
- Or point to the larger significance of your topic, possibly future implications or possibilities.

Revising the Classification

Revise your paper by following the guidelines in Chapters 4 and 5 as well as by asking yourself these questions:

How could the purpose and audience for the classification be more clear? Does my principle of classification accord with my purpose?

Do any of my categories overlap? If so, can I redefine a category or cut any that do not fit?

Have I chosen an appropriate number of categories, or I have forgotten some that should at least be mentioned?

Are these categories developed with sufficient details or examples that will interest a reader?

Are the categories and details arranged in an effective order? Can I rearrange them more effectively—maybe by building up to the most significant or important one?

Where can I improve the focus, coherence, or development of paragraphs? Do I need better transitions to get from one point to the next?

EXAMPLE OF A STUDENT ESSAY USING CLASSIFICATION

Get Used to It

Luke Kingma

1   In the world of education, there are those that are meant to teach, and there are those that should stay away. The poor teachers mix with the good and form the education system that we are acquainted with today. Unfortunately, those individuals who have yet to find the right job for their talents can add to the frustrations of student life. I suppose it could be argued that students must learn to deal with all personality types and levels of competence when interacting with others throughout life. Indeed, students owe a debt of gratitude to all those teachers who can take even the most ill-shaped mind and mould it into an objective-thinking unit; however, struggling students should be aware that teachers often fall into the following categories before they sign up for a class.

> Identifies thesis that will interest student audience.

The Genius

2   Viewed by average students as second only to Einstein, this mastermind is primarily a knowledge-focused individual who ignores all other aspects of life. A teacher like this is hired for credentials, not for an amazing teaching record. This teacher's intellect is on display each class in a plethora of mind-boggling detail. Imagine someone who can explain the Standard Model of Quantum Mechanics on the blackboard in ten seconds or less. This person may be smart, but intelligence alone does not make a teacher.

> Topic sentence clearly identifies first category.

3   Although naturally intelligent, this teacher does not comprehend how some students do not understand the lecture. A question directed at a genius teacher from a perplexed student will result in a confused and slightly frustrated look, followed by an explanation exactly like the one given before. This teacher puts forth no effort to make certain a student understands the material before progressing. Students who understand what is being taught are able to move on; those who do not are left grasping at straws. Lecturing is the teacher's job; students must teach themselves if they are to keep up.

> Develops key point with detail.

The Hider

4   Hiders are excessive introverts. Why these people chose teaching as a career is beyond most students. They shy away from the limelight and avoid communication as best they can. Chameleon-like, they blend in with the chalkboard, quietly scribbling notes for the class to copy down. They avoid eye contact when

> Topic sentence identifies second category.

students attempt to ask questions. The floor, the lecture notes, or the wall behind the students often make for a better target. An excellent tactic they use for avoiding questions is directing the struggling student back to the textbook. Unfortunately, the textbook is usually the source of the student's confusion. There is only one thing worse than a two-hour class with a hider—a three-hour one. Through these gruelling hours, students can only strive to stay awake and not miss anything for the big exam. Morning and evening classes worsen the dryness of the session. The drone of the fan, tapping on the chalkboard, and lack of enthusiasm entice students into a long nap.

The Crammer

> Third category is introduced, then developed throughout this paragraph.

5   <u>These tough guys assume that students are only taking one class each semester: theirs.</u> They often begin the semester by telling the class in an almost evangelistic way, "This will be the one most important and interesting class in all of your schooling . . . and perhaps provide your greatest lesson in life." A summary of grades for a past class is also given, and the particular focus is on those who failed or barely passed. The audience is not given any encouragement that they will achieve their usual grade average in this class. Students are left to try their best to keep up in the class, with no time for questions—they can review at home. The pile of homework given every night assumes that every other class is unimportant, so grades in the other classes may suffer. To top it off, this teacher often wears a slight, arrogant smirk while watching students frantically jot down notes and scramble to raise a seemingly "un-raisable" grade. Nothing is ever good enough for crammers.

The Know-It-All

> Note the lightly ironic tone in this topic sentence identifying the fourth category of teachers to avoid.

6   <u>Often spotted in universities, these instructors know everything there is to know about everything—except the subject they supposedly majored in.</u> More often than not, these teachers establish their authority on the first day about how many and which kinds of high-profile institutions they have taught at. Of course, these biographies never include reasons why they moved from one university to another; we are left to assume that they came to their current position of their own accord.

7   Somehow, these often loud attention-seekers get away with teaching nothing of the subject, and they justify leaving half-way through a class to let students "discuss their studies and work on projects." Often, if a student manages to gather up enough nerve to ask a Know-It-All a question about the course, the Know-It-All shoots back: "It's in the textbook. READ IT!" After struggling through the course, those students who survived move on without a secure foundation, often wondering what they actually learned and floundering in subsequent classes.

The Class Master

8   This may be the first undesirable teacher a grade-school student will encounter, and perhaps is the most damaging to a young mind. These teachers love to point out the obvious faults of their students—small or large—both in schoolwork and in personality. The tough survive; the weak get pounded. Every word that comes out of Class Master's mouth is undeniable, undisputable truth—at least in this teacher's own mind. These educators are on a mission: to make clones of themselves. Really, it's a "god complex," as many students have put it. These teachers want to save the world from drowning in its own stupidity. They seem to stick with the job simply because of the power it holds: a reign of terror over quivering students. When Class Masters step outside their classroom, they're just regular "schmos" walking down the street. Of these five undesirable types, the Class Master is the one students could do without the most.

> This fifth kind of teacher is potentially the "most damaging" and therefore is brought in last, following an order of climax.

9   Students encounter these types of undesirable teachers all too often, so students and administrators should be on the alert. Sadly, it is probably a fact of life that these types will forever be in our education system, so we might as well get used to it and learn from our experiences. In fact, no matter where we end up in life, we will have to deal with people such as these, so we might as well learn how to deal with them while we are growing up.

> Conclusion contains warning and recommendation.

> Final wrap-up statement in the conclusion relates this discussion to the larger world outside school.

DISCUSSION QUESTIONS

1. What is the writer's purpose in developing this classification? Where does he state it?
2. In what order has the writer arranged his categories? Refer to the essay when answering.
3. What is the writer's tone? Find support for your answer related to each kind of teacher discussed.
4. How might the writer have refined further the categories of undesirable teachers?

SUGGESTIONS FOR WRITING

1. *If you have or have had a job working with the public, write an essay classifying types of customers, service workers, waiters or waitresses, etc. based on their attitudes toward others. Use labels, similar to what the student above has done in his essay about teachers.*

2. *Write a classification paper on one of the topics below or one approved by your instructor. Determine your purpose and audience, select appropriate categories, decide how many you'll discuss, develop them with specific details, and arrange them in an effective order.*

   1. University pressures
   2. Motivation for learning
   3. Video game players
   4. Yoga

5. Reasons for surfing the Internet

6. Alternative energy sources

7. Extreme sports

8. Jokes

9. Attitudes toward death

10. Lies

11. Canadian TV sitcoms

12. Ways to break off a relationship

13. Ways to handle stress

Stepping Up to Synthesis

Classification provides an effective tool for organizing material into categories. Sometimes you will be able to draw on your own knowledge or experience to determine or develop categories, but often you will supplement what you bring to a writing assignment with research.

PREWRITING FOR SYNTHESIS

Suppose that for an introductory business course you're asked to prepare a paper that explores major types of investments. After consulting a number of books and magazines, you conclude that stocks, bonds, and real estate represent the three main categories of investments and that each category can be divided into several subcategories. Bonds, for example, can be grouped according to issuer: corporate, municipal, provincial, and federal.

At this point, you recognize that the strategy of classification would work well for this assignment. Reading further, you learn about the financial risks, rewards, and tax consequences associated with ownership. For example, Canada Savings Bonds offer the greatest safety, while corporate bonds, as well as stocks and real estate, entail varying degrees of risk, depending on the financial condition of the issuer and the state of the economy. Similarly, the income from the different categories and subcategories of investments is subject to different kinds and levels of taxation.

After assimilating the information you've gathered, you could synthesize the views expressed in your sources as well as your own ideas about investments. You might organize your categories and subcategories according to probable degree of risk, starting with the least risky investment and ending with the most risky. For your conclusion you might offer purchase recommendations for different groups of investors such as young workers, wealthy older investors, and retirees.

CRITICALLY EVALUATING YOUR SOURCES

When preparing to use the material of others in your writing, be sure to examine its merits. Do some sources seem more convincing than others? Why? Do any recommendations stem from self-interest? Are any sources overloaded with material that is irrelevant to your purpose? Which sources offer the most detail? Asking and answering questions such as these will help you write a more informed paper.[1]

---

[1] Because you rely on published sources for your information, it is important to read the sections on research in Chapters 14 and 15 and those on handling quotations and avoiding plagiarism in Chapter 16 before you start to write. As always, follow your instructor's guidelines for documenting sources.

SUGGESTIONS FOR WRITING

1. Examine professional essays on gender issues or cultural diversity in this text, and then write a paper that classifies their content.

2. Reflect on the professional essays that you've studied. Then write a paper that presents an appropriate classification system for them, perhaps based on the writers' levels of diction, tone, or reliance on authorities.

CLASSIFICATION ESSAYS: PROFESSIONAL MODELS

READING STRATEGIES

1. Identify your purpose for reading the essay and the writer's purpose for the classification.
2. Identify the principle of classification that is being used and the distinguishing features of each category. It can be useful to make a table that identifies each major classification and identifies the distinctive features of each category.

READING CRITICALLY

1. Determine the purpose for the classification.
2. Try to come up with an alternative classification system.
3. Check whether the categories of the classification are clear and distinct, or whether they overlap.
4. Note whether the principle of classification is logically consistent. Note whether it is a complete system, or whether some categories are omitted.

READING AS A WRITER

1. Note whether the essay arranges categories in a logical sequence, such as largest to smallest or least desirable to most desirable.
2. Observe whether the writer gives each category about the same amount of space and gives similar kinds of information for each category.

Marion Winik

What Are Friends For?

Marion Winik (born 1958) is a graduate of Brown University and of Brooklyn College, where she earned an M.F.A. in Creative Writing. She has written poems, short stories, essays, and memoirs; her shorter pieces have appeared in a variety of major newspapers and popular magazines. Her 1998 book, Lunch-Box Chronicles: Notes from the Parenting Underground, *discusses her experiences of being a single mom; her 2001 book,* Rules for the Unruly: Living an Unconventional Life, *is a book of advice; her 2005 book, a collection of essays, is called* Above Us Only Sky; *her 2008 book,* The Glen Rock Book of the Dead, *is a collection of short pieces about people who have touched her life; and her 2013 memoir is called* Highs in the Low Fifties. *In this selection, Winik takes a humorous look at the different categories of friends and the benefits derived from each one.*

<table>
<tr><td>Introduction describes the value of friends.</td><td>1</td><td>I was thinking about how everybody can't be everything to each other, but some people can be something to each other, thank God, from the ones whose shoulder you cry on to the ones whose half-slips you borrow to the nameless ones you chat with in the grocery line.</td></tr>
</table>

1   I was thinking about how everybody can't be everything to each other, but some people can be something to each other, thank God, from the ones whose shoulder you cry on to the ones whose half-slips you borrow to the nameless ones you chat with in the grocery line.

Introduction describes the value of friends.

Body begins. (Paragraphs 2 to 14)

First category: buddies.

2   Buddies, for example, are the workhorses of the friendship world, the people out there on the front lines, defending you from loneliness and boredom. They call you up, they listen to your complaints, they celebrate your successes and curse your misfortunes, and you do the same for them in return. They hold out through innumerable crises before concluding that the person you're dating is no good, and even then understand if you ignore their good counsel. They accompany you to a movie with subtitles or to see the diving pig at Aquarena Springs. They feed your cat when you are out of town and pick you up from the airport when you get back. They come over to help you decide what to wear on a date. Even if it is with that creep.

Second category: relatives.

3   What about family members? Most of them are people you just got stuck with, and though you love them, you may not have very much in common. But there is that rare exception, the Relative Friend. It is your cousin, your brother, maybe even your aunt. The two of you share the same views of the other family members. Meg never should have divorced Martin. He was the best thing that ever happened to her. You can confirm each other's memories of things that happened a long time ago. Don't you remember when Uncle Hank and Daddy had that awful fight in the middle of Thanksgiving dinner? Grandma always hated Grandpa's stamp collection; she probably left the window open during the hurricane on purpose.

Third category: co-workers.

4   While so many family relationships are tinged with guilt and obligation, a relationship with a Relative Friend is relatively worry-free. You don't even have to hide your vices from this delightful person. When you slip out Aunt Joan's back door for a cigarette, she is already there.

5   Then there is that special guy at work. Like all the other people at the job site, at first he's just part of the scenery. But gradually he starts to stand out from the crowd. Your friendship is cemented by jokes about co-workers and thoughtful favors around the office. Did you see Ryan's hair? Want half my bagel? Soon you know the names of his turtles, what he did last Friday night, exactly which model CD player he wants for his birthday. His handwriting is as familiar to you as your own.

6   Though you invite each other to parties, you somehow don't quite fit into each other's outside lives. For this reason, the friendship may not survive a job change. Company gossip, once an infallible source of entertainment, soon awkwardly accentuates the distance between you. But wait. Like School Friends, Work Friends share certain memories which acquire a nostalgic glow after about a decade.

Fourth category: faraway friends.

7   A Faraway Friend is someone you grew up with or went to school with or lived in the same town as until one of you moved away. Without a Faraway Friend, you would never get any mail addressed in handwriting. A Faraway Friend calls late at night, invites you to her wedding, always says she is coming to visit but rarely shows up. An actual visit from a Faraway Friend is a cause for celebration and binges of all kinds. Cigarettes, Chips Ahoy, bottles of tequila.

8   Faraway Friends go through phases of intense communication, then may be out of touch for many months. Either way, the connection is always there. A conversation with

your Faraway Friend always helps to put your life in perspective: when you feel you've hit a dead end, come to a confusing fork in the road, or gotten lost in some crackerbox subdivision of your life, the advice of the Faraway Friend—who has the big picture, who is so well acquainted with the route that brought you to this place—is indispensable.

9   Another useful function of the Faraway Friend is to help you remember things from a long time ago, like the name of your seventh grade history teacher, what was in that really good stir-fry, or exactly what happened that night on the boat with the guys from Florida.

10   Ah, the Former Friend. A sad thing. At best a wistful memory, at worst a dangerous enemy who is in possession of many of your deepest secrets. But what was it that drove you apart? A misunderstanding, a betrayed confidence, an unrepaid loan, an ill-conceived flirtation. A poor choice of spouse can do in a friendship just like that. Going into business together can be a serious mistake. Time, money, distance, cult religions: all noted friendship killers . . . .

Fifth category: former friends.

11   And lest we forget, there are the Friends You Love to Hate. They call at inopportune times. They say stupid things. They butt in, they boss you around, they embarrass you in public. They invite themselves over. They take advantage. You've done the best you can, but they need professional help. On top of all this, they love you to death and are convinced they're your best friend on the planet.

Sixth category: love-to-hate friends.

12   So why do you continue to be involved with these people? Why do you tolerate them? On the contrary, the real question is, What would you do without them? Without Friends You Love to Hate, there would be nothing to talk about with your other friends. Their problems and their irritating stunts provide a reliable source of conversation for everyone they know. What's more, Friends You Love to Hate make you feel good about yourself, since you are in so much better shape than they are. No matter what these people do, you will never get rid of them. As much as they need you, you need them too.

13   At the other end of the spectrum are Hero Friends. These people are better than the rest of us, that's all there is to it. Their career is something you wanted to be when you grew up—painter, forest ranger, tireless doer of good. They have beautiful homes filled with special handmade things presented to them by villagers in the remote areas they have visited in their extensive travels. Yet they are modest. They never gossip. They are always helping others, especially those who have suffered a death in the family or an illness. You would think people like this would just make you sick, but somehow they don't.

Seventh category: hero friends.

14   A New Friend is a tonic unlike any other. Say you meet her at a party. In your bowling league. At a Japanese conversation class, perhaps. Wherever, whenever, there's that spark of recognition. The first time you talk, you can't believe how much you have in common. Suddenly, your life story is interesting again, your insights fresh, your opinion valued. Your various shortcomings are as yet completely invisible.

Eighth category: new friends.

15   It's almost like falling in love.

Conclusion uses a memorable observation that meshes stylistically with rest of essay.

DISCUSSION QUESTIONS

1. Comment on the effectiveness of Winik's title.

2. Characterize the level of diction that Winik uses in her essay.

3. What elements of Winik's essay interest you the most? What elements interest you the least?

TOWARD KEY INSIGHTS

What traits characterize the various types of friends that you have?

In what ways are these friendships mutually beneficial or healthy?

If you have a number of friends on a social media site such as Facebook, are some of these people you see rarely or not at all? If so, how would you say that these virtual friendships do or do not serve you?

SUGGESTIONS FOR WRITING *Another short essay by Marion Winik called "Husbands: A Field Guide" that can be found online categorizes the kinds of husbands her married female friends have. After reading this essay as well as the essay here, write your own short essay in a similar light style, drawing from personal observation, classifying types of dates, parents, or romantic relationships that people have. Choose an appropriate number of categories and support them with appropriate and specific details.*

Geoff Dembicki

The Four Tribes of Climate Change

Geoff Dembicki, an Alberta-born writer, has published articles on energy, climate change, and sustainability that have appeared in Foreign Policy, Salon, Alternet, *the* Toronto Star, *and* The Walrus. *He is a lead reporter on energy issues for* The Tyee, *from which this essay is taken. A 2012 Asia Pacific Foundation of Canada media fellow, Dembicki is now writing a book about the new models for North American society in response to climate change.*

1   People have always disagreed about climate change. But for two fleeting years starting in 2006, it really seemed like most North Americans had accepted the climate narrative pushed into the mainstream by Al Gore and Lord Nicholas Stern: that in global warming humankind faced its greatest ever challenge, but solving it would make us all richer and stronger.

2   That worldview was so compelling, you may recall, that it won Gore the Nobel Peace Prize and elevated environmental worries to the top of North America's political agenda. It also caused Canada's Conservative Prime Minister, Stephen Harper, to assert in 2007 that global warming is "perhaps the biggest threat to confront the future of humanity today." Well, we all know what happened next.

3   Wall Street collapsed. So did climate talks in Copenhagen. Americans elected a Congress more polarized than any other in U.S. history. Cap-and-trade legislation fell to pieces. Activists declared war on Canada's oil sands. Harper's government declared war on activists. Media mostly ignored a global boom in climate-saving technology. And humankind's carbon emissions continued their inexorable rise.

4   It now seems improbable that a single, compelling climate narrative could recreate the environmental zeitgeist of 2006 and 2007. Instead, four influential subcultures have risen in the intervening years, each with its own story to tell about the limits and

opportunities of a warming planet. Taken together, they represent the fears and hopes of a generation living through tumultuous global change.

THE CIVILIZATION CYNICS

5   Imagine waking up one day suddenly unconvinced by western society's founding myths. You realize human progress is a sham. Endless growth, impossible. Your middle-class lifestyle? Built atop a battery of horrors: factory farming, rainforest destruction, mass extinctions and a dangerously warming climate. How would your world look if you admitted civilization is teetering on collapse?

6   "The funny thing is, as soon as you say it's not going to be all OK, that's a huge weight off your shoulders," Paul Kingsnorth, a widely published U.K. writer and former environmental campaigner, told *The Tyee*. "It allows you to be way more honest." That idea is central to the Dark Mountain Project, a network of writers and artists seeking new meaning in a civilization they're convinced is falling to pieces. Kingsnorth co-founded it in 2009.

7   "Lots of things are collapsing around us, but we still need to get on with our lives," Kingsnorth explained. Unconvinced the "green growth" promised by new clean technologies can save civilization, but dubious of an imminent "zombie apocalypse," Dark Mountain attempts to envision a humbled human existence more closely connected to nature. "We're not looking for a program to save the world," he said.

8   Kingsnorth spent much of his earlier career as a green activist trying to do just that. Over time he grew dismayed with the movement. "A lot of greens are not being honest about the causes of environmental destruction," he said. Oil firms like Shell are indeed ruining the planet, he agrees. But so are the regular people who buy their products. "We've seen the enemy and it's us," Kingsnorth said. "We're all complicit."

9   Since launching Dark Mountain in 2009, and publishing four anthologies of "Uncivilized" writing, Kingsnorth has watched the project grow into a "minor global movement," giving voice to fellow Civilization Cynics around the world. "We've tapped into a current," he said, "a sense of hopelessness and doom, and more interestingly than that, a positive desire to engage with what comes next."

THE FOSSIL FIGHTERS

10   For years you've felt an uneasy disconnect between your low-carbon lifestyle and the rising global temperatures it seems to have no impact on. Your home is lit by energy-efficient lightbulbs. You bike to work each morning. The produce in your fridge is organically grown and sourced from farms less than 100 miles away. What more can one person possibly do?

11   "Those things are all incredibly important," Phil Aroneanu, co-founder of 350.org, a leading opponent of the Keystone XL pipeline, said. "But they won't alone solve climate change."

12   Ultimate control over Earth's fate, he believes, resides in the corporate boardrooms of Shell, Exxon and other producers of fossil fuels. "We really need these companies to keep 80 per cent of the [oil, gas and coal] reserves they have in the ground," he said.

13   That won't happen without a fight. Ruining the planet makes those firms filthy rich. Since they can purchase political influence at the highest levels, the only recourse for regular people, Aroneanu is convinced, is to hit the streets en masse like the civil rights protesters of an earlier generation. "We need a huge societal shift," he said, "and only a social movement where everybody's involved" can achieve it.

14   Social movements require symbols. And few are more potent these days than the Keystone XL pipeline. The campaign by 350.org to defeat it could prevent a huge new source of carbon emissions. But Keystone, Aroneanu said, "is also a microcosm of what's wrong with our energy economy." It makes climate change feel real. "You can understand what it means to have a pipeline in your backyard," he said.

15   The same goes for tap-water lighting on fire. Tankers sailing through sacred rainforest. Boreal landscapes torn to shreds. Severed mountaintops. Oil-smothered ducks. These are the icons uniting Fossil Fighters across North America in battle. "We don't have the money to compete with the fossil fuel industry," Aroneanu said, "but we do have our creativity, our diversity and our bodies."

THE DOGMA DISRUPTERS

16   At a family reunion you make the mistake of arguing with your conservative uncle about climate change. The whole thing is a hoax, he claims—liberal junk science used to justify government intrusion into the lives of hardworking North Americans. Your uncle's an intelligent guy. Why does he think the 97 per cent of climate scientists who say the Earth is warming are wrong?

17   "On one level the debate is not really about climate change," Ted Nordhaus, co-founder of the Breakthrough Institute, a California-based environmental think-tank, told The Tyee. "It's about what society should look like." For years global warming has been conflated with tough controls on industry and big subsidies for clean energy. "Not surprisingly," he added, "a whole bunch of people on the right said, well, 'I don't think I believe your science.'"

18   Dismissing those people as idiots won't fix the situation. But changing the terms of the climate debate just might. Instead of hard limits on economic growth, think ultra-efficient buildings, widespread electric cars and power grids that resemble the Internet. "You get into very different mindset when you understand this as technological problem," Nordhaus said. "It's the politics of possibility."

19   That model sees government as the catalyst for a cleantech revolution, the same way federal policy helped create technology like the iPhone. It prioritizes coalition-building over conflict. "So much of the model on the left comes from the civil rights movement and protest politics," Nordhaus said. "You would think that's the only way social change has ever happened, and it's just not the case."

20   For now U.S. Republican denial of global warming shows little sign of changing. Same for the Canadian government's fixation on oil profits. But the answer for Dogma Disrupters isn't to hit the streets. They'd rather transform the assumptions that led us here. "What we're trying to do with climate change," Nordhaus said, "is force it out of the ideological frames that have defined the issue for a generation."

THE INDUSTRY IMPROVERS

21   You've just invented an incredible new product you're convinced will stop global warming. It promises to transform one of the world's dirtiest industries into the cleanest. But nobody in that dirty industry seems to care. You watch the eyes of executives glaze over as you talk carbon emissions and rising sea levels. Finally one of them asks you: "How will this new product save us money?"

22   "The adoption of clean products and services is being driven by economics," said Dallas Kachan, founder of Kachan & Co., an international cleantech consultancy based in Vancouver. Corporations, in other words, don't run on benevolent green ideals. They're interested in shrinking their ecological footprint if it makes them more profitable. "Saving the planet is kind of a pleasant after-effect," Kachan said.

23   Never has it been easier to do both at once. Kachan points to recent technology advances in sectors like clean energy, low-carbon transportation, water recycling, sustainable agriculture and green buildings. Cleantech, he explained, "is now built into more or less everything." In business parlance such innovations are referred to as "efficiencies." "It's not about carbon," he said. "It's about doing more with less."

24   Lately cleantech firms themselves have been forced to do more with less. Global clean energy investment peaked in 2011 at $302 billion, and has fallen steadily since. It's evidence of a maturing industry, Kachan believes, the same temporary slump faced by dot-com firms in the late 1990s. Politics are also a factor. "We've had completely underwhelming policy support for clean technology" in North America, he said.

25   Yet the "fundamental drivers" for cleantech remained unchanged: a world population set to hit 10 billion. Looming shortages of food, water and other vital resources. Rising global temperatures. Across the planet, Industry Improvers are looking for cheaper, better and less harmful ways to run human civilization. "The demand for clean products and services," Kachan said, "isn't going away anytime soon."

DISCUSSION QUESTIONS

1. In the first four paragraphs, Geoff Dembicki recounts what he calls a changing "climate change narrative" by way of introduction. What does he mean by this term? Why does he include this historical background about the "environmental zeitgeist" from 2005 to 2007? What does he suggest about the way the state of the economy shapes popular attitudes toward climate change?

2. Geoff Dembicki uses an example of what he calls a "civilization cynic" named Paul Kingsnorth, who is nevertheless a "green activist" (paragraphs 6 to 9). In what sense is Kingsnorth a "green activist," and how does his activism seem like a surprising, even paradoxical result of his pessimism about the planet's future?

3. Introducing "fossil fighters" in paragraph 10, the writer says, "For years you've felt an uneasy disconnect between your low-carbon lifestyle and the rising global temperatures it seems to have no impact on." Whom does he seem to be imagining as his audience here?

4. How do even "fossil fighters" who feel their personal efforts to conserve energy make no large impact have any hope of influencing large companies that make profits from exploiting energy resources?

5. In paragraphs 14 and 15, Dembicki uses an example of a "fossil fighter" named Phil Aroneanu, who in turn uses examples to illustrate that "social movements require symbols" (paragraph 14). What powerful symbols does he offer in paragraphs 14 and 15 that make "climate change feel real"?

6. What does the writer mean by "dogma disrupters" (paragraphs 16 to 20) and how does Ted Nordhaus argue that such people should "change the terms of the climate debate" (paragraph 18)?

7. What are "industry improvers" and why do you think Dembicki ends with this category?

TOWARD KEY INSIGHTS

In his discussion of what he refers to as "dogma disrupters," Dembicki seems to support the notion that "changing the terms of the climate debate" could be more effective than protest to persuade people who disagree that climate change is a real threat. Can you think of another issue, either from your personal life or from the larger culture, where changing the terms of the debate might influence people more than overt challenges to their position? Your examples could range from something as personal as a decision to get married or leave home to something as broad as immigration policies.

Of the four types of attitudes toward climate change that Dembecki describes, do you see a category where you or people you know might fit, or might like to fit—or do you think that Dembecki left out categories? If so, what would they look like?

It is always difficult to categorize people based on our limited knowledge. What risks do you see associated with these categories or perhaps with other ways of classifying types of people or kinds of attitudes?

SUGGESTION FOR WRITING *This article, which can be found online at http://thetyee.ca/News/2013/11/04/Climate-Change-Four-Tribes/, generated a great deal of online conversation. Read through the comments on the article, group the comments into four categories, and then name the categories in a way that is similar to what Dembicki did with his names, such as "fossil fighters." Write an essay in which you describe different types of comments on this or another article of your choice. Use specific examples to illustrate the types of comments you are describing.*

CHAPTER 13

Strategies for Convincing Others: Argument and Persuasion

"What did you think of that movie?"

"Great!"

"What do you mean, *great?* I thought the acting was wooden and the story completely unbelievable."

"That's about what I'd expect from you. You wouldn't know a good movie if it walked up and bit you."

"Oh yeah? What makes you think you're such a great . . . ?"

"Well, that's my opinion!"

Argument or quarrel? Many people would ask, "What's the difference?" To them, the two terms both suggest two angry people in a heated shouting match. However, in academic writing, the word *argument* stands for something quite different: a paper, grounded in logical, structured evidence, that attempts to convince the reader to accept a claim, take some action, or do both. Argument is different than a mere statement of opinion or personal taste that cannot really be debated or defended ("Well, that's what I think, so how can you challenge that?"). As the Monty Python's Flying Circus "Argument Clinic" sketch shows in a humorous way, a man who goes to the clinic to buy an argument protests that an argument is not just a game of contradiction ("It is!" "It isn't!"). Instead, it is a process by which one works to persuade an audience of a central claim through the strategic use of logic, relevant evidence, and consideration of other points of view.

Unlike some television talk show hosts, successful arguers do not work to inflame the passions of their audience by sensationalizing the topic and polarizing people. They avoid inflammatory statements, particularly those that attack the character of the opposition. Even when writers of academic argument have strong passions, they demonstrate respect for their audience and for the complexities of the issue. They do not oversimplify or distort evidence in order to score points or advance a claim. They convey a sense of being reasonable and fair people by presenting honest, logically sound arguments that display knowledge of the subject and understanding of their audience.

Some arguments do not have only the two clear-cut opposing sides of classical debate. Some are more about promoting awareness of an issue, or attempting to persuade a neutral audience to a new point of view or course of action. A salesperson who tries to convince someone to try a new product or a political activist who tries to influence people to sign a petition draws on the strategies of argument.

Some arguments may even take the form of exploratory dialogues, in which people test different perspectives or possibilities. Exploratory arguments allow you to air doubts about your own position, explain why certain reasons and evidence have weight with you, and address alternative positions and arguments that attract you. Before you craft a more committed and focused argument, exploratory arguments can help clarify your assumptions and values as you consider other points of view and acquire new information. Engaging in exploratory argument as a social conversation can also be an enjoyable and enlivening experience.

If you are writing about a complex issue, you will be more persuasive when you demonstrate that you understand there are alternative perspectives that reasonable people may reasonably hold. However, you do not want to be wishy-washy, so that readers cannot figure out where you stand. For most formal academic writing, you will need to find the balance between using enough qualifications to show you are not oversimplifying and taking a committed position using a confident, even authoritative tone.

When you write an argument, you don't simply sit down and dash off your views as though they came to you prefabricated. Instead, argument represents an opportunity to think things through, to gradually and often tentatively come to some conclusions, and then, in stages, to begin to draft your position with the support you have discovered. You should try to keep an open mind as you formulate and then express your views. And remember, you rarely start from scratch. Instead, you join a conversation where ideas and evidence have already been exchanged. As a result, you need to be thoughtful and informed.

Imagine that you have been asked to write an argumentative or persuasive paper. You decide that you will start with your opinion that development of the Alberta tar sands should be stopped at once. However, after you start researching your subject, you discover that the issue is more complicated than you realized. As you examine different sides of the issue, including opposing arguments, your opinion may become a more reasoned and nuanced proposition—the central claim of your argument that names the issue and indicates which position the writer will take:

> Multinational oil companies that are profiting from oil reserves in Alberta should pay much higher taxes.

As you investigate further, it is possible that your original idea will shift its focus considerably:

> The Canadian government should start investing more heavily in alternatives to fossil fuels in order to reduce carbon emissions.

When preparing to write an argument, you need to be aware that certain kinds of topics, such as questions of personal taste or preference, are just not debatable. An argumentative essay should not be confused with a factual report either, although arguers use facts as evidence to support their central claims. We turn to argument only when there is room for debate.

The most successful arguments rest on a firm foundation of solid, logical support. In addition, many arguments include emotion because it can play an important part in swaying reader opinion. Furthermore, writers often make ethical appeals by projecting favourable images of themselves as fair-minded people since readers form conclusions based on their judgments of the writer.

To write any essay, including an argumentative essay, you need to clarify for yourself why you are writing. What do you want your audience to think, believe, or do? Academic arguments may attempt to convince others to accept a proposal, to support a cause, or to take action. At the very least, a formal argument is a sincere attempt to persuade the audience that a particular point of view or judgment is worthy of consideration.

THE ART OF ARGUMENT AND PERSUASION

Argument is a form of persuasion. The word *argument* connotes an emphasis on logic and reason. The word *persuasion* has a broader meaning, suggesting an emphasis on swaying the reader's attitudes by appealing more to values and emotions. In some circumstances, argumentative propositions may be established through logical inference alone, drawing on common understanding of meaning in a language, general principles, or mathematical facts, rather than direct observation or other experiential evidence (*a priori*). However, argumentation that attempts to persuade usually requires the presentation of compelling empirical evidence drawing on one's own experience as well as the second-hand experience or expertise of others (*a posteriori*).

Arguments about practical issues, such as the need for civic improvements, may emphasize reasons, evidence, and rational appeals. Other arguments that seek to persuade people to do something voluntary, such as register for organ donation or take in a foster child, may emphasize emotional appeals. Effective arguments are grounded in logical, structured evidence—rational appeals known as *logos*—but since people are not just thinking machines, most also include appeals to people's emotions; emotional appeals in argument are classically referred to as *pathos*. Ethical appeals known as *ethos* are based on the ethical implications of the case being argued, often an appeal to the reader's sense of fairness and the common good. Ethical appeals are also based on the character of the speaker or writer, which is conveyed through the language and tone of the argument. Since readers often form conclusions based on their judgments of the writer's trustworthiness, effective arguers convey attitudes of authority, accuracy, and integrity.

Using Qualifiers to Strengthen Your Credibility

One way to convey your trustworthiness as a writer is to ensure that the claims you make are suitably limited and accurate rather than overgeneralized; most people know how resistant they feel when a family member accuses them of *never* cleaning up or *always* making a mess. Be careful not to make overly general, sweeping claims. For example, a student writing about the problem of alcohol abuse among teens originally claimed: "Drinking parties offer the opportunity for young people to find the acceptance and sense of belonging they cannot find anywhere else." After reflection, though, the student carefully revised this sweeping claim, inserting qualifiers: "*Many* teens who go to drinking parties and drink to excess *may be* seeking a sense of belonging and acceptance they cannot find *as easily* elsewhere." Rather than making blanket claims that the reader may take exception to, academic arguers often qualify their claims with words such as *may*, *seem*, and *perhaps* or phrases such as *often appears*. When you are making large claims that could be disputed, consider using qualifiers such as *it seems that*, *often*, *may*, or *perhaps* to limit your claim and thus make it more persuasive. For example, if you are arguing about the importance of manners for young people, you do not want to charge all young Canadians with rudeness. Instead, you could qualify your claim by saying something like "*Many* young people are not aware of the societal rules that can smooth out social interactions."

Using Primary and Secondary Research in Argument

While it is possible to use your own experience, observations, and skills in logic to build a strong argument in a personal writing assignment, for formal academic writing you will often be expected to draw on research to support your claims. Let's say that you're taking an education course and are asked to write a paper arguing for or against the use of iPads as an educational tool in elementary schools. Obviously, this assignment would require you to synthesize (see pages 356–357) the results of your outside reading as well as your own conclusions drawn from your observations of computer use in classrooms. It would, in short, require both secondary research (external sources from books, articles, or databases in the library) and direct observation, which is itself a form of primary research. Remember that before you use library and Internet sources, you will need to read the section on taking notes in Chapter 14 and the sections on handling quotations and avoiding plagiarism in Chapter 16. As always, follow your instructor's guidelines for documenting sources.

RATIONAL APPEALS

Among family, friends, and your community, and certainly in professional circles, you are usually expected to reach your conclusions on the basis of sound reasons and appropriate evidence. Reasons are the key points you use to defend your conclusions. For instance, if you support safe injection sites for intravenous drug users, one reason might be the reduction in AIDS-related deaths that could result. You could cite figures that project the number of deaths likely to be prevented by safe injection sites. If you oppose safe injections sites, one reason might be the drug dependency that will continue.

To convince readers, your reasons must be substantiated by evidence. If you favour needle exchange, you could cite figures that project the number of deaths that will be prevented. If you're against needle exchange, you might quote a respected authority who verifies that drug dependency will become entrenched.

Even if you do not entirely convince your audience, they should at least be able to see your position as a plausible one. If you or your readers have rigid, unmovable assumptions, there can be no real argument, because you are not really listening to one another. Argument presupposes that both you and your readers are reasonable people who have a vested interest in reaching some kind of common ground. You and your audience need to have some shared understanding about what counts as evidence.

Evidence falls into several categories: established truths, opinions of authorities, primary source information, statistical findings, and personal experience. The strongest arguments usually combine several kinds of evidence.

Established Truths

These are facts that no one can seriously dispute. Here are some examples:

Historical fact: The Canadian Charter of Rights and Freedoms prohibits racial discrimination.

Scientific fact: The layer of ozone in the earth's upper atmosphere protects us from the sun's harmful ultraviolet radiation.

Geographical fact: Alberta has the largest oil reserves in Canada.

Established truths aren't arguable themselves but do provide strong backup for argumentative propositions. For example, citing the abundant oil supply in the western regions could support an argument that Canada should promote the increased use of Canadian oil to supply its energy needs.

Some established truths basically amount to enlightened common sense, the result of careful observations and thinking over many years. The notion that everyone possesses a unique combination of interests, abilities, and personality characteristics illustrates this kind of truth. Few people would seriously question it.

Opinions of Authorities

An authority is a recognized expert in some field. Authoritative opinions help win readers to your side. Quotations from metropolitan police chiefs and criminologists could support your position on ways to control urban crime. Citing the research of scientists who have investigated the effects of air pollution could help you argue for stricter smog-control laws. Whatever your argument, use credible, recognized authorities from the field and, when possible, mention their credentials to your reader. This information makes their statements more persuasive. Consider the following statement from an argument about helping children develop a kind of internal self-monitoring referred to as self-regulation: "Dr. Stuart Shankar, a Distinguished Research Professor of Philosophy and Psychology at York University who has researched optimal brain development in childhood, urges school districts to promote self-regulation which allows children to manage energy, emotions, stressors, and attention effectively." Of course, citing the opinions of experts will sway readers only if the audience accepts the expert as authoritative.

The following paragraph, from an article arguing that extra-high-voltage electric transmission lines pose a health hazard, illustrates the use of authority:

> Robert Becker, a physician and director of the Orthopedic–Biophysics Laboratory at the Syracuse, New York, Veterans Administration Hospital–Upstate Medical Center, has been researching the effects of low-frequency electric fields (60 Hz) for fifteen years. Testifying at health and safety hearings for proposed lines in New York, he said that exposure to the fields can produce physiological and functional changes in humans—anything from increased irritability and fatigue to raised cholesterol levels, hypertension and ulcers. Studies of rats exposed to low-level electric fields showed tumor growths and abnormalities in development. Dr. Becker believes we are performing unauthorized medical experiments by exposing people to the electromagnetic fields surrounding the transmission lines.
>
> Kelly Davis, "Health and High Voltage: 765 KV Lines"

Beware of biased opinions. The agribusiness executive who favours farm price supports or the labour leader who opposes any restrictions on picketing may be writing merely to guard old privileges or garner new ones. Unless the opinion can stand close scrutiny, it will weaken rather than strengthen your case. Be especially careful with Internet sources. If you are using a general search engine such as Google, the first results of your key-word search may be those sites that have paid for priority placement on the list. If you are writing a formal academic argument, you might want to search scholarly databases such as Academic Search Premier or Canadian Periodical Index for articles that have been juried by specialists in the field. Follow your instructor's guidelines for citations and documentation.

Primary Source Information

Some arguments are supported and strengthened with primary source information—first-hand descriptions or original materials produced by people who witnessed the event you are writing about, or who were directly involved with the issue. Primary sources could include letters, maps, trial transcripts, or diaries. To make a claim about media coverage of a political protest or terrorist act, you would want to read the newspaper and magazine accounts of correspondents who were on the scene. This type of information can help you reach sound conclusions and build strong support for your position. Most university and college libraries contain a significant amount of primary source materials that you can draw on for an argument, some of which can be accessed through online archives such as the portal at ARCHIVESCANADA.ca. Document the sources you use according to your instructor's guidelines.

Statistical Findings

Statistics—data showing how much, how many, or how often—can also buttress your argument. Most statistics come from books, magazines, newspapers, handbooks, encyclopedias, and reports, but you can use data from your own investigations as well. The Statistics Canada website is a good source of authoritative statistics on many different topics.

Because statistics are often misused, many people distrust them, so any you offer must be credible and reliable. First, make sure your sample isn't too small. Don't use a one-day traffic count to argue for a traffic light at a certain intersection. City Hall might counter by contending that the results are atypical. To make your case, you'd need to count traffic for perhaps two or three weeks. You must have a large enough representative sampling to support the kinds of conclusions you draw. In addition, do not push statistical claims too far. You may know that two-thirds of Hamilton's factories are polluting the lake, but don't argue that the same figures probably apply in a different town. There's simply no carry-over. Also, keep alert for biased or poorly researched statistics; they can cause as serious a credibility gap as biased opinions. Generally, recent data are better than old data, but either must come from a reliable source. For example, older information from *The Globe and Mail* would probably be more accurate than current data from tabloid newspapers. Note how the following writer uses statistics to support her argument about the relative affordability of ending homelessness in Canada:

> According to Statistics Canada the average Canadian household spends $7,739 on food annually. This includes $5,572 in stores and $2,167 at restaurants. This works out to $3,095.60/person—$2,228.80/person in stores and $866.80/person in restaurants.
>
> Other Canadian expenditures (all indicated per person) include $1,384.40 for clothing, $1,493.20 for recreation, $80.80 on games of chance and $873.20 for household furnishings and equipment.
>
> For many households, one of their biggest expenses is probably their car. The Canadian Automobile Association calculates the cost of driving different types of cars (compact, mid-size and cross-over) for different lengths of distance. Using the average of the three cars driven 18,000 kms annually, the average Canadian driver spends $10,469.92/year. This works out to $872.49/month and $201.34/week. (At 24,000 km—average annual cost is $11,704.08, monthly cost is $975.34 and weekly cost is $225.08.)
>
> Tanya Gulliver-Garcia, "How Much Does It Cost to End Homelessness in Canada?"

Statistics from newspaper or journal articles, graphs, tables, and charts can help strengthen your case, but be sure to select data responsibly from credible sources and to document them correctly.

Personal Experience

You yourself may be a credible authority on some issues. Personal experience can sometimes deliver an argumentative message more forcefully than any other kind of evidence. Suppose that two years ago a speeder ran into your car and almost killed you. Today you're arguing for stiffer laws against speeding. Chances are you'll rely mainly on expert opinions and on statistics showing the number of people killed and injured each year in speeding accidents. However, describing the crash, the slow, pain-filled weeks in the hospital, and the months spent hobbling around on crutches may well provide the persuasive nudge that wins your reader over.

Often reports of others' experiences and observations, gathered from books, magazines, or interviews, can support your position. If you argue against chemical waste dumps, the personal stories of people who lived near them and suffered the consequences—filthy ooze in the basement, children with birth defects, family members who developed a rare form of cancer—can help sway your reader.

Despite its usefulness, personal experience generally reinforces but does not replace other kinds of evidence for more formal academic papers. Some readers may discount personal experience as biased or atypical. It is wise to make sure you understand your instructor's preferences regarding the use of personal experience in arguments.

EVALUATION OF EVIDENCE

Once you have gathered the appropriate evidence, you need to use certain standards to evaluate that evidence before you use it. That a piece of information is in some way connected to your topic does not automatically make it good evidence or qualify it for inclusion in your paper. Readers won't be convinced that trains are dangerous merely because you were in a train wreck. You should not reach a conclusion based on such flimsy evidence either. To reach a reasonable conclusion and defend a position with suitable evidence, you should apply the following principles.

Evaluation Criteria	**Explanations**
How credible are the sources of the information? How reliable is the evidence?	Not all sources are equally reliable. For example, Statistics Canada data about population change are more credible than a local newspaper's estimate, and both are likely more valid than your own estimate.
How much confirming evidence is there?	With evidence, more is better. One scientific study on the efficacy of high-protein diets would be good, but several would be better. One authority who claims that global warming is a reality becomes more credible when confirmed by several other authorities.
How much contradictory evidence is there?	If several scientific studies or authorities point to the efficacy of high-protein diets while several other studies find such diets harmful, clearly you would need to weigh the evidence carefully. To present the evidence honestly, you would have to include evidence from both sides in your paper.
How well established is the evidence?	Extremely well-established evidence, such as the evidence for atoms, becomes the basis for textbooks and is assumed in most other research. This evidence is usually unquestionable (although occasionally it can be overturned). Such evidence makes a solid foundation for arguments.
How well does the evidence actually fit or support the claim?	False connections between ideas weaken arguments. For example, the fact that most Canadians are immigrants or descendents of immigrants has no bearing on whether the country is admitting too many or too few immigrants. To make a case for or against some policy on immigration, the evidence would have to focus on good or bad results, not numbers.
What does the evidence actually allow you to conclude?	Conclusions should flow from the evidence without exaggeration. For example, studies showing that TV violence causes children to play more aggressively do not warrant the conclusion that it causes children to kill others.

Sometimes unwarranted conclusions result because a writer fails to take competing claims and evidence into consideration. You need to weigh the credibility, quantity, reliability, and applicability of all available evidence to reach and defend a conclusion.

REASONING STRATEGIES

An argument, then, consists of a conclusion or claim that you want to support, your reasons for arriving at that conclusion, and the evidence that supports your reasons. But how are reasons and evidence fitted together? Arguments with different purposes and audiences are constructed differently. Many arguments depend on inductive reasoning—that is, they move from specific pieces of evidence to a general conclusion, or from the bottom up. Other arguments emphasize deductive logic—that is, they are top-down arguments that follow from a general, commonly agreed-upon principle to a specific argument. Arguments may also employ all of the strategies of development, such as illustration, definition, comparison, or causal analysis, covered earlier in this text. It will often be necessary for arguers to use examples, to explain how a particular process works, to define unfamiliar or abstract terms, to compare two models, or to use a special kind of comparison called an analogy, which compares two seemingly unlike things that nevertheless have one or more features in common. It could be argued, in fact, that arguments underlie almost any kind of writing we do.

Inductive Reasoning

An argument that uses inductive reasoning proceeds from specific evidence—observations, statistical data, testimony of experts, or scientific studies—to a general claim or conclusion. We use inductive reasoning in our daily lives when we form expectations based on patterns of repeated observations or experiences that lead us to expect similar results. For example, we expect that we will feel more energy after exercise when we have experienced this result many times. When we conclude that a movie is worth watching because our friends liked it, when we decide that a university program is effective because most of the graduates get jobs, or even when we support a scientific hypothesis based on formal experimentation, we are drawing inductive generalizations from accumulated bits of evidence. After observing many specific instances of lung cancer seen in smokers, and noting that there were significantly fewer cases of lung cancer in non-smokers, scientists reasoned inductively that smoking was a contributing cause of lung cancer. We might think of inductive argument as building from the bottom up, from bits of evidence to a broad conclusion that is probable, given the evidence. Inductive conclusions are based on probability, not absolute certainty. To be absolutely certain of our conclusions, we'd have to check each possible case or piece of evidence, and that's not usually feasible. If you ask 10 out of 15 000 students whether they like the school's meal plan, you cannot draw a conclusion about the tastes of the entire student body, but the greater the number of observations and the larger the sample, the stronger your conclusion will be. Of course, we need to be thoughtful about our conclusions and carefully consider the trustworthiness of the evidence we use to make our case.

For some arguments that your reader may be skeptical about, it can be strategic to withhold your thesis until you have established some common ground with readers and answered possible objections they may have. The strategy of withholding the thesis can be especially effective if the argument is a solution to a problem that readers need to be convinced exists before they will be receptive to hearing your recommendations. Also, if possible, try to show how the evidence fits the conclusion you want to reach.

The body of the paper provides the supporting evidence for your claims. When you make a claim, you cannot simply expect that readers will take your word for it. To prove your point, you may need to draw on many kinds of evidence, including examples, references to authorities, illustrations, facts and statistics, and even charts and graphs in some kinds of papers. Some successful arguers call on narratives at times to help them reinforce a point and draw the audience closer. The body of your paper will also address possible objections to your argument.

In the conclusion, you reaffirm your position or suggest the consequences of that position. You can also raise a general question, evaluate how your evidence answers that question, and then draw your conclusion from that answer.

The following short example illustrates inductive argument.

States claim to be proven.	Systematic phonics, the method of reading instruction that shows children how to sound out letters, is an effective method of teaching word reading in the
Identifies justification of study.	first three grades. A large study, sponsored by the federal government in the 1970s, compared how effective different instructional methods were in helping
Provides results of evidence that supports major claim.	disadvantaged children. The direct instruction program resulted in children, otherwise expected to fall below the norm, to meet or be close to the national
Offers a second study to strengthen support.	standard for reading (Stebbins et al., 1977). Another study compared the effect of the whole-language instruction, embedded phonics, and direct code instruc-
States results that support claim.	tion on 285 students in a district with a high risk of reading failure. The university researchers found that the children taught by direct instruction improved in word reading much faster than students in the other groups. In fact, most taught with the whole-language approach had no measurable gains in word reading, even if they did have a more positive attitude towards reading (Stahl et al., 1994).
Provides qualification to support credibility.	While these studies may not fully demonstrate that systematic phonics is the best method for teaching reading, the fact that in experiments students taught with direct code instruction demonstrated greater gains in word reading than
Connects evidence clearly as support for claim.	those taught by other methods at least shows that systematic phonics can help students make gains in word reading.

Marjorie Hawkins

When writing an inductive argument, in addition to presenting the available evidence, you should demonstrate the credibility of your evidence. Here the student writer identified that the first study was large and sponsored by the federal government and gave the exact number of subjects in the second study, as well as the information that the researchers were from a university.

Deductive Reasoning

Unlike inductive reasoning, which follows a bottom-up strategy from the specific to the general, deductive reasoning follows a top-down strategy, arguing from the general rule or observation to the specific instance. Instead of formulating a general conclusion after considering pieces of evidence, deductive arguments begin with an observation that most people accept as true and then show how certain conclusions follow from that observation. For example, to convince a friend to study harder, you begin with the assumption that a profitable career requires a good education; proceed to argue that for a good education, students must study diligently; and conclude that, as a result, your friend should spend more time with the books. Of course, if your friend does not agree with what seems to you a self-evident truth (that a profitable career requires a good education), then your friend will not accept the conclusion that follows from that premise either. It is important that the premises from which you argue are indeed ones that your audience will accept. When politicians draw on the agreed-upon premise that we all want to act in ways that will be beneficial to future generations and then point out how the policies they favour will ensure that outcome, they are using deductive reasoning; most people will accept general premises based on principles of obvious ethical fairness—for example, the idea that community or long-term values are more important than short-term self-interest. However, arguments are weakened when people argue from premises they wrongly assume to be self-evident and commonly shared; for example, a person who argues from the premise that "everyone agrees" that all couples who have children should get married assumes an agreement that is not justified, and will likely not convince an alert audience.

Here is a short example of a deductive argument:

> The Canadian Charter of Rights and Freedoms specifies freedom of conscience and religion as a fundamental human right. Reasonable Canadians agree that this freedom to follow one's conscience and religion is a central tenet of our multicultural democracy. Therefore since traditional Sikh males wear turbans and do not cut their hair for religious reasons, they should be able to wear turbans in the hockey arena or in the workplace. It is vitally important that we as Canadians uphold religious freedoms and not open the door to discrimination or racist profiling.

Establishes basic shared assumption or premise.

Clarifying example follows logically.

Suggests negative consequences if argument is not accepted.

Syllogism   Sometimes a deductive argument is built around a three-part formula called a syllogism, a set of three statements that follow a fixed pattern to ensure sound reasoning. The first statement, called the major premise, names a category of things and says that all or none of them share a certain characteristic. The minor premise notes that a thing or group of things belongs to that category. The conclusion then states that the thing or group logically must share the characteristics of the category. Here are two examples:

Major premise:	All persons are mortal.
Minor premise:	Sue Davis is a person.
Conclusion:	Therefore, Sue Davis is mortal.
Major premise:	No dogs have feathers.
Minor premise:	Spot is a dog.
Conclusion:	Therefore, Spot does not have feathers.

Note that in each case, both major and minor premises are indisputably true, and so the conclusion follows logically.

Syllogisms frequently appear in stripped-down form, with one of the premises or the conclusion implied but unstated. The following example omits the major premise: "Because Wilma is a civil engineer, she has a strong background in mathematics." Obviously, the missing major premise is: "All civil engineers have strong backgrounds in mathematics."

Consider how the following syllogism works and then finds its way into a short piece of writing:

Major premise:	All stereotypes are damaging.
Minor premise:	Female sex objects shown in the media are stereotypes.
Conclusion:	Therefore, female sex object stereotypes are damaging.

The ideal of physical beauty portrayed by female stereotypes in the media is unattainable and unrealistic. Most women do not have this idealized body shape: full breasts, tiny waist, and narrow hips that air-brushed models appear to have. To attain these features, most women would have to resort to surgical alterations or starvation diets. Even so, all women must ultimately fail this beauty test in time, for the sex object is, above all else, young. Mere mortals cannot compare with these perpetually young, air-brushed, and ano-rexic visions of beauty. Like other stereotypes, the unrealistic images of female beauty reflected in the media are damaging to women and to the larger society.

To accept the deductive argument above, you would have to accept both the major premise listed above (the common-sense notion that stereotypes are damaging) and the minor premise (female sex objects in the media are stereotypes).

When arguing from deduction, you need to make clear how your conclusions follow from the agreed-upon premises. One student who wrote a persuasive paper cautioning people about the risks of cosmetic surgery organized her paper partly around the following syllogism:

All surgery carries risks.
Cosmetic procedures done under the knife are surgeries.
Therefore, cosmetic surgeries carry risks.

The student then proceeded to give examples of risks from respected medical authorities. These examples led to inductive conclusions such as "There are psychologi-cal risks after cosmetic surgery" and "There is a risk that some men and women can become addicted to plastic surgery." This essay, like many, blended inductive and deduc-tive reasoning.

As with induction, you have several options when organizing a deductive argu-ment. You might begin with the position you intend to prove, with a question that will be answered by the argument, or with a synopsis of the argument. The body of the paper works out the implications of your assumption. In the conclusion, you could directly state (or restate, in different words) your position, suggest the consequences of adopting or not adopting that position, or pose a question that is easily answered after reading the argument.

Avoiding the Misuse of Syllogisms Two cautions about the use of syllogisms are in order. *First*, make sure any syllogism you use follows the proper order. The writer of the following passage has ignored this caution.

> Furthermore, Robinson has stated openly that he supports a ban on all clear-cut logging practices. For many years now, the Green Party has taken the same environmentalist stand. Robinson's position places him firmly in the Green Party camp. I strongly urge anyone supporting this man's candidacy to reconsider. . . .

Restated in syllogistic form, the writer's argument goes like this:

> Green Party members support a ban on all clear-cut logging practices.
>
> Robinson supports a ban on all clear-cut logging practices.
>
> Therefore, Robinson is a supporter of the Green Party.

The last two statements reverse the proper order, and as a result the syllogism proves nothing about Robinson's politics: He may or may not be "in the Green Party camp."

Second, make sure the major premise of your syllogism is in fact true. Note this example:

> All Conservatives are opposed to environmental protection.
>
> Mary is a Conservative.
>
> Therefore, Mary is opposed to environmental protection.

But *is* every Conservative an anti-environmentalist? In some communities, political conservatives have led fights against air and water pollution, and most Conservatives agree that some controls are worthwhile. Mary's sympathies, then, may well lie with those who want to heal, rather than hurt, the environment.

EXERCISE *Which of these syllogisms is satisfactory, which have false major premises, and which is faulty because the last two statements reverse the proper order?*

1. All singers are happy people.

   Mary Harper is a singer.

   Therefore, Mary Harper is a happy person.

2. All cowards fear danger.

   "Chicken" Cacciatore is a coward.

   Therefore, "Chicken" Cacciatore fears danger.

3. All cats like meat.

   Towser likes meat.

   Therefore, Towser is a cat.

4. No salesperson would ever misrepresent a product to a customer.

Sabrina is a salesperson.

Therefore, Sabrina would never misrepresent a product to a customer.

Analogy in Argument

An analogy, touched on in Chapter 11 on comparison, that compares two unlike situations or things can be useful not only to clarify, but also to persuade. Arguers often use analogies to contend that, because two items share one or more likenesses, they are also alike in other ways. Familiar analogies assume that humans respond to chemicals as rats do and that success in school predicts success on the job.

However, because its conclusions about one idea rest on observations about a different idea, analogy is the weakest form of rational appeal. Analogies never prove anything, but they often help explain and show probability and therefore can be quite persuasive.

For an analogy to be useful, it must feature significant similarities that bear directly on the issue. In addition, it must account for any significant differences between the two items. It is often helpful to test an analogy by listing the similarities and differences. Here's an effective analogy, used to back an argument that a liberal education is the best kind to help us cope successfully with life:

> Suppose it were perfectly certain that the life and fortune of every one of us would, one day or other, depend upon his winning or losing a game of chess. Don't you think that we should all consider it to be a primary duty to learn at least the names and the moves of the pieces; to have a notion of a gambit, and a keen eye for all the means of giving and getting out of check? Do you not think that we should look with a disapprobation amounting to scorn, upon the father who allowed his son, or the state which allowed its members, to grow up without knowing a pawn from a knight?
>
> Yet it is a very plain and elementary truth, that the life, the fortune, and the happiness of every one of us, and, more or less, of those who are connected with us, do depend upon our knowing something of the rules of a game infinitely more difficult and complicated than chess. It is a game which has been played for untold ages, every man and woman of us being one of the two players in a game of his or her own. The chessboard is the world, the pieces are the phenomena of the universe, the rules of the game are what we call the laws of Nature. The player on the other side is hidden from us. We know that his play is always fair, just, and patient. But also we know, to our cost, that he never overlooks a mistake, or makes the smallest allowance for ignorance. To the man who plays well, the highest stakes are paid, with that sort of overflowing generosity with which the strong shows delight in strength. And one who plays ill is checkmated—without haste, but without remorse. . . .
>
> Well, what I mean by Education is learning the rules of this mighty game. In other words, education is the instruction of the intellect in the law of Nature, under which name I include not merely things and their forces, but men and their ways; and the fashioning of the affections and of the will into an earnest and loving desire to move in harmony with those laws. For me, education means neither more nor less than this. Anything which professes to call itself education must be tried by this standard, and if it fails to stand the test, I will not call it education, whatever may be the force of authority, or of numbers, upon the other side.

Thomas Henry Huxley, "A Liberal Education and Where to Find It"

Margin notes:

Establishes basis of analogy.

Finishes defining analogy by indicating how life is like a game.

Details the comparison of life and chess.

Completes the argument by demonstrating the rules that need to be learned and how that is an education.

To develop an argument by analogy, brainstorm the two items being compared for significant similarities and prepare a chart that matches them up. The greater the number and closeness of these similarities, the better the argument by analogy.

EMOTIONAL APPEALS

Although effective argument relies mainly on reason, an emotional appeal can lend powerful reinforcement. Indeed, emotion that wins hearts can move people who would otherwise passively accept a logical argument but take no action. Each Christmas, newspapers raise money for local charities by running stark case histories of destitute families. Organizations raise funds to fight famine by displaying brochures that feature skeletal, swollen-bellied children. Still other groups use emotion-charged stories and pictures to solicit support for environmental protection, to combat various diseases, and so on. Less benignly, advertisers use emotion to play upon our hopes, fears, and vanities in order to sell mouthwash, cars, clothes, and other products. Politicians paint themselves as fiscally responsible, trustworthy toilers for the public good while lambasting their opponents as being callous and unconcerned with social justice. In evaluating or writing an argument, ask yourself whether the facts warrant the emotion. Is the condition of the destitute family truly cause for pity? Is any politician unwaveringly good, any other irredeemably bad?

The following passage from a student argument favouring assisted suicide for the terminally ill represents an appropriate use of emotion.

> When I visited Grandpa for the last time, he seemed imprinted on the hospital bed, <u>a motionless, skeleton-like figure tethered by an array of tubes to the droning, beeping machine at his bedside.</u> The <u>eyes that had once sparkled with delight as he bounced grandchildren on his knee now stared blankly at the ceiling, seemingly ready to burst from their sockets.</u> His mouth, frozen in an open grimace, emitted raspy, irregular <u>noises as he fought to breathe. Spittle leaked from one corner of his mouth and dribbled onto the sheet. A ripe stench from the diaper around his middle hung about the bedside, masking the medicinal sickroom smells.</u> As I stood by the bedside, my mind flashed back to the irrepressible man I once knew, and tears flooded my eyes. Bending forward, I planted a <u>soft kiss on his forehead, whispered "I love you,</u> Gramps," and walked slowly away.
>
> Dylan Brandt Chafin

Annotation
Description indicates dependency and weakness.
Contrast shows change in quality of life.
Identifies degradation.
Shows narrator's love, which makes subsequent argument more credible.

To develop an effective emotional appeal, let yourself recall or think about stories, scenes, or events related to your topic that arouse the strongest emotional response within you. Try some free writing around these images, memories, or scenes, and choose whatever section seems most evocative. Sometimes the emotional appeal is especially effective if it is placed at the beginning or end of your paper.

ETHICAL APPEALS

Before logic can do its work, the audience must be willing to consider the argument. If a writer's tone offends the audience, perhaps by sounding arrogant or mean-spirited, the reasoning will fail to penetrate. But if the writer comes across as pleasant, fair-minded, and decent, gaining reader support is much easier. The writer who conveys a sense of integrity uses an ethical appeal.

If you write with a genuine concern for your topic, a commitment to the truth, and a sincere respect for others, you will probably come across reasonably well. When you finish writing, check whether occasional snide comments or bitter remarks slipped unnoticed onto the page. In the following passage from a website devoted to issues related to homelessness, the writer makes an ethical appeal when she asks Canadians if they would be willing to make a modest sacrifice to help the larger cause of ending homelessness.

> Tim Hortons, Canada's favourite coffee purveyor, serves 2 billion cups of coffee per year. Your daily coffee fix will run you over $500, even if you skip the weekends.
> Would you give up a coffee or two if it meant contributing towards ending homelessness?
>
> Tanya Gulliver-Garcia, "How Much Does It Cost to End Homelessness in Canada?"

By showing her own sensitivity to the plight of homeless people and appealing to the reader's empathy and sense of fairness, this writer uses an ethical appeal.

FERRETING OUT FALLACIES

As a critical reader and writer, it is helpful to be able to spot holes in logic called fallacies. The lapses or jumps in logic weaken your case. The fallacies described below are among the most common. Correct any you find in your own arguments, and if you are engaged in a debate, call attention to those used by the opposition.

Hasty Generalization

Hasty generalization results when someone bases a conclusion on too little evidence. The student who tries to see an instructor during one of her office hours, finds her out, and goes away muttering, "She's never there when she should be" is guilty of hasty generalization. Perhaps the instructor was delayed by another student, or had gone home ill. However, the student who fails to find the instructor during office hours several times is more justified in drawing such a generalization.

Non Sequitur

From Latin, meaning "it does not follow," this fallacy draws unwarranted conclusions from seemingly ample evidence. Consider this example: "Bill's been out almost every night for the last two weeks. Who is she?" These evening excursions, on their own, point to no particular conclusion. Bill may be studying in the library, participating in campus organizations, taking night classes, or walking. Of course, he could be with a new girlfriend, but that conclusion requires other evidence.

Stereotyping

A person who commits this fallacy attaches one or more supposed characteristics to a group or one of its members. Typical stereotypes include "Latins make better lovers," "Blondes have more fun," and "Teenagers are lousy drivers." Stereotyping groups of people based on race, ethnicity, age, gender, ability, or sexual orientation can destroy an argument. Thoughtful, fair-minded listeners and readers are offended by stereotyping, which is often meant as a slur.

Card Stacking

In card stacking, the writer presents only part of the available evidence on a topic, deliberately omitting essential information that would alter the picture considerably. Consider the following claim: "University students have a very easy life; they attend classes for only 12 to 16 hours a week." This statement ignores the many hours that students must spend studying, doing homework and research, writing papers, and earning enough money to pay tuition.

Either/Or Fallacy

The either/or fallacy, sometimes referred to as a false dilemma, asserts that only two choices exist when in fact other options are possible. A salesperson who wants you to buy snow tires may claim: "Either buy these tires or plan on getting stuck a lot this winter." But are you really that boxed in? You might drive only on main roads that are plowed immediately after every snowstorm. You could use public transportation when it snows. You could buy radial tires for year-round use, or you could buy tires from another dealer. If very little snow falls, you might not need special tires at all.

However, not all either/or statements are fallacies. The instructor who checks a student's record and then issues a warning, "Make at least a C on your final, or you'll fail the course," is not guilty of a reasoning error. No other alternatives exist. Most situations, however, offer more than two choices.

Begging the Question

A person who begs the question asserts the truth of some unproven statement. Here is an example of how such faulty reasoning may go around in circles: "Vitamin A is harmful to your health, and all bottles should carry a warning label. If enough of us write to the Minister of Health, we can get the labelling we need." But how do we know vitamin A does harm users? No evidence is offered. When someone begs the question, they simply restate the argument in other language: "Pauline is a good manager because she runs the company effectively" says, in effect, that "something is because something is." Repetition replaces evidence.

Arguing off the Point

The writer who commits this fallacy, which is sometimes called "ignoring the question" or "a red herring," sidetracks an issue by introducing irrelevant information. To illustrate, "Vancouver has a more moderate climate than Toronto. Besides, too many Torontonians are moving to Vancouver. They are creating congestion and driving up the price of real estate. Many Vancouverites are angry that the cost of buying a home is so high." The writer sets out to convince the reader that Vancouver offers a more enjoyable climate than Toronto, but then abruptly shifts to increasing congestion and rising house prices in Vancouver—a trend that has no bearing on the argument.

The Argument *ad Hominem*

The Latin term meaning "to the man" designates an argument that attacks an individual rather than that individual's opinions or qualifications. Note this example: "Sam Bernhard doesn't deserve promotion to personnel manager. His divorce was a disgrace, and he's always writing critical letters to the editor. The company should find someone more suitable." This attack completely skirts the real issue—whether Sam's job performance entitles him to the promotion. Unless his personal conduct has caused his work to suffer, it should not enter into the decision.

Appeal to the Crowd (also called Bandwagon Appeals)

An appeal of this sort arouses an emotional response by playing on the irrational fears and prejudices of the audience. This kind of appeal is based on the idea that because so many others are doing it, you should too. The term "bandwagon" comes from the practice of people jumping or climbing into a brightly coloured wagon that was big enough to hold a band of musicians, who would play music during political rallies or circus parades. People would jump into the wagon, thus showing support for a popular politician. It is a common form of manipulation used by politicians and advertisers. For example, an ad on YouTube for Tim Hortons starring Sidney Crosby appeals to the audience in an interesting way, showing a crowd descending on a hockey game and then adding a postscript naming Tim Hortons as "Proud to be part of our game".

Guilt by Association

This fallacy points out some similarity or connection between one person or group and another. It tags the first with the sins, real or imagined, of the second. The following excerpt from a letter protesting a speaker at a lecture series illustrates this technique:

> The next slated speaker, Dr. Sylvester Crampton, was for years a member of the Economic Information Committee. This foundation has very strong ties with other ultra-right-wing groups, some of which have been labelled fascistic. When he speaks next Thursday, whose brand of patriotism will he be selling?

Post Hoc, ergo Propter Hoc

From Latin, meaning "after this, therefore because of this," refers to the fallacy of assuming that because one event follows another, the first caused the second. Such weak thinking underlies many popular superstitions ("If a black cat crosses your path, you'll have bad luck") and many connections that cannot be substantiated ("Since video games have become so popular, childhood obesity rates have risen. Therefore, video games cause childhood obesity"). Sometimes one event does cause another: A sudden thunderclap might startle a person into dropping a dish. At other times, coincidence is the only connection. Careful research and thinking will help determine whether A caused B, or whether these two events just happened to occur at about the same time.

Faulty Analogy

Although analogies can sometimes be useful to explain unfamiliar or difficult concepts, at times analogies do not support the argument in some crucial way. These faulty or weak analogies assume that just because two things are similar in one respect, they are in fact similar in all respects. An example of a faulty analogy would be saying that someone who reaches every day for a cup of coffee in the morning is no different than an addict looking for his next fix. While both the coffee drinker and the addict are taking substances that affect their brains, there are important differences that this analogy overlooks. Another example is: "Toddlers are like puppies. They need a clear sense of who's in charge. They must be disciplined and housebroken." Obviously, while both toddlers and puppies are immature and dependent, there are many differences that make this analogy a weak one.

EXERCISE *Identify and explain the fallacies in the following examples. Remember that understanding the faulty reasoning is more important than merely naming the fallacy.*

1. After slicing a Golden Glow orange, Nancy discovers that it is rotten. "I'll never buy another Golden Glow product," she declares emphatically.
2. A campaigning politician states that unless the federal government appropriates funds to help people living in poverty, they will all starve.
3. A husband and wife see an X-rated movie called *Swinging Wives*. A week later the husband discovers that his wife, while supposedly attending an evening class, has been unfaithful to him. He blames the movie for her infidelity.
4. "Look at those two motorcycle riders trying to pick a fight. All those cycle bums are troublemakers."
5. "Bill really loves to eat. Someday he'll have a serious weight problem."
6. "Because no-fault divorce is responsible for today's skyrocketing divorce rate, it should be abolished."
7. "This is the best-looking picture in the exhibit; it's so much more attractive than the others."
8. "I am against the proposed ban on smoking in public places. As long as I don't inhale and I limit my habit to 10 cigarettes a day, my health won't suffer."

ETHICAL ISSUES

When writing an argument, we may wish to raise awareness, change attitudes, or spark some action. These objectives create an ethical responsibility for both the quality and the possible consequences of our arguments. Suppose that a doctor writing a nationally syndicated advice column recommends an over-the-counter product that may cause a serious reaction in users who also take a certain prescription drug. Clearly this writer has acted irresponsibly and risks legal action if some readers suffer harm. Asking and answering the following questions can help you avoid any breach of ethics.

- *Have I carefully considered the issue I'm arguing and the stance I'm taking?* Since you're trying to get others to adopt your views, you'll need to make sure they are very credible or make clear that your position is tentative or dependent on certain conditions.
- *Am I fair to other positions on the issue?* Careless or deliberate distortion of opposing views is ethically dishonest and could raise doubts about your credibility.
- *Are my reasons and evidence legitimate?* It is unethical to present flawed reasons as if they were credible or to falsify evidence.
- *Do I use fallacies or other types of faulty thinking to manipulate the reader unfairly?*
- *What consequences could follow if readers adopt my position?* Say that a writer strongly opposes genetically modified foods and advocates disruption of installations that help develop them. If some who are convinced by the argument then proceed to act on the writer's advice, innocent people could be injured.

WRITING AN ARGUMENT

Planning and Drafting the Argument

Some instructors assign argumentative topics, and some leave the choice of topic to you.

Prewriting the Argument

FINDING YOUR TOPIC

- Take notes on current disputes on television, the radio, and other media.
- Write down the major issues you and others find yourselves discussing or posting about.
- Select from your class notes issues touched on that interest you.

Focusing Your Question

When you explore a topic for an argument, take time to think things through, to gradually work toward some conclusions, and then begin to draft your position in stages with the support you have discovered. If you are using outside sources to find support for your argument, you need to use your active-reading and critical-thinking skills as you sift through and evaluate potential supporting materials. You need to weigh the merits of different writers' opinions, look for evidence of bias, weigh the type and amount of support backing each assertion, and select the key points to include in your paper. Try to keep an open mind as you are formulating your thesis.

Some instructors assign argument topics, and some leave the choice of topic to you. If you are choosing, many options are available. Interesting issues—some local, some of broader importance—crowd our newspapers, TV airways, and the Internet, vying for attention. Several of these may have piqued your interest; if not, you can always refer to the strategies discussed on pages 37–43 to help you choose your topic.

Some students approach an argument with such strong attitudes that they ignore evidence that contradicts their thinking. Don't make this mistake. Instead, maintain an open mind as you research different perspectives on the issue and then, after careful thought, clarify the position you'll take, keeping in mind that your preliminary thesis may be modified as you explore further.

Exploring Your Topic

You never really start an argument with a blank page. There is almost always an ongoing conversation about issues, so when you know that an argumentative paper will be assigned, it helps to be alert to controversies as you surf the Internet, read the news, and go about your daily life. Once you decide on a general subject, it helps to be informed by researching the topic. If your paper is based on sources, you may want to look at Chapter 14 for ideas and Chapter 16 for information about proper documentation. You may want to talk to others to get their views on the matter, or you might make your own formal or informal observations.

As you investigate possible positions, ask and answer the following questions about each.

What are the reasons for the various positions?

What values are at stake, and what conclusions do they imply?

What common ground or shared principles exist among various positions?

What kinds of evidence support the position?

How substantial is the evidence?

If the evidence includes statistics and authoritative opinions, are they reliable? Or are they flawed for some reason?

What are the objections to each position, and how can they be countered?

If the issue involves taking some action, what might be its consequences?

To help with this stage of the process, prepare a chart that summarizes your findings for each position; then examine it carefully to identify the best position to argue for. The example below illustrates a three-position issue:

Position 1	Position 2	Position 3
Evidence and evaluation	Evidence and evaluation	Evidence and evaluation
Objections and how countered	Objections and how countered	Objections and how countered
Consequences	Consequences	Consequences

One effective technique for developing an argument is to first write a dialogue between two or three people that explores the various sides of an issue without trying to arrive at any conclusion. Writing such a dialogue can help start your mental energy flowing, reveal the issue from many sides, and give you ideas about developing effective material for your paper.

DEVELOPING YOUR ARGUMENT

- Research your topic, examining all sides of the issue.
- Create a table with the major options on your position with the available reasons and evidence.
- Create a dialogue that tries to represent different sides of the issue to try out your argument.
- Write down your major reasons and link to evidence and justification for evidence.
- Identify the purpose and audience for your argument and use that to select reasons, evidence, and approach.
- Create a draft outline to help see how the reasons and evidence fit together and brainstorm for possible objections, then answer objections.

Arguments for Different Purposes

Arguments take many different forms, depending on the purpose, audience, situation, and genre for the argument. Whether you are posting online or writing an argument for a class, you may find yourself drawing on all of the different writing strategies you have previously learned. As you contemplate your position and evidence, consider the purpose of your argument and how the purpose will affect the strategies you choose to employ. An argument that takes the form of a critique may include a comparative analysis that demonstrates the relative merits of one item over another. An argument that takes the form of a complaint letter may use causal analysis to outline a problem and then propose a solution. An argument in a business context may also establish that something is a problem, and then recommend a new policy. An argument that takes the form of a formal academic research paper is likely to use a blend of strategies—definition and illustration, comparison and causal logic—as it makes its case, usually with the help of information from primary and secondary sources.

Purpose for Argument	**Strategy**
Demonstrating something is a fact—nursing is hard work, dormitories are poor study places, phonics increases word recognition.	- Depends on the appropriate evidence—examples, statistics, authoritative claims, personal experience. - Nursing is demanding: give an overview of a typical nursing day, cite city hospital nursing supervisors on the job, give statistics of turnover because of stress.

Defend or oppose some policy, action, or project—first-year students should be allowed cars, a company should drug-test employees, Wi-Fi should be added to the entire campus.	■ Identify need for policy or action, how it can be met, cost or feasibility of recommendation, and the resulting benefit. ■ Adding Wi-Fi: students with laptops need to connect to the Internet between classes and as part of class projects, the available technology and cost, the actual usefulness for students in connecting to course material between class and use in classrooms.
Assert the greater or lesser value of someone or something—a supervisor ranking candidates for promotion.	■ Indicate what you are trying to prove, criteria or points for evaluation, reasons along with evidence (details, examples, or statistics). ■ May be deductive, showing how conclusions follow from agreed-upon values. ■ Candidate may be shown to have more years of experience, greater skills such as more programming languages, more examples of leadership.

Directing Arguments to Readers   With an argument, as with any essay, purpose and audience are closely linked. For example, imagine that your audience is a group of readers who are neutral or opposed to your position; there's no point in preaching to the converted. Take a little time to analyze these readers so that you can tailor your arguments appropriately. Pose these questions as you proceed:

What are the readers' interests, expectations, and needs concerning this issue?
What evidence is most likely to convince them?
What objections and consequences would probably weigh most heavily with them?
How can I answer the objections?

Sometimes students think that their argument papers are being marked on whether or not the professor agrees with their point of view, but in fact your academic argument will be assessed on how successfully you win the reader over, in part by anticipating and countering possible objections, and making concessions where necessary. For example, when you offer your recommendations to change a current practice, you might need to admit that the new approach will be expensive in the short run. However, you may also be able to add that not accepting your proposals will cost more in the long run, or that the costs of not following these recommendations will be social, emotional, or environmental.

Even though you are unlikely to convince everyone, it is best to adopt the attitude that most readers are willing to be convinced if your approach is appealing and your evidence is sound.

Building Bridges with a Rogerian Argument

As you reflect on the issues that concern you, consider which people have the power to change things, why they might resist change, and how you could overcome their resistance. If your audience is likely to be resistant or even hostile, you may want to use a *Rogerian argument*. Named for psychologist Carl Rogers, this type of argument emphasizes the ability to look at things from someone else's point of view. To reduce the antagonism that people with opposing views might feel toward your position, you need to show that you understand and respect the opposing position as well as acknowledge its good points. You try to establish some common point of agreement, then show how the conclusion you want really follows from the reader's own values and assumptions without compromising your own. For example, if you are arguing about emotionally charged issues that affect people directly, such as physician-assisted suicide or user fees in Canada's health care system, you can acknowledge in your introduction that these challenging issues have troubling ethical implications that people are right to worry about. After you build a bridge of shared values and respect with your audience, you can then present a position that addresses opposing concerns without compromising your views.

You can also reduce audience resistance if you acknowledge possible objections early on, responding to them if you can or making concessions where necessary. For example, if you are arguing that the province needs to allocate more money for autistic children's therapy, you can acknowledge that these therapies are costly, but then emphasize that the long-term benefits include a more equitable society.

If your argument is highly controversial or your audience is highly resistant, delay stating your thesis until you have built a case by establishing common ground, anticipating possible objections, providing necessary background, and using other strategies such as humour or an apt illustrative narrative to draw your audience to your side.

In addition, you can adapt the language of your argument to the audience's concerns and interests. To convince an audience of farmers that organic farming is viable, you might stress the added income they would gain from selective consumers willing to pay more for organic food; for an audience of people interested in health, you might note the health benefits that would result from eating organic food. Even though you are unlikely to convince everyone, it is best to adopt the attitude that most readers can be convinced if your approach is appealing and your evidence is sound.

Argument as Problem and Solution

If you want to propose a change to an existing structure or policy, you must first prove that a problem exists before your audience will be receptive to hearing about a solution. As you investigate the extent of the problem, you may decide that it does not really need solving, or even that the real problem is different than you originally thought. As you attempt to convince your audience to accept your solution, you are likely to blend different writing strategies into your argument. You may use description and illustration to identify the problem and cause and effect analysis as you examine causes, including hidden causes, and possible effects. Sometimes you can come up with effective solutions by addressing the causes, or you can explore new ways to improve the situation. In some cases, you may have to explain the process of implementing your solution and/or defend (argue) its feasibility by showing that it will not have unacceptable consequences.

Arguments that propose a new action or policy may identify a need or a problem, and they generally recommend the implementation of a practical project, program, or action that will meet existing needs. For example, if there is no place on campus where students can gather to meet informally or study, a writer might propose the construction of a study lounge for students. Arguments that defend or oppose a broader social, political, or cultural policy—for example, the question of whether Canadian ports should have stricter security measures—must demonstrate the need for a new policy, how that need can best be addressed, and the benefits that will result. Arguments that propose a new policy or recommend a new action often use verbs such as *should, need,* or *ought.*

Argument as Evaluation and Critique

Reviews and critiques are arguments that evaluate something against specific criteria. Some reviews provide a short summary of content as background information, but the overall thesis should reflect your judgment and the rest of the review should develop reasons for this judgment. If you are asked to critique a movie, you need to commit yourself to a point of view on the quality of that movie rather than simply summarizing what happened. For example, your thesis for a movie review might be something like "The latest Star Wars movie does not live up to the hype it has generated." If you are looking at criteria such as the quality of acting, special effects, music, and pacing, use specific examples and details for each criterion you are evaluating. Remember to establish criteria for your evaluation that are in accord with what the movie, or restaurant, or writer is trying to do; you can't fault the movie for not being a book, a café for not being a five-star restaurant, or an essay for not having music. Moreover, if you are evaluating a text, you need to establish that you have not come to it with preformed judgments, but have tried to understand and appreciate it on its own terms.

If you are evaluating a text or comparing two texts, your evaluation does not have to be absolutely negative or positive, but you do have to decide whether to emphasize strengths or weaknesses. Typically the evaluation of a text, movie, or essay is mixed, something like "Although this movie features amazing chemistry between the two stars, other weaknesses seriously compromise its quality." If you want to emphasize weaknesses, subordinate the strengths and put the weaknesses afterwards, since whatever you end with makes the greatest impression on the reader. If you want to emphasize positives, end on a positive note. By the way, evaluations of texts and works of art usually employ the present tense throughout, except in the beginning when you are describing your experiences of entering a movie theatre, or picking up a book. If you are asked to write a comparative evaluation, in which you assert the greater value of someone or something as compared to a similar person or thing, you can refer to Chapter 11 on structuring comparisons.

Short Arguments with Visuals   The image on the next page with its caption makes a quick point about lectures. Photographs, cartoons, or a few pithy phrases can make powerful arguments. A photo of a river clogged with litter makes a strong environmental point. A cartoon showing a rich person picking the pocket of a poor person quickly presents a political argument. A short phrase like "your latte could have fed five children today" concisely appeals to our charity. While these short arguments are rarely appropriate to a university setting where reasons and evidence are more carefully weighed, they are part of how we communicate to persuade. For shorter arguments to be effective, the image needs to be easily understood, directly illustrate the point, and have emotional punch.

Drafting the Argument

When you have a good grasp on your position, reasons, evidence, and the approach you want to take, you're ready to draft your paper. Because arguments can be complex, it can be very useful to start by creating an outline of your main reasons, evidence, possible

Lectures don't always promote learning.

objections to your position, and an answer to those objections. Or you may wish to more informally write out your reasons in order with supporting evidence, possibly even initially labelling them to ensure that the reasons are supported.

> Reason 1
> Evidence:
> Evidence:
> Reason 2
> Evidence:
> Objection
> Answer to objection

The more detailed the outline, formal or informal, the easier it will be to draft the paper.

The **thesis statement** for an argument often indicates which position the writer will take, sometimes including the major reasons for that position. It can declare that something is a fact, support a policy, call for a certain action, or assert that something has greater value than something else. The following are examples.

1. Carron College does not provide adequate recreational facilities for its students. *(Declares something is fact.)*
2. Our company's policy of randomly testing employees for drug use has proved effective and should be continued. *(Supports policy.)*
3. Because the present building is overcrowded and unhealthy due to problems with mould, the people of Midville should vote funds for a new middle school. *(Calls for action.)*
4. The Toyota Prius is more fuel efficient and versatile than the Honda Civic hybrid. *(Asserts value.)*

To formulate your thesis, review your main reasons and focus on the claim you may want to make. Avoid making a claim broader than you want to support. If you believe students need to enhance their computer literacy to be employable, you would overreach if you suggested that students need to become computer *experts*.

The following are strategies for drafting your argument:

Introduction

- Jolt your reader, for example by describing a teen paralyzed in a car accident to argue against texting and driving.
- Or start with defining an unfamiliar term, "Why oppose oligarchy?"
- In a longer essay, preview main points.
- In a Rogerian argument, affirm the readers' core beliefs or values.
- In an exploratory essay, you might raise the question you will discuss without taking a position.

Body

- Define the issue and possible positions.
- Present contrary position and its evidence and reasons, offer your contrary reasons and evidence.
- Provide your reasons with evidence (often a major reason constitutes a paragraph).
- Identify possible objections to your position and answer with reasons and evidence.

Conclusion

- Possibly restate you main point and summarize main points.
- Or predict the consequences if your position doesn't prevail.
- Or offer a powerful example or story that clinches your position.
- Or make an emotional appeal for action.

After the introduction comes the evidence, arranged in whatever order you think will work best. If one of your points is likely to arouse resistance, hold it back and begin by making points your reader can more easily accept. Argument always goes more smoothly if you first establish some common ground of agreement that recognizes the values of your reader. Where strong resistance is not a factor, you could begin or end with your most compelling piece of evidence.

Many argument papers blend the different strategies of development discussed in earlier chapters. Let's see how you might combine several in an argument against legalized casino gambling.

- You might open with a brief *description* of the frantic way an all-too-typical gambling addict keeps pulling the lever of a slot machine, his eyes riveted on the spinning dials, his palms sweating, as flashing lights and wailing sirens announce winners at other machines.
- Next, you could offer a brief *definition* of gambling fever so that the writer and reader are on common ground, and, to show the dimensions of the problem, *classify* the groups of people who are especially addicted.

- Then, after detailing the negative *effects* of the addiction, you might end by *comparing* gambling addiction with drug addiction, noting that both provide a "high" and both kinds of addict know their habits hurt them.

Whatever strategies you use, make sure that substantiating evidence is embedded in them. To illustrate, in discussing the negative effects of gambling, you might cite statistics that show the extent and nature of the problem. An expert opinion might validate your classification of addicts. Or you might use personal experience to verify gambling's addictive effects.

Besides presenting evidence, use this part of your paper to refute; that is, to point out weaknesses or errors in the opposing position. You might try the following:

- Point out any evidence that undermines that position.
- Identify faulty assumptions and indicate how they are faulty: They don't lead to the implied conclusion, they lack the effectiveness of an alternative, or they are false or unsupported.
- Identify problems in the logic of the argument.

You can place refutations throughout the body of the paper or group them together just ahead of the conclusion. Whatever you decide, don't adopt a gloating or sarcastic tone that will alienate a fair-minded reader. Resist the urge to engage in *straw man* tactics—calling attention to imaginary or trivial weaknesses of the opposing side so that you can demolish them. Shrewd readers easily spot such ploys. Finally, don't be afraid to concede secondary or insignificant points to the opposition. Arguments have two or more sides; you can't have all the ammunition on your side. (If you discover you must concede major points, however, consider changing your position.)

Conclude in a manner that will sway the reader to your side.

There can be more than one pattern for an argument. Below are three examples.

Example 1	**Example 2**	**Example 3**
Introduction	Introduction	Introduction
Definition of the issue (optional)	Definition of the issue (optional)	Definition of the issue (optional)
Your reasons and evidence (can be a large number of paragraphs)	Alternative positions and reasons for those positions Objections and contrary evidence and reasons for those positions (can be several paragraphs)	Common objections or questions and answers to both
Objections or questions and answers to both (can be several paragraphs)	Restatement of your position and reasons and evidence for that position Objections or questions and answers to both	Your reasons and evidence
Conclusion	Conclusion	Conclusion

You are not limited to these patterns. Alternative positions and objections can be discussed and answered within the context of presenting your own reasons. An argument can be built around answering common questions. A Rogerian argument starts by affirming the reader's core values and beliefs and then shows deductively and by supporting evidence how those values and beliefs yield the conclusion you hope to support.

Revising the Argument

Review the guidelines in Chapter 4 and ask yourself these questions as you revise your argument paper:

Appropriate topic and thesis. Is my topic debatable one? Have I narrowed my topic to a clearly defined thesis that runs throughout the essay? Is my proposition clearly evident and of the appropriate type—that is, one of fact, policy, action, or value?

Focus. Do I have a clear purpose that I want to achieve through my argument, and do I maintain this sense of purpose and direction throughout? Is my thesis clear and strategically positioned? Are my main points clearly related to my thesis?

Awareness of audience. Is the paper aimed at the audience I want to reach? Have I tailored my argument to appeal to that audience? Have I kept a respectful tone throughout, even when dealing with possible objections to my argument?

Thoroughness. Have I examined the main positions? Have I assessed the evidence supporting each one? Have I considered the objections to each position and either countered these objections or made concessions where necessary?

Rational appeal. Do I have enough solid evidence to support my claims? Is my evidence sound, adequate, and appropriate to the argument? Are my authorities qualified? Have I established their expertise? Are they biased? Will my audience accept them as authorities? Do my statistics adequately support my position? Have I pushed my statistical claims too far?

Emotional appeal. If I've included an emotional appeal—perhaps by including a short narrative or story that fits with my larger purpose—does it centre on those emotions most likely to sway the reader? Have I addressed possible reader resistance by adequately refuting opposing arguments? Have I avoided sentimentality and self-pity?

Ethical appeal. Have I made a conscious effort to present myself as a fair and reasonable person? Have I weighed the possible consequences if my paper were to persuade someone to take action?

Logic. Have I established logical links between my claims and my evidence? Have I avoided overly broad claims and sweeping generalizations, especially ones that contain words such as *all* and *never*? If the proposition takes the form of a syllogism, is it sound? If faulty, have I started with a faulty premise, or reversed the last two statements of the syllogism? If I've used analogy, are my points of comparison pertinent to the issue? Have I noted any significant differences between the items being compared? Is my argument free of fallacies?

Organization. Does my argument follow an effective organizational plan, such as the order of climax? Have I developed my position with one or more writing strategies? Are transitions smooth, from one point to the next? Do I end with an effective conclusion, rather than going on too long or stopping short?

EXAMPLE OF A STUDENT ESSAY USING PERSUASION

The Prestige of Presenting with Prezi

Jesse Foley

1   For many years PowerPoint, from Microsoft's Office Suite, was the undisputed champion of presentation tools with, according to the Official Microsoft Office Blog, over 500 million users back in 2010 (Case, J). Lately, however, with greater adoption of the "cloud" and larger online storage capabilities, many competitors such as SlideRocket, Slideshare, and Google Docs have entered the ring. Probably the best well-known of these competitors is Prezi, which was launched in 2009 and now has over 250 million views on their "prezis," which are online presentations (Prezi). In this paper, I will analyze the two most popular presentation tools, identify their advantages and shortcomings, and make recommendations for students who may be wondering what presentation tools will best serve their needs.

Gives readers a map of the essay, and identifies audience of students.

2   Prezi has many benefits, but the most immediately obvious advantage is that the basic presentation creating tool is widely accessible. The site is monetized on a "freemium" platform, which means that customers can use the free service or upgrade to enhanced offerings and privacy. The program is also hosted in a browser, although there is a desktop application for those who want it. This means that users don't have to download/install a large software file, but need only an internet connection to access their presentations. Another part of its accessibility is the relatively short learning curve needed to use it. Users can become proficient in a matter of minutes and start creating.

Topic sentence identifies first advantage of Prezi— accessibility.

3   Another major benefit of Prezi is that it much more dynamic than the static slide-to-slide presentation that audiences have become used to. The platform allows people to design unique paths for their stories, and zoom in/out of text and images to create a more visually stimulating experience than most Power Point presentations provide. Prezi uses a Google search to find images, which can quickly be resized and placed into the proper location in the prezi. The ability to insert YouTube videos as well adds an extra degree of customization. The user can also add a soundtrack, and then move through the path in time with the music to create a more multisensory powerful experience for viewers/listeners.

Topic sentence identifies second advantage.

4 <u>Prezi also facilitates team collaboration.</u> Since the tool is used in-browser, teams don't need multiple product licenses of the same version of a software to be able to use it. Also, since it is hosted in the cloud, students or other users can quickly reach all of their files from anywhere and collaborate with each other as long as everyone has the right passwords. Instead of each member having to download a copy, edit and save it, and then reshare it, they can simply save it and continue working on it together. Under the free version, they can use the online presentation tool to share their presentation with audiences or stakeholders, or simply send them the link to the prezis.

| Topic sentence identifies third advantage. |

5 <u>Prezi does have some shortcomings, though.</u> Since all prezis made under the free version are publicly available, <u>the risk of plagiarism and information leaking does exist.</u> Especially in a classroom setting, where other students might be looking for inspiration or information on a project, they might search for their classmates' prezis for some ideas. <u>Another downside is the constricted formatting.</u> Although there are many design possibilities in terms of paths and images for the flow of the story there are limited texts and fonts available to users, and no system for adding in tables or rich-formatting aside from bulleted lists.

| Acknowledges possible objections. |
| Acknowledges first possible shortcoming. |
| Acknowledges second possible shortcoming. |

6 <u>PowerPoint, while often viewed as the large corporate enemy, does have some good features.</u> Unlike Prezi, it has an enormous amount of backend possibilities since it is a part of the Microsoft Office Suite. It has the capability to create tables and smart art through Excel compatibility, and easy Copy/Pasting through Microsoft Word. There are also tons of add-ons and PowerPoint enhancement options available for free. The program also comes with clip art and stock images that the user has the legal right to use, since they were paid for with the license. In a professional setting, where copyright issues come into play, this is a big advantage.

| Concedes opposing point of view on the virtues of PowerPoint. |

7 <u>Another benefit of PowerPoint is the complete control that the user has over the presentation.</u> Even if it takes a while to learn, users of PowerPoint can create precise animations and timing, and rich media may be built into presentation decks. Most images and videos can be placed into the presentation, and the user can create their own designs and templates that they can save and reuse later.

| Shows fairness by acknowledging other benefits of PowerPoint in this comparison. |

8 PowerPoint also lends itself to a professional context. The presents are private and secure, and teams can track changes and make edits. There are tools such as a spell-checker that come standard with Microsoft products. Lastly, PowerPoint's large user base is an advantage, since so many people are comfortable with using it.

Notes shortcomings of PowerPoint here and in subsequent paragraphs, as promised.	9 <u>There are many drawbacks that come with PowerPoint, though, which is probably why there is so much backlash against it.</u> The major problem is its cost. A user license is expensive; many people simply can't afford to pay that much for tools when there are free alternatives. Another problem is its massive size. While it can be simple for someone to make a barebones presentation, making something unique and interesting is quite difficult and time consuming. Most users will never use most of what PowerPoint can do, because it gets very technical, very quickly.

10   There is also the issue of compatibility. Many people use PowerPoint, but many of them are using different versions, and on different operating systems. A lot of formatting can be lost switching between PowerPoint 2007 and PowerPoint 2013 and even more between Apple and PCs. Files can also be corrupted or not save correctly during the download/upload stages necessary to share presentations, which is a panic-inducing moment that nearly everyone who has used Microsoft Office has experienced.

11   Lastly, Office formatting can be very stubborn. Often, people get frustrated with the time it takes to get the right things in the right places, all because PowerPoint has tricky formatting rules.

Writer is careful not to overgeneralize with a blanket claim.	12 In conclusion, I believe that <u>both products are better in a certain environment.</u> PowerPoint, with its professional settings and vastness, is often
Returns to the idea of student needs.	better in a corporate setting where, with enough money and time, people can create amazing presentations. However, <u>since Prezi is free, easy to learn, and visually exciting, it is usually a more effective tool for students and smaller scope projects.</u> In my view, Prezi is a better tool because anyone can use it anywhere. Located simply on a browser, it can be accessed and edited by anyone with a password. Its future looks relatively secure after landing a $14 million investment to accelerate the startup (Venture Beat).
After a balanced comparison, writer makes clear recommendation for students.	13 <u>So the next time you have to present in class, you might want to zoom away with Prezi instead of trotting out yet another oh-so-familiar PowerPoint, with one slide following another in dreary predictable order.</u>
Speculates about future directions for presentations, and leaves the reader with something to ponder.	14 And don't forget, that any presentation tool is just that—a tool to help you get your message across to real people. Who knows? <u>The next new thing may be one person talking to other people, without any technological glitz.</u>

WORK CITED

Case, J. *New Ways to Try and Buy Microsoft Office*. Microsoft Corp. 7 Oct. 2009. Web. 19 June. 2013.

Prezi. *Prezi Inc.* 2013. Web. 19 June. 2013.

Venture Beat. *Prezi 14 Million in Funding*. 15 Dec. 2011. Web. 19 June. 2013.

DISCUSSION QUESTIONS

1. The writer outlines three main advantages of Prezi as a presentation tool. What are these advantages?

2. It can be difficult to write about something as technical as online presentation tools for a rather general audience. Find a place where the writer assumes understanding, and one where she explains a term that a general reader might not know. Are there any places where you feel lost, or where you think she overexplains?

3. What strategies does the writer use in her introduction and conclusion (see Chapter 5, pages 95–101)?

TOWARD KEY INSIGHTS

Have you ever used PowerPoint, Prezi, or other presentation tools? If so, what was your experience with these tools?

If you have watched others using tools such as PowerPoint, what was your impression? To what degree have they helped the speaker communicate a message, and to what extent, if any, have they gotten in the way?

SUGGESTION FOR WRITING *If you are knowledgeable about a particular type of product, activity, or approach to learning that students or another group of people would appreciate, write an essay persuading this audience to consider trying it out. You might follow an approach similar to the one the writer here uses, comparing and evaluating the relative benefits of two things, and coming down clearly on the side of one over the other. Some examples to get you thinking include the following: why a hand-held camera has advantages over a phone camera when travelling; why full spectrum lighting is superior to standard lighting; ways in which a staycation trumps a vacation when you have only one week; why Montessori schooling has more educational benefits for a child than traditional public schooling.*

Stepping Up to Synthesis

By its very nature, a successful argument requires critical thinking. This chapter has given you the tools you need to test the logic and evaluate the evidence of argumentative positions. After all, rarely are writers assigned to generate an idea on their own and then argue for it. Instead, because most important issues have already been debated in print, they enter a discussion that's already under way. Sometimes it's on a topic of national interest, such as the desirability of politically correct speech and writing or the need to limit the number of terms elected officials can serve. At other times, the topic may be more localized: Should your province outlaw teacher strikes, your company install new equipment to control air pollution, or your university reduce its sports programs? On any of these issues, form your view as you read and assess the arguments of other writers.

A good way to take stock of conflicting opinions is to make a chart that summarizes key reasons and evidence on each side of the argument. Here is a segment of a chart that presents opposing viewpoints on whether industrial air pollution is related to the threat of global warming:

Pro-threat Side

Industrial emissions of carbon dioxide, methane, and chlorofluorocarbons let sun's rays in but keep heat from escaping.

Andrew C. Revkin, student

Atmospheric levels of carbon dioxide are now 25 percent higher than in 1860. Computer models indicate continuing rise will cause temperature increase of 2–5°C (3–9°F).

Revkin

No-threat Side

Natural sources account for almost 50 percent of all carbon dioxide production.

Dixy Lee Ray

The computer models are inaccurate, don't agree with each other, and fail to account for the warming effects of the oceans.

H.E. Landsberg

Even though you investigate the reasons and evidence of others, deciding what position to take and how to support it—that is, establishing your place in the debate—is the real work of synthesis (see pages 356–357). Therefore, after evaluating your sources, outline the main points you want to make. You can then incorporate material that supports your argument. Let's say that you're considering the issue of global warming. After examining the differing viewpoints, you might conclude that, although those who believe that global warming is occurring sometimes overstate their case, those who disagree tend to dismiss important scientific evidence. Moreover, when comparing the credentials of the pro-threat group against the no-threat group, you discover that many of the researchers in the no-threat group are indirectly members of lobby groups and are not scientists themselves. Since you have decided that global warming is a serious threat, you decide to argue for immediate environmental action. You might begin your paper by pointing out the dire environmental consequences of global warming if it is proved beyond the shadow of a doubt, then offer evidence supporting this possibility, acknowledge and answer key opposing viewpoints, and finally offer your recommendations for averting a crisis.[1]

SUGGESTIONS FOR RESEARCH-BASED ARGUMENTS

1. Read several sources that explore the best solution to the challenges around temporary foreign workers in Canada, and then write an argument supporting your own position based on those differing responses.

2. Use primary and secondary sources to investigate the placement of students with mental and emotional disabilities (special needs) in mainstream rather than special classes in your community. To gather primary information, you might interview people who work in the school system, or visit classrooms with and without students who have special

---

[1] Note that research-based arguments on topics such as those listed below must be documented correctly. Make sure that you understand your instructor's guidelines and expectations before starting to write this type of paper. You will need to be familiar with the sections on handling quotations and avoiding plagiarism in the research chapters that follow this chapter. As always, follow your instructor's guidelines for documenting sources.

needs. To gather secondary research, you might consult educational journals or websites. After researching this issue, write a paper addressed to the school board or other stakeholder arguing for a change in the present policy.

3. Read several sources that explore the issue of our legal and ethical responsibility regarding what we say and how we present ourselves on various social media networks, and write an argument that takes a position on this issue, drawing on the available sources.

4. Using outside sources, investigate a current social problem in your community, such as an increase in homelessness, drug abuse, or reckless street racing. Then write a paper addressed to a community council recommending a new course of action or policy.

5. Identify something you consider to be a problematic law or policy. Perhaps you view this law or policy as unjust, unfairly applied, outdated, or too expensive to enforce. Examine several sources that discuss this law, and then write a paper that identifies the problem and proposes a reasonable solution.

6. Analyze the rhetorical strategies used in a recent influential speech by a major politician. If you prefer, you might choose to analyze an article from a website, such as the Canadian Centre for Policy Alternatives (www.policyalternatives.ca), the Fraser Institute (www.fraserinstitute.org), or the Canadian Federation of Students (www.cfs-fcee.ca). Draw on your knowledge of argument and other writing strategies to show why you think the article or speech is or is not persuasive. Remember that your purpose is not simply to say whether or not you agree with the speaker or writer, but to evaluate the quality of the logic and other persuasive techniques in this speech or article.

7. If your instructor gives you a free choice of topics, you could consult a Canadian website, such as one of the following, that features articles on controversial issues for ideas to get you started.

www.policyalternatives.ca (Canadian Centre for Policy Alternatives)

www.Canadians.org (The Council of Canadians—a citizens' watchdog group devoted to social and environmental concerns)

www.rabble.ca (progressive alternative to mainstream media)

Alternatively, you could look for topical ideas in opinion pieces, columns, or commentary available on the websites of Canadian newspapers. Here are some examples:

www.canada.com (contains daily newspapers from Canadian cities; the section called "Forums" features colloquial debate from ordinary Canadians that might trigger an idea for you if you're stuck)

www.theglobeandmail.com/globe-debate

SUGGESTION FOR ORAL ARGUMENTATION

Oral argumentation through formal debate is an enjoyable and effective exercise that promotes research and argumentation skills, a commitment to honesty and truth, and an attitude of respect for others and their ideas. In preparing for a formal debate, the debaters must first conduct primary and/or secondary research on the proposition they will be addressing so that they will be able to defend either a pro or a con position. Because the debaters do not know which position they will take on the proposition while conducting their research, their priority is to establish clear facts and specific arguments that could be offered as proofs for either side of the proposition. Once debaters know which side of the proposition they will argue, they can draw from their research to develop a clear and concise argument for or against the proposition. Since the debaters have conducted their research prior to taking a pro or con position, they should be able to advance either argument with a thorough understanding of opposing views. This knowledge encourages an atmosphere of respect and tolerance.

After the debaters have completed their research on a proposition, they divide into teams representing pro and con positions. Each team then prepares opening statements outlining its arguments and compiles a set of proofs or examples that defends its positions. The actual debate can be structured in the following way.

Structuring a Debate (about 60 minutes)

- The moderator asserts the resolution and invites speakers from each team to direct opening statements to the audience.
- Each side gives opening statements outlining its argument (3 to 5 minutes each).
- Speakers from each team give proofs.
- A short break allows students to prepare statements and questions for cross-examination.
- Cross-examination: Each side presents responses and rebuttals in turn (may also include questions from audience).
- The moderator asks the audience to render a written decision assessing the debate teams according to these criteria:
  - Clarity of expression
  - Thoroughness of research
  - Effective use of rational, emotional, and/or ethical appeals
  - Effectiveness of oral delivery
- The moderator announces the results at the end of the debate.

Propositions for Debate

Propositions for debate can be found after the readings classified as "argument." Alternatively, try one of the following propositions.

- Canada's policy on refugees should be stricter (or more liberal).
- Decriminalization of marijuana for recreational use is (or is not) justifiable.
- Victims of crimes should (not) be compensated by the perpetrator.
- The Internet should be subject to stricter (looser) controls.
- Animal testing should (not) be banned.
- Grading for university English classes should (not) be abolished.
- Government invasion of personal privacy in cyberspace is (un)justifiable.
- Exclusive corporate advertising on university campuses is (un)ethical.
- High schools should (not) put stronger emphasis on trades and apprenticeships.
- E-cigarettes should (not) be banned.

ARGUMENT AND PERSUASION ESSAYS: PROFESSIONAL MODELS

READING STRATEGIES

1. Identify the background of the author, if possible. Does the author bring any expertise or experience that helps make the argument credible?
2. Read the introduction and conclusion to gain a sense of the thesis and main points of the argument.
3. Read the argument quickly to gain an overall sense of the major points of the essay.
4. Look for the organizational pattern of the essay and keep an eye out for transition sentences. Be aware of weak organizational patterns. Sometimes an inexperienced author argues by first presenting the viewpoints of several other authors, then pointing out limitations of those views, then presenting his or her own position and offering support, and finally admitting possible limitations and problems with this position (and possibly answering these objections). This pattern makes it difficult to understand the writer's position.
5. Read carefully to identify the major claims of the argument, the reasons for the author's position, and any evidence presented for any of the claims. It can be very helpful to outline the argument, making a special note of the major reasons and evidence for the claim. Note the author's approach. Is the argument mostly deductive or inductive? Does the author try to show the negative consequences of opposing views? Does the author base the argument on authority?

READING CRITICALLY

1. Check whether the author demonstrates any overt bias.
2. Determine whether the reasons given really support the author's thesis.
3. Test whether the evidence is adequate. Does the evidence support the claims? Is the source of the evidence trustworthy and unbiased? Is the evidence extensive or scanty? Could contrary evidence be offered?
4. Check the essay for logical fallacies.
5. Try to offer objections to the author's claims. Write objections in the margins or on a separate piece of paper.
6. Formulate alternative conclusions to those proposed by the author.
7. Formulate reasons and concerns that the author may have neglected.
8. Read essays that present other viewpoints and compare.

READING AS A WRITER

1. Note the organizational pattern of the argument. Identify how you might use the pattern in one of your argument papers.
2. Examine how the writer connects the reasons with the major thesis.
3. Identify how the evidence is presented and connected to arguments in support of the thesis.
4. Notice effective word choices that help cement the emotional argument.
5. Evaluate how the author establishes tone and ethos.
6. Examine how the author answers possible objections.

Margaret Webb

Canada Needs a National Food Strategy

Margaret Webb is the author of Apples to Oysters: A Food Lover's Tour of Canadian Farms. *She has written on food for the* Toronto Star, The Globe and Mail, More Magazine, *and* Canadian Geographic. *She teaches magazine writing at Ryerson University.*

Narrows the scope of her essay by identifying concerns that are valid, but not her focus.

1   What is most disturbing about Canada's food system is not the degraded quality, the impact on health, the devastation of natural resources from industrial fishing and farming, the impoverishment of food producers, the inequitable access that leaves so many Canadians undernourished, or even the safety scares that have us checking for recalls along with prices.

Thesis statement includes previous two sentences.

2   These travesties can be righted, if we act. But we have lost so much control over our food system that our ability to act is diminishing. Indeed, we can hardly imagine that we can act, that food should be a public good, like health care, to serve people foremost. That the public should decide what food Canada produces, how it's produced, and how we share that harvest.

Reason for loss of public control over food supply.

3   We have largely left those decisions to the market. Consequently, food has been cheapened into a tool for generating massive profits. And an increasingly small group of companies have gained enormous power over Canada's food supply.

Statistics buttress claim that a very few companies have gained enormous power.

4   A snapshot: four retailers control more than 70 per cent of grocery sales; two companies control 95 per cent of finished cattle slaughter; two control two-thirds of flour production; globally, just 10 multinationals control two-thirds of proprietary seeds, the basis of food.

Ethical claim.

5   Many Canadian farmers, abandoned to compete globally against appalling labour standards, see little future in independent food production here, which is shocking given increasing world hunger. More than a third of our farmers, holding half of all farm assets, are set to retire and most don't want their children to farm. Corporations are most likely to snap up those farms.

6   But demand for a citizen-led food fix is building.

Use of authority as well as ethical appeal.

7   This past summer, Canadians flocked to political meetings and community talks to discuss our increasingly sick food system and present ideas for a national food policy. Wayne Roberts of Toronto's Food Policy Council said such a policy could be this generation's medicare—a gift of healthy food, and sustainable farming and fishing to future generations.

8   The People's Food Policy Project held a series of "kitchen table meetings" in rural, fishing, northern and urban communities to gather ideas for a national platform on food sovereignty.

Causal chain gives effects of changing our food policy.

9   This would mean changing our current export-oriented agriculture to a "feed the family first and trade the rest" policy. It would shift support to local producers and give municipalities and their residents more of a voice in food choices. It would also entail a shift toward ecological food production to protect the natural resources on which future harvests depend. And through fair trade, Canada would extend the same right to other countries to protect their farmers and natural resources.

Ethical and emotional appeals.

10   Finally, it would reposition food as a public good rather than primarily a profit driver, and ensure all citizens affordable access to nutritious food.

11   Food sovereignty was a key recommendation of the first international assessment of agriculture, the IAASTD report, delivered last year. Of 62 countries participating,

59 signed the agreement. The agriculture policies of the three countries that dissented—Canada, the United States, and Australia—are strongly influenced by multinational food and agribusinesses.

12   "Our food system is controlled by large and frequently multinational corporations," said Cathleen Kneen, chair of Food Secure Canada. "This is about citizens having a real say in how the system functions. It's food democracy."

13   Currently, responsibility for food nationally is diced and sliced across ministries, with no coordinated strategy. Agriculture is a minor ministry, oriented to export commodities. Transportation pays for moving it over vast distances. Health picks up the tab for bad food.

14   Canada needs a national policy on food, say leading thinkers such as Dr. Harriet Friedmann, who contributed to the IAASTD report. She says the policy needs to integrate health, environment and accessibility goals.

15   In Parliament, the opposition parties have been stirring up ideas for a national food policy. And Canada's major farming organizations have all called for a national strategy for food and farming.

16   While a national policy is essential, municipalities and cities must drive it, by establishing food councils with responsibility for protecting food sheds. In the inevitable food fight with corporations resisting a local-first strategy, local power wields a particular strength. Roberts, of Toronto's food council, said the city's anti-pesticides legislation passed "rather easily" because the forces opposing it were national players, with little power in the city.

17   Toronto's Food Policy Council, created in 1992, was just the third in North America. Now there are some 35, many following Toronto's model. Operating under the Department of Public Health, the council has coordinated food action in the city, supporting community food centres, food banks, urban gardening and farmers markets.

18   The Stop Community Food Centre in Toronto serves as another model. Housed in the historic Wychwood streetcar barns, it runs a community kitchen, food bank, two farmers markets, urban gardens, a 3,000-square-foot greenhouse and teaches new and vulnerable Canadians food self sufficiency—to cook, grow and choose healthy foods.

19   Its director, Nick Saul, believes there should be a centre in every riding in Canada, adapted to local needs. That might include a farmers' co-op to sell food, an abattoir, processing facilities, a commercial-grade kitchen to incubate new businesses or even community catering of healthy meals for busy families and those in need.

20   "We don't have a prescription for how another community might wrap its arms around this," said Saul, "but we've developed the core elements." The concept, he says, is about using food to increase health, civic engagement, self-reliance, local economies, social justice and community.

21   It's about shifting more food into the public domain and returning the value to farmers and fishers and the food itself, where it belongs.

22   It's food that serves people, exactly the food policy Canada needs.

Statistics support claim that Canadian food production policies need reform.

Use of authority.

Cites experts on benefits of local food self-sufficiency.

Conclusion reinforces thesis.

DISCUSSION QUESTIONS

1. In the first paragraph, the writer cites a number of problems she sees with Canada's food system. In your own words, explain what she means by such concerns as a "degraded quality," "inequitable access" or "safety scares." Why do you think she does not spend time on proving that these areas are truly problems? What is the relationship between these problems and the idea of more public control of Canada's food system?

2. What are the reasons, according to Margaret Webb, that Canadian farmers do not increase mobilization for more local, independent food production (paragraph 4)?

3. In some ways, this argument follows a problem/solution model. What are some of the problems, as Webb sees it, with Canada's present food policy, and what solution does she propose? Explain in your own words the two models of greater "food sovereignty" in Toronto that Webb refers to (paragraphs 17 and 18). What other possibilities does she mention in paragraph 19?

4. Identify where this argument brings in such emotionally charged words as *travesties*, *appalling*, *sick*, or *healthy*. What is the effect on you when you read such words? Can you find other examples of such connotative language? Does the writer seem to be using emotional and/or ethical appeals? Explain.

TOWARD KEY INSIGHTS

What are the main sources of food production in your community? Where do you and others you know shop for food? Are the sources of food production controlled by corporations, or are there also examples of local food production and distribution in your community?

With a topic that is of such universal relevance, what other kinds of appeals might the author have used?

SUGGESTIONS FOR WRITING *Find out what you can about food policies in your community or province, and write to a local newspaper, magazine, or your member of Parliament about a specific proposal to improve "food democracy" or sustainability—for example, new grants, loans, and tax breaks for urban community gardens or green roofs, or the planting of fruit trees and vegetables on city boulevards; more public education about why people should grow their own food; more support for locally sourced street foods; stricter control of pesticide use.*

Tamsin McMahon

Is Local Food Bad for the Economy?

Tamsin McMahon reports on business and real estate for The Globe and Mail. *She has a Bachelor of Arts (B.A.) in Journalism from Ryerson University. She has also written for the* National Post *and* Maclean's, *from which this article is taken.*

1   The North American farm is experiencing a cultural renaissance, or so say the stories of urban twentysomethings swapping the comforts of the city for overalls and buckets of manure, of municipal bylaw officials debating the merits of backyard chicken coops, to say nothing of the explosion of farmers' markets, community gardens, high-end restaurants specializing in local food, and the home-delivery services of fresh produce from nearby farms.

2   The push for sustainable agriculture and local food trumpeted by everyone from Michelle Obama to the Canadian authors of *The 100-Mile Diet* seems innocuous enough as a way for us to end our dependence on a corn-based diet of junk food and soft drinks,

as well as curb rising rates of childhood obesity by teaching us to appreciate how our food gets from the farm to the table.

3 Know your farmer, proponents of local food say, and you'll make better choices about what you put in your mouth, support the local economy and save the environment in the process. As Michael Pollan, the *New York Times* writer and champion of the local food movement, is fond of saying, "Pay more, eat less."

4 Enter two previously little-known Canadian academics with a controversial new book that argues that, far from making our communities healthier and more self-sufficient, the local food movement will destroy our economies, ruin our environment and probably lead to more wars, famine and incidences of food poisoning.

5 *The Locavore's Dilemma*—the title is a play on Pollan's bestselling *The Omnivore's Dilemma*—by University of Toronto geography professor Pierre Desrochers and his wife, Hiroko Shimizu, who has a master's in international public policy, argues that much of the gains the world has made in food security and standards of living have come from the evolution of our food system from small-scale subsistence agriculture to international trade among large and specialized producers, the corporate-driven agribusiness that so many food activists despise.

6 To Desrochers and Shimizu, corporations that control huge swaths of the North American food supply—the McDonald's and Wal-Marts of the world—have made food safer and cheaper by creating economies of scale that can help support technological advancements such as more sophisticated automated farm equipment, safer pesticides and fertilizers, genetically modified seeds that produce higher yields, and more advanced food-safety practices that have cut the rate of outbreaks of food-borne illness by a hundredfold in the past century.

7 Food activists, they contend, would rather turn back the clock on those modern developments, close the doors to trade and return to a world where families toiled the land, pesticide- and fertilizer-free, and then squeaked by on what they could earn from selling their goods at the local farmers' market. It's a recipe, the authors say, for economic and social disaster.

8 Today's locavores—the term for those who support local food—"don't ask the most obvious question, which is, if things were so great in our great-grandmothers' time, why did things change so much since then?" Desrochers says in an interview. "If it was only an educational movement, I wouldn't have any problem with it. But increasingly, it's becoming a way to stick it to the man. What are activists going to do when Wal-Mart offers fair trade coffee and organic food? They will have to find another way to get back at corporations."

9 Local food movements have a long history, as successive generations rediscover the romantic idealism of living off the land as their ancestors did, from Henry David Thoreau heading to the woods in *Walden*, to Depression-era policies to turn vacant city lots into urban potato patches, to wartime "Victory Gardens." These movements were all popular for a few years and usually floundered when government funding ran out or farmers found living off the land too difficult. Today's movement, which Desrochers traces back to the economic boom times of the 1990s, is all well and good, he says, until the tumultuous global economy eventually forces us to spend less on groceries. "The main message we want to send to idealistic young farmers is don't count on charity to build your business. The movement might be popular right now, but I'm not sure it will last down the road."

10   Desrochers's and Shimizu's argument is largely a treatise on the benefits of the free market and globalization, the belief that the only way to feed an ever-growing global population is to produce more food on less land with fewer resources, which means the family farm will continue to die a gradual death in favour of corporate agribusiness.

11   To understand just how far we've come, they argue, consider that in a "short" several thousand years we've gone from needing 1,000 hectares (nearly 2,500 acres) of land to feed a single person to just one-tenth of an acre in today's globalized food chain. In the past 60 years, the world's population has exploded from 2.5 billion to seven billion, and the percentage of the population going hungry on a daily basis has dropped from 40 per cent to less than 15 per cent. Desrochers and Shimizu argue that if we were still using 1950s technology to produce our food, we would need to plow an extra land mass the size of South America just to feed the world's population.

12   Take local food to its most extreme conclusion, Desrochers says—grow only food that's truly native to North America—and we'd all be eating a lot of blueberries, seeds, squash, and not much else. The most dramatic examples of economic and social destruction from policies to promote local food over international trade, he says, include the nationalist policies of Mussolini's Italy, Hitler's Germany, and Japan of the 1930s, when rice prices rose 60 per cent above the international rate as the country pursued agricultural self-sufficiency.

13   Not surprisingly, an argument that compares locavores to Hitler has attracted its fair share of critics, who mostly accuse Desrochers and Shimizu of either being in the pockets of corporate agribusiness—Desrochers says the couple's only remuneration came from their publisher—or of harbouring a personal vendetta. Shimizu was born and raised near Tokyo and the couple wrote *The Locavore's Dilemma* after they took issue with a Toronto speech by a visiting professor from the University of British Columbia, in which he said Japan was one of the world's most "parasitic" countries because it imported so much of its food. Desrochers grew up in a farming community in Quebec's St. Lawrence Valley and worked for a time at the Quebec Farmers' Union ferrying new immigrants from Montreal out to the countryside to pick berries. Among his biggest supporters, he says, have been people who grew up on a farm and later left it. Two of his biggest detractors have been his brother, François Desrochers, a former Quebec MLA for the Action démocratique du Québec, who represented the rural riding of Mirabel, and his father, whom he describes as a "typical Quebec nationalist who wants Quebec to be self-sufficient."

14   Local food supporters say the authors have painted an unfair picture of the locavore movement by focusing on its most extreme elements. "The book is very, very manipulative," says Debbie Field, executive director of FoodShare, a Toronto community food program that sells about 4,000 local food boxes and feeds about 141,000 children in a school nutrition program. "It does not bring us light, it is throwing oil on the fire. It's just making things more complicated." Field says critics of the local movement too often assume that local food always has to cost more and that all locavores are against using modern technology on the farm. "I know a lot of young farmers in Ontario and they're some of the most technically sophisticated people in the world," she says. "They're not about going back to some mythical slavery past. It's about creating new, environmentally sustainable food."

15   Most local food supporters take a more balanced approach between promoting local and imported fair trade food, she says. For instance, FoodShare, which is supported by

private donations and government funding, bought $1.5 million worth of produce last year, with $500,000 of it from local producers. Only about half of the food in Food-Share boxes and 30 per cent of the food sent to schools is local. This year, FoodShare included imported strawberries and apples because unseasonably warm and wet weather wreaked havoc with local crops. "I don't want a child eating potato chips from southern California instead of strawberries and apples from southern California if our strawberry and apple crops are destroyed," Field says. "We're not saying, 'Don't eat the mango,' but they're saying, 'I'm not going to eat that local strawberry, even if it's the same price.'"

16   Among the most popular and controversial aspects of today's local food movement is the concept of "food miles," the distance food travels from the farm to the table, which serves as a rallying cry for environmentalists concerned over greenhouse gas emissions and climate change. Desrochers calls the food-miles argument a "misleading distraction" in the debate over food policy. Research from the U.K. comparing local tomatoes with those imported from Spain showed the U.K. tomatoes, which had to be grown in heated greenhouses, emitted nearly 2,400 kg of carbon dioxide per ton, compared to 640 kg for the Spanish tomatoes, which could grow in unheated greenhouses.

17   Other studies have found that food miles represent just four per cent of total emissions related to food, with most of the emissions coming from producing food and from consumers driving to the grocery store to buy it. Air transportation accounts for just one per cent of food miles, with much food transported in the cargo holds of passenger jets, while marine container ships are one of the most fuel efficient ways to transport large shipments of food, Desrochers says.

18   Studies on food miles need to be taken with a grain of salt since many are industry-funded, says Don Mills, president of Local Food Plus, which certifies local organic and sustainable farms in Ontario. Those studies also assume that produce shipped to Canada in the winter hasn't been kept in cold storage elsewhere, he says. Critics willing to dismiss the food-miles argument also ignore the tax dollars spent building the infrastructure to ship food long distances. "An awful lot of public infrastructure and public policy goes into food no matter how you shake it out, and that's why you see huge money being spent lobbying by large agricultural producers to get some policy outcome," he says.

19   A better measure than food miles or even food prices, he says, is the amount of energy, in fuel, put into growing food compared to the energy, in calories, that people get from eating it. By that standard, Mills says, research shows large, highly automated farms use more fossil fuel energy than small farms that use manual labour. "Small subsistence fallow farming is incredibly productive from a [fuel] calorie perspective," he says. "There's lots of ways to measure the world, and we may have to balance the predominance of economic measurement with a notion of energy balance."

20   Like it or not, Mills says, the debate around food policy is here to stay, mostly because food represents a core part of society's value system that eclipses the traditional economic arguments of industries such as manufacturing. "I would argue that food is different. It has a more important place in humanity and in culture than widgets," he says. "If we can figure out issues around food transportation, around energy, around how we treat our produce with pesticides, around how we treat our [farm] labour, we'll be well on our way to sorting through a number of other spheres as well. If we get food right, we'll get a lot of other things right."

21   Such arguments are one of the biggest dangers of the local food movement, counters University of Manitoba agricultural professor Ryan Cardwell. It's one thing for food activists to want to spend more on groceries at their local farmers' markets. It's another when they push governments to use tax dollars to support local agricultural production, either through direct subsidies or through programs that require public institutions such as schools, prisons and military bases to buy and serve only local food. "My concern is when advocates of local food try and influence policy and government money and regulations to address a policy objective," he says. "If you want to address an issue like urban poverty or greenhouse gas emissions, then you should pick the policy that best addresses them, and local food really doesn't answer any of them."

22   Another argument of the local food movement that Desrochers disputes is that local farming is inherently healthier and safer than the mass-produced counterpart, since farmers tend to use fewer pesticides and they have a duty to their local community. In contrast, he says, large corporations have brands to protect and budgets to devote to scrupulous food safety practices, compared to small farms, which usually aren't worth suing if they cause outbreaks of food-borne illnesses like E. coli or salmonella. He cites Jensen Farms, the family farm in Colorado whose pesticide-free cantaloupes were linked to an outbreak of listeria last year that killed at least 30 people.

23   Large farms and food processing plants are also susceptible to outbreaks of food-borne illness—Maple Leaf Farms paid $25 million to settle claims from a 2008 listeria outbreak—but Desrochers argues they're easier to trace and correct than illnesses caused by small farms since they generate more media coverage and government oversight.

24   "You see young organic farms grow their stuff in manure and bring it to the barn where all the doors are open and wash everything with a hose, all the various vegetables together," he says. "As [Loblaw executive chairman] Galen Weston said, farmers' markets are beautiful places, but eventually they will kill people."

25   Getting to know your farmer is a noble aim, but most visitors to farmers' markets have very little understanding that the food they buy from local growers is often not produced under the same conditions as those they can find at the grocery store, says Mary Shelman, director of Harvard University's agribusiness program. "Most people assume you can take it home and eat it out of the bag before they wash it," she says. "That's actually frightening to me because people don't respect that it actually came out of a field full of rabbits and deer and birds who aren't too discriminating about where they take a bathroom break." Larger commercial farms tend to have fewer problems of animal contamination because they're required to fence off animal pathways.

26   One of the advantages of the decline of the family farm has been to move agriculture away from the large population centres, where diseases can easily spread back and forth between humans and animals, Shelman says. "If everyone had chickens in their backyard and there was an outbreak of bird flu, that would take care of every chicken."

27   Neither, says Desrochers, is local food inherently more secure than that from commercial farms or foreign exports, as many food activists argue. Historically, societies that relied solely on their own agriculture were more susceptible to famine than those who opened their doors to international trade, mainly because if one country had a poor harvest it could always import food from a country that had a good season. Advancements in transportation—first the railway and later the airplane—have only helped eradicate food shortages and famines in developed countries by ensuring that fresh food can always be readily shipped anywhere.

28   Rather than closing borders or encouraging more local agriculture, Desrochers and others argue, food security requires encouraging economic development, so consumers can spend less of their incomes on food. Already the amount of disposable income spent on food has dropped from 23 per cent in 1930s America to 9.4 per cent today. By promoting less productive, small-scale agriculture, Desrochers says, locavores are encouraging a type of farming that will require huge tracts of wilderness to be destroyed to create farms in order to accommodate an anticipated doubling in the global food supply needed to feed the world's population by 2050. As it stands, he says, each year more agricultural land is reverting to wilderness than is consumed by urban sprawl.

29   True North American food security, says Shelman, would mean converting large parcels of urban land to agriculture use. "If you look at all the land that is devoted to huge houses and driveways and pools in the backyard and beautiful landscaping, you can make the argument that ultimately for food security we have to be willing to give up other parts of the way we live," she says.

30   Ultimately, though, Shelman says the local food movement is driven less by nationalism and more by consumers' need to connect with their food and have confidence in how it's produced, whether locally or abroad. That will keep the movement a potent force for years to come. "Local could mean it has to be in my backyard, or it could be local in the same sense that I have confidence in my food even if I'm eating artisan cheese that's been produced in Ireland and Italy," she says. "As long as I know the story, that is local. That's really what people are looking for, somebody to put a face on agriculture and farming. We're more confident in people than we are in faceless institutions."

DISCUSSION QUESTIONS

1. While this article reviews a book entitled *The Locavore's Dilemma*, it also makes points of its own about the local food movement. Find three places where the writer seems to agree with the points made in the book, and three places where McMahon questions the book's arguments.

2. Analyze paragraphs 14, 15, and 16 to see how they are structured. Identify the topic sentence of each paragraph. What kind of evidence supports this topic sentence?

3. One of the strongest arguments to support the local food movement relates to health benefits. From what you read here, explain the way in which the authors of *The Locavore's Dilemma* counter this argument.

4. *The Locavore's Dilemma* apparently argues that having more local foods does not contribute to food security (paragraph 5). In your own words, explain what food activists seem to mean by food security, and the counter-argument put forward in the book.

5. How does the writer conclude the review in the last paragraph? What impression are you left with?

TOWARD KEY INSIGHTS

Economics often trump ethics when we make consumer choices. Where and why might you choose to pay a bit more for a consumer item in order to support ethical aims?

SUGGESTIONS FOR WRITING *After reading this essay and the essay by Margaret Webb, make a list of points that support buying local food and points that argue against it. Then decide what arguments have most weight with you, and where you stand on this issue. Write an essay persuading a slightly resistant audience to your point of view. Be sure to use proper documentation if you quote from or use ideas in these or other articles.*

Read at least three sources about the issues surrounding food labels such as "organic" or "GMO." Then formulate an argument related to this issue. For example, you might argue that such labels need to be strictly regulated, or that they are unnecessary. Be sure to use proper documentation if you quote from or use ideas in these or other articles.

Neil Bissoondath

No Place Like Home

Neil Bissoondath has written several critically acclaimed books of fiction and non-fiction that explore themes of migration, alienation, multiculturism, and identity. His works of fiction include A Casual Brutality, The Worlds within Her, *and* The Unyielding Clamour of the Night. *Bissoondath's provocative discussion of identity politics and multiculturalism,* Selling Illusions: The Cult of Multiculturalism in Canada *(1994), provides a broader and more in-depth discussion of the ideas and concerns raised in his essay "No Place Like Home."*

1   Three or four years into the new millennium, Toronto, Canada's largest city, will mark an unusual milestone. In a city of three million, the words "minorities" and "majority" will be turned on their heads and the former will become the latter.

2   Reputed to be the most ethnically diverse city in the world, Toronto has been utterly remade by immigration, just as Canada has been remade by a quarter-century of multiculturalism.

3   It is a policy which has been quietly disastrous for the country and for immigrants themselves.

4   The stated purpose of Canada's *Multiculturalism Act* (1971) is to recognize "the existence of communities whose members share a common origin and their historic contribution to Canadian society." It promises to "enhance their development" and to "promote the understanding and creativity that arise from the interaction between individuals and communities of different origins." The bicultural (English and French) nature of the country is to be wilfully refashioned into a multicultural "mosaic."

5   The architects of the policy—the Government of then–Prime Minister Pierre Elliot Trudeau—were blind to the fact that their exercise in social engineering was based on two essentially false premises. First, it assumed that "culture" in the large sense could be transplanted. Second, that those who voluntarily sought a new life in a new country would *wish* to transport their cultures of origin.

6   But "culture" is a most complex creature; in its essence, it represents the very breath of a people. For the purposes of multiculturalism, the concept has been reduced to the simplest theatre. Canadians, neatly divided into "ethnic" and otherwise, encounter each

other's mosaic tiles mainly at festivals. There's traditional music, traditional dancing, traditional food at distinctly untraditional prices, all of which is diverting as far as it goes—but such encounters remain at the level of a folkloric Disneyland.

7   We take a great deal of self-satisfaction from such festivals; they are seen as proof of our open-mindedness, of our welcoming of difference. Yet how easily we forget that none of our ethnic cultures seems to have produced poetry or literature or philosophy worthy of our consideration. How seductive it is, how reassuring, that Greeks are always Zorbas, Ukrainians always Cossacks: we come away with stereotypes reinforced.

8   Not only are differences highlighted, but individuals are defined by those differences. There are those who find pleasure in playing to the theme, those whose ethnicity ripens with the years. Yet to play the ethnic, deracinated and costumed, is to play the stereotype. It is to abdicate one's full humanity in favour of one of its exotic features. To accept the role of ethnic is also to accept a gentle marginalization. It is to accept that one will never be just a part of the landscape but always a little apart from it, not quite belonging.

9   In exoticizing and trivializing cultures, often thousands of years old, by sanctifying the mentality of the mosaic-tile, we have succeeded in creating mental ghettos for the various communities. One's sense of belonging to the larger Canadian landscape is tempered by loyalty to a different cultural or racial heritage.

10   When, for instance, war broke out between Croatia and Serbia, a member of the Ontario legislature, who was of Croatian descent, felt justified in declaring: "I don't think I'd be able to live next door to a Serb." That he was speaking of a fellow Canadian was irrelevant. *Over there* mattered more than *over here*—and the cultural group dictated the loyalty. Ironic for a country that boasted about its leading role in the fight against apartheid.

11   Often between groups one looks in vain for the quality that Canadians seem to value above all—tolerance. We pride ourselves on being a tolerant country, unlike the United States, which seems to demand of its immigrants a kind of submission to American mythology. But not only have we surrendered a great deal of ourselves in pursuit of the ideal—Christmas pageants have been replaced by "Winterfests"; the anti-racist Writers Union of Canada sanctioned a 1994 conference which excluded whites—but tolerance itself may be an overrated quality, a flawed ideal.

12   The late novelist Robertson Davies pointed out that *tolerance* is but a weak sister to *acceptance*. To tolerate someone is to put up with them; it is to adopt a pose of indifference. Acceptance is far more difficult, for it implies engagement, understanding, an appreciation of the human similarities beneath the obvious differences. Tolerance then is superficial—and perhaps the highest goal one can expect of Canadian multiculturalism.

13   Another insidious effect of this approach is a kind of provisional citizenship. When 100-metre sprinter Ben Johnson won a gold medal at the Seoul Olympics, he was hailed in the media as the great Canadian star. Days later, when the medal was rescinded because of a positive drug test, Johnson became the Jamaican immigrant—Canadian when convenient, a foreigner when not. Tolerated, never truly accepted, his exoticism always part of his finery, he quickly went from being one of *us* to being one of *them*.

14   This makes for an uneasy social fabric. In replacing the old Canada, based on British and French tradition, with a mosaic (individual tiles separated by cement), we have shaken our sense of identity. In a country over 130 years old, we are still uncertain who we are.

15   A major 1993 study found that 72 per cent of the population wants, as one newspaper put it, "the mosaic to melt." Canadians were found to be "increasingly intolerant" of demands for special treatment made by ethnic groups—a Chinese group who wanted a publicly funded separate school where their children would be taught in Chinese by Chinese teachers; a Muslim group who claimed the right to opt out of the Canadian judicial system in favour of Islamic law. Canadians wanted immigrants to adopt Canada's values and way of life.

16   Many immigrants agree. They recognize that multiculturalism has not served their interests. It has exoticized, and so marginalized, them, making the realization of their dreams that much harder. The former rector of the Université du Québec à Montréal, Claude Corbo, himself the grandson of Italian immigrants, has pointed out that multiculturalism has kept many immigrants "from integrating naturally into the fabric of Canadian and Quebec society. . . . We tell people to preserve their original patrimony, to conserve their values, even if these values are incompatible with those of our society."

17   Which leads to the other false premise on which multiculturalism is based. It assumes that people who choose to emigrate not only can but also *wish to* remain what they once were.

18   The act of emigration leaves no one unscathed. From the moment you board a plane bound for a new land with a one-way ticket, a psychological metamorphosis begins—and the change occurs more quickly, more deeply and more imperceptibly than one imagines.

19   I arrived alone in Toronto from Trinidad in 1973, an 18-year-old with dreams but no experience of the world. A year later, I returned to Trinidad to visit my parents. Within days I realized the extent of the change that had come not only to me, but to all I had left behind. Even after so short a time, old friends had become new strangers, and old places remained only old places. Already Trinidad—its ways, its views, its very essences—was receding, becoming merely a memory of place and childhood experience. *Feeling* had already been wholly transferred to the new land, to this other country which had quickly become my home. Certainly, for others the process is slower and often less evident—but it is inexorable. The human personality is not immutable.

20   Multiculturalism, which asked that I bring to Canada the life I had in Trinidad, was a shock to me. I was seeking a new start in a land that afforded me that possibility. I was *not* seeking to live in Toronto as if I were still in Trinidad—for what would have been the point of emigration? I am far from alone in this. As the political scientist Professor Rias Khan of the University of Winnipeg put it: "People, regardless of their origin, do not emigrate to preserve their culture and nurture their ethnic distinctiveness. . . . Immigrants come here to become Canadians; to be productive and contributing members of their chosen society. . . . Whether or not I preserve my cultural background is my personal choice; whether or not an ethnic group preserves its cultural background is the group's choice. The state has no business in either."

21   The immigrant dream—of financial and social success; of carving out a place within the larger society—is grand in its simplicity. Requiring great courage, it is self-limiting on no level. All one asks is the freedom and fairness—through anti-discrimination legislation, if necessary—to fulfill one's potential. A vital part of that freedom is the latitude to recognize and welcome inevitable change in society and the migrant. One may treasure a private, personal identity built from family lore and experience, all the while

pursuing the public integration vital to wider success. To be put in the position of either obliterating the past or worshipping it is, for the individual, an unnecessary burden that leads to a false and limiting theatre of the self.

22   Not long ago, my daughter's teacher wanted to know what kind of family the children in her first-grade class came from. For most of the children, born in Quebec City into francophone families that have been here for over 200 years, the answer was straightforward.

23   Then it was my daughter's turn. Her father, she explained, was born in Trinidad into an East Indian family; having lived in Canada for a long, long time, he was Canadian. Her mother was born in Quebec City, a francophone. She herself was born in Montreal.

24   "Ahh!" the teacher exclaimed brightly, "So you're from a West Indian family!"

25   My daughter returned home deeply puzzled. At six years of age she had been, with the best of intentions, handed an identity crisis.

26   In some ways she was lucky. We were able to sort out her confusions. In other parts of the country—in Toronto or Vancouver—where ethnic identity has become a kind of fetish, my daughter would have had to deal with a far more complex proposal. To be true to her inherited ethnicities, she would be: Franco-Québécoise-First Nations-Indian-Trinidadian-West Indian-Canadian. Indeed, for her to describe herself as simply "Canadian" with no qualifying hyphen would be almost antagonistic.

27   The weight of this hyphen was signalled as far back as 20 years ago by the feminist writer Laura Sabia when she said: "I was born and bred in this amazing land. I've always considered myself a Canadian, nothing more, nothing less, even though my parents were immigrants from Italy. How come we have all acquired a hyphen? We have allowed ourselves to become divided along the line of ethnic origins, under the pretext of the 'Great Mosaic.' A dastardly deed has been perpetuated upon Canadians by politicians whose motto is 'divide and rule'. . . I am a Canadian first and foremost. Don't hyphenate me."

28   Or, one might add, future generations.

29   Canadian multiculturalism has emphasized difference. In so doing, it has retarded the integration of immigrants into the Canadian mainstream while damaging Canada's national sense of self. Canada has an enviable record in dealing with racism; our society, while hardly perfect (we too have our racists of all colours), remains largely free of racial conflict. And yet we do ourselves a disservice in pursuing the divisive potential in multiculturalism. With an ongoing battle against separatism in Quebec, with east-west tensions, we are already a country uncomfortably riven. Our "mosaic" does not help us.

30   In recognition of its growing unpopularity, official multiculturalism has had its status downgraded from a ministry, to a directorate, to a department. Canada, for the foreseeable future, will continue to be a nation open to immigrants—and one committed to combating racism, sexism and the various other forms of discrimination we share with other societies. Beyond this, because of the damage already inflicted by multiculturalism, we need to focus on programs that seek out and emphasize the experiences, values and dreams we all share as Canadians, whatever our colour, language, religion, ethnicity or historical grievance. And pursue *acceptance* of others—not mere *tolerance* of them.

31   Whatever policy follows multiculturalism, it should support a new vision of Canadianness. A Canada where no one is alienated with hyphenation. A nation of

cultural hybrids, where every individual is unique and every individual is a Canadian, undiluted and undivided. A nation where the following conversation, so familiar—and so enervating—to many of us will no longer take place:

32   "What nationality are you?"

33   "Canadian."

34   "No, I mean, what nationality are you *really*?"

35   The ultimate goal must be a cohesive, effective society enlivened by cultural variety; able to define its place in the world. Only in this way might that member of the Ontario legislature and his neighbour no longer see each other as Serb and Croat but as Canadians with a great deal more in common than their politically sanctioned blindness allows them to perceive.

36   In the end, immigration is a personal adventure. The process of integration that follows it is a personal struggle within a social context that may make the task either more or less difficult. Multiculturalism in Canada has the latter effect but it may matter very little, because integration—the remaking of the self within a new society with one's personal heritage as invaluable texture—is finally achieved in the depths of one's soul. Many Canadians, like me, have simply ignored multiculturalism, by living our lives as fully engaged with our new society as possible, secure in the knowledge of the rich family past that has brought us here.

37   I will never forget the bright summer evening many years ago when, fresh off the plane from a trip to Europe, I stood on my apartment balcony gazing out at the Toronto skyline, at the crystal light emanating off Lake Ontario and beyond. I took a deep breath of the cooling evening air and knew, deep within my bones, that it was good to be home.

DISCUSSION QUESTIONS

1. In your own words, explain the rationale for Canada's *Multiculturalism Act* (paragraph 4). Why does the writer say the policy is an "exercise in social engineering" (paragraph 5)?

2. What does the writer see as the "two essentially false premises" (paragraph 5) or flawed assumptions embedded in the policy of multiculturalism? Identify places where he uses rational, emotional, and ethical appeals throughout the essay to convince readers that these premises are mistaken.

3. What is the distinction that the writer makes between "tolerance" and "acceptance" (paragraph 12)? How does the example of Ben Johnson (paragraph 13) support his claim that tolerance does not necessarily translate into acceptance?

4. How does the writer gain credibility and authority from the inclusion of his personal background (paragraphs 19 and 20)? How might his point of view be affected by his country of origin, his marriage, and his social class? How might you have read this essay differently if the writer did not have the experience of being an immigrant?

5. What is the point of Bissoondath's anecdote about his daughter's school experience (paragraphs 22 to 25)? What does Bissoondath mean when he refers to "the weight of this hyphen" (paragraph 27)?

6. What positive alternatives to multiculturalism does Bissoondath envision (paragraphs 30 to 36)?

TOWARD KEY INSIGHTS

Do you agree that ethnic festivals are a kind of "folkloric Disneyland" (paragraph 6), or do you think they have value that Bissoondath does not discuss?

How do you respond to the idea of melting the cultural mosaic?

What, in your view, has Bissoondath left out of his argument that might have made it more persuasive?

SUGGESTION FOR ORAL ARGUMENT *After researching both sides of the argument on the Internet or elsewhere, come to class prepared to argue either side of the following proposition:*

To promote social justice, the Canadian government should implement an affirmative action program for ethnic minorities.

SUGGESTIONS FOR WRITING *Read government policy on multicultural-ism at www.cic.gc.ca/english/multiculturalism/citizenship.asp. Then write an essay weighing the claims of both Bissoondath and the statement put out by the Canadian government. Demonstrate that you understand the arguments for and against the policy of multiculturalism, but take a position and emphasize either the advantages or the disadvantages of the policy. You may choose to elaborate on, or to refute, arguments made in either piece of writing.*

Will Kymlicka

Immigrants, Multiculturalism and Canadian Citizenship

Will Kymlicka received his B.A. in Philosophy and Politics from Queen's University in 1984 and his D.Phil. in Philosophy from Oxford University in 1987. He is the author of six books: Liberalism, Community, and Culture (1989); Contemporary Political Philosophy (1990 and 2002); Multicultural Citizenship (1995), which was awarded the Macpherson Prize by the Canadian Political Science Association and the Bunche Award by the American Political Science Association; Finding Our Way: Rethinking Ethnocultural Relations in Canada (1998); Politics in the Ver-nacular: Nationalism, Multiculturalism and Citizenship (2001); and Multicultural Odysseys: Navigating the New International Politics of Diversity (2007). His works have been trans-lated into 30 languages. He served a three-year term as president of the American Society for Political and Legal Philosophy (2004–2006).

1   In 1971, Canada embarked on a unique experiment by declaring a policy of official "multi-culturalism." According to Pierre Trudeau, who introduced the policy in the House of Commons, the policy had the following four aims: to support the cultural

development of ethnocultural groups; to help members of ethnocultural groups to overcome barriers to full participation in Canadian society; to promote creative encounters and interchange among all ethnocultural groups; and to assist new Canadians in acquiring at least one of Canada's official languages.

2   Although the policy of multiculturalism was first adopted by the federal government, it was explicitly designed as a model for other levels of government, and indeed it has been copied widely. "Multiculturalism programs" can now be found, not just in the multiculturalism office of the federal government, but also at the provincial or municipal levels of government, and indeed within a wide range of public and private institutions, such as schools or businesses.

3   These policies are now under attack, perhaps more so today than at any time since 1971. The debate has heated up lately, in part because of two recent critiques of the multiculturalism policy: Neil Bissoondath's *Selling Illusions: The Cult of Multiculturalism in Canada* (Penguin 1994), and Richard Gwyn's *Nationalism Without Walls: The Unbearable Lightness of Being Canadian* (McClelland and Stewart 1995). Both make very similar claims about the results of the policy. In particular, both argue that multiculturalism has promoted a form of ethnic separatism amongst immigrants.

4   Thus Bissoondath says that multiculturalism has led to "undeniable ghettoization" (111). Rather than promoting integration, multiculturalism is encouraging the idea that immigrants should form "self-contained" ghettos "alienated from the mainstream." This ghettoization is "not an extreme of multiculturalism but its ideal: a way of life transported whole, a little outpost of exoticism preserved and protected" (110). He approvingly quotes Arthur Schlesinger's claim that multiculturalism rests upon a "cult of ethnicity" which "exaggerates differences, intensifies resentments and antagonisms, drives even deeper the awful wedges between races and nationalities. The endgame is self-pity and self-ghettoization" (98), or what Schlesinger calls "cultural and linguistic apartheid." According to Bissoondath, multiculturalism policy does not encourage immigrants to think of themselves as Canadians, and indeed even the children of immigrants "continue to see Canada with the eyes of foreigners. Multiculturalism, with its emphasis on the importance of holding on to the former or ancestral homeland, with its insistence that There is more important than Here, encourages such attitudes" (133).

5   Gwyn makes the same claim in similar language. He argues that "official multiculturalism encourages apartheid, or to be a bit less harsh, ghettoism" (274). The more multiculturalism policy has been in place, "the higher the cultural walls have gone up inside Canada" (8). Multiculturalism encourages ethnic leaders to keep their members "apart from the mainstream," practising "what can best be described as monoculturalism." In this way, "Our state encourages these gatekeepers to maintain what amounts, at worst, to an apartheid form of citizenship" (234).

6   If these claims were true, it would be a serious indictment of the policy. Unfortunately, neither Bissoondath nor Gwyn provide any empirical evidence for their claims. In order to assess their claims, therefore, I have tried to collect together some statistics which might bear on the question of whether multiculturalism has promoted ethnic separatism, and discouraged or impeded integration. I will start with evidence from within Canada, comparing ethno-cultural groups before and after the adoption of the multiculturalism policy in 1971. I will then consider comparative evidence, to see how Canada compares with other countries, particularly those countries which rejected the principle of official multiculturalism.

THE DOMESTIC EVIDENCE

7   How has the adoption of multiculturalism in 1971 affected the integration of immigrant groups in Canada? To answer this question requires some account of what "integration" involves. It is one of the puzzling features of the Gwyn/Bissoondath critique that they do not define exactly what they mean by integration. However, we can piece together some of the things which they see as crucial ingredients of integration: adopting a Canadian identity rather than clinging exclusively to one's ancestral identity; participating in broader Canadian institutions rather than participating solely in ethnic-specific institutions; learning an official language rather than relying solely on one's mother-tongue; having inter-ethnic friendships or even mixed-marriages rather than socializing entirely within one's ethnic group. These sorts of criteria do not form a comprehensive theory of "integration," but they seem to be at the heart of Gwyn and Bissoondath's concerns about multiculturalism, so they are a good starting-point.

8   *Citizenship:* I will start with the most basic form of integration—the decision of immigrants to become Canadian citizens. If the Gwyn/Bissoondath thesis were true, one would expect naturalization rates to have declined since the adoption of multiculturalism in 1971. In fact, however, naturalization rates have increased since 1971. This is particularly relevant since the economic incentives to naturalize have lessened over the last 25 years. Taking out Canadian citizenship is not needed to gain access to the labour market in Canada or to have access to social benefits. There are virtually no differences between citizens and permanent residents in their civil rights or social benefits—the right to vote is the only major legal benefit gained by naturalization. The primary reason for immigrants to take out citizenship, therefore, is that they identify with Canada: they want to formalize their membership in Canadian society and participate in the political life of the country.

9   Moreover, if we examine which groups are most likely to naturalize, we find that it is the "multicultural groups"—that is, immigrants from non-traditional sources for whom the multiculturalism policy is most relevant—which have the highest rate of naturalization. By contrast, immigrants from the United States and United Kingdom—neither of whom are seen in popular discourse as an "ethnic" or "multicultural" group—have the lowest rate of naturalization. In other words, those groups which fall most clearly under the multiculturalism policy have shown the greatest desire to become Canadian, while those groups which fall outside the multiculturalism rubric have shown the least desire to become Canadian.

10   *Political Participation:* If the Gwyn/Bissoondath thesis were true, one would expect the political participation of ethnic groups to have declined since the adoption of multiculturalism in 1971. After all, political participation is a symbolic affirmation of citizenship and reflects an interest in the political life of the larger society. In fact, however, there is no evidence for a decline in participation. To take one relevant indicator, in the period prior to the adoption of multi-culturalism between Confederation and the 1960s, non-British, non-French groups became increasingly underrepresented in Parliament, but since then the trend has been reversed, so that today they have almost as many MPs as one would expect given their share of the population.

11   Moreover, it is important to note the way ethnocultural groups participate in Canadian politics. They do not form separate ethnic-based parties, either on a group-by-group basis or even on a coalition basis. Instead, they participate overwhelmingly within pan-Canadian parties. Indeed, the two parties in Canada which are closest to

being ethnic parties were created by and for those of English or French ancestry—namely, the Parti/Bloc Québécois, whose support is overwhelmingly found amongst Quebecers with French ancestry; and the Reform party, whose support is concentrated amongst WASPs. And perhaps the purest case of an ethnic party in Canada—the COR Party—was exclusively a WASP-based party. By contrast, immigrants have shown no inclination to support ethnic-based political parties and instead vote for the traditional national parties.

12   This is just one indicator of a more general point—namely, that immigrants are overwhelmingly supportive of, and committed to protecting, the basic political structure in Canada. We know that, were it not for the "ethnic vote," the 1995 referendum on secession in Quebec would have succeeded. In that referendum, ethnics overwhelmingly expressed their commitment to Canada. More generally, all the indicators suggest that immigrants quickly absorb and accept Canada's basic liberal-democratic values and constitutional principles, even if they came from countries which are illiberal or non-democratic. As Freda Hawkins puts it, "the truth is that there have been no riots, no breakaway political parties, no charismatic immigrant leaders, no real militancy in international causes, no internal political terrorism . . . , immigrants recognize a good, stable political system when they see one."

13   In short, if we look at indicators of legal and political integration, we see that since the adoption of multiculturalism in 1971 immigrants are more likely to become Canadians, and more likely to participate politically. And when they do participate, they do so through pan-ethnic political parties which uphold Canada's basic liberal democratic principles.

14   This sort of political integration is the main aim of a democratic state. But I suspect that individual Canadians are often more concerned with the social integration of immigrants than their political integration. Immigrants who participate in politics may be good democratic citizens, but if they can't speak English or French or are socially isolated in self-contained ethnic groups, then many Canadians will perceive a failure of integration. So let us shift to two indicators of societal integration: namely, official language acquisition and intermarriage rates.

15   *Official Language Competence:* If the Gwyn/Bissoondath thesis were true, one would expect the desire of ethnocultural minorities to acquire official language competence to have declined since the adoption of multiculturalism in 1971. If immigrant groups are being "ghettoized" and "alienated from the mainstream," and are attempting to preserve their original way of life intact from their homeland, then presumably they have less reason to learn an official language. In fact, however, demand for ESL and FSL classes has never been higher, and indeed exceeds supply in many cities. Recent census statistics show that 98.6% of Canadians say that they can speak one of the official languages. This is a staggering statistic when one considers how many immigrants are elderly and/or illiterate in their mother-tongue, and who therefore find it extremely difficult to learn a new language. It is especially impressive given that the number of immigrants who arrive with knowledge of an official language has declined since 1971. If we set aside the elderly—who form the majority of Canadians who cannot speak an official language—the idea that there is a general decrease in immigrants' desire to learn an official language is absurd. Immigrants want to learn an official language, and do so. Insofar as their official language skills are lacking, the explanation is the lack of accessible and appropriate ESL classes, not the lack of desire.

16   *Intermarriage Rates:* One final indicator worth looking at is intermarriage rates. If the Gwyn/Bissoondath thesis were true, one would expect intermarriage rates to have declined since the adoption of multiculturalism in 1971, since the policy is said to have driven "even deeper the awful wedges between races and nationalities," and encouraged groups to retreat into their "monocultural" ghettoes, and hide behind "cultural walls." In fact, however, intermarriage rates have consistently increased since 1971. We see an overall decline in endogamy, both for immigrants and their native-born children. Moreover, we see a dramatic increase in social acceptance of mixed marriages. For example, whereas 52% of Canadians disapproved of black-white marriages in 1968, 81% approved of them in 1995.

17   In short, whether we look at naturalization, political participation, official language competence, or intermarriage rates, we see the same story. There is no evidence to support the claim that multiculturalism has decreased the rate of integration of immigrants or increased the separatism or mutual hostility of ethnic groups.

18   If we examined other indicators, we would get the same story. As Orest Kruhlak puts it, "In sum, irrespective of which variables one examines, including [citizenship acquisition, ESL, mother-tongue retention, ethnic association participation, intermarriage] or political participation, the scope of economic involvement, or participation in mainstream social or service organizations, none suggest a sense of promoting ethnic separateness."

THE COMPARATIVE EVIDENCE

19   I can make the same point another way. If the Bissoondath/Gwyn thesis were correct, we would expect Canada to perform worse on these indicators of integration than other countries which have not adopted an official multiculturalism policy. Both Gwyn and Bissoondath contrast the Canadian approach with the American approach, which exclusively emphasizes common identities and common values and refuses to provide public recognition or affirmation of ethnocultural differences. If Canada fared worse than the U.S. in terms of integrating immigrants, this would provide some indirect support for the Bissoondath/Gwyn theory.

20   In fact, however, Canada fares better than the United States on virtually any dimension of integration. Canada has higher naturalization rates than the United States—indeed, much higher, almost double. We also have higher rates of political participation, higher rates of official language acquisition, and lower rates of residential segregation. Canada also has higher rates of inter-ethnic friendships, and much greater approval for intermarriage. Whereas 72% of Canadians approved of inter-racial marriages in 1988, only 40% of Americans approved of them, and 25% felt they should be illegal!

21   In short, on every indicator of integration, Canada, with its multiculturalism policy, fares better than the United States, with its repudiation of multiculturalism. We would find the same story if we compared Canada with other immigration countries which have rejected multiculturalism in favour of an exclusive emphasis on common identities—e.g., France.

22   Canada does better than these other countries, not only in our actual rates of integration, but also in our day-to-day sense of ethnic relations. In a 1997 survey, for example, people in twenty countries were asked whether they agreed that "different ethnic groups get along well here." The percentage of people who agreed was far higher in Canada (75%) than in the United States (58%) or France (51%).

23   This should not surprise us, since Canada does better than virtually any other country in the world in the integration of immigrants. The only comparable country is Australia, which is interesting, since it too has an official multiculturalism policy. Indeed, its multiculturalism policy was largely inspired by Canada's policy, although of course it has been adapted to Australia's circumstances. The two countries which are head and shoulders above the rest of the world in the successful integration of immigrants are the two countries with official multiculturalism policies. They are much more successful than any country which has rejected multiculturalism.

24   In short, there is not a shred of evidence to support the claim that multiculturalism is promoting ethnic separateness or impeding immigrant integration. Whether we examine the trends within Canada since 1971, or compare Canada with other countries, the conclusion is the same—the multiculturalism program is working. It is achieving what it set out to do: it is helping to ensure that those people who wish to express their ethnic identity are respected and accommodated, while simultaneously increasing the ability of immigrants to integrate into the larger society. Along with our fellow multiculturalists in Australia, Canada does a better job of respecting ethnic diversity while promoting societal integration than any other country.

EXPLAINING THE DEBATE

25   This raises a genuine puzzle. Why do so many intelligent and otherwise well-informed commentators agree that multiculturalism policy is impeding integration? Part of the explanation is that many people have simply not examined the policy to see what it actually involves. For example, Gwyn and Bissoondath claim that *multiculturalism* tells new Canadians that they should practice "monoculturalism," preserving their inherited way of life intact, while not interacting with or learning from the members of other groups, or the larger society. According to Gwyn and Bissoondath, this sort of self-ghettoization is not so much an unintended consequence of the policy, but rather one of its explicit aims. Yet neither author quotes a single document published by the multiculturalism unit of the federal government to support this claim—none of their annual reports, demographic analyses, public education brochures, or program funding guidelines.

26   In reality, most of the focus of multiculturalism policy (and most of its funding) has been directed to promoting civic participation in the larger society and to increasing mutual understanding and cooperation between the members of different ethnic groups. More generally, the multiculturalism policy has never stated or implied that people are under any duty or obligation to retain their ethnic identity/practices "freeze-dried," or indeed to retain them at all. On the contrary, the principle that individuals should be free to choose whether to maintain their ethnic identity has been one of the cornerstones of the policy since 1971, and continues to guide existing multiculturalism programs. Multiculturalism is intended to make it possible for people to retain and express their identity with pride if they so choose, by reducing the legal, institutional, economic or societal obstacles to this expression. It does not penalize or disapprove of people who choose not to identify with their ethnic group, or describe them as poor citizens or as lesser Canadians.

27   One could multiply examples of these sorts of misinterpretations of the basic guidelines and purposes of the policy. But I think these are just symptoms of a deeper problem. The real problem, I think, is that critics of multiculturalism view the policy in

isolation, as if it was the only government policy affecting the integration of immigrants. But multiculturalism is not the only, or even the primary, policy affecting the integration of immigrants. Instead, it is a modest part of a larger package of policies, which includes citizenship, education and employment policies. It is these other policies which are the major engines of integration. They all encourage, pressure, even legally force immigrants to take steps towards integrating into Canadian society.

28   For example, it is a legal requirement for gaining citizenship that the immigrant know an official language (unless they are elderly), as well as some basic information about Canadian history and institutions. Similarly, it is a legal requirement under provincial education acts that the children of immigrants learn an official language and learn a common core curriculum. Moreover, immigrants must know an official language to gain access to government-funded job training programs. Immigrants must know an official language in order to receive professional accreditation or to have their foreign training recognized. The most highly skilled pharmacist won't be granted a professional license to practice pharmacy in Canada if she can only speak Portuguese. And of course knowledge of an official language is a precondition for working in the bureaucracy or for gaining government contract work.

29   These citizenship, education and employment policies have always been the major pillars of government-sponsored integration in Canada, and they remain fully in place today. Moreover, if we examine the amount of money spent on these policies, it eclipses the money spent on multiculturalism. The government spends billions of dollars a year on language training and job training for immigrants, and on education for their children, compared to under $20 million a year for multiculturalism programs.

30   So Canada spends billions of dollars encouraging and pressuring immigrants to integrate into common educational, economic and political institutions operating in either French or English. This is the context within which multiculturalism operates, and multiculturalism can only be understood in this wider context. With such a tiny budget, multiculturalism could not possibly hope to compete with this government-sponsored integration, and does not try to do so. On the contrary, from the very beginning, multiculturalism has explicitly gone hand-in-hand with government measures to promote societal integration.

31   For example, one of the guiding principles of multiculturalism has been to promote official bilingualism in Canada. This is reflected in the very terminology which Trudeau employed when introducing the policy—namely, "multiculturalism within a bilingual framework." It has been explicit from the beginning that multiculturalism works alongside the linguistic and institutional integration of immigrants.

32   Some critics see the phrase "multiculturalism within a bilingual framework" as incoherent or meaningless. But I think it has a very simple and compelling meaning. The idea is this: If Canada is going to pressure immigrants to integrate into common institutions operating in English or French, then we need to ensure that the terms of integration are fair. To my mind, this has two basic elements:

33   (a) we need to recognize that integration does not occur overnight, but rather is a difficult and long-term process which operates intergenerationally. Hence special accommodations are often required for immigrants on a transitional basis. For example, certain services should be available in the immigrants' mother tongue, and support should be provided for those groups and organizations within immigrant communities which assist in the settlement/integration process;

34   (b) we need to ensure that the common institutions into which immigrants are pressured to integrate provide the same degree of respect, recognition and accommodation of the identities and practices of ethnocultural minorities as they traditionally have been of WASP and French-Canadian identities. Otherwise, the promotion of English and French as official languages is tantamount to privileging the lifestyles of the descendants of the English or French settlers.

35   This requires a systematic exploration of our social institutions to see whether their rules, structures and symbols disadvantage immigrants. For example, we need to examine dress-codes, public holidays, or even height and weight restrictions to see whether they are biased against certain immigrant groups. We need to examine the portrayal of minorities in school curricula or the media to see if they are stereotypical or fail to recognize the contributions of ethnocultural groups to Canadian history or world culture. And so on.

36   These measures are needed to ensure that Canada is offering immigrants fair terms of integration. The idea of multiculturalism within a bilingual framework is, I think, precisely an attempt to define such fair terms of integration. And in my view, the vast majority of what is done under the heading of multiculturalism policy, not only at the federal level, but also at provincial and municipal levels, and indeed within school boards and private companies, can be defended as promoting fair terms of integration. Others may disagree with the fairness of some of these policies. The requirements of fairness are not always obvious, particularly in the context of people who have chosen to enter a country. How to define fair terms of integration is a debate that we can and should have. The claim that multiculturalism is anti-integrationist, however, is a red herring.

DISCUSSION QUESTIONS

1. What claims does the writer identify as ones made by Bissoondath and Gwyn that "would be a serious indictment of the policy" if they were accurate?

2. What evidence does the writer offer countering the claims made by Bissoondath and Gwyn?

3. Identify some of the argumentative techniques used by the writer to persuade the audience of the inaccuracy of the claims made by Bissoondath and Gwyn.

4. The author chooses to end and not begin his essay with a section entitled "Explaining the Debate." What possible reasons might he have had for the positioning of this section here? Would the essay be more or less effective if organized differently? Explain.

5. In your own words, explain what you think the writer means by "fair terms of integration," and how he thinks that the multiculturalism policy promotes "fair terms of integration."

TOWARD KEY INSIGHTS

Do you agree that Canada more successfully integrates immigrants into society than do most other countries? Explain.

Explain the author's assertion that "the requirements of fairness are not always obvious . . . in the context of people who have chosen to enter the country." Do you agree or not?

In your view, what has Kymlicka left out of his argument that might have made it more persuasive?

SUGGESTION FOR ORAL ARGUMENT *Review the Canadian Multiculturalism Act and research statistics on the cultural diversity of Canada's population over the past 40 or so years. Also consider evidence on the level of acceptance and tolerance of cultural diversity in Canada. Come to class prepared to argue either side of the following proposition:*

> The *Canadian Multiculturalism Act* has been successful in contributing to the development of Canada as a country that encourages and welcomes cultural diversity.

SUGGESTIONS FOR WRITING *Write a persuasive essay directed to people in a particular community about one of the following topics.*

1. The value, for the individual or for the larger Canadian society, of people retaining their ethnic heritage.

2. The need for more inclusiveness and acceptance of cultural differences.

3. The need for more governmental support of English-language training and/or other services for immigrants.

4. The need for Canada to welcome more refugees.

MyWritingLab

How Do I Get a Better Grade?

Go to **www.mywritinglab .com** for additional help with your grammar, writing, and research skills. You will have access to a variety of exercises, instruction, and videos that will help you improve your basic skills and help you get a better grade.

CHAPTER 14

Strategies for Writing a Research-Based Paper

WHY USE RESEARCH?

If you had the time and money to plan a European vacation this summer, how would you make decisions about countries to visit or places to stay? Would you begin by consulting travel books in a store or library? Would you Google online travel forums and websites? Would you talk to people who had travelled to places you were considering?

Whether we are planning a vacation, deciding which cellphone to buy, or trying to figure out the best ways to get fit, most of us conduct research in one way or another. Yet in this age of information overload, many students feel an understandable anxiety when they are asked to write academic research-based papers. Some worry that they will not have anything interesting to say about a topic that hasn't already been said. Strangely enough, however, the more deeply you explore a question or topic, the more likely you are to find a perspective that is yours—the result of combining what you are learning about; information from sources, whether primary or secondary; and your own unique interpretation or slant.

As you read what others have written about your topic or research question, you will develop new ideas and begin to formulate your own conclusions. Writing takes work, but it can be a very enjoyable process as you become more of a relative expert in a particular area.

Learning how to select information that is relevant to your topic, organize it, filter it through your own language, document it correctly, and present it is one of the most useful things you can learn in university. Researchers are like detectives or investigative journalists who follow a trail where it leads them, changing course if necessary. The experience of doing your own research helps you to make a topic your own.

Research writing can also help you in future courses and at work:

- A criminology instructor might ask you to examine the results of using restorative justice in sexual harassment cases.

- A business instructor might ask you to trace the history of a company, evaluate an advertising campaign, or review the latest styles of management.

- A building trades instructor might call for a short report that compares the effectiveness of several new insulating materials.

- At work, a marketing analyst might report on the development costs, sales potential, and competition for a product the company is considering introducing.

- A physical therapist might prepare a seminar paper that evaluates different exercise programs following arthroscopic surgery.

As for any kind of writing project, let your purpose guide your research and determine the information you elect to use. When you write your draft, do not attempt to cram in everything just because it vaguely pertains to your topic; select only the material that is relevant to your larger purpose and to the points you want to make.

CHOOSING A TOPIC

It is important that you make sure you understand the research paper assignment, as well as your instructor's expectations. Some library research assignments may ask for explanatory papers that help readers get a better grasp of a topic, but most require you to develop a thesis that communicates a clear point of view on a complex topic. Many research papers are, in essence, arguments or persuasive papers that aim to influence readers to adopt a certain perspective. In order to influence readers to accept a controversial idea—for example, the argument that sex trade workers should be protected by the government—a writer would need to draw on research, whether primary or secondary sources, or possibly both. Even an essay that is primarily informative may have a persuasive angle; for example, an essay that describes the advantages of wind power as an energy source may aim to clear up certain popular misconceptions.

Some instructors specify not only the type of paper but also the topic, while others give students a general subject area from which they are asked to choose a topic. If you have been given a topic that you feel is too restrictive, you can still search for an angle on it that interests you—it often happens that the more you investigate and learn about something, the more you begin to find it rather fascinating.

Some instructors give students the freedom to choose to research whatever interests them. While this free choice may seem alluring, it also means that you are the one responsible for zeroing in on what you want to talk about, and for limiting the scope of your discussion. Fearing that they will not be able to find enough information on a given topic, many students begin with an overly broad, general idea that soon mushrooms out of control, and then find that they need to start all over again, this time concentrating on something much narrower.

If you are free to choose your own topic, let your interests guide your choice. A long-standing interest in hockey might suggest a paper on the pros and cons of expanding the number of teams in the National Hockey League. An instructor's lecture might spark your interest in an economic crisis, a scientific development, a sociological trend, or an ethical question in medicine or law. An argument with a friend might spur you to investigate carbon taxes. A television documentary might arouse your curiosity about the psychological or cultural impact of residential schools on First Nations communities.

Be practical in selecting a topic, and choose something that will interest you or serve your needs. You could, for example, get a head start on a particular aspect of your major field by researching it now. Think about your audience, the availability of information, and the instructor's guidelines for your paper.

Topics to Avoid

If you are free to pick your own topic, how should you proceed? To begin, rule out certain types of topics that will take you to a dead end.

- Those based entirely on personal experience or opinion, such as "The Thrills I Have Enjoyed Snowboarding" or "Nova Scotia Has More [or Less] Scenic Beauty Than Prince Edward Island."
- Those fully explained in a single source. An explanation of a process, such as cardiopulmonary resuscitation, or the description of a place, such as the Alberta Badlands, does not require coordination of materials from various sources. Although you may find several articles on such topics, they will basically repeat the same information.
- Those that are overly broad. Don't try to tackle such elephant-sized topics as "The Technology of War" or "Recent Medical Advances." Instead, find an interesting angle on these topics, such as "The Need for a New Legal Framework for the Use of Drones in Warfare" or "Eye Surgery with Laser Beams: Risks and Benefits."
- Those that have been worked over and over, such as abortion and the legal drinking age. Why bore your reader with information and arguments that are all too familiar?

EXERCISE

The use of electronic monitoring systems with nonviolent offenders

Benefits of monitoring
- reduces jail population
- less expensive than prison
- effective for nonviolent offenders
- several systems available

Problems associated with monitoring
- signal interference problems
- legal concerns

Using the advice on topics to avoid, explain why each of the following would or would not be suitable for a library research topic.

1. Ethical, psychological, and legal issues with in vitro fertilization (IVF) in Canada
2. The challenges of cybersecurity
3. Canadian minor hockey
4. Tweeting as a marketing strategy for non-profit organizations
5. Social problems related to poverty

Finding a Focus

As you begin developing the focus of your paper, a quick search of online resources, encyclopedias, and other reference works may help determine possible directions for your research, or provide a broader context for the subject. Many students begin by checking Wikipedia entries for some quick general background, but keep in mind that because Wikipedia is edited by users and may have inaccuracies, it has uneven quality control and many faculty members do not want it used as a formal source. However, even if Wikipedia or other more casual articles, blogs, and online comments are not going to be used later as formal sources, skimming them may help you generate ideas. In addition, Wikipedia and other articles may have links to other information that can guide your search. Sometimes quickly skimming books, even their tables of contents, can offer ideas as well. During this preliminary search, you are simply scouting the terrain in order to focus your topic, determine the different issues that you want to address, and gain some sense of the resources available on your topic. Move fast and cover a lot of ground. You can always go back later to something you found interesting.

At this early stage, some students clarify their focus by brainstorming and sketching ideas using branching or clustering techniques. For example, if you were exploring the topic of child abuse, preparing a clustering diagram like the one in Figure 14.1 could help you decide how to narrow your topic, and uncover some promising areas to research.

The more you brainstorm, the richer your map will be. Brainstorming often yields a set of questions, perhaps based on the writing strategies discussed earlier, that can guide your research. Often it is helpful to write down your main research question, followed by a series of related questions that elaborate on it. For example, a student wishing to explore the topic of psychological abuse might use a clustering diagram to develop the following set of questions:

What can be done to help victims of psychological abuse?

What is psychological abuse?

What long-term and short-term effects does it have on a child?

How can a child living at home be helped?

Are there services to help limit the abuse?

Is family therapy an option?

What is family therapy, and what does it do?

What psychological help is available for an adult who experienced childhood abuse?

What therapies work best?

What do they do?

How effective are they?

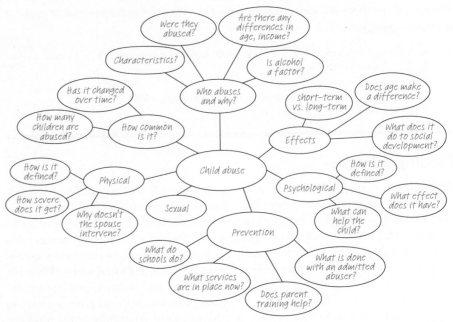

FIGURE 14.1 Clustering Diagram on Child Abuse

These questions make research easier; after all, the purpose of conducting research is to answer questions. Later, as you examine source material, you will seek specific answers to specific questions, instead of randomly generating information. Don't be discouraged by false starts and blind alleys, as you will need to try out various possibilities as you probe for a topic and a focus.

FINDING YOUR TOPIC	■ Make a list of your major interests that prompt questions. ■ Identify issues or questions raised in class or the media. ■ Brainstorm questions related to your initial question for focus. ■ Do some initial readings around your topic to get an overview to focus your topic.

Consider how a student named Keith Jacques had to change and refine his ideas for a paper in his criminology class. The assignment he had was fairly general, as he was asked to explore a possible solution to a social problem related to the prison system. When he finally landed on the problem of prison overcrowding, he thought it would be smooth sailing with this fairly focused idea. However, once he began to write about the problem of prison overcrowding, he realized he had to zero in more and more. He had begun by looking at several possible solutions: the development of early release programs for non-violent offenders, setting up house arrest programs verified by electronic monitoring systems, using halfway houses more effectively, and re-evaluating legal codes to determine which offences should require incarceration. After his paper began to get more and more unwieldy, Keith realized that he could not do justice to these various options in a relatively short paper. He decided to concentrate on the one option that intrigued him the most. Since his interest in electronic monitoring had been sparked by a recent television report he had watched, he decided to dive into this topic.

We often have to explore several possible approaches before we alight on one that really works. The process of narrowing a topic, finding a research question, selecting relevant sources, organizing, drafting, and revising often takes longer than students anticipate. Breaking down the steps of writing a research paper into smaller steps and following a schedule for the various stages of your paper will save you stress later and result in a better paper. Such a timetable helps you plan your work and allows you to check your progress at a glance. You can use the following sample schedule as a guide, but you will likely modify the stages or add other ones as necessary; for example, many people choose to do a flexible outline only after they have written a first draft.

Sample Schedule for a Library Research Paper

Activity	Targeted	Completion Date
Topic Selection	_____	_____
Preliminary Research to		
Narrow Research Question	_____	_____
Working Bibliography	_____	_____
Research Question and		
Tentative Thesis	_____	_____
Library and Online Research	_____	_____
Take Notes	_____	_____
Flexible Notes, Working Outline, or		
Research Proposal and/or		
Working Outline	_____	_____
Write First Draft	_____	_____
Prepare Works Cited List	_____	_____
Revise Drafts	_____	_____
Proofread (preferably after a day or two)	_____	_____
Final Draft Date Due	_____	_____

DISCOVERING YOUR SOURCES

Once you have a topic, you're ready look into possible resources that you might use in your paper. As you begin, perhaps by skimming information in print or online reference works, be sure you understand what kind of sources your instructor wants you to use in your paper. Have you been asked to bring in a certain number of sources, or certain kinds of sources? Articles from journals that have been "peer reviewed" or "refereed" have been reviewed by experts in the discipline, and usually contain references or a list of "Works Cited." Articles from magazines, which usually have appealing photos and are written for more general audiences, are considered popular sources. Some instructors want you to use scholarly sources only; others may ask for one or two scholarly sources; and still others do not specify.

Assembling a Working Bibliography

While you are searching, keep a set of notes, with accurate publishing information recorded, so that you begin a working bibliography—a list of promising sources of information—since you will need it later to cite your references. A discussion of some common reference tools and how to use them follows.

Online Catalogue

What It Is   Your library's online catalogue, which lists all of the library's holdings—books, magazines, newspapers, government documents, videos, and electronic recordings—is a good place to start your academic research. The online catalogue probably also offers additional information, such as whether a book has been checked out and, if so, the return date. Many networked catalogues that include the holdings of nearby libraries may have sources that you can order through interlibrary loan. Of course, since interlibrary loan sources may take a few days to arrive, it's a good idea to get started on your research as soon as you can.

Often, a key word or subject term search can be the most helpful way to approach a topic. In this type of search, the computer checks the titles and descriptions of books for the key terms you enter and lists any that it finds. Different key terms will produce varying strings of publications, so it is a good idea to try different words or phrases for the same topic. For example, if you're searching for material on "electric cars," you might also try similar words or word combinations—"electronic cars," "alternative fuels," and so on. Because such searches are very rapid, you can experiment with different combinations of terms to focus your search. If, for instance, you're asked to write a paper on some aspect of Japanese culture, you might investigate such combinations as "Japanese business," "Japan and education," and "Japanese feminists." If the list that turns up is too long to fit on the screen, narrow it down; for example, *Japan* AND *education* might be narrowed to *Japan* AND *primary arts education*. Because key-term searches allow you to use logical terms like *and, or, but,* and *not,* they are especially useful for narrowing a broad focus. If you know the exact phrase you are searching for, you can use quotation marks around the term to get exactly what you want.

Subject searches are more focused than key-word searches. However, when searching with subjects, rather than key words, you may be surprised that the subject you entered yields very little. Consider for a moment the vast number of possible wordings that exist for each subject. For example, if you were looking for resources on end-of-life choices, you could also try *euthanasia, assisted suicide,* or *doctor-assisted death* as you look for potentially relevant material. No library system could sort all of their books under all possible headings, so the subject you enter must exactly match the subject headings that the library system uses, commonly those used by the Library of Congress. You can sometimes find the *Library of Congress Subject Headings* (LCHS) manual on the subject page, or you can ask a librarian for help.

Obtaining Books   When you have found a promising title, click on the appropriate command to call up the relevant information. Most systems indicate whether the book is in the library or checked out and allow you to reserve a book by entering the request into the computer.

If you cannot print a list of results or email the list to yourself, record the following information in your electronic notes or in the upper left corner of a note card:

Author(s)

Title

Editor(s) and translator(s), as well as author(s) of any supplementary material

Total number of volumes (if more than one) and the number of the specific volume you want to use

City of publication

Name of publisher

Date of publication

Call number (for future reference)

Next, go to the stacks to scan the books themselves. Once you find your book, spend a few extra minutes browsing in the general area around it. Since all books on a topic are shelved together, you may discover other useful sources.

Skim each book's table of contents and any introductory material, such as a preface or introduction, to determine its scope and approach. Also check the index and note the pages with discussions that relate to your topic. Finally, thumb through any portions that look promising. If the book isn't relevant, place it in the reshelving area and discard the reference information.

Note that if a book is missing from the shelf and the computer indicates that nobody has checked it out, it's probably on reserve or in the reshelving area. Check at the circulation desk. If the book is on reserve, go to that section and examine it there. For a book in reshelving, you may need to return the next day to see if it shows up. Also, you can check the catalogue to see if another library location has a copy of the book or you can put a hold on the book so that the library will contact you as soon as it is available.

EXERCISE

1. *Select five of the following topics. Go to the online catalogue and find one book about each topic. List each book's call number, author, title, publisher, and date of publication. Because subject headings may vary, use more than one subject search. For example, if you find nothing under* mountaineering, *check* mountain climbing *or* backpacking.

   a. Adolescent emotional development　　　　**h.** Sports acupuncture

   b. Medical marijuana　　　　**i.** Tattoos

   c. Violence against Aboriginal women　　　　**j.** CUSO opportunities

   d. Extreme drought　　　　**k.** Professional hockey wages

   e. Multiple intelligences　　　　**l.** Canadian health supplements

   f. Mountaineering　　　　**m.** Honour killings

   g. Zombies in popular culture　　　　**n.** Benefits of mindfulness

2. *Provide your instructor with a list of three to five books that could be useful for developing a paper on one of the topics above. For each book, furnish the information specified in Exercise 1 above, along with a brief note of no more than one sentence indicating why you think the book will be useful.*

Database Indexes

What They Are   Databases are searchable online collections of stored information that provide access to articles published in popular and academic journals as well as other materials. They may cover multiple disciplines or a single subject. Some provide access to full-text articles from academic journals or popular sources such as newspapers. Some contain only abstracts (short summaries of articles) or citation information that you can use to locate the article in another location or in print form. Databases may also provide links to ebooks or to images for which your library has paid a licensing fee.

General database indexes such as *Academic Search Premier* or *JSTOR* catalogue articles from journals. The *ARTstor* database offers downloadable art images from museums, photographers, photo archives, and others that can be used for educational purposes. There are many specific databases for newspapers, business, and other disciplines that can help you find articles in specific subject areas such as Canadian Studies, Journalism, Nursing, Public Health, and so on. Databases such as *PsychINFO* (index for peer-reviewed sources in psychology and behavioural sciences), *ERIC* (Education Resources Information Center), and *Medline* (National Library of Medicine) give you access to citations of articles appearing in professional journals that are written by experts for experts. Since these articles are aimed at a specialized audience, they may sometimes be difficult to comprehend.

Databases allow you to search a wide range of topics by key word or subject, and many provide access to the full article online. Other times they identify the actual print version you are searching for and where you can locate it. In general, it is helpful to explore the available databases and the kind of information they make available. Their listings allow you to examine new topics, follow developments in older ones, and explore your topic in greater depth than you could by using books alone.

Perhaps the best place to start a search is with a general multidisciplinary database such as Academic Search Premier, where you can find academic articles on a wide range of topics. Other useful academic databases include *Project Muse, Sage Premiere, Springerlink, E-Journals Database, and Cambridge Journals Online.* DOAJ, the Directory of Open Access Journals, can be accessed on the web.

While you can sometimes obtain a full article directly online, other times the database entry instead offers only an abstract—a brief summary of the article's main points. *A word of caution: Don't mistake an abstract for the full article; an abstract is a 200- to 300-word summary of a journal article and should not be used as a source. Always take notes from the full article.* Also, do not restrict your research to articles that are available only online, as you may be able to find them in print or through interlibrary loan.

Subject Search   Because most indexes are organized around subject headings, it's a good idea to try a variety of subject terms because each will yield different articles. With indexes, as with the online catalogue, don't give up if a subject heading you're exploring yields few or no entries. Instead, explore related headings. For example, if your topic is teenage marriages, look also under *adolescence, divorce, teen pregnancies,* and the like. Browse through the system and try a variety of key words. Use this browsing time as an opportunity to gain different perspectives on your research project.

Often your key-word search results will suggest subject headings. If your entry matches a subject heading or you are referred to a cross-reference, the computer will use a series of screens to direct you to a list of articles.

Along the way, one of the screens may list subdivisions of the request being searched, as in the following example:

Acquaintance Rape, subdivisions of

—analysis
—cases
—investigation
—laws, regulations, etc.
—media coverage
—moral and ethical aspects
—personal narratives

—prevention
—psychological aspects
—research
—social aspects
—statistics
—studying and teaching
—use

Such a list can uncover facets of your topic that you hadn't considered and that could enrich your final paper. For example, the subdivision "personal narratives" might contain an experience that would provide a powerful opening for the paper. Similarly, articles catalogued under "statistics" could provide information on the scope of the acquaintance rape problem.

Advanced Search   The final result of any search is a list of articles. Several of the sources may be available directly online. If the database provides the full text of an article, the notation "Full text available" will appear after the citation. Other articles may include only an abstract in the database. The results list may also show whether the materials are available in your library either in print or on microfilm—if not, you may be able to request the material through interlibrary loan.

Obtaining the Articles   If the article you want is available online, the database often allows you to email the article to yourself or save the article to your computer. For references without complete articles, print a copy of each promising reference you find, including the abstract, if available. Otherwise, copy the following information into your notes.

Author(s), if identified
Title of article
Name of periodical
Volume or issue number (for professional and scholarly journals only)
Date of periodical
For newspapers, the edition name (city, metro) if more than one published, and section letter
The page range of the entire article

Obtain printouts of whatever articles you can and check the topic sentences of paragraphs for essential points. Also, scan any accompanying abstracts or summaries. If an article appears useful, check to see whether it has a bibliography, which might include additional useful sources. Keep the notes for articles that seem promising—and any useful articles—and discard the others.

If the database does not indicate whether the library has the article and periodical (journal or publication such as a magazine that appears at regular intervals), check the remaining references against the library's periodical catalogue, which is often part of the online catalogue, to see which periodicals are available and where they are located. Libraries frequently keep current issues in a periodical room or some other special section. Back issues of magazines are often kept on microfilm or bound into hardcover volumes and shelved. Most newspapers are on microfilm. Check the articles for which you don't have printouts in the same manner that you checked the others.

EXERCISE

Select two of the following topics. Using three different databases, such as Academic Search Premier, Humanities Index, Social Sciences Index, *or* JSTOR, *find links to three different relevant full-text articles on each topic. Record the name of the index you used, the name of the journal or magazine where the article can be found, the title of the article in quotation marks, the name of the author if given, the date of publication, and the page range of the article. Because subject categories may vary, investigate related categories, if necessary, to find an entry. To illustrate, if you find nothing under "bioengineered foods," check "genetically modified foods" or "bioaltered foods."*

1. Physician-assisted suicide
2. Identity theft
3. Black holes
4. Sexting
5. Collective bargaining
6. 3D printers
7. Polygamy
8. Plea bargains
9. Bioengineered foods
10. Wearable technology
11. Euthanasia
12. Drones
13. Racial profiling
14. Teen homelessness
15. Gluten-free diets
16. Sidney Crosby

Searching the World Wide Web

The Internet includes a stupendous amount of information. As a result, finding just the material you want can be difficult. To solve this problem, several *search engines* have been developed that can connect any search term or terms with potentially millions of sites that include the key words. While studies have found that most students automatically use Google for searches, Figure 14.2 provides the addresses of several other search engines. Because the various search engines often select differently and produce different results, it's a good idea to use several engines while conducting your search.

While each search engine works in a slightly different manner, they all provide similar sorts of information. If your search terms are overly general, search engines often

Search Engine	Address
Google	www.google.com
Bing	www.bing.com
Yahoo	www.yahoo.com
Ask	www.ask.com

FIGURE 14.2 Popular Search Engines

provide far too much irrelevant information to sort through. For that reason, you may want to narrow your search when you begin. Single terms such as "health," "cancer," or "crime" could give you a million possible sites; instead, you may want to search for "ovarian cancer" or even "ovarian cancer cures." Most search engines also let you add key words that will further narrow what has already been found. Different words or phrases can produce different results, so try a variety of words for the same topic. It is important to be patient. Often you might find a very helpful article only after scrolling through several pages of results.

You can scroll through the list of sites the engine has found. The sites are usually accompanied by a short description that may help you decide whether they are useful. If you select any highlighted words, the search engine will connect you to the selected web page.

Evaluating Internet Material   Because anyone can post anything on the Internet, it is crucial that you check the accuracy and validity of any information you obtain from it. A source that sounds like a research centre—for example, the Institute for Social Justice—could be a political or even a cult organization giving out one-sided or false information for its own purposes. While articles for professional journals are reviewed by experts to ensure that the information is reliable, no such safeguard exists on the Internet. Carelessly researched or ethically questionable material can and does appear. Here are some guidelines for checking the validity of an Internet source:

1. Is the source a reputable professional organization, such as the Canadian Medical Association, McGill University, or the Canadian Counselling and Psychotherapy Association? Keep in mind that anyone can make up a professional-sounding name, so be alert. If you are relying on the information from this source to make a controversial case, check whether the source is linked with a company that earns profits, or whether it is nonpartisan.
2. Is there an identified author whose credentials you can check and who speaks with some authority? If there is no email contact listed, or if you can't find another way to verify the contents of the website, don't use it.
3. Is the tone of the site professional? Does it maintain an objective stance and support its position with credible evidence?
4. Is the information consistent with the other material you have found? If the site disagrees with the standard information, does it offer adequate support for its claims?
5. Does the site explain how the data were obtained?
6. Does the site appear to misuse any data? For instance, is the sample too small? Are the claims pushed too far? Are the statistics biased?

Sometimes, of course, you may want to check out web pages that present the views of individuals or organizations with strong but slanted positions to gain a better understanding of their thinking, but don't consider such pages to be reliable sources. When using the Internet, "Reader beware" is prudent advice.

Email   You probably have your own email address as well as an email address provided to you by your university. You can use email to ask knowledgeable people about your research topic and get swift answers to your questions. If you must contact experts, don't bother them with questions that you could easily answer by reading background material. Reserve email for specific queries that defy answer after extensive research. If you do get a response to your query, evaluate its relevance carefully before deciding to include it in your paper.

Forums, Discussion Lists, and Social Media   Sometimes you can find current, topical information through online forums or threads in discussion groups that you can search. Increasingly, online news stories or blogs are followed by a number of comments by those interested in the topic. While such discussions may offer ideas, remember that almost anyone can post comments without correction, so the comments may be very inaccurate.

FAQs   Whenever you find a promising website, you will often see a line for FAQs (frequently asked questions). It's a good idea to read the FAQs first, since they may well answer your questions.

EXERCISE

Using an appropriate search engine, find information on each of the following topics:

   a. Solar power
   b. Current crime statistics in your region
   c. Sexual harassment
   d. Current government immigration policy

Creating an Annotated Bibliography

Your instructor may ask you to create an annotated bibliography, a list of sources following a documentation style such as the MLA (Chapter 16) or APA (Chapter 17) formats along with a brief summary of the article or book. Scholars sometimes produce annotated bibliographies for publication to give other scholars an overview of the research on a particular topic. Below is a sample entry for an annotated bibliography in MLA style.

> Anzaldua, Gloria. "La Conciencia De La Mestiza: Towards a New Consciousness" in *Making Face, Making Soul/Haciendo Caras*, ed. by Gloria Anzaldua, 377–389. San Francisco: Aunt Lute Books, 1990. Print. Gloria Anzaldua explores the concept of the mestiza, a borderlands figure pulled in multiple directions. Anzaldua narrates how this figure is simultaneously present in multiple spaces, having a foot in multiple cultures. The result of this experience, Anzaldua claims, is a tolerance for ambiguity and contradiction. Furthermore, the mestiza is here articulated as a powerful cultural figure, able to embody possibilities for change.

Primary Research Findings

Besides relying on library materials, you may wish to use information obtained by conducting primary research. Chapter 15 offers guidelines for conducting interviews, sending out questionnaires, and making direct observations. In addition, the scholarly article in the Reader titled "Community: Use It or Lose It" exemplifies a blending of primary findings based largely on interviews and secondary sources.

Evaluating Your Sources

Evaluate your sources by considering these factors.

The Expertise of the Author   Judge an author's expertise by examining his or her professional status. Let's say you're searching for information on a new cancer treatment drug. An article by the director of a national cancer research centre would be a better source than one by a staff writer for a popular magazine. Similarly, a historian's account of a national figure will probably have more balance and depth than a novelist's popularized account of that person's life. Gauging a writer's credentials is not difficult. Articles in periodicals often note authors' job titles along with their names. Some even supply thumbnail biographies. For a book, check its title page, preface or introduction, and—if it's been left on—the dust jacket. Finally, notice whether the writer has other publications on this general subject. If your sources include two or more items by one person, or if that person's name keeps cropping up as you take notes, you're probably dealing with an expert.

The Credibility of the Publication   A book's credibility hinges on its approach and its reception by reviewers. Cast a cautious eye on books that take a popular rather than a scholarly approach. For research papers, scholarly treatments are more reliable. In addition, examine what reviewers said when a book first appeared. There are two publications that excerpt selected reviews of new books and provide references to others. *Book Review Digest* (1905 to present) deals mainly with non-technical works, while the *Technical Book Review Index* (1935 to present) covers technical and scientific books. Turn first to the volume for the year in which the book came out. If you don't find any reviews, scan the next year's index. Often books published in the fall are not reviewed until the following year.

Like books, periodical articles can take either a scholarly or a popular tack. Editors of specialized journals and of some wide-circulation magazines—for example, *Equinox* and *The Atlantic*—publish only in-depth, accurate articles. Most newsstand publications, however, popularize news to some extent, and some deliberately strive for sensationalism. Popularizing may result in overly broad claims unsupported by sufficient evidence or details. There are times, however, especially when writing about a current topic, when you may want to use material from more popular sources; as always, be sure you understand your instructor's expectations and the nature of the assignment.

TAKING NOTES

Notes are the raw materials for your finished product, so develop them accurately. To take notes, read your references carefully and record significant information. Some people take notes on their tablets or computers, and many still use note cards or regular notebooks. If you don't have a laptop, you may find it works best to take notes on cards, and then type up the notes and bibliographical references at a computer afterwards. You can type notes into one central file and distribute them later to separate files by topic or distribute them as you go along. Remember to save your work after every entry.

If you are using cards, note each important point on a large index card to avoid confusion with the smaller bibliography cards. Record only one note per card, even when you take several notes from a single page of a book, because you may use the notes at different points in your paper. If you can't fit a note on a single card, continue the note on a second card and attach the two with a paper clip or staple them together. Cards allow you to test different arrangements of notes and use the best arrangement to write the paper.

If you are taking notes on your computer, create a new file called something like "Notes" in your new essay's main folder. Keep it distinct from your bibliography file. Record each piece of information in its own paragraph or point-form paragraph, skipping a line in between. Separating paragraphs allows you to move information around later to find the best arrangement.

Before you take a note, indicate its source at the bottom of the card or at the beginning (or end) of each paragraph or chunk of information. You will then have all of the details necessary for documenting the information if you use it in your paper. Usually the author's last name and the page number suffice, since the bibliography card or file contains all other details. To distinguish between two authors with the same last name or between two works by the same author, add initials or partial titles. *Don't forget to include the page number or numbers for each note,* otherwise you'll have to waste time looking them up when you cite your sources in your paper.

Summarize briefly the contents of the note at the top of the card. If using a computer, you may want to highlight key phrases. Later, when you construct an outline, these notations will help you sort your points into categories and subcategories.

As you proceed, take great care to distinguish between your notes and your thoughts about them. One good way to do this is to establish some system, such as using colour-coding if you are recording notes on a card, or using the Highlight feature to help organize notes on your computer. To avoid inadvertently using the exact words of others without giving proper credit, always put quotation marks around directly quoted material. As an added safeguard, you might also use different spacing or a different font for quotations. To identify the sources of your notes, you could number them to match the number of the source or end each note with the author's name. Finally, if you are recording your notes on a computer, be sure to keep printouts of your notes and bibliography to guard against accidental erasure or a power surge.

Whatever method of note taking you prefer, you need to make certain that all of your notes remain undividable, are linked to their source, and will be easy to organize later. Table 14.1 presents some strategies.

Thinking Critically as You Take Notes

As you take notes, reflect on your topic and try to come up with new ideas, see connections to other notes, and anticipate future research. Think of yourself as having a conversation with your sources, and jot down your responses on the backs of your note cards; in a separate, clearly labelled file; or next to or beneath your computer notes in italics or other distinct fonts. Ask yourself these questions: Does this information agree

Table 14.1 Note-Taking Strategies

Medium	Taking Notes	Linking to Source	Organization
Computer or Tablet	Most people end up taking notes from an article on a single page.	Identify the article's bibliographical information on the top of the page.	Identify the subject of the note directly above the note.
	Separate notes on the page.	Next to each note, indicate the author's name, an abbreviation of the source name, and the information's page number.	Later, it can be helpful to use the find function of your program to find all related notes and group them together by subject on the same page.
	Some people use a note-taking program that makes it easy to connect notes.		
	Avoid cutting and pasting from the source and clearly indicate all quoted material with quotes.		
Note Cards (4 × 6 cards)	Take one note per card.	Use a number linking to a bibliography with all information.	Identify the subject of the note card at the top for easy arrangement.
	Staple two cards with the same note together.	Identify author and abbreviated title on the bottom of the card.	Sometimes people assign a number or color to major topics.
	Be sure to mark quoted material with quotes.	Always record page number of information.	
Notebook or Yellow Pad	In many ways similar to computers.	Same as computers.	It can be difficult to try out different groupings using a notebook or yellow pad.
	Some people organize their notebooks by topic and take notes accordingly.		Some people cut out the notes to rearrange them.

with what I have learned so far? Does it suggest any new avenues to explore? Does it leave me with questions about what's been said? Although it may take a few minutes to record your responses to a note, this type of analysis will help you write a paper that reflects *your* opinions, decisions, and evaluations, not one that smacks of notes merely patched together from different sources.

Types of Notes

A note can be a summary, paraphrase, or quotation. *Whenever you use any kind of note in your paper, give proper credit to your source. Failure to do so results in plagiarism—that is, literary theft—a serious offence even when committed unintentionally. Just as a note can be in these forms, the draft of your paper may also include a summary, paraphrase, or quotation.*

Summary   A summary condenses original material, presenting its core ideas *in your own words.* In order to write an effective summary, you must have a good grasp of the information, and this comprehension ensures that you are ready to use the material in your paper. You may include brief quotations if you enclose them in quotation marks. A properly written summary presents the main points in their original order without distorting their emphasis or meaning, and it omits supporting details and repetition. Summaries, then, gather and focus the main points.

Begin the summarizing process by asking yourself, "What points does the author make that have an important bearing on my topic and purpose?" To answer, note especially the topic sentences in the original document, which often provide essential information. Copy the points in order; then condense and rewrite them in your own words. Figure 14.3 summarizes the John Stuart Mill passage that follows.

Such being the reasons which make it imperative that human beings should be free to form opinions, and to express their opinions without reserve; and such the baneful consequences to the intellectual, and through that to the moral nature of man, unless this liberty is either conceded, or asserted in spite of prohibition; let us next examine whether the same reasons do not require that men should be free to act upon their opinions—to carry these out in their lives, without hindrance, either physical or moral, from their fellow-men, so long as it is at their own risk and peril. This last proviso is of course indispensable. No one pretends that actions should be as free as opinions. On the contrary, even opinions lose their immunity, when the circumstances in which they are expressed are such as to constitute their expression a positive instigation to some mischievous act. An opinion that corn-dealers are starvers of the poor, or that private property is robbery, ought to be unmolested when simply circulated through the press, but may justly incur punishment when delivered orally to an excited mob assembled before the house of a corn-dealer, or when handed about among the same mob in the form of a placard. Acts, of whatever kind, which, without justifiable cause, do harm to others, may be, and in the more important cases absolutely require to be, controlled by the unfavourable sentiments, and, when needful, by the active interference of mankind. The liberty of the individual must be thus far limited; he must not make himself a nuisance to other people. But if he refrains from molesting others in what concerns them, and merely acts according to his own inclination and judgment in things which concern himself, the same reasons which show that opinion should be free, prove also that he should be allowed, without molestation, to carry his opinions into practice at his own cost. That mankind are not infallible; that their truths, for the most part, are only half-truths; that unity of opinion, unless resulting from the fullest and freest comparison of opposite opinions, is not desirable, and diversity not an evil, but a good, until mankind are much more capable than at present of recognising all sides of the truth, are principles applicable to men's modes of action, not less than to their opinions. As it is useful that while mankind are imperfect there should be different opinions, so is it that there should be different experiments of living; that free scope should be given to varieties of character, short of injury to others; and that the worth of different modes of life should be proved practically, when any one thinks fit to try them.

It is desirable, in short, that in things which do not primarily concern others, individuality should assert itself.

John Stuart Mill. *On Liberty*. 1859.

Individuality and society

According to John Stuart Mill, people should be able to form their own opinions and speak them freely. They should also be free to act upon these opinions without physical or moral interference from others as long as they are the only ones to pay the price for doing so. However, freedom of action and even of expression is not limitless; for example, a person should not be allowed to incite an agitated mob to violence. Society should leave people alone to follow their own desires unless their actions or speech cause harm to others. Assuming that people are not hurting others with their actions, having diverse ways of living is beneficial to a society.

Mill (100–102)

FIGURE 14.3 Summary

EXERCISE

1. Select two passages that your instructor approves from an essay in the Reader, and prepare summary note cards or computer notes for them.

2. Submit summaries of three pieces of information that you plan to use in writing your paper, along with complete versions of the original.

Paraphrase   To paraphrase is to restate material *in your own words* without attempting to condense it. Unlike a summary, a paraphrase allows you to present an essentially complete version of the original material. Be careful not to copy the original source nearly verbatim, changing only a word here and there. To do so is to plagiarize. To avoid this offence, follow a read, think, and write-without-looking-at-the-original strategy when you take notes so that you concentrate on recording the information in your own words. Then verify the accuracy of your notes by checking them against the original source. Here is a sample passage; Figure 14.4 is its paraphrase.

> Over time, more and more of life has become subject to the controls of knowledge. However, this is never a one-way process. Scientific investigation is continually increasing our knowledge. But if we are to make good use of this knowledge, we must not only rid our minds of old, superseded beliefs and fragments of magic, but also recognize new superstitions for what they are. Both are generated by our wishes, our fears, and our feelings of helplessness in difficult situations.
>
> Margaret Mead, "New Superstitions for Old," *A Way of Seeing*,
> New York: McCall, 1970, 266.

Combatting Superstitions

As time has passed, knowledge has asserted its sway over larger and larger segments of human life. But the process cuts two ways. Science is forever adding to the storehouse of human knowledge. Before we can take proper advantage of its gifts, however, we must purge our minds of old and outmoded convictions, while recognizing the true nature of modern superstitions. Both stem from our desires, our apprehensions, and our sense of impotence under difficult circumstances.

Mead (266)

FIGURE 14.4 Paraphrase

EXERCISE *Paraphrase a short passage from one of your textbooks. Submit a complete version of the passage with the assignment.*

Quotation   A quotation is an exact copy of a phrase, line, or passage of original material. Since your paper should demonstrate that you've mastered your sources, don't rely on quotations too much, and be careful not to string quotations together. The language and style of the quoted material will be different from your language and style, so you want to be sure that the quotation is smoothly integrated with your own language. Avoid overly long quotations where possible, and do not expect quotations to make your points for you. As a general rule, use quotations only when

- You really need support from an authority
- You need to back up your interpretation of a passage
- You need to show exactly what someone else has said in order to clarify how your perspective is different
- The original displays special elegance or force

Paraphrasing a passage as well written as the one below would rob it of much of its force.

> Man is himself, like the universe he inhabits, like the demoniacal stirring of the ooze from which he sprang, a tale of desolation. He walks in his mind from birth to death the long resounding shores of endless disillusionment. Finally, the commitment to life departs or turns to bitterness. But out of such desolation emerges the awful freedom to choose beyond the narrowly circumscribed circle that delimits the rational being.
>
> Loren Eiseley, *The Unexpected Universe,*
> New York: Harcourt Brace Jovanovich, 1969, 88.

Whether your instructor has asked for a full-blown research paper or an essay that incorporates a modest amount of research, you will want to ensure that the quotations you bring in are relevant, and you will also want to explain carefully how the quoted material relates to your larger point. When you introduce a quotation, do *not* simply say "My argument is supported by the following quotation," but alert the reader to what he or she should be looking for in the quotation.

- Alert the reader to the context of your quotation rather than dropping it in out of the blue. You might mention the occupation or credentials of the person or authority you are citing, as well as its significance for the point you are making. For example, if you were attempting to draw from a point that Neil Bissoondath makes in his essay "No Place Like Home" (Chapter 13), you might lead into the quotation as follows:

  > In his reflection on cultural identity, writer Neil Bissoondath argues that we need something much stronger than mere tolerance in Canadian society. While tolerance is passive, "acceptance is far more difficult, for it implies engagement" (quoted in Chapter 13 on page 308).

- Give your reader some idea of the issue or theme you are addressing *before* you include a long quotation. That way, the reader can be looking for the issue or theme as she or he reads the evidence. Consider the following:

  > While it may seem efficient to heat up frozen and instant foods for dinner, this efficiency comes at a price. As writer Sasha Chapman points out in her article titled "Manufacturing Taste," immigrants soon learn that Canadian "food culture doesn't leave much time for tradition at the table" (quoted in Chapter 7 on page 213).

Do not expect quotations to speak for themselves. In addition to leading into a quotation with your own words, follow a quotation with your own commentary, integrating it into your larger argument. Allow yourself to elaborate on the quotation rather than leaving it to dangle in mid-air. When you begin to do this, you may find that you think of more examples of your own to reinforce your argument. You may also notice subtle ways in which your ideas are different from those you are quoting. As you begin to explore more in this way, your essay will develop more richness and texture.

ORGANIZING AND OUTLINING

After taking notes from different sources, you may begin to envision a possible shape for your paper and plan the arrangement of your ideas. Some people work with a system of flexible notes (discussed earlier) to help them visualize a logical order for their chunks of material. Especially for longer papers, some find a formal outline to be a useful tool. The outline is a blueprint that shows the divisions and subdivisions of your paper, the order of your ideas, and the relationships between ideas and supporting details.

A formal outline follows a pattern such as the one shown below:

I.
   A.
   B.
      1.
      2.
         a.
         b.
II. . . .

You can see the significance of an item by its numeral, letter, or number designation and by its distance from the left-hand margin; the farther it's indented, the less important it is. All items with the same designation have roughly the same importance.

Developing Your Outline

Developing an outline involves arranging material from various sources in an appropriate manner. Sorting and re-sorting your notes is a good way to proceed. First, determine the main divisions of your paper, and then sort the notes by division. Next, review each grouping carefully to determine further subdivisions and sort it into smaller groupings. Finally, use the groupings to prepare your outline.

Many software programs, such as Word, provide options that facilitate outlining. With some programs you can compare two arrangements side by side; others enable you to call up your stored and organized notes on one side of the screen and create your outline on the other side.

Don't let software limitations cramp your exploration of possibilities. If your program allows you to compare two outlines but you'd like to compare more, make a second and, if necessary, a third printout; then examine them side by side. Similarly, if an outline includes more items than a single screen can accommodate, continue on a second screen and use printouts to check the complete product.

There are two types of formal outlines: *topic* and *sentence*. A topic outline presents all entries as words, short phrases, or short clauses. A sentence outline presents them as complete sentences. To emphasize the relationships among elements, items of equal importance have parallel phrasing. Although neither form is better than the other, a sentence outline includes more details and also your perspective on each idea. Many students first develop a topic outline, then do additional research, and finally polish and expand this version into a sentence outline. While it's easy to be sloppy in a topic outline, forming a sentence outline requires you to reach the kinds of conclusions that will become the backbone of your paper. The following segments of a topic outline and a sentence outline for a paper on prescription drug abuse illustrate the difference between the two.

Sample Topic Outline on Prescription Drug Abuse

   I. Prescription drug abuse problem
      A. Reasons for the problem
         1. Overpromotion
         2. Overprescription
         3. Easy availability from friends, Internet

      4. Multiple prescriptions from doctor-shopping
      5. Lack of awareness about dangers
   B. Ways to address the problem
      1. Education
      2. More monitoring of prescriptions

Sample Sentence Outline on Prescription Drug Abuse

II. Prescription pills such as anti-anxiety drugs, stimulants, and painkillers are being abused in Canada.
   A. Several factors account for the abuse of prescription drugs.
      1. Drug companies overpromote their products.
      2. Doctors may unnecessarily prescribe anti-anxiety pills, stimulants, and painkillers.
      3. People find these pills easily available from friends or the Internet.
      4. Some shop for doctors so they can get multiple prescriptions.
      5. Many perceive prescription drugs as safer than street drugs.
   B. The problem of prescription drug abuse can be addressed in two ways.
      1. People can become more educated about the potential dangers of prescription drugs.
      2. There can be more monitoring of prescriptions.

Note that the items in the sentence outline are followed by periods, but that those in the topic outline are not.

An outline can be a guide, but you will likely need to re-sort and rearrange your ideas as you try out various options. Here is a flexible notes outline that the criminology student Keith Jacques came up with for the first draft of his paper on electronic monitoring.

   I. Reasons why monitoring is used
     A. Serious crime problem and number of people in prisons
     B. High cost of prisons

  II. Brief history of electronic monitoring

 III. Types of monitoring systems
     A. Programmed-contact systems
     B. Continuous-contact systems
     C. Hybrid systems

 IV. Problems with these systems
     A. Practical problems
        1. Offenders' problems
        2. Transmission difficulties
     B. Legal problems
        1. Do the systems violate constitutional rights?
        2. "Net-widening" effect

  V. Effectiveness of electronic monitoring
     A. Effectiveness with low-risk offenders
     B. Cost effectiveness

 VI. Expanded use of monitoring likely

This version is marked by non-parallel structure and inadequate attention to some points. However, despite these weaknesses, it provided an adequate blueprint for the first draft of Keith's paper. After he wrote a draft, Keith was able to come up with a detailed formal sentence outline that helped him see where different ideas would be most strategically placed.

Sample Sentence Outline for Student Research Paper on Electronic Monitoring

Thesis statement: House arrest offers a choice of several monitoring systems, presents no insurmountable problems, proves effective in controlling low-risk offenders, and costs less than incarceration.

I. The use of house arrest stems from serious crime problems in both Canada and the United States.
   A. Extensive use of prisons in Canada and the United States has led to economic and social problems.
   B. Violent crimes committed by chronic offenders have led to tougher crime-control legislation.
   C. This legislation has increased the country's prison population and the cost of incarceration.
   D. As a result, many jurisdictions have adopted house arrest programs for low-risk offenders.

II. Electronic monitoring has a short history.
   A. The idea first appeared in the comic *Spider-Man*.
   B. A New Mexico judge asked computer companies to develop an electronic bracelet.
   C. Monitoring was first used in 1984 to control offenders, and the concept quickly spread across the United States.

III. Electronic monitoring devices fall into three categories.
   A. A programmed-contact system calls the offender's home during curfew periods and reports absences.
      1. A computer may simply record the offender's voice.
      2. A computer may compare the voice heard over the phone to a recording of the offender's voice.
      3. The offender may wear an encoded bracelet and insert it into a special telephone transmitter.
      4. A camera may transmit photos of the offender over telephone lines.

Sentence outline: Note use of complete sentences throughout, the periods following section and subsection markers, and the indentation arrangement.

B. A continuous-signal system requires the offender to wear a transmitter that sends uninterrupted electronic signals.

C. A hybrid system combines programmed-contact and continuous-signal techniques.

    1. The programmed-contact component usually includes voice- and photo-transmission units.

    2. Jurisdictions can tailor systems to their needs.

IV. Electronic systems have created practical and legal problems.

A. Practical problems include both difficulties experienced by offenders and transmission difficulties.

    1. Encoded bracelets can cause offenders discomfort and embarrassment.

    2. Telephone lines and objects in the offender's home can interfere with signal pickup.

B. Legal problems include possible infringement of rights and the net-widening effect.

    1. Charging surveillance fees and limiting surveillance to the least dangerous persons may infringe on offenders' equal protection rights.

    2. Monitoring may violate the right to privacy of others in offenders' homes.

    3. Net-widening can result in an excessive number of individuals under house arrest.

V. Electronic monitoring has proved effective with low-risk offenders.

A. Offenders successfully completed monitoring programs in B.C.

B. Monitoring costs less than incarceration.

VI. The advantages of house arrest over prison sentences should increase the use of this humane alternative in Canada.

AVOIDING PLAGIARISM

Plagiarism occurs when a writer uses another person's material without proper acknowledgement. Sometimes plagiarism is deliberate, but often it happens because students simply don't understand what must be acknowledged and documented. Deliberate or not, plagiarism is absolutely unacceptable. *Any summary, paraphrase, quotation, statistic, or graphic you include in your paper must be documented.* The only types of information that escape this requirement are those listed below.

1. *Common knowledge.* Common knowledge is information that most educated people would know. For instance, there's no need to document a statement that the Disney theme parks in California and Florida attract thousands of visitors each year. However, if you include precise daily, monthly, or yearly figures, then documentation is necessary.

2. *Your own conclusions.* As you write your paper, you'll incorporate your own conclusions at various points. Such comments require no documentation. The same holds true for your own research. If you polled students on a campus issue, simply present the findings as your own.

3. *Facts found in many sources.* Facts such as the year of Shakespeare's death, the size of the 2001 national budget surplus, and the location of the Taj Mahal need not be documented. However, where there may be disputes about the facts in question (such as the size of the 2003 deficit) or some need to enforce the credibility of your figures, provide the source for your facts. If you are not certain that something is common knowledge, indicate your source.

4. *Standard terms.* Terms widely used in a particular field require no documentation. Examples include such computer terms as *mouse*, *CD-ROM*, and *download*.

Any piece of information not set off with quotation marks must be in your own words. Otherwise, even though you name your source, you plagiarize by stealing the original phrasing.

The following passages illustrate the improper and proper use of source material.

Original Passage

One might contend, of course, that our country's biological diversity is so great and the land is so developed—so criss-crossed with the works of man—that it will soon be hard to build a dam anywhere without endangering some species. But as we develop a national inventory of endangered species, we certainly can plan our *necessary* development so as to exterminate the smallest number possible.

> James L. Buckley, "Three Cheers for the Snail Darter,"
> *National Review*, September 14, 1979: 1144–45. Print.

■ Plagiarism

Our country's biological diversity is so great and the land is so developed that it will soon be hard to build a dam anywhere without endangering some species. But as we develop a national inventory of endangered species, we certainly can plan our necessary development so as to exterminate the smallest number possible.

This writer clearly plagiarizes. The absence of Buckley's name and the failure to enclose his words in quotation marks create the impression that this passage is the student's own work.

■ Plagiarism

Given the extensive diversity of species in America, development such as the construction of dams is likely to endanger some species, whether it is a rare plant, a species of frog, or a rare variety of fish. By creating a database of endangered species, however, we can facilitate a planning process that will place the minimum number of species at risk.

Although this writer uses original language, the absence of documentation suggests that these ideas are the student's without any recognition of Buckley's contribution. Despite the paraphrase, this is still plagiarism.

■ Plagiarism

> Our country's biological diversity is so great and the land so developed that in the near future we may pose a threat to some creature whenever we construct a dam. By developing a national inventory of endangered species, however, we can plan necessary development so as to preserve as many species as possible (Buckley 1144).

This version credits the ideas to Buckley, but the student has plagiarized by failing to put quotation marks around the phrasing (underlined here) that was copied from the original. As a result, readers will think that the passage represents the student's own wording.

■ Proper Use of Original

> America has so many kinds of plants and animals, and it is so built up, that in the near future we may pose a threat to some living thing just by damming some waterway. If, however, we knew which of our nation's plants and animals were threatened, we could use this information to preserve as many species as we can (Buckley 1144).

This student has identified the author and used her own words. As a result, no plagiarism occurs.

Plagiarism is a serious offence because it robs the original writer of recognition. Students caught plagiarizing risk failure in the course or perhaps suspension from school. Whenever you are unsure whether material requires documentation, supply a reference.

Integrating Sources

Two main systems for formatting and documenting library research papers are in common use: the Modern Language Association (MLA) system, favoured by many English and humanities instructors, and the American Psychological Association (APA) system, used by many social science and psychology instructors. Chapters 16 and 17 provide technical guidelines for using these two styles, and you can also refer to a number of online links such as formatting and style guides at OWL (online writing lab at Purdue). Help with formatting a third style of documentation—the Chicago Manual of Style, which is used mainly in history—can be found online.

Whatever style of documentation you are using, there are some general principles to follow. You should consistently seek to avoid plagiarism by indicating where you got your information from even if you did not quote it. The following observations are related to the MLA format. You can signal the author before the information. For a more detailed account of summarizing and paraphrasing, see the section on note taking on pages 332–334.

Document Paraphrases as Well as Quotations   If you paraphrase a section, be careful not to directly quote large sections. You can document paraphrases similar to other information, but it is important to clearly indicate where the paraphrase ends. Sometimes it is useful to signal that you are paraphrasing.

> To paraphrase Mark Twain, . . . (32)

Quotations are always documented. Shorter quotations of less than five lines, are marked by quotation marks. You may start by signalling the author of the quote: The economist John Mayer argues that ". . ." (46). Or you may place the identifying information directly after the quotation . . . (Mayer 46).

Longer quotations are indented (ten spaces for MLA and five for APA) without quotation marks. Again, you should provide the identifying source information. Refer to the appropriate chapter for the documentation style you are using.

Provide Context for Quotations   Always provide some context for material that you quote. Various options exist. When you quote from a source for the first time, you might provide the author's full name and the source of the quotation, perhaps indicating the author's expertise as well. The passage just above omits the author's expertise; the passage below includes it.

> Writing in *Newsweek* magazine, Riena Gross, chief psychiatric social worker at Illinois Medical Center in Chicago, said, "Kids have no real sense that they belong anywhere or to anyone as they did ten or fifteen years ago. Parents have loosened the reins, and kids are kind of floundering" (74).

Or you might note the event prompting the quotation and then the author's name.

> Addressing a seminar at the University of Toronto, Dr. Joseph Pomeranz speculated that "acupuncture may work by activating a neural pain suppression mechanism in the brain" (324).

On other occasions, you might note only the author's full name and expertise.

> Economist Richard M. Cybert, president of Carnegie Mellon University, offers the following sad prediction about the steel industry's future: "It will never be as large an industry as it has been. There are a lot of plants that will never come back and many laborers that will never be rehired" (43).

When quoting from a source with no author given, introduce the quotation with the name of the source.

> Commenting on the problems that law enforcement personnel have in coping with computer crime, *Credit and Financial Management* magazine pointed out, "A computer crime can be committed in three hundredths of a second, and the criminal can be thousands of miles from the 'scene,' using a telephone" ("Computer Crime" 43).

ETHICAL ISSUES

When you present information you've gathered from a variety of sources, you want to proceed in an ethically responsible way. Just as you must give credit to the sources that you use, it is also important not to distort the meaning of other people's words or ignore evidence with which you don't agree. As you consider the ethical dimension of your argument, consider the following questions.

- Have I carefully researched my topic so that my conclusions are well founded? Imagine the consequences if slipshod testing by an automobile company led to the erroneous conclusion that the steering mechanism on one of its models met current safety standards.

- Have I adequately acknowledged any evidence that runs counter to the conclusions I draw? A paper that stresses the advantages of charter schools but deliberately avoids mentioning their disadvantages is unbalanced somewhat deceptive.

- Have I properly documented my sources? Using someone else's words or ideas without giving proper credit is a form of academic dishonesty.

- Have I honestly represented the authority of my sources? If you read an article touting almond extract as a cure for cancer that was written by a practising foot doctor, it would be dishonest to suggest that the article was written by a "prominent research scientist." Refer to someone as an "expert" only when that person's credentials warrant the label.

- Could my information have an undesirable effect on readers? If so, how can I address their concerns? A report describing a new antibiotic-resistant strain of tuberculosis might alarm some readers, and therefore the writer could provide appropriate reassurances of the limited risk to most people.

WRITING YOUR RESEARCH PAPER

A research paper is not simply a series of quotations, paraphrases, and summaries strung together. Certainly, you use the material of others, but *you* select and organize it according to *your purpose*. *You* develop insights, and *you* draw conclusions about what you've read. You can best express your conclusions by setting your notes aside, stepping back to gain some perspective, and then expressing your sense of what you've learned. Like all forms of writing, research papers are written for a clearly defined purpose and aimed at a particular audience.

Writing the First Draft

As with other essays you have written, you will need to clarify a thesis for your research paper. You have already drafted a tentative thesis, and now you need to refine or revise it to accommodate any changes in your perspective on the topic. Position the thesis in the introductory part of your paper unless you're analyzing a problem or recommending a solution; then you might hold back the thesis until later in the essay. If you do hold it back, state the problem clearly at the outset. Because of the paper's length, it's a good idea to reveal your organizational plan in your introductory section.

Students follow different approaches when writing a draft. Some follow the outline section by section, entering their notes and any thoughts that previously occurred to them, then go through everything again and add material. Others finish off one section before moving on to the next. Some develop ideas by focusing on their notes and then developing thoughts that elaborate on them; others develop their ideas first and then plug in their notes afterwards. Follow the procedure that works best for you.

If you discover that it might be better to introduce an item earlier than you intended, go ahead. Just be sure to check your organization later. As you write, think of selecting appropriate material from your notes to support your conclusions, not just throwing your quotations and summaries together willy-nilly. Blend the material from your notes with your own assessments and commentary, but be sure to distinguish between your ideas and other people's ideas throughout.

Don't worry if the style bumps along or connections aren't always clear at first. When you revise, you can improve coherence by connecting major sections with transitional paragraphs to bridge the material already discussed and prepare the reader for what will follow. You can also plug in transitional or topic sentences at the beginning of paragraphs that need more focus. Of course, you will need to know how to document your sources properly, handle quotations, and avoid plagiarism—that is, failing to give credit to others for their words or ideas, as discussed earlier.

On occasion you may want to include supplementary information that would interrupt the flow of thought if you placed it in the paper. When this happens, use an *explanatory note*.[1] A typical explanatory note might clarify or elaborate on a point, discuss some side issue, or define a term used in a specialized way.

When you finish writing, let this version sit for a day or two. Then revise it, just as you would with a shorter essay. Keep track of all your sources so that preparing the bibliography goes smoothly.

DEVELOPING YOUR RESEARCH PAPER	■ Identify audience and purpose. ■ Brainstorm related questions. ■ Research using available index. ■ Narrow or adjust your topic based on initial research and reading. ■ Identify key related material and take appropriate notes. ■ Label notes by subject. ■ Consider writing a quick draft without looking at notes to discover your direction. ■ Create an outline. ■ Connect notes to outline and organize notes. ■ Begin writing a draft from your outline.

[1] This is an explanatory note. Position it at the bottom of the page, spaced four lines away from the main text. If more than one note occurs on a page, double-space between them. If the note carries over to the next page, separate it from your text with a solid, full-length line. Put two spaces above the line and two spaces below it.

Using Images, Illustrations, and Graphs

Computer programs make it easy to import photographs, illustrations, and graphs into an essay and report. Visuals can be useful. An essay on different kinds of cats would be enhanced by pictures of cats. The best way to explain the bones in the skull is by using a labelled drawing. Complicated numbers can be presented best through appropriate graphs or charts.

General Principles for Using Visuals

- **Use visuals only when they help.** Excess visuals detract from a text; visuals should be used when they are the best way of presenting the information. Clichéd clip art only detracts from important messages.
- **Visuals should fit the text.** Visuals shouldn't just be thrown in. Instead, they should have a connection to nearby text so that the meanings are related.
- **Visuals need to be explained.** Visuals don't always stand on their own. You need to explain to readers why they should look at the visual and direct their attention to what they should notice. With graphs and tables, it is helpful to explain first what to look for in the visual and then, after the visual, identify the major conclusion the readers could reach from the visual.
- **Visuals often need a title.** To direct the reader's attention, label all visuals. The title should tell the story of the visual.
- **Place visuals so they don't break up the text.** You want your page to be attractive but not distracting. Visuals need to be positioned so the page looks good but the flow of the text is not seriously interrupted.
- **Visuals should be honest.** It is important to represent the data fairly and not distort the image or graph to slant the information.

Pictures The use of a scanner or digital camera makes it easy to import pictures, which can spice up the text. It is very easy to find images on the Internet related to your topic that you can download and incorporate into your paper. If you use pictures, make certain they are clear and simple. Readers shouldn't have to spend time trying to decipher the picture. Always document the source of any image you use.

Tables Including tables with columns and rows is an excellent way of comparing information such as the features of different computers, the quantity of sales, or even the quality of different employees. Make certain your table is clearly labelled. See Table 14.2 for an example.

Pie Charts Pie charts are an excellent way to present percentages or quantities of a whole. Figure 14.5 is a sample pie chart.

Bar Graphs Bar graphs can help you present and compare data that aren't a continuous trend, as Figure 14.6 shows.

Line Graphs Line graphs are an excellent way to show data that are continuous over time and show trends effectively. See Figure 14.7 for an example.

Table 14.2 Use Different Classroom Media for Different Purposes

Features	Blackboard	Overhead	PowerPoint
Class Time Used	Extensive; text written out in class	Minimal; prepared before class	Minimal; prepared before class
Equipment Required	Usually in every classroom	In most classrooms or easily obtained	Limited by number of computers and screens
Information Presented	Text and hand-drawn images or low-resolution graphs	Text and images or graphs; variable resolutions	All text and visuals with good resolution
Flexibility in Classroom Environment	Plans can be easily changed; readily accepts new direction and student input	Limited flexibility: order can be varied between overheads; can write on blank overheads	Limited: hard to change order of presentation or enter new input

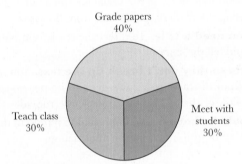

FIGURE 14.5 How Teachers Use Their Time

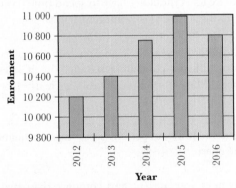

FIGURE 14.6 Student Enrolment by Year

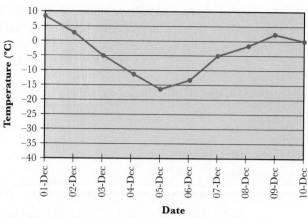

FIGURE 14.7 Temperatures at Noon Show Cold Spell

Headers, Numbered Lists, and Bullets

Information in longer reports is not always presented in an unbroken stream of text. You can use a number of devices to help readers navigate and understand the information.

- **Bold headings and subheadings can guide the reader to different sections of the text.** When the sections of a longer report, or even a shorter business memo, can be broken into distinct sections, it can be helpful to label those sections with bold words or phrases that will direct the reader's attention. This text uses headings and subheadings, and so do some of the articles in the Reader.

- **Lists can be a useful way to present organized information.** Steps in a process, several recommendations, or the identification of important qualities can all be well represented by an indented list. The discussion questions in this text are all presented as numbered lists.

- **Bullets are used when listed information shouldn't be numbered because there is no implied sequence.** The general principles for using visuals in this section are presented as a bulleted list. Lists and bullets should use parallelism, the same grammatical form.

Revising and Formatting

Students often hesitate to revise research papers because their length makes the task seem daunting, but the cut and paste functions on programs such as Word allow you to isolate sections and experiment with them; move large sections of the text around; or, if you used separate files for different sections, change transitions to reflect different orders. When you make such changes, check to see that you maintain the flow of the paper. An adjustment in one section must mesh logically and stylistically with what precedes and follows. Reviewing a printout offers the best opportunity to check your paper's continuity. As you revise, always keep copies of earlier versions. Some part that seemed ineffective may fill a gap or take on a new look in view of your changes.

Finally, be sure to take advantage of the formatting capabilities of your software. Most programs will position page numbers, set margins properly, and add your name at the top of each page. Some programs will also indent bibliographic entries properly. However, don't neglect your instructor's specifications with regard to spacing, print style, and the like.

Follow the revision guidelines in Chapter 4. In addition, verify that you have:

- Included all key information
- Clearly organized your material
- Not overloaded your paper with quotations
- Worked in your own observations
- Put in-text documentation and source information in the proper form

Writing Your Research Paper Checklist

Search Checklist

- Brainstorm to focus your topic.
- Get an overview by searching general references such as encyclopedias.
- Search your library for books.
     Use either key-term or subject searches using a computer catalogue.
     Copy or print out the call number that locates the book.
     Scan the books in your located section for unexpected finds.

- Search databases that fit your topic and assignment.
     Use either key-term or subject searches.
     Use the headings you find to narrow or guide your search.
     Print or copy the title of the articles, the author, the magazine, the volume number, the page number, the medium of publication of your source, and the date.

- Find the hard copy, microfiche, or microfilm version of your article.
- Search the Internet using a search engine such as Google or Yahoo.

     Try several combinations of terms or modify them to narrow a search.
     Assess the credibility of all Internet material based on the source for the site, author, quality of the web pages, and consistency with other credible information.
     Be sure to copy or print out the URL, author (if any), and title (if any).

Taking Notes Checklist

- Evaluate your source by author's qualifications, publication's credibility, and obvious bias.
- Take notes using index cards or in an electronic file.
     Record the date of access.
     Keep track of source and page number for each note.
     Record the medium of publication for each source.
     Cross-reference notes with bibliography cards.
     Give a title to each note card that identifies the note's topic.

■ Respond as you take notes with your own thoughts and observations.

■ Consciously summarize, paraphrase in your own words, or quote in your notes.

 If you are quoting directly, be sure to set off the beginning and ending of the quote.

■ Always consciously work to avoid plagiarism.

 Always carefully record your sources for notes.
 Do not simply change a few words in a paraphrase.
 Do not forget to identify the beginning and end of quotations when you quote.

Drafting Your Paper Checklist

■ Take steps to integrate your information.

 Read over your notes.
 Possibly write a brief draft without looking at your notes.

■ Write an outline.

 Determine the main divisions of your paper.
 Read note cards for subdivisions.
 Detail either a sentence outline or a topic outline.

■ Key your note cards to your outline.

■ Determine if you need to perform additional research.

■ Draft your paper in sections.

 Work to keep the paper in your own voice.
 Don't get stuck on the introduction. Just write.
 Use your notes to support your claims, but don't just cut and paste.
 Be sure to document as you write.
 Avoid plagiarism.
 Create deliberate transitions between sections.
 Go back and rework the introduction and conclusion.
 Document everything carefully using the instructions provided in Chapter 16.

Revising Your Draft Checklist

■ Do not be afraid to make extensive changes.

■ Read and change the paper with an eye to your original purpose.

■ Get feedback from other readers.

■ Check for material that doesn't fit and needs to be cut.

■ Check for holes that may require additional research, and do it if needed.

■ Check your notes to see that you didn't leave out something important.

■ Check to see that the paper is easy to follow.

■ Smooth your transitions and add transition paragraphs where needed.

■ Make certain the draft is in a consistent voice.

SAMPLE MLA STUDENT RESEARCH PAPER

Sample Student Research Argument Using MLA Style

Bottled Troubled Water

Scott Lemanski

1   A disease has swept over our nation. It's called consumeritis, and its symptoms, among many others, include sluggishness, chronic apathy, alienation, obesity, and a constant, nagging feeling that there is something missing from our lives. We temporarily relieve these symptoms, or at least distract ourselves from them, by seeing or hearing an advertisement, label, or slogan that convinces us that we absolutely need some useless product, then call a toll-free number to place an order or drive over to the local megamart to buy it, along with a few other superfluous items we feel that we just can't do without. Perhaps the most senseless product with which we've been treating our consumeritis in recent years is that clear, cool, tasteless drink that comes in a plastic container—bottled water. It comes in many attractive shapes and sizes from mountain springs and glaciers all over the world, promising us better health and a convenient way to attain it. The thought of drinking tap water for some people today is simply ridiculous because of the commonly held belief that it's just not pure enough. But do we really know how pure our beloved bottled water is? How often do we think about the impact our obsession with bottled water is having on the world or how much we actually benefit from such a product? The harm done to our environment, the waste of our resources, and the potential health risks caused by bottled water's mass production, distribution, and consumption far outweigh its possible benefits.

2   Our thirst for bottled water has become seemingly unquenchable, and as it grows, so does its impact on our environment. According to Tony Azios in his article "The Battle over Bottled vs. Tap Water," over 25 billion plastic water bottles per year are sold in the United States (3). Since 2002, production has increased an average of 9% per year; and since 2003, water has become the highest-selling commercial drink, second only to soft drinks (Azios 1). In "Bottled Water: Pure Drink or Pure Hype?" the National Resources Defense Council (NRDC) reports that "in 2006, the equivalent of 2 billion half-liter bottles of water were

shipped to U.S. ports, creating thousands of tons of global-warming pollution and other air pollution" (par. 7). The transport of bottled water that year from eastern Europe to New York contributed approximately 3,800 tons of global-warming pollution to the atmosphere, while the shipping of 18 million gallons of bottled water from Fiji to California produced about 2,500 tons of such pollution (par. 7).

Uses statistical evidence from more than one source for support. Identifies consequence of practice.

3   Given the virtually incomprehensible quantities of bottled water manufactured, transported, bought, and sold, it is no surprise that the waste from it amounts to alarmingly large numbers. In some U.S. states, we are required by law to pay a small deposit when purchasing plastic soda bottles, which works quite well as an incentive to bring them back for recycling. The same is not true for bottled water, although the bottles are recyclable. The NDRC notes that, "only about 13% of the bottles we use get recycled. In 2005, 2 million tons of plastic water bottles ended up clogging up landfills" (par. 7). Oil, however ultimately damaging to the future of our world it may be, is an ever-increasingly precious resource, now perhaps more than ever, and we're wasting that on bottled water, too. Azios points out that in 2006, "more than 17 million barrels of oil (not including fuel for transportation) were used in plastic bottle production" (3). Even water, arguably our most precious resource, is used in copious amounts in the production. Water is necessary to cool machinery in power plants and molds that form plastic parts, so when taking into account the huge volume of plastic water bottles made every year, it's no wonder that "it takes about 3 liters of water to produce 1 liter of bottled water" (3). It's also no wonder, with all the energy and resources wasted, that we end up paying 2,000 times more for a liter of bottled water than we would a liter of tap water (2).

Topic sentence identifies the problem of large quantities of waste.

Blends paraphrase and quoted phrase from source.

When this source is identified, only author's last name is used since the full name was given earlier.

Documents statistics concerning quantity of waste.
Blends paraphrase and quoted phrase from source.

4   While it's obvious we are willing to pay entirely too much money for it, are we also willing to gamble our health on bottled water? Since so many different brands of bottled water have words on their labels such as pure or natural, we are led to believe that drinking bottled water is a choice that will be a benefit to our health. It would be prudent, then, to become educated on some of the risks involved. According to Janet Jemmott in "Bottled Water vs. Tap Water," most of the bottles are made of a plastic called polyethylene terepthalate, or PET, which is supposed to be generally safe, but if heated, the plastic could leach chemicals into the water (3). There are hazards linked to these chemicals, but "the exact health risks are unknown" (3). Consequently,

Uses question in student writer's own voice to suggest next possible negative consequence.

Uses introductory tag before paraphrase.

Provides causal analysis of possible health risk.

we are taking a chance with our health if we, for example, leave a bottle in a hot car all day long and later return to drink it. Though a consensus hasn't been reached on the risks of PET chemicals, Jemmott notes that some findings may be unsettling.

Develops causal analysis of possible health risk further.

5   In the meantime, experts have raised a warning flag about a few specific chemicals. Antimony is a potentially toxic material used in making PET. Last year, scientists in Germany found that the longer a bottle of water sits around (in a store, in your home), the more antimony it develops. High concentrations of antimony can cause nausea, vomiting, and diarrhea. In the study, levels found were below those set as safe by the EPA, but it's a topic that needs more research (Jemmott 3).

Identifies reader's objection and raises questions for reader to ponder.

6   Many of us are willing to take our chances with the possible health risks associated with bottled water because, if nothing else, we see it as such a convenient way to obtain the water we need to drink every day. Is it really more convenient to go to the store and spend entirely too much money on a bottle of water than it is to simply fill a glass at home at the faucet? If we want to take it with us while we're out, there are plenty of containers that we can purchase for just such a purpose. Advertisers have cleverly convinced us that somehow it's more convenient to go out of our way to buy what they're selling than it is to take a moment and think about whether we truly need it or not. Do we really need to buy a product such as bottled water?

Acknowledges next possible objection.

Acknowledges legitimacy of reader's concerns.

Answers objection with sentence that introduces key passage from official report.

7   Many of us cite the most compelling reason to drink bottled water, besides convenience, is the concern over impurities in the water that comes out of our faucets and drinking fountains. It is a legitimate concern but one that doesn't necessarily have to result in the automatic response of reaching for the bottle. In "Water Quality: Bottled Water," the Cornell University Cooperative Extension says that tap water can and often does contain contaminants in varying concentrations, such as microorganisms, including pathogens, and sulfur compounds, including metals and metalloids, such as arsenic, lead and iron, just to name a few. However, the regulation of tap water is somewhat more reliable and transparent:

Block quotation longer than four lines of text has no quotation marks, but is set off from text, indented 10 spaces from the margin, and double spaced. Note different placement of period before author's name.

Tap water from municipal drinking water treatment plant is regulated by the U.S. Environmental Protection Agency (EPA) ... for close to a hundred chemicals and characteristics, [while] bottled water sold across state lines is regulated by the U.S. Food and Drug Administration (FDA). Your supplier must notify the community if there are problems with the water supply. Municipal plants are generally subject to much more frequent testing and inspection and must report test results to the public. (Cornell)

Furthermore, since more than 25% of the bottled water comes from a municipal source (Jemmott 4), there is a sizable chance that the water in the bottles from which we drink is just as contaminated as the water that comes out of the faucet in our kitchen sink.

8   The fluoridation of tap water is another positive health benefit. Most of us have seen enough television toothpaste commercials go uncontested for long enough to be reasonably confident in fluoride's ability to help prevent tooth decay. Tap water is generally fluoridated, while most bottled water is not, and since many children are drinking more bottled water than tap water, this could explain the current rise in tooth decay among children (Jemmott 5).

9   Recently in the *USA Today* article "AP: Drugs Show Up in Americans' Water," it has been reported that quite a few pharmaceuticals, "including antibiotics, anti-convulsants, mood stabilizers and sex hormones have been found in the water supply of at least 41 million Americans" (Donn, Mendoza, and Prichard). Though utilities say their water is safe and that the levels of the drugs found are measured in parts per billion or trillion, "far below the levels of a medical dose … [their presence is] heightening worries among scientists of long-term consequences to human health" (Donn, Mendoza, and Pritchard). Though these concerns are certainly valid, they still don't warrant turning to bottled water as the solution to the problem. Going back to the point Cornell University made about water regulation, it follows that it is unlikely that bottled water companies are doing the sort of rigorous testing of their water for substances such as pharmaceuticals that could ease our concerns on this matter; and even if they were, would they report it to the public? Also, if over 25% of bottled water comes from municipal sources, what percentage of that percentage might contain such pharmaceuticals?

10   "In general, toxins in drinking water don't exceed EPA limits" (Jemmott 5). However, there are steps we can take to inform ourselves of and reduce the risks of tap water contamination. A water quality or consumer confidence report is generally sent out to all customers of local water companies once a year, and it will show if any contaminants

---

Author is identified within the text.

Topic sentence in writer's own words helps make transitions easier to follow.

Offers evidence for claim that may surprise many.

Further acknowledges concern.

Uses logic to raise question about whether bottled water would be subjected to rigorous testing.

Topic sentence the recommends ways to reduce risk of health hazards with tap water.

have gone over the maximum allowable levels (5). We can also have our water tested by a state-certified lab (5). There are also many varieties of tap-water filters we can buy to purify the water coming out of our taps, but in order to ensure their effectiveness, they should be "approved by NSF, Underwriters Laboratories, or the Water Quality Association" (5). If after taking all this information into account, you still feel it necessary to replace tap water with bottled water, you can at least look for a brand that comes from a local source, so as to at least limit the environmental impact and waste or resources caused by long-distance mass transport. Also, look for brands with "NSF certification or [those that] belong to the IBWA. Check out the lists at NSF.org or bottledwater.org, or look at the bottle itself" for the NSF logo (5).

11   In our consumerist society, where so many things are available to us and convenience often seems to be of the greatest importance, it's easy to forget that everything we do in our personal lives has a direct or indirect effect on the rest of the world and our planet. According to scientist and environmentalist David Suzuki, the practice of shipping water from France to Canada is absurd: "I don't believe for a minute that French water is better than Canadian water. I think that we've got to drink the water that comes out of our taps, and if we don't trust it, we ought to be raising hell about that." If we go on ignoring growing environmental threats and the resources we're wasting, the consequences will affect us all. No absolute cure has been found for consumeritis, but we can take steps to minimize its impact by taking a little time out from our overly busy lives and trying to think rationally about the implications of something so seemingly harmless as drinking bottled water. The convenience and minimal, if any, health benefits we receive from drinking bottled water don't come close to justifying the harm it causes the earth and perhaps ourselves.

Offers alternative recommendation for readers who may not be quite willing to give up habit altogether.

Returns to the term con-sumeritis introduced in the first paragraph and makes recommendation to reader.

Reinforces thesis that the costs of drinking bottled water outweigh any perceived benefits.

Work Cited

Azios, Tony. "The Battle over Bottled vs. Tap Water." *Christian Science Monitor*. 17 Jan. 2008. Web. 17 Mar. 2008.

Cornell University Cooperative Extension. "Water Quality: Bottled Water." *Cornell University Cooperative Extension*. 13 Feb. 2008. Web. 20 Mar. 2008.

Donn, Jeff, Martha Mendoza, and Justin Prichard. "AP: Drugs Show Up in Americans' Water." USAToday.com. 9 Mar. 2008. Web. 20 Mar. 2008.

Jemmott, Janet Majeski. "Rethink What You Drink: Growing Thirst." *Reader's Digest*. 10 Jan. 2008. Web. 17 Mar. 2008.

"National Resources Defense Council: Bottled Water FAQ." NRDC: The Earth's Best Defense. 12 Sept. 2007. Web. 17 Mar. 2008.

Suzuki, David. "Buying Bottled Water Is Wrong, says Suzuki." *CBC News*. 1 Feb. 2007. Web. 14 July 2011.

DISCUSSION QUESTIONS

1. This essay tries to convince many readers to give up a common habit. Often readers can be defensive with such an approach. How does this writer lessen the possibility of reader resistance and defensiveness?

2. How does this author's argument appeal to his readers' concerns and values, assuming that many who drink bottled water are concerned about the environment and are health conscious?

3. Identify the forms of evidence that the writer uses.

4. Why does the writer offer some suggestions for buying bottled water in paragraph 10 when the entire paper is dedicated to discouraging the practice?

5. Notice where the writer proceeds, in part, by the use of questions and answers. To what extent does this questioning strategy seem effective? Explain.

TOWARD KEY INSIGHTS

What are the reasons that you or others you know do or do not drink commercially bottled water? Does this essay make you think about bottled water in a new way? Why or why not?

It is not only laws, but also social norms that govern certain habits that we do or do not find culturally acceptable on a large scale. These norms may change over time—for example, norms around smoking in public places, drinking while driving, wearing a seat belt, picking up after your dog, or spanking children as a form of discipline. Are there other examples you can think of? What contributed to these changing cultural norms?

SUGGESTION FOR WRITING
Do some research around a habit of convenience or consumption that many in our culture have fallen into, but that you find troubling for environmental or other reasons. Then draw up an argument similar to the one above, in which you use rational, ethical, and/or emotional appeals to persuade your audience to rethink or even stop this habit. Some examples include an argument against the regular purchase of takeout food in plastic containers, casual wasting of water in everyday tasks, buying canned goods or some other kind of product, or using chemicals to kill weeds on your lawn.

APA STUDENT RESEARCH PAPER

Running head in all caps is used on the top of pages.

Author's name.

Affiliation, which could be your course and instructor name.

INSTANT COMMUNICATION   1

Instant Communication Does Not Ensure Good Communication

Bruce Gilchrist

Ferris State University

Abstract Page

A separate page for abstract.

Running head.

Abstract, a brief objective summary of the paper's main argument.

Key words. Words that would help reader find the article if they were searching on a database.

INSTANT COMMUNICATION   2

Abstract

This review of the literature finds that increased rates of communication from voice mail, cellular phones, e-mail, and other sources results in increased levels of stress and decreased productivity. Technostress includes interruptions and the perceived demand for immediate response to the stress. Studies have found that the interruption negatively affects productivity and even IQ. Defense mechanisms for instant communication need to be adopted as coping strategies.

Keywords: instant communication, e-mail, text messaging, technostress, productivity.

Start of body, repeats running head.

Title at top of page.

Establishes broad context and leads into thesis.

Support with short quote, so documented authors' last names, date of publication, and page number.

1

INSTANT COMMUNICATION   3

Instant Communication Does Not Ensure Good Communication

The technological revolution ushered many new communications technologies and devices into the modern office over the past 25 years. "Every day brings yet another new communication device, software program, or piece of computer hardware that workers have to know, need to use, or must have to do their job" (Weil & Rosen, 1999, p. 56). The popularity of these devices at the office and declining costs eventually led to their acceptance for personal use outside the office. After all, who wouldn't want to take advantage of the benefits they offer? The fax machine reduces dependence on the postal system for moving paper documents. Voice mail, pagers, and cell phones make it possible to communicate with labour- and others even when they are away from their home or office telephones: Newer technologies such as e-mail and electronic text messaging allow individuals to remain connected with business associates, family, and friends on an almost perpetual basis.

Each new electronic communications gadget is hyped by its creator as yet another labor- and time-saving device. Marketing efforts and corporate management describe these devices almost as if they possess magical powers. Simply by using these devices, one is suddenly able to do more with less. Less time, less manual labor, lower costs, and so on. But are the users of these communications technologies really reaping the benefits that they were promised? Or have the negative aspects of these technologies been masked by clever marketing campaigns and corporate policies? Whether used professionally, personally, or both, many end users of these technologies are unaware of the negative effects to which they are subjecting themselves. Excessive or uncontrolled use of fax machines, voice mail, pagers, cellular phones, e-mail, and text messaging can lead to increased stress levels and decreased productivity.

Speaking in general terms, the first problem presented by instant communication technologies is that they contribute to a specialized form of stress known as technostress. The term was first defined in 1983 by clinical psychologist Craig Brod as "a modern disease of adaptation caused by an inability to cope with the new computer technologies in a healthy manner" (as cited in Genco, 2000, p. 1). Brod's original definition was primarily addressing the personal computer revolution and has since been modified to be more inclusive of newer forms of technology. In 1997, clinical psychologists Michelle Weil and Larry Rosen enhanced the definition of technostress to include "'any negative impact on attitudes, thoughts, behaviors, or body psychology caused directly or indirectly by technology'" (p. 1). Weil further explains technostress as "our reaction to technology and how we are changing due to its influence" (p. 1). Using these expanded definitions it is not difficult to conclude that instant communication technologies can indeed be a source of technostress.

2

3

States common knowledge rationale for new technologies.

Uses questions to hook reader and offer transition to main point.

Introduces thesis statement.

Transition, offers topic for first section. Definition is offered in this paragraph using a narrative history of the term.

Short quotation documented.

4

Topic sentence identifies effect of speed in communication that is also a cause of stress.

Draws on personal evidence, with clarification of credentials to make claims credible.

The simplest form of technostress produced by instant communication technologies is the stream of constant interruptions they ultimately produce. As an information technology support specialist, I often find myself working on complex technical problems that require my full attention and mental concentration. Interruptions from pagers, cell phones, and text messaging are distracting, as they force me to break away from the task at hand to deal with the incoming communication. Not only do these distractions lengthen the time necessary to complete a task, but they can also introduce errors, as my attention is not fully focused on a single task.

5

Transition to discussion of effect.

Introduces support from interviews and personal communication to develop claim.

Adding to this stress is the prevailing attitude that because these technologies provide for instant communication, one should receive an instant response to any messages they send. For me, having to interrupt the task at hand and respond to these incoming messages is indeed disruptive and can lower my productivity when the volume of messages becomes excessive. Personal interviews revealed that my views are shared by others as well. One interviewee stated his biggest complaint is that the constant stream of interruptions brought on by pagers, cell phones, and e-mail make it difficult for him to prioritize or sometimes even complete tasks (L. Murphy, personal communication, March 25, 2005). He further added that not only does everyone think their message is a top priority, they are also unaware of how many other messages the recipient already has waiting for a response. Another respondent criticizes overzealous management for adding to the problem. In a crisis situation, management frequently requests status updates via some form of instant communication. What they fail to realize is that every message they send requires the recipient to divert their focus away from the crisis situation and only lengthens the time it takes to resolve the problem (J. Tice, personal communication, March 25, 2005).

6

Transition and topic.

Identifies effect of technology.

Summarizes research to strengthen argument.

Newly published research supports these individuals' claims that the constant interruptions resulting from instant communications technologies are not only disruptive but detrimental to productivity. In one study, more than 1,000 individuals were subjected to persistent interruptions either through e-mail or text messaging. Monitoring and testing of the subjects allowed researchers to

INSTANT COMMUNICATION　　　　　　　　　　　　　　　　　6

determine that such interruptions produce a temporary but measurable drop in intelligence (Burnett & Ortiz, 2005). The *Houston Chronicle* summarized the study by reporting, "Constant e-mailing and text messaging reduces mental ability by 10 IQ points, a more severe effect than smoking cannabis, by distracting the brain from other tasks" (Moore, 2005). By comparison, a sleepless night will produce the same effect while smoking marijuana only causes a 4 point reduction (Moore, 2005).

> Offers a documented comparison to strengthen claim.

> Transition to next identified cause of stress.

Even more troubling is that the disruptions produced by instant communications technologies extend outside the professional and laboratory environments as well. Because pagers and cell phones with text messaging are portable devices and most employees have Internet access to their corporate e-mail from home, their reach is extended far outside the office. These devices have invaded the home and are eating away at our personal time. Research indicates somewhere between one-half and three-quarters of office professionals use business-related communication technologies outside the office for up to 2 hours per day (Weil & Rosen, 1999). A recent article in *Today's Parent* discusses how time spent working outside of office hours is taken away from other activities such as time parents should be spending with their families (Lopez-Pacheco, 2003).

> Draws from two studies to strengthen argument.

Psychologists concur that all this electronic communication is contributing to a wide array of undesirable psychological changes and increasing personal stress levels. People are becoming more isolated as they choose to use electronic means of communicating over traditional interpersonal methods (Rizzo, 1999). It is becoming increasingly more difficult for people to define their personal space boundaries and separate their personal and professional lives. According to Terrie Hienrich Rizzo (1999), "This boundary breakdown leads to a feeling of never being able to get away and contributes to an inability to relax" (p. 1). That anyone may be watching TV or reading a good book when a pager or cell phone beckons with a work-related problem clearly demonstrates this lack of separation and its consequences.

> Topic sentence introduces another effect through a causal chain.

> Sums up the problem in the student's own words.

I do not argue that instant communication technologies can offer benefits to the busy professional. However, the growing body of

> Anticipates possible objections and counters them.

Uses personal experience as support.

research supports my belief that these devices can elevate stress levels and reduce productivity when used inappropriately. I know from personal experience that I was a victim of the negative effects that these technologies can manifest. The experts call it technostress, multitasking mania, or information overload, but for me, the end result was career burnout regardless of what term is used to define how or why it happened. In fact, I am probably one of the statistics cited in an *Information Week* report stating that information technology professionals are burning out in ever-increasing numbers (Lally, 1997).

Strengthens support from personal experience with claim from an authority.

Makes prediction as to why this topic will be increasingly significant.

10

The reality is that not only are these electronic communication technologies a current problem we must deal with, but if left unchecked, the problem will only grow worse in the future. The number one recommendation of experts to reduce the stress manifested by instant communication devices and technologies is to limit their use. While this seems like an obvious solution, few people fail to put it into practice. Implementing some basic defense strategies to manage the interruptions of instant messages can go a long way toward reducing the stress they can produce (Rizzo, 1999). One is to disable notification of new voice mail and e-mail so that users can check it on their own schedule rather than when it demands their attention. Another is for users to take regular time-out periods where they inform others that they will not be reachable via a pager or cell phone. This will ensure that today's professionals have some time available to redefine personal space boundaries, spend (time) with their family, or just read a good book (Rizzo, 1999).

Offers possible solution.

Acknowledges possible problems with implementing main recommendation, and offers additional suggestions.

Summarizes main recommendations

References

Burnett, J. H., & Ortiz, V. (2005, April 23). Does more IM = a lower IQ? *Milwaukee Journal Sentinel*, p. A3.

Genco, P. (2000, September/October). Technostress in our schools and lives. *Book Report*, pp. 42–43. Retrieved from WilsonSelectPlus database.

Lally, R. (1997, October 6). Managing techno-stress. *Getting Results—for the Hands-On Manager*, 6, 5–6. Retrieved from WilsonSelectPlus database.

Two-author newspaper article.

Electronic-based source.

Electronic journal.

INSTANT COMMUNICATION   9

Lopez-Pacheco, A. (2003, February). Baby, baby, don't get hooked on me. *Today's Parent*, 110–112.

| Article from popular magazine in print. |

Moore, K. J. (2005, April 23). Constant e-mail harms intellect [Electronic version]. *The Houston Chronicle*, p. B3.

| Newspaper article, electronic version. |

Rizzo, T. H. (1999, November/December). Taming technostress. IDEA Health & Fitness. Retrieved from InfoTrac Onefile database.

| Single-author article in online journal retrieved from a database. |

Weil, M., & Rosen, L. (1999). Don't let technology enslave you. *Workforce*, 78(2), 56–60.

| Two-author article from print journal. |

DISCUSSION QUESTIONS

1. In paragraph 3, the author defines "technostress." What is it, in your own words, and how does the writer use authorities to enhance his own credibility in this discussion?
2. In paragraph 5, what are two negative effects the author says are the result of the speed and ease of instant communication? How does the author blend in primary source material to support this argument?
3. To what extent does this argument follow a problem/solution model?
4. How does the conclusion contain warnings and recommendations?

TOWARD KEY INSIGHTS

What stresses have you experienced in association with technological communication such as email, texting, social media status updates, and so on?

If you agree that there is such a thing as "technostresss," do you think it has been getting worse since this essay was written? Why or why not?

Some people have suggested that our mental health could be improved with an "electronic fast" at least one day a week. What do you think of the idea of abstaining from all technological communication or viewing for one day a week?

SUGGESTIONS FOR WRITING *After researching the phenomenon of multitasking, write an essay using correct documentation of the style your instructor prefers to argue that multitasking is not as effective or as efficient as many people might imagine.*

Write a research essay using correct documentation of the style your instructor prefers to explore the costs and benefits of doing something very quickly—such as eating fast food, shopping quickly, or driving fast—compared to the costs and benefits of slowing down in the same area.

CHAPTER 15

Strategies for Researching: Using Primary Research

The library and Internet aren't the only sources of information for research writing. Investigators also gather information through *primary research*, which includes such activities as consulting public records in local, provincial, and federal archives; performing experiments; conducting interviews; sending out questionnaires; and making direct observations of various kinds.

This chapter focuses on the latter three types, which are the most common primary research strategies.

THE VALUE OF PRIMARY RESEARCH

What makes primary research so valuable? First, it allows individuals and organizations to collect recent information that precisely suits their needs. A company that has developed a new product can't turn to published data to estimate its sales prospects; such information simply doesn't exist. However, polling test users with a well-crafted questionnaire could suggest some answers and also some tips for improving the product. Similarly, someone wanting to gauge the success of an ongoing clothing drive by a local charitable organization might interview its director.

Even when published material exists, it may not contain desired information. Although numerous articles discuss student attitudes about required courses, you probably wouldn't find a report that explores student reaction to a new general education requirement at your university. However, you could assemble this information by distributing a questionnaire. The findings might even contradict and, therefore, cause you to question the conclusions of others.

Primary research can also yield unexpected and significant material. Suppose you're investigating adult literacy needs and you interview a professor with a specialty in this area of study. She explains the reasons why people who can't read often resist help and supplies several relevant examples. Such information might not appear anywhere in print. Certainly the resulting report would carry more weight and elicit more interest than one without such insights.

Primary research can be used to supplement secondary research from external sources. In the final chapter of the Reader, the article by Ross Gordon on homelessness in Edmonton is strengthened by the inclusion of quotations from interviews with homeless people. In this case, the writer blended interview material with material from other secondary sources, but it sometimes happens that writers detail the findings of primary research in separate reports. This would be the case if, for example, your employer asked you to interview users of a new online collaboration tool at work in order to determine their degree of satisfaction with it.

GENERAL PRINCIPLES FOR PRIMARY RESEARCH

Like all research, primary research requires well-formulated questions. Such questions must be specifically focused, contain clearly defined terms, and be answerable by the actual research. A vague, general question such as "What attitudes do Canadians have about their government?" lacks the necessary precision and can't be resolved. What kinds of attitudes? What level or branch of government? Which Canadians? How would you gather their opinions? A more realistic question might be "According to Concordia University students, how adequate is the new federal government proposal for student loan funding in this country?" You could easily develop and distribute to students a questionnaire addressing the different provisions of the proposal. However, keep in mind that you can't resolve ethical or philosophical questions through primary research. While you could use a questionnaire to determine public attitudes about the police using sobriety spot checks, such information won't decide the ethical issue of whether the police should use such spot checks.

For valid results, approach primary research with an open mind rather than trying to justify your beliefs or opinions. Your questions should have no built-in bias. If you poll students and ask them to tell you "how teachers in English courses mark their papers unreasonably hard," those responding might falsify their answers to give you what you want. Instead, use neutral phrasing such as "To what extent do you believe the grades on your English essays are a fair assessment of quality? Explain." As well, don't rely on atypical sources and situations for your data. If you investigate the adequacy of parking space on campus, don't deliberately observe the parking lots on a day when some special event has flooded the campus with visitors. Thoughtful readers will see what you have done and reject your findings.

Just as you avoid bias when gathering information, don't force interpretations of your findings to make them agree with the conclusions you're after. If you believe that peer editing produces questionable results, don't claim that the students in a class you observed spent their time sneering at one another's work when in fact they were offering constructive criticism. Similarly, don't report conclusions that are unsupported by your actual research. If you observe several incidents of violence in early-morning television cartoons, you can't assume a causal relationship between the violence in the cartoons and children's bullying behaviour later that day. You simply don't have the necessary evidence to demonstrate a link between cartoon violence and bullying.

Finally, don't conveniently ignore results that you don't like. If your survey of teachers' marking practices shows that most of your respondents believe instructors mark fairly, don't hide the fact because it doesn't match what you expected to discover. Instead, report your findings accurately and rethink your original position. The following section further explores ethical matters.

ETHICAL ISSUES

Today, most people chuckle at an advertising ploy for a product recommended by "nine out of ten doctors." We recognize that the doctors were handpicked and don't represent an objective sample of adequate size. As a result, little harm occurs. With primary research, however, distorted investigating and reporting are sometimes hard to detect and can have significant consequences.

Let's say that the officials of Hafford, Saskatchewan, alarmed at a sharp rise in car accidents caused by distracted drivers, schedule a meeting attempting to ban cellphone use by those driving within city limits. It would be unethical for a reporter opposed to the ban to write a supposedly objective feature article on the issue but include interviews only with people who share his or her views. Now suppose that a presumably neutral group in the city of Winnipeg, Manitoba, distributes a questionnaire to residents to gauge their reaction to a proposed gambling casino. It would be unethical to include a biased question such as "Should the city deprive its residents of the revenue that a casino can provide?" Finally, imagine that a city manager, concerned by reports of motorists running a red light at a major intersection, asks the Department of Transportation to investigate. A department employee conducts a 20-minute observation and then writes a report indicating that surveillance cameras are not needed there. Clearly, the employee has acted unethically in drawing a conclusion after such a limited observation. To help ensure that your primary research reports are ethically responsible, ask and answer the following questions:

- Have I attempted to avoid bias in gathering and evaluating information?
- Are my data based on an adequate sample size? If not, have the limitations of the sample been clearly indicated?
- Have I presented my complete findings, with no intentional effort to omit findings that run counter to my position or hypothesis?
- Are the people involved, whether I'm preparing an interview, questionnaire, or direct observation report, aware that they are part of a study and how the information will be used? Are they protected from harm that might result from their inclusion?
- Do I have permission to include the names of persons interviewed or observed in my report?

- In an interview report, would the interviewee recognize and accept statements attributed to him or her?
- Have I noted any apparent bias in the interviewee?
- In a questionnaire report, have I avoided any biased questions?

INTERVIEWS

During an interview, questions are asked and answered. Sometimes short, informal interviews that are conversational in nature may still yield something of use for your paper—perhaps a quotation or brief anecdote that could enliven your paper. Other more formal interviews may feature extended conversations, involve a series of questions, and require careful preparation. Interviewing an expert or a person knowledgeable about your topic may provide you with first-hand, up-to-date information and allow you to ask follow-up questions.

If you major in a business program, an instructor may require you to question a personnel manager about the company's employee relations program. If your field is social work, you might have to interview a case worker as part of your study of some kind of family problem. On the job, you might have to talk with prospective employees and then assess their suitability for a position in the company. Police officers routinely interview witnesses to accidents and crimes, and journalists do the same in pursuit of stories. Sometimes excerpts from interviews can be threaded into academic essays.

Choosing the Interviewee

Professional and technical personnel are a rich source of interview candidates. The faculty of any university can provide insights into a wide range of subjects. If you were doing research on a specific issue related to health care, for example, you might interview doctors, nurses, pharmacists, and other health professionals who could give you perspective on the issue you are exploring.

The person you interview depends, of course, on what you wish to know. For information on the safe disposal of high-level nuclear waste, you might consult a physics professor. If you want an expert view on the causes of homelessness, contact an authority such as a sociologist, who could provide objective information. If, however, you want to gain a sense of what it's like to be homeless, you might interview the manager of a shelter or one or more homeless people. For interviews closer to home, it may be enlightening to interview a close family member, as the sample student essay in this section illustrates.

Preparing for the Interview

If you don't relish the thought of phoning to request an interview, keep in mind that most interviewees are eager to discuss their areas of expertise and are often flattered by the opportunity. The worst that can happen is that you get turned down; and in that event, you can always find someone else in the same field.

Before contacting the person you want to interview, review your own upcoming commitments and try to determine which ones you could reschedule if necessary. You may need to make an adjustment to accommodate the schedule of a busy person. When you call, indicate who you are, why you are calling, what you wish to interview about, and how much time you'd like.

If the person agrees to meet with you, ask when would be convenient. Carefully record the time, day, and place of the interview; if you need to cancel for any reason, be sure to call well in advance.

Before the interview, do as much background reading as possible. This reading will help you develop a list of key questions and avoid those with obvious and readily available answers. Write out your questions to help ensure that the interview will proceed smoothly.

Open-ended questions that permit elaboration are more effective than closed questions that ask for simple "yes" or "no" answers.

A closed question:	Is it difficult to work with adults with low literacy skills? (The obvious answer is simply "yes" or "no," but the answer may stop there.)
A more promising open-ended question:	What have you found most challenging about working with adults who have low literacy skills?

On the other hand, don't ask overly broad questions that can't be answered in a relatively brief interview.

Too broad:	What's wrong with primary school education?
Suitably narrow:	Why do you think so many children have trouble paying attention in class?

Avoid questions that are biased and may insult the interviewee.

Poor:	Why do you bother to work with adults with low literacy skills?
Better:	Why did you decide to work with adults with low literacy skills?

Likewise, avoid questions that restrict the interviewee's options for answering.

Poor:	What do you think accounts for the poor academic performance of some Canadian high school students—too much screen time with TV and video games or overly large classes?
Better:	People often blame the poor academic performance of some Canadian high school students on factors such as too much screen time or overly large classes. What importance do you attach to these factors? What other factors do you think might contribute to the problem?

The number of questions you prepare depends on the length of the interview. It's a good idea to draft more questions than you think you'll have time to ask and then arrange them in order of importance. If the interviewee keeps to the schedule, you'll obtain your desired information. If you find that you are both enjoying the interview process and discovering new ideas as you talk, you may uncover more information that you had originally anticipated.

Conducting the Interview

Naturally you'll want to arrive on time and bring a notepad and pen or a device to record the interview, depending on what your interviewee is comfortable with. If you want to record the interview, be sure to ask permission first. Because most people warm up slowly, you might start with one or two brief, general, non-threatening questions that provide you with useful background. Possibilities include "When did you start working in this area?" and "What changes have you seen in this field since you started in it?"

Proceed by asking your most important questions first. If you believe that a question hasn't been answered or that an answer is incomplete, don't hesitate to ask follow-up questions. You can check with your interviewee if he or she is comfortable with being recorded, but often it is better to take notes, simply jotting down key phrases and ideas that will serve as memory prompts. If you want to capture an essential explanation or some other important material in the interviewee's own words, ask the person to speak slowly while you copy them down. When the interview is over, thank the person for talking to you and, depending on the relationship and context, you might also offer to supply a copy of the finished report or send a follow-up thank you. With the answers to your questions fresh in your mind, expand on your notes by filling in details, supplying necessary connections between points that were made, and noting your reactions.

Writing about the Interview

The project you're working on determines how to handle your interview information. If you're preparing a research paper, identify and blend the relevant interview material into your other research and document it properly (see Chapters 16 and 17 for MLA and APA styles). The way you present your findings will depend on your rhetorical situation, audience, and purpose. Is this expected to be a relatively objective report in which you establish the context of the interview, determine the audience, and present the information accurately in a neutral manner? Or is the interview the basis for a more interpretive discussion or narrative? The sample student essay that follows shows how an interview can provide material for a personal narrative essay that includes a sense of personal discovery.

SAMPLE STUDENT ESSAY BASED ON PERSONAL INTERVIEW

Getting Schooled by My Pakistani Mother

Filza Ahmar

It seemed as if with age and time, the communication gap between my mother and me was widening with dishearteningly speed. I never had to come to terms with it because I always thought it was just a phase. Recently I had a chance to look more deeply into it.

I'm twenty, full of energy, and growing up in North America. You could say that the world is my oyster. Then there's my mother, who's not so twenty and most definitely not growing up in North America. She holds a degree in Science which she earned back home. She prides herself over her interest in Home Economics and her achievements in that elective.

> Paragraph 1: establishes context for interview.

> Paragraphs 2 to 4: identify interviewee, writer's relationship to interviewee, and context for assignment.

Contrast between cultural
values creates narrative
tension

You see, we used to live in Karachi, Pakistan, almost the New York City of Pakistan. As modernized as it is, it's still not the West, of course. If I am of the West, my mother is of the East. She grew up in a society with an excess number of rules and regulations that women had to abide by. There were social rules, cultural rules, and religious rules, to name a few.

When I recently received the assignment to interview an elder about their experiences, I decided to interview my mother about her experience in high school because she's always so judgemental about the Canadian education system. I saw it as an opportunity to connect, communicate, and maybe try to understand her point of view.

Writer blends direct and
indirect quotations, using
detail.

We sat across from each other in our living room. I sat in an armchair, legs crossed, notebook in hand, and a polite smile on my face. I was trying to settle into a zone of calm. My mother sat across from me with one arm resting on the arm of the couch and her hands resting on her knees. "If you could, would you go back in time and pursue an education in Canada or Pakistan?" I asked.

She smiled and said immediately, "Pakistan. It was more strict there." As a rule-detesting, free spirited woman, I was baffled. Why would she prefer a stricter environment over a more relaxed one? I had a sick feeling at the bottom of my stomach that this interview was going to be difficult.

"How strict and what were they strict about?" I was hungry for answers. What was it in her background that caused her to judge me so much?

"We weren't allowed to wear makeup or jewelry like you people. We could only wear black hair ties, black hair clips, black shoes and white socks," she explained. She told me that there would be severe consequences if any of those rules were broken. Students would be asked to leave the class and stand in the hallway as punishment. Later on they would get a call home. Getting a phonecall home was probably the most humiliating thing any parent would have to face back then. I tried to imagine what that would be like.

My mother kept sitting tall with a small smile on her face. It wasn't hard to tell that she was enjoying reminiscing. I cleared my throat and tried to focus on her, not on what I was thinking.

"How do you think your life would have been different if you had experienced schooling here, in Canada, and not in Pakistan?" I was curious to know how she thought she would have turned out if she grew up here, within this multicultural society with fewer rules, more acceptance of difference, and greater gender equality. In Pakistan, the men were much more free, with no curfew, no social or cultural obligations whereas the women were handed a to-do list the moment they hit puberty.

My mother sank back into the couch and looked down at her hands. I could tell that she had never reflected on that thought. She was quiet and I was patient. When she finally spoke, her gaze was still on her hands, "I would have been so much more than I am now." She exhaled almost like she'd been holding her breath the entire time she had been sitting quietly. "I would have been more outspoken, more educated—and fearless. I would have ended up with someone of my choice." She shifted a little in her seat and straightened her back as if she was accepting, with some difficulty, what and who she was at this moment. Her eyebrows furrowed and she pursed her lips almost as if she was trying to injest the bitter truth.

That answer alone was sufficient enough to satisfy me, but she continued. I realized that by answering this one question of mine, she was answering some of her own. I didn't interrupt, but listened to every word she had to say. Her body language gradually seemed to look more relaxed. She finally looked up at me and told me how she was so glad that I was growing up here and becoming the woman she never had a chance to be. She was happy that I would be in control of my own fate and that I will inevitably take life by the horns.

Now I had the choice to continue with clichéd questions or meaningful ones. I chose quality over quantity. "So you had an arranged marriage? Would you want the same for me?" Since she and I frequently bickered about the value of arranged marriage vs. a love marriage, I thought that this was the perfect time for me to listen to her on this sensitive topic.

"It was time. I was twenty two, educated, young, and I could cook. I was ready for marriage, I guess. I didn't have anyone in mind at that time. Time is everything and no man wants an old wife."

That one answer and the simple way she worded it gave me a vivid snapshot into the time she lived in back then. I was struck, as I had been before, by the double standard in a society where males were treated like crown jewels from day one, and females groomed for marriage and the basic duties of a housewife the moment they hit menarche.

> Writer offers necessary background information to help readers understand cultural context better

It wasn't anything I hadn't thought about or heard before. But this time, it sounded different to me. I was listening to her as an interviewee instead of as her daughter. I could imagine how it would have been considered culturally unacceptable to be any different than anyone in your age group. If they were all following a certain trend, you either did or you didn't. You couldn't do anything extraordinary without being a social pariah. My mother was timid, shy, and reserved. She had to follow that traditional duty because back then, that's what every twenty two-year-old was doing. They were finishing their education with no plans of pursuing a career and getting married.

> Writer's ability to see things differently now indicates a turning point

I laid my pen down, and leaned in a bit, taking a deep breath to clear my mind. Calmly I asked, "Would you suggest arranged marriage for me or any girl growing up in Canada?" I tried to quiet my inner rebel, who was standing up to protest with a bright red flag; chest out, and chin up, ready for war. My mother looked at me and seemed almost ready to pounce. Then she eased up a bit, smiling a "Yeah right" sort of smile at me. She tilted her head to the side with her eyes fixed on me and said, "I wish! I pity the fool who would agree to an arranged marriage with you. You'd eat him alive so good that you won't even spare his bones!"

I fell back into the couch, laughing because she was so right. My inner rebel let out a "phew!" as a sign of relief.

"Sweetie, there's pros and cons to everything in life." I sat up straight immediately and listened. Her tone was serious and she spoke almost matter-of-factly. "In an arranged marriage, your mate is chosen by your parents. They get to decide who they think can treat their child the best. Here, you people don't ever get close to your parents so we don't really have the same connection with our kids compared to what we had with our parents." The gravity of what she said sank in fast. It was true. I had never tried to sit down with either of my parents to really express my thoughts to them simply because I don't think that they would understand. We are from such different worlds. They come from the east, where the sun rises. I am of the west, where the sun sets. "It's scary to not know some-one and have to spend the rest of your life with them. But, mind you, we're not exactly blindfolded and pushed into marriage. I know that that is the misconception of you youngsters these days." Thank God she cleared that up because I was starting to believe it. "But how long does it really take to know someone? A few days?" She smiled at me.

"Forever?"

| New paragraph indicates change of speaker. |

"The pro to a love marriage is that you have a bit of history with that person. You know them and you feel that they can take care of you. And the con, well, like in any relationship, there's that chance that they might change after mar-riage," she said.

That particular answer did not satisfy me. But I knew that I couldn't possibly expect her to give me an answer that I wanted to hear given that she had never really known a "love" interest or even had social interactions with a male outside of marriage. I decided to try a lighter question.

"How were you different than me or most other Canadian girls at the age of twenty?" I asked. I knew that this answer would be priceless. She scoffed and raised an eyebrow. "Well, for starters, I could cook." She smiled at me teasingly.

"I could sew, knit, cook various cuisines, speak in Sindhi and I wasn't half as hard-headed and opinionated as you and your generation are." I laughed and shook my head. I should have seen this one coming.

She had sparked a fire in me. "Are you saying that being opinionated and aware of what you want and what you deserve is not a positive thing?" I saw her let out a small sigh, as if she were noticing an unwelcome thought.

"I wish I could do that," was all she said. I knew what she meant, but I needed for her to say it out loud. "I wish I could voice my opinion and demand what I deserve. I wish I could study more and have a career I love. I wish I had half the confidence you do." She was smiling as if she was enjoying an inside joke. She set her gaze on me and looked at me lovingly. "You are what I would have wanted to be if I was given the chance. As much as I prefer that education system, they could never teach us confidence, self-esteem—and ignite that will-power in our hearts that you have so effortlessly."

This was the time to end the interview. Although I would forget in the future, I would also know, when we bickered again, that we were both dealing with our own versions of culture shock in our own ways. She hasn't really settled into this culture yet, and likely I would never really settle into hers.

> Writer wraps up by returning to a theme mentioned earlier, but now it has gathered larger significance.

But the best part was finally realizing that I am learning from her as much as she is from me. I am her West and she is my East.

> Clarifies the larger point the writer has discovered.

QUESTIONNAIRES AND SURVEYS

Questionnaires and surveys, in which people are asked to respond to a series of statements or questions, can be a useful way to get information from several people or a specific group. Questionnaires and surveys can help assess trends. Organizations and businesses use surveys to find out what select groups of people think about particular products, services, issues, and personal matters. You have probably completed a variety of questionnaires yourself, including teacher evaluations and market surveys.

Developing the Questionnaire

Just as you need to think about your purpose and audience when you write an essay, you also need to consider your purpose and the population sample you want to survey when you draw up a questionnaire. What precisely do you want to learn? What will be your target population? Do you want to survey students in your school's cafeteria to determine their degree of satisfaction with the variety of food offerings? Or do you want to survey the service workers, faculty, and students who are in the cafeteria? Are you interested in what they think about the quality of the food, the cost of the food, or the variety of offerings? Zero in on your area of interest, and then explore it with appropriate questions.

Begin the questionnaire with a clear explanation of what you intend to accomplish, and supply brief but clear instructions on how to respond to each part. Keep the questionnaire short, preferably no longer than a page or two. The longer the survey is, the less likely people are to answer all of the questions.

As you draw up your questions, take care to avoid these common errors:

1. Don't ask two questions in the same sentence. Their answers may be different.

    Confusing: Do you find that your new Toyota Corolla is more reliable and fuel efficient than the Nissan you had before?

    To correct this fault, use separate sentences.

    Better: Do you find that your new Toyota Corolla is more reliable than the Nissan you had before?

    Better: Do you find that your Toyota Corolla is more fuel efficient than the Nissan you had before?

2. Don't include vague or ambiguous questions. Since people won't understand your intent, their answers may not reflect their beliefs.

    Unacceptable: Is carbon trading a good idea?

    Better: Will a federally monitored carbon trading protocol help Canada reduce emissions significantly in the next five years?

3. Avoid biased questions. They might antagonize those who don't share your views and cause them not to complete the questionnaire.

    Biased: Should taxpayers continue to waste money on renovating the Lion's Gate Bridge?

    Better: Should taxpayers spend an additional $10 million to complete the Lion's Gate Bridge renovation?

Most questionnaire items fall into the categories that follow. The information you want determines which you choose. Often you need to include several or all of the categories in your questionnaire.

Two-Choice Items   Some items have two possible responses: yes/no, true/false, male/female.

    Example: Do you plan to repaint your house during the summer months?
       ☐   yes
       ☐   no

Multiple-Choice Items   Often there are several possible responses to a questionnaire item. When you prepare this type of item, make sure that you include all significant choices and that the choices share some common ground. Don't ask if someone's primary vehicle is subcompact, compact, full-sized, automatic, or manual, because size and type of transmission are unrelated. To determine whether the vehicle is automatic or manual, use a separate item.

Example: Check the income group that describes your combined family income.
  ☐ less than $10 000 a year
  ☐ $10 000–$20 000 a year
  ☐ $20 001–$30 000 a year
  ☐ $30 001–$40 000 a year
  ☐ $40 001–$50 000 a year
  ☐ more than $50 000 a year

Ranking Lists   Sometimes you may need to ask people to rank their preferences. This information allows them to select the most suitable option from among several possibilities.

Example: Designating your first choice as "1," please rank your preferences in music from 1 through 5.
  ☐ classical
  ☐ country
  ☐ jazz
  ☐ rock
  ☐ rap

Using the responses to this item, the manager of a local radio station could broadcast the type of music that listeners clearly prefer.

Scale Items   When you are trying to determine the extent to which members of a group support or oppose some issue, using a scale can be helpful. Be sure to have people respond to a statement, *not* a question.

Example: Please circle the response that best reflects your feelings about the statement below.
SA = strongly agree, A = agree, N = no opinion,
D = disagree, SD = strongly disagree
Women should be allowed to fly combat aircraft in times of war.
SA   A   N   D   SD

Open-Ended Items   When you want to gather ideas from other people, you might turn to open-ended items—those that don't limit the reader's response. If you do, keep such items narrow enough to be manageable. However, you should know that readers are less likely to complete open-ended items and that they are difficult to sort and tally.

Example: Please list the three improvements you would most like to see in Point Grey's high school curriculum.

  _____

  _____

  _____

Administering the Questionnaire

To ensure that you obtain an accurate assessment, make certain that you select an appropriate cross-section of recipients. For example, assume that you and many of your friends dislike early-morning classes. You decide to draw up a questionnaire to sample the attitudes of other students. You suspect that many students share your dislike, and you plan to submit your findings to the university president for possible action. To obtain meaningful results, you would have to sample a sizable group of students. Furthermore, this group would need to include representative numbers of first-year and upper-year students, since these classes may not share a uniform view. Failure to sample properly can call your results into question and cause the administration to disregard them. Proper sampling, on the other hand, pinpoints where dissatisfaction is greatest and suggests a possible response. Thus, if first-year students register the most objections, the administration might decide to reduce the number of first-year classes meeting at 8 a.m.

Managing the Responses

When the recipients have finished marking the questionnaire, you need to total the responses. Even without computer scoring, this job is easier than you might think. Simply prepare a table that lists the questionnaire items and the possible responses to each; then go through the questionnaire and add up the number of times each response is marked.

When you finish, turn your numbers into percentages, which provide an easier-to-understand comparison of the responses. Simply divide the number of times each possible response is checked by the total number of questionnaires, then multiply the result by 100.

Writing the Questionnaire Report

When you write your report, don't merely fill it with numbers and responses to the questionnaire items. Instead, look for patterns in the responses and try to draw conclusions from them. Follow the order of the questionnaire items in presenting your findings.

Typically, a questionnaire report consists of two or three sections. The first, *Purpose and Scope*, explains why the survey was performed, how many questionnaires were distributed and returned, and how the recipients were contacted. The second section, *Results*, reports the conclusions that you have drawn. Finally, if appropriate, a *Recommendations* section offers responses that seem warranted based on the survey findings.

SAMPLE STUDENT QUESTIONNAIRE REPORT

Findings from a Smoking Questionnaire Distributed to Bartram College Students

Kelly Reetz

Purpose and Scope of Survey

> Provides background details on project, profile of respondents.

This survey was carried out to determine the smoking habits and attitudes toward public smoking of Bartram College's male students. The assignment was one of my requirements for completing Public Health 201. Each of the 240 male students in Crandall Hall received a copy of the questionnaire in his mailbox, and 72 completed questionnaires were returned. This latter number represents 10 percent of the college's male student population and therefore can be considered a representative sample. Of those responding, 37 students (or 51 percent) were cigarette smokers, and the remaining 49 percent were non-smokers. Of the smokers, all but 11 percent smoked more than a pack of cigarettes a day.

> Discusses responses to questionnaire items 1 and 2.

Results of Survey

Smokers seemed fairly considerate of non-smokers in public places. Only 16 percent said they would smoke freely. In fact, 51 percent said they wouldn't smoke at all. The remaining 33 percent indicated they would either look around to see whether they were bothering others or ask others whether they objected to cigarette smoke.

> Discusses responses to questionnaire item 3.

Surprisingly, all respondents seemed aware that second-hand smoke poses a health risk. Seventy-six percent believe that such smoke contains the same ingredients as directly inhaled smoke, and an amazing 100 percent believe that anyone exposed to second-hand smoke may be at risk.

> Discusses responses to questionnaire item 4.

Opinions were strongly divided on the matter of banning all public smoking, with 79 percent strongly opposed and 20 percent strongly in favour. As might be expected, all of the smokers fell into the first group, but just over 50 percent of the non-smokers did too. A sharp division was equally apparent between supporters and opponents of the ban on smoking in cars with children in them, with 81 percent for or strongly for a ban and 19 percent against or strongly against the idea. There was a similar division in supporters and opponents of the smoking ban on outdoor patios: 80 percent supported the ban, while 20 percent voted against or strongly against the ban.

> Discusses responses to questionnaire item 5.

Responses to items 3–5 reveal an awareness among smokers and non-smokers alike of the dangers posed by second-hand cigarette smoke. Both the light and heavy smokers showed concern for the well-being of non-smokers and a willingness to accept restrictions, though not an outright ban, on public smoking. For their part, about half the non-smokers showed a tolerant attitude by supporting smoking restrictions but rejecting an outright ban on all public smoking.

> Discusses patterns in responses to questionnaire items 3 to 5.

No smokers, but 71 percent of the non-smokers, responded to the request to provide one or two additional comments. All of these comments dealt with how the respondents would act if bothered by someone else's smoke, even on a patio or near a building entrance or exit. Half said they would move to another place, one said he would ask the smoker to stop, and the other one said he would remain silent rather than risk an argument.

> Discusses responses to questionnaire item 6.

Recommendations

As noted previously, this survey included only male students. To determine how its results compare with those for females, the same questionnaire should be administered to a similar group of female students. Perhaps a larger sample of respondents might allow us to better evaluate the proposal for a complete smoking ban on campus.

DIRECT OBSERVATIONS

Often direct observation can be an effective means of answering research questions. If you want to know the extent and nature of violence in children's TV cartoons, watching a number of shows tells you. Similarly, a researcher who seeks information about living conditions in a low-income urban area can learn by visiting that locale. Such observations furnish first-hand answers to our questions.

At school and on the job, you may need to report your own observations. If you're majoring in business, an instructor might require a report on the work habits of employees at a small local company. If your field is biology, you might need to assess and report on the environmental health of a marsh, estuary, or other ecological area. On the job, a factory superintendent might observe and then discuss in writing the particulars of some problem-plagued operation. Police officers routinely investigate and report on accidents, and waste management specialists inspect and report on potential disposal sites.

The following suggestions can help you make your observations, record them, and then write your report.

Preparing to Make the Observations

First, determine the purpose of your observations and keep the purpose firmly in mind as you proceed. Otherwise, you'll overlook important details and record less-than-helpful information.

Next, establish the site or sites that can best supply you with the information you need. If you're trying to determine how students interact in the classroom, then the time of day, kind of class, and types of students all make a difference. You might have to visit more than one class to observe the different types of behaviour.

If your observations take place on private property or involve an organized group, you need to obtain permission and make an appointment. Also, you might want to supplement your observations with an interview. Ordinarily, the interview takes place after you have made your observations so that you can ask about what you've seen. If technical information is needed in advance, the interview should precede the observations. However, you should have done research first so that you do not waste the expert's time and goodwill by asking about information that is reasonably available.

Making the Observations

If your visit involves a scheduled appointment, be sure to arrive on time and be ready to take notes. Select a location where you can observe without interfering. If you are observing people or animals, remember that they need time to adjust to you before they behave naturally.

Before you begin taking notes, record any pertinent general information. If you're observing a class, you might note the time it is meeting, its size, the name of the instructor, and whether he or she is present when you arrive. If you're observing an apartment, record the location and condition of the building, the time of the visit, and the general nature of the environment.

Take enough notes so that you can produce a thorough report. Try to follow some logical pattern in your note taking. When observing something physical such as the condition of an apartment, you could proceed from room to room, following a spatial order as you jot down your observations. When you finish, thank the person(s) who made your observations possible or helped you in other ways.

When you leave the observation site, expand your notes by adding more details. Supply any needed connections and record your overall impressions. For example, suppose you are expanding your notes on student interactions in an English class. You might note that the greatest number of interactions occurred before and immediately after the instructor arrived, that all student–student interactions involved individuals seated together, that student–instructor interactions included students in all parts of the room, and that all of the latter interactions were about subject-related matters. This information might stimulate interesting speculation concerning the student–student and student–instructor relationships in the class, causing you to conclude that the students were hesitant about having exchanges with the instructor. As you proceed, record only what you actually observed, not what you wanted or expected to observe.

Writing the Report

Once your notes are in final form, you can start writing your report. On the job, your employer may specify a certain form to follow.

Usually you begin by explaining the reason for the investigation, noting any preliminary arrangements that were made, and, if appropriate, providing an overview of the observation site. Depending on the nature of the report, use one of the following methods of organization:

Narration. A report on the changing conduct of a child over a three-hour period in a daycare centre would probably be organized chronologically.

Description. A report assessing the storm damage in a large urban area could present its details in spatial order.

Classification. A visit to a toxic-waste dump suspected of violating government regulations might produce a report classifying the types of wastes improperly stored there.

Point-by-point comparison. If you're comparing two possible sites for a baseball stadium, shopping mall, or other structure, a point-by-point comparison probably best suits your purpose.

Cause and effect. This pattern works well for reporting events whose effects are of special concern, such as the testing of a new siren intended to scare birds from an airport runway.

Process. This arrangement is indicated when readers want to know step by step how a process is carried out—for example, a new test for determining the mineral content of water.

Conclude the report by discussing the significance of the findings and making any other comments that seem justified.

CHAPTER 16

Strategies for Documentation: MLA Style

In order to acknowledge and handle sources, you must know how to (1) prepare proper bibliographic references, (2) document sources within your text, (3) integrate quotations, paraphrases, and summaries, and (4) avoid plagiarism.

The kind of information included in bibliographic references depends on the type of source and the documentation system. Two systems are in common use: the Modern Language Association (MLA) system, used mainly in the humanities such as English and philosophy, and the American Psychological Association (APA) system, used mainly in the social sciences.

This chapter provides a framework for use of the MLA system.

There are also a number of useful online links to help you with your documentation needs; the Online Writing Lab (OWL) at Purdue University is very reader-friendly, and your own university most likely has links through the campus library that you can use. For more information, consult the *MLA Handbook for Writers of Research Papers*, 7th ed., 2009. Citation generators such as EasyBib and Citation Machine can also be helpful, but as with spell- and grammar-checks, you need to know what you're doing and not depend on the computer alone.

MLA Citation Style

[2] LIBERTÉ, EGALITÉ, SORORITÉ

Women of the French Revolution

[1] JAN S. CARSON

City University Press
[3] Toronto [4]

CITY UNIVERSITY PRESS
First published 1996

[5] Copyright © 1996 by Jan S. Carson

All rights reserved.
No part of this publication may be reproduced, stored or transmitted in any form or by any means (electronic, mechanical, photocopying, recording or otherwise), without the prior written permission of both the copyright owner and the above publisher of this book.

Printed and bound in Canada

Canadian Cataloguing in Publication Data

Carson, Jan S.

Liberté, Egalité, Sororité: women of the French revolution

ISBN 0-194-21021-X

1. France—History—Revolution, 1789–1799.
2. France—Women—Influence. I. Title.

FC131.K23 1996 293.03'016

C96-951786-4

[1] Author—last name first
[2] Title in italics
[3] Place of publication followed by a colon
[4] Publisher
[5] Date of publication
[6] Medium

Carson, Jan S. *Liberté, Egalité, Sororité: Women of the French Revolution.* Toronto: City UP, 1996. Print.

---

[6] [3] [4] [5]

12   THE FUTURIST, VOL. 36 NO. 1 (2002)

[1] **Mark Zwelling**

[2] **The Blended Economy**

The traditional way to innovate is to carve a specialized niche. Some building contractors specialize in renovating nineteenth-century homes. Lawyers practice trade law, criminal law, family law, labor law, immigration, copyright, or libel. Doctors can be ear-nose-throat specialists, gerontologists, or pediatricians. Specialization is efficient; specialists do their jobs faster because they know them better than non-specialists. And a niche is usually more profitable than the mass market from which someone sliced it. The trouble with a niche is that when competitors recognize it's profitable they rush in.

Blending is the opposite of specialization. Instead of burrowing deeper into a field or product to specialize, blending creates a new market category. The secret in the technique is to unite different, not similar, ideas, products, or services. Minivans and sport-utility vehicles, for example, grew from blending cars and trucks, creating whole new categories of consumer vehicles.

Companies can continually generate new ideas by blending. Most new products today are simply extrapolations of successful products, such as a faster microprocessor, a cheaper airline ticket, a smaller camera, and so on. These innovations eventually run out of possibilities. Blending different ideas instead produces limitless new directions for innovative products.

A food company searching for a new product for kids might think of blending different items from a list of opposites like "frozen or unfrozen," "milk or cola," "peanut butter or peanuts," "salad or soup." Perhaps kids who love peanuts would savor them in a soup. And perhaps a cola could be frozen so it would stay cold longer, requiring no ice. The ideas may prove impractical, nonsensical, or just plain awful, but the point is to generate more ideas because they can lead to practical products.

Blending also operates within social and economic trends. For instance, barriers are falling between work and leisure, devastating some retail clothing chains and department stores as employees don the same outfits at home and the office.

In the job market, there is vast potential to create opportunities by combining apparently unrelated occupations. Consider the number of specialists you must work with to buy or sell a house: There is a real estate agent, the loan officer, the building inspector, an insurance agent, and the mover. One specialist hands you off to another. The blending opportunity here is for, perhaps, a "home transitions" professional who can manage all these different steps.

Some employees may have over-specialized. Specialization narrows a worker's opportunities in a slowly growing economy and causes bottlenecks in a booming economy. Blending avoids these problems.

Zwelling, Mark. "The Blended Economy." *The Futurist* 36.1 (2002): 12–33. Print.

[1] Author—last name first
[2] Title of article in quotation marks with period inside quotation marks
[3] Title of journal in italics
[4] Volume and issue number
[5] Date of publication
[6] First page number
[7] Number of final page of article
[8] Medium

Who were the *filles du roi?*

CENTRE FOR   CITY UNIVERSITY
CANADIAN HISTORY   [3]

[2] Who were the *filles du roi?*

Hundreds of young girls and women braved the unknown to come to New France, and turned the male-dominated economic outposts into real self-sustaining colonies; they are quite literally the founding mothers of Quebec and Canada.

[1]

© Dr. Kathleen J. Carson, Assistant Professor of History, City University, March 2005.   [4]

[1]Gagné, Peter J. King's Daughters and Founding Mothers: The Filles du Roi, 1663–1673. Orange Park, Fla.: Quintin Publications, 2001.

[2]This list was originally compiled by Elmer Courteau and Joy Reisinger and is available online at http://www.ziplink.net/~24601/roots/sources/KINGGIRL.htm.

http://www.cityuniversity.ca/centrecanhis/fillesduroi.html

Carson, Kathleen J. "Who were the *filles du roi?*" *Centre for Canadian History at City University.* March 2005. n. pag. Web. 16 Jan. 2011.

[1] Author–last name first (Identification as historian gives source credibility)
[2] Title of article in quotation marks
[3] The periodical or source location
[4] The date the article was published
[5] The page numbers of the article
[6] Medium of publication
[7] The date it was retrieved

MLA SYSTEM FOR PREPARING PAPERS

- Number each page in the upper right corner, one-half inch (1.27 cm) from the top. Precede each page number with your last name.
- Starting one inch (2.54 cm) from the top of the first page, type your full name, the instructor's name, the course designation, and the date, all flush with the left margin.
- Double-space the entire paper, including block quotations and "works cited" entries.
- Use the 12-point Times New Roman font.
- Leave one-inch (2.54 cm) margins on all four sides except at the top of the first page. Indent the first line of each paragraph five spaces or one-half inch (1.27 cm).
- The MLA system does not require a title page.
- Titles of longer works such as books, journals, newspapers, movies, and websites are in italics. Titles of shorter works such as poems, articles, and short stories are in quotation marks.
- Begin the bibliography on a new page that follows the text of the paper, and give it the heading "Works Cited," without quotation marks. Centre the heading on the page.
- List each "Works Cited" entry alphabetically according to the author's last name or, if no author is given, by the first significant word in the title. For a work with more than one author, alphabetize by the name that comes first. If there is more than one entry for an author, substitute three unspaced hyphens, followed by a period and a double space, for the author's name in the second and subsequent entries.
- Begin the first line of each entry at the left margin and indent subsequent lines five spaces.

It is important to note two changes to the MLA style for bibliographic references.

1. The MLA now uses italics instead of underlining for independently published works such as books, periodicals, websites, and television and radio broadcasts. You still use quotation marks for shorter works such as articles or poems that appear in a larger publication.
2. At the end of each entry, the MLA requires you to indicate the medium through which you retrieved it. The categories are Print, Web, CD, Performance, etc. An electronic version of a book retrieved online would be Web, and a copy of an article retrieved from a bound volume would be Print.

PREPARING A "WORKS CITED" LIST OF BIBLIOGRAPHIC REFERENCES

For papers that use the MLA style of documentation, you will need to list all sources you have used at the end. These sources are not numbered, but they are listed in alphabetical order, following the first author's last name. If no author is identified, use the title of the work to alphabetize the source.

Books

The basic bibliographic reference for a book includes the name of the author, the title of the book, the place of publication, the name of the publisher, the date of publication, and the medium of publication (Print or Web). Other information is added as necessary.

■ A Book with One Author

Ondaatje, Michael. *The English Patient.* Toronto: Vintage Books, 1993. Print.

■ A Book with Two Authors

Finnbogason, Jack, and Al Valleau. *Canadian Writer's Pocket Guide.* 5th ed. Toronto:
  Nelson, 2014. Print.

■ A Book with Three Authors

Poole, Gary, Deborah Matheson, and David Cox. *The Psychology of Health and
  Health Care: A Canadian Perspective.* 4th ed. Toronto: Pearson, 2012. Print.

■ A Book with More Than Three Authors

The MLA system permits the use of "et al." for four or more authors or editors (listing all authors is also permitted).

Sniderman, Pat R., et al. *Managing Organizational Behavior in Canada.* Toronto:
  Nelson, 2007. Print.

■ A Book with Corporate or Association Authorship

Canadian Public Health Association. *Assessment Toolkit for Bullying, Harassment and
  Peer Relations at School.* Ottawa: CPHA Publications, 2004. Print.

■ An Edition Other Than the First

Reinking, James, et al. *Strategies for Successful Writing: A Rhetoric, Research Guide,
  Reader, and Handbook.* 6th Canadian ed. Toronto: Pearson, 2017. Print.

■ A Book in Two or More Volumes

Vandendool, Grace. *Keyboard Theory.* 2nd ed., 3 vols. Mississauga: The Frederick
  Harris Music Co., Limited, 2010. Print.

■ A Book with an Editor Rather Than an Author

Toye, William, ed. *The Concise Oxford Companion to Canadian Literature.* 2nd ed.
  Toronto: Oxford University Press, 2012. Print.

MLA

■ **A Book with Both an Author and an Editor**

Conrad, Joseph. *Heart of Darkness.* Ed. Robert Hampson. London: Penguin,
     2007. Print.

■ **A Translation**

de Beauvoir, Simone. *All Said and Done.* Trans. Patrick O'Brian. New York: Putnam,
     1974. Print.

■ **An Essay or Chapter in a Collection of Works by One Author**

Woolf, Virginia. "The Lives of the Obscure." *The Common Reader.* New York:
     Harcourt, 1925. 111–18. Print.

■ **An Essay or Chapter in an Edited Anthology**

Blaise, Clark. "A Class of New Canadians." *Pens of Many Colours: A Canadian
     Reader.* Ed. Eva C. Karpinski and Ian Lea. Toronto: Harcourt Brace Jovanovich,
     1993. 218–26. Print.

■ **A Reprint of an Older Work**

Crimp, Douglas. "AIDS: Cultural Analysis/Cultural Activism." *AIDS: Cultural Analysis/
     Cultural Activism.* Ed. Crimp. Cambridge: MIT Press, 1988. 3–16. Rpt. from
     AIDS: Cultural Analysis/Cultural Activism. Ed. Crimp. Spec. issue of October 43
     (1987): 237–71. Print.

■ **A Book with a Title That Includes Another Title**

The MLA offers two options: You may omit italicizing the embedded title, or you may
set it off with quotation marks.

Tanner, John. *Anxiety in Eden: A Kierkegaardian Reading of* Paradise Lost. Oxford,
     UK: Oxford University Press, 1992. Print.

Tanner, John. *Anxiety in Eden: A Kierkegaardian Reading of "Paradise Lost."* Oxford,
     UK: Oxford University Press, 1992. Print.

Periodicals

Periodicals refer to newspapers, popular magazines, and specialized occupational and
scholarly journals. Whether you are using material from an academic journal or a popular magazine, the basic information for a periodical article includes the name of the
article's author, the name of the periodical, the title of the article, the date of publication, the page range of the entire article, and, for scholarly journals, the volume number and issue number (if there is one). Finally, you will include the medium of

publication—print or web. The MLA system capitalizes periodical titles, but omits an introductory *The* from these titles.

■ An Article in a Scholarly Journal

Pfennig, David. "Kinship and Cannibalism." *Bioscience* 47.10 (1997): 667–75. Print.

■ An Article in a Scholarly Journal That Uses Only Issue Numbers

Zine, Jasmin. "Honour and Identity: An Ethnographic Account of Muslim Girls in a
    Canadian Islamic School." *Topia* 19 (2008): 35–62. Print.

■ An Unsigned Article in a Scholarly Journal

"Baby, It's Cold Inside." *Science* 276 (1997): 537–38. Print.

■ A Signed Article in an Occupational or Popular Magazine

Gopnik, Adam. "Dog Story." *New Yorker* 8 Aug. 2011: 47–53. Print.

■ An Unsigned Article in an Occupational or Popular Magazine

"Robot Productivity." *Production Engineering* May 1982: 52–55. Print.

■ A Signed Article in a Daily Newspaper

Abma, Derek. "Competitiveness of Video Games Linked to Aggression." *Edmonton
    Journal* 4 Sept. 2011: A5. Print.

■ An Unsigned Article in a Daily Newspaper

"Delays in Oil Spill Response Don't Inspire Confidence." *Vancouver Sun* 11 April
    2015: B8. Print.

■ Editorial Comment

Holmes, John Haynes. "Editorial Comment." *Unity* Sept. 1945: 99. Print.

Encyclopedia Articles

When documenting familiar works, such as *The Canadian Encyclopedia*, the basic information for the MLA system includes the name of the article's author if known, the title of the article, the name of the encyclopedia, the edition number (if provided), and the date of the edition.

Henderson, William. "Aboriginal Self-Government." *The Canadian Encyclopedia*.
    2000 ed. Print.

The MLA system requires additional information for encyclopedia citations when less familiar publications are documented.

MLA

Fears, J. Rufus. "Emperor's Cult." *Encyclopedia of Religion.* Ed. Mircea Eliade. 16
vols. New York: Macmillan, 1987. Print.

For an anonymous article, references begin with the article's title.

Government Documents

The basic information for a federal, provincial, or foreign government publication that
is documented using the MLA system includes the name of the author, the title of the
publication, the name of the government and the agency issuing the publication,
the place of publication, the name of the printing group (if known), the date, and the
medium of publication. If no author is named, begin by identifying the government
and then cite the government agency as the author.

Centre of Expertise in Marine Mammalogy. *Marine Mammal Research: An Overview.*
Communications Branch, Fisheries and Oceans Canada. Ottawa, 2006. Print.

Helix, Jefferson. *Environmental Impact of Fish Farming in British Columbia.* British
Columbia Ministry of Environment. Victoria: Queen's Printer for British
Columbia, 1997. Print.

United States. Cong. Office of Technology Assessment. *The Biology of Mental
Disorders.* 102nd Cong., 2nd sess. Washington: GPO, 1992. Print.

Other Sources

■ Review

Caine, Ken. "Natural Resources and Aboriginal Peoples in Canada: Readings,
Cases, and Commentary 2nd ed." Rev. of *Natural Resources and Aboriginal
Peoples in Canada,* 2nd ed., eds. Robert Anderson and Robert Bone. *Northern
Review* Spring 2011: 138–42. Web. 9 Sept. 2011.

If the review is untitled, follow the above format but omit the missing element.

■ Published Interviews

Noriega, Manuel. "A Talk with Manuel Noriega." By Felipe Hernandez. *News Report*
20 Mar. 1997: 28–30. Print.

■ Personal Interviews

If you conducted the interview yourself, start with the name of the person interviewed
(last name first) and follow it with the kind of interview and the date on which it was
conducted.

Trudeau, Justin. Personal interview. 19 Nov. 2015.

MLA

■ Audiovisual Media

Frankenstein. Dir. James Whale. Perf. Boris Karloff, John Boles, Colin Clive, and Mae
Clarke. Universal, 1931. Film.

If you are interested in the contribution of a particular person, start with that person's
name. Use the same model for videocassette and DVD recordings, and add release dates
and distributors.

Whale, James, dir. *Frankenstein.* Perf. Boris Karloff, John Boles, Colin Clive, and Mae
Clarke. Universal, 1931. Film.

Whale, James, dir. *Frankenstein.* Perf. Boris Karloff, John Boles, Colin Clive, and Mae
Clarke. 1931. Universal, 1999. DVD.

■ Television and Radio Programs

The Independent Eye. Prod. M. Paris and J. Robertson. Knowledge Network. Know,
Burnaby. 13 Feb. 1999. Television.

Use this format when additional information is pertinent:

Peril at End House. By Agatha Christie. Dir. Renny Rye. Prod. Brian Eastman. Perf.
David Suchet and Hugh Fraser. *Mystery.* Introd. Diana Rigg. PBS. WKAR, East
Lansing. 12 Aug. 1993. Television.

■ Music and Sound Recordings

Smith, Bessie. *The World's Greatest Blues Singer.* Columbia, 1948. LP.

Give the recording date, followed by the medium (CD, Audiocasette, Audiotape, or LP).
If you mention the name of a particular item on the sound recording, set it off with
quotation marks, as shown below.

Smith, Bessie. "Down Hearted Blues." By Alberta Watson. *The World's Greatest Blues
Singer.* Columbia, 1948. LP.

■ Computer Software

Data Desk. Vers. 6.0. Data Description, 1997. Computer software.

■ CD-ROMs and Other Databases

Norman, J. L. "Barcelona." *Software Toolworks Multimedia Encyclopedia.* Disc 1.
Danbury: Grolier, 1996. CD-ROM.

Online Sources

Because data from the Internet are often incomplete—perhaps lacking an author, a title,
or any recognizable page or paragraph number—ask your instructor what format to

MLA

follow and then use that format consistently. Provide all available information, and include the online address if your reader couldn't find it otherwise.

■ Books on the Web

The basic information for a book on the web includes the name(s) of the author(s), if known; the title of the book; the place, publisher, and date of the original publication, if applicable; the electronic site, if named; the date of electronic publication if the online version has never been published in print, or if it is part of a scholarly project; the sponsor of the site; the medium of publication (*Web*); and the date on which the material was retrieved.

Locke, John. *An Essay Concerning Human Understanding.* London, 1690. Institute of
    Learning Technologies. 1995. Columbia U. Web. 24 June 2012.

When some of the basic information is not provided, use whatever is available.

Chaney, Walter J., William J. Diehm, and Frank Seeley. *The Second 50 Years: A
    Reference Manual for Senior Citizens.* Weed, CA: London Circle Publishing,
    1999. Web. 8 Aug. 2012.

To cite part of an electronic book, place the part's title after the name(s) of the author(s).

Dawson, Marie. Introduction. *Methods of Sociological Investigation.* New York:
    Harmon, 1997. Web. 6 Sept. 2011.

■ Periodicals on the Web

Periodicals online include specialized occupational and scholarly journals, popular magazines, newspapers, and newsletters. The basic information for a periodical is much the same as for a print publication: include the author's name, if known; the title of the article; the title of the periodical; the volume and issue numbers; the date on which the article was published; the page numbers (either print pages or online pages, or *n. pag.* if none are given); the medium of publication (*Web*); and the date on which the material was retrieved.

■ Article from Online Scholarly Journal

Ricciardelli, Rosemary. "Masculinity, Consumerism, and Appearance: A Look at Men's
    Hair." *Canadian Review of Sociology* 48.2 (2011): 181–201. Web. 8 Sept. 2011.

Meyers, Eric M., Lisa P. Nathan, and Kris Unsworth. "Who's Watching Your Kids?
    Safety and Surveillance in Virtual Worlds for Children." *Journal of Virtual Worlds
    Research* 3.2 (2010): n. pag. Web. 20 Apr. 2014.

■ Article from Online Newspaper

Fiorito, Joe. "Homeless Middle Class Tell a Story." *Toronto Star* 15 July 2011. GT2.
    Web. 9 Sept. 2011.

Hammer, Kate, and Tamara Baluja. "War on Child Obesity: Out of the Cafeteria and
onto the Playground." *Globe and Mail.* 23 May 2012. Web. 1 May 2014.

■ Periodicals Accessed through an Online Library Service or Large Network Provider

Many full-text articles are available online at libraries or at home through services provided by private institutions such as LexisNexis and ProQuest Direct or by public institutions such as governments that maintain extensive databases. For a work in a periodical in an online database, cite the author's name, if known; the title of the article; the title of the periodical; the date on which the article was published; the page numbers for the article; the name of the database, in italics; the medium of publication (*Web*); and the date on which the material was accessed.

Clemetson, Lynette. "A Ticket to Private School." *Newsweek* 27 Mar. 2000. n. pag.
LexisNexis. Web. 5 May 2012.

■ Government Documents

The basic information for a government document includes the name of the author, if known; the title; the name of the government and agency issuing the document; the place of publication and printing group, if known; the date of publication; the medium of publication (*Web*); and the date on which the material was retrieved. If no author is given, begin by identifying the government and then give the government agency as the author.

Nova Scotia Department of Education. Cyberbullying Task Force. *Bullying and
Cyberbullying.* 2011. Web. 9 Sept. 2011.

Shackell, Nancy, and John Lodger. *Climate Change and Its Effects on Ecosystems,
Habitats and Biota.* State of the Scotian Shelf Report. Fisheries and Oceans
Canada. Ottawa, April 2015. Web. 14 April 2015.

■ Personal Home Page

The basic information for a personal home page documented includes the name of its originator, if known; the title of the site, if any (use *Home Page* or other such description if no title is given); the medium of publication (*Web*); and the date on which the material was retrieved from the site.

Lanthrop, Olin. Home page. Web. 24 June 2000.

■ Online Postings and Email

For online postings such as newsgroups or mailing lists, use the label "Online posting" where the title would go. For an email message, give the name of the writer; the subject line of the message, if there is one, as the title in quotation marks; the words *Message to* and the name of the recipient; the date of the message; and the medium.

Corelli, Aldo. "Colleges and Diversity." Online posting. *Learninghouse,* 20 Apr. 1993.
Web. 24 June 2000.

Nicholson, Brad. "Casino Gambling." Message to author. 2 Feb. 2001. Email.

EXERCISE

1. **Using the MLA system, write a proper reference for each of the unstyled sets of information that follow.**

   a. A book by Melanie Watt entitled Chester, published by Kids Can Press in 2007 in Toronto.

   b. An essay by Patrick Lane called Counting the Bones in the second edition of a book titled Addicted: Notes from the Belly of the Beast, published first in 2001, then in 2006 by Greystone Books in Vancouver, B.C. The essay can be found on pages 1–15. The editors of this book are Lorna Crozier and Patrick Lane.

   c. A scholarly essay Uncritical Reading by Michael Warner published by Routledge in an anthology edited by Jane Gallop called Polemic: Critical or Uncritical in 2004. The essay can be found on pages 13–38.

   d. An unsigned article titled Global Warming Fears on Rise. The article was published in the October 25, 1997, issue of Newswatch magazine. It appears on pages 29 to 31.

   e. A book written by Guy Vanderhaeghe and titled The Englishman's Boy. The book was published in 1996 by McClelland & Stewart Inc. in Toronto.

   f. A scholarly article by James Dubinsky titled Service-Learning as a Path to Virtue: The Ideal Orator in Professional Communication. This article was published in a print book Writing and Community Engagement: A Critical Sourcebook by Bedford/St. Martins Press in 2010. The editors of this book are Tomas Deans, Barbara Roswell, and Adrian Wurr. The article can be found on pages 256–276.

   g. An email message about local food sources by John Menke that you received on June 2, 2015.

   h. A scholarly article titled Physical activity, screen time and self-rated health and mental health in Canadian adolescents, published on April 1, 2015, in an online journal Preventive Medicine, Volume 73, on pages 112–116. The authors of the article are Katya Herman, Wilma Hopman, and Catherine Sabiston. The article was accessed through the ScienceDirect data base on April 16, 2015.

   i. A film titled Casablanca. The film was directed by Michael Curtiz and starred Humphrey Bogart, Ingrid Bergman, Claude Rains, and Paul Henreid. It was released in 1942 by Warner Brothers.

   j. A CBC-TV documentary from the show Doc Zone called Faking the Grade. It aired on April 11, 2015.

2. **Prepare four or five "Works Cited" entries for web and print sources that you might use in writing a paper that draws on research.**

HANDLING IN-TEXT CITATIONS

The general rule of thumb is that any information you provide from external sources in your paper, unless it is common knowledge that can easily be found in multiple sources, should be cited. The MLA system requires you to use parenthetical citations for any quotations, paraphrases, and summaries from outside sources you have used within the body of the paper. In addition to giving credit where it is due, these citations also allow readers to follow a thread from the paper to the "Works Cited" list at the end. Then they might seek out further information if they so desire.

Unless you have included the author's name in your own sentence, the in-text citations start with the last name of the author and the page number of the publication in which the material originally appeared. If there is no author given, use the title or a short form of the title.

As you introduce an idea or quotation from an outside source, you will decide whether it sounds smoother to name the author in a signal phrase or introductory tag ("According to the philosopher Mark Kingwell" or "As the philosopher Mark Kingwell argues"), or whether you will simply include the name in a parenthetical citation.

Always provide some context for material that you quote. Various options exist. When you quote from a source for the first time, you might provide the author's full name and the source of the quotation, perhaps indicating the author's expertise as well, as the passage below illustrates:

> Writing in **Newsweek** magazine, Riena Gross, chief psychiatric social worker at Illinois Medical Center in Chicago, said, "Kids have no real sense that they belong anywhere or to anyone as they did ten or fifteen years ago. Parents have loosened the reins, and kids are kind of floundering" (74).

Or you might note the event prompting the quotation and then the author's name.

> Addressing a seminar at the University of Toronto, Dr. Joseph Pomeranz speculated that "acupuncture may work by activating a neural pain suppression mechanism in the brain" (324).

Note how the following passage identifies the author's full name and expertise and introduces the quotation by summing up the author's main idea.

> Economist Richard M. Cybert, president of Carnegie-Mellon University, offers the following sad prediction about the steel industry's future: "It will never be as large an industry as it has been. There are a lot of plants that will never come back and many laborers that will never be rehired" (43).

After first citing an author's full name, use only the last name for subsequent references.

> In discussing the value of reading literature, Frye claims, "Only literature gives us the whole sweep and range of the human imagination as it sees itself" (42).

When quoting from a source with no author given, introduce the quotation with the name of the source.

> Commenting on the problems that law enforcement personnel have in coping with computer crime, Credit and Financial Management magazine stated,

In-Text

"A computer crime can be committed in three hundredths of a second, and the criminal can be thousands of miles from the 'scene,' using a telephone" ("Computer Crime" 43).

Book with One Author

■ Bibliographic Reference for Book

Kingwell, Mark. *Better Living: In Pursuit of Happiness from Plato to Prozac.* Toronto: Penguin, 1998. 94–143. Print.

■ Paraphrased passage and citation with author's name and page number in parentheses

In our consumerist culture, it is easy to confuse it with having fun or finding pleasure, and to assume that feeling good is our natural human condition. Any pleasure that is prolonged eventually subsides, and may become a form of emptiness (Kingwell 107).

■ Paraphrased passage and citation with author identified in signal phrase

The philosopher Mark Kingwell claims that in our consumerist culture, we tend to confuse happiness with finding pleasure or having fun, and to assume that feeling good is our natural human condition. However, any pleasure that is prolonged eventually subsides, and may become a form of emptiness (107).

Online Newspaper Article

■ Bibliographic Reference

Goar, Carol. "Bringing Higher Education into the 21st Century." *Toronto Star* 5 April 2015. n. pag. Web. 16 April 2015.

■ Passage from newspaper source with signal phrase

In a column titled "Bringing Higher Education into the 21st Century," Carol Goar cites a Saskatchewan professor's report on recommendations to promote stronger links between university policies and the needs of the workforce.

■ Passage with parenthetical citation

A report that recommends stronger links between university policies and the needs of the workforce can help universities refocus their aims (Goar).

Authors with the Same Last Name

If your citations include authors with the same last name, use the initials of their first names to distinguish them.

In-Text

■ Bibliographic Reference

Adler, Jerry. "Search for an Orange Thread." *Newsweek* 16 June 1980: 32–34. Print.

Adler, William L. "The Agent Orange Controversy." *Detroit Free Press* 18 Dec. 1979,
    state ed.: B2. Print.

■ Passage and Citation (uses initial of author's first name to clarify)

As early as 1966, miscarriages, liver abscesses, and nerve damage were identified
(J. Adler 32).

Separate Works by the Same Author

If your references include two or more works by the same author, add shortened forms
of the titles to your in-text citation. Put shortened book titles in italics, and use quotation
marks around article and essay titles.

Two Sources for the Same Citations

If two sources provide essentially the same information and you wish to mention both in
one parenthetical citation, alphabetize them according to their authors' last names, list
them with a semicolon between them, and position the citation as you would any other
citation. Citations in MLA style do not need to be listed alphabetically.

■ Bibliographic Reference

Bryce, Bonnie. "The Controversy over Funding Community Colleges." *Detroit Free
    Press* 13 Nov. 1988, state ed.: A4. Print.

Warshow, Harry. "Community College Funding Hits a Snag." *Grand Rapids Press* 15
    Nov. 1988, city ed.: A2. Print.

■ Passage and Citation

In contending that a 3% reduction in state funding, . . . enrolment was expected to
jump by 15% during the next year (Warshow A2; Bryce A4).

Unsigned References

When you use a source for which no author is given, the in-text citation consists of all or
part of the title, and the appropriate page numbers.

■ Bibliographic Reference

"Money and Classes." *Progressive* Oct. 1997: 10. Print.

■ Passage and Citation

According to the General Accounting Office, repairing . . . many billions more
    ("Money and Classes" 10).

In-Text

CITING QUOTATIONS

Set off quotations fewer than five lines long with quotation marks, blending them into the text of the paper.

Be very sparing with longer quotations, using them only when they seem especially memorable or important. For these quotations longer than five lines, follow this format: Omit the quotation marks and indent the material 10 spaces from the left margin. If you quote part or all of one paragraph, don't further indent the first line. If you quote two or more consecutive paragraphs, indent each one's first line three additional spaces.

Use single quotation marks for a quotation within a shorter quotation and double marks for a quotation within a longer, indented quotation. Position the citation as shown in the following examples.

■ Bibliographic Reference

Schapiro, Mark. "Children of a Lesser God." *Harper's Bazaar* Apr. 1996: 205+. Print.

■ Passage and Citation

U.N. investigators who have studied the extent of child labour in developing countries estimate that "as many as 200 million children go to work rather than to school . . . making everything from clothing and shoes to handbags and carpets" (Schapiro 205).

■ Bibliographic Reference

Kymlicka, Will. "Immigrants, Multiculturalism and Citizenship." *Strategies for Successful Writing.* 2nd Canadian ed. Ed. James A. Reinking et al. Toronto: Pearson, 2006. 46–63. Print.

■ Passage and Citation

One commentator offers this assessment of the focus of Canada's multiculturalism policy, which is often misunderstood by its critics:

> In reality, most of the focus of multiculturalism policy (and most of its funding) has been directed to promoting civic participation in the larger society and to increasing mutual understanding and co-operation between the members of different ethnic groups. More generally, the multiculturalism policy has never stated or implied that people are under any duty or obligation to retain their ethnic identity/practices "freeze-dried," or indeed to retain them at all. On the contrary, the principle that individuals should be free to choose whether to maintain their ethnic identity has been one of the cornerstones of the policy since 1971 and continues to guide existing multiculturalism programs. Multiculturalism is intended to make it possible for people to retain and

express their identity with pride if they so choose, by reducing the legal, institutional, economic or societal obstacles to this expression. It does not penalize or disapprove of people who choose not to identify with their ethnic group, or describe them as poor citizens or as lesser Canadians. (Kymlicka 46)

Indirect Citations

In MLA style, if you use a quotation from person A that you obtained from a book or article written by person B, or if you paraphrase such a quotation, put "qtd. in" before the name of the publication's author in the parenthetical reference.

■ Bibliographic Reference

Goldstein, Joshua S. "World Peace Could Be Closer Than You Think." *Foreign Policy* 188 (Sept. Oct. 2011): 53+. *Canadian Periodicals Index Quarterly*. Web. 9 Sept. 2011.

■ Passage and Citation

The peace researcher Randall Forsberg imagined "'a world largely without war,'" one in which "'the vanishing risk of great-power war has opened the door to a previously unimaginable future—a future in which war is no longer socially-sanctioned and is rare, brief, and small in scale'" (qtd. in Goldstein 53+).

AVOIDING PLAGIARISM

While documenting your sources properly strengthens the authority of your writing, failing to document properly weakens your personal and academic or professional credibility. As discussed in Chapter 14, this failure to document, whether intentional or not, is a form of academic dishonesty referred to as plagiarism.

Plagiarism occurs when a writer uses another person's material without proper acknowledgement of the source. Almost all students know that the most obvious forms of plagiarism—such as buying a paper from a paper mill—are unethical. However, plagiarism often happens because students are careless in their note taking, or because they simply don't understand what must be acknowledged and documented. In our computerized world, where we have become used to downloading music and sharing software, it might be tempting to rationalize that material from the Internet is free for the taking. Some students might imagine that they can escape the obligation to cite sources by changing a word here or there, or cutting and pasting information from different sources. However, unless the material is clearly common knowledge that will not ever be questioned or challenged, any material from external sources, including the Internet, must be cited. Even if it is unintentional, plagiarism is unacceptable.

The consequences of plagiarism are often severe. Depending on the school policy, students caught plagiarizing risk getting a zero for that assignment, failing the course, or even being suspended or expelled. In 2002, 44 business and economics students at a major B.C. university were suspended for plagiarizing a tutor's work; the suspensions were noted on the students' transcripts. Large groups of students at other Canadian universities have been suspended for academic dishonesty. Instructors who are used to reading student essays can usually notice when the voice of the writer changes, or when the quality of the writing is inconsistent. In addition, many schools have plagiarism detection software that helps instructors track plagiarism, even if it is just a few sentences that have been raided from a source. It's easy for professors to use search engines to check whether particular phrases, sentences, or paragraphs have been copied from websites—and many do.

Students who are uncertain about what constitutes plagiarism are responsible for educating themselves. They may consult resources available through online sources, such as various documents available at www.plagiarism.org. Whenever you are unsure whether material requires documentation, supply a reference.

CHAPTER 17

Documenting Sources: APA Style

The APA (American Psychological Association) style is used mainly for papers in the social and behavioural sciences. The latest sixth edition of the APA style now has a broadened scope, as it is often used by students and researchers in areas such as business, nursing, and education. Changes in this edition reflect the growing dominance of electronic and online sources. For further information, see www.apastyle.org, or for an APA style tutorial, see www.apastyle.org/learn/tutorials/basics-tutorial.aspx. Other online sources, including YouTube videos, can help you with formatting and page layout when creating an APA research paper.

APA SYSTEM FOR PREPARING PAPERS

- **Title page:** The first page is a title page. On the title page, two inches (5.08 cm) from the top of the page, type the words "Running Head" in capital letters without quotation marks, flush with the left margin; then type a colon and a word or phrase that is an abbreviated version (fewer than 50 characters, including spaces) of your title in capital letters. Type the full title itself with the first letter of key words capitalized in the upper half of the title page, followed by your name, the course number, the instructor's name, and the date below. Place the page number in the upper right corner and number pages consecutively beginning with this title page.

- **Running Head:** The shortened version of your title should appear on the header of every page, in the left corner, typed in upper-case letters. Software programs such as Word have automatic header features that you can use to set the running head at the top left of the page.

- **Abstract:** The second page contains the abstract, a concise one-paragraph summary of the main points of your argument. Repeat the title of the paper on the first page, centred at the top of the page and typed in capital and lower-case letters. The heading "Abstract" is centred on the first line below the running head. It does not have quotation marks around it or a paragraph indent. Double-space here and throughout the paper.

- **Body:** The text of your essay begins on the third page. Type the title of the paper in upper- and lower-case letters under the running head. Indent each paragraph five to seven spaces.

- **Headings:** For longer papers, five levels of headings and subheadings are available to indicate the relative importance of different sections. Your shorter papers are unlikely to use more than two levels of headings: level 1 headings for main sections (centred, bold, key words beginning with a capital letter) and level 2 headings for subheadings (flush left, bold, key words beginning with a capital letter).

- **References:** The list of all sources used begins on a new page. The heading is centred, and the list of references is organized alphabetically by the surnames of the first authors. Begin the first line of each entry at the left margin, and use a hanging indent to indent subsequent lines five spaces. Double-space all entries.

- **Supplemental Material: Footnotes, Tables, Figures, and Appendixes:** If you have additional information to support the information in your text in the form of footnotes, you can include each footnote at the bottom of the page on which it is mentioned, or at the end of your paper on a separate page after the References. If you have tables to present data, or figures to present graphs or photographs, these begin on a separate page. Each appendix that presents additional information begins on a separate page at the end of your paper.

APA

PREPARING APA BIBLIOGRAPHIC CITATIONS FOR A REFERENCE LIST

The reference list you include at the end of your paper allows readers to locate the information you have quoted or paraphrased. As you are doing your research, be sure to keep careful notes, tracking all of the bibliographic information you will need for your reference list at the end of your paper: names of authors, editors, and translators; dates of publication; relevant titles, along with volume and issue numbers for journal articles; and page numbers.

To better meet the challenges of locating online publications, the APA style now recommends that the unique work you are referencing in print and electronic form be identified by the digital object identifier (DOI), a unique identification sequence assigned by the International DOI Foundation. The DOI can often be found near the copyright notices of electronic journal articles or in some cases at the top of the first page of the article. When the DOI is used, there is no need to indicate the URL of the reference.

■ **Sample**

Mesmer-Magnus, J. R., & DeChurch, L. A. (2009). Information sharing and team
    performance: A meta-analysis. *Journal of Applied Psychology, 94*(2), 535–546.
    doi:10.1037/a0013773

Books

The APA system uses initials rather than first and middle names for authors, editors,
and translators (for example, Ondaatje, M. rather than Ondaatje, Michael). If there are
different years of publication, give the most recent one. Note that only the first word
and proper nouns and adjectives such as names are capitalized in titles and subtitles.
Italicize the titles of books and other longer works. For the place of publication, give the
city followed by the province or state, then the name of the publisher in a shortened
form. The reference list for sources used begins on a new page at the end of the essay.

APA

■ **A Book with One Author**

Ondaatje, M. (1993). *The English patient.* Toronto, ON: Vintage Books.

■ **A Book with Two Authors**

Finnbogason, J., & Valleau, A. (2014). *A Canadian writer's pocket guide* (5th ed.).
    Toronto, ON: Nelson.

■ **A Book with Three Authors**

Poole, G., Matheson, D., & Cox, D. (2012). *Psychology of health and health care: A
    Canadian perspective* (4th ed.). Toronto, ON: Pearson.

The APA system gives up to and including six author or editor names in the reference
list. Substitute "et al.," meaning "and others," for the seventh or more.

■ **A Book with a Title That Includes Another Title**

Words that would be italicized on their own should be set roman as part of an italicized title.

Tanner, J. (1992). *Anxiety in Eden: A Kierkegaardian reading of* Paradise Lost. Oxford,
    England: Oxford University Press.

■ **A Book with Corporate or Association Authorship**

Canadian Public Health Association. (2004). *Assessment toolkit for bullying, harassment
    and peer relations at school.* Ottawa, ON: CPHA Publications.

United Nations, Public Administration Division. (1968). *Local government training.*
    New York, NY: Author.

When the author of the work is also the publisher, the APA system uses the word "Author" following the place of publication. If the work is published by another organization, its name replaces "Author."

■ An Edition Other Than the First

Reinking, J., von der Osten, R., & Cairns, S. (2016). *Strategies for successful writing: A rhetoric, research guide, reader, and handbook* (6th Canadian ed.). Toronto, ON: Pearson.

■ A Book in Two or More Volumes

Vandendool, G. (2010). *Keyboard theory* (2nd ed.) (Vols. 1–3). Mississauga, ON: The Frederick Harris Music Co., Limited.

■ A Reprint of an Older Work

Matthiessen, F. O. (1970). *American renaissance: Art and expression in the age of Emerson and Whitman.* New York, NY: Oxford University Press. (Original work published 1941)

■ A Book with an Editor Rather Than an Author

Toye, W. (Ed.). (2011). *The concise Oxford companion to Canadian literature* (2nd ed.). Toronto, ON: Oxford University Press.

■ A Book with Both an Author and an Editor

Conrad, J. (2007). *Heart of darkness* (R. Hampson, Ed.). London, England: Penguin. (Original work published 1902)

■ A Translation

de Beauvoir, S. (1974). *All said and done* (P. O'Brian, Trans.). New York, NY: Putnam. (Original work published 1972)

■ An Essay or Chapter in a Collection of Works by One Author

Woolf, V. (1925). The lives of the obscure. In *The common reader, first series* (pp. 111–118). New York, NY: Harcourt.

■ An Essay or Chapter in an Anthology

Blaise, C. (1993). A class of new Canadians. In E. C. Karpinski & I. Lea (Eds.), *Pens of many colours: A Canadian reader* (pp. 218–226). Toronto, ON: Harcourt.

Periodicals

Periodicals include newspapers, popular magazines, and specialized occupational and scholarly journals. The basic information for a periodical article includes the name of the article's author, the date of publication, the title of the article, the name of the periodical, the page range of the entire article, and, for scholarly journals, the volume number of the periodical.

Italicize the titles of journals, as you would the titles of books. Capitalize the first and last words and all key words for journal titles. For page numbers, include p. or pp. for newspaper articles, but not for articles from journals and magazines.

■ An Article in a Scholarly Journal Consecutively Paged through the Entire Volume

Pfennig, D. (1997). Kinship and cannibalism. *Bioscience, 47,* 667–675.

■ An Article in a Scholarly Journal That Pages Each Issue Separately

Block, J. W. (1976). Sodom and Gomorrah: A volcanic disaster. *Journal of Geological Education, 23*(5), 74–77.

■ An Unsigned Article in a Scholarly Journal

Baby, it's cold inside. (1997). *Science, 276,* 537–538.

■ A Signed Article in an Occupational or Popular Magazine

Gopnik, A. (2011, August 8). Dog story. *The New Yorker.* 47–53.

■ An Unsigned Article in an Occupational or Popular Magazine

Zoomsafer app stops texting. (2010, October 1). *The Province,* p. A12.

■ A Signed Article in a Daily Newspaper

Derek, A. (2011, Sept. 4). Competitiveness of video games linked to aggression. *Edmonton Journal,* p. A5.

■ An Unsigned Article in a Daily Newspaper

Delays in oil spill response don't inspire confidence. (2015, April 11). *Vancouver Sun,* p. B8.

Encyclopedia Articles

The APA system requires publication information for all encyclopedia citations.

Fears, J. R. (1987). Emperor's cult. In *The encyclopedia of religion* (Vol. 5, pp. 101–102). New York, NY: Macmillan.

APA

For an anonymous article, references for the APA system begin with the article's title. Position the publication date, within parentheses, after this title. The remaining format is identical to citations with an author.

Government Documents

The APA system includes the name of the author, the date of publication, and the place of publication and adds a cataloguing code where one exists.

Helix, J. (1997). *Environmental impact of fish farming in British Columbia.* British Columbia, Ministry of Environment. Victoria, BC: Queen's Printer for British Columbia.

Canadian Department of Finance. (1993). *Annual report 1991–1992.* Ottawa, ON: Queen's Printer.

U.S. Congress, Office of Technology Assessment. (1992). *The biology of mental disorders* (SUDOCS Report No. Y3.T22/2:2/B57/10). Washington, DC: Government Printing Office.

Other Sources

■ Book Reviews

Koenig, R. (1989, February 20). Billy the Kid [Review of the book *Billy Bathgate*]. *New York, 21*, 20–21.

Caine, K. (2011, Spring). Natural resources and Aboriginal peoples in Canada: Readings, cases, and commentary 2nd ed. [Review of the book *Natural resources and Aboriginal peoples in Canada,* 2nd ed. by R. Anderson and R. Bone]. *The Northern Review,* 138–142.

If the review is untitled, follow the above format but omit the missing element.

■ Published Interviews

Hernandez, F. (1997, March 20). A talk with Manuel Noriega. *News Report, 15*, 28–30.

If the interview is untitled, follow the example above, omitting mention of a title.

■ Personal Interviews or Emails

For the APA system, a personal interview or email message is considered personal correspondence and is not included in the References list. Instead, use an in-text parenthetical citation. Include the name of the person interviewed, the notation "personal communication," and the date: (J. Trudeau, personal communication, June 18, 2015).

■ Audiovisual Media

APA citations begin with an individual's name and his or her contribution to the *motion picture* (use this term, not *film*). The country of origin (where it was made and released) is now required.

Whale, J. (Director). (1931). *Frankenstein* [Motion picture]. United States: Universal.

■ Television and Radio Programs

Paris, M., & Robertson, J. (Producers). (1999, February 13). *The independent eye* [Television broadcast]. Burnaby, BC: Knowledge Network.

Use the following format when additional information is pertinent.

Exton, C. (Writer), & Rye, R. (Director). (1993). Peril at End House [Television series episode]. In B. Eastman (Producer), *Mystery*. Washington, DC: Public Broadcasting Service.

With the APA system, the name of the scriptwriter appears in the author's position, followed by the director. Any in-text references begin with the first name in the bibliographic reference (for example, Exton, 1993).

■ Music and Sound Recordings

The APA format requires identification of all formats, including a CD.

Smith, B. (1997). *The essential Bessie Smith* [CD]. New York, NY: Columbia Records.

Smith, B. (1948). Down hearted blues. On *The world's greatest blues singer* [CD]. New York, NY: Columbia Records. (Original recording February 17, 1923)

Recording dates, if different from the copyright year, follow the entry, enclosed in parentheses, with no final period.

■ Computer Software

Data Desk (Version 6.0) [Computer software]. (1997). Ithaca, NY: Data Description.

In the APA system, only specialized software or computer programs are listed in the References. Standard commercial software and languages should be cited by their proper name and version in the text itself.

■ CD-ROMs and Other Databases

Norman, J. L. (1996). Barcelona. In *Software toolworks multimedia encyclopedia* [CD-ROM]. Boston, MA: Grolier.

The APA Manual (6th ed.) takes the view that all aggregated databases are the same type of source, regardless of the format or manner of access (CD-ROM, library or university server, or online web supplier). Follow the model above when you need to cite an entire CD-ROM (not a document from it). In a reference to information

APA

taken from a database (even a CD-ROM), give a "retrieval statement" containing the date you retrieved the document, article, or piece of data, as well as the full, correct name of the database. When you retrieve information from an online database, end the entry with a correct and complete URL for the specific document or version. In this case, the name of the database is omitted, unless this information will help in retrieval from a large or complex site. (See online models in the next section.)

Online Sources

The most recent edition of the *Publication Manual of the American Psychological Association* provides the APA's latest guidelines for documenting online sources. You can also consult the association's website (www.apastyle.org/elecref.html) for its most up-to-date information about citing electronic sources.

When citing electronic sources, follow the models for print sources, using the author-date style. If the data from the Internet are incomplete, perhaps lacking an author, a title, or a recognizable page or paragraph number, include all available information. If the date is missing, use n.d. to indicate "no date."

■ Retrieval Date Only for Material Likely to Change

Include the date you retrieved material only if it is likely to be updated or altered, such as a blog or a wiki. A retrieval date is usually not needed for journal articles or books.

■ Include Name and Location of Source

Because Internet content often changes frequently, some academic publishers now assign a digital object identifier (DOI) to scholarly documents. A DOI is a unique string of numbers and letters assigned by a registration agency, is more stable than a URL, and should be used instead of a URL when available. It can usually be found on the first page of the article. If there is no DOI, include the URL, such as this example of the URL for the Social Sciences and Humanities Research Council of Canada: http://www.sshrc-crsh.gc.ca/home-accueil-eng.aspx

For convenience and accuracy, you can copy and paste the DOI, if one is available, or the URL. Because your goal is to allow the reader to locate the source you have used, you should test URLs in a new browser session to ensure that they work.

■ Books on the Web

Follow the general guidelines for a printed book, and conclude with appropriate electronic source information, as modelled here, or use the DOI, if known.

Locke, J. (1995). *An essay concerning human understanding.* New York, NY: Columbia University. Retrieved from http://www.ilt.columbia.edu/projects/digitexts/locke/understanding/title.html (Original work published 1690)

When some of the basic information is not provided, use whatever is available.

APA

Chaney, W. J., Diehm, W. J., & Seeley, F. (1999). *The second 50 years: A reference manual for senior citizens.* Weed, CA: London Circle. Retrieved from http://www.londoncircle.com/2d50.html

To cite part of an electronic book, place the part's title after the date of publication. The APA system also cites a chapter or section identifier following the title of the complete document.

Canadian Food Inspection Agency. (2008). Nutrition labelling. In *Guide to food labelling and advertising* (chap. 5). Retrieved from http://www.inspection.gc.ca/english/fssa/labeti/guide/ch17e.shtml

■ Periodicals on the Web

The APA recommends using the models for print periodicals when documenting online articles. When the article has a DOI assigned, no retrieval date, database name (if one is used), or URL is necessary. If the article does not have a DOI assigned, give the exact URL if access to the journal is open, and give the home page of the journal if the article is accessible only by subscription. A retrieval date is not necessary.

■ Journal Article with DOI Assigned

Raver, C., Li-Grining, C., Metzger, M., Jones, S., Zhai, F., & Solomon, B. (2009). Targeting children's behavior problems in preschool classrooms: A cluster-randomized controlled trial. *Journal of Consulting and Clinical Psychology, 77,* 302–316. doi:10.1037/a0015302

■ Journal Article with No DOI Assigned

Sprott, J., & Doob, A. (2008). Youth crime rates and the youth justice system. *Canadian Journal of Criminology and Criminal Justice, 50,* 621–639. Retrieved from http://www.ccja-acjp.ca/en/cjc.html

■ Periodicals Accessed through an Online Library Service or Large Network Provider

Increasingly, full-text articles are available online at libraries or at home through services such as LexisNexis, ProQuest Direct, and America Online. These services may or may not provide an online address for accessed material. In the APA documentation system, cite the author's name, if known; the date the article was published; the title of the article; the title of the periodical; and the page numbers for the article, if available. Do not include the name of the database.

Clemetson, L. (2000, March 27). A ticket to private school. *Newsweek.* Retrieved from http://www.newsweek/com.icl/83469

APA style prefers that the URL that leads directly to the document file be provided, following the word *from.*

APA

■ Book Reviews and Peer Commentaries

Galbo, J. (2008). Anxious academics: Mission drift and sliding standards in the modern Canadian university [Review of the book *Ivory tower blues: A university system in crisis*]. *Canadian Journal of Sociology, 33*, 404–417. Retrieved from http://ejournals.library.ualberta.ca/index.php/CJS/article/viewFile/4548/3694

Beare, M. (2008). [Response to David Hicks's peer comment on *Money laundering in Canada: Chasing dirty and dangerous dollars*]. *Canadian Journal of Sociology, 33*, 1065–1067. Retrieved from http://ejournals.library.ualberta.ca/index.php/CJS/ article/view/4546/3693

■ Newspaper or Newsletter Articles

Laucius, J. (2009, March 26). Students need real civics lessons: Educator. *Ottawa Citizen*. Retrieved from http://www.ottawacitizen.com/Life/Students+need+real+civics+lessons+educator/1428192/story.html

Oakes, J. (1999, January–February). Promotion or retention: Which one is social? *Harvard Education Letter*. Retrieved from http://www.edletter.org/pst/issues/1999-jf-promotion.shtml

APA style prefers that the URL that leads directly to the document file be provided, following the word *from*.

■ Encyclopedia Articles

The basic information for an encyclopedia article accessed through the web includes the author's name, if known; the title of the article; the name of the encyclopedia; the date of the edition, if known; and the URL of the home or index page.

Greene, G., & Spier, S. Banff Centre for the Arts. (2012). In *The Canadian encyclopedia/the encyclopedia of music in Canada*. Retrieved from http://www.thecanadianencyclopedia.com/articles/emc/banff-centre-for-the-arts

■ Bibliography from Website

Library and Archives Canada. (2006). *Aboriginal stories: English annotated titles*. Retrieved from Read Up on It 2006–2007, Library Archives Canada website: http://www.collectionscanada.gc.ca/read-up-on-it/015020-062000-e.html#a

■ Government Documents

The basic information for a government document includes the name of the author, if known; the date of publication; the title; a cataloguing code if one is available; and the online address. If no author is given, begin by identifying the government agency as the author.

Statistics Canada. (2008). *Educational portrait of Canada, 2006 census.* Retrieved
from http://www12.statcan.ca/english/census06/analysis/education/pdf/97-560-
XIE2006001.pdf

■ Annual Report

Petro-Canada. (2008). *Petro-Canada annual report: Strength to deliver.* Retrieved
from http://www.petro-canada.ca/pdfs/investors/2008_annual_report-e.pdf

■ Personal Home Page

The APA Manual offers no specific guidelines for personal home pages. We suggest
that you use the following pattern, which conforms to general APA practice. Note
that the APA system includes the date of the latest web page revision, if known,
in parentheses.

Lanthrop, O. (2000, May 28). Home page. Retrieved from http://www.cognivis.com/
olin/photos.htm

■ Alternative Media Sources such as Podcasts and Photographs

McDonald, B. (Producer). (2009, February 28). The evolution of moral disgust.
Quirks and Quarks [Audio podcast]. Retrieved from http://www.cbc.ca/quirks/

Hicker, R. (Photographer). (2011). *Moss rain forest* [Photograph]. Retrieved from
http://www.canadaphotos.info/picture/moss-rain-forest-378.htm

■ Newsgroups, Online Forums, and Email

APA style treats email as personal communications, which are cited in parentheses in
the text only (Cairns, S. November 30, 2015). Newsgroups, online forums, discussion
groups, and electronic mailing lists that maintain archives can be cited in the References,
but the APA advises that you do so with caution. With these electronic forms, indicate
the author's full last name and initials (screen name if the full name is not available), the
exact posting date, the name of the thread or blog, a label in brackets describing the
type of message, *Retrieved from* followed by the name of the list if not in the URL, and
the address for the archived message. Categories include Online forum comment (messages posted to newsgroups, online forums, or discussion groups), Electronic mailing list
message (a message on an electronic mailing list or listserv), Web log message (for a blog
post), and Video file (for a video blog post).

Raskin, R. (2009, March 4). Should learning be rewarded with "stuff"? [Web log mes-
sage]. Retrieved from http://www.robinraskin.com/blog/category/your-digital-kids/

Trehub, A. (2002, January 28). Re: The conscious access hypothesis [Online forum
comment]. Retrieved from http://listserv.uh.edu/cgi-bin/
wa?A2=ind0201&L=psyche-b&F=&S=&P=2334 APA

APA

EXERCISE

1. **Using the APA system, format a reference for each of the unstyled sets of information found below.**

   a. A book by Melanie Watt entitled Chester, published by Kids Can Press in 2007 in Toronto.

   b. An essay by Patrick Lane called Counting the Bones in the second edition of a book titled Addicted: Notes from the Belly of the Beast, published first in 2001, then in 2006 by Greystone Books in Vancouver, B.C. The essay can be found on pages 1–15. The editors of this book are Lorna Crozier and Patrick Lane.

   c. A scholarly essay Uncritical Reading by Michael Warner published by Routledge in an anthology edited by Jane Gallop called Polemic: Critical or Uncritical in 2004. The essay can be found on pages 13–38.

   d. An unsigned article titled Global Warming Fears on Rise. The article was published in the October 25, 1997, issue of Newswatch magazine. It appears on pages 29 to 31.

   e. A book written by Guy Vanderhaeghe and titled The Englishman's Boy. The book was published in 1996 by McClelland & Stewart Inc. in Toronto.

   f. A scholarly article by James Dubinsky titled Service-Learning as a Path to Virtue: The Ideal Orator in Professional Communication. This article was published in a print book Writing and Community Engagement: A Critical Sourcebook by Bedford/St. Martins Press in 2010. The editors of this book are Tomas Deans, Barbara Roswell, and Adrian Wurr. The article can be found on pages 256–276.

   g. An email message about local food sources by John Menke that you received on June 2, 2015.

   h. A scholarly article titled Physical activity, screen time and self-rated health and mental health in Canadian adolescents, published on April 1, 2015, in an online journal Preventive Medicine, Volume 73, on pages 112–116. The authors of the article are Katya Herman, Wilma Hopman, and Catherine Sabiston. The article was accessed through the ScienceDirect data base on April 16, 2015.

   i. A film titled Casablanca. The film was directed by Michael Curtiz and starred Humphrey Bogart, Ingrid Bergman, Claude Rains, and Paul Henreid. It was released in 1942 by Warner Brothers.

   j. A CBC-TV documentary from the show Doc Zone called Faking the Grade. It aired on April 11, 2015..

2. **Format five APA references for print and online books or articles that you might use in a research-based paper.**

HANDLING IN-TEXT CITATIONS

You need to identify all of the sources you have used in your paper—for paraphrases and summaries as well as quotations—in parenthetical citations within the text. These identify the last name of the author or authors and the year of publication. The APA style also includes the page number with quotations and also when the information is so specific that it is important to reference the specific page. To see an example of a how a student research paper uses the APA system of parenthetical citations within the text, view the essay on pages 358–363 in Chapter 14.

The following examples illustrate how one writer used APA citations for paraphrased passages from a book.

Book with One Author in Reference List

▪ Bibliographic Reference

Kingwell, M. (1998). *Better living: In pursuit of happiness from Plato to Prozac*. Toronto, ON: Penguin.

▪ Paraphrased or summarized passage from book with author's name, date, and page number in parentheses

In-Text

In our consumerist culture, it is easy to confuse it with having fun or finding pleasure, and to assume that feeling good is our natural human condition. Any pleasure that is prolonged eventually subsides, and may become a form of emptiness (Kingwell, 1998, p. 107).

▪ Paraphrased or summarized passage with author and year identified in signal phrase

The philosopher Mark Kingwell (1998) claims that in our consumerist culture, we tend to confuse happiness with finding pleasure or having fun, and to assume that feeling good is our natural human condition. However, any pleasure that is prolonged eventually subsides, and may become a form of emptiness (p. 107).

Online Newspaper Article in Reference List

▪ Bibliographic Reference

Goar, C. (2015, April 16). Bringing higher education into the 21st century. *Toronto Star*. Retrieved from http://www.thestar.com/opinion/commentary/2015/04/05/bringing-higher-education-into-the-21st-century-goar.html

▪ Paraphrased or summarized passage with parenthetical citation

A report that recommends stronger links between university policies and the needs of the workforce can help universities refocus their aims (Goar, 2015).

■ **Paraphrased or summarized passage with author and year identified in signal phrase**

In a column titled "Bringing Higher Education into the 21st Century," Carol Goar (2015) cites a Saskatchewan professor's report on recommendations to promote stronger links between university policies and the needs of the workforce.

Book with Two Authors in Reference List

■ **Bibliographic Reference**

Weider, B., & Hapgood, D. (1982). *The murder of Napoleon.* New York, NY: Congdon.

■ **Passage and Citation**

In-Text

Four different autopsy reports were filed. . . . Nevertheless, cancer has become accepted as the cause (Weider & Hapgood, 1982).

Note: If the source has more than five authors, use "et al." for all but the first named author.

Authors with the Same Last Name

If your citations include authors with the same last name, distinguish them by using the initials of their first names.

■ **Bibliographic References**

Adler, J. (1980, June 16). Search for an orange thread. *Newsweek*, 32–34.

Adler, W. L. (1979, December 18). The Agent Orange controversy. *Detroit Free Press*, state ed., p. B2.

■ **Passage and Citation**

As early as 1966, government . . . miscarriages, liver abscesses, and nerve damage (J. Adler, 1980).

Two Sources for the Same Citations

If two sources provide essentially the same information and you wish to mention both in one parenthetical citation, alphabetize them according to their authors' last names, list them with a semicolon between them, and position the citation as you would any other citation.

■ Bibliographic References

Bryce, B. (1988, November 13). The controversy over funding community colleges. *Detroit Free Press*, state ed., p. A4.

Warshow, H. (1988, November 15). Community college funding hits a snag. *Grand Rapids Press*, city ed., p. A2.

■ Passage and Citation

In contending that a 3% reduction in state funding . . . enrolment was expected to jump by 15% during the next year (Bryce, 1988; Warshow, 1988).

Unsigned References

When you use a source for which no author is given, the in-text citation consists of all or part of the title, the appropriate page numbers, and the date.

CITING QUOTATIONS

Set off quotations that are fewer than 40 words with quotation marks and run them into the text of the paper. For longer quotes, omit the quotation marks and indent the material five spaces. Double-space the typing. If you quote part or all of one paragraph, don't indent the first line. If you quote two or more consecutive paragraphs, indent each one's first line five additional spaces, except for the first paragraph in the quote, which should not be indented. Use single quotation marks for a quotation within a shorter quotation and double quotation marks for a quotation within a longer, indented quotation.

When the quotation is blended into the text of your paper, position the citation as shown in the following example.

■ Bibliographic Reference

Schapiro, M. (1996, April). Children of a lesser god. *Harper's Bazaar*, 205+.

■ Passage and Citation

UN investigators who have studied the extent of child labour in developing countries estimate that "as many as 200 million children go to work rather than to school . . . making everything from clothing and shoes to handbags and carpets" (Schapiro, 1996, p. 205).

With longer, indented quotations, skip one space after the end punctuation and type the citation in parentheses.

In-Text

■ **Bibliographic Reference**

Kymlicka, W. (2016). Immigrants, multiculturalism and citizenship. In *Strategies for successful writing: A rhetoric, research guide, reader, and handbook* (6th Canadian ed.) (pp. 46–63). Toronto, ON: Pearson. (Original work published 1998)

■ **Passage and Citation**

Kymlicka (2016) offers this assessment of the focus of Canada's multiculturalism policy, which is often misunderstood by its critics:

Multiculturalism is intended to make it possible for people to retain and express their identity with pride if they so choose, by reducing the legal, institutional, economic or societal obstacles to this expression. It does not penalize or disapprove of people who choose not to identify with their ethnic group, or describe them as poor citizens or as lesser Canadians (p. 46).

In-Text

Indirect Citations

If you refer to a source that is cited in another source, name the author or title of the original work and include a parenthetical phrase "as cited in" to show that you are referring to a work that the original author mentions. In your reference list, use only the source you consulted directly (the secondary source).

The peace researcher Randall Forsberg imagined "'a world largely without war'" (as cited in Goldstein, 2011, p. 53).

For further help, consult the APA website, which includes a tutorial, sample references, and sample papers, at www.apastyle.org. The *Publication Manual of the American Psychological Association* (6th ed., 2nd printing) is a good resource to have if you expect to be doing a number of research papers in this style.

Always, be careful with your documentation in order to ensure your credibility and to avoid plagiarism. If you have any questions about when to cite, consult Chapter 16, pages 395–396, the resource on plagiarism at the OWL website (https://owl.english.purdue.edu/owl/resource/589/2/), or links at your own university library.

John Gimlette

Down Labrador

John Gimlette is an award-winning author who practises law in London, England. He regularly contributes articles on travel to Condé Nast Traveler. *This selection is from the author's second book,* Theatre of Fish: Travels through Newfoundland and Labrador.

1   Jim Jones steered a thoughtful path through the last of the season's ice.

2   "This is all frozen over in the winter," he said, distractedly. "When I was a child they used to drop the mail over Mary's Harbour, and then a dog-slide would bring it out to Battle."

3   It was a twelve-mile journey. After the open water, we shrank into the flanks of Great Caribou Island, the *Iceberg Hunter* creaking and groaning with the surge. Jim said she was launched in the sixties, but with her funnels and copper pipes she seemed so much more Vintage Steam than Space Age. I thought of Curwen belting up here on the *Albert*, a record four days out of St. John's. Two days behind him was Grenfell, lurching along in his steam-launch, not unlike our own.

4   Great Caribou rolled and sprawled, and cracked and frothed, and then ended in a full stop. This was Battle Harbour, a third of a mile long and an eighth wide. Between the islands was a channel, big enough for a hundred schooners, too shallow for the icebergs to get among them.

5   *Batal*, the Portuguese called it, the Boat. Then came the horse-faced Basques and the scraggy livyers, landless Scots and bony Norwegians, merging their fortunes with the Esquimaux girls. By 1862, Battle was the capital of fish, and "the most lawless and disorderly place on the whole coast." By the time Curwen appeared, there were three hundred permanent residents—"the Wintermen"—and ten times that in summer. There was no law, no police, no representation, and the place was terrorized by dogs. But the killing and "making" of cod was industrial; over two-and-a-quarter million pounds of "Labrador Cure" were being shipped out every year, along with 5,000 barrels of herring for New York. The stink of fish pip and gurry carried way out to sea, and the rocks were rotten with slime.

6   But—despite itself—Battle had never ceased to please. Grenfell was so delighted that he chose it as the centre for his Labrador, even though it was solid half the year. Curwen was more circumspect in his praise: "An odd-looking place," he wrote, "but picturesquely situated on the rock."

7   But what was merely surprising for Curwen left me gaping with disbelief. Of course, I'd lived with his photographs all my life, and now here it was, almost exactly as he'd left it. I had a feeling not unlike homecoming, even though the place I'd known was fogged with sepia and age. Now here was Battle transfused with colour; seal-oil scarlet, cavernous white fish-sheds, wharves, salt warehouses, a tiny church, and the hillside writhing with sundew and vetch. It was like memory in reverse, faint recollections bursting into life.

8   "They nearly burnt it all down," he told me, "in 1992."

9   With the cod gone, pretty Battle was almost lost. Even the Spearings had stopped visiting their old home, and Victorian woodwork had begun to flap apart. But then, unable to watch it perish, the Labradorians had restored it. A handful of them had even stayed on—cooks, boatmen, joiners and clerks—to feed the curious and sustain the myth. It was an uncanny resurrection; Battle much as Curwen had described it but without the fish, of course, and the tuberculosis. Someone had hung copies of his photographs in the net shed, a reminder that life hadn't always been so quaint.

10   I climbed upwards, through a mercantile complex known as "The Room."

11   "It was all made in England," said the carpenter, "two hundred years ago." Every knee and joint was shipped over, he said, and slotted together without a nail.

12   Most of the stores still smelt of industry, of seals and pine, salmon, flour and herrings. "No spitting," said the signs, although the salt had gone; drifts of seven hundred tons once loomed out of the darkness like alps. Curwen had often held services in here, among the stench and grind. It was a bleak ordeal, he noted, the men "sleepy and unresponsive." The floorboards still bore the mark of their exhaustion, furrows sculpted by seaboots and heavy feet.

13   "Most think of nothing," wrote Curwen, "but fish, fish, fish."

14   Only a fraction of the fish flake had survived, a platform of latticed spruce. In 1893, it had sprawled up the hill like a basketwork rash. To the armies and workers of Europe, it truly was a bread basket, crusts of fish warming in the sun. Three-quarters of each fillet would evaporate, leaving a husk of concentrated protein (it took 75 lbs. of salt and 225 lbs. of fish to produce 112 lbs. of Labrador Cure). The Spearings explained the metamorphosis. First, they said, the fish was pitch-forked from the boats, split and lightly salted for twenty-one days. Then, the "beach women" spread it on the flake, flipping it skin-up if it rained. There it dried for up to four days, until an aromatic amber.

15   "Too much salt, she burns," said Levi. "Too little she had redshanks."

16   Finally, the fish was sorted for export: Choice and Prime for Europe, and the broken cullage for the Caribbean. Battle carried on like this until the age of fridges. "We stopped makin' fish in about the fifties," said Alfred. "After that, people wanted it frozen, see."

. . .

17   Elsewhere, there'd been a few refinements since Curwen's day.

18   The Doctors' House, I noticed, was new. As the Mission had grown, Grenfell had had it shipped out from England, complete with gingerbread gables and leather-buttoned chairs. The "Big House" too was enjoying a little splendour; there was William Morris wallpaper, and linen for the guests, and polish and caribou cutlets. Even the Battle Store was in the throes of renaissance. There was still the old counter, of course, and the brass scales and bags of split peas and hard tack, but there were apples too, and tins of meat. Curwen would remember just the caplin and "porpoise chops," all emphatically fishy.

19   "Anything by way of fresh meat," reported Grenfell, "is a treat in this country."

20   Only Curwen's tiny hospital was missing. In his photographs, it's all new; walls of rough-hewn planks caulked, or *chinsed* with straw and felt, eight iron beds, biblical

tracts and a shelf of unguents. It will be the first hospital outside St. John's, but already things aren't right; they realise—too late—that it'll have to close for winter, and the *Albert* has brought the bacon instead of the drugs. It's an inauspicious start, but the hospital will do brave work—until it's carbonised by a careless cigarette in 1930. The Spearings had watched it burn.

21   "It was a bit o' fun," said Albert, "'til we heard about the gun-powder . . ."

22   "Then we was running," said Levi, "like pigs before thunder . . ."

23   But the Rooms didn't blow. The fire moved off harmlessly, into Battle's miniature barrens. The only other casualty was the Marconi station. "Battle Harbour Burning . . ." it squeaked as it melted into the rock. Now, there was nothing left but four blobs of metal in the moss.

24   I often took the same path as the fire, out into the muskeg. Battle's barrens made up for their size with their ferocity. There were always signs of struggle; kittiwakes bombing the sea, fierce goldenrod and snarly dogwood, pieces of an aircrash, and the icebergs booming like artillery. It was easy to see how Grenfell had been ignited by such beauty. Curwen was different; his curiosity endlessly stimulated, but deep affection never aroused. I decided that nowadays it was possible to feel all these things; Battle had ironed out its cruelty, but was still as savage as ever.

25   That night, I slept out on the headland, above the battle of the hulks. They fought through until dawn, roaring and imploding, and collapsing in clouds of diamond dust. Then there was a lull, and a new cathedral floated into the bay.

DISCUSSION QUESTIONS

1. How does the writer appeal to different senses such as hearing, touch, smell, and taste?

2. What is the point of the reference to the history of Battle and the island?

3. There are quite a few changes of time frame, from the present to the past to the present. Identify signal words that help orient the reader in time and transitions that indicate a shift in the time frame.

4. What concrete images or verbs are vivid enough to create a picture in your mind? Look especially at paragraphs 4, 12, and 15.

5. The writer includes several quotations from the locals he encounters (see paragraphs 8, 11, 13, 15, 16, 19, 21, and 22). What do these quotations of direct speech contribute to the overall effect of the writing?

TOWARD KEY INSIGHTS

This author places his description of Battle in a historical context, indicating how it was viewed in the past, and the changes it experienced. In what ways can the appearance of things be related to their history?

In paragraph 7, the author contrasts his experience of Battle through a photograph and its appearance when he visits it in person. How do the actual environments the author visits in person differ from his impression of those environments from their pictures?

SUGGESTION FOR WRITING *Write an essay about a place near you that you can visit and where you can talk to at least one person about its local history, whether that history is related to labour, resources, politics, or migration patterns—whatever interests you. Write an account of your visit, providing historical background as well as narrative material such as quotations, where appropriate.*

Michael Harris

Clearing House

The writer and editor Michael Harris has won the Governor General's Award for English language nonfiction in 2014 for his book *The End of Absence: Reclaiming What We've Lost in a World of Connection.* In this book he explores questions related to what we have lost in a wired world. He has also written about issues related to digital life, civil liberties, and the arts for publications such as *Wired, Salon, The Globe and Mail,* the *National Post,* and *The Walrus.* In 2012 he published a young adult novel, *Homo,* about a gay teenager struggling to come out.

1   My boyfriend and I have seen the future. It looks like this: two guys sitting cross-legged in the middle of a creaky room, surrounded by forty-two dusty sherry glasses, a pile of crumpled newspaper and a tower of cardboard boxes marked "Salvation Army." One of these guys takes a piece of his mother's crockery out of the other guy's hands and says, "Not yet."

2   Holed up in the Greek end of Kitsilano, in Vancouver, my man and I have been clearing out his parents' house—making room for our own lives in the home they bought for $18,000 in the 1960s, when they moved here from Athens. The home they raised their son in.

3   His parents never imagined that he'd invite another man to live with him here. They certainly never imagined that another man would help pack up their fancy glasses or cuddle with their son on the good floral-print sofa—which nobody was allowed to sit on—while watching old movies on VHS. And what would his mother, in her prime, have said about that new ring of water damage on the living room's solid-teak table? What would she say about the kitten-scratched upholstery? Would she scowl as we rapidly undo a half-century's worth of careful preservation? The floor gets scuffed or the rug gets stained and these signs of carelessness become fuel for self-condemnation. We aren't suited to a life of doilies and slipcovers. And neither, anymore, is she. She sits, ravaged by Alzheimer's, in her institutional home, and no longer has the luxury of caring about the state of her teak table. We couldn't even manage to care about it for her.

4   And so it goes—for us, for our friends, for the country. We come downstairs each morning, feed the cats and stare at room after room of a ghost life. This scene is becoming familiar for more and more Canadians. Never before have there been so

many people over the age of eighty in this country—1.2 million at the last census. Statistics Canada predicts that in a few years there will be more senior citizens here than children. Demographers tell us this trend will continue for decades. So, just as the previous generation was defined by the activism and celebration of youth, mine will be defined by its care for the elderly. It will be our unglamorous lot to settle accounts, sort through the leftovers—to clean up, as it were, after the party. By the time I enter the later years of my own life, a full quarter of Canada's population will be over sixty-five years old. That's an awful lot of cardboard boxes.

5   On day one of all this, we had ducked into the basement, past wooden shelves of canned preserves that will never be opened, to check out the crawl space. And there we found the steamer trunk. It was a grimy, beaten-up old thing, the kind of container that once carried people's lives over from Europe. Dragged upstairs, its contents (all unused) started to tell a story: a frying pan with the label still on, a set of pea-green containers, eight tiny wine glasses, three pressed dresses from Woodward's, two pairs of men's socks and ten pairs of hose, still in their packaging. Why was it all untouched? Why abandoned there, wrapped in pages of a 1969 copy of the *Vancouver Sun*?

6   To find out, my forty-two-year-old boyfriend called his ninety-three-year-old dad in the retirement home. They spoke in Greek about bowel movements, their next visit, his mother's Alzheimer's and how the house must never, ever be sold. While they spoke, I lugged a few more vases (decorated with "antique" Greek tableaus) down to the new Vase Annex in the basement. To make room, I rearranged his mother's sewing station, with its giant unworkable machinery and thousand spools of tangled threads.

7   Later I learned that the trunk is a genuine hope chest (though my boyfriend and I began to call it the "hopeless chest"). It belonged to a young woman, an acquaintance of his parents, who had collected all the things she needed for some future married life. But then she got herself pregnant while failing to collect a husband. She fled to Europe to have an abortion, promising to come back soon for the trunk. My boyfriend's parents were thriving immigrants then, and they wanted to reach out and help this wayward, unwed girl. She never came back for her things.

8   They didn't throw out her trunk, nor did they pack her intended life into cardboard boxes for the Salvation Army. They kept it all just as she'd left it, because she had said she would return.

9   But people never do return, not really. They get married, they move on to new lives and they grow, irrevocably, old. When my boyfriend's father was brought back to the house on a visit, he sat (mostly blind, mostly deaf) on the sofa and clumsily stroked one of the cats. Standing, he started to rifle through papers in a drawer and nervously took to asking, "What's this? Is this dealt with? What's this?"

10   While his wife is now ignorant of her own past, he is forced to give things up. "It's nothing," said my boyfriend, taking his dad back to the sofa. "That's nothing." The things they've left are mostly junk to the modern eye, not particularly noble, or collectible, or precious. Just something you hold up for a moment before placing it in the box to give to charity.

11   I took a picture of the two of us with my iPhone, surrounded by stacks of cloudy crystal and framed pictures of unrecognizable saints. I emailed it to my mother: "Please start throwing things out." While it's easy enough for me to be ruthless with junk at my boyfriend's house, I know I would be pitiful if I ever tried to clear the house that I grew up in. How do you hold a garage sale for your parents' lives? How

do you haggle with some early-bird shopper who wants to take your dad's croquet set off your hands for a few bucks? I'd end up a class-one hoarder, surrounded by stacks of earthenware dishes and telling my boyfriend, "Not yet."

12   Or I would for about a year or two. Ultimately, life finds ways to force a razing. (A job in another city, a needful sale of the house.) And then what does anyone hold onto? A picture or two. A favourite set of teacups. Maybe one of dad's old jackets. But otherwise the flotsam is just that—debris from some other adventure. My boyfriend's parents, after all, didn't carry trappings from their parents across the ocean, except in haversacks of memory. They cut loose and sailed for a new world. They bought shiny things from big department stores and filled their home with a million choices of their own. They had an idea of a new life, and each seemingly random purchase from Woodward's or the Bay became part of that larger picture. Almost every part of life has its objective correlative. Each daily act leaves behind some tool, some object now imbued with foggy meaning.

13   I should know; I've packed enough of them. We wrapped the plastic measuring cups, the cheap glassware from gas stations, the ridiculous gifts that may or may not have been cherished. We wrapped it all in pages of that day's newspaper and fit it all into boxes, muttering, "What the hell is this? Why did they need this?" And still the house feels full, stuffed with a life that's (to me) illegible and (to him) so heavy. Just the other day, when I tried to throw out a plastic container with "Greek Coffee" written on the side, my boyfriend stopped my hand and said, "What are you doing?" like I'd committed an act of treason.

14   We drove our first load down to the Salvation Army. A week's work popped out of the car in a couple minutes. In the receiving area at the back of the store, a few nice old women tugged open boxes, pulled out napkin holders, figurines, creamers, and tagged them with prices. I peeked inside the shop and shuddered at row after row of sherry glasses. Where will it all go in five years, when the baby boomers, now senior boomers, begin downsizing, and their millions of hard-won purchases are orphaned and unwanted? Where will nostalgia force us to store the almost-okay brass lamps, the chipped platters, the twenty-year collections of National Geographic? When the thrift stores are finally gorged, where goes all the stuff, the stuff, the stuff?

15   My boyfriend and I have seen the future. Looking in on a room that will one day be the master bedroom, he tells me, "I want just a bed in here. Just a bed and nothing else."

16   "Well, maybe some bookshelves, yeah?"

17   He gives me a look. "Just. A bed."

18   Either way, I don't imagine we'll live here long. Someday the whole thing will be sold (likely, this time around, to an immigrant from Asia rather than Europe). A letter recently came in the mail announcing that the house, initially purchased for less than $20,000, had risen in value by $250,000 in just one year. The value, of course, is all in the land. The house itself is what they call a "tear-down."

DISCUSSION QUESTIONS

1. The writer does not report his feelings or attitude about clearing out the house of his boyfriend's mother, but you can infer his attitude and feelings from the specific details he provides. How is his tone, or attitude, conveyed through the selection of details he reports? What words would you use to describe his tone?

2. How does this essay bring in an imagined future at the beginning and end, and what does this allusion to the future contribute to the effectiveness of the piece?

3. How does the writer use the tension of contrast between then and now in paragraphs 2, 3, 5, and elsewhere? What other contrasts are brought in?

4. How do paragraphs 3, 11, and 14 bring in an accumulation of details to build their effect? What does the image of the steamer trunk that turns out to be a hope chest (paragraphs 5 and 7) suggest to you? How does the writer use questions to encourage reflection and develop a theme? What questions, if any, strike you as especially poignant?

5. How, in paragraph 4, does the writer enlarge the significance of his personal account so that it becomes about something more than his own experience? Where else does he make his story relevant to others by going beyond his own story and raising questions that will touch most thoughtful readers?

6. How does the reference to immigration stories in paragraphs 7, 8, and 9 reinforce the theme? What is the relevance of the boyfriend's call to his father in the retirement home?

7. How does the writer develop his ideas partly by raising questions in paragraphs 4, 5, and 14? What is the effect of these questions on the reader?

8. Examine the last paragraph to see how the writer closes this unfinished story. What is the tone of the last sentence, and how does it leave you feeling?

TOWARD KEY INSIGHTS

It is clear from the beginning that the writer is in a gay relationship, and while that is not a major focus here, does our knowledge of this relationship as something the mother likely did not imagine affect how we respond to his story? Discuss.

In paragraph 14, Michael Harris asks what will happen as the senior boomers begin to shed possessions as they downsize. How do you respond to the question "When the thrift stores are finally gorged, where goes all the stuff, the stuff, the stuff?" Do you have any experience similar to the writer's of clearing out someone else's once-treasured possessions? How did that experience affect your perspective on our attachments—or time?

SUGGESTION FOR WRITING *Write a narrative account of your own about a time when you cleared out possessions, either your own or someone else's, during a significant life transition. Use concrete, sensory details that create a picture in the reader's mind, and consider raising questions, as Michael Harris does in paragraphs 4, 5, and 14, to develop a theme. If appropriate, consider also using brief narrative vignettes set in the past, present, and imagined future.*

Jeffrey Andreoni

Why Can't I Feel What I See?

Jeffrey Andreoni, a freelance writer, artist, and activist, was born in Rhode Island but now lives mainly in Rome. He has studied at Moscow State University, La Sapienza University of Rome, and University of Rhode Island. He began an artistic career while designing posters for political parties in Rome and also established an artists' and activists' collective there. He has done installation art and performance pieces focused on social issues in both the United States and Italy, and he is the creator of the bilingual cartoon Exxxtraman, posted on YouTube, about a superhero who defends the rights of immigrants in Italy. The article below was published in Adbusters, a magazine based in Vancouver devoted to "culture jamming"—"the attempt to change the way information flows, the way corporations wield power, and the way meaning is produced in our society."

1   I can't keep up with my grandfather. Whenever I see him, he's rushing off to the gym, going on a fishing trip or taking his "baby doll" out on a date. My grandfather is 87 (his baby doll is 90) and he's one of the happiest people I know. At 32, my gleeful disposition seems to decrease in inverse proportion to my years, and I'm left wondering how my grandfather, who grew up poor in Hell's Kitchen and fought overseas, is so much more youthful and energetic than I am.

2   Psychologist Martin Seligman conducted two studies in the 70s in which people of different age groups were asked about depression. Comparing the responses of different generations, Seligman found that younger people were far more likely to have experienced depression than older people. In fact, one study found that those born in the middle third of the 20th century were ten times more likely to suffer from severe depression than those born in the first third. So statistically, my grandfather is more likely to be happy than me.

3   I don't get it. I was the first kid on my block to have a Nintendo. I got a car on my 16th birthday. I didn't have to work a single day in college (unless you count selling homemade bongs at Phish concerts). My grandfather grew up with nothing. He had to drop out of high school during the Depression to help his family get by, earning money shining the shoes of drunks at a local saloon. Why is my generation, one of relative privilege and wealth, experiencing higher rates of depression than any previous generation?

4   I turned to French philosopher Jean Baudrillard for some illumination on this conundrum. It seems that in the 19th century, for the first time in history, humans began to require *observable proof* of happiness. According to Baudrillard, happiness became something that had to be measurable in terms of material gain, something that would be evident to the eye. But I'm surrounded by stuff and yet I'm still glum. At my age, my grandfather had fewer possessions and more happiness. So what do you make of that, Mr. Baudrillard? Maybe people from previous generations—whose lives were characterized by the greater effort required to survive—were, paradoxically, mentally healthier (even though they didn't have iPods). I guess that means that by simply looking around at all my lovely nonessential belongings (acquired with relative ease), I don't feel as happy as I would if I was busting my hump just to put food in my belly. Or maybe the anxiety I feel has nothing to do with my possessions, perhaps the problem is in my brain.

5   The nucleus accumbens is a tiny structure of the brain located within the striatum, which controls movement, and next to the limbic system, which is involved with emotion and learning. The accumbens is the main junction between our emotions and our actions. These closely linked motor and emotive functions also extend to the prefrontal cortex, which controls our thought processes. It is this accumbens-striatal-cortical network (the crucial system that links movement, emotion and thinking) that has been dubbed the "effort-driven rewards circuit."

6   This effort-driven rewards circuit is a proposed neuroanatomical network that underlies most symptoms associated with depression. It is actually possible to correlate every symptom of depression with a brain part on this circuit. Loss of pleasure? The nucleus accumbens. Sluggishness and slow motor responses? The striatum. Negative feelings? The limbic system. Poor concentration? The prefrontal cortex. The brain is also programmed to derive a deep sense of satisfaction and pleasure if physical effort produces something tangible, visible and necessary for survival. So if I go out in the field and harvest my own food, my effort-driven rewards circuit will be stimulated, causing neurogenesis (the production of new brain cells), which is believed to be an important factor in recovering from depression. Unfortunately I have no field to harvest.

7   But surely there must be some other means to labor my way to happiness. Apparently the key factor in the effort-driven-rewards scenario is the use of the hands. Our hands are so important that moving them activates larger areas of the brain's cortex than moving much larger parts of our bodies, like our back or legs. What if I were to try constructing some of my own possessions: building some of that observable proof of happiness that Baudrillard talks about? My grandfather worked as a craftsman his whole life, building and upholstering furniture. Instead of harvesting food, he produced objects.

8   I considered trying something similar, perhaps by going to work in a factory. But then I read Guy Debord, who claimed that "the general separation of worker and product tends to eliminate any direct personal communication between the producers and any comprehensive sense of what they are producing." Coincidentally, my grandfather made furniture for people he knew. Most of his work was commissioned—he designed a unique product for a specific need. If I were to work in a factory, I would be assembling mass-produced goods for anonymous consumers. The fruits of my labor would no doubt be added to the crowded apartment of some other melancholic modern soul. This is what Debord calls the "vicious circle of isolation."

9   Unlike people of my generation who are increasingly defined by their possessions, my grandfather never owned much. But he never complained about not *having* because he was too busy *being*. Perhaps I'm unhappy because my concerns are reversed—I'm too worried about *having* to focus on *being*. Human fulfillment is no longer equated with what I *am*, but with what I *possess*. Debord says this is the second stage of modernization, "in which social life becomes so completely dominated by accumulated products that it causes a shift from *having* to *appearing*, wherein all 'having' must now derive its immediate prestige from appearances." So all I need to do to fit modern society is to appear to be a possessor of a lot of stuff, but in reality I will *be* and *have* nothing. I need a personal image. Perhaps this is the visible sign of happiness Baudrillard was talking about. I have to create an image to hide behind, and this image seems to be the only thing I'm able to produce. Have I really been reduced to an image whose sole purpose is to mix and mingle with other *seemingly* compatible images? Is modern life really so complex?

10   If we ask Gilles Deleuze and Felix Guattari, modernization is "a process by which capitalism uproots and makes mobile that which is grounded, clears away or obliterates that which impedes circulation, and makes exchangeable what is singular." This applies as much to bodies, signs, images, languages, kinship relations, religious practices and nationalities as it does to commodities, wealth and labor power. So this image of myself that I have created can be bought, sold or traded—but where does it go?

11   It goes to the spectacle. The voracious insatiable beast that consumes all images and leaves nothing to waste. The spectacle *is* society, it's a looking glass that absorbs your image and gives you nothing in return: no reflection, no impression, just a representation that is beyond your control. The image you projected joins the other images of the "spectacular" society. You'll never see your image again. You'll never see the spectacle because it, like you, is just a shadow on the wall of the Platonian cave. The image I've projected in this essay isn't me. It's the image of a person claiming to be me. All that was once directly lived has become mere representation. You are no longer surrounded by objects, writes Debord, but by a spectacle:

12   "Where the real world changes into simple images, the simple images become real beings. The spectacle, as a tendency to make one see the world by means of various specialized mediations, is not identifiable with mere gazing, even combined with hearing. It is that which escapes the activity of men, that which escapes reconsideration and correction by their work. It is the opposite of dialogue. Wherever there is independent representation, the spectacle reconstitutes itself."

13   So how do we find the happiness that has eluded our generation? By drugging ourselves into mass status quo submission or by defeating the spectacle that robs us of our singular essence. Be unique. Use your hands. Go out and create.

DISCUSSION QUESTIONS

1. What examples does the writer offer of his "relative privilege and wealth"—compared to his grandfather (paragraph 3)—and what is the relevance of these examples?

2. What two examples does the writer provide to show how human efforts that result in something tangible, "*observable proof* of happiness," may produce more satisfaction and pleasure than the easy acquisition of many "nonessential belongings" (paragraph 4)?

3. Why does the writer emphasize that his "grandfather made furniture for people he knew" (paragraph 8)?

4. In paragraph 9, Andreoni quotes Guy Debord's claim that in a second stage of modernization, "social life becomes so completely dominated by accumulated products that it causes a shift from *having* to *appearing*, wherein all 'having' must now derive its immediate prestige from appearances." How would you put this idea into your own words?

5. In paragraphs 11 and 12, Andreoni discusses society as a "spectacle" that "consumes all images." In your own words, explain what he means by the concept of society as a "spectacle." What does he mean when he suggests in his conclusion that we might be able to defeat "the spectacle that robs us of our singular essence"?

TOWARD KEY INSIGHTS

In paragraph 2, Andreoni cites a study that suggests young people are more likely to be depressed than older people born earlier in the twentieth century. Does this claim seem plausible to you? If so, what possible reasons do you imagine there could be for this increased rate of depression? If not, what do you find problematic about the claim?

Andreoni says that in contemporary life, image becomes all-important, the one thing we can all produce. How, in your view, do you or others you know construct an image, either through social media such as Facebook, through writing, or in some other way?

SUGGESTIONS FOR WRITING

1. Write an essay that either supports or argues with the proposition that we feel happiest when we are producing elemental, basic things related to survival. Use examples.

2. Read or review the short essay in Chapter 2, "Teen Angst, RIP," which has a different slant on the relative happiness of the younger generation. Then, drawing from these essays and your own experiences and observations, write an essay on which argument seems more compelling to you.

3. Andreoni says, "The image I've projected in this essay isn't me. It's the image of a person claiming to be me." Read the essay in the Reader—"Fostering Multiple Identities through Teaching Cyborg Writing" (pages 462–467)—that discusses the ways in which self-representations projected through writing are constructed and illusory. If you are interested, you might also wish to read the actual text referred to in paragraph 11 as the "Platonian cave." This excerpt from *The Republic* by Plato is easily found on the Internet by searching "Plato's Parable of the Cave" or "Plato's Allegory of the Cave." Then, drawing from one or more of these pieces as well as Andreoni's article, write an essay using examples to support the thesis that the image we project in writing, or through social media, is just that—an image, not a true and essential self.

Remember to review documentation and citation guidelines, given in Chapter 16–17, when you bring in quotations or ideas from these writers.

> **MyWritingLab**
>
> **How Do I Get a Better Grade?**
>
> Go to **www.mywritinglab .com** for additional help with your grammar, writing, and research skills. You will have access to a variety of exercises, instruction, and videos that will help you improve your basic skills and help you get a better grade.

Beth Wald

Let's Get Vertical!

Beth Wald (born 1960) first felt the attraction of the mountains when, at age 16, she took a backpacking trip to Canada. A native of Minnesota, she studied botany and Russian at the University of Minnesota and then, in the mid-1980s, began a dual career as a freelance writer and photographer. Her career and her love of climbing have taken her around the world. Her articles have appeared in a variety of climbing and outdoor magazines, as have her photographs, which include environmental and cultural subjects as well as sports and travel. From 1988 to 1992, she was a contributing editor for Climbing Magazine. *In recent years she has turned from photographing adventure sports to documenting at-risk cultures. In our selection, Wald acquaints potential recruits with the sport of rock climbing.*

1   Here I am, 400 feet up on the steep west face of Devil's Tower,[1] a tiny figure in a sea of petrified rock. I can't find enough footholds and handholds to keep climbing. My climbing partner anxiously looks up at me from his narrow ledge. I can see the silver sparkle of the climbing devices I've jammed into the crack every eight feet or so.

2   I study the last device I've placed, a half-inch aluminum wedge 12 feet below me. If I slip, it'll catch me, but only after a 24-foot fall, a real "screamer." It's too difficult to go back; I have to find a way up before my fingers get too tired. I must act quickly.

3   Finding a tiny opening in the crack, I jam two fingertips in, crimp them, pull hard, and kick my right foot onto a sloping knob, hoping it won't skid off. At the same time, I slap my right hand up to what looks like a good hold. To my horror, it's round and slippery.

4   My fingers start to slide. Panic rivets me for a second, but then a surge of adrenalin snaps me back into action. I scramble my feet higher, lunge with my left hand, and catch a wider crack. I manage to get a better grip just as my right hand pops off its slick hold. My feet find edges, and I regain my balance. Whipping a chock (wedge) off my harness, I slip it into the crack and clip my rope through a carabiner (oblong metal snaplink). After catching my breath, I start moving again, and the rest of the climb flows upward like a vertical dance.

5   **The Challenges and Rewards** I've tried many sports, but I haven't found any to match the excitement of rock climbing. It's a unique world, with its own language, communities, controversies, heroes, villains, and devoted followers. I've lived in vans, tepees, tents, and caves; worked three jobs to save money for expenses; driven 24 hours to spend a weekend at a good rock; and lived on beans and rice for months at a time—all of this to be able to climb. What is it about scrambling up rocks that inspires such a passion? The answer is, no other sport offers so many challenges and so many rewards.

---

[1]A large, flat-topped rock formation, 876 feet high, in northeastern Wyoming.

6   The physical challenges are obvious. You need flexibility, balance, and strength. But climbing is also a psychological game of defeating your fear, and it demands creative thinking. It's a bit like improvising a gymnastic routine 200 feet in the air while playing a game of chess.

7   Climbers visit some of the most spectacular places on earth and see them from a unique perspective—the top! Because the sport is so intense, friendships between climbers tend to be strong and enduring.

8   **Anyone Can Climb** Kids playing in trees or on monkey bars know that climbing is a natural activity, but older people often have to relearn to trust their instincts. This isn't too hard, though. The ability to maintain self-control in difficult situations is the most important trait for a beginning climber to have. Panic is almost automatic when you run out of handholds 100 feet off the ground. The typical reaction is to freeze solid until you fall off. But with a little discipline, rational thinking, and/or distraction tactics such as babbling to yourself, humming, or even screaming, fear can change to elation as you climb out of a tough spot.

9   Contrary to popular belief, you don't have to be superhumanly strong to climb. Self-confidence, agility, a good sense of balance, and determination will get you farther up the rock than bulging biceps. Once you've learned the basics, climbing itself will gradually make you stronger, though many dedicated climbers speed up the process by training at home or in the gym.

10   Nonclimbers often ask, "How do the ropes get up there?" It's quite simple; the climbers bring them up as they climb. Most rock climbers today are "free climbers." In free climbing, the rope is used only for safety in case of a fall, *not* to help pull you up. (Climbing without a rope, called "free soloing," is a *very* dangerous activity practiced only by extremely experienced—and crazy—climbers.)

11   First, two climbers tie into opposite ends of a 150-foot-long nylon rope. Then one of them, the belayer, anchors himself or herself to a rock or tree. The other, the leader, starts to climb, occasionally stopping to jam a variety of aluminum wedges or other special gadgets, generically referred to as protection, into cracks in the rock. To each of these, he or she attaches a snaplink, called a carabiner, and clips the rope through. As the leader climbs, the belayer feeds out the rope, and it runs through the carabiners. If the leader falls, the belayer holds the rope, and the highest piece of protection catches the leader. The belayer uses special techniques and equipment to make it easy to stop falls.

12   When the leader reaches the end of a section of rock—called the pitch—and sets an anchor, he or she becomes the belayer. This person pulls up the slack of the rope as the other partner climbs and removes the protection. Once together again, they can either continue in the same manner or switch leaders. These worldwide techniques work on rock formations, cliffs, peaks, even buildings.

13   **Rocks, Rocks Everywhere** Some of the best climbing cliffs in the country are in the Shawangunk Mountains, only two hours from New York City. Seneca Rocks in West Virginia draws climbers from Washington, D.C., and Pittsburgh, Pennsylvania. Chattanooga, Tennessee, has a fine cliff within the city limits. Most states in the U.S. and provinces in Canada offer at least one or two good climbing opportunities.

14   Even if there are no large cliffs or rock formations nearby, you can climb smaller rocks to practice techniques and get stronger. This is called bouldering. Many climbers who live in cities and towns have created climbing areas out of old stone walls and buildings. Ask someone at your local outdoor shop where you can go to start climbing.

15   **Get a Helping Hand** There's no substitute for an expert teacher when it comes to learning basic techniques and safety procedures. One of the best (and least expensive) ways to learn climbing is to convince a veteran climber in your area to teach you. You can usually meet these types at the local crag or climbing shop.

16   As another option, many universities and colleges, some high schools, and some YMCAs have climbing clubs. Their main purpose is to introduce people to climbing and to teach the basics. Other clubs, such as the Appalachian Mountain Club in the eastern U.S. and the Mountaineers on the West Coast, also provide instruction. Ask at your outdoor shop for the names of clubs in your area.

17   If you live in a place completely lacking rocks and climbers, you can attend one of the fine climbing schools at the major climbing area closest to you. Magazines like *Climbing*, *Rock & Ice*, and *Outside* publish lists of these schools. Once you learn the basics, you're ready to get vertical.

18   In rock climbing, you can both lose yourself and find yourself. Life and all its troubles are reduced to figuring out the puzzle of the next section of cliff or forgotten in the challenge and delight of moving through vertical space. And learning how to control anxiety, how to piece together a difficult sequence of moves, and how to communicate with a partner are all skills that prove incredibly useful back on the ground!

DISCUSSION QUESTIONS

1. Discuss the effectiveness of Wald's title.
2. At the beginning of the essay, Wald notes that she is 400 feet up one side of Devil's Tower and positioned above her climbing partner. What do you think these statements accomplish?
3. In which paragraphs does Wald detail the actual process of climbing? What do the remaining paragraphs in the body of the essay accomplish?
4. Point out two places in the first four paragraphs where Wald cites reasons for her actions.
5. What qualities does Wald believe a rock climber must have? Refer to paragraphs 6, 7, 8, and 18 when answering.
6. After reading this essay, are you ready to begin rock climbing? Does your answer stem from Wald's content, the manner of presentation, or both? Discuss.

TOWARD KEY INSIGHTS

What challenging activities appeal to you?

What level of risk are you willing to accept in an activity?

How do you account for your attitude about taking risks?

SUGGESTION FOR WRITING *Think of a sport or recreational activity you know well. Then write an essay explaining the personal qualities needed to engage in this activity, the steps involved in learning it, and the rewards and challenges it offers. Address your essay, as Wald does, to people who are unfamiliar with the activity you are discussing.*

Tim Falconer

Autoholics

Tim Falconer is an award-winning journalist and freelance writer whose non-fiction books include That Good Night: Ethicists, Euthanasia and End-of-Life Care; Drive: A Road Trip through Our Complicated Affair with the Automobile; Watchdogs and Gadflies: Activism from Marginal to Mainstream; *and* Bad Singer. *He is also the co-author of* Drop the Worry Ball: How to Parent in the Age of Entitlement. *In this essay, in which he recommends a 12-step program for breaking our addiction to the automobile, he draws from process analysis as well as cause-and-effect analysis.*

1   As individuals and as a society, we love our automobiles—even as we hate how they screw up our planet, our cities, and our lives. Environics Research Group, a Toronto-based research firm, found that 32 percent of Canadians see their wheels as an extension or reflection of their style and image. For the other 63 percent, it's an appliance, a tool used to get from A to B. Recreational driving may seem, in an age of climate change, to be a destructive pastime. But the auto collectors and recreational drivers aren't the problem, just as connoisseurs of fine wine, who prize quality over quantity, aren't necessarily problem drinkers. It's the people who drive (or drink) all the time—mindlessly, compulsively, because they can't help themselves—who do the real damage to themselves and others. That's addiction—and collectively, we're pretty close to hitting bottom. The automobile has wasted our time, choked our air, and destroyed many downtowns while spurring sprawl in the suburbs. Obviously, cars aren't about to go away completely (though we can certainly hope they change dramatically over the next few years). But let's never forget: the fault, dear drivers, lies not in our cars, but in ourselves.

2   As with all addictions, change will only occur if we want to change, both individually and collectively. This handy 12-step program for car dependency may help, but in the end only you can decide when it's best to leave the keys at home and go another way.

1. Accept That We Have a Problem

3   Let's be honest: cars are cool, sexy, and fun and provide us with speed, power, and freedom. Some of them offer gorgeous styling, luxurious comfort, and advanced engineering (not to mention great sound systems). And then there are the memories. Having suffered through the motion sickness of family road trips, we finally turn 16 and start hanging out in cars with friends, reveling in our first taste of freedom from our parents, and fumbling through early experiments with sex—good times many of us spend the rest of our lives wishing we could recapture. So cars come with a lot of positive baggage. But we've gone too far and designed our existence around the automobile. You may hear some dreamers talk about a car-free world. Don't believe them. Fortunately, breaking our addiction doesn't have to mean never driving our wheels again—a recovering alcoholic may never be able to drink again, and people who've given up the cancer sticks may envy the social smokers, but being an occasional driver is nothing to be ashamed about.

2. Educate Ourselves about the Alternatives

4   Sometimes the car, a really convenient device, can't be beat for getting around. In fact, there's no better way to whisk a gaggle of kids and their oversized hockey bags to a far-flung arena. And while high-speed trains are long overdue in this country, you'll still want to travel to cottages, campgrounds, and mountains. But if you never go anywhere unless it's in a car, you need to consider walking, cycling, and public transit. Sure, buses can be crowded, inconvenient, and unreliable—I thought my wife, Carmen, had stood me up on our first date, though to this day she blames Ottawa's OC Transpo for her tardiness—but they are also economical, encourage reading, and let you feel more virtuous. Of course, these alternatives only work in places where there are stores, restaurants, and other spots worth walking to, where cyclists can travel safely and where the population density is enough to support public transit.

3. Start with the Most Basic Form of Transportation—Walking

5   Aside from being the most pleasant places to live and encouraging other ways of getting around, walkable neighbourhoods create better communities. It's no coincidence that Calgary is both the most sprawled and the most conservative large city in Canada, while the two densest big cities south of the border—New York and San Francisco—are the most liberal American ones. When we live in sprawl and spend so much time cooped up in our cars, we develop strange notions about life. But when we walk around our neighbourhood we soon discover that other races, religions and socio-economic classes aren't scary after all. Sprawl stokes fear; density fosters tolerance.

4. Admit the Harm Our Actions Have on Ourselves

6   Every year, 1.2 million people die on the world's roads. But even when we survive our drive, sitting sedentary behind a steering wheel is no way to go through life. Drive-through windows at fast-food joints are just the beginning: there are now drive-through pharmacies, banks, and even libraries. Meanwhile, parenting has become little more than glorified chauffeuring as we raise a generation of kids who never walk anywhere.

5. Understand the Wrongs of the Past

7   Urban sprawl—dominated by cloned homes, lowslung strip malls, and clogged arterial roads—forces people to drive more and makes no aesthetic, economic, or environmental sense. Among other sins, sprawl encourages drunk driving: partiers will take the car when they live so far from bars, restaurants, and friends' homes that walking is too daunting, public transit is too inconvenient, and taking a cab is too expensive. Decades of short-sighted urban planning have put us in this mess, and fixing the problem will take time, but we need to start intensifying our neighbourhoods now.

6. Treat Others as We Would Like to Be Treated

8   Sure, cruising down an open highway can be a blast, but lurching along in bumper-to-bumper traffic is no fun. A tense commute is, at best, dispiriting and exhausting; at

worst, it can lead to road rage, which is an extension of the increase in aggressive driving (including following too closely, travelling at excessive speeds, weaving through traffic, running stop lights) and the decline in civility on the road.

9   We behave differently (read: more irrationally) when we're behind the wheel of a car, which—especially if it's a big SUV—can create a sense of isolation and invincibility. The anonymity of riding in a living room on wheels, an extension of the anonymity of suburban life, can weaken common sense and self-discipline so much that even upstanding citizens can act in ways they never would in a grocery store lineup. "Road-ragers are an unpredictable group," Sgt. Cam Woolley, who recently retired from the Ontario Provincial Police, told me. "They've timed their commute down to the last second, and if anybody goes too slow or doesn't drive the way they'd like, they go nuts."

7. Don't Be Part of the Problem

10   The typical commute has lengthened substantially—to more than an hour for the average round trip in Canada—as people seek cheaper homes and larger lawns. This is not just bad for air quality, it's bad for quality of life. You've probably heard drivers rationalize that their commute is their only alone time: a chance to think, to listen to their favourite music, or to simply enjoy some rare silence. But if you're like me, you want to yell, "Get a life, pal."

8. When You Must Drive, Do It Well

11   Bad driving doesn't just cause more collisions, it exacerbates congestion and increases commute times. Even a bad lane change can slow down everyone behind you. To Carlos Thomas, who runs Shifters, a school for drivers who want to learn the joys of stick shifts, the two biggest mistakes we make are not looking far enough ahead and following too closely. "The most common crash is the rear-end collision," according to Thomas, "and it's the most easily preventable crash." Paradoxically, the easiest way to avoid smashing into the car in front of you is to look well ahead. When you tailgate you can't see as far down the road so you miss advance warnings that you need to hit the brakes, and when you don't look down the road you're more likely to tailgate because it's so easy to become fixated on the bumper in front of you. Seeing is crucial: Thomas says weak observation skills lead to poor lane changes, bad turns, loss of control in slippery conditions, and failure to recover after losing control. The other danger of becoming fixated on that bumper ahead is that your mind begins to wander and too often that ends badly.

12   Most tailgaters are cocky enough to believe they'll have no trouble stopping in time, but the dynamics of traffic are more complex than most of us realize. In *Traffic: Why We Drive the Way We Do (and What It Says About Us)*, author Tom Vanderbilt explains what happened when seven cars had to stop suddenly on a Minneapolis highway: the seventh car crashed into the sixth because the third car reacted too slowly—it didn't hit the second car, but it reduced the stopping time available to those behind it. As Vanderbilt points out, tailgaters "increase their risk not only of striking the vehicle they're following but of being struck by the car following them."

9. Make Amends to the Planet

13   Given that we've located planets in distant solar systems, mapped the human genome, and put an iPod in every pocket, the inability of automakers to come up with something better than the internal combustion engine suggests they haven't tried that hard. They're paying for it now, but we're going to have to pony up more than bailout money. For environmental—and geopolitical—reasons, North Americans need a revenue-neutral carbon tax. Aside from being the simplest and fairest way to make the most egregious energy gluttons pay the most, the behavioural changes would be dramatic: we would drive less often, buy smaller, more fuel-efficient cars, and insist automakers build cleaner vehicles. After the last election, the nation's punditry pronounced the idea rejected once and for all, but what the voters really balked at was Stéphane Dion. True, there was little enthusiasm for his "Green Shift," but the hopeless Liberal leader showed he couldn't sell cheap gas on a long weekend in the summer. If we're lucky, a more talented politician will prove more adept because the cap-and-trade schemes favoured by the Obama and Harper regimes are, as Paul Wells, the country's smartest and funniest pundit (faint praise, I realize), described them, "massively interventionist, cumbersome, harrowingly difficult to design, prone to loopholes and investor confusion, destined to take forever to implement." While writing about this on Inkless Wells, his blog at macleans.ca, he also asked: "If you believe climate change is real and catastrophic; that human agency can inflect its course; that Canada has something to contribute to the search for a solution; and that dawdling is no longer permissible—then what better idea do you have?"

10. Renounce Free Parking

14   When I'm hunting for a place to leave my car—all the while burning fossil fuels and adding to the traffic congestion—it never occurs to me how much space cities devote to parking. But the typical driver has a spot at home, one at work (usually bigger than the cubicle he or she spends all day in), and shared spaces everywhere, including at malls, churches, and fairgrounds. Spoiled by abundant free parking, we resist paying for it, hate looking for it, and, most of all, dread tickets. As Donald Shoup, America's parking guru, told me, "Everybody thinks parking is a personal problem, not a policy problem." But everybody is wrong.

15   A professor at UCLA's urban planning department and the author of *The High Cost of Free Parking*, Shoup has a growing band of followers who call themselves Shoupistas even though the market-oriented policies he advocates could best be summed up by the battle cry, "Charge whatever the traffic will bear." Shoup, who rides a bike two miles to campus, is convinced that free parking is unattractive, expensive (subsidizing it costs the U.S. economy more than Medicare), and encourages driving: "Parking is the single biggest land use in almost any city, and almost everybody has ignored it." California adopted Shoup's proposal that companies that pay for employees' parking had to offer the cash equivalent to non-parkers. After the law passed, 13 per cent of workers took the money (most switched to car pools or public transit, though a few started cycling or walking). The harm free parking does feeds on itself: all that land dedicated to parking, which often sits empty for much of the day,

increases sprawl, and that sprawl makes alternatives such as public transit and walking less feasible, which forces more people into cars, which increases the need for more parking. And so on.

11. Embrace Road Pricing

16   Although all drivers can figure out what they pay for gas, insurance, and other car-related expenses, and some may even put a value on their time, few ever think about the public cost of traffic. London has the world's most famous congestion charge, a measure introduced by "Red Ken" Livingstone, the now former mayor. Although the aims of road pricing are largely progressive, it still remains a fundamentally market-driven policy. Such policies were actually debated, decades ago, by the likes of Alan Walters, who went on to be chief economic advisor to Margaret Thatcher. These thinkers realized that when we travel a crowded road, we don't consider the price we impose on others when we slow them down. By paying tolls, we face the true cost of our decision, reducing demand and increasing the efficiency of the roads. This makes far more sense than simply building more roads, which just attracts more traffic anyway.

12. Spread the Gospel (and Practice What We Preach)

17   Although we should push the carmakers—and our politicians, who now own a chunk of them—to come up with more fuel-efficient products, even the cleanest vehicles will do nothing to fix sprawl. So we need to convince developers, politicians, and urban planners that we actually want to live in mixed-use walkable neighbourhoods. We can do that by moving to such places. And we must encourage walking, cycling, public transit, and car sharing, for ourselves and for others. Our credo should be: driving, if necessary, but not necessarily driving.

DISCUSSION QUESTIONS

1. An essay about breaking any addiction could easily sound preachy and alienate readers. How does the writer seek to establish a common ground with readers from the first sentence on? How does he show empathy and understanding of why people rely on cars in each step? Give examples.

2. Identify points from the introduction in paragraphs 1 and 2 where you find Tim Falconer making the case that we have a collective addiction to the automobile, and then follow the thread of this analogy throughout his essay. To what extent do you find the use of this analogy to be an effective rhetorical strategy?

3. Even though the subject matter is serious, how does the writer keep his tone fairly casual, even light at times? How does he also bring in rational appeals such as statistics, examples, and quotations from people knowledgeable about traffic problems? Do you recognize the allusion at the end of paragraph 1, and if so, does it seem effective? Why or why not?

4. The essay weaves in cause and effect analysis throughout—for example, in paragraph 1, the writer cites the effects of the automobile on our society: "The automobile has wasted our time, choked our air, and destroyed many downtowns while spurring sprawl

in the suburbs." Locate three other examples of cause-and-effect reasoning, and one example of reasoning that employs a causal chain.

5. The writer identifies problems with what he calls an addiction to the automobile as well as potential solutions that can help ameliorate these problems. Name three problems besides traffic congestion that he identifies and describe the potential solutions he recommends.

6. Falconer brings in arguments that might seem incidental to the main argument about freeing ourselves as much as possible from depending on our automobiles; for example, he argues for more walkable communities and that these kinds of denser neighbour-hoods decrease social isolation and foster greater tolerance (paragraph 5). What additional secondary arguments does he bring in (see paragraphs 6 to 12 especially), and how are these relevant to his overall thesis?

TOWARD KEY INSIGHTS

To what extent do you agree with the claim in paragraph 9 that people often act less rationally when they are behind the wheel of a car? Explain.

Some of Falconer's suggestions that cost money (renouncing free parking, embracing road pricing) may raise resistance in readers who are watching their budgets very closely (that includes most students). How does Falconer address potential resistance?

Whether you are an automobile lover or not, identify the part of the argument that is most effective here, and what part you find least convincing.

SUGGESTIONS FOR WRITING *Write an essay using process analysis and cause and effect that makes a similar case that some other cultural phenomenon is a collective addiction that could be addressed with a 12-step program. Some examples could include cellphone or Internet addiction, shopping mall addiction, and a certain kind of relationship addiction.*

Write an essay focused on how one of the secondary problems that Falconer discusses (free parking that causes people to drive more) or secondary solutions (bicycling instead of driving) might be addressed in your local community. Define the problem clearly before making recommendations, and also consider how to anticipate and answer potential objections that readers could have.

Joe Kelly

Go Take a Hike

Joe Kelly, a writer and educator who teaches at Capilano University, is interested in positive change in the world. In this article from the Vancouver Sun, *he explores the ways in which a simple walk in the forest can deepen our sense of connection with and appreciation for nature. Follow him at www.joe-kelly.com or @drjoekelly.*

1   The Japanese have a wonderful expression for spending time in the woods: Shinrin-yoku, or forest bathing.

2   Widely practised in Japan, forest bathing involves visiting a forest expressly for its health benefits. Advocates of Shinrin-yoku claim that breathing in the volatile organic compounds produced from trees, called phytoncides or wood essential oils, helps to promote relaxation and reduce stress. It works just like aromatherapy, set in the great outdoors.

3   Whether or not you buy into the aromatherapeutic effects of trees, the general health benefits of nature are well founded. Studies show that spending time in nature can help to enhance your mood, increase energy levels and heighten your overall well-being. In fact, being outside for just 20 minutes a-day is sufficient for boosting your vitality levels. Spending time in nature can also increase your resistance, to illnesses, promote longevity and decrease the risks of mental illness.

4   It might not be a surprise that time spent in nature is good for your health. However, have you ever considered how spending time in nature can help to make the world around you a better place?

5   To explore this question, I challenged myself to spend one hour in nature every day in March. In the most primitive sense, nature is any natural setting untouched and uninfluenced by civilization. Strictly speaking, a park with a maintained trail system and other amenities is not truly in a natural state. For me, however, spending time every day in authentically wild places is impractical. So, for the purpose of this challenge, I relaxed the definition of nature to include some minor human influences (a park with trails and picnic areas is considered to be nature; a soccer pitch is not).

6   One way that spending time in nature benefits the broader community is by promoting positive social interactions with others. Free of the distractions and background noise present in the city, the serenity of nature provides a perfect venue to connect with others. Even strangers seem more willing to exchange pleasantries in natural settings than in urban ones. These interactions can help to build stronger social ties and connectedness in a community. When social ties are strong, people feel less isolated and more inclined to help and support one another.

7   Whenever I was joined by friends or colleagues on my excursions, our conversations seemed more genuine, thoughtful and inspiring than had they occurred in a busy downtown café. One reason why nature promotes more, enriching social interactions is that fresh air and natural light help to elevate people's mood. Additionally, the physical activity from walking or hiking has been shown to improve the functioning of your brain, reduce stress and increase energy levels. Quite simply, nature puts you in a better frame of mind for engaging in positive, interactions with others.

8   Spending time in nature can also make communities safer. The sights and sounds of nature help to reduce mental fatigue by restoring the mind's ability to concentrate and pay attention. When mental fatigue is relieved, people are better equipped to manage their problems calmly and thoughtfully rather than with anger and aggression. This can help to reduce the propensity for violence and crime in a community.

9   This month, I experienced the benefits of a calmer disposition first-hand. As a result of a computer glitch, and quite possibly some human error, I lost four hours' worth of work from my laptop. I was surprised at how calmly I responded. A more stressed-out version of me would have slammed my desk and hailed my computer with expletives. This time, I simply took a breath and then recreated all my lost work over the next two hours. I'd like to think my daily jaunts through nature were at least partly responsible for my calmer disposition.

10   One of the more surprising benefits of nature is its power to change our outlook on life. Research has shown that exposure to nature can shift a person's values and priorities from personal gain to a broader focus on community and connections with others. Simply put, nature has the intrinsic ability to make people more caring and empathetic. I personally find it uplifting to know that nature brings out the best in people.

11   Spending time in nature is good for the planet, too. It can enhance our sense of connection and appreciation for the natural environment. A stronger environmental ethos can promote more environmentally friendly choices and behaviours in our daily life, such as recycling, conserving energy or taking transit. In addition, time spent in nature means less time spent on more materialistic and resource-intensive pursuits like watching TV or shopping.

12   Imagine if every one of us spent some time each day in nature. It's not a stretch to say our communities would be more connected, less stressed, healthier and more caring. We'd likely treat each other, and the natural environment, a lot better than we do now. Knowing that you are helping the world around you, while enjoying the scenic beauty of nature, provides extra incentive to get outdoors more often.

DISCUSSION QUESTIONS

1. The writer begins with a definition of the lovely metaphor "forest bathing" as a walk in the woods. What personal benefits does he suggest are associated with this practice? What might be the broader social benefits of this practice?

2. Joe Kelly posits that spending time in nature not only improves personal health, but also may promote healthier communities (paragraphs 6 to 8) and a more ecological ethos (paragraph 11). What kind of support does he offer for these claims?

3. Analyze the causal chain of logic in paragraphs 6 to 8. How does one cause lead to an effect that then becomes a cause of another effect?

TOWARD KEY INSIGHTS

What is your response to the writer's claim that being in nature can "change our outlook on life" in a positive way?

In paragraph 9, the writer says that spending an hour a day in nature, helped him to deal better with stress. Have you had similar experiences in the forest or in nature that have calmed your stress?

SUGGESTIONS FOR WRITING   *Write an essay that employs a causal chain of logic to argue for the damaging effects of too much noise—or write an essay using cause and effect logic to show that some aspect of exposure to nature is beneficial. Narrow your focus— for example, you might show that playing outdoors in a natural environment helps children in a number of ways, or you might explore the ways that being outside, even for a few minutes a day, can help soothe anxiety.*

Krissy Darch and Fazeela Jiwa

Beyond Bullying

Krissy Darch is a writer and visual artist based in Vancouver. She has published in the Vancouver Observer, Megaphone, This Magazine, *and* TRIVIA: Voices of Feminism.

Fazeela Jiwa is an educator and writer from Vancouver. Her words can be found in independent and mainstream media, academic journals, creative anthologies, spoken performances and pamphlets, and on websites and walls.

1   The day after Nova Scotia high school student Rehtaeh Parsons took her life in April, a headline read: "Bullying to blame in death of NS teen." Months earlier, on the other side of the country, Amanda Todd hung herself to death in Port Coquitlam after posting a YouTube video discussing her torturous school life. In this case, mainstream media pointed to cyberbullying as the culprit. It doesn't take much digging, however, to learn that both young women experienced sexual harassment or assault by young men.

2   Here, the language of bullying papers over the systemic realities of misogyny and gendered violence. Elsewhere, the term conceals racism, homophobia, and ableism. This terminology frustrates us: *bullying* obscures the effects of asymmetrical social structures and power relations, cloaking them as kids' issues. Its vagueness lends itself to the emotional, hand-wringing responses we saw in the media after these suicides. Expressions of shock and outrage, while understandable, negate that experiences of sexual violence like Rehtaeh and Amanda's happen all the time, though less visibly, to girls and women who are perhaps less relatable—less white, less pretty, less middle-class.

3   Vague terms and superficial reactions in the media match vague and superficial institutional responses like anti-bullying campaigns. These reactions barely hint at the systemic degradation and disempowerment encountered by young women such as Amanda and Rehtaeh. In her essay "White Privilege: Unpacking the Invisible Knapsack," Peggy McIntosh says she "was taught to see racism only in individual acts of meanness, not in invisible systems conferring dominance on my group." Similarly, in these young women's cases, sexist actions are understood as individual instances of bullying rather than as being part of a system of dominance that privileges boys and men. We must demand more than anti-bullying campaigns from educators and ourselves if we're serious about challenging the patterns of rape culture.

4   Anti-bullying campaigns and suggested changes to legislation invite us, further, to place our faith in bureaucratic solutions and systems of authority. We are troubled by this reflex to defer to state "experts"—services, programs, and government agencies—during moments that might otherwise spark constructive, critical dialogues about systemic problems.

5   Such knee-jerk reactions are readily folded into the conservative law-and-order discourse that prescribes criminalization and mandatory minimums in lieu of preventative measures and community-based initiatives. Rape and sexual assault are already serious and highly stigmatized crimes, yet according to Statistics Canada there are over 500,000 sexual assaults a year. Less than one in 10 is ever reported, with women between the ages of 15 and 24 the most frequent targets.

6   Many commentators acknowledge that the police failed to bring justice when it mattered for Rehtaeh and Amanda, as is routine in the "he said, she said" police interpretation of many rape cases. Even with photographs of the rape in the Rehtaeh Parsons case, the evidence was deemed insufficient. Nova Scotia Justice Minister Ross Landry did ask for a review of the case but stressed: "It's important that Nova Scotians have faith in the justice system." Here, the impetus for reviewing the case is to bolster trust in the justice system instead of addressing the cultural logic that makes rape endemic in spite of its criminalization.

7   We believe hands-off funding for independent rape crisis centres and community initiatives aimed at critical re-education would be more effective than legalistic tinkering. But our proposals emphasize collectivity in a society where collective action is an abstraction.

8   Anti-bullying discourse is appealing because it is apolitical and individualistic, emphasizing free will and agency: each person can change their surroundings by simply being nicer. Ironically, this discourse can result in blaming and shaming, putting the onus on victims or people who are structurally disadvantaged to correct the situation.

9   The idea of bullying relegates violence to something that people grow out of in the ostensibly unlimited agency of adulthood. But we only have agency within given systems and embodied histories. Agency is social, uneven, conditional.

10   Before even posing the question—"How can we prevent this?"—that sparks so many anti-bullying campaigns, we wonder if it's more useful to ask ourselves whether we're open to the kind of change that far-reaching prevention requires. We can prevent these deaths and the injustice that leads to them. The question is, are we really willing to change not only ourselves but also the social systems in which we participate?

DISCUSSION QUESTIONS

1. Why are the writers unsatisfied with the notion that cyber-bullying led to the suicides of teenagers Amanda Todd in 2012 and Rehtaeh Parsons in 2013? How do they try to revise and expand the popular definition of bullying?

2. What do the writers say about the ways in which race, physical attractiveness, socio-economic status, or other factors intersect with gendered violence and assault?

3. Why do the writers focus more on promoting "critical dialogues about systemic problems" (paragraph 4) and "hands-off funding for independent rape crisis centres and community initiatives aimed at critical re-education" (paragraph 7) than changes in the law?

4. Examine paragraph 9, and explain what the writers seem to mean by the word *agency* and why they claim that "agency is social, uneven, conditional."

5. How do the writers use questions to help readers reflect on large, troubling social issues?

TOWARD KEY INSIGHTS Much of this essay attempts to redefine what is often called bullying, arguing that this term is too vague and ignores the broader systemic injustices, particularly misogyny and other forms of oppression, that lie beyond so-called bullying. What kind of language have you heard related to anti-bullying campaigns? In your view, does this language fall short?

The writers seem to focus more on assault and violence toward females in what they refer to as "rape culture." In your view, how relevant would a discussion of violence against males be in this essay? Would it strengthen or weaken the overall argument?

SUGGESTIONS FOR WRITING *Write an essay in which you define a term that the writers only mention, such as "ableism," using illustrations to show how this form of injustice is something that many people overlook.*

After analyzing this essay, write your own essay in which you explain how a term such as "honour killings," which commonly target females, is inadequate for what it refers to.

Drawing from the paper "White Privilege: Unpacking the Invisible Knapsack" by Peggy McIntosh referred to in this essay, which you can easily find on the Internet, write a paper defining "white privilege" or another kind of privilege or cultural blindness such as "speciesism." Use examples. Unlike the essay here, your essay will have to include documentation (see Chapter 16–17) if you bring in any material from outside sources, since you are writing for an academic audience, not a popular audience.

Laura Trethewey

Screen Saver

Hailing originally from Toronto, Laura Trethewey has lived in Halifax, Nova Scotia, and Banff, Alberta, and currently resides in Vancouver. She writes fiction and non-fiction for Geist, *the* National Post, *and other publications. Her work has been nominated for a National Magazine Award and a Western Magazine Award.*

1   Online media has monetized humanity's rubbernecking reflex like never before. "Clickbait," as defined by Urban Dictionary, is an "eye-catching link on a website which encourages people to read on. It is often paid for by the advertiser or generates income on the number of clicks." Clickbait is now a widespread phenomenon. These highly clickable links to videos, articles or images thrive on the lowest forms of controversy and intrigue, attracting an audience in the same manner as a bar fight or a car accident.

2   Back in September of 2013, a viral image spread across the internet: Miley Cyrus in a leather bikini, with knobby pigtails and lascivious red lips, twerking into Robin Thicke's black-and-white Beetlejuice pants. I saw it paired with an ostensibly feminist headline drubbing the performer. Eager to hear what new lows Cyrus had sunk to, I clicked.

3   Days later, it seemed, I emerged from the haze of Cyrusbait now repulsed by the image, much the way you might react to the sight of tequila the morning after a binge. Had I learned anything new about the exploitation of female performers? No, I'd gorged on sugary listicles like "22 Things That Miley Cyrus Looked Like at the 2013 VMAs." Had I ruminated on contemporary approaches to feminism? No, I'd

watched as discussion devolved into mud-slinging between Miley Cyrus, Sinead O'Connor, and Amanda Palmer. And I was primed for the new Miley Cyrus video "Wrecking Ball" when it came out—with artful timing—just a few days after the controversy. I clicked, yet again, along with millions of other viewers.

4   Once we were through with Miley, more highly clickable stories arose in her wake: David Gilmour teaching only "serious heterosexual guys"; the Rob Ford crack circus; Brazilian prostitutes taping Justin Bieber sleeping; a toy company suing the Beastie Boys—to name just a few.

5   Some of these stories touch on important issues—the pervasive power of straight white men in the literary world, dangerously irresponsible civil servants—but mainly it's a bunch of people doing stupid shit. Why are we giving them so much attention?

6   The answer, of course, is money. Websites like BuzzFeed, Upworthy, and Huffington Post are figuring out the best way to pair journalism with ads that are designed so that you can barely distinguish the two. BuzzFeed uses an algorithm to determine what people click on, and then marries successful campaigns with "BuzzFeed Partners" like Virgin Mobile. *New York* magazine estimates this new "advertorial" approach to journalism nets BuzzFeed around $40 million a year in ad revenue (BuzzFeed does not release official numbers). Jonah Perretti, BuzzFeed's founder, described the relationship between his company and Facebook by saying, "They own the railroad tracks, we drive the trains."

7   Upworthy employs a team to run randomized tests and determine the most clickable headlines. The formulaic nature of these headlines has spawned imitators and parodies, but remains shockingly effective. Before the site was two years old, it had 22 million visitors a month and had raised $8 million from investors—cash that these investors want to see returned. Naturally, Upworthy is trying out its own forays in sponsored stories. Unlike BuzzFeed, Upworthy produces no original content at all; it functions through aggregation and reframing, and as of March, partnerships with hard-news sites like ProPublica. Huffington Post uses the same mixed editorial/advertorial approach—also called "native advertising"—as Upworthy and BuzzFeed, and was sold to AOL for $300 million in cash.

8   We may think we're getting a great deal with all this free and fun clickbait, but we're paying for it dearly in other ways. Tech start-ups and advertising companies are colluding to turn us into a bunch of rats in Skinner boxes, primed to click for the next sugary reward, while they make big bucks off "sponsored content" stories about the new Xbox or Chevy Corvette. In a world of narcissistic articles like, "23 Signs You're Secretly an Introvert," hard-hitting journalism becomes an endangered species. War reporters in Aleppo can't afford health insurance and are paid $70 per article—barely enough for a night's room and board in the war-torn region.

9   You can fight back by doing one simple thing: think before you click. Don't click or share what will only make you or others uselessly angry. (No more Margaret Wente columns—we only have ourselves to blame for her continued career.) You can employ online tools, like Rather (GetRather.com), which allow you to filter out clickbait generators and stories. You can follow Twitter feeds like @Huffpospoilers and @Upworthyspoilers which skewer leading tweets and reveal the banal answers behind mysterious headlines. You can support quality journalism. You can choose not to stop and gawk at the spectacle.

DISCUSSION QUESTIONS

1. Explain in your own words the meaning of the first sentence: "Online media has monetized humanity's rubbernecking reflex like never before." What is the definition of "clickbait" that the writer defines in the opening paragraph? How does the writer return to the idea of "rubbernecking" in the concluding sentence?

2. What is the definition of "a mixed editorial/advertorial approach" or "native advertising" (paragraph 7)?

3. In addition to using definition, this essay employs other rhetorical strategies for development, including illustration, cause and effect, and argument. Find an example of each of these.

4. What can you infer about the writer's identity and values from the diction, tone, and use of examples in this piece? What kind of audience would be most interested in it? Examine this essay in terms of the writing persona it projects, as well as the kind of audience it seems to address.

5. What other dangers, in addition to causing us to waste time, does the writer associate with such a glut of clickbait or "sponsored content" (paragraph 8)?

TOWARD KEY INSIGHTS What "clickable headlines" have drawn you in to read more and more recently? If you have access to the Internet, take a look at some of the headlines that pop up in a casual search and explain how they work.

SUGGESTION FOR WRITING *Many people have had the experience of falling into a kind of Internet vortex similar to what the writer describes, where one search leads to many distractions. Write an essay illustrating this phenomenon, drawing from your own experiences and observations.*

Richard Rodriguez

Private Language, Public Language

Richard Rodriguez (born 1944) is a native of San Francisco who is of Mexican ancestry. After learning English in the elementary grades, he went on to earn a baccalaureate degree in English at Stanford University (1967) and graduate degrees at Columbia University (1969) and the University of California at Berkeley (1975). Rejecting job offers from several major universities, he spent the next six years writing Hunger of Memory: The Education of Richard Rodriguez *(1982), a book that traces his educational odyssey.* Days of Obligation *was published in 1992, and* Brown: The Last Discovery of America *was published in 2003. His articles have appeared in a variety of scholarly magazines. In the following essay, Rodriguez explores his contrasting childhood perceptions concerning English and his native Spanish.*

1   I remember to start with that day in Sacramento—a California now nearly thirty years past—when I first entered a classroom, able to understand some fifty stray English words.

2   The third of four children, I had been preceded to a neighborhood Roman Catholic school by an older brother and sister. But neither of them had revealed very much about their classroom experiences. Each afternoon they returned, as they left in the morning, always together, speaking in Spanish as they climbed the five steps of the porch. And their mysterious books, wrapped in shopping-bag paper, remained on the table next to the door, closed firmly behind them.

3   An accident of geography sent me to a school where all my classmates were white, many the children of doctors and lawyers and business executives. All my classmates certainly must have been uneasy on that first day of school—as most children are uneasy—to find themselves apart from their families in the first institution of their lives. But I was astonished.

4   The nun said, in a friendly but oddly impersonal voice, "Boys and girls, this is Richard Rodriguez." (I heard her sound out: *Rich-heard Road-ree-guess.*) It was the first time I had heard anyone name me in English. "Richard," the nun repeated more slowly, writing my name down in her black leather book. Quickly I turned to see my mother's face dissolve in a watery blur behind the pebbled glass door.

5   Many years later there is something called bilingual education—a scheme proposed in the late 1960s by Hispanic-American social activists, later endorsed by a congressional vote. It is a program that seeks to permit non-English-speaking children, many from lower-class homes, to use their family language as the language of school. (Such is the goal its supporters announce.) I hear them and am forced to say no: It is not possible for a child—any child—ever to use his family's language in school. Not to understand this is to misunderstand the public uses of schooling and to trivialize the nature of intimate life—a family's "language."

6   Memory teaches me what I know of these matters; the boy reminds the adult. I was a bilingual child, a certain kind—socially disadvantaged—the son of working-class parents, both Mexican immigrants.

7   In the early years of my boyhood, my parents coped very well in America. My father had steady work. My mother managed at home. They were nobody's victims. Optimism and ambition led them to a house (our home) many blocks from the Mexican south side of town. We lived among *gringos* and only a block from the biggest, whitest houses. It never occurred to my parents that they couldn't live wherever they chose. Nor was the Sacramento of the fifties bent on teaching them a contrary lesson. My mother and father were more annoyed than intimidated by those two or three neighbors who tried initially to make us unwelcome. ("Keep your brats away from my sidewalk!") But despite all they achieved, perhaps because they had so much to achieve, any deep feeling of ease, the confidence of "belonging" in public was withheld from them both. They regarded the people at work, the faces in crowds, as very distant from us. They were the others, *los gringos*. That term was interchangeable in their speech with another, even more telling, *los americanos*.

8   I grew up in a house where the only regular guests were my relations. For one day, enormous families of relatives would visit and there would be so many people that the noise and the bodies would spill out to the backyard and front porch. Then, for weeks, no one came by. (It was usually a salesman who rang the doorbell.) Our house stood

apart. A gaudy yellow in a row of white bungalows. We were the people with the noisy dog. The people who raised pigeons and chickens. We were the foreigners on the block. A few neighbors smiled and waved. We waved back. But no one in the family knew the names of the old couple who lived next door; until I was seven years old, I did not know the names of the kids who lived across the street.

9   In public, my father and mother spoke a hesitant, accented, not always grammatical English. And they would have to strain—their bodies tense—to catch the sense of what was rapidly said by *los gringos*. At home they spoke Spanish. The language of their Mexican past sounded in counterpoint to the English of public society. The words would come quickly, with ease. Conveyed through those sounds was the pleasing, soothing, consoling reminder of being at home.

10   During those years when I was first conscious of hearing, my mother and father addressed me only in Spanish; in Spanish I learned to reply. By contrast, English *(inglés),* rarely heard in the house, was the language I came to associate with *gringos.* I learned my first words of English overhearing my parents speak to strangers. At five years of age, I knew just enough English for my mother to trust me on errands to stores one block away. No more.

11   I was a listening child, careful to hear the very different sounds of Spanish and English. Wide-eyed with hearing, I'd listen to sounds more than words. First, there were English *(gringo)* sounds. So many words were still unknown that when the butcher or the lady at the drugstore said something to me, exotic polysyllabic sounds would bloom in the midst of their sentences. Often the speech of people in public seemed to me very loud, booming with confidence. The man behind the counter would literally ask, "What can I do for you?" But by being so firm and so clear, the sound of his voice said that he was a *gringo;* he belonged in public society.

12   I would also hear then the high nasal notes of middle-class American speech. The air stirred with sound. Sometimes, even now, when I have been traveling abroad for several weeks, I will hear what I heard as a boy. In hotel lobbies or airports, in Turkey or Brazil, some Americans will pass, and suddenly I will hear it again—the high sound of American voices. For a few seconds I will hear it with pleasure, for it is now the sound of *my* society—a reminder of home. But inevitably—already on the flight headed for home—the sound fades with repetition. I will be unable to hear it anymore.

13   When I was a boy, things were different. The accent of *los gringos* was never pleasing nor was it hard to hear. Crowds at Safeway or at bus stops would be noisy with sound. And I would be forced to edge away from the chirping chatter above me.

14   I was unable to hear my own sounds, but I knew very well that I spoke English poorly. My words would not stretch far enough to form complete thoughts. And the words I did speak I didn't know well enough to make into distinct sounds. (Listeners would usually lower their heads, better to hear what I was trying to say.) But it was one thing for *me* to speak English with difficulty. It was more troubling for me to hear my parents speak in public: their high-whining vowels and guttural consonants; their sentences that got stuck with "eh" and "ah" sounds; the confused syntax; the hesitant rhythm of sounds so different from the way *gringos* spoke. I'd notice, moreover, that my parents' voices were softer than those of *gringos* we'd meet.

15   I am tempted now to say that none of this mattered. In adulthood I am embarrassed by childhood fears. And, in a way, it didn't matter very much that my parents could not speak English with ease. Their linguistic difficulties had no serious

consequences. My mother and father made themselves understood at the county hospital clinic and at government offices. And yet, in another way, it mattered very much—it was unsettling to hear my parents struggle with English. Hearing them, I'd grow nervous, my clutching trust in their protection and power weakened.

16   There were many times like the night at a brightly lit gasoline station (a blaring white memory) when I stood uneasily, hearing my father. He was talking to a teenaged attendant. I do not recall what they were saying, but I cannot forget the sounds my father made as he spoke. At one point his words slid together to form one word—sounds as confused as the threads of blue and green oil in the puddle next to my shoes. His voice rushed through what he had left to say. And, toward the end, reached falsetto notes, appealing to his listener's understanding. I looked away to the lights of passing automobiles. I tried not to hear anymore. But I heard only too well the calm, easy tones in the attendant's reply. Shortly afterward, walking toward home with my father, I shivered when he put his hand on my shoulder. The very first chance that I got, I evaded his grasp and ran on ahead into the dark, skipping with feigned boyish exuberance.

17   But then there was Spanish. *Español:* my family's language. *Español:* the language that seemed to me a private language. I'd hear strangers on the radio and in the Mexican Catholic church across town speaking in Spanish, but I couldn't really believe that Spanish was a public language, like English. Spanish speakers, rather, seemed related to me, for I sensed that we shared—through our language—the experience of feeling apart from *los gringos.* It was thus a ghetto Spanish that I heard and I spoke. Like those whose lives are bound by a barrio, I was reminded by Spanish of my separateness from *los otros, los gringos* in power. But more intensely than for most barrio children—because I did not live in a barrio—Spanish seemed to me the language of home. (Most days it was only at home that I'd hear it.) It became the language of joyful return.

18   A family member would say something to me and I would feel myself specially recognized. My parents would say something to me and I would feel embraced by the sounds of their words. Those sounds said: *I am speaking with ease in Spanish. I am addressing you in words I never use with* los gringos. *I recognize you as someone special, close, like no one outside. You belong with us. In the family.*

19   *(Ricardo.)*

20   At the age of five, six, well past the time when most other children no longer easily notice the difference between sounds uttered at home and words spoken in public, I had a different experience. I lived in a world magically compounded of sounds. I remained a child longer than most; I lingered too long, poised at the edge of language—often frightened by the sounds of *los gringos,* delighted by the sounds of Spanish at home. I shared with my family a language that was startlingly different from that used in the great city around us.

21   For me there were none of the gradations between public and private society so normal to a maturing child. Outside the house was public society; inside the house was private. Just opening or closing the screen door behind me was an important experience. I'd rarely leave home all alone or without reluctance. Walking down the sidewalk, under the canopy of tall trees, I'd warily notice the—suddenly—silent neighborhood kids who stood warily watching me. Nervously, I'd arrive at the grocery store to hear there the sounds of the *gringo*—foreign to me—reminding me that in this world so big, I was a foreigner. But then I'd return. Walking back toward our house, climbing the steps from the sidewalk, when the front door was open in summer, I'd

hear voices beyond the screen door talking in Spanish. For a second or two, I'd stay, linger there, listening. Smiling, I'd hear my mother call out, saying in Spanish (words): "Is that you, Richard?" All the while her sounds would assure me: *You are home now; come closer; inside. With us.*

22   "*Sí,*" I'd reply.

23   Once more inside the house I would resume (assume) my place in the family. The sounds would dim, grow harder to hear. Once more at home, I would grow less aware of that fact. It required, however, no more than the blurt of the doorbell to alert me to listen to sounds all over again. The house would turn instantly still while my mother went to the door. I'd hear her hard English sounds. I'd wait to hear her voice return to soft-sounding Spanish, which assured me, as surely as did the clicking tongue of the lock on the door, that the stranger was gone.

24   Plainly, it is not healthy to hear such sounds so often. It is not healthy to distinguish public words from private words so easily. I remained cloistered by sounds, timid and shy in public, too dependent on voices at home. And yet it needs to be emphasized: I was an extremely happy child at home. I remember many nights when my father would come back from work, and I'd hear him call out to my mother in Spanish, sounding relieved. In Spanish, he'd sound light and free notes he never could manage in English. Some nights I'd jump up just at hearing his voice. With *mis hermanos* I would come running into the room where he was with my mother. Our laughing (so deep was the pleasure!) became screaming. Like others who know the pain of public alienation, we transformed the knowledge of our public separateness and made it consoling—the reminder of intimacy. Excited, we joined our voices in a celebration of sounds. *We are speaking now the way we never speak out in public. We are alone—together,* voices sounded, surrounded to tell me. Some nights, no one seemed willing to loosen the hold sounds had on us. At dinner, we invented new words. (Ours sounded Spanish, but made sense only to us.) We pieced together new words by taking, say, an English verb and giving it Spanish endings. My mother's instructions at bedtime would be lacquered with mock-urgent tones. Or a word like *sí* would become, in several notes, able to convey added measures of feeling. Tongues explored the edges of words, especially the fat vowels. And we happily sounded that military drum roll, the twirling roar of the Spanish *r.* Family language: my family's sounds. The voices of my parents and sisters and brother. Their voices insisting: *You belong here. We are family members. Related. Special to one another. Listen!* Voices singing and sighing, rising, straining, then surging, teeming with pleasure that burst syllables into fragments of laughter. At times it seemed there was steady quiet only when, from another room, the rustling whispers of my parents faded and I moved closer to sleep.

DISCUSSION QUESTIONS

1. What does Rodriguez accomplish in his first four paragraphs? What connection do you see between these paragraphs and later parts of the essay?

2. What is Rodriguez's main point? Where is it stated?

3. Discuss the significance of paragraphs 7 to 9.

4. Why did his parents' difficulties with English cause Rodriguez such concern?

5. In paragraph 16 Rodriguez tells us that he "looked away to the lights of passing automobiles" and that he "ran on ahead into the dark . . ." Explain these actions.

6. Rodriguez does not begin to develop his discussion of Spanish—the private language—until paragraph 17. Why do you think this discussion didn't occur earlier in the essay?

7. Explain why the concluding paragraph is effective.

TOWARD KEY INSIGHTS

In what ways other than those noted by Rodriguez do children and their families create or inhabit private worlds that are separate from their public worlds?

What are some of the benefits and problems that result from this dichotomy?

How important is language to a person's identity and social world?

SUGGESTION FOR WRITING *Write an essay comparing and contrasting the languages you use in two different discourse communities. These may be altogether different languages such as English and Mandarin, Spanish, or Punjabi; or they may be languages that have fairly subtle differences—for example, the language you use in your home and the one you use with your friends or at school.*

Scott Russell Sanders

The Men We Carry in Our Minds

Scott Russell Sanders was born in 1945 in Memphis, Tennessee. After earning a B.A. degree from Brown University in 1967 and a Ph.D. from Cambridge University in 1971, he joined the English faculty at Indiana University, where he is a full professor. Sanders is the author of numerous books of fiction and non-fiction. These books span a wide range of genres, including science fiction, historical novels, children's stories, folk tales, biographies, and personal essays. He has contributed to several essay anthologies, and his articles have appeared in literary journals and popular magazines. He has won several awards for his writing. In this essay, Sanders, in light of what he knows about the lives of working men, examines the view that power is rooted in gender.

1   The first men, besides my father, I remember seeing were black convicts and white guards, in the cottonfield across the road from our farm on the outskirts of Memphis. I must have been three or four. The prisoners wore dingy gray-and-black zebra suits, heavy as canvas, sodden with sweat. Hatless, stooped, they chopped weeds in the fierce heat, row after row, breathing the acrid dust of boll-weevil poison. The overseers wore dazzling white shirts and broad shadowy hats. The oiled barrels of their shotguns flashed in the sunlight. Their faces in memory are utterly blank. Of course those men, white and black, have become for me an emblem of racial hatred. But

they have also come to stand for the twin poles of my early vision of manhood—the brute toiling animal and the boss.

2   When I was a boy, the men I knew labored with their bodies. They were marginal farmers, just scraping by, or welders, steel workers, carpenters; they swept floors, dug ditches, mined coal, or drove trucks, their forearms ropy with muscle; they trained horses, stoked furnaces, built tires, stood on assembly lines wrestling parts onto cars and refrigerators. They got up before light, worked all day long whatever the weather, and when they came home at night they looked as though somebody had been whipping them. In the evenings and on weekends they worked on their own places, tilling gardens that were lumpy with clay, fixing broken-down cars, hammering on houses that were always too drafty, too leaky, too small.

3   The bodies of the men I knew were twisted and maimed in ways visible and invisible. The nails of their hands were black and split, the hands tattooed with scars. Some had lost fingers. Heavy lifting had given many of them finicky backs and guts weak from hernias. Racing against conveyor belts had given them ulcers. Their ankles and knees ached from years of standing on concrete. Anyone who had worked for long around machines was hard of hearing. They squinted, and the skin of their faces was creased like the leather of old work gloves. There were times, studying them, when I dreaded growing up. Most of them coughed, from dust or cigarettes, and most of them drank cheap wine or whiskey, so their eyes looked bloodshot and bruised. The fathers of my friends always seemed older than the mothers. Men wore out sooner. Only women lived into old age.

4   As a boy I also knew another sort of men, who did not sweat and break down like mules. They were soldiers, and so far as I could tell they scarcely worked at all. During my early school years we lived on a military base, an arsenal in Ohio, and every day I saw GIs in the guardshacks, on the stoops of barracks, at the wheels of olive drab Chevrolets. The chief fact of their lives was boredom. Long after I left the Arsenal I came to recognize the sour smell the soldiers gave off as that of souls in limbo. They were all waiting—for wars, for transfers, for leaves, for promotions, for the end of their hitch—like so many braves waiting for the hunt to begin. Unlike the warriors of older tribes, however, they would have no say about when the battle would start or how it would be waged. Their waiting was broken only when they practiced for war. They fired guns at targets, drove tanks across the churned-up fields of the military reservation, set off bombs in the wrecks of old fighter planes. I knew this was all play. But I also felt certain that when the hour for killing arrived, they would kill. When the real shooting started, many of them would die. This was what soldiers were *for*, just as a hammer was for driving nails.

5   Warriors and toilers: those seemed, in my boyhood vision, to be the chief destinies for men. They weren't the only destinies, as I learned from having a few male teachers, from reading books, and from watching television. But the men on television—the politicians, the astronauts, the generals, the savvy lawyers, the philosophical doctors, the bosses who gave orders to both soldiers and laborers—seemed as remote and unreal to me as the figures in tapestries. I could no more imagine growing up to become one of these cool, potent creatures than I could imagine becoming a prince.

6   A nearer and more hopeful example was that of my father, who had escaped from a red-dirt farm to a tire factory, and from the assembly line to the front office. Eventually he dressed in a white shirt and tie. He carried himself as if he had been

born to work with his mind. But his body, remembering the earlier years of slogging work, began to give out on him in his fifties, and it quit on him entirely before he turned sixty-five. Even such a partial escape from man's fate as he had accomplished did not seem possible for most of the boys I knew. They joined the Army, stood in line for jobs in the smoky plants, helped build highways. They were bound to work as their fathers had worked, killing themselves or preparing to kill others.

7   A scholarship enabled me not only to attend college, a rare enough feat in my circle, but even to study in a university meant for the children of the rich. Here I met for the first time young men who had assumed from birth that they would lead lives of comfort and power. And for the first time I met women who told me that men were guilty of having kept all the joys and privileges of the earth for themselves. I was baffled. What privileges? What joys? I thought about the maimed, dismal lives of most of the men back home. What had they stolen from their wives and daughters? The right to go five days a week, twelve months a year, for thirty or forty years to a steel mill or a coal mine? The right to drop bombs and die in war? The right to feel every leak in the roof, every gap in the fence, every cough in the engine, as a wound they must mend? The right to feel, when the layoff comes or the plant shuts down, not only afraid but ashamed?

8   I was slow to understand the deep grievances of women. This was because, as a boy, I had envied them. Before college, the only people I had ever known who were inter-ested in art or music or literature, the only ones who read books, the only ones who ever seemed to enjoy a sense of ease and grace were the mothers and daughters. Like the menfolk, they fretted about money, they scrimped and made-do. But, when the pay stopped coming in, they were not the ones who had failed. Nor did they have to go to war, and that seemed to me a blessed fact. By comparison with the narrow, ironclad days of fathers, there was an expansiveness, I thought, in the days of mothers. They went to see neighbors, to shop in town, to run errands at school, at the library, at church. No doubt, had I looked harder at their lives, I would have envied them less. It was not my fate to become a woman, so it was easier for me to see the graces. Few of them held jobs outside the home, and those who did filled thankless roles as clerks and waitresses. I didn't see, then, what a prison a house could be, since houses seemed to me brighter, handsomer places than any factory. I did not realize—because such things were never spoken of—how often women suffered from men's bullying. I did learn about the wretchedness of abandoned wives, single mothers, widows; but I also learned about the wretchedness of lone men. Even then I could see how exhausting it was for a mother to cater all day to the needs of young children. But if I had been asked, as a boy, to choose between tending a baby and tending a machine, I think I would have chosen the baby. (Having now tended both, I know I would choose the baby.)

9   So I was baffled when the women at college accused me and my sex of having cornered the world's pleasures. I think something like my bafflement has been felt by other boys (and by girls as well) who grew up in dirt-poor farm country, in mining country, in black ghettos, in Hispanic barrios, in the shadows of factories, in Third World nations—any place where the fate of men is as grim and bleak as the fate of women. Toilers and warriors. I realize now how ancient these identities are, how deep the tug they exert on men, the undertow of a thousand generations. The miseries I saw, as a boy, in the lives of nearly all men I continue to see in the lives of many—the body-breaking toil, the tedium, the call to be tough, the humiliating powerlessness, the battle for a living and for territory.

10   When the women I met at college thought about the joys and privileges of men, they did not carry in their minds the sort of men I had known in my childhood. They thought of their fathers, who were bankers, physicians, architects, stockbrokers, the big wheels of the big cities. These fathers rode the train to work or drove cars that cost more than any of my childhood houses. They were attended from morning to night by female helpers, wives and nurses and secretaries. They were never laid off, never short of cash at month's end, never lined up for welfare. These fathers made decisions that mattered. They ran the world.

11   The daughters of such men wanted to share in this power, this glory. So did I. They yearned for a say over their future, for jobs worthy of their abilities, for the right to live at peace, unmolested, whole. Yes, I thought, yes yes. The difference between me and these daughters was that they saw me, because of my sex, as destined from birth to become like their fathers, and therefore as an enemy to their desires. But I knew better. I wasn't an enemy, in fact or in feeling. I was an ally. If I had known, then, how to tell them so, would they have believed me? Would they now?

DISCUSSION QUESTIONS

1. Why is the essay titled "The Men *We* Carry in *Our Minds*" rather than "The Men *I* Carry in *My Mind*"?

2. Other than starting the essay, what does paragraph 1 accomplish?

3. What primary categories of men does Sanders discuss? What principle of classification does he use?

4. Sanders uses a number of comparisons, such as "zebra suits, heavy as canvas" in paragraph 1, to enhance his writing. Point out other comparisons and comment on their effectiveness.

5. The last sentence of paragraph 10 and the second, sixth, and eighth sentences of paragraph 11 are short statements. What do you think Sanders accomplishes with these statements?

6. In paragraphs 9-11, how does Sanders suggest that social class greatly influences how we judge wealth and privilege? What does he mean when he says toward the end that he "wasn't an enemy" but "an ally"? What do his final two questions cause you to reflect upon?

TOWARD KEY INSIGHTS

To what extent do you imagine that the views expressed by women in this essay are similar to the views of women you know at university?

How do you account for any changes you might note?

SUGGESTION FOR WRITING *Write an essay classifying the different high school teachers, former friends, or former partners that you carry in your mind. Develop your categories with specific, informative details.*

MyWritingLab

How Do I Get a Better Grade?

Go to **www.mywritinglab .com** for additional help with your grammar, writing, and research skills. You will have access to a variety of exercises, instruction, and videos that will help you improve your basic skills and help you get a better grade.

Patrick Moore

Going Nuclear

Patrick Moore was born in 1947, received a Ph.D. in ecology from the University of British Columbia, and served as an environmental activist with Greenpeace from 1971 to 1986. Since then, he has taken very different views from Greenpeace, suggesting that climate change may not be man made and that nuclear power is an important environmental solution. He is co-founder and chief scientist for the consulting firm Greenspirit Strategies. He is also a paid lobbyist for the Nuclear Energy Institute. One question readers need to consider is whether his history and current affiliations should influence how his article is evaluated. "Going Nuclear" appeared as an opinion piece in the Sunday edition of The Washington Post *on April 16, 2006.*

1   In the early 1970s when I helped found Greenpeace, I believed that nuclear energy was synonymous with nuclear holocaust, as did most of my compatriots. That's the conviction that inspired Greenpeace's first voyage up the spectacular rocky northwest coast to protest the testing of U.S. hydrogen bombs in Alaska's Aleutian Islands. Thirty years on, my views have changed, and the rest of the environmental movement needs to update its views, too, because nuclear energy may just be the energy source that can save our planet from another possible disaster: climate change.

2   Look at it this way: More than 600 coal-fired electric plants in the United States produce 36 percent of U.S. emissions—or nearly 10 percent of global emissions—of CO_2, the primary greenhouse gas responsible for climate change. Nuclear energy is the only large-scale, cost-effective energy source that can reduce these emissions while continuing to satisfy a growing demand for power. And these days it can do so safely.

3   I say that guardedly, of course, just days after Iranian President Mahmoud Ahmadinejad announced that his country had enriched uranium. "The nuclear technology is only for the purpose of peace and nothing else," he said. But there is widespread speculation that, even though the process is ostensibly dedicated to producing electricity, it is in fact a cover for building nuclear weapons.

4   And although I don't want to underestimate the very real dangers of nuclear technology in the hands of rogue states, we cannot simply ban every technology that is dangerous. That was the all-or-nothing mentality at the height of the Cold War, when anything nuclear seemed to spell doom for humanity and the environment. In 1979, Jane Fonda and Jack Lemmon produced a frisson of fear with their starring roles in "The China Syndrome," a fictional evocation of nuclear disaster in which a reactor meltdown threatens a city's survival. Less than two weeks after the blockbuster film opened, a reactor core meltdown at Pennsylvania's Three Mile Island nuclear power plant sent shivers of very real anguish throughout the country.

5   What nobody noticed at the time, though, was that Three Mile Island was in fact a success story: The concrete containment structure did just what it was designed

to do—prevent radiation from escaping into the environment. And although the reactor itself was crippled, there was no injury or death among nuclear workers or nearby residents. Three Mile Island was the only serious accident in the history of nuclear energy generation in the United States, but it was enough to scare us away from further developing the technology: There hasn't been a nuclear plant ordered up since then.

6   Today, there are 103 nuclear reactors quietly delivering just 20 percent of America's electricity. Eighty percent of the people living within 10 miles of these plants approve of them (that's not including the nuclear workers). Although I don't live near a nuclear plant, I am now squarely in their camp.

7   And I am not alone among seasoned environmental activists in changing my mind on this subject. British atmospheric scientist James Lovelock, father of the Gaia theory, believes that nuclear energy is the only way to avoid climate change. Stewart Brand, founder of the "Whole Earth Catalog," says the environmental movement must embrace nuclear energy to wean ourselves from fossil fuels. On occasion, such opinions have been met with excommunication from the anti-nuclear priesthood: The late British Bishop Hugh Montefiore, founder and director of Friends of the Earth, was forced to resign from the group's board after he wrote a pro-nuclear article in a church newsletter.

8   There are signs of a new willingness to listen, though, even among the staunchest anti-nuclear campaigners. When I attended the Kyoto climate meeting in Montreal last December, I spoke to a packed house on the question of a sustainable energy future. I argued that the only way to reduce fossil fuel emissions from electrical production is through an aggressive program of renewable energy sources (hydroelectric, geothermal heat pumps, wind, etc.) plus nuclear. The Greenpeace spokesperson was first at the mike for the question period, and I expected a tongue-lashing. Instead, he began by saying he agreed with much of what I said—not the nuclear bit, of course, but there was a clear feeling that all options must be explored.

9   Here's why: Wind and solar power have their place, but because they are intermittent and unpredictable they simply can't replace big baseload plants such as coal, nuclear and hydroelectric. Natural gas, a fossil fuel, is too expensive already, and its price is too volatile to risk building big baseload plants. Given that hydroelectric resources are built pretty much to capacity, nuclear is, by elimination, the only viable substitute for coal. It's that simple.

10   That's not to say that there aren't real problems—as well as various myths— associated with nuclear energy. Each concern deserves careful consideration:

11   *Nuclear energy is expensive.* It is in fact one of the least expensive energy sources. In 2004, the average cost of producing nuclear energy in the United States was less than two cents per kilowatt-hour, comparable with coal and hydroelectric. Advances in technology will bring the cost down further in the future.

12   *Nuclear plants are not safe.* Although Three Mile Island was a success story, the accident at Chernobyl, 20 years ago this month, was not. But Chernobyl was an accident waiting to happen. This early model of Soviet reactor had no containment vessel, was an inherently bad design and its operators literally blew it up. The multi-agency U.N. Chernobyl Forum reported last year that 56 deaths could be directly attributed to the accident, most of those from radiation or burns suffered while fighting the fire. Tragic as those deaths were, they pale in comparison to the more

than 5,000 coal-mining deaths that occur worldwide every year. No one has died of a radiation-related accident in the history of the U.S. civilian nuclear reactor program. (And although hundreds of uranium mine workers did die from radiation exposure underground in the early years of that industry, that problem was long ago corrected.)

13   *Nuclear waste will be dangerous for thousands of years.* Within 40 years, used fuel has less than one-thousandth of the radioactivity it had when it was removed from the reactor. And it is incorrect to call it waste, because 95 percent of the potential energy is still contained in the used fuel after the first cycle. Now that the United States has removed the ban on recycling used fuel, it will be possible to use that energy and to greatly reduce the amount of waste that needs treatment and disposal. Last month, Japan joined France, Britain and Russia in the nuclear-fuel-recycling business. The United States will not be far behind.

14   *Nuclear reactors are vulnerable to terrorist attack.* The six-feet-thick reinforced concrete containment vessel protects the contents from the outside as well as the inside. And even if a jumbo jet did crash into a reactor and breach the containment, the reactor would not explode. There are many types of facilities that are far more vulnerable, including liquid natural gas, plants, chemical plants and numerous political targets.

15   *Nuclear fuel can be diverted to make nuclear weapons.* This is the most serious issue associated with nuclear energy and the most difficult to address, as the example of Iran shows. But just because nuclear technology can be put to evil purposes is not an argument to ban its use.

16   Over the past 20 years, one of the simplest tools—the machete—has been used to kill more than a million people in Africa, far more than were killed in the Hiroshima and Nagasaki nuclear bombings combined. What are car bombs made of? Diesel oil, fertilizer and cars. If we banned everything that can be used to kill people, we would never have harnessed fire.

17   The only practical approach to the issue of nuclear weapons proliferation is to put it higher on the international agenda and to use diplomacy and, where necessary, force to prevent countries or terrorists from using nuclear materials for destructive ends. And new technologies such as the reprocessing system recently introduced in Japan (in which the plutonium is never separated from the uranium) can make it much more difficult for terrorists or rogue states to use civilian materials to manufacture weapons.

18   The 600-plus coal-fired plants emit nearly 2 billion tons of CO_2 annually—the equivalent of the exhaust from about 300 million automobiles. In addition, the Clean Air Council reports that coal plants are responsible for 64 percent of sulfur dioxide emissions, 26 percent of nitrous oxides and 33 percent of mercury emissions. These pollutants are eroding the health of our environment, producing acid rain, smog, respiratory illness and mercury contamination.

19   Meanwhile, the 103 nuclear plants operating in the United States effectively avoid the release of 700 million tons of CO_2 emissions annually—the equivalent of the exhaust from more than 100 million automobiles. Imagine if the ratio of coal to nuclear were reversed so that only 20 percent of our electricity was generated from coal and 60 percent from nuclear. This would go a long way toward cleaning the air and reducing greenhouse gas emissions. Every responsible environmentalist should support a move in that direction.

DISCUSSION QUESTIONS

1. In the introductory paragraph 1, the author identifies his role in Greenpeace and his initial opposition to nuclear power before discussing his current support for nuclear power. Why does the author start by discussing his background as an environmentalist?

2. After reading the biographical information about the author at the top of his essay, how do you evaluate his argument in light of his affiliation with the Nuclear Energy Institute?

3. Who is the target audience for this argument? Why did the writer choose this target audience? What particular parts of the argument are used specifically for that audience?

4. The author attempts to answer what he refers to as common "myths" about nuclear power. Why does he employ this strategy? What point seems strongest to you? What argument seems weakest? Explain.

TOWARD KEY INSIGHTS

Often we face not the best possible answer have to choose but rather the least undesirable option. Consider the ways that in this and other situations we may face such unfortunate choices.

The discussion of nuclear power often comes down to an assessment of risk. How much risk is there? How can risk be evaluated in determining whether we should expand the number of nuclear power, plants?

SUGGESTIONS FOR WRITING

1. After reading this essay, do additional research and write an argument either supporting or opposing the use of nuclear power as a solution to global warming.

2. If you oppose nuclear power, write to people who are unsure of their position on nuclear power, countering key points in this author's argument.

Alexis Rowell

Ten Reasons Why New Nuclear Was a Mistake—Even Before Fukushima

Alexis Rowell was born in 1965. He was for a time a BBC journalist. He was the founder of the consulting group cuttingthecarbon and was elected member of Camden Council in 2006. He has been appointed to be Camden Eco Champion and is Chair of the council's All-party Sustainability Task Force. He is the author of Communities, Councils and a Low Carbon Future. *The article below was posted on March 15, 2011, on the website* Transition Culture: an Evolving Exploration into the Head, Heart, and Hands of Energy Descent.

1   It's hardly a surprise that building nuclear power stations on seismic fault lines, as Japan has done, turns out to be a foolish thing. In the pause for reflection about the safety of nuclear power that the Fukushima disaster is bound to create, here are ten reasons why it's a mistake to build a new round of nuclear power stations in the UK.

NUCLEAR POWER IS TOO EXPENSIVE

2   Nuclear has always been an expensive white elephant. UK taxpayers currently subsidise nuclear directly to the tune of more than £1bn per year.[1] But the indirect subsidies such as decommissioning and insurance are far greater.

3   The cost of decommissioning old nuclear in the UK is now estimated to be at least £73bn.[2] Surely anyone wishing to provide new nuclear should have to put that sort of sum into an up-front clean-up fund. But of course they won't. They can't possibly afford to.

4   If there's a nuclear accident in the UK, then who will pay? An insurance company? Not a hope. Existing UK reactors are insured to the tune of £140m each, which the government is talking about increasing to £1.2bn, but that's still nothing like enough to cover a serious accident like Fukushima or Three Mile Island or Chernobyl.[3]

5   Nuclear power is uninsurable. It's too risky and the potential payouts are too big. The government, meaning the UK taxpayer, will have to pay as we did to bail out the banks. The free market will never bear the true costs of nuclear.

6   A report published by the US Union of Concerned Scientists last month said nuclear power had never operated in the United States without public subsidies.[4] The existence of an Office of Nuclear Development at the Department of Energy and Climate Change (DECC) makes a mockery of Chris Huhne's claim that no public money will be spent on new nuclear.[5]

7   Only two atomic power stations are under construction in Western Europe: one in France and one in Finland. The Finnish reactor, which was supposed to be the first of a new generation of "safe" and "affordable" units, has been subsidised by the French nuclear industry (and therefore the French state) as a loss leader in the hope that it will spark a new nuclear building boom. When the decision was announced Standard & Poor instantly downgraded to "negative" the stock of the Finnish utility commissioning the reactor. The project has been plagued with cost overruns and delays (it was due to open in 2009), is under investigation by the Finnish nuclear safety regulator STUK and is probably the single best reason why new nuclear is a mistake.[6]

---

[1]www.psiru.org/reports/2008-03-E-nuclearsubsidies.doc

[2]http://news.bbc.co.uk/1/hi/business/4859980.stm; http://www.guardian.co.uk/environment/2008/jan/30/nuclearpower.energy

[3]http://www.decc.gov.uk/en/content/cms/news/pn11_007/pn11_007.aspx

[4]Koplow, D. (2011). http://www.ucsusa.org/assets/documents/nuclear_power/nuclear_subsidies_report.pdf

[5]www.decc.gov.uk/en/content/cms/what_we_do/uk_supply/energy_mix/nuclear/new/office/office.aspx

[6]Thomas, S. (2010). "The Economics of Nuclear Power: An Update." http://boell.org/downloads/Thomas_UK_-_web.pdf

NEW NUCLEAR POWER STATIONS WON'T BE READY IN TIME

8   According to the 2007 Energy White Paper the earliest the first new nuclear power station could possibly be ready is 2020.[7] Chris Huhne occasionally says it might be possible by 2018 but most observers disagree. However we need to replace 40% of our energy generation by 2015 because old nuclear and coal-fired plants are set to close. New nuclear will come too late.

NUCLEAR DOES NOT AND WILL NOT SAFEGUARD OUR ENERGY SECURITY

9   Nuclear power currently provides 18% of our electricity but only about 1% of our total energy needs.[8] Three quarters of the UK's primary energy demand comes from gas and oil.[9] Gas is used for most of our space heating and hot water. Oil is used for virtually all forms of transport. Indeed the vast majority of our oil and gas consumption is for purposes other than producing electricity. Nuclear power cannot replace that energy, while gas and oil deliveries are threatened by tightening supply (peak oil) and political instability. A 2008 Sussex University study concluded: "we are not convinced that there is a strong security case for new nuclear, especially if the costs and risks of strategies that include new nuclear are considered alongside those of strategies that do not."[10]

NUCLEAR POWER IS NOT GREEN

10   Mining uranium requires fossils fuels. So does building a nuclear power station. And so does trying to dispose of radioactive waste. Over its lifecycle a nuclear power station produces as much carbon dioxide as a gas-fired power station.[11] Better than oil or coal but not carbon-free. And it will get worse. In the not too distant future uranium will become so hard to mine that it will require more fossil fuels to extract it than the energy that will be produced from it.[12]

NUCLEAR POWER WILL DO LITTLE TO REDUCE OUR CARBON EMISSIONS

11   Even if Britain built ten new reactors, nuclear power would only deliver a 4% cut in carbon emissions some time after 2025.[13] But that's too late. We need the carbon reductions now. We'd do better to ban standby buttons on electrical appliances than to develop new nuclear power.

[7]http://www.decc.gov.uk/en/content/cms/legislation/white_papers/white_paper_07/white_paper_07.aspx

[8]http://www.decc.gov.uk/en/content/cms/what_we_do/uk_supply/energy_mix; http://www.decc.gov.uk/assets/decc/Statistics/publications/dukes/348-dukes-2010-printed.pdf

[9]http://www.oilandgasuk.co.uk/economics.cfm

[10]Watson, J. & Scott, A. "New Nuclear Power in the UK: A Strategy for Energy Security?" http://www.sussex.ac.uk/Users/prpp4/Supergen_Nuclear_and_Security.pdf

[11]Van Leeuwen, J. & Smith, P. (2008). "Nuclear power the energy balance." http://www.stormsmith.nl/

[12]http://en.wikipedia.org/wiki/Peak_uranium

[13]http://www.greenpeace.org.uk/climate/nuclear-power

NUCLEAR POWER STATIONS ARE INEFFICIENT

12   We really need to stop producing electricity in huge power stations hundreds of miles away which waste 60% of the energy they produce as heat through cooling towers and another 7–9% in transmission losses across the national grid. If we produce energy locally and use Combined Heat and Power (CHP), then we can reach efficiencies of 80–90%.[14] Nuclear cannot and never has been made to work with CHP because to distribute the heat you need residents or businesses to be close by. But how many people want to live near a nuclear power station?

PLANE CRASHES ARE A RISK TO NUCLEAR POWER STATIONS

13   In February 2011 a Loughborough University aviation expert suggested the chance of a plane crashing into a UK reactor was 20% higher than official estimates and *The Guardian* reported that a Health & Safety Executive internal report had admitted that a crash could trigger "significant radiological releases."[15] Finally, if you can fly a plane into the Twin Towers, then you can certainly fly one into a nuclear power station.

NUCLEAR POWER KILLS

14   Miscarriage rates by women living near the Sellafield nuclear reprocessing facility are higher than would be expected.[16] Billions of fish are killed every year when they get trapped in the cooling water intake pipes of nuclear reactors.[17]

IT'S A MYTH THAT RENEWABLES CANNOT PROVIDE BASELOAD

15   There has never been a day on record when the wind has not blown somewhere in the UK. The point about baseload is that what you need is enough people in enough places producing electricity. The more you decentralise electricity generation the more secure the baseload becomes. The same principle holds for investing in shares—it's much more risky to invest everything in a couple of big companies than it is to invest in a basket of shares that reflect all aspects of the market. The real reason why proponents of nuclear are obliged to talk about baseload is that it's uneconomic to do much with atomic reactors other than run them continuously, whether or not the energy is needed. And in the UK that has usually meant prioritising nuclear over available wind energy.

GLOBAL EXPANSION COULD LEAD TO NEW NUCLEAR SECURITY RISKS

16   In February 2011 the Royal Society launched an inquiry into nuclear non-proliferation saying that a global expansion of nuclear power "could lead to the wider

---

[14]http://en.wikipedia.org/wiki/Cogeneration

[15]http://www.guardian.co.uk/environment/2011/feb/21/nuclear-risk-plane-crashes

[16]Jones, K. & Wheater, A. (1989). "Obstetric outcomes in West Cumberland Hospital: a risk from Sellafield?" http://www.ncbi.nlm.nih.gov/pmc/articles/PMC1292295/

[17]Speight, M. & Henderson, P. (2010). *Marine Ecology—Concepts and Applications.* p. 186

proliferation of nuclear weapons, as well as creating new nuclear security risks," which could "impact on international progress towards nuclear disarmament."[18] Look at the problems the international community is having with the Iranian nuclear power programme. Many observers believe the US and Israel recently collaborated on a cyber sabotage project to slow the Iranian development up and prevent it from developing atomic weapons.[19]

AND WE STILL HAVE NO IDEA WHAT TO DO WITH NUCLEAR WASTE

17   All those arguments against new nuclear and not one of them was about nuclear waste. The 2003 Energy White Paper said one of the reasons why the then government wasn't proposing new nuclear was because there were "important issues of nuclear waste to be resolved." Have they been? No.

18   There are perfectly good non-nuclear solutions but they all require a lot more government intervention than the coalition government seems prepared to contemplate. They are:

1) Energy Efficiency

19   As it stands, the government's Green Deal—under which householders can borrow funds for energy efficiency measures to be repaid out of energy bill savings—is set to be a completely inadequate sticking plaster solution. It feels like the government has decided that existing buildings are too difficult to deal with seriously which is why they're so gung-ho about new nuclear—to fuel electric radiators the energy from which will then be wasted through leaky windows, walls, roofs and floors. The only way to create genuinely low energy buildings is by-using Passivhaus design.[20] Asking the UK's building sector to refurbish buildings using a proper engineering standard will be a challenge, but it is at least a coherent approach. Unlike new nuclear and the Green Deal.

2) Renewables (and possibly combined heat & power in urban areas if we can find enough non-fossil fuels to run it)

20   Nuclear has taken up a huge amount of civil servant time over the last few years. That's time that could have been spent on renewables. Britain has by far the most potential for wind and tidal power in Europe because of our geography. 40% of Europe's wind passes through these isles.[21] Yet in 2010 we produced just 3.2% of our electricity from wind. Germany obtained 9.4% of its electricity from wind in 2010, Spain generated 14.4% and Denmark managed a whopping 24%.[22]

---

[18]http://royalsociety.org/nonproliferation/

[19]http://www.reuters.com/article/2011/02/07/us-nuclear-iran-idUSTRE71622Z20110207

[20]http://www.cuttingthecarbon.co.uk/home/passivhaus-standard

[21]http://www.energysavingtrust.org.uk/Generate-your-own-energy/Wind-Turbines

[22]http://ewea.org/fileadmin/ewea_documents/documents/statistics/EWEA_Annual_Statistics_2010.pdf

21   The reason the Danes are so far ahead on wind is because they learnt the right lessons from the oil shocks of the 1970s and started planning for a renewably-powered future back then. The UK, by contrast, was blinded by the discovery of North Sea Oil.

3) Tradable Energy Quotas (TEQs)

22   Tradable Energy Quotas (TEQs) are a way of using the market to reduce fossil fuel energy consumption.[23] Every adult is given an equal free entitlement of TEQs units each week. Other energy users (government, industry etc.) bid for their units at a weekly auction. If you use less than your entitlement, you can sell your surplus. If you need more, you can buy them. All trading takes place at a single national price, which will rise and fall in line with demand. When you buy energy, such as petrol for your car or electricity for your household, units corresponding to the amount of energy you have bought are deducted from your TEQs account, in addition to your money payment. The total number of units available in the country is set out in the TEQs Budget, which goes down each year.

23   *There are greener, cheaper, more secure, quicker to install, safer alternatives to new nuclear so don't let yourself be persuaded that it's the only solution. It's not.*

DISCUSSION QUESTIONS

1. The writer offers ten reasons against nuclear power and organizes them with bold headers. What might be his rhetorical reason for organizing them in this way?

2. Why do you think the writer focused more on refuting the argument that nuclear power is too expensive rather than on the argument that nuclear power is too unsafe?

3. In paragraph 12, the writer makes a very technical point about efficiency. What did you understand might be the writer's point here? How could this paragraph be made more clear for less knowledgeable readers?

4. In rejecting nuclear power, is it important for the writer to suggest other alternatives? How effective do you find his argument for alternatives such as wind power in paragraphs 15 and 20?

5. The article documents its sources and presents them in footnotes. To what extent, if at all, does this strengthen or weaken the argument of the article? Explain.

TOWARD KEY INSIGHTS

Like many arguments today, this one was posted on a blog rather than published as a newspaper opinion piece. How might writing for a blog differ from writing for print media, and in what ways is it the same?

The article is written about England's nuclear program for an English audience. To what extent are or aren't the arguments applicable to other countries such as Canada and the United States that may face different situations?

---

[23] http://www.teqs.net

SUGGESTIONS FOR WRITING

1. Identify one key issue raised by the article, such as the problem of disposing of nuclear waste; then research the topic and write an argument about it.

2. Research the safety of nuclear power and write an argument on whether nuclear power is or is not safe.

3. Having read both articles on nuclear power in the Reader, do additional research and write an argument to concerned Canadian readers on whether or not Canada should support the construction of new nuclear power plants to meet our energy needs.

4. Wind power has also come in for a certain amount of criticism related to health and environment. Research the drawbacks and the benefits of wind power; then write an essay choosing a point of view on this issue but also showing your awareness of different perspectives.

Julie Traves

The Church of Please and Thank You

Julie Traves has spent several years in the publishing industry in roles ranging from promoting writers to promoting her own writing. She is currently based in Toronto, where she is part of The Globe and Mail's *editorial team and contributes pieces on the arts and society and ideas to newspapers and magazines including* The Globe and Mail, *the* Toronto Star, *the* National Post, Maisonneuve, The Walrus, Canadian Business, *and* This Magazine.

1   Michelle Szabo smiles encouragingly as a young businessman talks about his hobbies in broken English. She is a Canadian teacher at Aeon's language school in Kawagoe, Japan. He is a prospective student she's charged to recruit as part of her job. The two meet in a drab five-storey office building outside the train station. The room is so small it fits only a table and two chairs. But making the sell to would-be learners has little to do with décor. What counts is Szabo's final handshake.

2   More than contact with an attractive young woman, her personal touch symbolizes a grasp on a better life. In the competitive marketplace of Japan, English test scores make or break job applications. Getting ahead means getting into classes with teachers like Szabo. "I would ask so many people, 'Do you expect to use English in your life?' And most people would say 'No, no, no, I just need this test score,'" says Szabo. "I think it's sort of a given for all families—it's like food, shelter, English." Some *sarariiman* (salarymen) were so excited they trembled when they took her hand.

3   In addition to the 380 million people worldwide who use English as their first language, it's estimated there are 350 million to 500 million speakers of English as a foreign language (EFL)—and the number is growing. For people from affluent and developing nations alike, it is clear that the secret passwords to safety, wealth and freedom can be whispered only in English. Even 66 percent of French citizens, linguistic protectionists *par excellence*, agreed they needed to speak English in a 2001 Eurobarometer poll. While thinkers such as John Ralston Saul proclaim the death of globalization, locals from countries around the world are clamouring for English training.

4   Enter thousands of Westerners who spread the English gospel overseas each year. Like the Christian missionaries who came before them, many are young, have a blind faith in the beliefs they've grown up with and, are eager to make their mark on the world. Unlike the 19- to 26-year-olds who proselytize for the Latter-day Saints, however, these new missionaries are also out for adventure, good times—and hard cash. Part of a $7.8-billion industry, instructors can earn $400 a month plus room and board in China and up to $4000 a month in Japan. That's a lot more than a McJob back home.

5   But students expect more than lessons in syntax and style. EFL teachers are also hired to share Western customs and values. "'Let's have lunch sometime' doesn't mean stop by my office tomorrow and we'll go out and have lunch. It means something more general, like 'It's been nice talking to you and maybe at some point I'd like to continue the conversation,'" says Diane Pecorari, a senior lecturer at the University of Stockholm. "When you're teaching formulae like 'Please,' 'Thank you,' 'Can I split the cheque?' you also have to teach the context in which they come up. That means teaching culture."

6   But what is the effect of that culture on students' dialects, customs—their very identity? Ian Martin, an English professor at York University's Glendon College in Toronto, points to a troubling precedent for the current explosion of EFL. "One of the big moments in the spread of English took place in India in 1835. [British politician] Thomas Babington Macaulay proposed that English be used to create a class of Indian middlemen who would be sympathetic to British interests, without the necessity of large numbers of British citizens coming out and running the show." Instead of invading India at great economic and human cost, English allowed the British to transform the country from within. With English on the tip of their tongues, Indians could much more easily swear allegiance to England.

7   Today's linguistic imperialism has a similar goal. Where once English facilitated the staffing of colonial offices, now it helps fill the cubicles of multinational corporations. Teaching locals Western speech and when it's appropriate to use it no longer transforms them into perfect Englishmen: it makes them into perfect businessmen and women. The politics of English haven't changed—the language simply serves a new corporate master.

8   To be sure, even those who are fascinated by the countries where they teach sometimes can't help transforming "the natives" as part of their work abroad. Canadian Michael Schellenberg, who taught in Japan more than a decade ago, loved learning about Japanese customs but also sheepishly admits he urged students to express themselves—quite against the Japanese grain. "One of the sayings in Japan is that the nail that sticks up will get pounded down. They wanted people to conform," he says. "I remember classes where I'd be like, 'Just be yourself!' As someone in my early 20s, I had a pretty good sense of how I thought the world should be. I felt pretty confident being forthright about that."

9   Teaching materials subtly suggest the superiority of Western values. Produced primarily in the US and UK, textbooks propagate the advantages of materialism, individualism and sexual liberation. For example, Ian Martin recalls an Indian friend's reaction to one textbook that showed Jack and Jane meeting in lesson one and dancing alone together by lesson three. "Where are the parents?" his friend wondered.

10   Some newer textbooks are more culturally sensitive. But in many of the books currently in circulation, says Martin, "there's nothing about environmentalism, nothing about spirituality, nothing about, say, respecting non-native [English] speakers. And there's very little realism in any of the language learning material that I've seen. It's this

mythic world of dream fulfillment through consumerism and Westernization." The Aeon language franchise in Japan uses Cameron Diaz and Celine Dion as its poster girls.

11   Of course, not all teachers aggressively peddle a mythic world—some have their soapbox thrust upon them. In her book *The Hemingway Book Club of Kosovo*, California writer Paula Huntley chronicles her experience teaching English to the survivors of the area's brutal ethnic clashes. Huntley doesn't believe her language and culture are better than any other. She wants to learn from the Kosovars as much as they want to learn from her. It's her students who are convinced that the American way is the way forward, that English is the true language of progress.

12   Before leaving for Kosovo, Huntley crams for four weeks to complete an English as a second language instructors' certificate. But this is not what impresses the owner of the Cambridge School in Kosovo, a man named Ahmet whose house and library of 5000 books were destroyed by the Serbs. Barely looking at her CV, he tells her she's hired. "'You are an American,'" he says. "'So you can teach our students more than English. You can teach them how to live together, with others, in peace. You can teach them how to work, how to build a democracy, how to keep trying no matter what the odds.'"

13   Then there is the conflicted experience of Kathy Lee. She teaches at Guangdong Industry Technical College in China. In a suburb called Nanhai, the school is putting up satellite facilities eight times larger than the main campus. Teaching labs have banks of computers and a plasma screen TV. But like so much of the country, there is such impatience to forge ahead that Lee conducts her three classes a week amid construction because the school is expanding so fast.

14   Her pupils are equally anxious to take part in the country's massive business boom. Though most of them have been studying English since primary school, their fluency is strained. They tell her: "The world is growing and many people speak English. If I want to do business with them, I must speak English well too!" What students want is a foreign teacher to help them get up to speed. That's why the college has hired the 23-year-old Canadian at 4000 RMB a month, two to three times the average salary for Chinese teachers.

15   The payoff is more than just monetary for Lee. Born in China but raised in Canada, she accepted the job so she could live in Hong Kong, within a short train ride from her sick grandmother. But now, her feelings have deepened. "When the schools were asking me why I wanted to teach in China, I BS'd and said it's because I wanted to learn about my 'other' culture," she says. "But the more I said it, the more I believed it. Now, I feel that I need to be here and learn what it means to be a Chinese person."

16   Yet the way of life Lee is trying to understand is challenged by her methodology in the classroom. By the end of term, her students will be well practised in communication modes that are entirely un-Chinese. Lee worries about this—and the general English fever sweeping the country that even includes television programs that aim to teach English.

17   "I know that if everyone spoke English in the world there would still be cultural differences, but the differences between cultures will become less and less," she says. "Why is China pushing English so hard? [My students] get the sense that their own language is not good enough. To prosper, they need English. What was wrong with the way it was before? Why do you have to be Western to be competitive in business?"

18   If it is tough for teachers to come to terms with these questions, it is even more complex for students. While some are in what Martin calls a "process of self-assimilation," others are much more ambivalent about the course they are on. These

students may be struggling with the political implications of learning English in places where the language is associated with American or British hegemony. Or they may simply recognize that as English proliferates, the survival of their own customs and dialects is under threat.

19   Take 27-year-old Sanghun Cho of South Korea. He is a graduate student in Toronto and has a Canadian girlfriend. But when he thinks of English, he also thinks of the US. "It's a kind of dilemma for Koreans," he says. "I don't like America in Korea because they want to control the Korean government; but to survive in this kind of competitive environment I have to speak English and I have to know what English culture is."

20   Another South Korean student puts it even more bluntly. Part of a multinational research project Martin has been conducting over the past five years to examine why students study English as a foreign language, the student was asked to draw a picture of his future with English and describe the picture. He sketched Uncle Sam extending a fishing line from the US across the Pacific Ocean, a hook dangling above the student's open mouth. His description: "English is the bait that Americans are using to catch Koreans in their net."

21   Marta Andersson is a part of the last generation of Poles forced to learn Russian in school. When she was able to study English after the fall of communism, she was thrilled. On the one hand, it paid off: she got a good job in Poland, is now studying abroad and speaks English at home with her husband. On another level, though, Andersson is aware that using English is eroding part of what her people fought for. "I have just started to lose the sense of my native language and just wait when it will become moribund," she says, "Yet I cannot imagine my future without the presence of English."

22   Swede Hélène Elg is also concerned about the fate of her language as English words invade it the way they do in "Chinglish" and "Franglais." "I think it's important to separate the languages in order to 'protect' our own," she says. "I realize that languages evolve, allowing new words to come into use, but we should be aware of that development and be cautious about it. The reason I feel this is because languages are so much more than just words. Words have cultural connotations. As with languages, cultures evolve, but that development should not be about adopting another culture."

23   Can students fight back? It's arguable that withdrawing from English would exact too high a cost for those who want to be a part of a global economy. Instead, what's changing is how people from around the world use English. Rather than simply conforming to an English steeped in Western values, many students are co-opting the language for themselves.

24   On an internet discussion board for EFL teachers, one teacher writes: "I feel the need of reminding our students and young colleagues that the purpose of learning English is not for us to 'speak and act' like an English person . . . but to 'speak English' as an educated Indonesian." Similarly, one Cuban who participated in Martin's project drew a picture of a rocket being launched into the sky with the description: "English is the rocket which will allow Cuba to tell its own stories to the world."

25   A new "global" English is emerging that is a bridge language between cultures, not simply a language that supplants other cultures. As Salman Rushdie is quoted as saying in the best-selling history *The Story of English*, "English, no longer an English language, now grows from many roots; and those whom it once colonized are carving out large territories within the language for themselves. The Empire is striking back."

26   Along with students, many teachers are joining the fight to create a more egalitarian English. They do not want to be cultural colonialists. As David Hill, a teacher in Istanbul, writes in *The Guardian Weekly*: "English is global for highly dubious reasons: colonial, military and economic hegemony, first of the British, now of the US. . . . If we are not to be imperialists then we must help our students to express themselves, not our agenda."

27   To do that, new programs are emerging, like the Certificate in the Discipline of Teaching English as an International Language, which Martin coordinates at Glendon College. It pays close attention to issues of cultural sensitivity and autonomy when training teachers. As Martin says, "We're trying to come to grips with the effect of globalization on language teaching. Do we want a globalization that is going to be assimilationist to Western models of communication only? Or do we want to help people gain a voice in English?"

28   Michelle Szabo is one teacher who has tried to give her students a voice. After her stint in Japan, she took a job at Chonbuk National University in South Korea from 2003 to 2004. On one November morning, she recalls encouraging discussion about the power of English. Her hope was to give pause to students who'd never considered the impact of studying English on their lives—as well as a place for those who had thought about it—a rare place to vent.

29   And there was plenty of venting as students heatedly debated face-to-face from desks arranged in a conversation-friendly horseshoe configuration. "One side was feeling very pressured and resentful," says Szabo, "and one side was saying, 'No, [English is] opening doors for us.'" Szabo tried to "equalize" the class by sitting among the students. She also said little. She wanted a forum that conveyed the message, "I'm not here to change you, to acculturize you, to force my beliefs on you," she says.

30   But even Szabo's new self-consciousness about what it is she is selling to her students along with English grammar has limits. English has irrevocably changed and acculturated the world already. Even if locals don't want to participate in the global capitalist machine, they need English to truly challenge it. As one of Szabo's students couldn't help but point out during the debate, "Isn't it ironic we're discussing the effect of English—in English?"

DISCUSSION QUESTIONS

1. Explain the significance of the title.
2. What do you think is the thesis of the essay? If it is explicit, where is it located? Why is it located where it is?
3. How does the writer build a bridge with her audience by showing that she understands the ambiguities and complexities of her issue? How does she avoid blaming English teachers and thus alienating potential readers (paragraphs 8, 10, and 11)?
4. Cite examples where the author uses rational appeals such as statistics or expert opinion, and where she uses emotional and ethical appeals in her argument.
5. This essay incorporates writing strategies such as illustration and cause and effect analysis. What is the point of illustrations such as those used in paragraphs 1, 2, 8, 9, 11 to 16, and 18 to 21? What is the point of the cause and effect analysis used in paragraphs 4, 6, 8, 13 to 16, and 19?

6. In some ways, this essay is structured as a problem and solution argument. What is the problem, and why does the author spend so much time establishing that there is a problem? What possible solutions are suggested for students of English and for teachers of English?

7. How effective is the concluding paragraph? What irony does it point out?

TOWARD KEY INSIGHTS

This essay argues that Westerners who teach English overseas cannot help but teach Western values along with teaching the language. How does learning a new language necessitate learning different ways of seeing, or different values? How can learning a new way of seeing bring losses as well as gains?

This essay criticizes the subtle bias of teaching materials that promote Western values (paragraph 9). Have you noticed any kind of bias in textbooks or teaching materials to which you have been exposed? Explain.

Think of jobs that you have done, or different kinds of work that you have considered pursuing. What unintended social consequences, negative or positive, might follow from doing this kind of work?

SUGGESTIONS FOR WRITING

1. If you have taught or studied English as a second or additional language, respond to Julie Traves's argument that teaching English is a form of "linguistic imperialism."

2. Write an argument that some other kind of activity that is usually viewed as positive— for example, travelling to a developing country or adopting a baby from a foreign country—may have negative effects on people's values or sense of identity.

3. Following the structure of Traves's argument, establish that something usually perceived as benign is actually a problem; then recommend some possible solutions.

Natalie 'Ilaheva Tua'one Gallagher

Fostering Multiple Identities through Teaching Cyborg Writing

Natalie 'Ilaheva Tua'one Gallagher was born and raised in Salt Lake City, Utah, and stayed to receive an Honour's Bachelor of Science in Gender Studies at the University of Utah. She currently lives in Dorchester, Massachusetts, teaching and studying toward a Ph.D. in English at Northeastern University. Her father is an immigrant from Tonga, and her mother is Scottish-Irish, but as a Utah native, she has multiple racial identities she can claim. Her identity is also influenced by her Mormon upbringing, which in turn comes into conflict with another of her identities: lesbian. She also has 7 sisters and 2 brothers, 16 nieces and nephews, and 75 first cousins. Her English name is Natalie, but she goes by her Tongan name 'Ila. She prefers 'Ila, but will still answer to Natalie.

1   My online self can fly, hovering near the ground or perhaps very high. She loves log tossing and prefers Vishnu to Siddhartha. He also loves recipe blogs and distasteful comic strips. They enjoy reading *The Onion* and *Newsweek*. We have been swayed by Branch Davidian homepages, and joined the Human Rights Coalition. My online selves rarely meet each other in cyberspace. We have several windows open at once. I am a fundamentalist capitalist on one page, a radical environmentalist on another. On this site she is a man, a woman, a genderless mule, and here they are a Minotaur. My online selves are multiple, varying, contradictory, and ironic. My online selves are subject to various, dynamic, evolving narratives. She also breaks the rules, transgresses boundaries. He sees things of which he should feel ashamed. Multiple, divided, limitless elf selves saving selves of soulless singularity.

2   My class/space-teacher/student self is less fragmented, less multiple, gesturing toward a whole that is "I," an identity mapped out in checked boxes on an application. As a graduate student getting close to my doctorate in Rhetoric and Composition, I have joined the professional organization *College Composition and Communication* (*CCCC*), whose membership, Victor Villanueva says, is 92% white (651). Gazing around my graduate seminars, I see that most of my cohorts have no doubt checked the box called White (non-Hispanic) on their membership forms if they chose to check a box at all, while their sexual orientation remains legally protected and unchecked. However, like me, they also have multiple selves, and separate, distinct, unknowable identities. Our online selves meet in cloistered chatrooms. I do not know who they are, but I know that a few of us share an affinity for Wurlitzer theatre pipe organs.

3   In this postmodern world, identities based on common interests and associations can be multiple, escaping the narrow definitions that limit the possibilities of being, and contribute to the perpetuation of dominating ideologies: "We cannot maintain oppositional notions of identity/difference without falling into a situation in which 'identity' gains (or attempts to gain) hegemonic control over difference" (McComiskey 70). In other words, as soon as I label my race, my gender, my sexual orientation, I am put into a category by which I am defined and fixed. Even the apparent simplicity of a label such as "female" is "itself a highly complex category constructed in contested scientific discourses and other social practices" (Haraway 14). In the field of Composition and Rhetoric, which is overwhelmingly represented by people who are white, middle class, and heterosexual, I posit that focusing on race, class, and gender politics, which limit the meanings and potentialities of identity, will not help to "fix" the problem of underrepresented identities. I read a lot about the under-representation of people of color in higher education, or from lower socio-economic backgrounds, but I rarely read about the lack of dirt-bikers. Binary oppositions that create identities out of differences constrict the individual and the writer. I do not want me or my students to be defined and limited in a category that is defined by what they are not: not male, not white, not heterosexual, and so on.

4   I argue that students, and the field of composition, would be better served by a move toward a postmodern pedagogy of multiplicity, a politics of "affinity not identity," and a postmodern approach to teaching writing that employs various genres, media, and voices, and aims more for multiplicity than for unity (Haraway 14). This kind of multimodal writing, what I will call Cyborg writing, helps students to discover the freedom of no fixed address in multiple identities.

5   I argue for the value of a multimodal postmodern approach to teaching writing that disrupts the ideologies of academia, disrupts writing, and disrupts the identity of

the "self." It is in this disruption wherein the cyborg lies. What we write about, and how we write about it, informs the narratives we tell ourselves about our various identities; as Jean-Francois Lyotard wrote: "If you are the narrator, the narratee or the narrated of a story in which you are implicated, you become dependent upon that story" (qtd. in Sim 87). As teachers and scholars of rhetoric and composition, we can help contribute to the formation of a queer, diverse, ambiguous, and multiple writing technique, a rhetoric that allows for the formation of a diverse identity, that "move[s] away from the discourse of mastery and assertion toward a more dialogic, dynamic, open-ended, receptive, nonassertive stance" (Olson 14).

6   In order to get to the problem of the whole of identity, we must begin with the problem of the whole. I instruct my students to at least have a point to their papers, even with the absence of a thesis statement. The words you are currently reading began from a prompt that said, "Yes, *say something* . . .". I ask how to teach forms of writing that moves away from the "rhetoric of assertion" that says all writing must reach a conclusion, creating the movement toward "wholeness" and "unity" which modern pedagogies support (Olson 9). Instead of focusing on the "whole" of truth-making language, rhetoric and composition should give students pedagogical access to writing that is dynamic, questionable, divided, and contradictory, allowing for the possibility of separate selves: a kind of open-ended Create Your Own Adventure Essay.

7   The notion of the whole, the One, and the Other dates back to Plato and *The Symposium*, when Aristophanes relates the story of the origin of love: the first humans had two faces, four arms and legs, split in two by gods who envied the unity, which is why subjects feel complete when they find their "Other half" (Plato 22). This concept of original unity is further explored in Marxist and psychoanalytic theory, where it has been argued, "their concepts of labor and of individuation and gender formation, depend upon the plot of original unity out of which difference must be produced" (Haraway 9). In Marxist ideology, the subject (laborer) is separated from her "whole" being because she is alienated from the fruits of her labor (Marx 401). The separation from her self relies on the assumption that "her/self" was once a whole. The same concept of the once-whole can be found in Freudian psychoanalysis wherein the subject separates from his phallic mother and becomes an incomplete, always desiring subject, whose superego keeps him longing for that early fantastical unity with the mother.

8   Jacques Lacan understands that the idea of the perfect unity and wholeness is a myth: "[a]t the same time 'identity' and 'wholeness' remain precisely at the level of fantasy. Subjects in language persist in their belief that somewhere there is a point of certainty, of knowledge and of truth" (qtd. in Rose 33). It is this fantasy of wholeness whose limiting effects on identity I wish to abolish. When Haraway proposes the image of the cyborg as a weapon that will help to abolish the myth of unifying identity, she describes it as an organism whose identity is fluid: human and machine, machine and animal, human and animal—a robotic furry squirrel-self:

9   A cyborg exists when two kinds of boundaries are simultaneously problematic: 1) that between animals (or other organisms) and humans, and 2) that between self-controlled, self-governing machines (automatons) and organisms, especially humans (models of autonomy). The cyborg is the figure of the interface of automaton and autonomy (Haraway qtd. in Gonzalez 264). As writers and teachers of writing, we

must move away from the idea of a unifying identity, toward acceptance of the poly-amorous and poly-identified. Writing instructors must teach multimodal composition as a means to break through simplistic binary constructions of identity such as male OR female; white OR non-white; heterosexual OR queer.

10   McComiskey writes: "We should begin, in other words, to abandon our alliance with an illusion of the universal, and we must merge the concerns of our own 'head-ing' with the concerns of the 'headings' of others" (74). Merging our "headings" can be found in online identification, such as the Hispanic, septuagenarian, queer, gen-dered subject whose username subject writes fan-fiction for *Gossip Girl*, diversifying and deconstructing the teenage upper-class endings. As we find affinity with different asso-ciations and communities, we can inhabit simultaneously, various, seemingly contra-dictory identities.

11   Jung claims that the writing teacher should accept "that knowledge is always par-tial, even contradictory," and should "build it into her writing through a self-reflexive consideration of her own knowledge-making" (30). She is calling for a writing that foregrounds its own access to power,[1] a writing that acknowledges its own limitations and capacities, a writing that causes "dis-identification" and "disrupts harmonious reading experiences by using textual strategies that delay immediate convergence of meaning," delaying the replacement of "being" with "meaning" (30). A postmodern, postprocess approach to writing, as represented in this paper by online identification, looks like the "absence of totality" championed by Lyotard: "the idea that I think we need today in order to make decisions in political matters cannot be the idea of the totality, or the unity, of the body. It can only be the idea of a multiplicity or diversity" (Sims 89). Multimodal, mulitgenred, multivoiced, multidentified writing creates spaces between meaning wherein the writer is forced to pause and "struggle to make meaning across a field of generic differences" (Jung 33).

12   Cyborg writing, the kind of approach to writing I am advocating, rejects the notion of the original whole, the idea that we can ever get back to that mythical garden. Multimodal writing, including online identification, is one such step toward cyborg writing. Within online identification, the subject releases the constraints of gender, race, and class that oppress and becomes simply a Username. A Username can roam freely, trying on different identities without fear of repercussions.

13   Those identities that have been "excluded from the knowledge-making" such as trapezists, avatars, and plumbers, hold their own "multiple, contesting narratives" that remain outside the dominant academic culture. They may indeed often speak their own language such as the leet speak preferred by gamers,[2] using a highly dynamic, ever-evolving cipher and grammar, "creating their own apparatus for the production of knowledge" (Haraway qtd in Olson 11); cyborgs that are "oppositional, utopian, and completely without innocence. No longer structured by the polarity of public and private. . ." (Haraway 9). Cyborg writing that moves away from unified, linear kinds of thinking that is traditionally valued in higher education and opens up

---

[1]At an attempt to foreground one of my accesses to power, I am stating that I used several different voices in this exploration: a multivoiced essay/opera, a weaving together of knowledges in the format, using one knowledge against another to create a multicolored coat of postknowledge. These voices have their own access to power that must be acknowledged—I draw on the voices of people who are Masters in their Field. Using another's words has its own implications, of course.

[2]Thank you Katherine Lang for introducing me to this concept. http://en.wikipedia.org/wiki/Leet_speak

room for multiplicity, supports imagination, and encourages creativity and invention. Sarah Arroyo asks that we promote a kind of cyborg writing that encourages multiple tangential thoughts, an ambiguous tree of meaning (699). Arroyo also envisions the writing classroom "as a scene for inventions" . . . "open[ing] up a gigantic space for the *potentiality* for writing" (695).

14   Cyborg writing is a diverse and daring writing, without conclusions and without a knowable truth, open to diverse discourse that leads to the recognition of sundry selves. Within multiple meanings of words lies the multiple meaning of selves; selves fusing together and dividing apart, into a dazzling amalgam of affinities. McComiskey writes: "A few cultural theorists . . . do not view 'identity' and 'difference' as oppositional terms; instead, they construct 'identity and difference' as a complementary pair, as an alliance rather than an opposition" (70). Those of us who teach and practice writing may envision the creation of a self or selves through an alliance in identity and difference that gestures toward the cyborg of the post-gender world, a self that can(not) be mapped out in the illimitable cyber/ world-cyborg/space.

15   There are inconsistencies in this line of argument, dangers in refuting identity politics, a thin line between racism and erase-ism. But this is the point, to live and write and teach within the contradiction of multiple identities: believe in God on Monday Night's football, and let your belief slide at your brother's funeral. Be a dainty princess who enjoys mudding, or a m(other) who is the World's Greatest Father. Flaunt your racial pride and abhor your racial downfalls, become an/other race, an/ other gender or gender/queer. Forget race politics, but never forget race politics. Always already remember (and forget) that the truth lied, the one is two, and within the whole is always already a hole.

Works Cited

Arroyo, Sarah J. "Playing to the Tune of Electracy: From Post-Process to a Pedagogy Otherwise." *JAC*. 25.4 (2005): 683–715. Print.

Gonzalez, Jennifer. "Envisioning Cyborg Bodies: Notes from Current Research." *Wolmark*. 264–79. Print.

Haraway, Donna. "Science, Technology, and Socialist Feminism in the 1980s." *The Haraway Reader*. New York: Routledge, 2004. 7–45. Print.

Jung, Julie. *Revisionary Rhetoric, Feminist Pedagogy, and Multigenre Texts*. Carbondale, IL: Southern Illinois UP, 2005. Print.

Marx, Karl. "Alienation of Labor from Economic and Philosophic Manuscripts of 1844." *The Critical Tradition: Classic Texts and Contemporary Trends*. 3rd ed. Ed. David H. Richter. New York: Bedford Books, 1997. 400–06. Print.

McComiskey, Bruce. "Composing Postmodern Subjectivities in the Aporia between Identity and Difference." *Teaching Composition as a Social Process*. Logan, UT: U of Utah P, 2000. 69–75. Print.

Olson, Gary A. "Toward a Post-Process Composition: Abandoning the Rhetoric of Assertion." *Post-Process Theory: Beyond the Writing-Process Paradigm*. Ed. Thomas Kent. Carbondale, IL: Southern Illinois UP, 1999. 7–15. Print.

Plato. *The Symposium.* London: Penguin Classics, 1999. Print.

Rose, Jacqueline. "Introduction-II." *Feminine Sexuality: Jacques Lacan and the Ecole Freudienne.* Eds. Juliet Mitchell and Jacqueline Rose. New York: W. W. Norton and Pantheon Books, 1985. 27–33. Print.

Sim, Stuart. *Beyond Aesthetics: Confrontations with Poststructuralism and Postmodernism.* Toronto: U of Toronto P, 1992. Print.

Villanueva, Victor. "On the Rhetoric and Precedents of Racism." *College Composition* and Communication. 50.4 (1999): 645–61. Print.

DISCUSSION QUESTIONS

1. In the first paragraph, why do you think the writer changes the number, point of view, and gender of the pronoun references?

2. How does the writer locate her professional and student identity in the second paragraph? Why is this identity "less multiple" than her online identities? Why do you think she includes the unusual detail that "a few of us share an affinity for Wurlitzer theatre pipe organs"?

3. In your own words, explain what the writer means by preferring "identities based on common interests and associations" to identities based on "race, class, and gender" (paragraph 3)? What do you understand by the term "binary opposition"?

4. The writer argues that "Writing instructors must teach multimodal composition as a means to break through simplistic binary constructions of identity such as male OR female; white OR non-white; heterosexual OR queer" (paragraph 9). Explain, in your own words, what multimodal composition might look like and how it is similar or different from the writing that is typically expected in a university class. Are you persuaded by the argument that teaching this form of writing can help people "break through" limiting notions of identity? Explain.

5. What examples of contradicting identities does the writer give in the final paragraph? Do you find these contradictions plausible or not? How does the writer play with words in the concluding paragraph or elsewhere?

TOWARD KEY INSIGHTS

To what extent is it possible, in your view, to move beyond viewing people in terms of "binary oppositions" such as male and female?

The writer claims that "As we find affinity with different associations and communities, we can inhabit simultaneously, various, seemingly contradictory identities." Consider the organizations or associations with which you are formally or informally involved. What different identities do you have in these different groups or associations? Are there places where the identity you present in one community is quite different from the identity you present in another group? Explain.

What is your understanding of "cyborg writing"? Is this essay an example of "cyborg writing" or can you think of other forms of writing that are?

The writer wonders how to teach forms of writing that move away from the "rhetoric of assertion" that says all writing must reach a conclusion, creating the movement toward "wholeness" and "unity." How does the writer demonstrate contradiction in her argument for a new way to teach writing, as well as a defense of her own contradictions? Track places where the writer brings in scholarly or other academic sources. How does she use these sources—as a point of departure to make her own argument; as reinforcement or an extension of her own ideas; as a position that she can take issue with; as a kind of proof for her own knowledge of the subject area—or in some other way? Explain.

SUGGESTIONS FOR WRITING

1. Write your own argument about how the idea of a unified identity is a myth, using examples based on personal experience or observation that demonstrate how we all have a tendency to "inhabit simultaneously, various, seemingly contradictory identities."

2. Respond to this writer by making a case for more traditionally structured academic writing that does strive for "wholeness," "unity," and a conclusion.

3. After looking at Haraway's "Cyborg Manifesto," cited in this paper look for a copy of Donna Haraway's essay "A Cyborg Manifesto"—try searching online or at the library. After reading the essay, write your own argument for a cyborg approach to another realm besides writing.

Ross Gordon

Community: Use It or Lose It?

After a career in business management, Ross Gordon, who is based in Edmonton, returned to university to finish his B.A. in Anthropology, and stayed on to complete his Ph.D. in Social and Cultural Anthropology. He has since published his scholarly work in journals such as Anthropologica, *from which this article is adapted. He has studied and published work on the environmental knowledge of people in Kadavu Province, Fiji, and is currently working on an extended study researching interactions between humans and their environment in the Aru Islands of Indonesia.*

1   What makes a Canadian community great? A special 2011 Canada Day feature that ran in the *Globe and Mail* newspaper (Agrell, 2011) profiled nine communities selected from reader submissions. Reviews of small communities and urban neighbourhoods often focused upon significant levels of neighbourhood social interaction. In urban environments, these interactions take place in areas with high walkability, multiculturalism, and diversity of shops and restaurants. Reader submissions often placed high value on practices of civic engagement, which address local crime and poverty issues. For smaller communities, positive social interaction with neighbours, family and friends is valued, along with the chance to enjoy the outdoors.

2   In recent years, both the academic media and popular works such as Robert Putnam's (2000) *Bowling Alone* have profiled the demise of traditional neighbourhood-based communities, but in actuality many North American physical neighbourhoods are nourishing communities which shape people's perceptions of themselves and their social worlds. While our communities do not always meet our needs for affiliation and

recognition, the majority of Canadians take for granted the advantages, including relative ease of access and movement, of belonging to a geographically defined community.

3   What happens to those on the fringes of society who cannot make these easy assumptions? Although most Canadians cannot imagine becoming homeless, 7 per cent of Canadians report being homeless at some point in their life, and 22 per cent have drawn support from food banks or charities. Despite the current fashion of anti-homelessness initiatives among North American government bodies, this issue seems unlikely to go away any time soon. In policy terms, homeless people are classed as either the "sheltered homeless" for those holding some employment or who are in temporary housing without a permanent lodging option, or the "absolute homeless" who have no housing and are often sleeping rough outside or in public buildings. In this paper, I will be demonstrating some very real boundaries to these 'taken for granted aspects' of our communities by examining the re-entry attempts of some people who spend substantial time in physical communities, but struggle for recognition as identifiable members of a group. Looking at individual and collective reactions to the salience of people often termed as "the homeless," as well as the reactions of some homeless people to broad community exclusion, sheds light on our broad collective notions of community in North American urban societies. This sense of exclusion suggests not only the necessity of considering the forms of association that people are in, but also the importance of broader notions of community that drive social policy makers.

4   What are some views that people in the dominant culture of Canadian society have toward this intractable problem of homelessness—and about the people who find themselves, for one reason or another, dislodged, displaced, disenfranchised?

5   A 2011 Salvation Army sponsored poll by Angus Reid queried prevailing attitudes of 1000 Canadians towards homelessness. Survey results show that while he majority of Canadians do see housing as a fundamental right that is required for a sense of dignity that everyone deserves, 39 per cent believe most homeless people want to live on the streets, 29 per cent believe that a good work ethic is sufficient to escape homelessness, 19 per cent believe that homeless people are always to blame for their situation, 35 per cent believe that homeless people can always find work if they want to, and 17 per cent attribute homelessness to chronic laziness.

6   The very presence of homeless people may make securely housed people anxious for the security of their person and possessions, and perhaps also make them feel guilty at these visible signs of economic disparity. The same survey reports that two thirds of Canadians have felt frightened of homeless people. The salience of absolute homeless people "sleeping and living rough" outside of community in economically competitive urban environments is a modern archetype for social failure, which warns children of the perils of ignoring parental instructions and life expectations.

7   Viewed in this harsh economic light, homeless people appear as an economic burden on the rest of society, trapped in a state of social evolutionary failure through their inabilities to achieve the financial independence necessary to maintain an economic joint commitment to contribute to and benefit from society in appropriate ratios. For the Alberta government, the key justifications given for addressing this problem as a "community issue" are both the moral and ethical obligations to ensure secure housing for all Albertans, and concern over the economic costs of providing emergency services to people who are homeless or at risk of homelessness. Thus, a "housing first model" is justifiable as a business case to control budgets for shelters,

healthcare and police services budgets, since estimates put provision of these services to homeless people at three times the cost of providing these services to the average housed Albertan (Alberta Plan, Alberta Plan News Release, 2011).

8   This economic justification for ending homelessness involves a different kind of reasoning than examining the less immediately tangible dimensions of this issue. Looking at homelessness in affective and ethical ways means more than responding to some people's fears of homeless people; it also entails examining homelessness in light of people's needs for what Vered Amit calls affect-belonging—a felt sense of being a member of an interdependent group (2010, p. 357). If we consider affect-belonging as a human right, then the notion of housing also becomes a right. Homeless people have little sense of affect-belonging in common with people in securely housed and identified communities. Thus, this variation in the affect-belonging of homeless people demonstrates the existence of this broader securely housed community with defined membership requirements and borders.

A DOWNWARD SPIRAL

9   On a practical as well as an affective level, people who are not recognized as members of a community where they have a sense of identity that is recognized by others may be caught in a downward spiral. Consider what an Albertan tradesman named John experienced when he lost his operator's license, his primary form of identification. After being caught driving under the influence of alcohol (DUI) and charged by the police, John, who had previous DUI convictions, has his operator's license confiscated, and is issued a twenty-one day paper temporary license to get his affairs in order. John then receives a mandatory license suspension of three months until his trial. John pleads guilty to expedite matters, receiving a year in prison and a further year's suspension of driving privileges. John serves his time and is released from prison. John attends Alcoholics Anonymous meetings as part of his sentencing. John had been paying child support to his ex-wife, but he lost his job when he went to prison and is now $15,000.00 behind in maintenance payments. John now has no photo identification and no driver's license. John visits a registry bureau to obtain an Alberta Identification Card (AIC), but he is denied services due to the child maintenance deficit. John would also be unable to obtain an AIC, as he has no photo identification or secondary support documents to prove who he is. During his time in prison his roommates have moved out of their apartment and his other papers are gone. John wants to get a job and pay up his maintenance to his ex-wife. He knows his Social Insurance Number, but employers want to see identification before they will hire him, and they require a bank account to make payroll deposits. John has a bank account, but no bankcard and his bank requires photo identification to give him account access. John has goods in a pawnshop, but cannot access them without photo identification. John leaves prison with good intentions, but without money or identification, he has limited options to re-enter any law-abiding community.

10   John's drunk driving is a bad practice, of course. Yet after serving his prison sentence, John was driving a car without a license or insurance to and from his under-the-table tradesman workplace. John exists within a community, but in an indeterminate place, much like a ghost in a haunted house. The house or community is real because John is trapped in the walls and denied entry or exit, but how real does John feel? John has limited access to participating in law-abiding communities,

regardless of what he chooses to imagine, perceive or interpret. Thus, the idea of community for John is very tangible. After he made some big mistakes, he lost his community membership card.

DO HOMELESS PEOPLE BELONG TO A COMMUNITY?

11   Designating homeless people as a definable social group is controversial. For some people, the term "homeless community," may imply that homelessness is a permanent and satisfactory situation, which is not the case for most homeless people.

12   In practice, many users of the term "homeless community," such as supporters of www.homelessnation.org, attempt to validate and connect the lives of homeless people, while creating broader awareness of associated social issues and soften more negative responses towards the homeless (2009). Leading researchers into homelessness issues refer to "community-based" preventative programs to stabilize people who are on the threshold of becoming homeless (Culhane, Metraux, & Byrne, 2011). These authors regard community as a jurisdiction where institutions share common cause in the necessity of supporting people who are at risk of homelessness or who have experienced a crisis precipitating the loss of their home. This suggests that being housed and belonging to a geographically defined community is so fundamental that most of us just take it for granted.

13   In 2008, in Edmonton I conducted a study of homeless people that demonstrates very clearly that physically bounded communities are very real both in practice and in people's understanding of their world, especially for those struggling on society's margins. Without a stable address, people who find themselves on the outside of society need a point of entry into community represented in both symbolic and real ways by photo identification. Without photo identification, people's range of choices and movements are severely restricted, as my study shows.

A RESEARCH STUDY INTO PHOTO IDENTIFICATION LOSS EXPERIENCES: METHODS AND RESULTS

14   In 2008, I interviewed 102 people who visited identity document (ID) clinics to receive a basic identification card from non-government run social support agencies in Edmonton (Gordon n.d.). I informally interviewed people in quiet corners of public spaces of the centres after they obtained their new ID card. Interviewees were willing to discuss the significant life challenge associated with identity loss issues. Most people launched into a relevant story as soon as they understood the topic of the interview.

15   As shown in Chart 1, most of the interviewees were in their thirties and forties. Younger people were well represented in the centres, but less likely to volunteer for interviews. 40 percent of the people interviewed were of First Nations heritage, a disproportionate percentage as they comprise only 5 percent share of Edmonton's population (Statistics Canada website, 2006). Twice as many men as women were interviewed for this study.

16   Interviews followed a loose structure around a few core questions, but answers often took a narrative or anecdotal form. Many people would be holding their new photo identity card in their hand during the interview and would frequently look at their picture. Getting this new photo ID appears to be a meaningful experience for many people, representing their aspirations for community membership.

Time Since Identity Loss

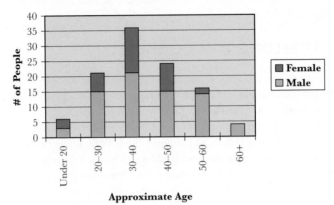

CHART I Interview Population: Age and Gender

17   Thirty percent of 72 people had lost their ID between one and five years ago. They were attending the ID clinics because government options were either inaccessible or unaffordable, or were perceived as such. Nine people spontaneously told me "you need ID to get ID," or similar words. This concept is part of oral street culture, reflecting people's frustration with and adaptation to alienation. Ten people either told me that "you can't do anything without ID," that they felt "stuck" or said that they felt "like you are nothing."

Reasons for Identity Loss

18   Of the 46 people who gave reasons for ID loss, many had lost it repeatedly, including one who had lost a health care card twenty times. Street people are vulnerable to theft and often have no secure means to store their photo identification. Primary loss factors are theft and carelessness. Common forms of theft include being: "jumped" and robbed, pick-pocketed, or having knapsacks and coats stolen in public places or shelters. Substance abuse was often associated with ID loss through carelessness.

19   Given that they may have been using drugs or alcohol, have criminal records or outstanding fines, interviewees seldom if ever made police report for events involving identification loss. Several people lost their photo identification during an interaction with police and others had it confiscated by child maintenance enforcement. Thirty-five of the interviewees stated in conversation that they could not access Alberta Registry services due to either unpaid maintenance or other provincial fines. Recent Alberta government policy changes for issuing photo identification to people with outstanding provincial fines may have reduced this problem somewhat.

Identity Loss: The Limiting Factors, Barriers and Problems

20   **Banking Services** access is the most significant problem for the interviewees without identification. Payday loan services charge high fees, but provide easy financial services access through client recognition by a picture in an electronic database.

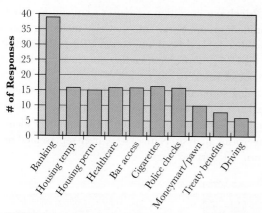

CHART 2 Identity Loss Limiting Factors

Note: The data in Chart 2 reflects the total number of factors mentioned, not factors per person.

In contrast, banks require a government issued photo-identification or a sponsor to open an account or to replace a lost bankcard. Interviewees might not be able to access money in their account or incoming electronic deposits. Some people who overdraw their accounts have their accounts frequently closed, given their high risk, low profit customer profiles coupled with post 9-11 anti-terrorism security regulations.

21 **Temporary Housing** includes the ability to rent hotel or motel rooms and access to some shelters. Renting a hotel room requires 40 to 100 dollars plus an equivalent damage deposit in cash. These interviewees do not have credit cards. Renting a room, when it is thirty-five degrees below zero and a person cannot access or handle the night in a shelter, is a major expense. Most hotels require photo identification upon check-in. Some interviewees are high-risk guests, who may sublet the room to a number of people, have parties, engage in drug use, damage the room or steal hotel room items. Most people just want a warm and safe bed, but without credit card recourse, they are likely to be turned away from hotel operators. Short-term room rental landlords face similar risks in renting to unknown people with limited financial options. Some shelters require photo identification.

22 **Permanent Housing** With questions about longer-term commitment and prospects of eviction, landlords are even more concerned with identification issues and financial stability. Interviewees described a variety of identification requirements by landlords. Many landlords run credit bureau checks on prospective tenants, although most people have a poor understanding of the workings of the credit bureau system. Most people reported that two pieces of government identification, including photo ID, are essential to obtain permanent housing.

23 **Healthcare Access** was a key issue, although Alberta Health Care (AHC) cards may have the lowest acquisition barriers. Interviewees from other provinces without photo ID and a permanent Alberta address have even more significant access issues. 62 percent of people indicating healthcare access problems were native: a disproportionate ratio that would benefit from further research. All responses from natives on this item came from people estimated as over thirty years old.

24   **Bar Access and Cigarette Purchase** limitation responses were concentrated among the thirty-year-old age estimate group. Some interviewees, including non-drinkers, were unable to access bars that are key social interaction settings for friends and family. Casual observation of the homeless people spending time in support centres suggests there is a high percentage of smokers.

25   **Police Checks** consisted of being stopped and questioned while people were walking, or after being in a vehicle that is pulled over for any reason. People who cannot produce acceptable photo ID may be taken into custody and held until their identity can be verified, perhaps by fingerprint analysis. Natives were over-represented in this category by 50 per cent as shown in Chart 3.

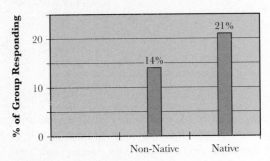

CHART 3 Police Check Problems

26   One native male had been detained in error in lieu of three different people who look like him and are often sought by police. Some interviewees with criminal records appreciate less frequent detainments due to the use of computers in cruisers to access people's pictures, tattoos and scars. This system uses the term "deadbeat dad" to identify men whose driver's license has been suspended for child maintenance debts. Ironically, people without criminal records had a harder time identifying themselves to the police. One person without photo ID who was pulled over in a vehicle late at night and after being held until 4:30 AM was late for work and lost his job. It is interesting to note that these respondents seldom admitted to doing anything wrong prior to their police interaction, although I became aware that at least three of these interviewees were active drug dealers. A key point is that the police do have a well-developed system for tracking people who lack formal photo identification.

27   People mentioned treaty benefits that require an Indian Status Card in order to access support programs, as well as funded education opportunities, band payments, and tax exempt purchasing. Treaty card replacement was a key issue for these primarily female respondents, who saw it as their core identification piece, but were unable to get back to their reserve to get a replacement. The treaty card system has since been modified.

28   **Driving Issues** arose six times. The lack of a driver's license limits employment options in particular for trades-people to get to jobsites with their tools. Driver's license reacquisition is complicated by unpaid traffic violations, criminal conviction fines, or unpaid alimony. Some people mentioned that they drive regularly without a license and by inference without insurance. One person received a $2800 fine for this offense to be added to other unpaid fines.

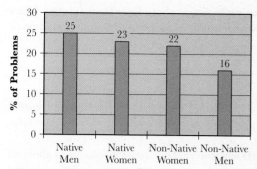

CHART 4 Average Number of Factors Per Interviewee and Ethnicity shows that native men and women reported more problems associated with ID loss than did Non-native men, which suggest a need for further research.

Table I Quotes from interviews about getting along without photo ID. Texts in italics are observations or questions asked by the interviewer.

"You can't do jack-shit without ID"

"You need ID to get ID"

"It's tough to wake up without ID" *How does it make you feel?* "shitty!"

"quite inconvenient to your life" (*after being picked up without ID and detained by police for 14 hours*)

"With picture ID, you are a person now" *In reference to his new photo ID clinic card.*

"What if you get hurt? With picture ID, the police and hospital can figure out who you are."

How does it make you feel not having ID? "Like you are nothing."

"without no ID or Birth Certificate you can't get ID or a Birth Certificate"

"I think about having no ID every day, I feel bad about it, it's stressful"

"I am at a total stop" "I'm stuck" "very frustrated, I can't get any more frustrated" "I can't go anywhere" (several years without photo ID), *Did you try the registry?* "No, you need picture ID to get picture ID"

Without ID "I didn't know who the hell I was"

"very excited to have ID" (photo clinic ID) "trying to get sober"

"If you don't have it, you can't get ID"

"Impossible to get ID without ID"

"It takes ID to get ID"

"How about using a chip implanted in people to replace ID cards?"

Without ID "You can't do anything." "You are nobody!" "You are lost!" "life is difficult" "Its a pain in the butt!"

"You can't do anything without ID."

Reactions to Living without Identification

29   As shown in Table 1, the prevalence of the use of the phrase, "you need ID to get ID" or similar words by a significant percentage of people interviewed suggests a

story that gets reinforced whenever people discuss photo identification issues. Many people interviewed face barriers to participating in society and community, some of their own making and some not.

NEGOTIATING BUREAUCRACY

30   Replacing one's identification when one has none requires negotiating complex bureaucratic structures. A nineteen-year-old University student who lost his wallet described his experiences as follows:

31   At my bank, I was without any ID whatsoever. They asked me questions about all my recent transactions, DOB, profession, who I'd worked for, who my father worked for, his DOB, if I knew any card numbers off hand, what my current balances were, and so on. I was convinced that they knew it was me, but it was a pretty lengthy interview process to verify, in order to get a new debit card. I (later) used my Passport to get my Driver's License again, and also to get a new university ID card. However, the people that I spoke with were all very wary to make sure that I had really lost my ID and wasn't just trying to make duplicates." [Personal email, March 16, 2008]

32   This well-spoken educated person had strong family ties to draw upon to establish his identity, along with a safely stored passport, and $113.00 in hand to pay for the replacements. Few people interviewed for this study had these resources. Some were chronic substance abusers or mentally ill and many lacked stable family ties for support. Interviewees reported aggressive venting of their frustrations about the poorly understood processes to the registry clerks. Complex requirements reinforce the hopeless mantra of "You need ID to get ID".

33   A secure identification card system necessitates strict card acquisition requirements. Herein lies the difficulty for those with limited resources. The government photo identification or AIC that could be available to many of the interviewees is not available to them for reasons of blocked access, lack of awareness, uncertainty or intimidation of the acquisition process, lack of support documents, oral street culture perceptions of difficulty, and perceived high expense. Lack of Internet access or use contributes to people's limited options and knowledge.

34   The approximate $100 cost of replacing identification was a significant problem for many people. For people dealing with the day-to-day challenges of eating and staying warm or paying rent, the idea of having $100.00 to spend on identification was an abstract one. Some people felt that if the government required citizens to carry photo identification in order to participate in society, then the government should pay for it. Few of the people interviewed had fulltime jobs; some received social assistance or treaty benefits.

OBSERVATIONS ON THE STUDY

35   When they received the photo identification at the clinic, its symbolic value was evident in many people's reactions. People would walk away from the ID station staring at it, not looking where they walked. People would keep it out during interviews, stealing glances at it as we talked. Comments such as, "with picture ID you are a person now," illustrate a high awareness of the symbolic nature of photo ID among people who lack it.

36   People who have no identification in our culture are stigmatized. Comments such as, "you can't do anything," "you are nobody," and "you are lost" demonstrate just how pernicious this stigma is. One man in his late fifties who had been without photo ID for many years explained to me that he restricted his movements to stay within a certain police district where the local officers knew him. This stigma highlights a contrast between our notion of a free society and abstract notions some people may hold of romance and freedoms of a lifestyle on the margins.

37   Most people interviewed were dissatisfied and frustrated with their life situation, which they recognized as isolated from the communities where they live. Of the 102 people who discussed their situation, ninety-five identified life limitations caused by their inability to obtain identification. These include access to money, shelter, healthcare and physical security. Possession of photo identification is a physical process, but the physical item is a symbol of membership in society and its loss invokes social isolation. If governments require citizens to have photo ID for them to operate in society, several interviewees emphasized that the government has an obligation to make photo identification accessible. Identification replacement programs must both improve access and incent people to take responsibility for their identification cards. Providing simple access to AICs for people leaving prison would seem an obvious place to begin. Instead of reintegration into society, people are estranged by their lack of photo identification. The same principles apply to those who have fallen, lacking shelter or stable social networks, to the margins of society.

38   The results of this study and a number of recommendations were presented in 2008 to the Alberta Cabinet Minister responsible for Service Alberta, the regulatory body for the province's photo identification cards and birth certificates. The Honourable Minister recognized the significance of the problem and has since supported a number of changes in provincial legislation and policy, which have simplified some of the barriers described here. People with unpaid fines and maintenance now have limited access to registry services and social agencies can sponsor identification applicants.

COMMUNITIES AND ANTI-HOMELESSNESS

39   People without ID recognize the practical and symbolic value of a photo identification card and desire this representation of community membership. My research with homeless people and identification loss issues shows that 70 per cent of 72 people had been without photo identification for more than six months. Comments such as "without photo ID, you are nothing . . . without it you are lost. . .you are lost, a nobody" illustrate the sense of hopelessness and isolation from community felt by people caught in these difficult situations. Identification replacement is difficult without a permanent address, family and adequate funds. People ask why institutions demand identification, but make it difficult to obtain.

40   For people without identification, obtaining new photo identification often draws strong positive reactions. Recipients walking blindly through a crowded room, staring at their new identification held with both hands in front of them, demonstrate just how much these people long to join a community. This is a clear identification of a community by people negotiating its borders. Researchers might question what communities people wish to belong to or wish they did not. What steps are people taking to get there or leave?

ANALYSIS THROUGH TRACKING MOVEMENTS NEAR BORDERS

41   Catherine Knowles' (2010) focus on using people's movement and journeys as analytical method expands upon Amit's (2010) ideas of community creation through a series of interactions by individuals. "People as the sum of their journeys" (Knowles 2010, p. 369), speaks to the notion of people's aspirations and the ongoing interaction between physical communities and less tangible forms of plural subject-hood. Hence, people without identification who are denied various interactions with other community members highlight the vital significance of community. The study of identification loss issues presented here is very much a study of movement or attempts at movement that are repeatedly blocked by community barriers.

42   Social scientists have long debated whether people exist as individuals who make choices, or as social beings who reflect their society. Louis Dumont characterized this as an opposition between holism, which validates the social whole, and individualism, which subordinates the social whole (1986, pp. 2, 279). The theologian, Paul Tillich (1952) describes individualism as self-affirmation without regard to worldly participation, as opposed to collectivism, a self-affirmation of being part of a larger whole without giving attention to the individual's character (pp. 113–114). Western thought stresses individualism as an ongoing production of a progressive social evolution; Tillich describes this so-called "rise of individualism" in the context of shifts in religious worship towards flexibility of faith or non-faith in tandem with economic liberalism, allowing increased financial and intellectual independence. However, this binary is symbolic as few of us in practice are extreme individualists or collectivists, but exercise our individualism within various communities and guidelines, whether explicitly named or not. Ironically, if one views increased individualism as a social evolutionary process, then we could see people living rough on the streets as near the top of the evolutionary ladder, often acting and making decisions quite at odds with broader conventions, while continuing to draw heavily upon services offered by society.

43   Concepts of community have analytical value for anthropology at both physical and less tangible levels. Researching the movements and interactions of marginalized groups such as the homeless, even though they are perceived by some as anti-communities, complements our understanding of Amit's tools of joint commitment, affect-belonging and other forms of association (2010). As we study how people's individual and collective aspirations to join or leave communities are reflected in their journeys and movements, we also need to keep in mind that we do not all move freely, and our identities, as well as our communities, may be bounded by the lack of official recognition that ID documentation confers.

ACKNOWLEDGEMENTS

44   I must acknowledge the assistance and generosity of time and thoughtfulness that I received from the staff and clients of the social support agencies, where the interviews summarized in this article took place. Many other people saw the value in this research and have drawn on it to make positive changes to social policy and helped disseminate these results into other channels for this purpose. In particular, in this regard, I would like to thank the Honorable Heather Klimchuk, Minister of Service Alberta, and

Jeannette Wright, Social Worker with the City of Edmonton. I appreciate the support of the Department of Anthropology at the University of Alberta and the encouragement and guidance of Associate Professor Kathleen Lowrey, who provided academic supervision of this research project.

References

Alberta Secretariat For Action On Homelessness. (2008). *A plan for Alberta: Ending homelessness in 10 years.* Retrieved from http://humanservices.alberta.ca/documents/PlanForAB_Secretariat_final.pdf

Amit, V. (2010). Community as "Good to Think With": The productiveness of strategic ambiguities. *Anthropologica, 52,* 357–363.

Culhane, D. P., Metraux, S., & Byrne, T. (2011). A prevention-centered approach to homelessness assistance: a paradigm shift? *Housing Policy Debate, 21*(2), 295–315. doi:10.1080/10511482.2010.536246.

Dumont, L. (1986). *Essays on individualism: Modern ideology in anthropological perspective.* Chicago, IL: University of Chicago Press.

Gordon, R. (2008). *You need ID to get ID* (Unpublished undergraduate thesis). University of Alberta, Edmonton, Canada.

Government of Alberta. (2011). *More homeless to be helped off the street and into housing* [Press release]. Retrieved from http://www.alberta.ca/release.cfm?xID=299967C502DE4-EA47-3AF6-17C5A14B45A6AAF3

Homeless nation. (2009). *About homeless nation.* Retrieved from http://www.homelessnation.org/en/node/16973.

Knowles, C. (2010). Response to "Community as 'Good to Think With'". *Anthropologica, 52,* 366–370.

Putnam, R. D. (2000). *Bowling alone: The collapse and revival of American community.* New York, NY: Simon & Schuster.

Salvation Army. (2011). *"Canada Speaks": Exposing persistent myths about the 150,000 Canadians living in the street.* Retrieved from http://salvationarmy.ca/DPresources/CanadaSpeaks_report_May2011.pdf

Tillich, P. (1952). *The courage to be.* New Haven, CT: Yale University Press.

DISCUSSION QUESTIONS

1. What is a negative stereotype, according to the author, that people associate with homeless people (paragraphs 5 and 6)? How do leading researchers suggest that people should support people "at risk of homelessness" (paragraph 7)?

2. How do the actual quotations from homeless people add to your understanding of their concerns?

3. How does the writer show his awareness of multiple audiences—Alberta political bodies, academics, especially urban anthropologists, and the broader Canadian and North American public?

4. The writer says that Aboriginal people are disproportionately represented among the homeless in Alberta. Why do you think this is?

5. Find at least two places where the writer attempts to defuse people's negative judgments and automatic dismissal of homeless people.

6. The writer invites us to look "at homelessness in affective and ethical ways" and examine "homelessness in light of people's needs for . . . affect-belonging" (paragraph 8). What does "affective" or "affect-belonging" appear to mean here, and why do you think the writer brings in this dimension?

7. How effective is the author's illustration of the downward spiral induced by homelessness (paragraphs 9 and 10)?

8. How does the writer prepare the reader for the discussion of his study of homeless people? What is the most important finding that emerges from his interviews?

9. After reviewing Chapter 13, pages 262–271, where several kinds of rational appeals are discussed, find examples of each of the following rational appeals: established truths, opinions of authorities, primary source information, and statistical findings.

10. How does the use of subtitles help you follow this rather complex argument? What else, either in the formatting or in the actual text, is most helpful for your understanding?

TOWARD KEY INSIGHTS

What is your understanding of the term *community* that the author discusses? What different communities do you belong to? Are there also communities that you feel excluded from but to which you wish to belong?

Have you ever had an experience of homelessness, or anything close to it? What was that like? Whether you have had this experience or not, how do you feel about homeless people you have seen on the streets?

SUGGESTION FOR WRITING A RESEARCH ARGUMENT

Research one of the ways in which the problem of homelessness has been addressed or could be addressed more effectively in your community—for example, an initiative such as Housing First, an alliance focused on ending, not just managing homelessness; a program for rapid rehousing or for increasing housing affordability; or a policy related to helping a vulnerable group such as homeless veterans, addicts, street youth, the mentally ill, or those who have been released from jail. Then write an argument that establishes one problem associated with homelessness and identifies at least one possible solution, following Ross Gordon's lead in anticipating prejudices and potential objections. Bring in ethical, emotional, and rational claims to persuade your audience. Your audience could be the general public in your community, or it could be more narrowly defined—for example, your essay could be directed to students to encourage them to volunteer, or it could be directed to people in a specific area of study such as social work or health care.

Learning the parts of English sentences will not in itself improve your writing, but it will equip you to gain more control over your writing as you learn to identify and repair errors at the sentence level. For example, before you can identify and correct unwarranted shifts from past to present time, you need to know about verbs and their tenses. Similarly, to recognize and correct pronoun case errors, you need to know what pronouns are and how they are used. This section first covers subjects and predicates; then complements, appositives, and the parts of speech; and finally, phrases and clauses.

SUBJECTS AND PREDICATES

The subject of a sentence tells who or what the sentence is about. A *simple subject* consists of a noun (that is, a naming word) or a noun substitute. A *complete subject* consists of a simple subject plus any words that limit or describe it.

The predicate tells something about the subject and completes the thought of the sentence. A *simple predicate* consists of one or more verbs (words that show action or existence). A *complete predicate* includes any associated words. In the following examples, the simple subjects are underlined <u>once</u> and the simple predicates <u>twice</u>. The subjects and predicates are separated with slash marks.

<u>Jason</u>/<u>laughed</u>.

<u>Harpreet</u>/<u>has moved</u>.

<u>Sarah</u>/<u>painted</u> the kitchen.

The <u>student</u> over there in the corner/<u>is majoring</u> in art.

Complex subjects can be very long; it is helpful to be able to pick the simple subject out of a complex subject.

The <u>storms</u> in March, which dropped a record rainfall in one week, <u>resulted</u> in fierce floods.

A sentence can have a compound subject (two or more separate subjects), a compound predicate (two or more separate predicates), or both.

The <u>elephants</u> and their <u>trainer</u>/<u>bowed</u> to the audience and <u>left</u> the ring.

Sentences that ask questions don't follow the usual simple subject–simple predicate order. Instead, the word order may be changed slightly.

When questions use forms of the verb *to be* (*is, am, are*), the verb appears before the subject while the rest of the predicate still follows the subject.

<u>*Is*</u>/<u>Angela</u>/*an experienced mountain climber?*

When the sentences include auxiliary, or helping, verbs, the auxiliary is moved in front of the subject while the rest of the predicate remains in the same place.

<u>Has</u>/<u>a package</u>/*arrived yet for me?*

Sometimes a question word such as *when, why, who,* or *where* appears in front of the sentence with the helping verb.

> When <u>will</u>/<u>we</u>/<u>be allowed</u> to park on campus?

Sometimes certain types of phrases and clauses can fall between the subject and the predicate. These should not be confused with the subject. They are usually easy to detect since they can be moved elsewhere in the sentence. The subject is underlined.

> <u>My dog</u>/, *since he has gotten old*, simply lies around the house.
> <u>My dog</u>/simply lies around the house *since he has gotten old*.

Sometimes a phrase that is not part of the subject can introduce the sentence. This phrase can also usually be moved.

> *After we have repaired the rock wall*/, <u>we</u>/ will begin to plant the new flowers.
> <u>We</u>/will begin to plant the new flowers *after we have repaired the rock wall*.

Usage Considerations   Because subjects are such important sentence elements, make sure that your subjects are clearly spelled out, not vague or misleading. Read the example below.

> *Our government* has failed to repeal the Goods and Services Tax.

This statement can be expressed more precisely:

> The *House of Commons* has failed to repeal the Goods and Services Tax.
>
> The *prime minister* has rejected proposals to repeal the GST.

Paying close attention to subjects lets you present your ideas more accurately and clearly.

EXERCISE *Place a slash mark between the complete subject and the complete predicate; then underline the simple subject once and the verb(s) twice. If a subject comes between two verbs, set it off with two slash marks.*

1. The full moon rose majestically over the mountain peak.
2. John was ill on the day of the big test.
3. The boys and girls laughed and splashed happily in the pool.
4. That man by the door is my uncle.
5. The judge revoked Rudy's parole and ordered him to jail.
6. The tall oak shaded almost the entire backyard.
7. My favourite subject is English.
8. Mr. Eames has bought a wicker chair for his living room.

sent

COMPLEMENTS

A complement is a word or word group that forms part of the predicate and helps complete the meaning of the sentence. Anything that comes after the verb is usually a complement. There are many kinds of complement, including phrases and clauses, which will be reviewed later in this chapter.

- I think *that Glenn Gould was the quintessential Canadian musician.*
- Robert hesitated *to trap the groundhog behind his house.*
- We were late *because our car would not start.*

sent

The four common complements of traditional grammar are direct objects, indirect objects, subject complements, and object complements.

A *direct object* names whatever receives, or results from, the action of a verb.

The millwright repaired the *lathe.* (Direct object receives action of verb *repaired.*)

Hilary painted a *picture.* (Direct object results from action of verb *painted.*)

They took *coffee* and *sandwiches* to the picnic. (Direct objects receive action of verb *took.*)

An *indirect object* identifies someone or something that receives whatever is named by the direct object.

Doris lent *me* her calculator. (Indirect object *me* receives *calculator,* the direct object.)

Will and Al bought their *boat* new sails. (Indirect object *boat* receives *sails,* the direct object.)

An indirect object can be converted to a prepositional phrase that begins with *to* or *for* and follows the direct object.

Doris lent her calculator *to me.*

Will and Al bought new sails *for their boat.*

A *subject complement* follows a linking verb—one that indicates existence rather than action. It renames or describes the subject.

Desmond is a *carpenter.* (Complement *carpenter* renames subject *Desmond.*)

The lights are too *bright* for Percy. (Complement *bright* describes subject *lights.*)

An *object complement* follows a direct object and renames or describes it.

The council named Misuk *treasurer.* (Object complement *treasurer* renames direct object *Misuk.*)

The audience thought the play *silly.* (Object complement *silly* describes direct object *play.*)

If a word is an *object complement,* you can form a short test sentence using *is.*

Misuk is *treasurer.*

The play is *silly.*

Usage Considerations   Like subjects, direct objects can be revised for greater precision, as these examples show:

John sent *a gift*.

John sent *a giant colouring book as a birthday gift*.

Often, you can carry the revision one step further by adding an indirect object, subject complement, or other complement to the sentence.

John sent his *niece* a giant colouring book as a birthday gift. (Indirect object added.)

sent

APPOSITIVES

An appositive is a noun, or word group serving as a noun, that follows another noun or noun substitute and expands its meaning. Appositives may be restrictive or non-restrictive. Restrictive appositives distinguish whatever they modify from other items in the same class. They are written without commas.

My sister *Heidi* is a professional golfer. (Appositive *Heidi* distinguishes her from other sisters.)

I have just read a book by the novelist *Henry James*. (Appositive *Henry James* distinguishes him from other novelists.)

Non-restrictive appositives provide more information about whatever they modify. This sort of appositive is set off by a pair of commas, except at the end of a sentence; then it is preceded by a single comma.

Anatoly Karpov, *the Russian chess player*, was interviewed on TV. (Appositive names *Karpov's* occupation.)

Todd plans to major in paleontology, *the study of fossils*. (Appositive defines the term *paleontology*.)

Usage Considerations   When a brief definition is necessary, appositives can help you improve your sentences.

John Cage wrote hundreds of pieces for prepared piano.

John Cage, *a twentieth-century avant-garde composer*, wrote hundreds of pieces for prepared pianos, *instruments with odds and ends stuck between their strings to provide unusual effects*.

However, avoid cluttering your writing with appositives that provide unneeded information; the flow overload will impede and irritate your reader.

EXERCISE   *Identify each italicized item as a direct object (DO), an indirect object (IO), a subject complement (SC), an object complement (OC), or an appositive (AP).*

1. Raj is a *student* in business administration.
2. Mr. Ames gave his *son* money for the movies.

3. The study group found Kant's philosophy *difficult*.

4. Dan lost his *umbrella* in the subway.

5. Speed Spedowski, *our best pitcher*, won 23 games last season.

6. Chelsea borrowed several *CDs* for the party.

7. The newspaper named Melissa *editor*.

8. Nelson was *overjoyed* at winning the essay contest.

PARTS OF SPEECH

noun

Traditional English grammar classifies words into eight parts of speech: *nouns, pronouns, verbs, adjectives, adverbs, prepositions, conjunctions,* and *interjections*. This section discusses these categories as well as verbals, phrases, and clauses, which also serve as parts of speech.

It is important to recognize that words that may look like one part of speech can function as another part of speech. For example, the verb *swim* can function as a noun:

Swimming is good for your health.

To identify a word as a part of speech is to identify how it functions in a sentence.

Noun

Traditional grammar defines nouns as words that name persons, places, things, conditions, ideas, or qualities. Most nouns can take a plural (*book, books*), possessive (*Andy, Andy's*), or article (*bench, the bench*).

Proper Nouns   Some nouns, called *proper nouns*, identify one-of-a-kind items like the following and are commonly capitalized.

France	Thanksgiving
Pacific Ocean	Saskatchewan
Man Booker Prize	Stanley Cup
Canadarm	Fantasy Corporation
Charter of Rights and Freedoms	Capilano University

Common Nouns   Common nouns name general classes or categories of items. Some common nouns are *abstract* and name a condition, idea, or quality that we can't experience with our five senses. *Abstract nouns* often cannot accept the plural; we cannot usually say we have *envies*. *Concrete nouns* identify something that we can experience with one or more of our senses and usually have plural forms.

Abstract Nouns	**Concrete Nouns**
arrogance	man
fear	bicycle
liberalism	desk
sickness	cartoon

Count and Non-Count Nouns   Most nouns identify things we can count, and such nouns usually can take the plural form: *three bananas, a book, two children.* Some nouns, including many abstract nouns, cannot accept a plural: *underwear, patriotism, honesty.*

Usage Considerations   Good writing demands precise, potent nouns that have been carefully chosen. Ill-chosen nouns suggest poor thinking. Note how the vague word *freedom* robs the following sentence of any specific meaning.

> Our *freedom* needs to be protected.

What did the writer have in mind? Here are a few possibilities:

> Our *right to free speech* needs to be protected.
>
> Our *private behaviour* needs to be protected.
>
> Our *national sovereignty* needs to be protected.

Even when meaning does not present problems, sentences can be sharpened by careful attention to nouns. Note the greater precision of the second sentence below:

> Our *dog* has a savage bite.
>
> Our *pit bull* has a savage bite.

pro

EXERCISE *Identify the nouns in the following sentences.*

1. Jeremy has undertaken the task of learning conversational German this summer.
2. Scrabble is a pleasant game to play on a cold, wet evening.
3. The chairperson will tell you about the decision of the committee.
4. The tree was covered with blossoms around which many bees buzzed.
5. My new apartment is in St. John's, Newfoundland.
6. Marcy Johnson jumped in her car, revved its engine, and roared off down the road.

Pronouns

Pronouns are a special class of words that can sometimes take the place of a noun in a sentence. Pronouns can help you avoid the awkward repetition of nouns.

Personal Pronouns   Personal pronouns refer to identifiable persons or things. Personal pronouns have different cases. The subjective case is used when the pronoun serves as the subject of the sentence or clause. **I** *helped Steve.* The objective case is used when the pronoun is the object of a verb or preposition. *Steve helped* **me.** *We spoke about* **him.** The possessive case shows possession or ownership. *That is* **my** *brief-case. My, your, our,* and *their* always precede nouns, as in *their car. Mine, hers, ours, yours,* and *theirs* do not precede nouns, as in *That book is mine. His* and *its* may or may not precede nouns.

	Subjective	**Objective**	**Possessive**
Singular			
First person	I	me	my, mine
Second person	you	you	your, yours
Third person	he, she, it	him, her, it	his, her, hers, its
Plural			
First person	we	us	our, ours
Second person	you	you	your, yours
Third person	they	them	their, theirs

pro

Relative Pronouns   A relative pronoun relates a subordinate clause—a word group that has a subject and a predicate but does not express a complete idea—to a noun or pronoun, called an antecedent, in the main part of the sentence. The relative pronouns include the following.

who	whose	what	whoever	whichever
whom	which	that	whomever	whatever

Who in its various forms refers to people, *which* to things, and *that* to either things or groups of people.

Mary Beth Cartwright, *who* was arrested last week for fraud, was Evansville's "Model Citizen" two years ago. (The antecedent of *who* is *Mary Beth Cartwright*.)

He took the electric razor, *which* needed a new cutting head, to the repair shop. (The antecedent of *which* is *electric razor*.)

David Bullock is someone *whom* we should definitely hire. (The antecedent of *whom* is *someone*.)

Montreal is a city *that* I've always wanted to visit. (The antecedent of *that* is *city*.)

Which typically introduces non-restrictive clauses—that is, clauses that provide more information about whatever they modify (see page 528).

The palace, *which* was in bad condition a century ago, is finally going to be restored. (Clause adds information about palace.)

That is typically used in other situations, especially to introduce restrictive clauses: those that distinguish the things they modify from others in the same class (see page 528).

The used car *that* I bought last week at Honest Bill's has already broken down twice. (Clause distinguishes the writer's used car from others.)

Interrogative Pronouns   Interrogative pronouns introduce questions. All of the relative pronouns except *that* also function as interrogative pronouns.

who	which	whoever	whichever
whom	what	whomever	whatever
whose			

What is the matter?

Who asked you?

Whatever do you mean?

pro

When *what, which,* and *whose* are followed by nouns, they act as adjectives, not pronouns.

Which movie should we see?

Demonstrative Pronouns   As their name suggests, demonstrative pronouns point things out. There are four such pronouns.

this	these
that	those

This and its plural *these* identify recent or nearby things.

This is the play to see.

These are difficult times.

That and its plural *those* identify less recent or more distant things.

That is Mary's house across the road.

Those were very good peaches you had for sale last week.

Reflexive and Intensive Pronouns   A reflexive pronoun is used when the pronoun refers back to the noun in the same clause. An intensive pronoun lends emphasis to a noun or pronoun. The two sets of pronouns are identical.

myself	herself	ourselves
yourself	itself	yourselves
himself	oneself	themselves

My father cut *himself* while shaving. (reflexive pronoun)

The premier *himself* has asked me to undertake this mission. (intensive pronoun)

Don't substitute a reflexive pronoun for a personal pronoun.

Faulty   Jill and *myself* are going to a movie.

Revision   Jill and *I* are going to a movie.

Indefinite Pronouns   These pronouns refer to unidentified persons, places, or things. One group of indefinite pronouns consistently acts as pronouns.

anybody	everything	one
anyone	nobody	somebody
anything	no one	someone
everybody	nothing	something
everyone		

A second group functions as either pronouns or adjectives.

all	any	most	few	much
another	each	either	many	neither

Here are some examples:

Everyone is welcome. (indefinite pronoun)

Many are called, but *few* are chosen. (indefinite pronouns)

Many men but only a *few* women attend the Air Force Academy. (adjectives)

Usage Considerations   Many students use vague or ambiguous pronouns that damage the clarity of their writing. Problems include letting the same pronoun stand for different nouns or using a pronoun where detailed, vivid language would be more effective. The following passage illustrates poor pronoun usage.

My brother loves fly-fishing. He thinks *it* is the only way to spend a summer weekend. In fact, whenever he's off work, he'll do *it*.

Rewritten as follows, the passage has been notably improved.

My brother loves fly-fishing. He thinks that *wading a stream and casting leisurely for trout* is the only way to spend a summer weekend. In fact, whenever he's off work, he *can be found up to his hips in water, offering his hand-tied flies to the waiting rainbow trout.*

EXERCISE *Identify each pronoun in the following sentences and indicate its type (personal, relative, interrogative, demonstrative, reflexive, intensive, and indefinite). If it is a personal pronoun, indicate if it is in the subjective (S), objective (O), or possessive (P) case.*

1. This is the kind of movie that I like.
2. Everyone in the class came to the party she gave at term's end.
3. If you feel thirsty, pour yourself a glass of lemonade.
4. That is a terrible-looking chair. Who would buy it anyhow?
5. What do you think Ashley and Bill bought each other for their wedding?
6. I myself will take the blame for anything that goes wrong with the experiment.

Verbs

A verb indicates action or existence. Main verbs fall into two classes: *action verbs* and *linking verbs*. A very different type of verb is the *auxiliary* (or *helping*) verb, which adds specific kinds of meaning to the main verb.

Action Verbs   As their name suggests, action verbs express action. Some action verbs are transitive, others intransitive. A transitive verb has a direct object that receives or results from the action and rounds out the meaning of the sentence.

The photographer *took* the picture.

Without the direct object, this sentence would not express a complete thought. In contrast, an *intransitive* verb requires no direct object to complete the meaning of the sentence.

Lee Ann *gasped*.

Little Tommy Tucker *sings* for his supper.

Many action verbs can play both transitive or intransitive roles, depending on the sentences they are used in.

> Kari *rode* her bicycle into town. (transitive verb)
>
> Karl *rode* in the front seat of the car. (intransitive verb)

Linking Verbs   A linking verb shows existence—what something is, was, or will be—rather than action. Linking verbs are intransitive and tie their subjects to subject complements. Some subject complements are nouns or noun substitutes that rename their subjects. Others are adjectives that describe their subjects.

> Ms. Davis *is* our new director. (Complement *director* renames subject *Ms. Davis.*)
>
> The soup *was* lukewarm. (Complement *lukewarm* describes subject *soup.*)

The most common linking verbs are forms of the verb *to be (is, are, am, was, were, be, being, been)*. Likewise, verbs such as *seem, become, appear, remain, feel, look, smell, sound,* and *taste* function as linking verbs when they do not indicate actual physical action. In such cases, they are followed by adjectives (see pages 496–498). Here is an example:

> Brian looked *angry.*

When such verbs do indicate physical action, they function as action verbs and are followed by adverbs (see pages 598–500).

> Brian looked *angrily* at the referee.

Linking verbs can also be followed by adverbial phrases of place or time.

> Your dinner is *on the table.* (adverb phrase of place)
>
> The meeting will be *at 8:00 a.m.* (adverb phrase of time)

Auxiliary Verbs   These helping verbs accompany action or linking verbs and provide information about time, possibility, or obligation. They also establish the passive voice. *Have, be,* and *do* can function as both auxiliary and main verbs.

The auxiliary verbs *have (has, had)* and *be (is, are, was, were)* can provide information about time.

> Halle *has* repaired your computer.
>
> Carol *is* reformatting your hard drive.

The auxiliary verb *do* is inserted to form the negative or interrogative (question form) when there is no other auxiliary.

> Ian *did* not resign.
>
> *Did* Ian resign?

Auxiliary verbs called modals show time, obligation, possibility, or ability: *shall, should, will, would, can, could, may, might.*

With questions, the auxiliary verb is often moved to the front.

> *Will* Ian *resign?*

vbs

Usage Considerations   Energetic writing requires precise verbs. Don't take verbs for granted; revise them as necessary in order to strengthen a sentence. Note the improved precision of the second example sentence.

I *gave* the maître d' a twenty-dollar bill.

I *slipped* the maître d' a twenty-dollar bill.

vbs

EXERCISE *Identify each verb in the following sentences and indicate its type.*

1. If Paul and Jim need transportation, my car will be available.

2. Please write your name on your quiz before you give it to me.

3. Marvin has been sitting in front of the TV all morning.

4. I will be watching the Toronto Raptors play tonight.

5. The movie offered lots of action, but the plot was poor.

6. Christine's assistance on this project has been invaluable.

Tense   Verbs change in form to show distinctions in time. Every main verb has two basic tenses: present and past.

The *present tense* shows present condition and general or habitual action, indicates permanent truths, tells about past events in the historical present, and sometimes denotes action at some definite future time.

Verbs in the present tense must agree with their subjects. If the subject of a verb is a singular noun or pronoun (*he, she, it*), add *s* or *es* (if the word ends with an *s, z,* or *ch* sound: *talk***s**, *teach***es**). If the subject is plural or a second-person pronoun (*you*), the verb takes no ending (*talk, teach*).

Helen *looks* beautiful in her new gown. (present condition)

John *works* on the eighteenth floor. (general action)

I *brush* my teeth each morning. (habitual action)

The earth *rotates* on its axis. (permanent truth)

On November 11, 1918, the guns *fall* silent, and World War I *comes* to an end. (historical present)

On Monday, I *begin* my new job. (future action)

The past tense shows that a condition existed or an action was completed in the past. This verb tense leaves the time indefinite, but surrounding words may specify it. Most verbs are regular and form the past tense by adding *ed: talk, talk***ed**. Some verbs are irregular and form the past by changing the vowel: *r***u***n, r***a***n*. A very few verbs do not change forms at all in creating the past: *set, set*.

Paul *was* angry with his noisy neighbours. (past condition, time indefinite)

Sandy *received* a long letter yesterday. (past action, time specified by *yesterday*)

Past Participle   In addition to the basic tenses, there is a *past participle* form of main verbs that is used to form the perfect form of the verb phrase (*He* **has talked** *to her*), as well as the passive voice (*the table* **was set**). For most verbs, the past participle form is identical to the past tense in form.

Present	Past	Past Participle
talk	talk**ed**	talk**ed**
stand	st**oo**d	st**oo**d
set	set	set

vbs

Some verbs have different past forms and past participles. This can often lead to errors, as less experienced writers may use the regular past (*He has* **swam** *this river before*) when the past participle form is required (*He has* **swum** *this river before*). Below is a table of many but not all of the irregular verbs for your reference.

Present Infinitive	Past	Past Participle
arise	arose	arisen
be	was, were	been
become	became	become
bite	bit	bitten
blow	blew	blown
break	broke	broken
choose	chose	chosen
come	came	come
do	did	done
draw	drew	drawn
drink	drank	drunk
drive	drove	driven
eat	ate	eaten
fall	fell	fallen
fly	flew	flown
freeze	froze	frozen
get	got	get *or* gotten
give	gave	given
grow	grew	grown
hide	hid	hidden
know	knew	known
ride	rode	ridden
see	saw	seen
shake	shook	shaken
slay	slew	slain
speak	spoke	spoken
spring	sprang	sprung
write	wrote	written

Time and Verb Forms

In addition to the tenses in English, many other forms of a verb are used to express time.

Future Time   *Future time* is frequently indicated by the auxiliary modals *shall* or *will* with the present tense form of the verb.

You *will feel* better after a good night's sleep. (future condition)

I *shall attend* the concert next week. (future action)

Perfect Verb Forms   The perfect form of a verb describes a past action or condition that continued. It is formed using the auxiliary verb *have* and the past participle of the verb.

The *present perfect* tense is formed with *has* or *have* and the past participle of the main verb. It shows that a past condition or action, or its effect, continues until the present time.

The players *have been* irritable since they lost the homecoming game. (Condition continues until present.)

Juanita *has driven* a truck for five years. (Action continues until present.)

William *has repaired* the snow blower. (Effect of action continues until present although the action itself was completed in the past.)

The *past perfect* tense combines *had* and the past participle of the main verb. It refers to a past condition or action that was completed before another past condition or action.

He *had been* in the army two years when the war ended. (Past perfect condition occurred first.)

Vivian moved into the house that she *had built* the summer before. (Past perfect action occurred first.)

The *future perfect* tense is formed from the verbs *shall have* or *will have* plus the past participle of the main verb. It shows that a condition or an action will have been completed at some time in the future. Surrounding words specify time.

Our sales manager *will have been* with the company 10 years next July. (Condition will end.)

By the end of this year, I *shall have written* the great Canadian novel. (Action will be completed.)

Progressive Verb Forms   Each verb form, including the basic tenses, has a *progressive form* that indicates action in progress. The progressive is always indicated by some form of the verb *to be* followed by a present participle (or progressive), a verb that ends in *ing*.

Present progressive	I am running.
Past progressive	I was running.
Future progressive	I will be running.
Present perfect progressive	I have been running.
Past perfect progressive	I had been running.
Future perfect progressive	I will have been running.

An easy way to identify the form of the verb phrase is to use the following formula (see page 510 for modal verbs):

(modal) + (have + en/ed) + (be + ing) + main verb

vbs

Simply read the first tense in the sentence. If the modal is *will*, then that designates future time. Then, if *have, has,* or *had* is present, the verb phrase is *perfect*. If a form of *be* is present and the main verb ends with *ing*, then the verb phrase is progressive.

| *will* | *have* | *been living* |
| future | perfect | progressive |

vbs

Usage Considerations   While most students use regular tenses and the progressive accurately, many less experienced writers do not always use the perfect verb form where appropriate. This is acceptable in informal writing; it is not acceptable in most formal writing.

Not acceptable	Jim *studied* accounting for the last three years.
	(This suggests that the action is over and done with.)
Acceptable	Jim *has studied* accounting for the last three years. (The present perfect verb form shows that the action comes right up to the present and may not be finished yet.)

Pages 527–528 discuss unwarranted shifts in tense and their correction.

Choosing the Right Verb Voice   A sentence's verb voice derives from the relationship between the subject and the action. A sentence is in the *active voice* when the subject carries out the action named by the verb.

Barry *planned* a picnic. (Subject *Barry* performs action.)

This pattern keeps the key information in the key part of the sentence, making it strong and vigorous and giving the reader a close-up look at the action.

The *passive voice* reverses the subject-action relationship by having the subject receive, rather than perform, the action. The performer may be identified in an accompanying phrase or go unmentioned.

A picnic *was planned* by Barry. (The phrase *by Barry* identifies the performer.)

The picnic *was cancelled*. (The performer goes unmentioned.)

A passive construction always uses a form of the verb *to be* and the past participle of an action verb. Like other constructions, the passive may show past, present, or future time.

Amy *is paid* handsomely for her investment advice. (present tense)

I *was warned* by a sound truck that a tornado was nearby. (past tense)

I *will be sent* to Ghana soon by the Canada Corps. (future tense)

I *have been awarded* a sizable research grant. (present perfect tense)

The city *had been shelled* heavily before the infantry moved in. (past perfect tense)

By the end of this month, the site for our second factory *will have been chosen*. (future perfect tense)

To convert a sentence from the passive to the active voice, make the performer of the action the subject, the original subject the direct object, and drop the form of *to be*.

The treaty *was signed* by the general. (passive)

The general *signed* the treaty. (active)

Occasionally passive voice can be useful. For example, it can emphasize the passivity of the subject (e.g., "The man was murdered."). Reporters may use it to conceal the identity of a source. Scientific writing customarily uses the passive voice since its flat, impersonal tone adds an air of scientific objectivity and authority. Consider how the passive voice in the following example of scientific writing provides a desirable objective tone and places the emphasis where it's most important: on the action, not the actor.

> In the production of steel, iron ore is first converted into pig iron by combining it with limestone and coke and then heating the mixture in a blast furnace. Pig iron, however, contains too many impurities to be useful to industry, and as a result must be refined and converted to steel.

vbs

On occasion, everyday writing also uses the passive voice.

The garbage is collected once a week on Mondays.

These caves were formed about 10 million years ago.

In the first case, there's no need to tell who collects the garbage; obviously, garbage collectors do. In the second case, the writer may not know what caused the formation, and saying "Something formed these caves about 10 million years ago" makes the sentence sound mysterious. In both situations, the action, not the actor, is paramount.

Usually, however, passive voice takes away from the energy of a piece of writing. It dilutes the force of the sentence, puts greater distance between the action and the reader, and almost always adds extra words to the message.

Most writers who overuse the passive voice simply don't realize how it bogs down their writing. Read this paragraph, written mainly in the passive voice:

> Graft becomes possible when gifts are given to police officers or favours are done for them by persons who expect preferential treatment in return. Gifts of many kinds may be received by officers. Often free meals are given to them by the owners of restaurants on their beats. During the Christmas season, they may be given liquor, food, or theatre tickets by merchants. If favoured treatment is not received by the donors, no great harm is done. But if traffic offences, safety code violations, and other infractions are overlooked by the officers, corruption results. When such corruption is exposed by the newspapers, faith is lost in law enforcement agencies.

This impersonal, wordy passage plods across the page. Now note the livelier, more forceful tone of this rewritten version.

> Graft becomes possible when police officers accept gifts or favours from persons who expect preferential treatment in return. Officers may receive gifts of many kinds. Restaurant owners often provide free meals for officers on the beat. During the Christmas season, merchants may give them liquor, food, or theatre tickets. If donors do not receive favoured treatment, no great harm is done. But if officers overlook traffic offences, safety code violations, and other infractions, corruption results. When the newspapers expose such corruption, citizens lose faith in law enforcement agencies.

EXERCISE *Identify each verb in the following sentences, indicate its tense, and note any use of the passive voice:*

1. They will have arrived in Tokyo by this evening.
2. This TV program is relayed to Europe by satellite.
3. The Krause Corporation's new headquarters building will be dedicated June 30.
4. The school psychologist was asked whether she had any explanation for Tim's odd behaviour.
5. We have been told we face yet another 15 percent staff cutback.
6. Leslie works in the sales department of Canadian Tire.

Adjectives

An adjective *modifies* a noun or pronoun by describing it, limiting it, or otherwise making its meaning more precise.

> The *brass* candlestick stood next to the *fragile* vase. (*Brass* modifies *candlestick*, and *fragile* modifies *vase.*)

> The cat is *long-haired* and *sleek*. (*Long-haired* and *sleek* modify *cat.*)

There are three general categories of adjectives: limiting, descriptive, and proper.

Limiting Adjectives   A limiting adjective identifies or points out the noun or pronoun it modifies. It may indicate number or quantity. Several categories of pronouns can serve as limiting adjectives, as can numbers and nouns.

> *Whose* briefcase is on the table? (interrogative adjective)

> The couple *whose* car was stolen called the police. (relative adjective)

> *This* restaurant has the best reputation for gourmet food. (demonstrative adjective)

> *Some* people have no social tact at all. (indefinite adjective)

> Heather swerved *her* car suddenly to avoid an oncoming truck. (possessive adjective)

> *Three* people entered the lecture hall late. (number as adjective)

> The *schoolgirl* look is fashionable this year. (noun as adjective)

Descriptive Adjectives   A descriptive adjective, which is the largest category of adjectives, names a quality, characteristic, or condition of a noun or pronoun. Two or more of these adjectives may modify the same noun or pronoun.

> He applied *clear* lacquer to the tabletop.

> The *slim, sophisticated* model glided onto the runway.

> The child was *active, happy,* and *polite.*

Proper Adjectives   A proper adjective is derived from a proper noun and is always capitalized.

> Harwell is a *Shakespearean* actor.

Articles as Adjectives   Articles appear immediately before nouns and can therefore be considered adjectives. There are three articles in English: *a, an,* and *the. The* points to a specific item; *a* and *an* do not. *A* precedes words beginning with consonant sounds; *an* precedes words with vowel sounds, making pronunciation easier.

> *The* right word at *the* right moment can save a friendship. (Definite articles suggest there is one right word and one right moment.)

> *A* right word can save a friendship. (Indefinite article suggests there are several right words.)

> I think I'd like *an* apple with my lunch. (No particular apple is specified.)

Sometimes the definite article refers to a class of items.

> *The* tiger is fast becoming an endangered species.

Context shows whether such a sentence refers to particular items or entire classes.

Comparison with Adjectives   Adjectives may be used to show comparison. When two things are compared, shorter adjectives usually add *-er* and longer adjectives add *more*. When three or more things are compared, shorter adjectives usually add *-est* and longer ones add *most*.

> John is *taller* than Tobias. (short adjective comparing two people)

> Sandra seems *more cheerful* than Jill today. (long adjective comparing two people)

> John is the *tallest* of the three brothers. (short adjective comparing three people)

> Sandra is the *most cheerful* girl in the class. (longer adjective comparing more than three people)

Some adjectives, like the examples below, have irregular forms for comparisons.

> good—better—best
> bad—worse—worst

Don't use the *-est* form of the shorter adjective for comparing just two things.

> *Faulty*   This is the *smallest* of the two castles.

Instead, use the *-er* form. (See pages 536–538 for revision of faulty comparisons.)

> *Revision*   This is the *smaller* of the two castles.

Position of Adjectives   Most adjectives come immediately before the words they modify. In a few set expressions (for example, heir *apparent*), the adjective immediately follows the word it modifies. Similarly, adjective pairs sometimes appear in a follow-up position for added emphasis (The rapids, *swift* and *dangerous*, soon capsized the raft). Adjectives can also serve as subject complements, where they follow their subjects (The puppy was *friendly*).

Usage Considerations   Some students overuse adjectives, especially in descriptions, but most underuse them. Review your sentences carefully to see where adding or cutting adjectives can increase the impact of your writing.

adj

My Cadillac is the talk of my friends.

My *old, dilapidated, rusty, fenderless 1985* Cadillac is the talk of my friends.

My *rusty, fenderless 1985* Cadillac is the talk of my friends.

The first sentence lacks adjectives that show why the car is discussed. The second sentence overcorrects this fault by including two adjectives that repeat the information provided by the others. The final sentence strikes the proper balance.

Determiners   Some words, called *determiners*, limit the noun or pronoun but do not name a quality or characteristic of the noun or pronoun. These words are sometimes classified with adjectives.

adj

Three sailboats raced around the island.

While we know how many sailboats are involved, there is no descriptive content added to the concept of sailboats.

There are many different kinds of determiners.

Determiners	Name
a, an	Indefinite article
the	Definite article
this, that, these, those	Demonstrative
one, two, three, four, five	Cardinal number
first, second, third, fourth	Ordinal number
my, our, your, his, her, hers, its, their	Possessive pronoun
some, any, no, every, another, enough	Indefinite pronoun
either, neither, all, both, each, less,	
other, many, more, most, few, several	
Kim's, Maria's	Possessive noun

EXERCISE *Identify the adjectives in the following sentences.*

1. Jasper is a very unhappy person.

2. Paul has an aunt who writes long, chatty letters to him regularly.

3. Sean ate an English muffin and drank a cup of black coffee.

4. Barton has an unusual sideboard in his dining room.

5. The tired carpenter tossed his tools into the red truck and drove home.

6. After buying a few gifts, Nicole and Audrey took a slow stroll around the resort town.

Adverbs

An adverb modifies a verb, an adjective, another adverb, or a whole sentence. Adverbs generally answer questions such as "How?" "When?" "Where?" "How often?" and "To what extent?"

The floodwaters receded *very* slowly. (Adverb modifies
adverb and answers the question "How?")

My sister will visit me *tomorrow*. (Adverb modifies
verb and answers the question "When?")

The coach walked *away from the bench*. (Adverb modifies
verb and answers the question "Where?")

The tire is *too* worn to be safe. (Adverb modifies
adjective and answers the question "To what extent?")

The teller is *frequently* late for work. (Adverb modifies
adjective and answers the question "How often?")

Unfortunately, the game was cancelled because of rain. (The adverb modifies
the whole sentence but does not answer any question.)

adv

Formation of Adverbs   Most adverbs are formed by adding -*ly* to adjectives.

The wind is *restless*. (*Restless* is an adjective modifying *wind*.)

He walked *restlessly* around the room. (*Restlessly* is an adverb modifying *walked*.)

However, many common adverbs (*almost, never, quite, soon, then, there,* and *too*)
lack -*ly* endings.

I *soon* realized that pleasing my boss was impossible.

This movie is *too* gruesome for my taste.

Furthermore, some words such as *better, early, late, hard, little, near, only, straight,* and
wrong do double duty as either adjectives or adverbs.

We must have taken a *wrong* turn. (*Wrong* is an adjective modifying the noun *turn*.)

Where did I go *wrong*? (*Wrong* is an adverb modifying the verb *go*.)

Comparison with Adverbs   Like adjectives, adverbs can show comparison. When
two things are compared, adverbs add *more*. When three or more things are compared,
most is used.

Harold works *more* efficiently than Don. (adverb comparing two people)

Of all the people in the shop, Harold works the *most* efficiently. (adverb comparing
more than two people)

Some adverbs, like some adjectives, use irregular forms for comparisons.

well—better—best

much—more—most

Position of Adverbs   Adverbs are more movable than any other part of speech. Usually,
adverbs that modify adjectives and other adverbs appear next to them to avoid confusion.

Her *especially* fine tact makes her a welcome guest at any party. (Adverb *especially*
modifies adjective *fine*.)

The novel was *very* badly written. (Adverb *very* modifies adverb *badly*.)

Adverbs that modify verbs, however, can often be shifted around in a sentence without causing changes in meaning.

Quickly, she slipped through the doorway.

She slipped *quickly* through the doorway.

She slipped through the doorway *quickly*.

prep

EXERCISE *Identify the adverbs in the following sentences.*

1. Anthony is late more frequently than any other member of the crew.
2. After dinner, the children went outdoors and played noisily.
3. Jason stepped quickly to the door and listened intently to the howling wind.
4. The pirate ship glided swiftly and silently toward the sleeping town.
5. The tired, perspiring runner staggered wearily across the finish line.
6. You'll have to work very fast to keep up with Huan.

Prepositions

A preposition links its object—a noun or noun substitute—to some other word in the sentence and shows a relationship between them. The relationship is often one of location, time, means, or reason or purpose. The word group containing the preposition and its object makes up a prepositional phrase.

The new insulation *in* the attic keeps my house much warmer now. (Preposition *in* links object *attic* to *insulation* and shows location.)

We have postponed the meeting *until* tomorrow. (Preposition *until* links object *tomorrow* to *postponed* and shows time.)

The tourists travelled *by* train. (Preposition *by* links object *train* to *travelled* and shows means.)

Warren swims *for* exercise. (Preposition *for* links object *exercise* to *swims* and shows reason or purpose.)

The following list includes the most common prepositions, some of which consist of two or more words.

above	beside	in	out of
after	between	instead of	over
against	by	into	since
along with	by reason of	like	through
among	contrary to	near	to
at	during	next to	toward
because of	except	of	under
before	for	on	with
below	from	onto	without

Many of these combine to form additional prepositions: *except for, in front of, by way of, on top of,* and the like.

Some prepositions such as *up, on,* and *in* can also function as a different part of speech called a *verb particle*. Here are two examples.

The instructor let Jeff make *up* the test.

The officer turned *in* his best friend.

The verb particle is closely associated with the verb and is a part of its meaning. If a word is used as a verb particle (rather than a preposition), it can usually be moved after the noun.

The instructor let Jeff make the test *up*.

The officer turned his best friend *in*.

Usage Considerations   It is easy to use a small group of prepositions over and over in your writing. This habit often results in imprecise or misleading sentences. To avoid this problem, think carefully about your choice of prepositions as you revise. Read the following example:

He walked *by* the railway tracks on his way home.

Note that two interpretations are possible.

He walked *along* the railway tracks on his way home.

He walked *past* the railway tracks on his way home.

Clearly you want to use the preposition that conveys your intended meaning.

EXERCISE *Identify the prepositions and their objects in the following sentences.*

1. I finally finished waxing the car just before the rainstorm.
2. Aloe lotion will give you instant relief from sunburn.
3. For reasons of security, this gate must be kept locked at all times.
4. Shortly after dark, the group arrived at the camp.
5. Across the street, Gillian was working on her roof.
6. At the end of the concert, everyone in the hall stood and applauded.

Conjunctions

Conjunctions serve as connectors, linking parts of sentences or whole sentences. These connectors fall into three groups: coordinating conjunctions, subordinating conjunctions, and conjunctive adverbs.

Coordinating Conjunctions   Coordinating conjunctions connect terms of equal grammatical importance: words, word groups, and simple sentences. These conjunctions can occur singly *(and, but, or, nor, for, yet, so)* or in pairs called correlative conjunctions *(either—or, neither—nor, both—and,* and *not only—but also)*.

conj

The elements that follow correlative conjunctions must be parallel—that is, have the same grammatical form.

conj

> Dylan *and* his cousin are opening a video arcade.
> (Coordinating conjunction connects nouns.)
>
> Shall I serve the tea in the living room *or* on the front porch?
> (Coordinating conjunction connects phrases.)
>
> I am going to Europe this summer, *but* Marjorie is staying home.
> (Coordinating conjunction connects simple sentences.)
>
> Amy *not only* teaches English *but also* writes novels.
> (Correlative conjunctions connect parallel predicates.)
>
> You can study nursing *either* at the University of British Columbia *or* at Kwantlen Polytechnic University. (Correlative conjunctions connect parallel phrases.)
>
> Friendship is *both* pleasure *and* pain. (Correlative conjunctions connect parallel nouns.)

Subordinating Conjunctions   Like relative pronouns, subordinating conjunctions introduce subordinate clauses, relating them to independent clauses, which can stand alone as complete sentences. Examples of subordinating conjunctions include *because, as if, even though, since, so that, whereas,* and *whenever* (see page 528 for more).

> I enjoyed the TV program *because* it was so well acted. (Conjunction connects *it was so well acted* to the rest of the sentence.)
>
> *Whenever* you're ready, we can begin dinner. (Conjunction connects *you're ready* to the rest of the sentence.)

Conjunctive Adverbs   Some connectors are adverbs that function as conjunctions. They serve as linking devices between elements of equal rank and as modifiers, showing such things as similarity, contrast, result or effect, addition, emphasis, time, and example.

> The job will require you to travel a great deal; *however,* the salary is excellent.
>
> Sean cares nothing for clothes; *in fact,* all of his socks have holes in their toes.

The following list groups the most common conjunctive adverbs according to function.

> *Similarity:* likewise, similarly
>
> *Contrast:* however, nevertheless, on the contrary, on the other hand, otherwise
>
> *Result or effect:* accordingly, as a result, consequently, hence, therefore, thus
>
> *Addition:* also, furthermore, in addition, in the first place, moreover
>
> *Emphasis or clarity:* in fact, in other words, indeed, that is
>
> *Time:* afterwards, later, meanwhile, subsequently
>
> *Example:* for example, for instance, to illustrate

Conjunctive adverbs should not be confused with coordinating conjunctions. Unlike other conjunctions and other adverbs, conjunctive adverbs can move, often to create a specific emphasis.

The job will require you to travel a great deal; the salary, *however*, is excellent.

The job will require you to travel a great deal; *however*, the salary is excellent.

Sean cares nothing for clothes; all of his socks, *in fact*, have holes in their toes.

Sean cares nothing for clothes; *in fact*, all of his socks have holes in their toes.

Because conjunctive adverbs can move, the second independent clause must be treated as a complete sentence and either be joined to the previous independent clause with a semicolon or be separated by a period.

Usage Considerations   You can add variety to your writing by varying the conjunctions you use. For example, if you consistently rely on the conjunction *because*, try substituting *as* or *since*. When you have choppy sentences, try combining them by using a conjunction.

> *Original*   You can buy smoked salmon at Sally's Seafoods. You can buy it at Daane's Thriftland as well.
>
> *Revision*   You can buy smoked salmon *either* at Sally's Seafoods *or* at Daane's Thriftland.

The revision is much smoother than the original sentence pair.

Interjections

An interjection is an exclamatory word used to gain attention or to express strong feeling. It has no grammatical connection to the rest of the sentence. An interjection is followed by an exclamation point or a comma.

> *Hey!* Watch how you're driving! (strong interjection)
>
> *Oh*, is the party over already? (mild interjection)

EXERCISE *Identify the coordinating conjunctions (CC), subordinating conjunctions (SC), conjunctive adverbs (CA), and interjections (I) in the following sentences.*

1. The car was not only dented but also dirty.
2. While Roger was at the movies, his brother bought a model airplane.
3. Rats! My computer ate my essay.
4. Although they felt under the weather, Tara and Laura went to the party.
5. The candidate's views matched those of his audience; consequently, he received warm applause.
6. Sandra is no academic slouch; indeed, she was valedictorian of her high school class.

PHRASES AND CLAUSES

Phrases

A phrase is a group of words that lacks a subject and a predicate and serves as a single part of speech. This section discusses four basic kinds of phrases: *prepositional phrases*, *participial phrases*, *gerund phrases*, and *infinitive phrases*. The last three are based on participles, gerunds, and infinitives, verb forms known as verbals. A fifth type of phrase, the verb phrase, consists of sets of two or more verbs (*has fixed, had been sick, will have been selected,* and the like).

Prepositional Phrases   A prepositional phrase consists of a preposition, one or more objects, and any associated words. These phrases serve as adjectives or adverbs.

> The picture *over the mantel* was my mother's. (prepositional phrase as adjective)
>
> He bought ice skates *for himself.* (prepositional phrase as adverb modifying verb)
>
> The toddler was afraid *of the dog.* (prepositional phrase as adverb modifying adjective)
>
> Our visitors arrived late *in the day.* (prepositional phrase as adverb modifying another adverb)

Frequently, prepositional phrases occur in series. Sometimes they form chains in which each phrase modifies the object of the preceding phrase. At other times, some or all of the phrases may modify the verb or verb phrase.

> John works *in a clothing store/ on Main Street/ during the summer.*

Here the first and third phrases serve as adverbs modifying the verb *works* and answering the questions "Where?" and "When?" while the second phrase serves as an adjective modifying *store* and answering the question "Where?"

Participial Phrases   A participial phrase consists of a participle plus associated words. Participles are verb forms that function as adjectives or adverbs when used in participial phrases. A present participle ends in *-ing* and indicates an action currently being carried out. A past participle ends in *-ed,- en, -e, -n, -d,* or *-t* and indicates some past action.

> The chef *preparing dinner* trained in France. (present participial phrase as adjective)
>
> The background, *sketched in lightly,* accented the features of the woman in the painting. (past participial phrase as adjective)
>
> She left *whistling a jolly melody.* (present participial phrase as adverb)

A perfect participial phrase consists of *having* or *having been* plus a past participle and any associated words. Like a past participial phrase, it indicates a past action.

> *Having alerted the townspeople about the tornado,* the sound truck returned to the city garage. (perfect participial phrase)
>
> *Having been alerted to the tornado,* the townspeople sought shelter in their basements. (perfect participial phrase)

Some participial phrases that modify persons or things distinguish them from others in the same class. These phrases are written without commas. Other phrases provide more information about the persons or things they modify and are set off with commas.

> The man *fixing my car* is a master mechanic. (Phrase distinguishes man fixing car from other men.)
>
> Mr. Welsh, *fatigued by the tennis game,* rested in the shade. (Phrase provides more information about Mr. Welsh.)

phr

Gerund Phrases   A gerund phrase consists of a gerund and the words associated with it. Like present participles, gerunds are verb forms that end in *-ing*. However, unlike participles, they function as nouns rather than as adjectives or adverbs.

> Kathryn's hobby is *collecting stamps*. (gerund phrase as subject complement)
>
> Kathryn's hobby, *collecting stamps*, has made her many friends. (gerund phrase as appositive)
>
> He devoted every spare moment to *overhauling the car*. (gerund phrase as object of preposition)

phr

Infinitive Phrases   An infinitive phrase consists of the present principal part of a verb preceded by *to (to fix, to eat)*, together with any accompanying words. These phrases serve as adjectives, adverbs, and nouns.

> This looks like a good place *to plant the shrub*. (infinitive phrase as adjective)
>
> Lenore worked *to earn money for tuition*. (infinitive phrase as adverb)
>
> My goal is *to have my own business some day*. (infinitive phrase as noun)

Gerunds can often be substituted for infinitives and vice versa.

> To repair this fender will cost two hundred dollars. (infinitive phrase as subject)
>
> Repairing this fender will cost two hundred dollars. (gerund phrase as subject)

At times the *to* in an infinitive may be omitted following verbs such as *make, dare, let*, and *help*.

> Kristin didn't dare *(to) move* a muscle.
>
> The psychiatrist helped me *(to) overcome* my fear of flying.

Verbals Not in Phrases   Participles, gerunds, and infinitives can function as nouns, adjectives, or adverbs, even when they are not parts of phrases.

> That *sunbathing* woman is a well-known model. (participle as adjective)
>
> *Dancing* is fine exercise. (gerund)
>
> The children want *to play*. (infinitive as noun)
>
> If you're looking for a job, Jamie is the person *to see*. (infinitive as adjective)
>
> I'm prepared *to resign*. (infinitive as adverb)

Usage Considerations   Phrases can often help clarify or develop the information in a sentence.

> | | |
> |---|---|
> | *Original* | My brother is fishing. |
> | *Revision* | My brother is fishing *for trout just below Barnes Dam on Sidewinder Creek*. (prepositional phrases added) |
> | *Original* | The boat barely made shore. |
> | *Revision* | The boat, *listing heavily and leaking badly*, barely made shore. (participial phrases added) |

cl

Testing a Phrase's Function   To determine whether a phrase is functioning as noun, adjective, or adverb, try this substitution test. Try replacing the phrase in question with a common noun (*something, someone,* or *it*), with an adjective or adjective phrase, or with an adverb. Whichever choice works will demonstrate the function of the phrase.

> *Walking at a brisk pace* is excellent exercise. (participial phrase)
>
> *Something* is excellent exercise. (therefore, a **noun** phrase)
>
> I am prepared *to finish the job.* (infinitive phrase)
>
> I am prepared *completely.* (therefore, an **adverb** phrase)
>
> He was a man *of unusual craftiness.* (prepositional phrase)
>
> He was a *crafty* man. (therefore, an **adjective** phrase)

EXERCISE *Identify the italicized phrases as prepositional, participial, gerund, or infinitive and tell whether each is used as a noun, an adjective, or an adverb.*

1. *Walking the dog in the rain* made me grouchy for the rest of the day.
2. *To ride the Orient Express* was Marian's fondest ambition.
3. *Opening the door a tiny crack,* Michelle stared with horror at the scene before her.
4. Sue Ellen works *in a grocery store* during the summer.
5. Darren couldn't decide which refrigerator *to buy for his mother.*
6. Old-fashioned in every way, Chester shaves *with a straight razor.*

Clauses

A clause is a word group that includes a subject and a predicate. An *independent clause,* sometimes called a main clause, expresses a complete thought and can function as a simple sentence. A *dependent clause,* or subordinate clause, cannot stand by itself. Subordinate clauses may serve as nouns, adjectives, or adverbs.

Noun Clauses   A noun clause can serve in any of the ways that ordinary nouns can.

> *What the neighbour told John* proved to be incorrect. (noun clause as subject)
>
> The woman asked *when the bus left for Sherbrooke.* (noun clause as direct object)
>
> I'll give a reward to *whoever returns my phone.* (noun clause as object of preposition *to*)

Noun clauses normally begin with one of the following words.

Relative Pronouns		**Interrogative Pronoun**
who	whoever	when
whom	whomever	why
whose	that	where
what	whatever	how
which	whichever	whether

The relative pronoun *that* is sometimes omitted from the beginning of a clause that acts as a direct object.

Dr. Kant thinks *(that) he knows everything.*

If a clause is serving as a noun, you can replace it with the word *something* or *someone,* and the sentence will still make sense.

Dr. Kant thinks *something.*

If the clause is serving as an adjective or an adverb, making the substitution turns the sentence into nonsense.

The person *who wins the lottery* will receive two million dollars.

The person *someone* will receive two million dollars.

cl

Adjective Clauses   Like ordinary adjectives, adjective clauses modify nouns and noun substitutes.

Give me one reason *that could sway my opinion.* (Adjective clause modifies noun.)

I'll hire anyone *that Dr. Stone recommends.* (Adjective clause modifies pronoun.)

Generally, adjective clauses begin with one of the following words.

Relative Pronouns

who	what
whom	which
whose	that

Sometimes the word that introduces the clause can be omitted.

The chair *(that) we ordered last month* has just arrived. (pronoun *that* omitted but understood)

The man *(whom) we were talking to* is a movie producer. (pronoun *whom* omitted but understood)

An adjective clause may be restrictive and distinguish whatever it modifies from others in the same class, or it may be non-restrictive and provide more information about whatever it modifies.

Flora wiped up the cereal *that the baby had spilled.* (restrictive clause)

Harriet Thomas, *who was born in Saskatchewan,* now lives in Alberta. (non-restrictive clause)

As these examples show, restrictive clauses are not set off with commas, but non-restrictive clauses are.

Adverb Clauses   These clauses modify verbs, adjectives, adverbs, and sentences, answering the same questions that ordinary adverbs do.

You may go *whenever you wish.* (Adverb clause modifies verb.)

Sandra looked paler *than I had ever seen her look before.* (Adverb clause modifies adjective.)

Darryl shouted loudly *so that the rescue party could hear him*. (Adverb clause modifies adverb.)

Unless everyone cooperates, this plan will never succeed. (Adverb clause modifies whole sentence.)

The word or word group that introduces an adverb clause is always a subordinating conjunction. Here are the most common of these conjunctions, grouped according to the questions they answer.

When? after, as, as soon as, before, since, until, when, whenever, while

Where? where, wherever

How? as if, as though

Why? as, because, now that, since, so that

Under what conditions? although, if, once, provided that, though, unless

To what extent? than

Usage Considerations   Like phrases, clauses can help develop sentences as well as smooth out choppiness.

Original	The old grandfather clock ticked loudly through the night.
Revision	The old grandfather clock *that my great-aunt gave me before she died* ticked loudly through the night. (Clause adds information.)
Original	The chemistry professor insisted on lab safety. He had been hurt in a lab explosion the previous year.
Revision	The chemistry professor, *who had been hurt in a lab explosion the previous year,* insisted on lab safety. (Clause adds smoothness.)

To avoid clumsiness, avoid overloaded sentences like the one below:

The old grandfather clock that my great-aunt gave me before she died *and that I took with me to England when my company transferred me there for two years* ticked loudly through the night.

EXERCISE *Identify the italicized clauses as noun, adjective, or adverb.*

1. Why do Neil's parents always give him *whatever he wants?*

2. Steve skated *as if an NHL scout were watching him.*

3. Gary is the only golfer *who putted well today.*

4. The dog barked loudly *because he was hungry.*

5. *Why anyone would want to skydive* is beyond me.

6. The administrator *Maria hired last month* has already received a raise.

Coordination and Subordination

Coordination and subordination are ways to rank ideas in sentences. Coordination makes ideas equal; subordination makes them unequal. To understand coordination and subordination, you need to know about four kinds of sentences: simple, compound, complex, and compound–complex.

crd

Simple Sentences   A simple sentence has one subject and one predicate. Some simple sentences consist merely of a single noun and a single verb.

Millicent shouted.

Others can include elements such as compound subjects, compound verbs, direct objects, indirect objects, and subject complements.

Jim and Charlotte have bought a car. *(compound subject, direct object)*

Lucretia Borgia smiled and mixed her guests a cocktail. *(compound verb, indirect object, direct object)*

Autumn is a sad season. *(subject complement)*

Most simple sentences are rather short and easy to understand. This trimness can add punch to your writing, but it can also make your writing sound childish and may waste words.

The audience was young and friendly. It was responsive. It cheered for each speaker.

Combined into a single simple sentence, the information is easier to follow and more interesting to read:

The young, friendly, responsive audience cheered for each speaker.

Compound Sentences   A compound sentence contains two or more independent clauses, each holding the same (coordinate) rank. As a result, the idea in the first clause receives the same emphasis as the idea in the second. In some cases, a comma and a coordinating conjunction *(and, but, or, nor, for, yet, so)* link successive clauses.

She named the baby William, *and* her mother approved.

The audience was young, friendly, and responsive, *so* it cheered for each speaker.

In others, a semicolon and a conjunctive adverb *(for example, however, in fact, likewise, meanwhile, instead,* and the like) furnish the connection.

Tod wants to see the play; *in fact,* he's talked about it for weeks.

Today, many young women do not rush into marriage and motherhood; *instead,* they spend several years establishing careers.

Finally, a writer may omit any connecting word and separate the clauses with a semicolon.

The sky grew pitch black; the wind died; an ominous quiet hung over the whole city.

Be sure to read this Robertson Davies novel; it shows the ramifications of a single small event.

As the preceding sentences show, compound sentences allow writers to express simple relationships among simple ideas. However, such sentences have an important limitation: They make it impossible to highlight one particular idea. To do this, we need to use complex sentences.

Complex Sentences   A complex sentence has one independent clause and one or more dependent clauses. Relegating an idea to a dependent clause shows that the writer wishes it to receive less emphasis than the idea in the main clause.

> *Because the young, friendly audience was responsive,* it cheered for each speaker.
>
> *After the ball was over,* Derek collapsed on the sofa.
>
> *Once they had reached the lakeshore,* the campers found a level spot where they could pitch their tent.

Unlike compound sentences, complex ones allow writers to vary the emphasis of ideas.

> While I watered the grass, I discussed stock options with Lee.
>
> I watered the grass while I discussed stock options with Lee.

The first sentence emphasizes the talk with Lee, the second watering the lawn. By shifting emphasis a writer can change the meaning of a sentence.

> *While his bicycle was damaged,* Pat walked to work.
>
> *While Pat walked to work,* his bicycle was damaged.

Furthermore, complex sentences signal *how* ideas relate. Note the various relationships in the following sentences.

> *Because she was swimming well,* Alysha did 200 laps today. *(reason)*
>
> The CN Tower is taller *than the Empire State Building. (extent)*
>
> Ms. Yoshira is the executive *for whom I am working. (relationship between persons)*

Compound–Complex Sentences   This type of sentence features two or more independent clauses and one or more dependent clauses. Here are two examples with the dependent clauses italicized:

> Ms. Shin works as an investment manager, and Mr. Grewal, *who lives next door to her,* owns a jewellery store.
>
> If you are to communicate properly, your thoughts must be clear and correct; thoughts are wasted when language is muddled.

With compound–complex sentences writers can present more intricate relationships than with other sentences. In the following example, three sentences—one compound and two simple—have been rewritten as a compound–complex sentence. Notice how subordination improves the compactness and smoothness of the final version.

Alison hated to be seen in ugly clothing, but she wore an ugly dress with red polka dots. She had received the dress as a Christmas present. Her Aunt Carmen had given it to her.

Alison hated to be seen in ugly clothing; nevertheless, she wore an ugly red-polka-dot dress that her Aunt Carmen had given her for Christmas.

The second version condenses 35 words to 26.

EXERCISE

crd

1. **Label the independent and dependent clauses in the sentences below. Then identify each sentence as simple, compound, complex, or compound–complex.**

   a. A career in broadcasting requires good verbal skills, an extensive wardrobe, and a dazzling smile.

   b. Because its bag was too full, the vacuum cleaner backfired, leaving the room dirtier than it had been before.

   c. When Dean arrived home, his roommate asked him where he had really gone; six hours seemed too long a time to spend in the library.

   d. My apple tree blossomed last week; however, the peach trees have withered, probably because of the freeze last month.

   e. It's risky to confide in a co-worker because one can never be sure that the confidence will be kept.

2. **Using coordination and subordination, rewrite the following passages to reduce words and/or improve smoothness.**

   a. He played the piano. He played the organ. He played the French horn. He did not play the viola.

   b. Life on Venus may be possible. It will not be the kind of life we know on Earth. Life on Mars may be possible. It will not be the kind of life we know on Earth.

   c. Albert lay in bed. He stared at the ceiling. Albert thought about the previous afternoon. He had asked Kathy to go to dinner with him. She is a pretty, blonde-haired woman. She sits at the desk next to his. They work at Hemphill's. She had refused.

   d. I went to the store to buy a box of detergent. I saw Joshua there, and we talked about last night's game.

   e. Connor went to the newsstand. He bought a magazine there. While he was on the way home, he lost it. He had nothing to read.

Accepted usage improves the smoothness of your prose, makes your writing easier to understand, and demonstrates that you are a careful communicator. These assets, in turn, increase the likelihood that the reader will accept your ideas.

When you've finished revising the first draft of a piece of writing, edit it with a critic's eye to ensure that you eliminate all errors. Circle sentences or parts of them that are faulty or suspect. Then check your circled items against this section of the Handbook, which deals with the most common errors in writing.

REVISING SENTENCE FRAGMENTS

A sentence fragment is a group of words that fails to qualify as a sentence but is capitalized and punctuated as if it were a sentence. To be a sentence, a word group must (1) have a subject and a verb and (2) make sense by itself. The first of the following examples has a subject and a verb; the second does not. Neither makes sense by itself.

> If you want to remain.

> His answer to the question.

frag

Methods of Revision   Eliminating a sentence fragment is not hard. Careful reading often shows that the fragment goes with the sentence that comes just before or just after it. And sometimes two successive fragments can be joined. Note how we've corrected the fragments (italicized) in the following pairs:

Faulty	*Having been warned about the storm.* We decided to stay home.
Revision	Having been warned about the storm, we decided to stay home.
Faulty	*After eating.* The dog took a nap.
Revision	After eating, the dog took a nap.
Faulty	Monique went to work. *Although she felt sick.*
Revision	Monique went to work although she felt sick.
Faulty	Dave bought a new suit. *Over at Bentley's.*
Revision	Dave bought a new suit over at Bentley's.
Faulty	*That bronze clock on the mantel. Once belonged to my grandmother.*
Revision	That bronze clock on the mantel once belonged to my grandmother.

Joining a fragment to a sentence or to another fragment works only if the problem is simply one of mispunctuation. If the fragment stems from an improperly developed thought, revise the thought into correct sentence form.

Punctuating Your Corrections   When you join a fragment to the following sentence, you need not place a comma between the two unless the fragment has six or more words or if omitting a comma might cause a misreading. When joining a fragment to the preceding sentence, omit a comma unless there is a distinct pause between the two items. The preceding examples illustrate these points.

Intentional Fragments   Fragments are commonly used in conversation and the writing that reproduces it. Professional writers also use fragments to gain special emphasis or create special effects. (See pages 104–105.)

CONNECTED DISCOURSE EXERCISE *Identify and correct the sentence fragments in the following letter.*

Dear Phone Company:

Recently I received a phone bill for over $500. While I do use the phone fairly extensively. Most of the calls I make are local ones. In this case, many of the calls on my bill were to other countries. Including a phone call to New Delhi, India. I can hardly be held responsible for these calls. Especially since I don't know anyone who lives overseas. Since the only long-distance call I made was to Sudbury, Ontario. I have deducted the charges for all the other long-distance calls from my bill and am sending you the balance. In order to prevent this type of error from happening again. Would you please have a representative determine why these charges appeared on my bill?

frag

Sincerely,

Desperate

EXERCISE *Eight main clauses paired with fragments are shown below. In each case identify the sentence (S) and the fragment (F) and then eliminate the fragment.*

1. The clerk handed the package to the customer. And walked swiftly away from the counter.
2. Exhausted by his efforts to push the car out of the snowbank. Paul slumped wearily into the easy chair.
3. The dinner honoured three retirees. One of them my father.
4. After tidying up the kitchen. My parents left for the movies.
5. If Dr. Frankenstein's experiment is a success. He'll throw a monster party to celebrate.
6. Even though Ned studied very hard. He had trouble with the test.
7. The dog barked at the stranger. And chased him from the property.
8. By leaving the arena before the last goal was scored. We avoided the after-game crowd.

REVISING FUSED SENTENCES AND COMMA SPLICES

A fused, or run-on, sentence occurs when one sentence runs into another without anything to mark their junction. A comma splice occurs when only a comma marks the junction. A comma is not strong enough punctuation to join independent clauses, or sentences. Here are several examples:

Fused sentence	Laura failed to set her alarm she was late for work.
Comma splice	Violets are blooming now, my lawn is covered with them.
Fused sentence	Rick refused to attend the movie he said he hated horror shows.
Comma splice	Tyler watched the road carefully, he still missed his turn.
Fused Sentence	Janet worked on her term paper her friend studied for a calculus test.
Comma splice	Janet worked on her term paper, her friend studied for a calculus test.

Testing for Errors   To check out a possible comma splice or fused sentence, read what precedes and follows the comma or suspected junction and see whether the two parts can stand alone as sentences. If *both parts* can stand alone, there is an error. Otherwise, there is not.

Darryl is a real troublemaker, someday he'll find himself in serious difficulty.

Examination of the parts preceding and following the comma shows that each is a complete sentence:

Darryl is a real troublemaker.

Someday he'll find himself in serious difficulty.

The writer has therefore committed a comma splice that needs correction.

Methods of Revision   You can correct fused sentences and comma splices in several ways.

1. Create two separate sentences.

Revision	Violets are blooming now. My lawn is covered with them.
Revision	Rick refused to attend the movie. He said he hated horror shows.

2. Join the sentences with a semicolon.

Revision	Violets are blooming now; my yard is covered with them.
Revision	Rick refused to attend the movie; he said he hated horror shows.

3. Join the sentences with a comma and a coordinating conjunction *(and, but, or, nor, for, yet, so).*

Revision	Laura failed to set her alarm, *so* she was late for work.
Revision	Tyler watched the road carefully, *but* he still missed his turn.

4. Join the sentences with a semicolon and a conjunctive adverb (see pages 522–523).

fs cs

Revision   Laura failed to set her alarm; *consequently*, she was late for work.

Revision   Violets are blooming now; *in fact*, my yard is covered with them.

5. Introduce one of the sentences with a subordinating conjunction (see page 522).

Revision   *Because* Laura failed to set her alarm, she was late for work.

Revision   Janet worked on her term paper *while* her friend studied for a calculus test.

As our examples show, you can often correct an error in several ways.

CONNECTED DISCOURSE EXERCISE *Identify and correct the comma splices and fused sentences in the following letter.*

Dear Desperate:

We are sorry to hear that you are having difficulty paying your bill, it is, however, your responsibility. Unfortunately we have no way to prevent you from making overseas calls, you have to curb your own tendency to reach out and touch your friends. Following your instructions, we are sending a technician to remove your phone. Please be home this Friday morning he will arrive then. Even though we will remove your phone, you are still responsible for the unpaid portion of your bill, it is your financial obligation. We would dislike referring this matter to a collection agency, it could ruin your credit rating.

Sincerely,

Your friendly phone representative

fs cs

EXERCISE *Indicate whether each item is correct (C), is a fused sentence (FS), or contains a comma splice (CS), and then correct the faulty items.*

1. Lee is a difficult person he becomes angry whenever he doesn't get his own way.

2. The student appeared puzzled by the instructor's answer to his question, but he said nothing more.

3. The doctor warned Allan about his high cholesterol level, he went on a high-fibre diet.

4. Anisa researched her topic thoroughly and wrote her report carefully as a result she received an *A*.

5. It's nice to see you again; we should get together more often.

6. The horse stumbled and nearly fell in the backstretch, nevertheless it managed to finish second.

7. Janice thought the exercises would be easy, after finishing them she found that her whole body ached.

8. I've just started to take up chess, you can hardly expect me to play well.

CREATING SUBJECT–VERB AGREEMENT

A verb should agree in number with its subject. Singular subjects should have singular verbs, and plural subjects should have plural verbs.

> *Correct*   My *boss is* a grouch. (singular subject and verb)
>
> *Correct*   The *apartments have* two bedrooms. (plural subject and verb)

Ordinarily, matching subjects and verbs causes no problems. However, the following special situations can create difficulties.

Subject and Verb Separated by a Word Group   Sometimes a word group that includes one or more nouns comes between the subject and the verb. When this happens, match the verb with its subject, not a noun in the word group.

> *Correct*   Our *basket* of sandwiches *is* missing.
>
> *Correct*   Several *books* required for my paper *are* not in the library.
>
> *Correct*   *Mr. Schmidt*, along with his daughters, *runs* a furniture store.
>
> *Correct*   The old *bus*, crammed with passengers, *was* unable to reach the top of the hill.

Two Singular Subjects   Most singular subjects joined by *and* take a plural verb.

> *Correct*   The *couch* and *chair were* upholstered in blue velvet.

Sentences like the one above almost never cause problems. However, in sentences with subjects like *restoring cars* and *racing motorcycles,* singular verbs are often mistakenly used.

> *Faulty*   *Restoring cars* and *racing motorcycles consumes* most of Frank's time.
>
> *Revision*   *Restoring cars* and *racing motorcycles consume* most of Frank's time.

When *each* or *every* precedes the subjects, use a *singular* verb in place of a plural.

> *Correct*   Every *book* and *magazine was* badly water-stained.

Singular subjects joined by *or, either/or,* or *neither/nor* also take singular verbs.

> *Correct*   A *pear* or an *apple is* a good afternoon snack.
>
> *Correct*   Neither *rain* nor *snow slows* our letter carrier.

Finally, use a singular verb when two singular subjects joined by *and* name the same person, place, or thing.

> *Correct*   My cousin and business partner is retiring next month. (*Cousin* and *partner* refer to the same person.)

One Singular and One Plural Subject   When one singular subject and one plural subject are joined by *or, either/or,* or *neither/nor,* match the verb with the closer of the two.

> *Correct*   Neither *John* nor his *parents were* at home.
>
> *Correct*   Neither his *parents* nor *John was* at home.

sv agr

As these examples show, the sentences are usually smoother when the plural subject follows the singular.

Collective Nouns as Subjects   Collective nouns (*assembly, class, committee, family, herd, majority, tribe,* and the like) are singular in form but stand for groups or collections of people or things. Ordinarily, collective nouns are considered singular and therefore take singular verbs.

Correct	The *class is* writing a test.
Correct	The *herd was* clustered around the water hole.

Sometimes, though, a collective noun refers to the separate individuals making up the grouping, and then it requires a plural verb.

Correct	The *jury are* in dispute about the verdict.

Sentences in Which the Verb Comes Ahead of the Subject   The verb comes before the subject in sentences that begin with words such as *here, there, how, what,* and *where.* In such sentences, the verb must agree with the subject that follows it.

Correct	Here *is* my *house.*
Correct	Where *are* my *shoes?*
Correct	There *is* just one *way* to solve this problem.
Correct	There *go* my *chances* for a promotion.

sv agr

CONNECTED DISCOURSE EXERCISE *Identify and correct the subject–verb agreement errors in the following letter.*

Regional Accounts Manager:

One of your area phone representatives have seriously misread a letter I submitted with my bill. I refused to pay for long-distance overseas calls since neither I nor my roommate know anyone who lives overseas. Instead of deducting the calls from my bill, she sent someone to remove my phone. Now my phone, along with many of my valuable possessions, have been removed. Unfortunately the technician, whom I allowed into my apartment only after carefully checking his credentials, were a thief. He locked me in a closet and cleared out the apartment. I have contacted the police, but I also expect the phone company to reimburse me for my losses. There is only two choices. Either the stolen items or a cheque covering the loss need to be sent to me immediately. Otherwise I am afraid I will be forced to sue. A jury are sure to rule in my favour. In addition, I expect to find that those overseas calls has been deducted from my bill.

Sincerely,

Desperately Desperate

EXERCISE *Choose the correct verb form from the pair in parentheses.*

1. The pictures in the drawing room of the mansion (has, have) been insured for twelve million dollars.

2. Every dish and piece of stainless that I own (is, are) dirty.

3. Look! There (is, are) Kathy and her friend Sheeba.

4. Reading novels and watching TV (takes, take) up most of Stanley's time.

5. Each of these proposals (represents, represent) a great amount of work.

6. Two hamburgers or a hot beef sandwich (makes, make) an ample lunch.

7. (Has, Have) either of the orchids blossomed yet?

8. The automobile with the broken headlights and dented sides (was, were) stopped by the police.

ACHIEVING PRONOUN–ANTECEDENT AGREEMENT

pa agr

The antecedent of a pronoun is the noun or pronoun to which it refers. Just as verbs should agree with their subjects, pronouns should agree with their antecedents: Singular antecedents require singular pronouns, and plural antecedents require plural pronouns. Ordinarily, you will have no trouble matching antecedents and pronouns. The situations below, however, can cause problems.

Indefinite Pronouns as Antecedents   Indefinite pronouns include words such as *each, either, neither, any, everybody, somebody,* and *nobody.* Whenever an indefinite pronoun is used as an antecedent, the pronoun that refers to it should be singular.

> *Faulty*   *Neither* of the actors had learned *their* lines.
>
> *Revision*   *Neither* of the actors had learned *his* lines.

As the revised example shows, this rule applies even when the pronoun is followed by a plural noun.

When the gender of the antecedent is unknown, you may follow it with *his or her;* if this results in awkwardness, rewrite the sentence in the plural.

> *Correct*   *Anyone* who has studied *his or her* assignments properly should do well on the test.
>
> *Correct*   *Those* who have studied *their* assignments properly should do well on the test.

Occasionally, a ridiculous result occurs when a singular pronoun refers to an indefinite pronoun that is obviously plural in meaning. When this happens, rewrite the sentence to eliminate the problem.

> *Faulty*   *Everybody* complained that the graduation ceremony had lasted too long, but I didn't believe *him.*
>
> *Revision*   *Everybody* complained that the graduation ceremony had lasted too long, but I didn't agree.

Two Singular Antecedents   Two or more antecedents joined by *and* ordinarily call for a plural pronoun.

> *Correct*   Her briefcase and umbrella were missing from *their* usual place on the hall table.

When *each* or *every* precedes the antecedent, use a singular pronoun.

> *Correct*   Every college and university must do *its* best to provide adequate student counselling.

Singular antecedents joined by *or, either/or,* or *neither/nor* call for singular pronouns.

> *Correct*   Neither Carol nor Irene had paid *her* rent for the month.

Applying this rule can sometimes yield an awkward or foolish sentence. When this happens, rewrite the sentence to avoid the problem.

> *Faulty*   Neither James nor Breanne has finished *his* or *her* term project.
>
> *Revision*   James and Breanne have not finished *their* term projects.

Singular antecedents joined by *and* that refer to the same person, place, or thing use a singular pronoun.

> *Correct*   My *cousin* and *business partner* is retiring to *his* condo in Florida next month.

Singular and Plural Antecedents   If one singular and one plural antecedent are joined by *or, either/or,* or *neither/nor,* the pronoun agrees with the closer one.

> *Correct*   Either Terrence James or the Parkinsons will let us use *their* chainsaw.
>
> *Correct*   Either the Parkinsons or Terrence James will let us use *his* chainsaw.

Sentences of this sort are generally smoother when the plural subject follows the singular.

Collective Nouns as Antecedents   When a collective noun is considered a single unit, the pronoun that refers to it should be singular.

> *Correct*   The *troop* of scouts made *its* way slowly through the woods.

When the collective noun refers to the separate individuals in the group, use a plural pronoun.

> *Correct*   The *staff* lost *their* jobs when the company shut down.

pa agr

CONNECTED DISCOURSE EXERCISE *Identify and correct the pronoun–antecedent agreement errors in the following letter.*

Dear Desperately Desperate:

We were sorry to hear about the theft from your apartment. Apparently a gang of con artists recently had their base of operations in your city. It posed as repair technicians and presented false credentials to anyone expecting their phone to be repaired. Someone also must have intercepted your mail and written their own response since we have no record of any previous letter from you. Clearly neither the representative you mentioned nor the phony phone technician could have held their position with our company. Every one of our technicians must provide us with their fingerprints and take periodic lie detector tests. Further, none of our representatives will answer correspondence since it is not a part of their job description. For these reasons, we do not believe we are responsible for your losses. However, a review of our records shows that you owe $500; we have included a copy of the bill in case you have misplaced the original.

Sincerely,

Accounts Manager

EXERCISE *Choose the right pronoun from the pair in parentheses.*

1. If everybody does *(his or her, their)* part, the pageant should go smoothly.
2. Neither Greg nor the Snows had remembered to make *(his, their)* reservations at the ski lodge.
3. The graduating class filed by the principal and received *(its, their)* diplomas.
4. Each of the performers nervously waited *(his or her, their)* turn to audition.
5. Every boot and shoe I own needs to have *(its, their)* laces replaced.
6. Either Laurie or Alicia will show *(her, their)* slides at the party.
7. Dave and Bill loudly voiced *(his, their)* complaints about the restaurant's service.
8. Pleased with the performance, the audience showed *(its, their)* pleasure by applauding loudly.

pr ref

USING EFFECTIVE PRONOUN REFERENCE

Any pronoun except an indefinite pronoun should refer to just one noun or noun substitute—its antecedent. Reference problems result when the pronoun has two or more antecedents, a hidden antecedent, or no antecedent. These errors can cause mix-ups in meaning as well as ridiculous sentences.

More Than One Antecedent   The following sentences lack clarity because their pronouns have two possible antecedents rather than just one.

Faulty   Take the screens off the windows and wash *them*.

Faulty   Carter told Eli that *he* was putting on weight.

The reader can't tell whether the screens or the windows should be washed or who is putting on weight.

Sometimes we see a sentence like this one:

Faulty   If the boys don't eat all the Popsicles, put *them* in the freezer.

In this case, we know it's the Popsicles that should be stored, but the use of *them* creates an amusing sentence.

Correct these faults by replacing the pronoun with a noun or by rephrasing the sentence.

Revision   Wash the windows after you have taken off the screens.

Revision   Take off the screens so that you can wash the windows.

Revision   Carter told Eli, "I am (you are) putting on weight."

Revision   Put any uneaten Popsicles in the freezer.

Hidden Antecedent   An antecedent is hidden if it takes the form of an adjective rather than a noun.

Faulty   The movie theatre is closed today, so we can't see *one*.

Faulty   As I passed the tiger's cage, *it* lunged at me.

To correct this fault, replace the pronoun with the noun used as an adjective or switch the positions of the pronoun and the noun and make any needed changes in their forms.

Revision   The theatre is closed today, so we can't see a movie.

Revision   As I passed its cage, the tiger lunged at me.

No Antecedent   A no-antecedent sentence lacks any noun to which the pronoun can refer. Sentences of this sort occur frequently in everyday conversation but should be avoided in formal writing. The examples below illustrate this error.

Faulty   The lecture was boring, but *they* took notes anyway.

Faulty   On the news program, *it* told about another flood in Quebec.

To set matters right, substitute a suitable noun for the pronoun or reword the sentence.

Revision   The lecture was boring, but the students took notes anyway.

Revision   The news program told about another flood in Quebec.

Sometimes *this, that, it,* or *which* will refer to a whole idea rather than a single noun. This usage is acceptable provided the writer's meaning is obvious, as in this example:

Correct   The instructor spoke very softly, *which* meant we had difficulty hearing him.

However, problems occur when the reader can't figure out which of two or more ideas the pronoun refers to.

Faulty   Ginny called Mia two hours after the agreed-upon time and postponed their shopping trip one day. *This* irritated Mia very much.

What caused Mia to be irritated—the late call, the postponement of the trip, or both? Again, rewording or adding a clarifying word will correct the problem.

Revision   Ginny called Mia two hours after the agreed-upon time and postponed their shopping trip one day. This *tardiness* irritated Mia very much.

pr ref

Revision   Ginny called Mia two hours after the agreed-upon time and postponed their shopping trip one day. Ginny's *change of plans* irritated Mia very much.

The first of these examples illustrates the addition of a clarifying word; the second illustrates rewriting.

CONNECTED DISCOURSE EXERCISE *Identify and correct any faulty pronoun references in the following memorandum.*

TO: Director of Food Services, Groan University

FROM: Vice-President of Services

DATE: February 19, 2008

SUBJECT: Student Complaints about Cafeteria

Complaints about food quality and cafeteria hours are common but easily resolved. They can be extended by simply installing vending machines. It might not make for a nutritious meal, but it certainly will undercut some of the dissatisfaction. Of course, no matter how good the food, they will complain. Still, you can partially defuse those complaints by having students list their major concerns and then meeting them. Of course, you can always increase student satisfaction by purchasing a soft ice cream machine and offering it for dessert.

shft

EXERCISE *Indicate whether each sentence is correct (C) or contains a faulty pronoun reference (F) and then correct any faulty sentences.*

1. Ann told Jennifer that the boss wanted to see her.
2. Because the ring hurt her finger, Ruth took it off.
3. At the farmers market they sell many kinds of produce.
4. I like the food in Thai restaurants because it is very spicy.
5. They tell me that the company's profits have risen 5 percent this quarter.
6. Knowing that my friends like hot dogs, I grilled them at the picnic.
7. When Liam rose to make his speech, they all started laughing.
8. In the paper, it told about the province's budget surplus.

MANAGING SHIFTS IN PERSON

Pronouns can be in the first person, second person, or third person. *First-person* pronouns identify people who are talking or writing about themselves, *second-person* pronouns identify people being addressed directly, and *third-person* pronouns identify persons or things that are being written or spoken about. The following table sorts pronouns according to person.

First Person	Second Person	Third Person	
I	you	he	its
me	your	she	one
my	yours	it	they
mine	yourself	him	them
we	yourselves	his	their
us		her	theirs
our		hers	indefinite pronouns
ours			
ourselves			

All nouns are in the third person. As you revise, be alert for unwarranted shifts from one person to another.

Faulty	I liked *my* British vacation better than *my* vacation in Italy because *you* didn't have language problems.
Revision	I liked *my* British vacation better than *my* vacation in Italy because *I* didn't have language problems.
Faulty	Holidays are important to *everyone*. They boost *your* spirits and provide a break from *our* daily routine.
Revision	Holidays are important to *everyone*. They boost *one's* spirits and provide a break from *one's* daily routine.
Faulty	The taller the *golfer*, the more club speed *you* will have with a normally paced swing.
Revision	The taller the *golfer*, the more club speed *he* or *she* will have with a normally paced swing.

As these examples show, the shift can occur within a single sentence or when the writer moves from one sentence to another.

Some shifts in person, however, are warranted. Read the following correct sentence.

Correct	*I* want *you* to deliver these flowers to Ms. Willoughby by three o'clock. *She* needs them for a party.

Here the speaker identifies himself or herself (*I*) while speaking directly to a listener *(you)* about someone else *(she)*. In this case, shifts are needed to get the message across.

shft

CONNECTED DISCOURSE EXERCISE *Identify and correct the unwarranted shifts in person in the following paragraph.*

Good health is clearly important to you. But it is one's responsibility to ensure our own good health. You can start with simple exercises. We would like to provide you with a low-impact aerobics DVD for only $9. We guarantee that the more out of shape the customer, the quicker you will notice the benefits. The way our bodies feel affects the quality of one's lives. Let our tape help you to a better life.

EXERCISE *Indicate whether the sentence is correct (C) or contains an unwarranted shift in person (S). Correct faulty sentences.*

1. Because many of our tour guides spoke very poor English, the tourists soon became quite frustrated.

2. We like the location of our new house very much; you are close to a couple of large shopping centres.

3. If you want me to invite Gary to the party, I'll call him right now.

4. Be sure you tell the bakery clerk that we will need the cake by tomorrow noon.

5. If you complete a degree in vocational education, anyone can expect a rewarding career.

6. Once we learn to ride a bicycle, a person never forgets how.

7. Anyone wishing to make the trip to Kelowna should make your own hotel reservations.

8. After we had finished the test, the instructor told the students she would return it on Thursday.

USING THE RIGHT PRONOUN CASE

case

Case means the changes in form that a personal pronoun (see page 487) undergoes to show its function in a sentence. English has three cases: the *subjective*, the *objective* (nonsubjective), and the *possessive*. The following chart shows the different forms.

Subjective Form	Objective Form	Possessive Form
I	me	my, mine
he	him	his
she	her	her, hers
we	us	our, ours
you	you	your, yours
they	them	their, theirs
who	whom	whose

The subjective case is used for subjects and subject complements, and the objective case is used for direct objects, indirect objects, and objects of prepositions. The possessive case shows ownership and is also used with gerunds.

The following pointers will help you select the proper pronoun as you revise.

We and Us Preceding Nouns   Nouns that serve as subjects take the pronoun *we*. Other nouns take the pronoun *us*.

Correct   *We* tourists will fly home tomorrow. (*We* accompanies the subject.)

Correct   The guide showed *us* tourists through the cathedral.
(*Us* accompanies an object.)

If you can't decide which pronoun is right, mentally omit the noun and read the sentence to yourself, first with one pronoun and then with the other. Your ear will identify the correct form.

My mother made *(we, us)* children vanilla pudding for dessert.

Omitting *children* shows immediately that *us* is the right choice.

> *Correct*　　My mother made *us* children vanilla pudding for dessert.

Pronouns Paired with Nouns　　When such a combination serves as the subject of a sentence or accompanies the subject, use the subject form of the pronoun. When the combination plays an object role, use the object form of the pronoun.

> *Correct*　　Arlene and *I* plan to join Katimavik. (*I* is part of the compound subject.)
>
> *Correct*　　Two people, Claire and *I*, will represent our school at the meeting. (*I* is part of a compound element accompanying the subject.)
>
> *Correct*　　The superintendent told Kevin and *him* that they would be promoted soon. (*Him* is part of a compound object.)
>
> *Correct*　　The project was difficult for Jeffrey and *him* to complete. (*Him* is part of a compound object.)

Again, mentally omitting the noun from the combination will tell you which pronoun is correct.

Who and Whom in Dependent Clauses　　Use *who* for the subjects of dependent clauses; otherwise use *whom*.

> *Correct*　　The Mallarys prefer friends *who are interested in the theatre.* (*Who* is the subject of the clause.)
>
> *Correct*　　Barton is a man *whom very few people like.* (*Whom* is not the subject of the clause but the object of the verb *like*.)

A simple test will help you decide between *who* and *whom*. First, mentally isolate the dependent clause. Next, block out the pronoun in question and insert *he* (or *she*), and then *him* (or *her*) at the appropriate spot in the remaining part of the clause. If *he* (or *she*) sounds better, *who* is right. If *him* (or *her*) sounds better, *whom* is right. Let's use this test on the sentence below.

> The woman who (m) Scott is dating works as a mechanical engineer. Scott is dating (she, her.)

Clearly *her* is correct; therefore, *whom* is the proper form.

> *Correct*　　The woman *whom* Scott is dating works as a mechanical engineer.

Pronouns as Subject Complements　　In formal writing, pronouns that serve as subject complements (see page 483) always take the subject form.

> *Correct*　　It is *I*.
>
> *Correct*　　It was *she* who bought the old Parker mansion.

However, this rule is often ignored in informal writing or casual speech.

> It's *her*.
>
> That's *him* standing over by the door.

case

Comparisons Using *Than* or *As . . . As*   Comparisons of this kind often make no direct statement about the second item of comparison. When the second naming word is a pronoun, you may have trouble choosing the right one.

> Harriet is less outgoing than (*they, them*).

> My parents' divorce saddened my sister as much as *(I, me)*.

Not to worry. Expand the sentence by mentally supplying the missing material. Then try the sentence with each pronoun and see which sounds right.

> Hannah is less outgoing than *(they, them)* are.

> My parents' divorce saddened my sister as much as it did *(I, me)*.

Obviously *they* is the right choice for the first sentence, and *me* is the right choice for the second one.

> *Correct*   Hannah is less outgoing than *they* are.

> *Correct*   My parents' divorce saddened my sister as much as it did *me*.

Pronouns Preceding Gerunds   Use the possessive form of a pronoun that precedes a gerund (see page 525).

> I dislike *their* leaving without saying goodbye.

> Ted can't understand *her* quitting such a good job.

This usage emphasizes the action named by the gerund instead of the person or persons performing it. Thus, in the above sentences, the possessive form of the pronoun signals that it's the *leaving* the writer dislikes and the *quitting* that Ted can't understand. The people involved are secondary.

When the pronoun precedes a participle (see pages 524–525), it should be in the objective case. The emphasis is then on the actor rather than the action.

> Jennifer caught *them* listening to CDs instead of studying.

In this example, Jennifer caught the listeners, not the listening.

If you have trouble deciding between the objective and possessive forms of a pronoun, ask yourself whether you want to emphasize the action or the actor; then proceed accordingly.

CONNECTED DISCOURSE EXERCISE   *Identify and correct the pronoun case errors in the following paragraph.*

Between my brother and I, we are always able to pull at least five good-sized trout a day from the creek behind our house. Us rural trout fishermen just seem to have the knack. Of course, those city fishermen whom insist on employing artificial flies won't appreciate our methods even if they can't do as well as us. We just let our bait, usually a juicy worm, float downstream to the waiting trout. Of course, my brother won't let the fishing interfere with him sleeping. In fact, it was him that developed the idea of looping the line around his toe so that he would wake up when a trout took the bait. Others have told my brother and I that this method is dangerous, but neither of us has lost a toe yet. Of course, the people who we invite to dinner don't complain about our methods, and they seem to enjoy the fish.

EXERCISE *Choose the right form of the pronoun for each of the following sentences.*

1. Cherie is the one student *(who, whom)* I believe has the potential to become a professional acrobat.
2. Two students, Carrie and *(I, me)*, scored 100 on the calculus test.
3. *(We, Us)* Greens pride ourselves on our beautiful lawns.
4. Ken Conwell is the only candidate *(who, whom)* I like in this election.
5. Brandon has richer friends than *(I, me)*.
6. The friendly student told *(we, us)* visitors that we were in the wrong building.
7. As children, Mason and *(I, me)* used to play Lego games.
8. My uncle has given Sandra and *(I, me)* tickets for tonight's Bach concert.

CREATING CONSISTENCY IN SHOWING TIME

time

Inconsistencies occur when a writer shifts from the past tense to the present or vice versa without a corresponding shift in the time of the events being described. The following paragraph contains an uncalled-for shift from the present tense to the past:

> As *The Most Dangerous Game* opens, Sanger Rainsford, a famous hunter and author, and his old friend Whitney are standing on the deck of a yacht and discussing a mysterious island as the ship passes near it. Then, after everyone else has gone to bed, Rainsford manages to fall overboard. He swims to the island and ends up at a chateau owned by General Zaroff, a refugee from the Communist takeover in Russia. Zaroff, bored with hunting animals, has turned to hunting humans on his desert island. Inevitably, Rainsford is turned out into the jungle to be hunted down. There were [shift to past tense] actually four hunts over a three-day period, and at the end of the last one, Rainsford jumped into the sea, swam across a cove to the chateau, and killed Zaroff in the general's own bedroom. Afterwards he sleeps [shift back to present tense] and decides "he had never slept in a better bed."

The sentence with the unwarranted shift in tense should read as follows:

> There are actually four hunts over a three-day period, and at the end of the last one, Rainsford jumps into the sea, swims across a cove to the chateau, and kills Zaroff in the general's own bedroom.

The time shift in the part of the final sentence in quotations is justified because the sleeping has occurred before Rainsford's thoughts about it.

A second kind of inconsistency results when a writer fails to distinguish the immediate past from the less immediate past. The following sentence illustrates this error.

Faulty   Emily *answered* all 30 test questions when the class ended.

This sentence states that Emily completed all 30 test questions during the final instant of the class. This is impossible. When you detect this type of error in your writing, determine which action occurred first and then correct the error by adding *had* to the verb. In this case, the first verb needs correcting.

Revision   Emily *had answered* all 30 test questions when the class ended.

Besides adding *had*, you may sometimes need to alter the verb form.

Faulty   Before he turned 20, John *wrote* two novels.

Revision   Before he turned 20, John *had written* two novels.

CONNECTED DISCOURSE EXERCISE *Identify and correct any inconsistencies in showing time through unwarranted and confusing shifts in verb tense.*

There is no better time to go swimming than at night. The summer after I had graduated from high school, I worked for a landscaping company. After a sweaty day mowing lawns and digging up gardens, all of us who worked there would jump into the back of Ryan's old pickup and rattle out to Woods Lake. It is just dark as we arrive. The moon is beautiful, reflected in that black mirror set in a frame of hills. We stumble down a small, sandy hill to the beach, where we strip off our dusty jeans and sweaty shirts before plunging into the cool reflection of stars.

*mis
adj/
adv*

EXERCISE *Indicate whether each sentence is correct (C) or contains an unwarranted shift (S) in tense. Correct the faulty sentences.*

1. Although the alarm rang, Owen continues to lie in bed.
2. When autumn arrives, we often go for long walks in the woods.
3. When the trapeze artist fell into the net, the audience gasps loudly.
4. When I baked the cake, I ate a slice.
5. Levi walks for half an hour before he ate dinner.
6. Sarah had many friends but sees them infrequently.
7. As Elaine walked toward the garden, a rabbit scampers quickly away.

USING ADJECTIVES AND ADVERBS EFFECTIVELY

Beginning writers often use adjectives when they should use adverbs, and they also often confuse the comparative and superlative forms of these parts of speech when making comparisons.

Misusing Adjectives as Adverbs   Although most adjectives can be misused as adverbs, the following five, listed with the corresponding adverbs, cause the most difficulty.

Adjectives	**Adverbs**
bad	badly
good	well
most	almost
real	really
sure	surely

The following sentences show typical errors.

Faulty   Bryan did *good* in his first golf lesson. (*good* mistakenly used to modify verb *did*)

Faulty   *Most* every graduate from our auto service program receives several job offers. (*most* mistakenly used to modify adjective *every*)

Faulty   The speech was delivered *real* well. (*real* mistakenly used to modify adverb *well*)

Because adverbs modify verbs, adjectives, and other adverbs (see pages 498–500), and adjectives modify nouns and noun substitutes (see pages 496–498), the above sentences clearly require adverbs.

Revision   Bryan did *well* in his first golf lesson.

Revision   *Almost* every graduate from our auto service program receives several job offers.

Revision   The speech was delivered *really* well.

If you can't decide whether a sentence requires an adjective or an adverb, determine the part of speech of the word being modified and proceed accordingly.

Confusing the Comparative and Superlative Forms in Comparisons   The comparative form of adjectives and adverbs is used to compare two things, the superlative form to compare three or more things. Adjectives with fewer than three syllables generally add -*er* to make the comparative form and -*est* to make the superlative form (tall, tall*er*, tall*est*). Adjectives with three or more syllables generally add *more* to make the comparative and *most* to make the superlative (enchanting, *more* enchanting, *most* enchanting), as do most adverbs of two or more syllables (loudly, *more* loudly, *most* loudly).

When making comparisons, beginning writers sometimes mistakenly use double comparatives or double superlatives.

Faulty   Jacob is *more taller* than James. (double comparative)

Faulty   The Shrangri-La Hotel has the *most splendidest* lobby I've ever seen. (double superlative)

mis
adj/
adv

The correct versions read as follows:

> *Revision*   Jacob is *taller* than James.
>
> *Revision*   The Shrangri-La Hotel has the *most splendid* lobby I've ever seen.

In addition, writers may erroneously use the superlative form, rather than the comparative form, to compare two things.

> *Faulty*   Barry is the *richest* of the two brothers.
>
> *Faulty*   Jeremy is the *most talented* of those two singers.

Here are the sentences correctly written:

> *Revision*   Barry is the *richer* of the two brothers.
>
> *Revision*   Jeremy is the *more talented* of those two singers.

Reserve the superlative form for comparing three or more items.

> *Correct*   Barry is the *richest* of the three brothers.
>
> *Correct*   Jeremy is the *most talented* of those four singers.

---

*mis
adj /
adv*

CONNECTED DISCOURSE EXERCISE *Identify and correct the adjective–adverb errors in the following paragraph.*

This year our football team is outstanding. Spike Jones, our quarterback, has been playing real good this past season. Stan Blunder, the most talented of our two ends, hasn't dropped a pass all season. The team can most always count on Stan to catch the crucial first-down pass. Of course, the team wouldn't be where it is today without John Schoolyard's good coaching. He has made this team much more better than it was a year ago. Only the kicking team has done bad this season. Of course, with this most wonderfulest offence, the defensive players haven't got much practice. The good news is, then, that we can sure expect to watch some terrific university football for years to come.

EXERCISE *For each of the following sentences, choose the proper word from the pair in parentheses.*

1. A person can become *(stronger, more stronger)* by lifting weights.
2. Canvasback Dunn is clearly the *(less, least)* formidable of the two main challengers for Killer McGurk's boxing crown.
3. Diane did *(good, well)* on her chemistry test.
4. Carol wore the *(silliest, most silliest)* hat I've ever seen to the masquerade party.
5. Don was hurt *(bad, badly)* in the auto accident.
6. Brad was the *(funniest, most funniest)* of all the performers at the comedy club.
7. Clear Lake is the *(deeper, deepest)* of the three lakes in our county.

POSITIONING OF MOVABLE MODIFIERS

Movable modifiers can appear on either side of the main statement or within it.

Modifiers after Main Statement   Sentences that follow this arrangement, frequently called *loose* sentences, occur more commonly than either of the others. They mirror conversation, in which a speaker first makes a statement and then adds further thoughts. Often, the main statement has just one modifier.

> Our company will have to file for bankruptcy *because of this year's huge losses.* (phrase as modifier)

Or the main statement can be followed by a series of modifiers.

> He burst suddenly into the party, *loud, angry, obscene.* (words as modifiers)

> The family used to gather around the hearth, *doing such chores as polishing shoes, mending ripped clothing, reading, chatting, always warmed by one another's presence as much as by the flames.* (words and phrases as modifiers)

> Zoey stared in disbelief, and then she smiled, *slowly, tremulously, as if she couldn't believe her good fortune.* (words and clause as modifiers)

> There are three essential qualities for buzzard country: *a rich supply of unburied corpses, high mountains, a strong sun.* (noun-base groups as modifiers)
>
> John D. Stewart, "Vulture Country"

A sentence may contain several layers of modifiers. In the following example, we've indented and numbered to show the different layers.

1. The men struggled to the top of the hill,
  2. thirsty,
  2. drenched in sweat,
  2. and cursing in pain
    3. as their knapsack straps cut into their raw, chafed shoulders
      4. with every step.

In this sentence, the items numbered 2 refer to *men* in the item numbered 1. Item 3 is linked to *cursing* in the preceding item 2, and item 4 is linked to *cut* in item 3.

The modifiers-last arrangement works well for injecting descriptive details into narratives and also for qualifying, explaining, and presenting lists in other kinds of writing.

Modifiers before Main Statement   Sentences that delay the main point until the end are called *periodic.* In contrast to loose sentences, periodic sentences lend a formal note to what is said, slowing its pace, adding cadence, and making it more serious.

> *If you can keep your head when everyone around you is panicking,* you can probably survive the situation. (clauses as modifiers)

> *From the outset of his journey to the heart of darkness,* Marlow witnesses many incidents that reveal the human capacity for evil. (phrases as modifiers)

> *The danger of sideswiping another vehicle, the knowledge that a hidden bump or hole could throw me from the dune buggy,* both of these things added to the thrill of the race. (noun plus phrase and noun plus clause as modifiers)

mm

When so many of our students admit to cheating, when so many professors practise grade inflation, and when administrators fail to face up to these problems, our schools are in serious trouble. (clauses as modifiers)

1.   *When the public protests,*
2.   *confronted with some obvious evidence of the damaging results of pesticide applications,* it is fed little tranquilizing pills of half truth. (clause and phrase as modifiers)

Rachel Carson, *Silent Spring*

As shown in the preceding examples, periodic sentences can also have layers of modifiers.

Positioning the modifiers before the main point throws the emphasis on the end of the sentence, adding force to the main point. The delay also lets the writer create sentences that, as in the first example, carry stings, ironic or humorous, in their tails.

Modifiers within Main Statement   Inserting one or more modifiers into a main statement creates a sentence with *interrupted order.* The material may come between the subject and the verb or between the verb and the rest of the predicate.

The young girl, *wearing a tattered dress and looking anything but well-off herself,* gave the beggar a 20-dollar bill. (phrases between subject and verb)

Dewey declared, *with a cheery flourish of his ticket,* that the concert was the best he'd ever heard. (phrase between verb and rest of predicate)

The bedsprings, *bent and rusted, festooned with spiderwebs,* lay on top of the heap. (words and phrase between subject and verb)

The evolutionists, *piercing beneath the show of momentary stability,* discovered, *hidden in rudimentary organs,* the discarded rubbish of the past. (one phrase between subject and verb, another between verb and rest of predicate)

By stretching out the main idea, the inserted modifiers in these sentences slow the forward pace, creating a more formal tone.

PLACING MODIFIERS CORRECTLY

A misplaced modifier is a word or word group that is improperly separated from the word it modifies. When separation of this type occurs, the sentence often sounds awkward, ridiculous, or confusing.

Usually, you can correct this error by moving the modifier next to the word it is intended to modify. Occasionally, you'll also need to alter some of the phrasing.

Faulty	There is a bicycle in the basement *with chrome fenders.* (The basement appears to have chrome fenders.)
Faulty	David received a phone call from his uncle *that infuriated him.* (The uncle appears to have infuriated David.)
Revision	There is a bicycle *with chrome fenders* in the basement.
Revision	David received an *infuriating* phone call from his uncle. (Note the change in wording.)

When shifting the modifier, don't inadvertently create another faulty sentence.

> *Faulty*   Fritz bought a magazine with an article about Taylor Swift *at the corner newsstand*. (The article appears to tell about Swift's visit to the corner newsstand.)
>
> *Faulty*   Fritz bought a magazine *at the corner newsstand* with an article about Taylor Swift. (The corner newsstand appears to have an article about Swift.)
>
> *Revision*   *At the corner newsstand*, Fritz bought a magazine with an article about Taylor Swift.

As you revise, watch also for *squinting modifiers*—that is, modifiers positioned so that the reader doesn't know whether they are supposed to modify what comes ahead of them or what follows them.

> *Faulty*   The man who was rowing the boat *frantically* waved toward the onlookers on the beach.

Is the man rowing frantically or waving frantically? Correct this kind of error by repositioning the modifier so that the ambiguity disappears.

> *Revision*   The man who was *frantically* rowing the boat waved toward the onlookers on the beach.
>
> *Revision*   The man who was rowing the boat waved *frantically* toward the onlookers on the beach.

dm

EXERCISE *Indicate whether each sentence is correct (C) or contains a misplaced modifier (MM). Correct faulty sentences.*

1. The boss asked me after lunch to type a special report.
2. Brenda returned the cottage cheese to the store that had spoiled.
3. The hikers tramped through the woods wearing heavy boots.
4. Mark mailed a package to his friend sealed with masking tape.
5. The woman packing her suitcase hastily glanced out the window at the commotion in the yard.
6. We bought a dictionary that was bound in leather at the local bookstore.
7. Jerry bought an Inuit carving for his bedroom in Regina.

REVISING DANGLING MODIFIERS

A dangling modifier is a phrase or clause that lacks clear connection to the word or words it is intended to modify. As a result, sentences are inaccurate, often comical. Typically, the modifier leads off the sentence, although it can also come at the end.

Sometimes the error occurs because the sentence fails to specify who or what is modified. At other times, the separation is too great between the modifier and what it modifies.

> *Faulty*   *Walking in the meadow,* wildflowers surrounded us. (The wildflowers appear to be walking in the meadow.)
>
> *Faulty*   Dinner was served *after saying grace.* (The dinner appears to have said grace.)
>
> *Faulty*   *Fatigued by the violent exercise,* the cool shower was very relaxing. (The cool shower appears to have been fatigued.)

These sentences are faulty because they do not identify who walked, said grace, or found the shower relaxing.

You can correct dangling modifiers in two basic ways. First, leave the modifier unchanged and rewrite the main part of the sentence so that it begins with the term actually modified. Second, rewrite the modifier so that it has its own subject and verb, thereby eliminating the inaccuracy.

> *Revision*   *Walking in the meadow,* we were surrounded by wildflowers. (The main part of the sentence has been rewritten.)
>
> *Revision*   *As we walked in the meadow,* wildflowers surrounded us. (The modifier has been rewritten.)
>
> *Revision*   Dinner was served *after we had said grace.* (The modifier has been rewritten.)
>
> *Revision*   *Fatigued by the violent exercise,* Ted found the cool shower very relaxing. (The main part of the sentence has been rewritten.)
>
> *Revision*   *Because Ted was fatigued by the violent exercise,* the cool shower was very relaxing. (The modifier has been rewritten.)

Ordinarily, either part of the sentence can be rewritten, but sometimes only one part can.

EXERCISE *Indicate whether each sentence is correct (C) or contains a dangling modifier (DM). Correct faulty sentences.*

1. Dancing at the wedding reception, my feet hurt.
2. Working in the yard, Pete was drenched by the sudden cloudburst.
3. Looking out the window, a velvety lawn ran down to the river's edge.
4. Having mangy fur, our parents wouldn't let us keep the stray cat.
5. Reminiscing about my school days, a run-in with my principal came to mind.
6. Unaware of what had happened, the confusion puzzled Nan.
7. At the age of eight, my father wrote a bestselling novel.

USING PARALLELISM

Parallelism presents equivalent ideas in grammatically equivalent form. Dressing them in the same grammatical garb calls attention to their kinship and adds smoothness and polish. The following sentence pairs demonstrate the improvement that parallelism brings.

Non-parallel	James's outfit was wrinkled, mismatched, and *he needed to wash it*. (words and independent clause)
Parallel	James's outfit was wrinkled, mismatched, and *dirty*. (words)
Non-parallel	Lucas likes reading books, attending plays, and *to search for antiques*. (different kinds of phrases)
Parallel	Lucas likes reading books, attending plays, and *searching for antiques*. (same kind of phrases)
Non-parallel	Beth performs her tasks quickly, willingly, and *with accuracy*. (words and phrase)
Parallel	Beth performs her tasks quickly, willingly, and *accurately*. (words)
Non-parallel	The instructor complimented me for taking part in class discussions and *because I had written a superb theme*. (phrase and clause)
Parallel	The instructor complimented me for taking part in class discussions and *for writing a superb theme*. (phrases)

As the examples show, revising non-parallel sentences smoothes out bumpiness, binds the ideas together more closely, and allows for faster comprehension.

Parallelism doesn't always stop with a single sentence. Writers sometimes use it in a series of sentences:

> He had never lost his childlike innocence. He had never lost his sense of wonder. He had never lost his sense of joy in nature's simplest gifts.

For an example of parallelism that extends over much of a paragraph, see page 945 (Chapter 5, excerpt from "What Is Poverty?").

Repeating a structure through several sentences of a paragraph adds intensity to meaning and rhythm to the prose. Balance, a special form of parallelism, positions two grammatically equivalent ideas on opposite sides of some pivot point, such as a word or punctuation mark.

> Hope for the best, and prepare for the worst.

> Many are called, but few are chosen.

> When I'm right, nobody ever remembers; when I'm wrong, nobody ever forgets.

Like regular parallel sentences, balanced sentences sometimes come in series. Balanced sentences can be especially resonant in speeches.

> We want to live in a country in which French Canadians can choose to live among English Canadians and English Canadians can choose to live among French Canadians without abandoning their cultural heritage.
>
> Pierre Elliott Trudeau, "Statement on Introduction of the Official Languages Bill"

Balance works especially well for pitting contrasting ideas against each other. It sharpens the difference between them while achieving compactness and lending an air of insight to what is said.

MAINTAINING PARALLELISM

Non-parallelism results when equivalent ideas follow different grammatical forms. One common kind of non-parallelism occurs with words or word groups in pairs or in a series.

Faulty	Althea enjoys *jogging, to bike,* and *to swim.*
Faulty	The superintendent praised the workers *for their productivity* and *because they had an excellent safety record.*
Faulty	The banner was *old, faded,* and *it had a rip.*

Note how rewriting the sentences in parallel form improves their smoothness.

Revision	Althea enjoys *jogging, biking,* and *swimming.*
Revision	The superintendent praised the workers *for their productivity* and *their excellent safety record.*
Revision	The banner was *old, faded,* and *ripped.*

Non-parallelism also occurs when correlative conjunctions *(either/or, neither/nor, both/and,* and *not only/but also)* are followed by unlike elements.

Faulty	That sound *either* was a thunderclap *or* an explosion.
Faulty	The basement was *not only* poorly lit *but also* it had a foul smell.

Ordinarily, repositioning one of the correlative conjunctions will solve the problem. Sometimes, however, one of the grammatical elements must be rewritten.

Revision	That sound was *either* a thunderclap *or* an explosion. (*Either* has been repositioned.)
Revision	The basement was *not only* poorly lit *but also* foul smelling. (The element following *but also* has been rewritten.)

EXERCISE *Indicate whether each sentence is correct (C) or non-parallel (NP). Correct faulty sentences.*

1. The lemonade was cold, tangy, and refreshing.
2. Although he had practised for several days, the scout could neither tie a square knot nor a bowline.
3. This job will involve waiting on customers, and you will need to maintain our inventory.
4. My summer job at a provincial park gave me experience in repairing buildings, the operation of heavy equipment, and assisting park visitors.
5. To maintain his rose bushes properly, Sam fertilizes, sprays, prunes, and waters them according to a strict schedule.
6. Once out of high school, Kylie plans either to join the navy or the air force.
7. My favourite sports are swimming, golfing, and to bowl.
8. Janice's leisure activities include collecting coins, reading, and she also watches TV.

REVISING FAULTY COMPARISONS

A faulty comparison results if you (1) mention one of the items being compared but not the other, (2) omit words needed to clarify the relationship, or (3) compare different sorts of items. Advertisers often offend in the first way.

> *Faulty*   Irish tape has better adhesion.

With what other tape is Irish tape being compared? Scotch tape? All other transparent tape? Mentioning the second term of a comparison eliminates reader guesswork.

> *Revision*   Irish tape has better adhesion than any other transparent tape.

Two clarifying words, *other* and *else*, are frequently omitted from comparisons, creating illogical sentences.

> *Faulty*   Sergeant McNabb is more conscientious than any officer in his precinct.
>
> *Faulty*   Stretch French is taller than anyone on his basketball team.

The first sentence is illogical because McNabb is one of the officers in his precinct and therefore cannot be more conscientious than himself. Similarly, because French is a member of his basketball team, he can't be taller than anyone on his team. Adding *other* to the first sentence and *else* to the second corrects matters.

> *Revision*   Sergeant McNabb is more conscientious than any *other* officer in his precinct.
>
> *Revision*   Stretch French is taller than anyone *else* on his basketball team.

Comparing unlike items is perhaps the most common kind of comparison error. Here are two examples:

> *Faulty*   The cities in Ontario are larger than Nova Scotia.
>
> *Faulty*   The cover of this book is much more durable than the other book.

The first sentence compares the cities of Ontario with a province, while the second compares the cover of a book with a whole book. Correction consists of rewriting each sentence so that it compares like items.

> *Revision*   The cities in Ontario are larger than those in Nova Scotia.
>
> *Revision*   The cover of this book is much more durable than *that of* the other book.

comp

CONNECTED DISCOURSE EXERCISE *Identify and correct the misplaced modifiers, dangling modifiers, non-parallelism, and faulty comparisons in the following memorandum.*

TO: All Residency Hall Advisors in Knuckles Hall

FROM: John Knells, Residence Hall Director

DATE: March 13, 2008

SUBJECT: Noise in Residence Hall

Recently I received a report from a student that deeply disturbed me. Apparently, after quiet hours students still have visitors in their rooms, are playing their stereos loudly, and are even staging boxing matches in the halls. The student who wrote me desperately tries to study. However, he is often forced to leave his room disturbed by the noise. He was not the only one to complain. You should know that we have had more complaints about Knuckles Hall than any residence on campus. Since discussing this problem with you at the last staff meeting, things haven't seemed to get any better. The rules are not only poorly enforced but also they are completely ignored. Your job performance is worse than the students. If you don't improve immediately, I will be forced to dismiss you.

comp

EXERCISE *Indicate whether each sentence is correct (C) or contains a faulty comparison (FC). Correct any faulty comparison.*

1. The houses on Parkdale Street are more modest than Windsor Terrace.
2. Maxine has more seniority than any other member of her department.
3. The finish on the dresser is not as smooth as the end table.
4. In contrast to your yard, I have an underground sprinkling system.
5. My mother's homemade jam has more flavour than any jam I've eaten.
6. The dresses sold at The Bay are much less expensive than the Tres Chic Shoppe.
7. The paint on the front of the house is much lighter than the back.

Punctuation marks are cues to readers that indicate how one part of the sentence is related to a different sentence element. These marks help clarify the meaning of written material. Similarly, a knowledge of mechanics—capitalization, abbreviations, numbers, and italics—helps you avoid confusing the reader with distracting inconsistencies or confusing signals.

This part of the Handbook covers some of the fundamentals of punctuation and mechanics.

APOSTROPHES

Apostrophes (') show possession, mark contractions, and occasionally indicate plurals singled out for special attention.

Possession Possessive apostrophes usually show ownership *(Mary's cat)*. Sometimes they identify the works of creative people *(Hemingway's novels)* or indicate an extent of time or distance *(one hour's time, one metre's distance)*.

The possessive form is easily recognized because it can be converted to a prepositional phrase beginning with *of.*

The collar of the dog (the dog's collar)

The whistle of the wind (the wind's whistle)

The intention of the corporation (the corporation's intention)

Possessive apostrophes are used with nouns and with pronouns such as *someone, no one, everybody, each other,* and *one another.* To show possession with these pronouns, with singular nouns, and with plural nouns that do not end in an *s,* add an apostrophe followed by an *s.*

Someone's car is blocking our driveway. (possessive of pronoun *someone*)

The *manager's* reorganization plan will take effect next week. (possessive of singular noun *manager*)

The *women's* lounge is being redecorated. (possessive of plural noun *women*)

Sentences that make comparisons sometimes include two possessives, the second coming at the very end. In such cases, be sure to use an apostrophe with the second possessive as well.

York's football team is much better than *Toronto's.*

With singular nouns that end in *s,* some people form the possessive merely by adding an apostrophe *(James' helmet)*. However, the preferred usage is to add another *s* to singular words that end in *s (James's helmet)* unless the additional *s* would make pronunciation awkward.

Charles's dog was afraid of the water. (awkward pronunciation of *Charles's*)

Charles' dog was afraid of the water. (non-awkward pronunciation of *Charles'*)

Plural nouns ending in *s* form the possessive by adding only an apostrophe at the end.

> All the *ladies'* coats are on sale today. (possessive of plural noun *ladies*)
>
> The *workers'* lockers were moved. (possessive of plural noun *workers*)

To show joint ownership by two or more persons, use the possessive form for the last-named person only. To show individual ownership, use the possessive form for each person's name.

> *Ronald and Joan's* boat badly needed overhauling. (joint ownership)
>
> *Laura's* and *Alice's* term projects are almost completed. (individual ownership)

Hyphenated nouns form the possessive by adding *'s* to the last word.

> My *mother-in-law's* house is next to mine.

Never use an apostrophe with the possessive pronouns *his, hers, whose, its, ours, yours,* or *theirs.*

> This desk is *his;* the other one is *hers.* (no apostrophes needed)

Contractions   Contractions of words or numbers omit one or more letters or numerals. An apostrophe shows exactly where the omission occurs.

> *Wasn't* that a disappointing concert? (contraction of *was not*)
>
> Around here, people still talk about the ice storm of *'98.* (contraction of *1998*)

Many people confuse the contraction *it's,* meaning *it is* or *it has,* with the possessive pronoun *its,* which should never have an apostrophe. If you're puzzled by an *its* that you've written, try this test. Expand the *its* to *it is* or *it has* and see whether the sentence still makes sense. If it does, the *its* is a contraction and needs the apostrophe. If the result is nonsense, the *its* is a possessive pronoun and does not get an apostrophe. Here are some examples:

> *Its* muggy today. Test: Expand *its* to *it is.*
>
> *It is* awfully muggy today. Correct: It's muggy today.
>
> *Its* been an exciting trip. Test: Expand *its* to *it is* or *it has.*

This sentence makes sense when the *its* is expanded to *it has.*

> *It has* been an exciting trip. Correct: It's been an exciting trip.
>
> Every dog has *its* day. Test: Expand *its* to *it is* or *it has.*

This last sentence, however, turns into nonsense when *its* is expanded.

> Every dog has *it is* day.
>
> Every dog has *it has* day.

In this case, *its* is a possessive pronoun and requires no apostrophe.

> Correct: Every dog has *its* day.

Plurals   Most nouns are made plural simply by adding *s* (for example, pen**s**, note-books, holiday**s**), but sometimes the spelling changes for nouns in the plural form. You probably know that common singular nouns such as man, woman, child, and person become men, women, children, and people in the plural form. For some other irregular plurals, the spelling changes in the plural form.

For nouns that end in *ch, s, sh, x* or *z*, the plural is formed by adding *es* (branch**es**, bus**es**, dish**es**, box**es**, buzz**es**). Some nouns that end in *o* (tomato, volcano) add *es* in the plural form; if there is more than one tomato, the spelling changes, and the plural form is tomato**es**. Some words that end in *fe* (life, knife) change the *fe* to *ves* in the plural form (li**ves**, kni**ves**), while a few words that end in *f* (half, wolf) change the spelling in the plural form (hal**ves**, wol**ves**).

If you are unsure of the plural form of a noun, you can consult an online dictionary.

In some situations, if there is a potential for confusion, such as with letters, numbers, symbols, and words being singled out for special attention, the plural is written with apostrophes.

Mind your *p's* and *q's*. (plurals of letters)

Your *5's* and *6's* are hard to tell apart. (plurals of numbers)

The formula was sprinkled with *¶'s* and *β's*. (plurals of symbols)

Don't use so many *however's* and *therefore's* in your writing. (plurals of words)

While apostrophes are sometimes used to form plurals for these few exceptions as well as for the plural form of abbreviations (the plural form of CD, an abbreviation for compact discs, can be either *CD's* or *CDs*), note that the apostrophe has a meaning. With nouns, it usually indicates possession, not that there is a plural. It is not used arbitrarily just because there is an *s* in the word.

If you are unsure of how to form the plural of a noun, check with an online dictionary.

EXERCISE *Supply apostrophes where necessary to correct the following sentences:*

1. This years winter promises to be significantly more severe than last years.
2. Everyones office will be furnished with the newest ergonomic chairs and workspaces.
3. Were attempting to determine how our students needs can best be met.
4. Somebodys purse was left in Dean Smiths office.
5. Cindys computer program was much more efficient than her peers programs.
6. There are two *Rs* and two *Ss* in the word "embarrassment."
7. Lets determine what caused the schools mainframe computer to fail before we panic.

CONNECTED DISCOURSE EXERCISE *Supply, delete, or relocate apostrophes as necessary in the following paragraph.*

Its very important to understand todays media environment. The three major network's market share has decreased significantly over the year's as the number of cable channels increased. Now as people turn to services like Hulu and Netflix, the Internet's impact on entertainment consumption has become almost as great as televisions. The Internet provides viewers' with the programs they want when and where they want them. With the numerous wireless devices, it's portability makes the Internet services especially attractive to younger audience. Television has been a staple in many North American homes since the 1950's; the question is whether television as we know it has a place in our future.

COMMAS

Since commas (,) occur more frequently than any other mark of punctuation, it's vital that you learn to use them correctly. When you do, your sentence structure becomes clearer, and your reader grasps your meaning without having to reread.

Commas separate or set off independent clauses, items in a series, coordinate adjectives, introductory elements, places and dates, non-restrictive expressions, and parenthetical expressions.

Independent Clauses   When you link two independent clauses with a coordinating conjunction (*and, but, or, nor, for, yet,* or *so*), put a comma in front of the conjunction.

> Arthur is majoring in engineering, *but* he has decided to work for a clothing store following graduation.

> The water looked inviting, *so* Darlene decided to go for a swim.

Don't confuse a sentence that has a compound predicate (see pages 000 and 000) with a sentence that consists of two independent clauses.

> Hunter watered the garden and mowed the lawn. (simple sentence with compound predicate)

> Hunter watered the garden, *and* Charlotte mowed the lawn. (sentence with two independent clauses)

Items in a Series   A series consists of three or more words, phrases, or clauses following on one another's heels. Whenever you write a series, separate its items with commas.

> *Sarah, Paul,* and *Anne* are earning A's in advanced algebra. (words in a series)

> Lily strode *across the parking lot, through the revolving door,* and *into the elevator.* (phrases in a series)

> The stockholders' report said *that the company had enjoyed record profits during the last year, that it had expanded its workforce by 20 percent,* and *that it would soon start marketing several new products.* (clauses in a series)

Coordinate Adjectives   Use commas to separate coordinate adjectives—those that modify the same noun or noun substitute and can be reversed without altering the meaning of the sentence.

> Andrea proved to be an *efficient, cooperative* employee.

> Andrea proved to be a *cooperative, efficient* employee.

When reversing the word order wrecks the meaning of the sentence, the adjectives are not coordinate and should be written without a comma.

> Many new models of hybrid cars have come on the market lately.

Reversing the adjectives *many* and *new* would turn this sentence into nonsense. Therefore, no comma should be used.

Introductory Elements   Use commas to separate introductory elements—words, phrases, and clauses—from the rest of the sentence. When an introductory element is short and the sentence will not be misread, you can omit the comma.

> *Correct*   After showering, Jack felt refreshed.
> *Correct*   Soon I will be changing jobs.
> *Correct*   Soon, I will be changing jobs.

The first example needs a comma; otherwise, the reader might become temporarily confused.

> After showering Jack . . .

A good rule of thumb is to use commas after introductory elements of six or more words.

> *Correct*   Whenever I hear the opening measure of Beethoven's *Fifth Symphony*, I get goose bumps.

Places and Dates   Places include mailing addresses and geographical locations. The following sentences show where commas are used:

> Sherry Delaney lives at 651 Daniel Street, Westmount, Quebec H4Z 6W5.
> I will go to Calais, France, next week.
> Chicoutimi, Quebec, is my birthplace.

Note that commas appear after the street designation and the names of cities, countries, and provinces, except when the name of the province is followed by a postal code.

Dates are punctuated as shown in the following example:

> On Sunday, June 8, 2008, Elaine received a degree in environmental science.

Here, commas follow the day of the week, the day of the month, and the year. With dates that include only the month and the year, commas are optional.

> *Correct*   In July 2015 James played chess for the first time.
> *Correct*   In July, 2015, James played chess for the first time.

Non-Restrictive and Restrictive Expressions   A non-restrictive expression supplies added information about whatever it modifies. This information, however, is *non-essential* and does not affect the basic meaning of the sentence. The two sentences below include non-restrictive expressions.

> Premier Stephen McNeil, Leader of the Nova Scotia Liberal Party, faced a tough campaign for re-election.
> My dog, *frightened by the thunder*, hid under my bed while the storm raged.

If we delete the phrase *the leader of the British Columbia Liberal Party* from the first sentence, we still know that Premier Christie Clark faced a tough re-election battle. Likewise, if we delete *frightened by the thunder* from the second sentence, we still know that the dog hid during the storm.

Restrictive expressions, which are written *without commas,* distinguish whatever they modify from other persons, places, or things in the same category. Unlike non-restrictive expressions, they are almost always *essential* sentence elements. Omitting a restrictive expression alters the meaning of the sentence, and the result is often nonsense.

Any person *caught stealing from this store* will be prosecuted.

Dropping the italicized part of this sentence leaves us with the absurd statement that any person, not just those caught stealing, faces prosecution.

Parenthetical Expressions　　A parenthetical expression is a word or a group of words that links one sentence to another or adds information or emphasis to the sentence in which it appears. Parenthetical expressions include the following:

Clarifying phrases

Names and titles of people being addressed directly

Abbreviations of degree titles

Echo questions

"Not" phrases

Adjectives that come after, rather than before, the words they modify

The examples that follow show the uses of commas:

All of Joe's spare time seems to centre around reading. Kevin, *on the other hand,* enjoys a variety of activities. (phrase linking two sentences together)

Myra Hobbes, *our representative in Calgary,* is being transferred to Halifax next month. (clarifying phrase)

I think, *Jill,* that you'd make a wonderful teacher. (name of person addressed directly)

Tell me, *Captain,* when the cruise ship is scheduled to sail. (title of person addressed directly)

Harley Kendall, *Ph.D.,* will be this year's commencement speaker. (degree title following name)

Alvin realizes, *doesn't he,* that he stands almost no chance of being accepted at McGill? (echo question)

Mathematics, *not drama,* was Tamara's favourite high school subject. ("not" phrase)

The road, *muddy and rutted,* proved impassable. (adjectives following word they modify)

Punctuating Conjunctive Adverbs　　Writers often mistakenly punctuate conjunctive adverbs with commas and create, as a result, a comma splice.

Vancouverites do not experience the snowfall of their northern neighbours, however, they do experience a lot of rainfall.

Conjunctive adverbs do not join sentences and can be moved, revealing the underlying comma splice.

> Vancouverites do not experience the snowfall of their northern neighbours, they do, however, experience a lot of rainfall.

To fix such comma splices, join the sentences with a semicolon or punctuate with a period and start a new sentence.

> Vancouverites do not experience the snowfall of their northern neighbours; however, they do experience a lot of rainfall.

> Vancouverites do not experience the snowfall of their northern neighbours. However, they do experience a lot of rainfall.

CONNECTED DISCOURSE EXERCISE *Add or delete commas as necessary in the following letter.*

Dear Loy Norrix Knight:

While we know you will be busy this summer we hope you will take time to join us for the 20-year reunion of the graduating class of 1996. Come reminisce with old friends and make new ones, you will enjoy visiting the Facebook photo gallery. The reunion will include a buffet dinner and a live band. John Mcleary who is now a well-known professional nightclub performer will serve as the emcee you may remember him hosting our grade 12 assemblies?

Yes many of your former, hard-working teachers will be at the reunion. You can thank them for the difference they made in your life or you can tell them what you've thought of them all these years. This reunion will also be your opportunity to catch up on the lives of your former friends and brag a little about your own successes.

We hope you will make plans, to join us here at the Penticton Hilton on July 28 2016 at 7 p.m. Wear your best retro clothes, remember that revisiting the past, can be fun.

Sincerely,
The Reunion Committee

EXERCISE *Supply commas as necessary to correct the following sentences.*

1. Before leaving Skyla stopped to say goodbye to Andrew.

2. Let us know Ms. Granger when you would like to enjoy your free stay at Rolling Hills Resort.

3. If you are interested in making a tax-deductible donation to the Stratford Festival please write Carla Darma treasurer at 165 University Avenue Suite 700 Toronto Ontario Canada M5H 3B8.

4. Stepping into the cool pleasant bake shop Annette bought a large cinnamon doughnut for a snack.

5. Mr. Kowalski was born in Warsaw Poland and became a Canadian citizen on February 15 1994.

6. For more information about the Scotland tour write Doreen Campbell 218 Riverdale Street Windsor Ontario M6T 3Y7.

SEMICOLONS

The main use of the semicolon (;) is to separate independent clauses, which may or may not be connected with a conjunctive adverb (see pages 000–000). Other uses include separating

- Two or more of a series of items
- Items containing commas in a single series
- Independent clauses that contain commas and are connected with a coordinating conjunction.

Independent Clauses   The examples that follow show the use of semicolons to separate independent clauses.

> The fabric in this dress is terrible; its designer must have been asleep at the swatch. (no conjunctive adverb)

> Steve refused to write a term paper; *therefore*, he failed the course. (conjunctive adverb *therefore* joining independent clauses)

Conjunctive adverbs can occur within, rather than between, independent clauses. When they do, set them off with commas.

> Marsha felt very confident. Jane, *on the other hand*, was nervous and uncertain. (conjunctive adverb within independent clause)

To determine whether a pair of commas or a semicolon and comma are required, read what comes before and after the conjunctive adverb. Unless both sets of words can stand alone as sentences, use commas.

Two or More Series of Items   With sentences that have two or more series of items, writers often separate the series with semicolons in order to reduce the chances of misreading.

> My duties as secretary include typing letters, memos, and purchase orders; sorting, opening, and delivering mail; and making plane and hotel reservations for travelling executives.

The semicolons provide greater clarity than commas would.

Comma-Containing Items within a Series   When commas accompany one or more of the items in a series, it's often better to separate the items with semicolons instead of commas.

> The meal included salmon, which was cooked to perfection; asparagus, my favourite vegetable; and brown rice, prepared with a touch of curry.

Once again, semicolons provide greater clarity than additional commas.

Independent Clauses with Commas and a Coordinating Conjunction   Ordinarily, a comma is used to separate independent clauses joined by a coordinating conjunction. However, when one or more of the clauses have commas, a semicolon provides clearer separation.

> The long black limousine pulled up to the curb; and Jerry, shaking with excitement, watched the prime minister alight from it.

The semicolon makes it easier to see the two main clauses.

EXERCISE *Supply semicolons wherever they are necessary or desirable in the following sentences. You may have to substitute semicolons for commas. If a sentence is correct, write C.*

1. When he visits the main office, Mr. Harmon would like to meet with the vice-president of marketing, Carol Chaffe, the personnel director, Carl Hart, and the vice-president of finance, Mary Angelo.

2. Donald Nathanson, a clinical psychologist, has written an insightful book on shame, ironically other psychologists, who at first were very critical of his work, have begun to use his ideas in their practice.

3. Email is a crucial part of most businesses; therefore you must learn to master email etiquette.

4. This year a number of new plays will be shown, this season should be exciting.

5. The reading for the course was eclectic, and included Leonard Cohen's *Beautiful Losers,* a book set in the 1960s; *Neuromancer:* and *The Heart Goes Last,* a more recent novel by Margaret Atwood.

6. Computers can crash at any time, therefore, it is important to back up your data frequently.

7. This has been a good year for raspberries, I've got more than 30 litres from my small patch of bushes.

CONNECTED DISCOURSE EXERCISE *Add and delete semicolons as appropriate in the following letter. You may have to substitute semicolons for commas.*

To: All Students

From: John Bits; IT Manager

Re: Improving Our Online Learning Environment

As many of you have pointed out, there have been a number of problems with GrendelUP, our online learning platform, and those problems, President Kleften agrees, have been severe enough to warrant a new system.

You deserve a system that offers consistent, reliable service, is compatible with recent Java Script, allows you to easily view Internet links, and makes it possible for you to review your grades, without changing systems. We believe that you should have an opportunity to have a say in the system we select,

;

therefore, you are invited to attend the demonstration sessions for the possible replacements.

We hope you will attend one or all of these sessions, the system we select should reflect your needs as students.

PERIODS, QUESTION MARKS, AND EXCLAMATION POINTS

Since periods, question marks, and exclamation points signal the ends of sentences, they are sometimes called *end marks*. In addition, periods and question marks function in several other ways.

Periods Periods (.) end sentences that state facts or opinions, give instructions, make requests that are not in the form of questions, and ask indirect questions—those that have been rephrased in the form of a statement.

Linda works as a hotel manager. (Sentence states fact.)

Dean Harris is a competent administrator. (Sentence states opinion.)

Clean off your lab bench before you leave. (Sentence gives instruction.)

Please move away from the door. (Sentence makes request.)

I wonder whether Raoul will be at the theatre tonight. (Sentence asks indirect question.)

Periods also follow common abbreviations, as well as a person's initials.

Mr.	p.m.	Ms.	s.a.p.
Dr.	St.	a.m.	Corp.
Sr.	P.S.	etc.	R.S.V.P.

Mark J. Valentini, Ph.D., has consented to head the new commission on traffic safety.

Periods are usually omitted after abbreviations for the names of organizations or government agencies, as the following examples show:

CBC	GST	RCAF	TD
PST	IBM	UPS	WTO

An up-to-date dictionary will indicate whether a certain abbreviation should be written without periods.

Periods also precede decimal fractions and separate numerals standing for dollars and cents.

0.81 percent	$5.29
3.79 percent	$0.88

Question Marks   A question mark (?) ends a whole or a partial sentence that asks a direct question (one that repeats the exact words of the person who asked it).

> Do you know how to operate this movie projector? (whole sentence asking a direct question)

> Has Cinderella scrubbed the floor? swept the hearth? washed the dishes? (sentence and sentence parts asking direct questions)

> The minister inquired, "Do you take this woman to be your lawful wedded wife?" (quotation asking a direct question)

Note that you if you are reporting in statement form that you had a question about something, this declarative statement will not take a question mark.

> I questioned whether I would be able to pass my finals.

> I asked myself if I could really go back there again.

Exclamation Points   Exclamation points (!) are used to express strong emotion or especially forceful commands. Do not imagine that you can use them simply to inject excitement and energy into any piece of writing. While they may be very common in promotional marketing and text messaging, they are rarely used in academic writing, which tends to be relatively serious and calm. They are most useful for narrative—sometimes for dialogue to indicate that someone is shouting, or for dramatic moments to indicate surprise or shock.

> Sam! Turn that radio down immediately!

> Help! Save me!

> I could hardly believe what I was seeing!

.?!

EXERCISE *Supply periods, question marks, or exclamation points wherever they are necessary. You may have to change existing punctuation marks. If a sentence is correct, write C.*

1. Be sure to proofread your paper before you submit it for a grade.
2. Sigmund Freud really established the concept of the unconscious.
3. Take action now to protect the sustainability of our water.
4. Great we will have to buy another battery.
5. When you shopped for a new computer, did you consider what programs you wanted to run, set a budget for yourself, check the reliability of the different brands.
6. The engineer wanted to know how much stress would be placed on the beams.
7. Has Dr Stevens read the research on the most recent anti-clotting medication.

CONNECTED DISCOURSE EXERCISE *Add, change, or remove end marks as necessary. You may want to do some slight rewording.*

Are you worried about being audited by the C.R.A. Stop worrying. Dr. Carl Sly, a C. A. from the Atlantic School of Chartered Accountants, will be available next

Friday afternoon in the Chomsky room to answer all of your questions! Many often ask, "Does using a tax preparation program protect you." No. Tax preparation software doesn't keep you from an audit. Only the kind of knowledge Carl Sly provides can make certain you avoid costly hours answering an audit! Learn how to itemize safely, avoid tax penalties, and even take legal deductions for home renovations?

COLONS, DASHES, PARENTHESES, AND BRACKETS

Colons, dashes, parentheses, and brackets separate and enclose, thereby clarifying relationships among the various parts of a sentence.

Colon   Colons (:) introduce explanations and anticipated lists following words that could stand alone as a complete sentence.

> His aim in life is grandiose: to corner the market in wheat. (explanation)
>
> Three students have been selected to attend the conference: Lucille Perkins, Dan Blakely, and Frank Napolis. (list)
>
> Three factors can cause financial problems for farmers: (1) high interest rates; (2) falling land values; and (3) a strong dollar, which makes global sales of crops difficult. (numbered list)

The first of the following sentences is incorrect because the words preceding the colon can't stand alone as a sentence:

> *Faulty*   The tools needed for this job include: a hacksaw, a file, and a drill.
>
> *Revision*   The tools needed for this job include a hacksaw, a file, and a drill.

Colons also frequently introduce formal quotations that extend beyond a single sentence.

> The speaker stepped to the lectern and spoke forcefully: "I am here to ask for your assistance. Today several African nations face a food crisis because drought has ruined their harvests. Unless we provide help quickly, thousands of people will die of starvation."

Colons also separate hours from minutes (8:20 a.m.), titles of publications from subtitles (*The Careful Writer: A Guide to English Usage*), numbers indicating ratios (a 3:2:2 ratio), and chapter from verse in scriptural references (Luke 6:20–49).

Dashes   Like colons, dashes (—) set off appositives, lists, and explanations but are used in less formal writing. A dash emphasizes the material it sets off.

> Only one candidate showed up at the political rally—Jerry Manders. (appositive)
>
> The closet held only three garments—an out-at-the-elbows sports coat, a pair of blue jeans, and a tattered shirt. (list)

I know what the baby's problem is—a wet diaper. (explanation)

Dashes set off material that interrupts the flow of thought within a sentence.

Her new car—didn't she get it just three months ago?—has broken down twice.

Similarly, dashes are used to mark an interrupted segment of dialogue.

"I'd like to live in England when I retire."

"In England? But what will your wife—?"

"My wife likes the idea and can hardly wait for us to make the move."

Dashes set off parenthetical elements containing commas, and a dash can set off comments that follow a list.

The comedian—short, fat, and squeaky-voiced—soon had everyone roaring with laughter. (parenthetical element with commas)

A brag, a blow, a tank of air—that's what the director is. (comment following a list)

Parentheses Parentheses () are used to enclose numbers or letters that designate the items in a formal list and to set off incidental material within sentences. Except in the kind of list shown in the first example below, a comma does not usually precede a parenthesis.

Each paper should contain (1) an introduction, (2) several paragraphs developing the thesis statement, and (3) a conclusion.

Some occupations (computer programming, for example) may be overcrowded in 10 years.

If the material in parentheses appears within a sentence, don't use a capital letter or period, even if the material is itself a complete sentence.

The use of genetic engineering (one cannot foresee its consequences) worries some people today.

If the material in parentheses is written as a separate sentence, however, then punctuate it as you would a separate sentence.

Paula's angry outburst surprised everyone. (She had seemed such a placid person.)

If the material in parentheses comes at the end of a sentence, put the final punctuation after the closing parenthesis.

This company was founded by Willard Manley (1876–1951).

In contrast to dashes, parentheses de-emphasize the material they enclose.

Brackets In quoted material, brackets [ ] enclose words or phrases that have been added to make the message clearer. They are also used with the word *sic* (Latin for "thus") to point out errors in quoted material.

"This particular company [Zorn Enterprises, Inc.] pioneered the safe disposal of toxic wastes," the report noted. (The bracketed name is added to the original.)

"[John Chafin's] expertise in science has made him a popular figure on the lecture circuit," his friend stated. (The bracketed name replaces *his* in the original.)

"The principle [*sic*] cause of lung cancer is cigarette smoking," the article declared. (The word *principal* is misspelled "principle" in the original.)

To call attention to an error, follow it immediately with the bracketed *sic*. The reader will then know that the blame rests with the original writer, not with you.

CONNECTED DISCOURSE EXERCISE *Supply any necessary or appropriate colons, dashes, parentheses, and brackets in the following letter.*

Wayout Auto Company

We at Oldfield Sales a subsidiary of Jip, Inc., have had a serious problem with the cars we ordered from your company for leasing to our customers who will probably never return to us again. Two major parts fell off while the cars were sitting in the customers' driveways the exhaust system and the transmission. If this had happened while they were driving thank goodness it didn't, our customers could have been killed. Just imagine what that especially once it got into the newspapers would have done to our business. We must hold you to your claim that "while our cars are the cheapest *sic* on the market, we garnishee *sic* every car we sell." We expect immediate reimbursement for all the cars we purchased from you plus one million dollars to cover the damage to our reputation. A menace, a rip-off, a bad business deal, that's what your cars are. If you don't issue a formal recall for all your vehicles by 530 p.m., Friday, July 23, we will be forced to forward this matter to the federal government.

Sincerely,

Ken Swindelle

Service Manager

EXERCISE *Supply colons, dashes, parentheses, and brackets wherever they are necessary.*

1. Worthington's new house mansion would be a better term has 28 rooms.
2. This resort offers unsurpassed facilities for three winter sports ice skating, skiing, and tobogganing.
3. Two long meetings, a shopping trip, a dinner engagement I've had a busy day!
4. The main parts of the pressure tester include 1 an indicator dial, 2 a hose connection, 3 a damper valve, and 4 a sensing unit.
5. The headline stated, "Students Voice They're *sic* Disapproval of Tuition Hike."
6. One major social problem will remain with us for years the need for more affordable housing.
7. Our city area offers many advantages to businesses a skilled workforce, a well-developed infrastructure, and relatively low taxes.

QUOTATION MARKS

Quotation marks (" ") set off direct quotations, titles of short written or broadcast works, subdivisions of books, and expressions singled out for special attention.

Direct Quotations   A direct quotation repeats a speaker's or writer's exact words.

> "Tell me about the movie," said Debbie. "If you liked it, I may go myself."

> The placement director said, "The recruiter for Procter and Gamble will be on campus next Thursday to interview students for marketing jobs." (spoken comment)

> "The trade deficit is expected to reach record levels this year," the *Financial Times* noted. (written comment)

> Jackie said the party was "a total flop."

As these sentences show, a comma or period that follows a direct quotation goes inside the quotation marks. When a quotation is a sentence fragment, the comma preceding it is omitted.

When an expression like "he said" interrupts a quoted sentence, use commas to set off the expression. When the expression comes between two complete quoted sentences, use a period after the expression and capitalize the first word of the second sentence.

> "Hop in," said James. "Let me give you a ride to school."

> "Thank you," replied Kelly, opening the car door and sliding into the front seat.

> "I can't remember," said James, "when we've had a worse winter."

Titles of Short Works and Subdivisions of Books   These short works include magazine articles, essays, short stories, chapters of books, one-act plays, short poems, songs, and television and radio episodes.

> The article was titled "The Real Conservatism." (article)

> Last night I read John Cheever's "The Enormous Radio," "Torch Song," and "The Swimmer." (short stories)

> Many Stompin' Tom Connors fans consider "Sudbury Saturday Night" to be his greatest piece of music. (song)

> The unsuccessful TV show *Pursued* ended its brief run with a segment titled "Checkmate." (TV episode)

Here, as with direct quotations, a comma or period that follows a title goes inside the quotation marks.

Expressions Singled Out for Special Attention   Writers who wish to call the reader's attention to a word or symbol sometimes put it inside quotation marks.

> The algebraic formula included a "p," a "Q," and a "D."

> "Bonnets" and "lifts" are British terms for car hoods and elevators.

More frequently, however, these expressions are printed in italics (page 000).

" "

Again, any commas and periods that follow expressions set off by quotation marks go inside the marks.

Quotation Marks within Quotation Marks   When a direct quotation or the title of a shorter work appears within a direct quotation, use single quotation marks (' ').

> "I heard the boss telling the foreman, 'Everyone will receive a bonus,'" John said.

> The instructor told the class, "For tomorrow, read Jack Hodgins' 'Separating.'"

Note that the period goes inside both the single and double quotation marks.

Positioning of Semicolons, Colons, and Question Marks   Position semicolons and colons that come at the end of quoted material *after*, not before, the quotation marks.

> Marcia calls Francine "that greasy grind"; however, I think Marcia is simply jealous of Francine's abilities.

> There are two reasons that I like "Babylon Revisited": the characters are interesting and the writing is excellent.

When a question mark accompanies a quotation, put it outside the quotation marks if the whole sentence rather than the quotation asks the question.

> Why did Cedric suddenly shout, "This party is a big bore"?

Put the question mark inside the quotation marks if the quotation, but not the whole sentence, asks a question or if the quotation asks one question and the whole sentence asks another.

> Marie asked, "What school is your brother planning to attend?" (The quoted material, not the whole sentence, asks the question.)

> Whatever possessed him to ask, "What is the most shameful thing you ever did?" (The whole sentence and the quoted material ask separate questions.)

CONNECTED DISCOURSE EXERCISE   *Use quotation marks correctly in the following paragraph.*

Mr. Silver recently lectured our class on Stephen Crane's The Bride Comes to Yellow Sky. One thing we shouldn't forget, Mr. Silver insisted, is that the town is deliberately named Yellow Sky. What is the significance of Crane's choice of the words Yellow Sky? Mr. Silver pointed out a number of possible associations, including cowardice, the setting sun, the open expanse of the West, freedom, and the sand in the concluding passage. The story, Mr. Silver stated, is drenched in colour words. For example, he pointed out, in the first three paragraphs alone Crane mentions vast flats of green grass, brick-coloured hands, new black clothes, and a dress of blue cashmere.

EXERCISE *Supply properly positioned quotation marks wherever they are necessary.*

1. Jeffrey called the novel's plot a hopeless mishmash.

2. I think, said Gabriel, I'll go to Niagara Falls for the weekend.

3. What poem has the lines Home is the sailor, home from the sea, / And the hunter home from the hills?

4. What did Yeats mean by the line in his famous poem The Second Coming, Things fall apart, the center cannot hold?

5. In his closing argument, the attorney challenged the jury. How would any of us act if accused of a crime we didn't commit?

6. At last my paper is finished, John said happily. Now I can start typing it.

7. I managed to read Faulkner's short story The Bear, Jennifer sighed, but I don't really know what I want to say about it in my paper for English.

HYPHENS

Hyphens (-) are used to join compound adjectives and nouns, compound numbers and word–number combinations, and certain prefixes and suffixes to the words with which they appear. In addition, hyphens help prevent misreadings and awkward combinations of letters or syllables and are used to split words between two lines.

Compound Adjectives   Hyphens are often used to join separate words that function as single adjectives and come before nouns. Typical examples follow:

Sophia is a very *self-contained* person.

The *greenish-yellow* cloud of chlorine gas drifted toward the village.

Alana's *devil-may-care* attitude will land her in trouble someday.

When the first word of the compound is an adverb ending in *-ly* or when the compound adjective follows the noun it modifies, no hyphen is used.

The *badly* burned crash victim was rushed to the hospital.

The colour of the chlorine gas was *greenish yellow.*

When two or more compound adjectives modify the same last term, the sentence flows more smoothly if that term appears just once, after the last item in the series. However, keep the hyphens accompanying the earlier terms in the series.

Many seventeenth-, eighteenth-, and nineteenth-century costumes are on display in this museum.

Compound Nouns   Hyphenated nouns include such expressions as the following:

secretary-treasurer   good-for-nothing   sister-in-law   man-about-town

Here is a sentence with a hyphenated noun:

Denton is *editor-in-chief* of the largest newspaper in this province.

Compound Numbers and Word–Number Combinations   Hyphens are used to separate two-word numbers from twenty-one to ninety-nine and fractions that have been written out.

Marcy has worked *twenty-five* years for this company.

One-quarter of my income goes for rent.

Similarly, hyphens are used to separate numerals from units of measurement that follow them.

This chemical is shipped in *200-litre* drums.

Prefixes and Suffixes   A prefix is a word or set of letters that precedes a word and alters its meaning. A suffix is similar but comes at the end of the word.

Although most prefixes are not hyphenated, the prefixes *self-* and *all-* do get hyphens, as does the suffix *-elect*. Also, the prefix *ex-* is hyphenated when it accompanies a noun.

This stove has a *self-cleaning* oven.

Let Claire Voyant, the *all-knowing* soothsayer, read your future in her crystal ball.

Ethel is the *chairperson-elect* of the club.

Several *ex-teachers* work in this department.

A prefix used before a capitalized term is always hyphenated.

The *ex-RCMP* officer gave an interesting talk on the operations of that organization.

Preventing Misreadings and Awkward Combinations of Letters and Syllables   Hyphens help prevent misreadings of certain words and also break up awkward combinations of letters and syllables between certain prefixes and suffixes and their core words.

The doctor *re-treated* the wound with a new antibiotic. (The hyphen prevents the misreading *retreated*.)

The company plans to *de-emphasize* sales of agricultural chemicals. (The hyphen prevents the awkward repetition of the letter *e* in *deemphasize*.)

EXERCISE *Supply hyphens wherever they are necessary. If the sentence is correct, write C.*

  1. The task of residing the house will take three days.

  2. Margaret is the most selfsufficient person that I've ever met.

  3. The piece of music ended with bird like sounds made by the entire woodwind section.

  4. Nearly three quarters of our chemistry majors go on to graduate school.

5. When I was thirty five years old, I quit my boring job and opened my own small business.

6. Most of my exsoldier friends belong to veterans' organizations.

CAPITALIZATION

Capitalize the first word in any sentence, the pronoun *I,* proper nouns and adjectives, titles used with—or in place of—names, and the significant words in literary and artistic titles.

Proper Nouns   A proper noun names one particular person, group of persons, place, or thing. Such nouns include the following:

Persons

Organizations

Racial, political, and religious groups

Countries, provinces and states, cities, and streets

Companies and buildings

Geographical locations and features

Days, months, and holidays

Trademarks

Languages

Ships and aircraft

Abbreviations for academic degrees

Titles used in place of names

cap

The sentences below show the capitalization of proper nouns (in italics).

Sigmund works for the *National Psychoanalytical Institute,* an organization that has done much to advance the science of psychiatry.

How much does this roll of *Saran Wrap* cost?

Gwen Greene moved to *Paris, France,* when her father became the consul there.

On *Friday, December 8,* 2016, *Dianna Krall* visited our city.

Larry has a master of arts degree, and his sister has a *Ph.D.*

My father works for the *Ford Motor Company,* but I work for *Toyota.*

Do not capitalize words such as *institute, college, company,* or *avenue* unless they form part of a proper name. Likewise, do not capitalize the names of educational courses unless they start a sentence, are accompanied by a course number, or designate a language.

I have a 95 average in *Economics* 112 but only a 73 average in sociology.

Alex plans to take intermediate *German* next year.

Do you plan to attend *Queen's University* or some other university?

Proper Adjectives　Adjectives created from proper nouns are called proper adjectives. Like the nouns themselves, they should be capitalized.

> Lolita Martinez, our class valedictorian, is of *Spanish* ancestry. (*Spanish* is derived from the proper noun *Spain*.)

ABBREVIATIONS OF TITLES, NAMES OF ORGANIZATIONS, AND TECHNICAL TERMS

Abbreviations for certain personal titles, names of organizations and agencies, Latin terms, and scientific and technical terms are capitalized.

Personal Titles　Abbreviate *Mister, Doctor,* and similar titles when they come just before a name, and *Junior, Senior,* and degree titles when they follow names.

> Will *Mr.* Harry Babbitt please come to the front desk?
>
> Arthur Compton, *Sr.,* is a well-known historian; his son, Arthur Compton, *Jr.,* is a television producer.
>
> This article on marital discord was written by Irma Quarles, *Ph.D.*

As a general rule, capitalize abbreviations only if the words they stand for are capitalized.

> Milton DeWitt works for the *NDP.* (*NDP* is capitalized because *New Democratic Party* would be.)
>
> The speed limit was just increased here from 110 km to 120 km. (The abbreviation *km* is not capitalized because *kilometres* would not be.)

A few abbreviations are capitalized even though all or some of the words they stand for aren't. Examples include TV (television) and CD (compact disc). Others are shown below in the section titled "Abbreviations."

Personal Titles　Capitalize a personal title if it precedes a name or is used in place of a name. Otherwise, do not capitalize.

> The division is under the command of *General* Arnold Schafer.
>
> The *dean* of our engineering division is Dr. Alma Haskins.

Many writers capitalize titles of high rank when they are used in place of names.

> The *Prime Minister* will sign this bill tomorrow.
>
> The *prime minister* will sign this bill tomorrow.

Either usage is acceptable.

Titles of Literary and Artistic Works　When citing the titles of publications, pieces of writing, movies, television programs, paintings, sculptures, and the like, capitalize the first and last words and all other words except *a, an, the,* coordinating conjunctions, and prepositions.

abr

Last week I played *Gone with the Wind* on my DVD player and read Patricia Cornwell's *Book of the Dead*. (The preposition *with*, the article *the*, and the preposition *of* are not capitalized.)

John is reading a book called *The Movies of Abbott and Costello*. (The preposition *of* and the coordinating conjunction *and* are not capitalized.)

Although I'm no TV addict, I watched every episode of *Murder, She Wrote*. (The major words in the title are capitalized.)

EXERCISE *Identify any word or abbreviation that should be capitalized in the following sentences.*

1. The recipe for this stew comes from *the canadian family cookbook*.

2. My cousin has accepted a job with the federal national mortgage association and will move to ottawa, ont., in july.

3. The announcement said that sergeant brockway had received a second lieutenant's commission.

4. The newest municipal judge in boyle city is judge martha berkowicz.

5. Unless sales increase markedly in the next quarter, the delta corporation will be forced into bankruptcy.

Names of Organizations and Agencies   Many organizations and agencies are known primarily by their initials rather than their full names; for example:

CAA	CTV	NATO	WHO
CARE	IMF	SPCA	WTO
CMA	IRA	UNESCO	CRTC

abr

Latin Terms   Certain Latin terms are always abbreviated; others are abbreviated when used with dates or times.

e.g. (*exempli gratia:* for example) Many writers (*e.g.,* Dylan Thomas and Malcolm Lowry) have had serious problems with alcohol.

i.e. (*id est:* that is)

etc. (*et cetera:* and [the] others)

vs. or v. (*versus:* against)

A.M. or a.m. (*ante meridiem:* before noon)

P.M. or p.m. (*post meridiem:* after noon) The play starts at 8 p.m.

Scientific and Technical Terms   For brevity's sake, scientists and technicians abbreviate terms of measurement that occur repeatedly. Terms that the reader would not know are written out the first time they are used, and they are accompanied by their abbreviation in parentheses. Unfamiliar organizations and agencies that are mentioned repeatedly are handled in like manner.

The viscosity of the fluid measured 15 centistokes (cs) at room temperature.

Common practice calls for writing such abbreviations without periods unless they duplicate the spelling of some word.

Standard dictionaries list common abbreviations. When you don't recognize one, look it up. Use abbreviations sparingly in essays. If you're unsure about what is appropriate, don't abbreviate.

EXERCISE *Supply abbreviations wherever they are necessary or are customarily used.*

1. The conference on poverty in the twenty-first century will be chaired by Donald Frump, Doctor of Philosophy.

2. When writing, don't use Latin terms such as *id est* and *exempli gratia* except as comments in parentheses and footnotes.

3. The United Nations Educational, Scientific, and Cultural Organization sponsors programs in primary education throughout developing countries.

4. The thermometer on my front porch says that the temperature is 19° Celsius.

5. At 10:20 *ante meridiem*, the local TV station announced that a tornado had been sighted near Leesville.

6. This fall, the Columbia Broadcasting System will air nine new sitcoms.

---

num

NUMBERS

Some instructors ask their students to express numbers larger than ninety-nine as figures and to spell out smaller numbers.

Banff is 100 kilometres from here.

Banff is *ninety-nine* kilometres from here.

Other instructors prefer that students switch to figures beginning with the number ten.

My son will be *nine* years old on his next birthday.

My son will be 10 years old on his next birthday.

With either practice, the following exceptions apply.

Numbers in a Series   Write all numbers in a series the same way regardless of their size.

Gatsby has *64* suits, *110* shirts, and *214* ties.

In just *one* hour the emergency room personnel handled *two* stabbings, *five* shootings, and *sixteen* fractures.

We have *150* salespeople, *51* engineers, and *7* laboratory technicians.

Dates   Use figures for dates that include the year.

February *14, 2005* (not February 14th, 2005)

When the date includes the day but not the year, you may use figures or spell out the number.

June 9

June ninth

the ninth of June

Page Numbers and Addresses   Use figures for page numbers and street numbers in addresses.

I live at *111* Cornelia Street, and my office is at *620* Victoria Avenue.

Numbers Beginning Sentences   Spell out any number that begins a sentence. If this requires three or more words, rephrase the sentence so that the number comes after the opening and numerals can be used.

The year *2004* was a good year for this wine.

Sixty thousand fans jammed the stadium.

An army of *265 000* troops assaulted the city. (If this number began the sentence, five words—an excessive number—would be needed to write it out.)

Decimals, Percentages, Times   Use figures for decimals and percentages as well as for expressions of time that are accompanied by a.m. or p.m.

The shaft has a *0.37*-millimetre diameter.

Last year the value of my house jumped *25* percent.

The plane leaves here at *9:50* a.m. and reaches Winnipeg at *2:30* p.m.

One Number Following Another   When two numbers directly follow each other (such as a quantity number followed by a measurement number), spell out the first number if it is smaller than 100 and use numerals for the second one. If the first number is larger than 100, use numerals for it and spell out the second one.

We ordered six 100-litre drums of solvent for the project.

The supplier shipped us 600 hundred-litre drums by mistake.

num

EXERCISE *Identify any miswriting of numbers in the following sentences and rewrite these numbers correctly.*

1. 50 000 people ride this city's buses each day.

2. The article on page fifty-nine of this week's issue of *Maclean's* discusses Alanis Morissette's latest CD.

3. Next Saturday at one-thirty p.m., the city will test its emergency warning sirens.

4. My grandparents' golden wedding anniversary was July seventeen, two thousand nine.

5. It is not uncommon for credit card holders to pay interest rates of eighteen percent or more.

6. The thickness of this piece needs to be increased by fifteen hundredths of a centimetre.

ITALICS

Italics are used for the titles of longer publications, the names of vehicles and vessels, foreign words and phrases, and expressions singled out for special attention. Use underlining to represent italics when writing by hand.

Titles of Longer Publications and Artistic Works   These items may include the following:

books	record albums	long musical works and poems
magazines	paintings	plays
newspapers	movies	sculptures

ital

As noted on page 553, quotation marks are used for the titles of *short* pieces—articles, short stories, short poems, and one-act plays. Longer, full-length works always take italics.

Last night I finished Michael Ondaatje's *The English Patient* and read two articles in *Geist*. (book, magazine)

Michelangelo's *David* is surely one of the world's greatest sculptures. (sculpture)

The Globe and Mail had praise for the revival of Tomson Highway's *The Rez Sisters*. (newspaper, play)

Stephen Vincent Benét's poem *John Brown's Body* won a Pulitzer Prize in 1929. (book-length poem)

Do not use italics when naming the Bible, Koran, Torah, other scriptural books, or any of their chapters.

Names of Vehicles and Vessels   Names of particular airplanes, ships, trains, and spacecraft are italicized.

The plane in which Charles Lindbergh flew over the Atlantic Ocean was named *The Spirit of St. Louis*.

Foreign Expressions   Use italics to identify foreign words and phrases that have not yet made their way into the English language.

The writer has a terribly pessimistic *Weltanschauung*. (philosophy of life)

This season, long skirts are the *dernier cri*. (the latest thing)

When such expressions become completely assimilated, the italics are dropped. Most dictionaries use an asterisk (*), a dagger (†), or other symbol to identify expressions that need italicizing.

Expressions Singled Out for Special Attention   These expressions include words, letters, numerals, and symbols.

The Greek letter *pi* is written π.

I can't tell whether this letter is meant to be an *a* or an *o* or this number a *7* or a *9*.

In England, the word *lorry* means truck.

As noted previously, quotation marks can replace italics for this purpose.

CONNECTED DISCOURSE EXERCISE *Use hyphens, capitalization, abbreviations, numbers, and italics properly in the following passage.*

The spy who could speak Russian fluently had been recruited by the central intelligence agency while still a student in Boston. Although the records are unclear, it may have been a certain professor Hogsbottom, a Political Science teacher, who had suggested that they consider him. After all, this professor had been a General during World War II and still had connections with the intelligence community. Soon this american spy found himself in England being asked, strangely enough, to spy on the english. For three years he posed as a british aristocrat who was a general bon vivant and man about town. He went by the alias of Mister Henry Higgins, Junior. Everyone, of course, wanted to know if he had seen My Fair Lady. The whole experience, in retrospect, seems like a monty python type of joke. He spied on the british and assumed that no one suspected he was american, and then later found out that that because of his fluent Russian, they had suspected him of being a russian spy, they had fed him false information all along.

ital

EXERCISE *Supply italics wherever they are necessary.*

1. To keep abreast of the business news, I read both Investor's Daily and Forbes.
2. Next week, Boris is taking the Siberian Express to Irkutsk, Siberia.
3. There are few artistic statements against war as powerful as Picasso's Guernica.
4. Because Pam lost her brother's copy of Moby Dick, she bought him a new one.
5. Sometimes when I try to print a b I make a d instead.
6. In Scotland, the term lum refers to a chimney.

"Why the big deal about accurate spelling?"

"Does it really make that much difference if I have an *i* and an *e* turned around or if I omit a letter when spelling a word?"

Students frequently question the importance of proper spelling. Perhaps the answer is suggested by the following sentence, taken from a student essay:

Children's video games are far too violet.

The omission of an *n* in *violent* makes this writer's criticism of video games sound absurd. Not only does inaccurate spelling suggest carelessness, but also it sometimes drastically alters meaning.

While there is no sure way of becoming a good speller, you can minimize difficulties by learning basic spelling rules, applying helpful spelling tips, and memorizing the proper spelling of troublesome words.

SPELLING RULES

The following four rules should ease many spelling pains.

Rule 1   If a word has the double vowels *ie* or *ei* and the combination has a long *e* sound (as in me), use *ie* except after *c*. If the combination has an *a* sound, use *ei*.

ie (as long *e*)	*ei* after *c*	*ei* (as *a*)
relieve	deceive	freight
belief	receive	neighbour
grieve	receipt	reign
piece	perceive	weigh

The main exceptions to this rule include *either, financier, leisure, neither, seize, species,* and *weird.*

Rule 2   If a one-syllable word (example: *sin*) ends in a single consonant preceded by a single vowel, double the consonant before adding a suffix that starts with a vowel. Apply the same rule to a word of two or more syllables: If the final syllable is accented (example: *admit, prefer*) and ends with a single consonant preceded by a vowel, or if the final consonant is *l, p, s,* or *t* (example: *travel*), double the final consonant.

Words with Single Syllables	Words with Two or More Syllables
rig—rigged	admit—admittance
sin—sinned	control—controller
stop—stopping	equip—equipped
counsel—counsellor	

If the accent does not fall on the last syllable, do not double the final consonant.

audit—audited   chatter—chattered   simmer—simmering

Rule 3   If a word ends in *y* preceded by a single consonant, change the *y* to an *i* unless you are adding the suffix *-ing*.

y **changed to** *i*	*y* **retained**
beauty—beautiful	copy—copying
fury—furious	defy—defying
easy—easily	dry—drying
vary—various	vary—varying

Rule 4   If a word ends in a silent *e*, the *e* is usually dropped when a suffix starting with a vowel is added.

blue—bluish   fame—famous

dense—density   grieve—grievous

In a few cases, the *e* is retained to avoid pronunciation difficulties or confusion with other words.

dye—dyeing (not dying)   singe—singeing (not singing)

shoe—shoeing (not shoing)

The *e* is also retained when it is preceded by a soft *c* sound (pronounced like the letter *s*) or a soft *g* sound (pronounced like the letter *j*) and the suffix being added starts with an *a* or an *o*.

peace—peaceable   courage—courageous

change—changeable   manage—manageable

HELPFUL SPELLING TIPS

Here are some tips that can further improve your spelling:

1. Examine each problem word carefully, especially prefixes (*im*probable, *intra*venous), suffixes (superintend*ent*, descend*ant*), and double consonants (sate*ll*ite, roo*mm*ate, and *coll*apsible).
2. Sound out each syllable carefully, noting its pronunciation. Words such as *height, governor,* and *candidate* are often misspelled because of improper pronunciation.
3. Make a list of your problem words and review them periodically. Concentrate on each syllable and any unusual features (*ar*ctic, ambig*uous*).
4. Use any crutches that will help: There is *gain* in *bargain;* to *breakfast* is to *break a fast;* a disease causes *dis-ease*.
5. When you copy anything from a blackboard or textbook, copy it carefully. Writing a word correctly helps you to spell it correctly the next time.
6. Buy a good dictionary and look up the words you don't know how to spell.

sp

7. Use the spell-checker of your word processor, but double-check the suggested corrections. Spell-checkers often use non-Canadian spellings, confuse parts of speech, and can't differentiate among homophones (e.g., *there, their, they're*).

LIST OF TROUBLESOME WORDS

Students frequently misspell the words in the following list. Study these words carefully until the correct spelling becomes automatic. Then ask a friend to read them to you while you write them down. Tag the ones you misspell, and whenever you revise a paper, check for these words.

sp

abandoned	alley(s)	bachelor	chauffeur
abbreviate	allot	balance	chief
absence	allotted	balloon	colloquial
absorb	allowed	barbarous	colonel
absorption	all right	barbiturate	column
absurd	already	beautiful	commission
academy	although	beggar	commit
accelerate	altogether	believe	commitment
accept	always	beneficial	committed
access	amateur	benefit	committee
accessible	ambiguous	benefited	committing
accident	among	biscuit	comparatively
accidentally	analysis/analyses	boundary	competent
accommodate	analyze	bourgeois	competition
accomplish	anonymous	breathe (v.)	concede
accumulate	anxiety	Britain	conceive
accustom	apartment	bulletin	condemn
achieve	apparent	bureau	condescend
achievement	appearance	bureaucracy	confident
acknowledge	appreciate	business	congratulations
acknowledgment	appropriate	cafeteria	connoisseur
acquaintance	architecture	calendar	conqueror
acquire	arctic	camouflage	conscience
acquit	argue	campaign	conscientious
acquitted	arguing	candidate	conscious
address	argument	carburetor	consistency
advice (n.)	arithmetic	carriage	consistent
advise (v.)	ascent	carrying	conspicuous
aerial	assassin	casual	contemptible
aggravate	assent	category	continuous
aggravated	assistance	causal	controversy
aggression	assistant	ceiling	convenience
aggressive	athlete	cellar	convenient
aging	athletics	cemetery	coolly
alcohol	attempt	changeable	cooperate
allege	attendance	changing	corollary
alleviate	average	characteristic	corps

sp

corpse
correlate
counterfeit
courteous
criticism
criticize
cruelty
curiosity
curriculum
dealt
deceit
deceive
decent
decision
defence
defendant
definite
definitely
dependent
descendant
descent
describe
description
desert
desirable
despair
desperate
dessert
develop
development
difference
dilemma
disappear
disastrous
discernible
disciple
discipline
discussion
disease
dissatisfied
dissipate
dominant
drunkenness
echoes
ecstasy
efficiency
efficient
eighth
eligible
eliminate
embarrass

emphasis
employee
engineer
enthusiastic
environment
equal
equip
equipment
equipped
equivalent
especially
exaggerate
exceed
excellent
except
excerpt
excess
excitement
exercise
existence
experience
extraordinary
extremely
fallacy
familiar
fascinate
fascist
February
fiery
finally
financier
foreign
foreword
forfeit
forward
friend
fulfill
gaiety
gases
gauge
genius
genuine
government
grammar
guarantee
guard
handkerchief
harass
height
heroes
hindrance

hygiene
hypocrisy
hysterical
illiterate
illogical
illusion
immediate
implement
impromptu
inadequate
incident
incidentally
independent
indict
indispensable
individual
inevitable
infinitely
ingenious
ingenuous
innocent
intelligent
interest
interfere
irresistible
irresponsible
jeopardy
judgment
judicial
knowledge
knowledgeable
laboratory
legitimate
leisure
library
licence (n.)
license (v.)
lightning
loneliness
loose
lose
magnificent
maintain
maintenance
manoeuvre
manual
marriage
mathematics
mattress
meant
medicine

medieval
mediocre
melancholy
miniature
minute
miscellaneous
mischievous
misspell
modifies
modify
modifying
moral
morale
mortgage
mosquitoes
muscle
mysterious
necessary
neither
nevertheless
niece
noticeable
obedience
occasion
occasionally
occur
occurred
occurrence
occurring
official
omission
omit
omitted
omitting
opinion
opponent
opportunity
optimistic
original
outrageous
pamphlet
parallel
paralysis
parliament
particularly
pastime
patent
peaceable
perceive
perfectible
perform

permanent
permissible
perseverance
persuade
physical
physician
picnic
picnicked
playwright
pleasant
pleasurable
politician
possess
possession
possible
potatoes
practice (n.)
practise (v.)
precede
precedent
precious
predominant
preference
preferred
prejudice
preparation
privilege
probably
procedure
proceed
professor
prominent
pronounce
pronunciation
propaganda
propagate
propeller
prophecy (n.)
prophesy (v.)
prostate
prostrate
protein
psychiatry
psychology
pursue
pursuit
quantity
questionnaire
quiet
quite
quiz

quizzes
realize
receipt
receive
recipe
recognizable
recommend
refer
reference
referring
reign
relevant
relieve
religious
remembrance
reminisce
reminiscence
reminiscent
rendezvous
repellent
repentance
repetition
representative
resemblance
resistance
restaurant
rhetoric
rhyme
rhythm
roommate
sacrifice
sacrilege
sacrilegious
safety
salary
sandwich
scarcely
scene
scenic
schedule
science
secretary
seize
sensible
separate
sergeant
severely
siege
similar
simultaneous
sincerely

skeptical
skiing
skilful (skillful)
skis
society
sophomore
source
specifically
specimen
sponsor
spontaneous
statistics
steely
strategy
studying
subtle
subtlety
subtly
succeed
success
successful
succinct
suffrage
superintendent
supersede
suppose
suppress
surprise
syllable
symmetry
sympathize
synonym
synonymous
tangible
tariff
technical
technique
temperament
temperature
temporary
tenant
tendency
thorough
thought
through
traffic
trafficking
tragedy
tranquility
transcendent
transcendental

transfer
transferred
transferring
translate
tries
truly
twelfth
tyrannical
tyranny
unanimous
unconscious
undoubtedly
unmistakable
unnecessary
until
unwieldy
urban
urbane
usage
useful
using
usual
usually
vacancy
vacillate
vacuum
valuable
vegetable
vengeance
victorious
village
villain
waive
warrant
warring
weather
Wednesday
weird
whether
whole
wholly
wield
wintry
wiry
worshipped
wreak
wreck
writing
written
yield

sp

The English language has many words and expressions that confuse writers and thereby lessen the precision and effectiveness of their writing. These troublesome items include the following:

Word pairs that sound alike or almost alike but are spelled differently and have different meanings

Word pairs that do not sound alike but still are often confused

Words or phrases that are unacceptable in formal writing

The following glossary identifies the most common of these troublemakers. Familiarize yourself with its contents. Then consult it as you revise your writing if you have even the slightest doubt about the proper use of a word, phrase, or expression.

a, an   Use *a* with words beginning with a consonant sound (even if the first written letter is a vowel); use *an* with words beginning with a vowel sound.

a brush, *a* student, *a* wheel, *a* risky situation, *a* once-in-a-lifetime opportunity

an architect, *an* apple, *an* unworthy participant, *an* interesting proposal, *an* honest politician

accept, except   *Accept* is a verb meaning "to receive" or "to approve." *Except* is used as a verb or a preposition. As a verb, *except* means "to take out, exclude, or omit." As a preposition, it means "excluding," "other than," or "but not."

She *accepted* the bouquet of flowers.

Linda *excepted* Sally from the list of guests. (verb)

All of Linda's friends *except* Sally came to the party. (preposition)

access, excess   *Access* is a noun meaning "means or right to enter, approach, or use." In the computer field, it is a verb meaning "gain entrance to." *Excess* is an adjective meaning "too much; more than needed; lack of moderation."

I have *access* to a summer cottage this weekend.

The code permits users to *access* the computer.

The airline booked an *excess* number of passengers on that flight.

adapt, adopt   To *adapt* is "to adjust," often by modification. To *adopt* is "to take as one's own."

He *adapted* to the higher elevations of the Rocky Mountains.

She *adopted* the new doctrine expounded by the prophet.

advice, advise   *Advice* is a noun meaning "a recommendation about how to deal with a situation or problem." *Advise* is a verb meaning "to recommend or warn."

The young man followed his sister's *advice*.

Mr. Smith *advised* John to buy 10 000 shares of the stock.

affect, effect   Although both words may function as nouns and verbs, usually *affect* is a verb and *effect* is a noun. The verb *affect* means "to influence, cause a change in, or arouse the emotions of." The noun *affect* is a technical term in psychology and refers to feeling. The noun *effect* means "result or outcome." The verb *effect* means "to bring about or achieve."

His speech *affected* me greatly. (verb)

The *effect* of the announcement was felt immediately. (noun)

The doctor was soon able to *effect* a cure. (verb)

aggravate   *Aggravate* is a verb meaning "to intensify or make worse" an existing situation. The use of *aggravate* to mean "annoy" or "anger" is colloquial.

Colloquial   Grace's behaviour at the dance really *aggravated* me.

Standard   Marcy's interference only *aggravated* the conflict between Bill and Nadine.

all ready, already   *All ready* means "completely prepared" or "everyone is ready." *Already* means "previously, even now, even then."

The scouts are *all ready* for the camp out.

When we arrived we found he had *already* gone.

The report is *already* a week overdue.

all together, altogether   *All together* means "all in one place" or "in unison." *Altogether* is an adverb meaning "completely, entirely."

The family was *all together* at the wedding.

All together, push!

Mr. Doe is *altogether* at fault for writing the letter.

allusion, delusion, illusion   An *allusion* is an indirect reference. A *delusion* is a mistaken belief, often part of a psychological condition. An *illusion* is a deceptive appearance presented to the sight or created by the imagination.

In his lecture, the professor made many *allusions* to *The Odyssey*.

He suffers from the *delusion* that he is a millionaire.

They wore makeup to give the *illusion* of beauty.

a lot, alot   *Alot* is an erroneous spelling of the two words *a lot*. The phrase *a lot* is usually colloquial; in formal writing replace it with *many*.

usage

already   See *all ready, already*.

alternately, alternatively   *Alternately* means "occurring by turns, one after the other." *Alternatively* means "providing a choice between two items."

> The British Columbian flag has three blue and two white wavy stripes, arranged *alternately*.

> Highway 5 offers the most direct route to Kelowna. *Alternatively*, Highway 3 is much more scenic.

altogether   See *all together, altogether*.

among, between   Use *between* when referring to two things and *among* when referring to more than two.

> He divided the candy *between* Allan and Stephanie.

> He divided the candy *among* the five children.

amoral, immoral   *Amoral* means "neither moral nor immoral; morally neutral." *Immoral* means "contrary to the moral code."

> The movie, which takes no clear position on the behaviour it depicts, seems curiously *amoral*.

> Murder is an *immoral* act.

amount, number   *Amount* refers to total quantities, things in bulk, or weight. *Number* refers to countable things. Never use *amount* when referring to people.

> Cassandra inherited a large *amount* of money.

> Cassandra now has a large *number* of friends.

an, a   See *a, an*.

and/or   Although often used in commercial and legal documents, this combination should be avoided in other writing.

angry, mad   *Mad* means "insane," although it is often used colloquially to mean "annoyed" or "angry." To be precise, use *mad* only to mean insane.

> *Colloquial*   I was *mad* at Serena.

> *Standard*   I was *angry* with Serena.

around   *Around* is colloquial use for "approximately" or "about."

> *Colloquial*   She arrived *around* 10:00 p.m.
>
> The blouse cost *around* $35.

> *Standard*   She arrived at *approximately* 10:00 p.m.
>
> The blouse cost *about* $35.

usage

as   *As* is frequently used as a weak substitute for *because, since, when,* and *while.*

> *Weak*   She ran out of the house *as* it was on fire.

> *Better*   She ran out of the house *because* it was on fire.

as, like   *As* may be used as a conjunction that introduces an adverb clause, but *like* should not be used this way.

> *Unacceptable*   *Like* my father always said, "You can fool some of the people all of the time."

> *Standard*   *As* my father always said, "You can fool some of the people all of the time."

However, *like* may be used as a preposition.

> In times *like* this, it's hard not to despair.

> Any woman *like* Jennifer can expect a successful career in business.

assure, ensure, insure   To *assure* is "to make safe from risk, to guarantee" or "to convince." *Ensure* and *insure* can be variant spellings meaning "to make certain." *Insure,* however, is now generally associated with the business of insurance.

> The counsellor tried to *assure* the students that they had made a wise choice.

> The captain *assured* them that they would be rescued.

> The father, wanting to *ensure* his son's higher education, applied for a federally *insured* loan.

awhile, a while   *A while,* consisting of the noun *while* and the article *a,* means "a period of time." *Awhile* is an adverb meaning "for a short time."

> Dinner will be served in *a while.*

> Sit *awhile* and tell me the latest gossip.

bad, badly   *Bad* is an adjective. *Badly* is an adverb. *Badly* is colloquial when used to mean "very much."

> *Unacceptable*   She feels *badly* about her mistake.

> Sean behaved *bad* at the hockey game.

> *Colloquial*   I want a new car *badly.*

> *Standard*   She feels *bad* about her mistake. (adjective as subject complement)

> Sean behaved *badly* at the hockey game. (adverb)

> I want a new car *very much.*

beside, besides   Both words are prepositions, but they have different meanings. *Beside* means "at the side of," and *besides* means "in addition to."

Sheila and Bill sat *beside* the trailer to eat their lunch.

Besides Harvey, Seymour is coming to dinner.

between   See *among, between*.

breath, breathe   *Breath* is a noun and *breathe* is its verb counterpart.

Nicole stepped outside the stuffy cabin for a *breath* of fresh air.

The cabin was so stuffy that Nicole could hardly *breathe*.

broke   *Broke*, when used to mean "without money," is colloquial.

    Colloquial   Because Shelley was *broke*, she had to miss the movie.

    Standard   Because Shelley *had no money*, she had to miss the movie.

can, may   *Can* refers both to permission and to the ability to do something, while *may* refers to permission only.

I think I *can* pass the exam on Friday. (ability)

My mother says I *can* go to the movies. (permission)

When used to denote permission, *can* lends a less formal air to writing than does *may*.

cannot, can not   The use of *cannot* is preferred unless the writer wishes to italicize the *not* for emphasis.

You *cannot* expect a raise this year.

No, you can *not* expect a raise this year.

can't help but   In formal writing, this colloquial phrase should be revised to the simpler I *can't help* or I *cannot help*.

    Colloquial   I *can't help but* wish that I were going to the concert.

    Standard   I *can't help* wishing that I were going to the concert.

capital, capitol   *Capital* means "a city that serves as a seat of government." *Capitol* means "a building in which a legislature meets" in the United States or "the building in which Congress meets."

Winnipeg is the *capital* of Manitoba.

The *capitol* in Washington is popular with visitors.

Capital can also refer to wealth or assets, to an offence punishable by death, or to something excellent or first-rate.

My *capital* consists entirely of stocks and bonds.

Canada does not have *capital* punishment.

That's a *capital* suggestion!

childish, childlike   Both of these terms mean "like a child." *Childish*, however, has a negative connotation.

> He is 52 years old, but he behaves in a *childish* manner.

> Jon's face has a *childlike* quality that everyone likes immediately.

cite, sight, site   *Cite* means "to mention or quote as an example," *sight* means "to see" or "a view," and *site* means "a location."

> Cheryl *cited* E.J. Pratt's *Towards the Last Spike* in her talk.

> He was able to *sight* the enemy destroyers through the periscope.

> The building *site* is a woody area south of town.

complement, compliment   Both words can act as nouns or verbs. As a noun, *complement* means "something that completes or makes up the whole." As a verb, it means "to complete or perfect." As a noun, *compliment* means "a flattering or praising remark." As a verb, it means "to flatter or praise."

> A *complement* of navy personnel boarded the foreign freighter. (noun)

> This fruit will *complement* the meal nicely. (verb)

> Scott paid Sara Jane a lovely *compliment* at the time of her graduation. (noun)

> My mother *complimented* me for cleaning my room. (verb)

usage

conscience, conscious   *Conscience* refers to the sense of moral right or wrong. *Conscious* refers to the awareness of one's feelings or thoughts.

> Edgar's *conscience* forced him to return the money.

> Basil was not *conscious* of his angry feelings.

Do not confuse *conscious* with *aware*; although these words are similar in meaning, one is *conscious* of feelings or actions but *aware* of events.

contemptible, contemptuous   *Contemptible* means "deserving of contempt." *Contemptuous* means "displaying contempt."

> Peter's drunkenness is *contemptible*.

> Mary is *contemptuous* of Peter's drunkenness.

could have, could of   *Could of* is an unacceptable substitute for *could have* because a preposition cannot substitute for a verb.

> *Unacceptable*   I *could of* gone with my parents to Portugal.

> *Standard*   I *could have* gone with my parents to Portugal.

council, counsel   A *council* is a group of people that governs or advises. *Counsel* can be used as both a noun and a verb. The noun means "advice," and the verb means "to advise."

The city *council* meets on the second Tuesday of every month.

The lawyer's *counsel* was sound. (noun)

The psychologist *counsels* many abused children. (verb)

couple   *Couple* denotes two things and should not be used to refer to more than that number.

criteria, criterion   *Criterion* is always singular, *criteria* always plural.

The primary *criterion* for performing this job is manual dexterity.

Manual dexterity is but one of many *criteria* on which you will be judged.

data   *Data* is the plural of *datum*. Although *data* is sometimes used with a singular verb, this use is considered incorrect.

> *Standard*   These *data* are incorrect.

> *Unacceptable*   This *data* is incorrect.

delusion   See *allusion, delusion, illusion*.

desert, deserts, dessert   *Desert* is land that is arid. With the accent on the last syllable, it is a verb meaning "to abandon." *Deserts* means "that which is deserved." *Dessert* is food served after dinner.

The Sonoran *desert* is full of plant life.

You'll get your just *deserts* if you *desert* me now.

They had cheesecake for *dessert* every Thursday night.

usage

different from, different than   *Different from* is preferred to *different than*.

His ideas on marriage were *different from* those of his wife.

Different than is accepted, however, when a clause follows and when the *from* construction would be wordy.

> *Acceptable*   Fiona looks *different than* she did last summer.

> *Wordy*   Fiona looks *different from* the way she looked last summer.

discreet, discrete   To be *discreet* means to be "prudent, tactful, or careful of one's actions." *Discrete* means "distinct or separate."

Jack was always *discreet* when he talked to his grandparents.

When two atoms of hydrogen combine with one atom of oxygen, they are no longer *discrete* entities.

disinterested, uninterested   A person who is *disinterested* is impartial or unbiased. A person who is *uninterested* is indifferent or not interested.

We need a *disinterested* judge to settle the dispute.

Joe is completely *uninterested* in sports.

due to *Due to* has always been acceptable following a linking verb.

> Her success was *due to* hard work.

Purists, however, object to *due to* when it is used in other situations, especially in introductory phrases.

> *Due to* the many requests we have had, not everyone who wishes tickets will receive them.

In such cases, you may wish to recast the sentence.

> *Because* we have had so many requests, not everyone who wishes tickets will receive them.

effect See *affect, effect*.

e.g. This abbreviation, from the Latin *exempli gratia*, means "for example." Avoid using it except in comments in parentheses and in footnotes.

elicit, illicit *Elicit* is a verb that means "to draw forth." *Illicit* is an adjective meaning "not permitted."

> A good professor can always *elicit* responses from students.

> He was engaged in many types of *illicit* activities.

emigrate, immigrate When people *emigrate*, they move out of a country. When people *immigrate*, they move into a country.

> The family *emigrated* from Poland.

> Many Russians *immigrated* to Canada.

ensure See *assure, ensure, insure*.

enthused, enthusiastic *Enthused* is a colloquial word and should not be used in place of *enthusiastic*.

> *Colloquial* John was *enthused* about the prospects for jobs in his hometown.
>
> *Standard* John was *enthusiastic* about the prospects for jobs in his hometown.

especially, specially The term *especially* means "particularly, notably." *Specially* means "for a specific purpose."

> He is an *especially* talented pianist.

> He was *specially* chosen to represent his group.

et al. This expression, from the Latin *et alia*, means "and others," referring to people. Ordinarily, the abbreviation should be used only in footnotes and bibliographic entries.

etc.   This abbreviation, from the Latin *et cetera*, means "and other things" and is used in reference to objects rather than people. It should be avoided except in comments in parentheses or in footnotes. It should never be preceded by *and*.

everyone, every one   *Everyone* means "every person." *Every one* means "every particular person or thing."

> *Everyone* who wants to go to the ball game should let me know today.

> If you carefully check *every one* of your paragraphs, you can improve your writing.

except   See *accept, except*.

excess   See *access, excess*.

explicit, implicit   *Explicit* means "clearly expressed" or "straightforward." *Implicit* means "implied" or "understood without direct statement."

> You must state your needs *explicitly* if you want them fulfilled.

> When I took on the project, I made an *implicit* commitment to see it through.

farther, further   The traditional distinction is that *farther* refers to physical distance and *further* to distance in time. Only *further* should be used to mean "additional" or "additionally."

> In the race for the Muscular Dystrophy Association, Janet ran *farther* than Cindy.

> If you think *further* on the matter, I am certain we can reach an agreement.

> Let me make one *further* point.

fewer, less   *Fewer* refers to countable items. *Less* refers to quantity or degree.

> Mrs. Smith has *fewer* dogs than cats.

> There is *less* money in Joan's chequing account than in Stanley's.

> Jack was *less* ambitious in his later years.

Never use *less* to refer to people.

> *Unacceptable*   *Less* people were there than I expected.

> *Standard*   *Fewer* people were there than I expected.

formally, formerly   *Formally* means "according to established forms, conventions, and rules; ceremoniously." *Formerly* means "in the past."

> The ambassador *formally* greeted his dinner guests.

> *Formerly*, smallpox was one of our most serious diseases.

usage

funny   *Funny* refers to something that is amusing. In formal writing it should not be used to mean "odd" or "unusual."

> *Colloquial*   I felt *funny* visiting my old grade 4 classroom.
>
> *Standard*   I felt *odd* visiting my old grade 4 classroom.

further   See *farther, further.*

get   *Get*, in any of its many colloquial senses, should not be used in writing.

> *Colloquial*   Her way of looking at a man really *gets* me.
>
> I'll *get* him if it's the last thing I do.
>
> *Standard*   Beth will *get* at least a B in this course.

good, well   Do not mistakenly use *good* as an adverb when an adjective is required.

> *Unacceptable*   John did *good* on his first test.
>
> *Standard*   John is making *good* progress on his report.
>
> John is a *good* student.

usage

Well can be used as an adjective meaning "in good health." Otherwise it should always be used as an adverb.

> Last week I had a bad cold, but now I am *well.* (adjective)
>
> John did *well* on his first test. (adverb)

got, gotten   Both are acceptable past-participle forms of the verb *to get.*

hanged, hung   People may be *hanged*. Objects may be *hung*.

> The prisoner was *hanged* at noon.
>
> Mavis *hung* the picture in the dining room.

hopefully   *Hopefully* means "in a hopeful manner." In informal speaking, it is used to mean "it is hoped" or "I hope," but this usage is not correct in formal writing. (Compare this with *carefully*, which means "in a careful manner"; no one uses *carefully* to mean "it is cared.")

> *Colloquial*   *Hopefully*, it will not rain during the class picnic.
>
> *Standard*   Sally walked *hopefully* into the boss's office to ask for a raise.

hung   See *hanged, hung.*

i.e.   This abbreviation, meaning "that is," comes from the Latin *id est.* Avoid using it except in comments in parentheses or footnotes.

if, whether   *If* is used to introduce adverb clauses, where it means "assuming that."

> *If* I finish my report on time, I'll attend the concert with you.

If and *whether* are often used interchangeably to introduce noun clauses that follow verbs such as *ask, say, doubt, know,* and *wonder.* In formal writing, however, *whether* is preferred.

Less Desirable	I don't know *if* we'll be able to see the North Star tonight.
More Desirable	I don't know *whether* we'll be able to see the North Star tonight.

illicit   See *elicit, illicit.*

illusion   See *allusion, delusion, illusion.*

immigrate   See *emigrate, immigrate.*

immoral   See *amoral, immoral.*

impact   Although *impact* is sometimes used in colloquial speech as a verb meaning "affect," this use is unacceptable in formal writing.

Colloquial	This new law will greatly *impact* political campaigning.
Standard	This new law will greatly *affect* political campaigning.

implicit   See *explicit, implicit.*

imply, infer   To *imply* is "to indicate indirectly or give implication." To *infer* is "to conclude from facts, evidence, or indirect suggestions."

Jack *implied* that he wanted a divorce.

Doris *inferred* that Jack wanted a divorce.

As these examples indicate, speakers and writers *imply*; listeners and readers *infer*.

incidence, incidents   *Incidents* are separate, countable experiences. *Incidence* refers to the rate at which something occurs.

Two *incidents* during childhood led to her reclusiveness.

The *incidence* of cancer in Japan is less than that in Canada.

incredible, incredulous   *Incredible* means "fantastic, unbelievable." *Incredulous* means "skeptical, disbelieving."

That she could run so fast seemed *incredible.*

Why is Bill wearing that *incredulous* look?

infer   See *imply, infer.*

in regards to   This is an incorrect use of *in regard to.*

insure   See *assure, ensure, insure.*

usage

inter-, intra-   *Inter-* means "between or among." *Intra-* means "within."

> From Calgary to Saskatoon is an *interprovince* drive of approximately 700 kilometres.

> From Osoyoos to Vancouver is an *intraprovince* drive of about 500 kilometres.

in terms of   Avoid this vague, overused expression.

> *Vague*   *In terms of* the price he is asking, I would not recommend purchasing Liam's car.

> *Preferred*   *Because* of the price he is asking, I would not recommend purchasing Liam's car.

irregardless   This nonstandard form of *regardless* includes the repetitive elements of *ir* and *less*, both of which mean "without."

is when, is where   *Is when* properly refers only to time.

> April *is when* our lilac bush blooms.

Is where properly refers only to place.

> Athens *is where* I met him.

The following sentences are *faulty* because of poorly phrased predicates which indicate that muckraking is a place and an abscess is a time:

> Muckraking *is where* someone investigates corporate or governmental abuses of power.

> An abscess *is when* some spot in body tissue fills with pus.

These sentences should be rephrased to eliminate the faulty assertion.

> Muckraking is the investigation of corporate or governmental abuses of power.

> An abscess is a spot in body tissue that fills with pus.

its, it's, its'   *Its* is a possessive pronoun. *It's* is a contraction of *it is* or *it has*.

> The gold chair was ruined, for someone had torn *its* seat.

> *It's* all I have to offer. (It is all I have to offer.)

> *It's* been a difficult day. (It has been a difficult day.)

There is no correct use for *its'*.

kind of, sort of   In formal writing, these are unacceptable substitutes for *somewhat*, *rather*, or *slightly*.

> *Colloquial*   She is *sort of* angry.

> I am *kind of* glad she went away.

Standard	She is *somewhat angry.*
	I am *rather* glad she went away.

When *kind* and *sort* refer to a type, use them with singular nouns and verbs. With their plural forms, *kinds* and *sorts*, use plural nouns and verbs.

Unacceptable	These *kind* of exams are difficult.
Standard	This *kind* of exam is difficult.
	These *kinds* of exams are difficult.

In such constructions, be certain that *kind of* or *sort of* is essential to your meaning.

later, latter, last *Later* refers to time; *latter* points out the second of two items. If more than two items are listed, use *last* to refer to the final one.

He arrived at the party *later* than he was expected.

Although professors Stein and Patterson both lectured during the course, only the *latter* graded the final exam.

Of my cats, Sheba, Tiger, and Spot, only the *last* needs the vaccination.

lay, lie *Lie* means "to recline" or "to remain in a particular position." It never takes a direct object. *Lay* means "to place" and always takes a direct object. These verbs are often confused, in part because the past tense of *lie* is *lay*. (The past tense of *lay* is *laid*.)

If I *lie* here a minute, I shall feel better.

As I *lay* asleep, a robber entered my apartment and stole my stereo.

Lay the book on the table, please.

He *laid* a hand on her shoulder.

leave, let *Leave* means "to depart," and *let* means "to allow." Never use *leave* when *let* is meant.

Unacceptable	*Leave* him figure it out alone.
Standard	*Let* him figure it out alone.

lend, loan Traditionally, *loan* has been classed as a noun and *lend* as a verb. Today, the use of *loan* as a verb is so commonplace that it is accepted as colloquial English.

Standard	I have applied for a *loan* so that I can buy a car. (noun)
	Please *lend* me your class notes. (verb)
Colloquial	Please *loan* me your class notes. (verb)

less See *fewer, less.*

like See *as, like.*

usage

literally   The word *literally* means "restricted to the exact, stated meaning." In formal writing, use *literally* only to designate factual statements.

> *Colloquial*   It was 15 degrees outside, but I was *literally* freezing.
>
> *Standard*   Our dog was *literally* foaming at the mouth.
>
> It was 15 degrees outside, but I felt *very* cold.

loan   See *lend, loan.*

loose, loosen, lose   *Loose* is used primarily as an adjective, meaning "unattached, unrestrained, not confined." *Loosen* is a verb meaning "undo or ease." *Lose* can be used only as a verb meaning "mislay, fail to win, fail to maintain."

> One should wear *loose* clothing when bowling. (adjective)
>
> When will Mrs. Brady *loosen* her control over young Jack?
>
> You would *lose* your nose if it were not attached to your face.

lots, lots of   *Lots* and *lots of* colloquially mean "many, much, a large amount, or a great amount." Avoid these expressions in formal writing.

> *Colloquial*   I've spent *lots of* money in my life.
>
> *Standard*   I have spent *much* money in my life.

mad   See *angry, mad.*

many, much   *Many* is used when referring to countable items; *much* is used when referring to an indefinite amount or to abstract concepts.

> There are *many* students in the biology class.
>
> How did Betty learn so *much* in so little time?

may   See *can, may.*

may be, maybe   *May be* is always used as a verb phrase. *Maybe* is an adverb meaning "perhaps."

> I *may be* chairman of the board by next June.
>
> *Maybe* we will see Jim at home.

medium, media   *Medium* is the singular form of this word; *media* is the plural.

> The Internet is the *medium* I use most to get the news.
>
> The *media* have given extensive coverage to the brain transplant story.

much   See *many, much.*

usage

myself   *Myself* is an intensive and a reflexive pronoun; it cannot substitute for a personal pronoun such as *I* or *me*.

> *Unacceptable*   Four other students and *myself* founded the club.
>
> *Standard*   Four other students and *I* founded the club.

number   See *amount, number*.

on account of   When used to begin an adverb clause (see page 528), this is a non-standard substitute for *because*.

> *Unacceptable*   The team was unable to practise *on account of* everyone was still upset over Tuesday's loss.
>
> *Standard*   The team was unable to practise *because* everyone was still upset over Tuesday's loss.

When *on account of* precedes a single word or a phrase, it is considered to be colloquial.

> *Colloquial*   The game was called *on account of* rain.

passed, past   *Passed* is a verb designating activity that has taken place. *Past* is a noun or an adjective designating a former time.

> The parade *passed* the reviewing stand at 10:30 a.m.
>
> In the *past*, few people were concerned about the environmental effects of pesticides.
>
> This *past* summer, I visited France.

personal, personnel   *Personal* is an adjective meaning "private, individual." *Personnel* are the people working in an organization.

> Age is a *personal* matter that you do not have to reveal during a job interview.
>
> The *personnel* of the sanitation department will not be involved in the city workers' strike.

precede, proceed   *Precede* means "to go before or ahead of." *Proceed* means "to go on" or "to go forward."

> The ritual of sharpening his pencils always *preceded* doing his homework.
>
> The guide then said, "If you will *proceed*, I will show you the paintings by da Vinci."

predominant, predominate   *Predominant* is an adjective meaning "chief, main, most frequent." *Predominate* is a verb meaning "to have authority over others."

> The *predominant* European influence on South American culture was Spanish.
>
> In Canada, the will of the people should *predominate*.

usage

principal, principle   *Principal*, which means "chief," "most important" (including as a noun referring to the chief administrator in a school), or "the amount of money on which interest is computed," is used as both an adjective and a noun. *Principle* is used only as a noun and means "truths, beliefs, or rules generally dealing with moral conduct."

> The *principal* suspect in the case was arrested last Friday by the police.

> The *principal* of Lewiston High School is Alison Cooperstein.

> At this interest rate, your *principal* will double in 10 years.

> His *principles* are unconventional.

proceed   See *precede, proceed*.

raise, rise   *Raise* is a transitive verb and therefore requires a direct object. *Rise*, its intransitive counterpart, takes no direct object.

> We plan to *raise* horses on our new farm.

> The temperature is expected to *rise* to 30°C tomorrow.

Raise can also be a noun meaning "an increase in pay."

> Tammy received a 25 percent *raise* last week.

real, really   *Real* is an adjective; *really* is an adverb.

> He had *real* plants decorating the bedroom.

When used as an adverb, *real* is a colloquialism and should be replaced with *really*.

> Colloquial   We had a *real* good time at the party.

> Standard   We had a *really* good time at the party.

reason is because, reason is that   The *reason is because* is colloquial and unacceptable in formal writing; the *reason is that* is the correct usage.

> Colloquial   The *reason is because* I love her.

> Standard   The *reason is that* I love her.

respectfully, respectively   *Respectfully* means "with respect." *Respectively* indicates that the items in one series are related to those in a second series in the order given.

> Joseph should treat his parents *respectfully*.

> Justin, Anna, and Evan were assigned *Bleak House*, *Great Expectations*, and *Dombey and Son*, *respectively*, for their reports.

rise   See *raise, rise*.

usage

sensual, sensuous   *Sensual* refers to bodily or sexual sensations. *Sensuous* refers to impressions experienced through the five senses.

Singles bars offered *sensual* pleasures without emotional commitments.

The Tivoli Garden provides many *sensuous* delights for visitors.

set, sit   Generally, *set* means "to place" and takes a direct object. *Sit* means "to be seated" and does not take a direct object.

Alice *set* her glass on the mantel.

May I *sit* in this chair?

When it refers to the sun, however, *set* is used without a direct object.

As the sun *set*, we turned homeward.

shall, will   *Shall* is used in first-person questions and in specialized forms of writing such as military orders and laws. Otherwise, *will* is generally used.

Shall we go to the movies tonight?

The company *shall* fall into formation at precisely 12 noon.

No family home *shall* be assessed at more than 50 percent of its actual value.

should have, should of   *Should of* is an unacceptable substitute for *should have* because a preposition cannot substitute for a verb.

> *Unacceptable*   I *should of* gone to the lake.

> *Standard*   I *should have* gone to the lake.

[*sic*]   This Latin word, always enclosed in brackets, follows quoted errors in grammar, spelling, or information. Inclusion of [*sic*] indicates that the error appeared in the original, which is being quoted exactly.

sight   See *cite, sight, site*.

sit   See *set, sit*.

site   See *cite, sight, site*.

so   *So* is an acceptable coordinating conjunction but tends to add an informal effect to writing and should therefore be used sparingly. For example, "Thomas said he was divorcing me, *so* I began to cry" would be more effective if restated as follows: "When Thomas said he was divorcing me, I began to cry." Do not use *so* as a substitute for *extremely* or *very* except with adverb clauses beginning with *that*.

> *Colloquial*   You are *so* careless in what you say.

> The discussion was *so* informative that I took many notes.

usage

> *Standard*   You are *very* careless in what you say.
>
> The discussion was *extremely* informative.

sometime, some time, sometimes   *Sometime* means "at a future unspeci-fied time," *some time* means "a span of time," and *sometimes* means "occasionally."

> We should get together *sometime* and play bridge.
>
> The weather has been hot for *some time.*
>
> *Sometimes* I go to dinner with Ethel.

sort of   See *kind of, sort of.*

specially   See *especially, specially.*

such, such . . . that   The use of *such* when it means "very" or "extremely" is unacceptable unless it is followed by a *that* clause completing the thought.

> *Colloquial*   They were *such* good cookies.
>
> *Standard*   They were *such* good cookies *that* I asked Steve for his recipe.

suppose to, supposed to   *Suppose to* is the nonstandard form of *supposed to.* In speech, it is difficult to hear the final *d* on *supposed,*and one may say *suppose to* without being detected; however, the correct written form is always *supposed to.*

than, then   *Than* is used to make comparisons; *then* means "at that time, in that case," or "after that."

> Jill is taller *than* her brother.
>
> First we will eat, and *then* we will discuss business.

that, which   These two words have the same meaning. *That* may refer both to things and groups of people; *which,* only to things. When referring to things, *that* is gen-erally used with clauses that distinguish the things they modify from others in the same class (restrictive clauses). *Which* is generally used with clauses that add information about the things they modify (non-restrictive clauses).

> Any book *that* she likes is certain to be trashy. (restrictive clause)
>
> The Winthrop Building, which cost two million dollars to construct, could not now be duplicated for ten times that much. (non-restrictive clause)

See page 567 of the Handbook for a more complete explanation of restrictive and non-restrictive expressions.

their, there, they're   These three separate words are often confused because they sound alike. *Their* is the possessive form of *they. There* is an expletive that appears at the beginning of a sentence and introduces the real subject, or it is an adverb meaning "in or at that place, at that point." *They're* is a contraction of *they are.*

usage

It is *their* basketball.

There are many reasons why I cannot come.

Put the sofa down *there*.

They're going to be here soon.

then   See *than, then*.

there   See *their, there, they're*.

thorough, through   *Thorough* means "careful, complete, exact, painstaking." *Through* means "in one side and out the other, from end to end, from start to finish, over the whole extent of, finished."

Brenda has done a *thorough* job.

Let's run *through* the plan again.

thusly   *Thusly* is a nonstandard form of *thus*.

to, too, two   *To* is a preposition meaning "as far as, toward, until, onto." *Too* is an adverb meaning "excessively" or "also." *Two* is a number.

I'm going *to* the store.

Are you going *too?*

This car is *too* expensive for me.

There are *two* characters in the play.

toward, towards   Both forms are correct. *Toward* generally is used in North America and *towards* in England.

two   See *to, too, two*.

uninterested   See *disinterested, uninterested*.

unique   *Unique* means "without an equal" or "extremely unusual" and thus should not be modified by an adverb such as *very*.

use to, used to   *Use to* is the nonstandard form of *used to*. In speech it is difficult to hear the *d* on *used*, and one may say *use to* without being detected; however, the correct written form is always *used to*.

way, ways   *Ways* may be used to refer to two or more means or methods but not to time or distance.

Unacceptable	Puerto Vallarta is a long *ways* from Canada.
Standard	There are two *ways* of thinking about that issue.
	Puerto Vallarta is a long *way* from Canada.

well   See *good, well*.

usage

were, where   *Were* is the past form of the verb *to be*. *Where* is an adverb or a pronoun meaning "in, at, to, from a particular place or situation" or "which or what place."

I'm sorry that you *were* ill yesterday.

Mr. Morris will show you *where* to register.

where . . . at, to   *At* and *to* are unnecessary after *where*.

Wordy	*Where* are you taking the car *to?*
	Where does she live *at?*
Standard	*Where* are you taking the car?
	Where does she live?

whether   See *if, whether*.

which   See *that, which*.

who, whom   In formal writing, *who* should be used only as a subject in clauses and sentences and *whom* only as an object.

Unacceptable	*Who* are you taking to dinner on Friday?
	I know *who* the boss will promote.
	John is the candidate *whom* I think will be elected.
Standard	*Whom* are you taking to dinner on Friday?
	I know *whom* the boss will promote.
	John is the candidate *who* I think will be elected.

See page 525 of the Handbook for a more detailed discussion of *who* and *whom*.

who's, whose   *Who's* is a contraction of *who is* or *who has*, and *whose* is the possessive form of *who*.

Who's coming to see us tonight?

I would like to know *who's* been dumping trash in my yard.

Whose book is that?

will   See *shall, will*.

wise   Do not randomly add *wise* to the ends of nouns. Such word coinings are ineffective.

Ineffective	Personality *wise*, Sheila is ideal for the job.
Standard	Sheila has an *ideal personality* for the job.

usage

would have, would of   *Would of* is an unacceptable substitute for *would have*. A preposition cannot substitute for a verb.

> *Unacceptable*   I *would of* enjoyed seeing the Picasso exhibit.

> *Standard*   I *would have* enjoyed seeing the Picasso exhibit.

would have been, had been   When *would* occurs in the main part of a sentence, use *had been* (not *would have been*) in an "if" clause.

> *Unacceptable*   If the engine *would have been* lubricated, the bearing *would not have* burned out.

> *Standard*   If the engine *had been* lubricated, the bearing *would not have* burned out.

your, you're   *Your* is a possessive form of *you; you're* is a contraction of *you are*.

> Where is *your* history book?

> Tell me when *you're* ready to leave.

usage

CREDITS

Suzanne Ahearne. "Monday Night in the Nickel Fields," *Maisonneuve Magazine,* 2013.

Filza Ahmar, "Getting Schooled by my Pakistani Mother." Used by permission of Filza Ahmar.

R.T. Allen, "The Porcupine." from *Children, Wives and Other Wildlife* by Robert Thomas Allen. (Toronto: Doubleday, 1970).

Mitchell Anderson, *Oil Wealth: Should Norway Be the Canadian Way?* The Tyee, 2012.

Jeffrey Andreoni. "Why Can't I Feel What I See? — What Is the Happiness that Eluded Our Generation?" Originally published in *Adbusters #89: The Ecopsychology Issue* (May/June 2010). Copyright © Jeffrey Andreoni. Used by permission of the author.

"Antigen," *Encyclopaedia Britannica,* 1974, I, 417.

Margaret Atwood, *Alias Grace.* Hachette UK., 2009.

Marilyn Baker, "Greed Works," *Vancouver Sun,* Sept. 15, 2004.

Andrew Beyak, "The Sweet Bird of Youth Is Showing Signs of Age," *Georgia Straight,* Jan. 1–8, 1998: 11.

Neil Bissoondath, "No Place Like Home." Reproduced with permission.

Dionne Brand, "Blossom: Priestess of Oya, Goddess of Winds, Storms and Waterfalls" from *Other Solitudes: Canadian Multicultural Fictions* (Oxford University Press, 1990).

Claude Brown, *Manchild in the Promised Land* (Simon and Schuster, Inc., 1965).

James L Buckley. "Three Cheers for the Snail Darter." Published by National Review Inc, 1979.

Ian Bullock, "What Do You See? Is Your Brain East or West?" Originally published in *Adbusters* Magazine, Jan. 4, 2010. Copyright © Ian Bullock. Used by permission of Ian Bullock.

Kyle Butt. Excerpt. Used by permission of Kyle Butt.

Sasha Chapman. Abridged from "Manufacturing Taste" first printed in *The Walrus.* Reprinted with permission from Sasha Chapman. © September 2012.

Wayson Choy, "I'm a Banana and Proud of It." Originally published in Canada by *The Globe and Mail.* Copyright © 1997 by Wayson Choy. Reprinted by permission of the author via The Bukowski Agency. All rights reserved.

"Computer Crime." Published by Schoolwires, Inc.

"Controlling Phobias through Behavior Modification." *USA Today,* August 1978.

Crozier, Lorna, *Small Beneath the Sky* (Vancouver: Greystone Books/D&M Publishers, 2009), pp. 38–39.

Krissy Darch and Fazeela Jiwa, "Beyond Bullying" *Briarpatch Magazine,* 2013. Used by permission of Briarpatch Magazine.

Robertson Davies, "Literature in a Country Without a Mythology," *The Merry Heart: Reflections on Reading, Writing, and the World of Books* (Toronto: Viking Penguin, 1997), p. 50.

Kelly Davis. *Health and High Voltage: 765 KV Lines.* Published by Kelly Davis, © 1978

Geoff Dembicki. "The Four Tribes of Climate Change," TheTyee.ca, Nov 4, 2013. Used by permission of TheTyee.ca.

Meeru Dhalwala and Vikram Vij, "Vij's at Home." Douglas and McIntyre, 2010. Reprinted with permission from the publisher.

Joan Didion, "On Self-Respect," in *Slouching Toward Bethlehem* (New York: Farrar, Strauss and Giroux, 1968), pp. 143–44.

Loren Eiseley, "The Unexpected Universe," Harcourt Brace Jovanovich College Publishers, 1969.

Howard Ensign Evans, *Life on a Little-Known Planet* (Big Earth Publishing 1968).

Harry Fairlie, "A Victim Fights Back," *The Washington Post,* Apr. 30, 1978.

Tim Falconer, "Autoholics," *THIS Magazine,* March/April 2009. Copyright © 2009 by Tim Falconer. Used by permission of Tim Falconer.

Will Kymlicka, "Immigrants, Multiculturalism and Canadian Citizenship." The material in this paper is drawn from the book *Finding Our Way: Rethinking Ethnocultural Relations in Canada*, by Will Kymlicka (Oxford University Press, 1998). Used by permission of the author.

Tara Lee, "Knife Skills: How to Choose the Right Knife and Wield it like a Pro." Georgia Straight, 2013. Used by the permission of Straight.com.

Scott Lemanski, "Bottled Troubled Water," 2013. Used by permission of Scott Lemanski.

Jamie Lockrey. "The Cleanse Cycle." 2015. Used by permission of Jamie Lockrey.

Barry MacDonald. "Help Your Son Think Positively," Boy Smarts Newsletter, page 4. Copyright © 2014 by Barry MacDonald. Used by permission of Barry MacDonald.

Marilyn Machlowitz, "Workaholism: What's Wrong with Being Married to Your Work?" *Working Woman*, May 1978, p. 51.

Rafe Mair, *Hard Talk* (Madeira Park, B.C.: Harbour Publishing, 2005).

Marya Mannes, "Wasteland," in *More in Anger*. Published by Marya Mannes, © 1958.

Alexander McIlwain, "Zero to Hero: A Comparative Analysis of Heroism in The Odyssey and Tale of Despereaux." Used by permission.

Tamsin McMahon, "Is Local Food Bad for the Economy?" *Maclean's*, 2012.

Margaret Mead. "New Superstitions for Old," McCallin, 1970.

Don Ethan Miller, "A State of Grace: Understanding the Martial Arts," *Atlantic Monthly*, Sept. 1980.

Moses Milstein, "Memories of Montreal — and Richness," Originally published in *The Globe and Mail*, 28 April 28 1998, A16. Copyright © Moses Milestein. Used by the permission of Moses Milstein.

Alanna Mitchell, *Seasick: Ocean Change and the Extinction of Life on Earth*. University of Chicago Press, 2009.

Susanna Moodie, *Roughing It in the Bush*.

Patrick Moore, "Going Nuclear," *The Washington Post*, 2006. Used by permission of Patrick Moore.

Peter C. Newman, "Seymour Schulich: Champion Philanthropist" in *Heroes: Canadian Champions, Dark Horses and Icons* by Peter C. Newman (Toronto: HarperCollins Canada, 2010) p. 364.

William Nichols, "Real vs. Fake Conversation." Used by permission of William Nichols.

Kristine Nyhout, "Send in the Clowns." Originally published in *Chatelaine*, Apr. 1998, pp. 165–166. Copyright © Kristine Nyhout. Reprinted by permission of Kristine Nyhout.

Jo Goodwin Parker, "What Is Poverty?" in George Henderson, *America's Other Children: Public Schools Outside Suburbia* (University of Oklahoma Press. 1971).

Quote by Dr. Joseph Pomeranz, Published by Schoolwires Inc.

Robert Rodreguez, "Private Language, Public Language" in ARIA: A MEMOIR OF A BILINGUAL CHILDHOOD by Richard Rodriguez. Copyright © 1980 by Richard Rodriguez. Originally appeared in *The American Scholar*. Reprinted by permission of Georges Borchardt, Inc., on behalf of the author.

Alexis Rowell, "Ten Reasons Why New Nuclear Was a Mistake- Even Before Fukushima," *Transtion Culture*, 2011. Used by permission of Alexis Rowell.

Scott Russell Sanders, "The Men We Carry in Our Minds." Copyright © 1984 by Scott Russell Sanders; first appeared in *Milkweed Chronicle*; collected in the author's *The Paradise of Bombs* (Bostom: Beacon Press, 1993); reprinted by permission of the author.

Mark Schapiro, "Children of a Lesser God," *Harper's Bazaar*, April 1996. Published by EBSCO Publishing, 1996.

John E. Shepler, *What Thoreau Knew: Walden and the Meaning of Voluntary Simplicity*. 1998. Reproduced by permission of John E. Shepler.

Carol Diggory Shields, *Larry's Party* (Toronto: Penguin Random House Canada Limited, 1997), pp. 242–243.

Elliott L. Smith and Andrew W. Hart, *The Short Story: A Contemporary Looking Glass* (New York: Random House, 1981).

Russell Smith, "Battered by Blandness," *The Globe and Mail*, Oct. 24, 2002: R7.

Adam Sternbergh. "Teen Angst, RIP: There's something disturbing about the overwhelming happiness of Canada's teenagers." Originally published in *The Walrus*, June 2010. Copyright © Adam Sternbergh. Reprinted by permission of the author.

John D. Stewart, "Vulture Country," *Atlantic Monthly*, 1959.

Joyce Susskind, "Surprises in a Woman's Life," *Vogue*, Feb. 1979, p. 252.

Gideon Sjoberg. "The Origin and Development of Cities," *Scientific American*, 1965.

Elle-Máijá Tailfeathers. "Fractured land, A first-hand account of resistance to fracking on Blood land," *Briarpatch Magazine*. 2012. Used by permission of Briarpatch Magazine.

Lewis Thomas, excerpt from "Societies as Organisms," in *The Lives of a Cell* by Lewis Thomas. Penguin, USA, 1971.

Douglas Todd, "Combating the 'Culture of Despair'," *Vancouver Sun*, Aug. 19, 2011: C5 (Weekend Review).

Richard Tomkins, "Old Father Time Becomes a Terror." *Financial Times*, Mar. 20, 1999.

Julia Traves, "The Church of Please and Thank You." *This Magazine*. Copyright © Julia Traves. Reprinted by permission of the author.

Laura Trethewey, "Screen Saver - Click Bait," *This magazine*, 2014. Used by permission of Laura Trethewey.

Pierre Elliott Trudeau., "Statement on Introduction of the Official Languages Bill," 1968.

Jon Turk, *Cold Oceans: Adventures in Kayaks, Rowboat, and Dogsled*. HarperCollins Publisher.

Chris Turner. Excerpt from *The Leap: How to Survive and Thrive in the Sustainable Economy*. Penguin Random House Canada Limited.

Bryan Wainright, "Lust and Gluttony." Used by permission of Bryan Wainright.

Beth Wald, "Let's Get Vertical!," *Climbing Magazine*. Used by permission of Beth Wald Photography.

Margaret Webb, "Canada needa a national food strategy." Originally published in *Toronto Star* (15 October 2009). Copyright © Margaret Webb. Used by permission of the author.

Steve Whysall, "Don't Let Emotion Guide Your E-Mail." Steve Whysall/*Vancouver Sun*, October 19, 2004: C1–C4.

Marion Winik, "What Are Friends For?" From *Telling* (New York: Vintage, 1995), pp. 85–89. Copyright © Marion Winik. Used by permission of Marion Winik.

Tom Wolfe, *The Pump House Gang*. Farrar, Straus & Giroux, Inc., 1966.

Chris Wood, *Dry Spring: The Coming Water Crisis of North America*. Vancouver: Raincoast Books, 2008. Used by permission of the author.

Orville Wyss and Curtis Eklund, *Microorganisms and Man* (New York: John Wiley and Sons, 1971), pp. 232–33.

Marc Zwelling, "The Blended Economy, Blending Ideas Offers an Alternative to Specialization, by Marc Zwelling from The Futurist. Copyright © 2002 by Marc Zwelling. Used by permission of Marc Zwelling.

INDEX

EDITING SYMBOLS

Symbol	Problem	Page	Symbol	Problem	Page
ab	improper abbreviation	558–60	nsu	nonstandard usage	569–89
agr pa	faulty agreement of pronoun and antecedent	518–20	¶	new paragraph needed	
			no ¶	new paragraph not needed	
agr su	faulty agreement of subject and verb	515–18	⊡	period needed	548–49
∛ or apos	missing or misused apostrophe	539–41	|| or para	nonparallelism	534–36
awk	awkward phrasing		? or ques	missing or misused question mark	548–49
bib	faulty bibliographic form		"/" or quot	missing or misused quotation marks	553–54
cap	capital letter needed	557–58	ref	unclear reference of pronoun to antecedent	520–22
case	wrong case	524–27			
cl	cliché	506–08	ro	run-on sentence	
⋀ or com	missing or misused comma	542–45	; or sem	missing or misused semicolon	546–47
cs	comma splice		sp	spelling error	564–68
comp	faulty comparison	536–38	shift p	shift in person	522–24
dm	dangling modifier	533–34	shift t	shift in tense	
⊙ or ellip	missing or misused ellipsis		sq	squinting modifier	
frag	sentence fragment	512–13	t or tense	wrong tense	
ital	missing or misused italics	562–63	trans	poor transition	
lc	lowercase (small) letter needed		vb	wrong verb form	489–95
ll or lev	wrong level of usage	12–15	wdy	wordiness	
log	faulty logic		ww	wrong word	
mm	misplaced modifier	532–33	⟨	delete (omit)	
num	use numerals	560–62	⋀	material omitted	
			⟨?⟩	meaning unclear or word illegible	